Lecture Notes in Computer Science 12388

More information about this subseries at http://www.springer.com/series/7409

Sara Hofmann · Oliver Müller ·
Matti Rossi (Eds.)

Designing for Digital Transformation

Co-Creating Services with Citizens and Industry

15th International Conference on Design Science Research
in Information Systems and Technology, DESRIST 2020
Kristiansand, Norway, December 2–4, 2020
Proceedings

Springer

Editors
Sara Hofmann 🆔
University of Agder
Kristiansand, Norway

Oliver Müller
University of Paderborn
Paderborn, Germany

Matti Rossi 🆔
Aalto University
Aalto, Finland

ISSN 0302-9743   ISSN 1611-3349 (electronic)
Lecture Notes in Computer Science
ISBN 978-3-030-64822-0   ISBN 978-3-030-64823-7   (eBook)
https://doi.org/10.1007/978-3-030-64823-7

LNCS Sublibrary: SL3 – Information Systems and Applications, incl. Internet/Web, and HCI

This Springer imprint is published by the registered company Springer Nature Switzerland AG
The registered company address is: Gewerbestrasse 11, 6330 Cham, Switzerland

Preface

Welcome to the proceedings of the 15th International Conference on Design Science Research in Information Systems and Technology (DESRIST 2020). There has been a surge of interest in design science research (DSR) in the last decade and DSR has developed into a mature research paradigm. The goal of the design science research paradigm is to extend the boundaries of human and organizational capabilities by designing new and innovative constructs, models, methods, processes, and systems. Scholars from different backgrounds – such as information systems, computer science, data science, software engineering, energy informatics, medical informatics, and operations research – are actively engaged in generating novel solutions to interesting design problems. The theme of DESRIST 2020 was "Designing for digital transformation – Co-Creating Services with Citizens and Industry."

The conference attracted different types of submissions, including completed research, ongoing research, research-in-progress, and prototype papers. In addition, the conference organized a PhD colloquium. DESRIST has brought together researchers and practitioners from the private and public sector to the conference to discuss and debate how to co-create services for citizens and industries. Participants engaged in all aspects of design science research, with a special emphasis on the design of services for digital transformation.

This year's preparation and execution of the conference have been heavily influenced by the COVID-19 pandemic. Originally planned to take place in June at the University of Agder in Kristiansand, Norway, DESRIST 2020 was eventually held as a fully digital conference during December 2–4, 2020. Authors of completed research papers prepared a five-minute presentation, which was followed by an intensive five-minute discussion. The research-in-progress and prototype contributions were presented in an entertaining one-minute design science research slam. In addition, interesting discussions took place during the two panel sessions on "Ethics in Design Science Research" and "The Role and Impact of Design Research on Digital Transformation." While we lost some of the ad-hoc meetings and informal gatherings, we managed to have much interaction and participation.

This volume contains 28 full research papers, 7 research-in-progress papers, and 9 prototype papers, which accounts for an acceptance rate of 47%. The contributions span across the overarching topics of Digital Public Services, Data Science, Design Principles, and Methodology.

We would like to thank all the contributors who have aided in making this year's conference a success. Our gratitude goes to the members of the Program Committee, including associate editors and reviewers for their effort in preparing the conference, and reviewing and selecting the accepted papers, as well as to the authors for submitting their papers. A special thanks goes to the local organizers at University of Agder for their preparation and their flexibility in these challenging times. The conference was only possible with the help and contribution of you all.

December 2020   Matti Rossi
                                                                 Oliver Müller
                                                                 Sara Hofmann

Organization

General Chairs

Bengisu Tulu   Worcester Polytechnic Institute (WPI), USA
Gondy Leroy   University of Arizona, USA
Soussan Djamasbi   Worcester Polytechnic Institute (WPI), USA

Conference Chairs

Leif Skiftenes Flak   University of Agder, Norway
Maung Kyaw Sein   University of Agder, Norway

Program Chairs

Matti Rossi   Aalto University, Finland
Oliver Müller   Paderborn University, Germany

Panel Chairs

Margunn Aanestad   University of Agder, Norway
Monica Chiarini Tremblay   Raymond A. Mason School of Business, USA
Polyxeni Vasilakopoulou   University of Agder, Norway

Doctoral Consortium Chairs

Devendra Bahadur Thapa   University of Agder, Norway
Sandeep Purao   Bentley University, USA

Prototypes Chairs

Amir Haj-Bolouri   University West, Sweden
Leona Chandra Kruse   University of Liechtenstein, Liechtenstein

Proceedings Chair

Sara Hofmann   University of Agder, Norway

Industry Relations Chair

Carl Erik Moe   University of Agder, Norway

Website

Amna Drace   University of Agder, Norway

Program Committee

Abayomi Baiyere	Copenhagen Business School, Denmark
Ahmed Abbasi	McIntire School of Commerce, University of Virginia, USA
Ahmed Elragal	Luleå University of Technology, Sweden
Alexander Herwix	University of Köln, Germany
Alexander Maedche	Karlsruhe Institute of Technology, Germany
Andreas Drechsler	Victoria University of Wellington, New Zealand
Arturo Castellanos	Baruch College, USA
Brian Donnellan	Maynooth University, Ireland
Christian Janiesch	University of Würzburg, Germany
Daniel Beverungen	Paderborn University, Germany
Dirk Hovorka	The University of Sydney, Australia
Dominik Gutt	Rotterdam School of Management, The Netherlands
Guido Schryen	Paderborn University, Germany
Heiko Gewald	Neu-Ulm University of Applied Sciences, Germany
Jan vom Brocke	University of Liechtenstein, Liechtenstein
Jason Thatcher	University of Alabama, USA
Jeffrey Parsons	Memorial University, Canada
Jens Pöppelbuß	Ruhr University Bochum, Germany
Jonas Sjöström	Uppsala University, Sweden
Kathrin Figl	University of Innsbruck, Austria
Kaushik Dutta	University of South Florida, USA
Ken Peffers	University of Nevada, USA
Konstantin Hopf	University of Bamberg, Germany
Martin Matzner	University of Erlangen-Nuremberg, Germany
Matthew Mullarkey	USF Muma College of Business, USA
Matthias Söllner	University of Kassel, Germany
Monica Chiarini Tremblay	Raymond A Mason School of Business, USA
Munir Mandviwalla	Temple University, USA
Netta Iivari	University of Oulu, Finland
Oliver Müller	Paderborn University, Germany
Rangaraja Sundarraj	Indian Institute of Technology Madras, India
Richard Baskerville	Georgia State University, USA
Robert Winter	University of St. Gallen, Switzerland
Roman Lukyanenko	HEC Montréal, Canada
Samir Chatterjee	Claremont Graduate University, USA
Sara Hofmann	University of Agder, Norway
Stefan Morana	Karlsruhe Institute of Technology, Germany
Stefan Seidel	University of Liechtenstein, Liechtenstein
Tuure Tuunanen	University of Jyväskylä, Finland

Reviewers

Abhinay Puvvala
Aleksi Aaltonen
Alexia Athanasopoulou
Alfred Benedikt Brendel
Alfred Castillo
Ali Sunyaev
Alois Paulin
Andrea Kayl
Andreas Weigert
Andy Nguyen
Anik Mukherjee
Anna Sigridur Islind
Ann-Kristin Cordes
Arto Lanamäki
Benedikt Berger
Benjamin Sturm
Brent Kitchens
Casandra Grundstrom
Christian Bartelheimer
Christian Hovestadt
Christian Kalla
Connor Esterwood
Craig A. Horne
Daniel Szopinski
Darwin Hale
David Harborth
David Schuff
Debra Vander Meer
Denis Dennehy
Denis Edwards
Dennis Kundisch
Dixon Prem Daniel
Djordje Djurica
Eli Hustad
Elin Uppström
Elina Annanperä
Elizabeth Sanders
Erol Kazan
Esko Penttinen
Florence Mwagwabi
Gerit Wagner
Guohou Shan
Gustaf Juell-Skielse

Steffi Haag
Hanlie Smuts
Hedda Lüttenberg
Hendrik Wache
Hossam Hassanien
Hossana Twinomurinzi
Hyung Koo Lee
James Wallace
Jan Holmström
Jan Niklas Dörseln
Jan Pries-Heje
Janine Hacker
Jan-Peter Kucklick
Jasper Feine
Jingjing Li
John Venable
Jonna Järveläinen
Joshua Peter Handali
Julian Prester
Jörg Becker
Kai Heinrich
Kai Klinker
Kai-Kristian Kemell
Karin Elisabeth Väyrynen
Karthikeyan Umapathy
Leena Arhippainen
Lena Otto
Lina Bouayad
Louise Harris
Mala Kaul
Manoj Thomas
Marcus Green
Marcus Rothenberger
Maria Cucciniello
Mariem Ben Rehouma
Marius Schmid
Markus Helfert
Mary Tate
Matthew Caron
Maximilian Haug
Maximilian Roeglinger
Mengcheng Li
Michael Fruhwirth

Michael Hausch
Michael Lee
Moutaz Haddara
Na Liu
Nadine Ogonek
Niall Connolly
Nicola Staub
Nicolai Bohn
Ning Yang
Oliver Posegga
Osmo Mattila
Padmal Vitharana
Patrick Delfmann
Patrick Zschech
Pengcheng Wang
Per Rådberg Nagbøl
Peter Fettke
Philipp Brune
Philipp Mazur
Philipp Zur Heiden
Ralf Laue
Roman Rietsche
Ron Deserranno
Ryan Murphy
Sabine Klein
Samuel Kießling
Sascha Lichtenberg

Scott Thiebes
Sebastian A. Günther
Sebastian Bräuer
Sebastian Hobert
Shane Mcloughlin
Shawn Ogunseye
Stefan Cronholm
Stephan Aier
Sumita Sharma
Susanne Strahringer
Thomas Friedrich
Thomas Schulz
Tiemo Thiess
Till J. Winkler
Tilo Böhmann
Tim Rietz
Tobias Brandt
Tobias Manner-Romberg
Tobias Pauli
Ulrike Lechner
Veda Storey
Verena Wolf
William Baber
Xuanhui Liu
Yomn Elmistikawy
Yunxuan Zhang

Contents

Data Science

Design Principles

Methodology

Platforms and Networks

Service Science

Digital Public Services

Delivering Effective Care Through Mobile Apps: Findings from a Multi-stakeholder Design Science Approach

Monica Chiarini Tremblay[1]([⊠]), Maria Cucciniello[2], Rosanna Tarricone[3], Gregory A. Porumbescu[4], and Kevin C. Desouza[5]

[1] William and Mary, Williamsburg, VA 23185, USA
Monica.tremblay@mason.wm.edu
[2] University of Edinburgh Business School, Edinburgh EH8 9JS, UK
maria.cucciniello@ed.ac.uk
[3] Bocconi University, 20136 Milan, Italy
rosanna.tarricone@unibocconi.it
[4] Rutgers University, Newark, NJ 07102, USA
greg.porumbescu@rutgers.edu
[5] Queensland University of Technology, Brisbane, Australia
kevin.c.desouza@gmail.com

Abstract. In this paper, we use a design science approach to develop a mobile app for lung cancer patients that facilitates their interactions with their clinicians, manages and reports on their health status, and provides them access to medical information/education. This paper contributes to the information systems literature by demonstrating the value of design science research to co-create solutions that advance health care outcomes through technological innovations. The design process engaged a diverse cast of experts and methods, such as a survey of oncologists and cancer patients, a workshop, roundtables and interviews with leading patient and clinician association representatives and focus groups, including two panels each of clinicians and cancer patients. Our approach also develops actionable knowledge that is grounded in evidence from the field, including design guidelines that recapitulate what we learned from the design-testing-redesign cycles of our artefact.

Keywords: Healthcare · m-Health · Cancer care · Value co-creation

1 Introduction

Mrs. Rossi[1] found it difficult to describe how angry, depressed, and betrayed by her own body she felt when she was initially diagnosed with lung cancer almost 3 years ago. These feelings intensified once she began therapy.

---

[1] The quotes are translated from Italian.

© Springer Nature Switzerland AG 2020
S. Hofmann et al. (Eds.): DESRIST 2020, LNCS 12388, pp. 3–14, 2020.
https://doi.org/10.1007/978-3-030-64823-7_1

"When necessary, I would prefer to easily communicate with my clinician because he's the only one who really understands how I feel and explains what I should do or expect. However, I know that he's very busy and takes care of many patients. I am embarrassed to call him whenever I feel like I need to speak to him".

Mrs. Rossi was one of the many participants who we interviewed during this research. Many of the patients we spoke with reflected upon numerous instances in which they wished they could have had closer contact with their physician. Patients noted feeling alone during this long and difficult journey. Given the demands on a physician's time, patients reported that they felt uncomfortable sharing updates on their condition or requesting information because they did not want to be a nuisance. Patients also regularly failed to measure key indicators (e.g., weight and temperature) due to the lack of real-time and personalized reminders between hospital visits (which could be 21–30 days apart). Thus, their ability to manage their care on a regular basis was limited.

The sentiments expressed by the cancer patients we interviewed are not surprising. Research shows that care models that are successful at improving outcomes and reducing costs succeed in enhancing patient and family engagement in self-care and coordinating care and communication among patients and providers [1]. For example, Singh, Drouin [2] conducted a scoping review[2] and found that self-management is essential to caring for high-need, high-cost populations. Furthermore, Hong, Siegel [3] found that successful care management programs 1) consider care coordination to be one of their key roles, 2) focus on building trusting relationships with patients and their primary care providers, 3) match the team composition and interventions to patient needs, 4) offer specialized training for team members, and 5) use technology to bolster their efforts. In general, patient understanding, trust, and clinician-patient agreement affect intermediate outcomes (e.g., increased adherence and better self-care skills) that in turn affect the health and well-being of the patient [4].

Identifying interventions capable of improving self-care and coordination with health care providers for cancer patients is a topic of growing importance in that chronic diseases, such as cancer, are a major reason for increased healthcare spending [5]. Among chronic diseases, cancer is the second leading cause of mortality and was responsible for 8.8 million deaths in 2015. Globally, nearly one in six deaths is due to cancer [6]. We focus on lung cancer, which is the most common cancer worldwide, accounting for 1.8 million new cases and more than 1.6 million deaths per year – more than breast, colon and prostate cancers combined [7].

Our goal was to develop an artifact that would reduce the amount of time a clinician spends gathering routine data from patients at the beginning of each visit and, but also simultaneously provide the clinicians with relevant and accurate information about the patients. We investigate the use of mobile phones, one of the most accessible forms of IT that has served as a platform for significant innovations that have impacted almost all aspects of society. According to the Pew Research Centre's 2017 report, more than three-quarters of American adults (77%) now own a smartphone, but the fastest growing demographic is people over 50, 74% of whom now own a device. In recent years, the

---

[2] For details on the scoping review, please see http://hlwiki.slais.ubc.ca/index.php/Scoping_reviews.

emergence of mobile health apps in health care management has helped to overcome geographical and organizational barriers to improve health care delivery [8]. In 2018, approximately 50% of mobile phone users had at least one mobile health app on their mobile phones [9].

Studies stress the importance of stakeholder input in mHealth application development for them to reach their potential. Unfortunately, many mHealth apps are designed without considering the needs of either patients or clinicians [10]. The literature lacks empirically validated guidelines or process models on how to design apps *with* stakeholders rather than *for* stakeholders [11]. We utilize a design science approach to develop a mobile app for lung cancer patients that facilitates their interaction with their clinicians, manages and reports on their health status, and provides them access to medical information/education. Our approach co-creates the IT artefact in collaboration with cancer patients and clinicians, who are the two important stakeholders. Our four aims are as follows: 1) identify what functionality is to be included in the mHealth app so the app is valuable for healthcare processes (improving patient-clinician relationships and the effectiveness of care delivery); 2) design an mHealth app that is valuable for patients and clinicians and includes them at the center of the design process; 3) test, redesign, and evaluate the validity of the mHealth app; and 4) identify generic design guidelines that can be utilized for the creation of mHealth apps for the management of chronic diseases. After completing the research process defined above, we conducted a reflective examination of our findings and identified emergent themes that we further developed into design guidelines. These design guidelines summarize what we learned from the design-testing-redesign evaluation cycles of our artefact and represent actionable knowledge that is grounded in evidence from the field.

2   Background

mHealth can be particularly important to cancer patients receiving treatments because they experience one or more side effects that can have a profound effect on their quality of life [12] and can also lead to dose delays, dose reductions, reductions in dose density and, in some cases, dose discontinuation. This reduces the effectiveness of chemotherapy and leads to worsening health for the patients [13]. Furthermore, these patients substantially increase the utilization of healthcare resources through increased hospitalization, emergency room visits, and the adoption of palliative treatments and ultimately increase the care-giving burden, which results in increased costs for healthcare systems, patients and care givers.

Mobile monitoring devices could allow patients who experience severe symptoms to measure and record their health conditions and send the data electronically to physicians or specialists without delay, which also empowers patients to increase their self-confidence and self-management [14]. Currently, mHealth solutions are used for limited purposes in cancer care, with a prevailing focus on treatment activities [15]. This underutilization may be due to several factors, including environmental, regulatory, technological, and organizational elements [14] or the distinctive characteristics of the target populations (patients and clinicians). For example, consumers are concerned about the use of their data when using mobile devices for health-related activities, which dilutes the potential to collect real-world data for research and development. Some medical doctors fear that mHealth may jeopardize the patient-physician relationship and increase their workload [16]. Providers are reluctant to adopt mHealth technologies unless these services are adequately reimbursed [17]. Huckvale and Car also noted that apps are normally designed without considering the needs of their users, including both patients and clinicians [10]. In fact, despite the important role physicians play in the success of mHealth initiatives, little empirical research has examined how physicians use mHealth to manage patient health outcomes [18].

3   Design-Test-Re-Design: The Case of LuCApp

We designed, tested, redesigned and evaluated LuCApp, an mHealth app for lung cancer. Our research process is described in Fig. 1.

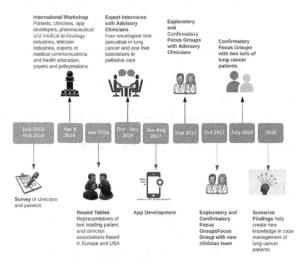

Fig. 1. Research process

We distributed two surveys targeting two populations of mHealth application stakeholders – randomly selected cancer clinicians and patients who use Internet-enabled mobile devices, such as smartphones. The two survey instruments were developed after consulting the literature and previous experiments on mHealth[3]. The results from the survey were shared with several stakeholder groups to solicit input and feedback. An international workshop was organized in Milan on April 8, 2016, to facilitate interactions with more than 100 stakeholders, including patients, clinicians, app developers, the pharmaceutical and medical technology industries, telecom industries, experts in medical communications and health education, payers and policymakers.

The feedback from the workshop was used to develop a set of questions that we posed to an expert roundtable. The roundtable consisted of four participants who represented

---

[3] The study survey is available upon request. Citation blinded for review.

two leading patients' and clinicians' associations based in Europe and the USA. The aim was to gather more specific insights and suggestions about the design and development of a lung cancer app. The discussion was moderated by a member of the research team. The roundtable was recorded and later transcribed for analysis. The moderator utilized probing questions to solicit suggestions from the participants concerning three main themes: 1) information content, 2) interface design, and 3) usability. The roundtable results were in turn used to create an interview script that was utilized to conduct five in-depth interviews with oncologists from different Italian hospitals. The participants included four oncologists that specialized in lung cancer and one clinician that specialized in cancer palliative care[4]. Each interview lasted approximately 60 min, was recorded and was analyzed by two independent coders using content analysis to identify the main themes. The clinicians helped us identify a specific type of cancer patient who could benefit from an mHealth app – patients diagnosed with small or non-small cell lung cancer that were eligible for chemotherapy, immunotherapy or biological therapy and the purpose of our mHealth application:

1) Improve the efficiency of the patient visit with real-time acquisition of critical data that can be useful for the clinician during patient visits. The app helps to collect and synthesize data for use by clinicians during a visit, which saves unnecessary collection time during appointments.
2) Improve the patient's quality of life (QoL) by helping to achieve better management of side effects caused by cancer therapies.
3) Achieve earlier detection of any worsening of the disease by bridging the gap between clinicians and outpatients.
4) Reassure patients by providing them with a means for supporting their continuity of care (which is particularly important for fragile persons).

4 LuCApp Development

The app was developed by an IT firm in collaboration with the team of researchers involved in this study. The preliminary version of the app was built for both the iOS and Android platforms. The lung cancer application was designed and developed to be used in Italy; thus, all of its features and functions are in Italian. Figure 2 shows the main screen of the app. LuCApp also includes automatic alerts, reminders and tips that complement the patient's therapy. The app was developed to comply with EU privacy regulations and the General Data Protection Regulation (GDPR). In addition, the development followed all of the guidelines from the Apple Store Review Guidelines and Android Market Guidelines. There are two versions of the app, one for clinicians and one for patients. After the feasibility assessment, the first prototype was released to the research team for trial and feedback. The overall development effort, which lasted eight months, was performed utilizing DevOps methods [19] to provide the following for all nine releases in parallel: integration with the validated platform, full execution of the full test suite, quality control (according to European regulatory standards), and

---

[4] Palliative care is any treatment that focusses on reducing symptoms, improving quality of life, and supporting patients and their families.

release reliability. By leveraging DevOps approaches, the team of researchers obtained rapid feedback throughout the development, test, and implementation processes, allowing them to evaluate all proposed improvements iteratively. In turn, the research team contributed feedback, thereby accelerating the review process in both the Apple and Android stores.

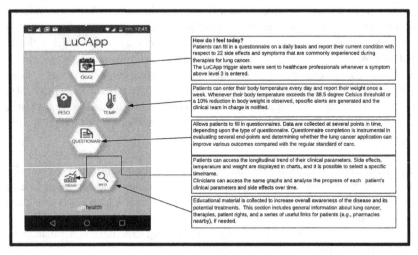

Fig. 2. Screenshot of LuCApp.

5   LuCApp Test and Redesign Using the Exploratory Focus Group

After careful consideration of several possible techniques that would allow us to test, redesign and evaluate [20] our LuCApp, we decided to use focus groups that consist of oncologists and patients [21]. The focus groups allowed us to probe them on key ideas – specifically, on the functionality and usefulness of the app. Furthermore, the interaction between the respondents allows for key insights that normally do not surface with other techniques. Tremblay, Hevner [21] described two types of focus groups: exploratory focus groups (EFGs) for the design and improvement of an artefact and confirmatory focus groups (CFGs) for evaluating the application in the field. We used the EFGs to provide feedback for the improvement of the design of the lung cancer application. In the second phase, no additional changes were made to the lung cancer application, and the CFGs were used to evaluate the app for usability and usefulness.

For the EFGs (as well as for the CFGs), the planning process included creating a carefully planned script. The main topics of both EFGs included understanding i) how using a mobile health app as part of the routine practice of managing cancer patients could affect how clinicians monitor and evaluate patient health outcomes and their decision-making process and ii) how the app could affect patient quality of life and the quality of services offered by healthcare institutions. Before each focus group, the moderators introduced the project, explained the objectives and provided general information about the focus group. Furthermore, possible improvements to the app were agreed upon, which was aimed at refining the app before the final release.

Specifically, sample screenshots were used to gather users' feedback on the overall usability (e.g., layout, font size, and color) and attractiveness of the functions (e.g., content and design). The focus group script was divided into several parts reflecting the main operational implications from a clinician's perspective (the script is in Italian and is available upon request). The focus groups (both the EFGs and the CFGs) were recorded and professionally transcribed. The transcripts were analyzed using computer-assisted qualitative data analysis software (CAQDAS). After the initial coding had highlighted relevant discussion themes, all of the text segments were iteratively analyzed. Themes were added or merged until they effectively represented all of the text segments and captured the essence of the discussion. The coding frame was refined with discussions about areas of disagreement and consensus, and any differences in interpretation were reconciled by the authors (the inter-rater reliabilities were 78% for EFG1, 76% for EFG2).

5.1 Feedback from Clinician Exploratory Focus Groups (EFG1 and EFG2)

The clinicians in both EFGs agreed that LuCApp could improve their ability to evaluate the patient's condition. Most of the focus group participants made similar comments and discussed several instances in which this app would be useful in their daily activities. The clinicians particularly appreciated the possibility of being informed in real time by patients about their symptoms and about the severity of their symptoms; this timeliness would allow them to quickly contact the patients and make suggestions for next steps. Furthermore, clinicians found the "trend" component of the app of major importance. One doctor focused on how the use of the app could change current standards, highlighting that instead of using email and WhatsApp, this approach could be a more systematic, innovative and effective solution. However, one clinician in the second focus group noted that the effectiveness of the solution could depend upon the stage of the disease and the type of cancer; patients often have serious symptoms, and as they become worse, it would be difficult for them to use LuCApp by themselves.

The findings from the clinicians can be summarized in two categories: *functionality* and *usefulness*. In terms of functionality, it was clear that the navigation and structure of the app must be evident for both patients and clinicians. Regarding the usefulness of the app, physicians want the ability to evaluate patient progress and monitor patient symptoms; they felt that they could improve the patient's quality of life if the app provided mechanisms to reassure the patient. It is also important to them that the app integrate all necessary clinical information. Finally, the physicians want the app to give them the ability to continuously evaluate patient progress and monitor patient symptoms.

5.2 Feedback from Patient Exploratory Focus Groups (EFG3)

The patients stated that LuCApp reminded them of a powerful diary that they could fill in every day and share in real time with clinicians. The clinicians could then access the patient's information and be in contact with the patient when necessary. The patients also emphasized the relevance of symptom monitoring. This functionality would provide a mechanism to collect data that could be used to improve therapeutic treatment plans, not only for themselves but also for other patients now and in the future. The patients noted that LuCApp would make them feel safer. By using LuCApp, they would be able to communicate their symptoms in real time in cases when the symptoms were mild, moderate, severe or extreme. This ability is particularly important when patients have mild and moderate symptoms that could be serious but are not usually communicated to the clinician. The participants stated that this reporting could also help advance science; clinicians could learn what mild and moderate symptoms could lead to adverse outcomes.

An important emergent theme is how LuCApp could influence the patient's relationship with caregivers. Stressing the importance of keeping their caregivers in the loop, some participants suggested that it could be useful to create a login and password to LuCApp for them to access important information about the patient's care. This ability would be helpful in reassuring the caregivers, particularly when the it is a spouse or son/daughter. The participants indicated that LuCApp would improve their relationship with the clinicians because the clinicians would be able to access all of the data and information in real time. The participants were aware that the app would not substitute for real contact with the clinicians during regular checks but felt that LuCApp would keep the clinician better informed and updated about what is happening with the patient.

We considered this initial feedback about the app from the patient EFG and particularly what this might mean for our design guidelines. Regarding the *functionality* and *usefulness* of the app, we learned from the patients that: 1) the navigation and structure must be clear; 2) the app must use fonts and colors that are appealing to patients; 3) patient quality of life can be improved if the app provides mechanisms to reassure the patient; and 4) the app must facilitate communication between clinician and patients.

5.3 Redesign of LuCApp

The comments on user needs and preferences and app functionality and usefulness from all three exploratory focus groups were classified using the following themes: content and information (e.g., features, functions and relevant symptoms), navigation and structure, and design and presentation (e.g., use of color, graphics, and amount of text). The considerations for selecting which modifications to apply included the number of participants who mentioned the app, the context of use, overlap/integration with existing information and technical feasibility.

6 LuCApp Evaluation Using Confirmatory Focus Groups

The same panel of clinicians was included in the two clinician EFGs. However, a new panel of patients was involved in CFG3. Like the EFGs, the CFGs were recorded and professionally transcribed (the inter-rater reliabilities were 79% for CFG2 and 77% for CFG3). We applied the same demo approach described for the EFGs; illustrating the revised version of the mobile app based on the comments and suggestions received in the EFGs. The participants were presented with a new list of symptom definitions. The list that was previously presented during the EFGs was revised and simplified using less medical jargon, a suggestion made by the clinicians during the EFGs to make the list less difficult for patients to understand. The clinicians (who had also participated in the EFGs) said the new labels were very clear. Moreover, the patients agreed even though they did not consider this issue to be a major one to be fixed because they considered themselves familiar with medical wording, and the issue was part of a single case; they did not request a specific modification to simplify the wording. The clinicians in EFG2 had suggested the elimination of graphs and trends because they were worried that they would unnecessarily scare the patient (e.g., if they saw that they vomited three times in one week). When we raised the issue to a different panel of clinicians (CFG1), they initially did not understand why the change was necessary, but after explaining the reasons, they eventually agreed that showing patients this type of information was of little use and could have a negative effect on their quality of life.

Conversely, EFG3 (patients) was enthusiastic about the trends section, finding it one of the most useful functions. When we presented this functionality to CFG3 (patients), we asked them to decide whether to keep the trends functionality or to remove it. We explained that the clinicians were worried that this information could scare or stress them. The patients did not agree with the clinicians and were in complete concordance with the patient EFG. They felt that the trend section was one of the most important and relevant features. The research team decided to keep this functionality in the latest version of LuCApp. Based on results from this phase, we conclude that the app was well received by the users.

7 Design Guidelines

We derived three categories of design guidelines based on a reflexive examination of the themes that emerged from the survey, workshop, roundtable, expert interviews and focus groups: *design process, functionality* and *usefulness.*

Our process design guidelines indicate the fundamental role of stakeholders in the development of the app. Our two functionality design guidelines are related to the usability and attractiveness of an mHealth application. Three usefulness design guidelines indicate the functionality necessary in the mHealth application to achieve our goal – better coordination in the management of chronic disease.

Design Process
DG1: *Stakeholder involvement.* Stakeholders must be involved not only in the requirement gathering stage but also throughout the entire iterative design process. Direct and active interaction and cooperation between users and developers of the app enhances the quality, functionality, usability, design and utility. Different stakeholders might perceive information elements differently; thus, including different viewpoints improves the design. The intentional inclusion of difficult-to-serve clients, such as severely ill patients may be the best way to improve the final artifact that will serve all types of customers better. While traditional approaches stress standardization typically from the perspective of the practitioner, our focus group interviews suggest that this orientation may result in designers excluding aspects or features that create the most value.

Functionality of mHealth App
DG2: *Navigation and structure must be clear for both patients and clinicians.* The typical lung cancer patient is elderly and needs an app that is easy to navigate through the

different sections and screens (i.e., scroll systems should be used). Conversely, clinicians do not want to spend too much time searching for information. Ease capturing of information (e.g., dropdown boxes) is important to minimize effort of use.

DG3: Presentation must use fonts and colors that are appealing to patients. The typical lung cancer patient is elderly; thus, the font size and spacing of text should ensure good readability, the text for labels and buttons should be clear and concise, and the colors should provide good readability and good contrast.

Usefulness of mHealth apps

DG4: Ability to evaluate patient progress and monitor patient symptoms. Symptom descriptions should be simple and clear. Symptoms list should be accurate, complete and disease-specific. Functionality should include the ability to monitor and assess side effects caused by cancer therapies.

DG5: Improve patient quality of life by providing mechanisms to reassure the patient. Provide the possibility of sharing patient's symptoms and side effects with clinicians in order to receive rapid feedback about what to do and facilitate earlier detection of worsening disease.

DG6: Integration of all clinical information. Provide the ability to port data directly into other systems and platforms they use.

DG 7: Ease of communication between clinician and patients, including the ability for the clinician to view patient history.

8   Contributions

In this study, we introduce a mixed-methods design process based on a combination of quantitative, qualitative, exploratory and evaluation activities, such as a survey, workshops, interviews, and focus groups. This approach allowed us to obtain nuanced understandings of both the clinicians' and patients' needs and of the challenges and intricacies of chronic disease management of a particularly complex chronic disease, lung cancer. Lung cancer patients tend to be elderly and have a high symptom burden, and the disease has both difficult and painful physiological and major psychological effects.

As a team, we reflected that without following the design-test-redesign design science approach highlighted in the paper, *we likely would have developed a completely different app.* The direct and active interaction and cooperation between the users and developers of the app enhanced its quality, functionality, usability, design and utility, as was emphasized during the interviews and the focus groups we conducted with the clinicians. The overall process of our research highlighted how a design science approach can be used to build useful mHealth applications using approaches that bolster user acceptance. We proposed a series of design guidelines that highlight the overall implications and contributions of this work. Our guidelines (or technological rules) were built as a reflective cycle [22]. We chose the case management of a chronic disease, specifically, cancer. Our design guidelines were a result of the research team reflecting on our journey and can be categorized as design knowledge that can be tested and refined in subsequent cases in other chronic disease management contexts and/or be directly used by practitioners [22].

We observed the transformative capacity of an IT intervention, LuCApp, on severely ill lung cancer patients. The information gleaned from focus group interviews allowed us to take a step toward opening up the black box of efficacious treatment for severely ill cancer patients. From the patient focus groups we learned how accounting for the perspective of extreme customers in the technology design phase may could enable designing an mHealth app that serve all types of customers better. Often the most vulnerable consumers are the least involved, which exacerbates the inequalities of care [23]. In our study, we focused on extreme cases of customers – lung cancer patients, many of whom were in their final stages of life – and found that these individuals were optimistic about the potential impacts of the mHealth app we designed with their input.

We acknowledge that in a perfect world, we would have had the opportunity to test the app live and collect feedback from a large number of users. However, we must reconcile this ideal with the realities of the world in which we live. The developed app was tested in a smaller group due to resource constraints. In addition, we believe that although the collected feedback might not be representative of every opinion of a potential user, is rich and informative. Another limitation of our study is that it was solely conducted in one country, Italy, which might hinder the generalizability of our results. Cultural beliefs and values might influence the opinions of both health professionals and patients. Therefore, further research is needed to investigate the validity of our work across different jurisdictions.

References

1. McCarthy, D., Ryan, J., Klein, S.: Models of care for high-need, high-cost patients: an evidence synthesis. Issue Brief (Commonwealth Fund) **31**, 1–19 (2015)
2. Singh, K., et al.: Patient-facing mobile apps to treat high-need, high-cost populations: a scoping review. JMIR mHealth uHealth **4**(4) (2016)
3. Hong, C.S., Siegel, A.L., Ferris, T.G.: Caring for high-need, high-cost patients: what makes for a successful care management program. Issue Brief (Commonwealth Fund) **19**(9), 1–19 (2014)
4. Street Jr., R.L., et al.: How does communication heal? Pathways linking clinician–patient communication to health outcomes. Patient Educ. Couns. **74**(3), 295–301 (2009)
5. Martin, A.B., et al.: Growth in US health spending remained slow in 2010; health share of gross domestic product was unchanged from 2009. Health Aff. **31**(1), 208–219 (2012)
6. Word Health Organization. Cancer (2018). http://www.who.int/news-room/fact-sheets/detail/cancer
7. American Cancer Society. American Institute for Cancer Research. American Institute for Cancer Research 2017. https://www.cancer.org/content/cancer/en/cancer/lung-cancer/about/key-statistics.html
8. Silva, B.M., et al.: Mobile-health: a review of current state in 2015. J. Biomed. Inform. **56**, 265–272 (2015)
9. Fox, S., Duggan, M.: Mobile Health 2012, in Internet and Technology. Pew Research Center (2012)
10. Huckvale, K., Car, J.: Implementation of mobile health tools. JAMA **311**(14), 1447–1448 (2014)
11. Labrique, A.B., et al.: mHealth innovations as health system strengthening tools: 12 common applications and a visual framework. Global Health: Sci. Pract. **1**(2), 160–171 (2013)

12. Sommariva, S., Pongiglione, B., Tarricone, R.: Impact of chemotherapy-induced nausea and vomiting on health-related quality of life and resource utilization: a systematic review. Crit. Rev. Oncol./Hematol. **99**, 13–36 (2016)
13. Tarricone, R., et al.: A systematic literature review of the economic implications of chemotherapy-induced diarrhea and its impact on quality of life. Crit. Rev. Oncol./Hematol. **99**, 37–48 (2016)
14. Nasi, G., Cucciniello, M., Guerrazzi, C.: The role of mobile technologies in health care processes: the case of cancer supportive care. J. Med. Internet Res. **17**(2) (2015)
15. Mooney, K.H., et al.: Telephone-linked care for cancer symptom monitoring. Cancer Pract. **10**(3), 147–154 (2002)
16. Steinhubl, S.R., Muse, E.D., Topol, E.J.: Can mobile health technologies transform health care? JAMA **310**(22), 2395–2396 (2013)
17. Schmeida, M., McNeal, R.: State policy action on Medicaid telemedicine reimbursement laws. Health Policy Technol. **5**(1), 32–39 (2016)
18. Illiger, K., et al.: Mobile technologies: expectancy, usage, and acceptance of clinical staff and patients at a university medical center. JMIR mHealth uHealth **2**(4) (2014)
19. Forsgren, N., Tremblay, M.C., VanderMeer, D., Humble, J.: DORA platform: DevOps assessment and benchmarking. In: Maedche, A., vom Brocke, J., Hevner, A. (eds.) DESRIST 2017. LNCS, vol. 10243, pp. 436–440. Springer, Cham (2017). https://doi.org/10.1007/978-3-319-59144-5_27

Design of a Machine Learning System for Prediction of Chronic Wound Management Decisions

Haadi Mombini[1]([✉]), Bengisu Tulu[1], Diane Strong[1], Emmanuel Agu[1], Holly Nguyen[1], Clifford Lindsay[2], Lorraine Loretz[3], Peder Pedersen[1], and Raymond Dunn[3]

[1] Worcester Polytechnic Institute, Worcester, MA, USA
{hmombini,bengisu,dstrong,emmanuel,hanguyen,pedersen}@wpi.edu
[2] UMass Medical School, Worcester, MA, USA
clifford.lindsaycbrad@umassmed.edu
[3] UMass Memorial, Worcester, MA, USA
{lorraine.loretz,raymond.dunn}@umassmemorial.org

Abstract. Chronic wounds affect 6.5 million Americans, are complex conditions to manage and cost \$28–\$32 billion annually. Although digital solutions exist for non-expert clinicians to accurately segment tissues, analyze affected tissues or efficiently document their wound assessment results, there exists a lack of decision support for non-expert clinicians who usually provide most wound assessments and care decisions at the point of care (POC). We designed a machine learning (ML) system that can accurately predict wound care decisions based on labeled wound image data. The care decisions we predict are based on guidelines for standard wound care and are labeled as: continue the treatment, request a change in treatment, or refer patient to a specialist. In this paper, we demonstrate how our final ML solution using XGboost (XGB) algorithm achieved on average an overall performance of F-1 $= .782$ using labels given by an expert and a novice decision maker. The key contribution of our research lies in the ability of the ML artifact to use only those wound features (predictors) that require less expertise for novice users when examining wounds to make standard of care decisions (predictions).

Keywords: Point-of-care decision · Machine learning · Design science · Chronic wounds · Non-expert clinicians

1 Introduction

Chronic wounds (also known as chronic ulcers) affect 6.5 million Americans [1], are complex conditions to manage [2], and cost \$28–\$32 billion annually [3]. Yet, the majority of patients with chronic wounds do not have access to evidence-based wound care services or certified wound clinicians [4]. As a result most wound assessments and care decisions are provided by non-expert clinicians (with no wound specialization training) who have limited chronic wound treatment expertise [5]. This lack of expertise results in uncertainty during wound care decision-making causing inaccurate treatments. If

© Springer Nature Switzerland AG 2020
S. Hofmann et al. (Eds.): DESRIST 2020, LNCS 12388, pp. 15–27, 2020.
https://doi.org/10.1007/978-3-030-64823-7_2

inaccurately diagnosed or inappropriately treated [6], wound healing may be delayed resulting in amputations [7], limited quality of life and even death [8]. Thus, patients must receive appropriate wound care to maintain normal healing process [9]. Although narrative wound care guidelines exist to support these clinicians [10–12], non-adherence to these guidelines is reported recurrently [13]. There is the burden of finding the right procedure for the right patients on the user of these guidelines. This burden becomes even heavier with having to cope with narrative descriptions that may not align with their current expertise and knowledge. However, there exist opportunities for using ML to support POC wound care decisions which is the focus of current paper.

In this paper we demonstrate the design and development of a ML solution that is envisioned for a smartphone clinical decision support system (CDSS) app. The envisioned CDSS app will take advantage of this ML solution that can predict decisions only by taking raw wound images using phone camera. These decisions are generalizable to contexts where both experts and novices make wound care decisions.

2 Background: Challenges and Opportunities for Chronic Wound Management

2.1 Accurate Diagnosis and Treatment

Chronic wounds are characterized as diabetic foot ulcers (DFUs), pressure ulcers (PUs), venous ulcers (VUs), and arterial ulcers (AUs) and surgical wounds. Each wound type has different assessment and management procedures. Despite the abundance of published chronic wound management studies (e.g., clinical trials and decision guidelines) on how to treat these wounds, non-expert clinicians delivering wound care still have major clinical uncertainties as to which decision to make when it comes to a particular wound [14]. This often leads to undesirable wound care outcomes [15], patients being harmed [16] and waste of healthcare resources [17]. Hence research is required to develop alternative decision support tools, such as digital wound care support using ML solutions, that enhance wound healing [18] and reduce costs [19].

2.2 Consistent and Collaborative Decision-Making

Wound care is known to lack standardization within and across institutions and among specialists [20]. Although models of collaborative reorganization and integrated care have been proposed [20], there still is a great need for more highly trained providers in the wound care community (registered and visiting nurses, wound practitioners and experts, vascular, podiatric and plastic surgeons). In the wound care community non-expert clinicians deliver most of the wound care, e.g. changing wound dressings and collecting wound measurements. Their assessment often requires judgment and decision-making in complex, challenging and uncertain circumstances [21]. Such a complexity in a dynamic wound care context [22] creates uncertainty for these non-expert clinician decision makers [23]. Uncertainty can also derive from lack of relevant wound care knowledge and expertise [22]. To help non-expert clinicians there should be alternative solutions such as digital support tools that simulate standard wound care guidelines for more consistent decision-making [24].

Non-expert clinicians may draw on their intuition to guide their judgments and decision-making by association with experience and expertise [22] which then increase their uncertainty. Hence, the digital support tool must use a generalizable solution based on standard wound care that is applicable to contexts where both expert and non-expert clinicians treat patients. Avoidance of inconsistent decision making across the wound care community will promote high-quality wound care and protect chronic wound patients.

2.3 ML Practices for Chronic Wound Management

Several ML studies have attempted to provide digital chronic wound care support for non-expert clinicians. For example, one study [25] proposed a telemedicine tissue segmentation (granulation, necrotic, slough) using linear discriminant analysis (LDA) to assist the clinicians to make better chronic wounds diagnostic decisions. Their model was trained on 60 digital images and used wound tissues in color images of both pressure and diabetic ulcers. When evaluated on ground truth images labeled by experts, the model could classify the tissue types with overall accuracy of 91.45%. Another study [26] used information collected during routine care in outpatient wound care centers and developed a digital predictive ML model for delayed wound healing. A total of 180,696 patient wounds were collected at 68 outpatient centers. The data from first and second wound assessments was used to construct predictors of delayed wound healing. The model achieved an area under the curve (AUC) of 0.842 for the delayed healing outcome. For wound assessment and efficient documentation, we found one recent study [27] that developed a smart-glass based POC solution using DSR methodology. Although their study demonstrated through user experiment a unique approach for efficient wound documentation, it did not utilize ML prediction to support non-expert decision making.

2.4 Uniqueness of the Current Study

Our study aims to design a ML solution artifact that can predict wound care decisions based on labeled wound image data. We use visual and descriptive features from the image as predictors and care decisions as target labels. The decisions we predict are based on standard wound care guidelines and are labeled as: continue with the current treatment (D1), request non-urgent change in treatment from a wound specialist (D2), or refer patient to a wound specialist (D3). Our ML solution artifact is unique in several ways: (a) It predicts care decisions for all main types of chronic wounds (DFUs, Pus, VUs, AUs and surgical), (b) It is trained and tested on a diverse collection of labeled image datasets (local hospital collection and publicly available web collection), (c) It has a knowledge base of predictors that are extracted from a collection of wound care guidelines, and (c) It uses a decision pathway that mitigates inconsistent decision labels for the training image datasets that lack information about current treatments for each image.

2.5 Use Scenario Addressed by the Artifact

The design process is inspired by the scenario where a wound non-expert clinician, who treats patients for various conditions within a clinical or non-clinical setting, encounters a patient with a lower extremity (LE) chronic wound. If this is a new undocumented LE chronic wound with no current treatment plan, this non-expert clinician will refer the patient to a wound specialist for initial treatments and timely plan of care (2-week/4-week follow-ups). Due to the patient's immobility, transportation time and costs, and lack of access to wound care clinics, regularly visiting a wound expert clinic becomes challenging. As a result, these patients will continue receiving their routine wound care (according to their current treatment prescribed by the wound specialist) through local non-expert clinicians. This routine wound care includes dressing changes, contacting the expert for type of dressing and replacement products (if any changes), reassessing and documenting the wound measurements (depths, height and width), controlling infections using antibiotics and providing non-sharp debridement.

The non-expert clinician must be able to identify healing wounds from those that require non-urgent change of current treatment and most importantly wounds that must be urgently referred to the wound specialist for surgical closure, debridement or surgical referral. The quality of these decisions will determine the progress of patient's wound and wound care outcomes. To address this use scenario, we ask the following design questions: *How can we design a ML system artifact that can accurately predict standard of care decisions for LE chronic wounds? Can this ML system artifact produce consistent decisions using labels given by expert and novice decision makers?*

3   Research Methodology and Design Process

When adherence to clinical guidelines is ignored, the treatment procedures clinicians (wound experts and non-experts) follow may differ considerably. This results in inconsistent decision-making across the chronic wound care community (i.e., some clinicians may be aggressive about debriding the wound, while others may be less concerned about regular debridement). A ML system that can provide generalizable decisions that follow the standard of care can address this issue. To do so, we defined the following design requirements (DR) for our ML artifact that predicts sensitive chronic wound management decisions: *DR* (1): The knowledge base for ML system artifact to predict wound care decisions should include the common features recommended by standard wound care practices. *DR* (2): The ML system artifact design should include procedures that ensure the accuracy and consistency of expert and non-experts' decisions when treating chronic wound patients. The process for designing the ML system artifact was followed by the design science methodology [28] and went through two phases and two design cycles as described below.

4   Design Phase One- Developing Standard of Care Knowledge Artifact for Wound Care

4.1   Cycle 1: Understand the Domain, Develop and Evaluate Knowledge Base

We began by developing the wound care knowledge base using requirements that we identified through (1) literature and (2) expert interviews as described below.

Literature. We collected information about visual characteristics of all the chronic wounds from published articles and Wound Union Wound Healing Society clinical guideline [29]. The main inclusion criteria for both published articles and guidelines were wound types and their diagnostic features (wound shape, etiology, tissue colors, etc.). Features were extracted for each wound and stored in spreadsheets. These features were then compared to each other by their visual and non-visual (patient history data, smell, warmth, etc.) characteristics. We also compared their terminologies since some guidelines used different names for similar wound features. This step was necessary to build an accurate wound feature table and then to classify wound features by their common terminologies. We reviewed and compared several wound assessment tools (Braden scale [30], Pressure Ulcer Scale for Healing (PUSH) [31], Wound, Ischemia and Foot Infection (WIfI) [32] and Photographic Wound Assessment Tool (PWAT) [33]) to find the one that uses more accurate yet visual features for our wound feature table. We selected PWAT, a validated visual wound assessment tool, as it was the only wound assessment tool designed to work with wound photos. The other tools in the literature were designed for bedside assessment and require inputs beyond what can be gleaned from an image including infection status and blood flow of the wound. PWAT has eight sub-scores each of which receives a score from 0 to 4 (0 represents conditions observed in a healing wound and 4 represents conditions observed in wounds that are not healing or degrading). The total score of the PWAT adds up to 32 which represents a wound in a very severe condition [33].

Wound expert interviews. Before the interviews, we selectively resampled two sets of wound images from two sources for which we had IRB approval. One set had 29 images (with high, middle and low PWAT scores) from chronic wound image repository of a local hospital. The second set had 6 images with doctors' notes and decisions from our ongoing data collection at a local hospital.

We conducted two rounds of semi-structured interviews with a dually credentialed podiatric surgeon/vascular nurse practitioner and a plastic surgeon from an academic medical center in the northeast (4 total interviews). Each interview took 1–2 h and was video recorded and transcribed.

At the beginning of each interview, wound experts were given clear explanations about the goals of the project. We asked our experts what a standard assessment tool would ideally include, how they assess a wound visually, and what suggestions they have for project improvement. We also requested our experts to visually assess only 15 images from set one (experts annotated all 29 images with decision labels) and give additional expert information. In the second round of interviews, we used the same wound images but asked both experts to visually assess and explain their assessment procedure for wound depths, underlying tissues and other clinical characteristics in detail. Transcriptions and videos were analyzed by one of the authors, and new findings were added to the wound feature table.

Developing decision rules. The review of literature, analysis of clinical guidelines and expert interviews helped us identify critical wound features required for assessing a chronic wound. These features were used to design IF-THEN rules that capture chronic wound conditions based on location and visual descriptors [34]. These rules were tested using a decision table to solve for overlapping rules.

Evaluation of the decision rules. We tested our decision rules on 14 remaining images in the set one annotated by the two wound experts (see Fig. 1 for an example of wound image). The goal was to check each of the assessment rules to see how visual features are presented and verify them when necessary. Out of 14 total instances, decision rules could not accurately assess two wound types (Diabetic and Venous ulcer) due to imprecise location and history features (85.7% accuracy). Each corresponding rule and the experts' descriptions for the wound images were analyzed and location information and patient history data were added based on guidelines. Modifications and changes were made to the rest of the rules to enhance the location rule.

4.2 Cycle 2- Rethinking the Domain Knowledge

In the second cycle we revisited the wound knowledge base and added extra features from a total of 14 guidelines to make the decision rules more comprehensive. The total predictive features from our wound feature table were raised to sixty-one visual and non-visual features. We used a decision table to find the best matching rules with no overlap (see Fig. 1 for example of a decision rule). This resulted in thirty-nine decision rules. These rules were validated further using 4 new wound images and their corresponding clinicians' notes extracted from the wound clinic EHR (clinicians' notes contained decision labels). When compared with the notes presented in patients' medical records, the rules provided consistent and detailed explanations regarding wound locations and wound tissues. We also found that VU rules required to have thin and thick slough descriptors for more accurate assessment. The revisions were made, and comprehensives of the rules were finally assured.

IF *C1* AND *C2* AND *C3* THEN *D3*

Fig. 1. Example of chronic wound image labeled using rules from decision table

5   Design Phase Two- ML System Artifact

5.1   Cycle 1- Designing ML System Artifact

Requirements. In the second phase as summarized in Table 1, we began the actual process of the ML artifact design using the following requirements:

Databank: A total of 2056 unlabeled wound images. There are 1695 images from a local wound clinic, 249 from publicly available web sources and 114 from previous study. Decision labels (predictions): D1 with 51 labels from expert and 25 labels from novice, D2 with 57 expert labels and 245 novice labels and D3 with 97 expert labels and 135 novice labels. *Labeling procedure*: The experts labeled the image data using their own expertise during a 3-h session which was video recorded. The novice researcher used the decision rules and labeled the 205 images with 61 features and decision labels separately (video recording was not necessary). *Included features*: We used 9 PWAT features (eight sub-scores and the total PWAT score), wound locations, and five wound types. These together resulted in 64 one-hot encoded features. Evaluation metrics: F-1 scores (weighted as suggested for the imbalance classification problems) and area under the receiver operating characteristics (AUC). We also applied SMOTE oversampling with 3 iterations of 10-fold cross validation. *Sample*: A total of 205 images were randomly selected and labeled with D1, D2, or D3.

Table 1. Phase two of DSR: designing ML system artifact

Relevance	A ML artifact can support non-expert clinicians with chronic wound management decisions at the point of care
Define objective	Instantiate ML artifact and demonstrate its use for non-experts
Design & develop	Trained ML artifact on 205 image samples with labels that have acceptable agreement level between expert and novice
Artifact	ML system capable of predicting wound decisions where all features are present
Evaluate & observe	Inaccurate decision labels from expert-novice inconsistency ML should be built based on the features expected to be available at the time of prediction and common to non-experts
Create knowledge	Not all expected features are available at the time of prediction
Current knowledge	Wound cleaning (debridement) is recommended for all wounds and must be included in assessment

ML Design. We experimented with most common ML algorithms that were used by several studies with promising results. These are decisions trees (DT), random forest (RF), support vector machine classifier (SVM) and XGB.

Evaluate and observe. The results from testing different ML algorithms showed above average performance for the main ML model (XGB) with overall F-1 = .806 when

Table 2. ML artifact prediction results - multiclass (Cycle 1)

Classifier	Expert		Novice	
	F-1	AUC	F-1	AUC
DT	.530	.777	.747	.817
RF	.556	.760	.756	.800
SVM	**.587**	.814	.782	**.876**
XGB	.543	**.844**	**.806**	.862

trained using novice data (given features and labels). When trained on expert data, the performance dropped to F-1 = .543. Table 2 depicts performance results for this initial set up of the ML artifact (XGB), recommended for fast deployment [35]).

To solve for the inconsistency, we calculated the agreement level between novice and expert (agreed on 144 images and disagreed on 61 images) and realized that lack of clear labeling procedure resulted in inconsistent decision-making between them and this may have caused 30% of the disagreement cases. We also analyzed the videos from the labeling sessions and realized there were two issues with our prior labeling procedure: First, there were times that the expert was inconsistent about giving two decision labels (D1 and D2) while referring to non-urgent and urgent cases. Second, the expert seemed troubled labeling some images due to lack of information about the current treatment the wound images were under. For example, for a wound located on the plantar foot, the expert was recommending both D1 ("I assume it is already in a cast to offload pressure") and D2 ("this wound needs to be offloaded"). This is a common issue with most medical image datasets especially for chronic wound management where no pre-existing image database is available for routine image collection from the provider.

5.2 Cycle 2- Refining ML Artifact Design

Requirements. In the second phase (Table 3), we reassessed and revised our protocol and added new assumptions that solve for current treatment ambiguities. We also resampled more images from our image databank and conducted and video recorded a new labeling session with the same expert. In that session, we used our new protocol and asked the expert to proceed with labeling based on the followings: (a) This is the first visit by the non-expert, (b) Non-expert clinician's expertise does not include sharp debridement (c) The current wound (image) was debrided/required no debridement when the patient was sent home from the wound clinic, (d) Patient's transportation to the wound clinic is costly, and (e) The patient has a current treatment plan based on the standard of care (control infection, perform daily dressing changes, offload, and VAC).

Table 3. Phase two of DSR: refining the ML artifact

Relevance	A strong ML system capable of predicting wound decisions with average high accuracy from both expert and novice labels
Define objective	Solve for inconsistent decision labels by expert and novice
Design & develop	Instantiate the generalizable ML artifact with less predictors
Artifact	XGB classifier
Evaluate & observe	Reevaluate using performance metrics to demonstrate overall capability of the ML artifact
Create knowledge	A highly accurate ML artifact can be developed based on most common factors of the wound healing as predictors
Use of the current knowledge	This ML artifact can be integrated into a smartphone App with the ability to solve for current treatment ambiguity

We also updated the wound knowledge base with new wound features from a recent guideline [29]. These features were recommended for wounds that can benefit from regular debridement and were based on appearance of wound bed, wound edge and surrounding skin. Using these new features and new knowledge gained from the cycle 1, we designed a decision pathway (see Fig. 2) to be used for next round of labeling.

Sampled Dataset: A total of random 375 images (338 training and 37 testing samples) were selected based on new criteria that matched current protocol and PWAT criteria. The images were labeled using new protocol and decision pathway shown in Fig. 2. Labeling procedure: The expert and novice used the new decision protocol and pathway to label 375 images. The expert was informed of our novel approach that solve for D1 and D2 ambiguities for POC due to lack of information about the current treatment (i.e. D1 and D2 as single decision under non-urgent class and D3 under urgent class).

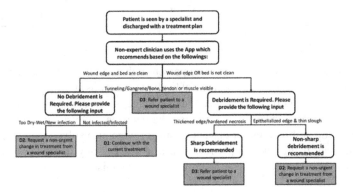

Fig. 2. The designed decision pathway used for wound assessment

The expert had this knowledge while labeling the images. There were 189 non-urgent and 186 urgent labels given by the expert and 152 non-urgent and 223 urgent labels given by the novice. The agreement between the novice and expert (Table 4) increased to nearly 85% (with 83% for 74 overlapping images with prior set). *Included features*: We used total PWAT, wound locations, gangrene, slough, hardened necrosis, thickened rolled edge, epithelialization, undermining and tunneling as predictors.

ML design and evaluation. We also analyzed how the algorithms perform comparing to a dummy classifier (DC) which relies on random predictions.

In the actual labeling session (which took about 2.5 h), wound expert had no trouble following new structured protocol and decision pathway and labeled all 375 images. We then asked the expert to label six new randomly sampled images from our ongoing image data collection from a local wound clinic (not previously known to/seen by the expert or novice) to evaluate the consistency of our new protocol and the decision pathway. After labeling these 6 new images, we revealed to our expert the clinicians' notes and actual decisions associated with those wounds seen in the clinic. The expert was in total agreement with the clinician's decisions. These 6 images were chosen to see whether "the decision pathway" is accurate and captures enough information required to make an informed decision.

Table 4. ML artifact prediction results- multiclass (Cycle 2)

Agreement when requesting for current treatment input			Expert		Novice		Both Avg.	
			F-1	AUC	F-1	AUC	F-1	AUC
		DC	.311	.500	.340	.500	.325	.500
		DT	.633	**.875**	**.926**	.976	.779	**.925**
Agreed	318	RF	.587	.799	.906	.929	.746	.864
Disagreed	57	SVC	.632	.812	.858	.975	.745	.893
Agreement	84.8%	XGB	**.641**	.791	.923	**.976**	**.782**	.883
The difference between expert and novice models for D1 and D2 before requesting for current treatment input is depicted							XGB Confusion Matrix	

When asked, the expert noted that the percent reduction in wound surface area has been demonstrated to be a strong predictor of healing for venous and diabetic foot wounds [36, 37]. Consideration of percent area surface reduction in comparing wound image sequences would be of value in determining the decision pathway, using the existing assumptions. The ambiguities for current treatment were also solved using our current decision pathway using one simple rule that ask whether any current treatment was already given. This simple input at the point of care can raise the confidence of the ML system's predictions.

6 Conclusion

This study demonstrated, through DSR, the development of a ML artifact that can predict wound care decisions generalizable to contexts where both novice and expert clinicians may be facing. Results of the artifact evaluation demonstrated the acceptable prediction performance of the ML artifact that uses XGB model with average F-1 = .782 for both novice and expert decision makers. All the algorithms performed better than the dummy classifier that uses random predictions. These results also demonstrate that this prediction capability for XGB ML artifact can be achieved using image data (common wound features as predictors and decisions as labels) that are given by either novice or expert. The most predictive features are *thick slough or hardened necrosis, thickened rolled edge, total PWAT, thin slough, anterior leg and dorsal toe*, respectively which confirm the usability of our designed decision pathway.

Comparing to the current wound care solutions that require experts to make treatment decisions [25–27], our ML solution provides POC decision support using wound features that non-expert clinicians commonly report when documenting wounds. Non-expert clinicians provide most of the wound care within the wound care community and their ability to determine wound conditions at the appropriate time directly affect the quality of treatment these patients receive. Although current solutions provide tools to efficiently document these common wound features, non-experts' inabilities to determine the correct decision pathway (when certain features are present) at different stages of chronic wound development results in delayed and thus more aggressive treatments (often surgical amputations) that cost a lot for the patients and their families.

7 Limitation and Future Research

This study has some limitations. First, our sample size of 375 wound images with no clinical notes (decisions and measurements) may not be enough to demonstrate generalizability of the ML artifact due to the wound care domain that has limited available image datasets with associated clinical notes. In this challenging environment, we showed several demonstrations prior and post development of a high performing ML artifact through iterative design cycles. Future research can address this by adding into the ML artifact database the wound surface area measurements and comparison with subsequent images to calculate the percent change. Moreover, user adoption and effective delivery of the predictions from our ML artifact to the final user provide rich opportunities for future research. Second, in current study a non-expert clinician was considered a novice researcher. Although this may be another threat to generalizability (when ML artifact is used by real-world users), we expect their agreement level with experts to be higher thereby allowing for higher ML performance. The next phase focuses on the design and evaluation of a smartphone App using image processing techniques that allow for automatic feature extraction of our predictors.

References

1. Fife, C.E., et al.: Wound care outcomes and associated cost among patients treated in US outpatient wound centers: data from the US wound registry. Wounds 24(1), 10 (2012)
2. Han, G., Ceilley, R.: Chronic wound healing: a review of current management and Treatments. Adv. Ther. 34(3), 599–610 (2017). https://doi.org/10.1007/s12325-017-0478-y
3. Nussbaum, S.R., et al.: An economic evaluation of the impact, cost, and medicare policy implications of chronic nonhealing wounds. Value Health 21(1), 27–32 (2018)
4. Benskin, L.: A review of the literature informing affordable, available wound management choices for rural areas of tropical developing countries. Ostomy/Wound Manage. 59(10), 20–41 (2013)
5. McIntosh, C., Ousey, K.: A survey of nurses' and podiatrists' attitudes, skills and knowledge of lower extremity wound care. Wounds UK 4(1) (2008)
6. Wu, S.C., Marston, W., Armstrong, D.G.: Wound care: the role of advanced wound healing technologies. J. Vasc. Surg. 52(3 Suppl), 59S–66S (2010)
7. Jeffcoate, W.J., van Houtum, W.H.: Amputation as a marker of the quality of foot care in diabetes. Diabetologia 47(12), 2051–2058 (2004)
8. Järbrink, K., et al.: The humanistic and economic burden of chronic wounds: a protocol for a systematic review. Syst. Rev. 6(1), 15 (2017)
9. Frykberg, R.G., Banks, J.: Challenges in the Treatment of Chronic Wounds. Adv. Wound Care (New Rochelle) 4(9), 560–582 (2015)
10. Kottner, J., et al.: Prevention and treatment of pressure ulcers/injuries: the protocol for the second update of the international Clinical Practice Guideline 2019. J. Tissue Viability 28(2), 51–58 (2019)

11. Franks, P.J., et al.: Management of patients with venous leg ulcers: challenges and current best practice. J. Wound Care **25**(Sup6), S1–S67 (2016)
12. Hingorani, A., et al.: The management of diabetic foot: a clinical practice guideline by the Society for Vascular Surgery in collaboration with the American Podiatric Medical Association and the Society for Vascular Medicine. J. Vasc. Surg. **63**(2), 3S–21S (2016)
13. Beeckman, D., et al.: A multi-faceted tailored strategy to implement an electronic clinical decision support system for pressure ulcer prevention in nursing homes: a two-armed randomized controlled trial. Int. J. Nurs. Stud. **50**(4), 475–486 (2013)
14. Christie, J., et al.: Do systematic reviews address community healthcare professionals' wound care uncertainties? Results from evidence mapping in wound care. PLoS ONE **13**(1), e0190045 (2018)
15. Thompson, C., Dowding, D.: Responding to uncertainty in nursing practice. Int. J. Nurs. Stud. **38**(5), 609–615 (2001)
16. Balsa, A.I., et al.: Clinical uncertainty and healthcare disparities. Am. JL Med. **29**, 203 (2003)
17. French, B.: Uncertainty and information need in nursing. Nurse Educ. Today **26**(3), 245–252 (2006)
18. Agu, E., et al.: The smartphone as a medical device: Assessing enablers, benefits and challenges. In: 2013 IEEE International Workshop of Internet-of-Things Networking and Control (IoT-NC). IEEE (2013)
19. Nasi, G., Cucciniello, M., Guerrazzi, C.: The role of mobile technologies in health care processes: the case of cancer supportive care. J. Med. Internet Res. **17**(2), e26 (2015)
20. Couch, K.S.: The Expanding Role of the Nurse & the NP in Chronic Wound Care
21. Logan, G.J.B.j.o.c.n.: Clinical judgment and decision-making in wound assessment and management: is experience enough? Br. J. Community Nurs. **20**(Sup3), S21–S28 (2015)
22. Gillespie, B.M., et al.: Health professionals' decision-making in wound management: a grounded theory. J. Adv. Nurs. **71**(6), 1238–1248 (2015)
23. Hedberg, B., Larsson, U.S.: Environmental elements affecting the decision-making process in nursing practice. J. Clin. Nurs. **13**(3), 316–324 (2004)
24. Jung, Hoill., Yang, JungGi., Woo, Ji-In., Lee, Byung-Mun., Ouyang, Jinsong., Chung, Kyungyong, Lee, YoungHo: Evolutionary rule decision using similarity based associative chronic disease patients. Cluster Comput. **18**(1), 279–291 (2014). https://doi.org/10.1007/s10586-014-0376-x
25. Chakraborty, C., et al.: Telemedicine supported chronic wound tissue prediction using classification approaches. J. Med. Syst. **40**(3), 68 (2016)
26. Jung, K., et al.: Rapid identification of slow healing wounds. Wound Repair Regener. **24**(1), 181–188 (2016)
27. Klinker, K., Wiesche, M., Krcmar, H.: Conceptualizing passive trust: the case of smart glasses in healthcare. in European Conference on Information Systems (2019)
28. Peffers, K., et al.: A design science research methodology for information systems research. J. Manage. Inform. Syst. **24**(3), 45–77 (2007)
29. (WUWHS), W.U.o.W.H.S.: Advances in Wound Care: The Triangle of Wound Assessment. Florence Congress: Wounds International (2016)
30. Bates-Jensen, B.M., Vredevoe, D.L., Brecht, M.-L.J.D.: Validity and reliability of the pressure sore status tool. Decubitus **5**(6), 20–28 (1992)
31. The National Pressure Ulcer Advisory Panel: Prevention and Treatment of Pressure Ulcers: Clinical Practice Guideline (2019). http://www.npuap.org/resources/educational-and-clinical-resources/prevention-and-treatment-of-pressure-ulcers-clinical-practice-guideline/
32. Mills, J.L., Sr., et al.: The Society for Vascular Surgery Lower Extremity Threatened Limb Classification System: risk stratification based on wound, ischemia, and foot infection (WIfI). J. Vasc. Surg. **59**(1), 220–34 e1-2 (2014)

33. Thompson, N., et al.: Reliability and validity of the revised photographic wound assessment tool on digital images taken of various types of chronic wounds. Adv. Skin Wound Care **26**(8), 360–373 (2013)
34. Mombini, H., et al.: Design of a rule-based decision model for assessment of chronic wounds. In: Online Proceedings of 14th International Conference on Design Science Research in Information Systems and Technology (2019)
35. Chen, T., Guestrin, C.: Xgboost: A scalable tree boosting system. In: Proceedings of the 22nd ACM SIGKDD International Conference on Knowledge Discovery and Data Mining (2016)
36. Sheehan, P., et al.: Percent change in wound area of diabetic foot ulcers over a 4-week period is a robust predictor of complete healing in a 12-week prospective trial. Diabetes Care **26**(6), 1879–1882 (2003)
37. Cardinal, M., et al.: Early healing rates and wound area measurements are reliable predictors of later complete wound closure. Wound Repair Regener. **16**(1), 19–22 (2008)

Designing a Real-Time Integrated First Responder Health and Environmental Monitoring Dashboard

Ann Fruhling[1]([✉]), Margeret Hall[1], Sharon Medcalf[2], and Aaron Yoder[2]

[1] University of Nebraska at Omaha, 1110 South 67th St, Omaha, NE 68182, USA
{afruhling,mahall}@unomaha.edu
[2] University of Nebraska Medical Center, 42nd and Emile Str, Omaha, NE 68198, USA
{smedcalf,aaron.yoder}@unmc.edu

Abstract. Between 2007 and 2016, there were 144,002 HAZMAT incidents on US highways, with damage totaling nearly \$600 M. The top two incident types in the past three years involved flammable-combustible liquids and corrosive materials. In 2016, 38% of firefighter fatality was a result of sudden cardiac death, making it one of the two leading causes of death among firefighters. Heat-related illness is directly linked to adverse cardiovascular events [5], but when detected early, recovery is likely. We propose a new system called **REaCH: Real-Time Emergency Communication System for HAZMAT Incidents.** The REaCH system will include real-time health monitoring of first responders through wearable devices that capture individual health parameters and exposure to hazardous materials. Individual health data and HAZMAT exposure data will be transmitted to a dashboard that integrates all of the information for the Incident Commander to monitor. The Incident Commander can evaluate if individuals need to be removed from the scene when his/her health status is being compromised.

Keywords: Real-time integrated dashboard · First responder health · Environmental monitoring system · HAZMAT incidents · Design science

1 Introduction

Hazardous materials traffic in the US exceeds 800,000 shipments per day and results in more than 3.1 billion tons of hazardous material shipped annually across approximately 300 million shipments within the US. Out of these, 94% of the HAZMAT shipments are moved by trucks [1]. Between 2007 and 2016, there were 144,002 HAZMAT incidents on US highways, with damage totaling nearly \$600 M.[1] The top two incident types in the past three years involved flammable-combustible liquids and corrosive materials.

Transporting hazardous materials safely, establishing requirements for real-time emergency response information, and monitoring human exposure from hazardous material incidents are critical national and global concerns. Human exposure are monitored

---

[1] Office of the Federal Register, National Archives and Records Administration. (2011, October 1). Code of Federal Regulations Title 49 (*Transportation*).

© Springer Nature Switzerland AG 2020
S. Hofmann et al. (Eds.): DESRIST 2020, LNCS 12388, pp. 28–34, 2020.
https://doi.org/10.1007/978-3-030-64823-7_3

through wearable sensors that capture bio and environmental data. Sensor data accuracy, validity, reliability, and security are especially important in HAZMAT situations where there is little room for error or variance. However, technical integration of heterogeneous sensor data is still drastically lacking even in the current information age. Figure 1 displays an example of a 2018 incident command coordination in the service district around Interstate 80; this is the current FEMA standard operating model today.

Fig. 1. This center was set up to coordinate strategies for all pictured responding units. https://twitter.com/OmahaFireDept/status/1062394307955621888; 13 Nov 2018

During HAZMAT emergencies, First Responders (FRs), including firefighters, police officers, state patrol, paramedics, and environmental quality representatives, are the first to reach the incident site. As the decision of the Incident Commander (IC) directly influences the safety of FRs at the incident site, correct and appropriate information delivered at the right time can be life-saving. Figure 2 displays incident command devices for reading various sensors. The data that is used by the IC to monitor the situation is heterogeneous and not integrated nor is it available in one application, multiple monitors and systems have to be used that do not communicate with each.

Fig. 2. Pictures of various devices and user interface currently used by the OFD demonstrated to the research team (November 2017).

We propose a new system called **REaCH: Real-Time Emergency Communication System for HAZMAT Incidents.** The main features from this project is an integrated IT system that includes mobile apps, wearable and sensory devices that capture human health conditions and environmental data, and a real-time communication network for all stakeholders (e.g., RFs, ICs, Safety and Environmental Services (SEMS), etc.) that can be used during hazardous materials incidents. The REaCH system will include real-time health monitoring of FRs through wearable devices that capture individual health parameters and exposure to hazardous materials. Individual health data and HAZMAT exposure data will be transmitted to a dashboard that integrates all of the information for the IC to monitor. The IC can evaluate if individuals need to be removed from the scene when his/her health status is being compromised. The main features of the system are derived from the use cases presented in Table 1.

Table 1. Finalized operation criteria the seven user type perspectives

Agent type	Minimum operating criteria
Team leader	1. *As a TL, I need to be able to* visualize the data for each FR, so that I can monitor the FR's HR, RR, and HI 2. - know when a FR has reached a threshold, so that I can take the appropriate action 3. - see the trends of the biodata, so I can have more details on the FR's health status
SEMS operator	1. *As a SEMS operator, I need to be able to* add/edit/remove people to the REaCH system 2. - assign devices, so that they are assigned to the correct person
Sys-admin	1. *As a SA, I need to be able to* add/edit/remove a device, so that the device can connect to the REaCH system 2. – add/edit/remove teams to the REaCH system 3. - create thresholds, so the REaCH system knows when the Sensor Data has reached one
Users	1. *As a FR, I need to be able to* send my biodata to the REaCH system 2. - see my historical data. The data should include the user's demographic, biodata, threshold data, potential exposures, and location
First responders	1. *As the REaCH system, I need to be able to* be accessible during a HAZMAT situation 2. - store the sensor data, so that I can display historical information 3. - compare the biodata of a FR to the threshold for each current sensor data, so that it can be determined if the threshold has been reached
REaCH system	1. *As a device, I need to be able to* have sensors, so I can collect data 2. - connect to the REaCH system, so I can transmit sensor data and status information 3. - tolerant enough to survive harsh conditions, so I can function within the PPE of a FR in a HAZMAT situation
Devices	1. *As a TL, I need to be able to* visualize the data for each FR, so that I can monitor the FR's HR, RR, and HI 2. - know when a FR has reached a threshold, so that I can take the appropriate action 3. - see the trends of the biodata, so I can have more details on the FR's health status

2 Significance to Research

Design Science enables the iterative reflection and construction of an artifact to define, develop, demonstrate, and evaluate in a way that is well-suited to the exploratory nature of this prototype [2]. Design Science is distinct from general system building not only because it sets it emphasis on the creation of innovative artifacts, but it also inherently considers the evaluation of results [3]. Context dependencies surrounding emergency incident management, critical safety aspects, and their various interactions need to be investigated in a manner that allows for rigorous evaluation to assure a theoretically and practically valuable instantiation.

Emergency response scenarios differ from traditional decision support systems in several key aspects [4]: system latency between sensors, and platform-to-IC is paramount; multiple displays from different devices (air pack level, air quality, two-way radio) cause additional cognitive load; and while scenario-based specialized knowledge required, the decision support system must be uniform and accommodate heterogeneous event data types. Finally, system maladaptation and/or failure carries the real risk of FR death. Addressing these challenges through innovative technology solutions such as an integrated Dashboard, wearable sensors, and specialized health threshold algorithms has the potential to make significant contributions to the scientific community.

Decision support systems for FR health management are largely missing in established literature. This is partially due to the critical nature of the process. Workshops can facilitate the ground-up gathering of design requirements (see e.g., [5]) that allows researchers to engage with emergency personnel in a way that does not distract from critical missions, nor put them at additional risk. Subsequently the PI and the chief system architect attended the 2018 Fire Department International Conference where the team interviewed dozens of vendors and learned that no system exists that integrates real-time environmental and human sensor data to monitor an individuals' health during a fire or hazardous material incident. We are designing a system that does not exist.

3 Significance to Practice

The significance of this research to practice is to improve FR safety and health through early recognition of health hazard indicators. In 2016, 38% of firefighter fatality was a result of sudden cardiac death, making it one of the two leading causes of death among firefighters [6]. Moreover, overexertion and strain (27.1%) was the largest cause of fire-related ground injuries [7]. Heat-related exposure in FR is not limited to just fire—it can be a result of hot weather and over exertion, which can increase core body temperature. Heat-related illness is directly linked to adverse cardiovascular events [8], but when detected early, recovery is likely. The research imperative is focusing on prevention. Real-time biometric health data collection is deemed the best predictor of impending adverse health events, and rapid intervention should be based on proven techniques for detecting impending illness [9].

We initially conducted an overall needs assessment of the most important concerns of the OFD [5, 10]. One of the foremost concerns identified was *shortened life expectancy of FRs* and a need to better monitor FRs during incidents. Several issues with current processes were identified: **1) Data integration problems.** The critical data about FRs and incident environment are displayed on two different screens because each system has its own user interface, which makes it difficult to make effective decisions during emergencies. **2) Outdated technology.** The user interface works on a Windows XP platform with limited processing capabilities that are updated in 45 s time intervals. This implies that the data available to IC about FRs is often not available until after the FR has taken 20 steps and thus potential exposure to hazardous materials may have already occurred before the FR or IC is aware. **3) Incident commander experiences cognitive overload.** There is a constant exchange of critical data between FRs and IC during emergencies. The visualization of so much data on separate displays leads to cognitive overload for IC. **4) System user interface usability issues.** The dated user interfaces for the current systems have several problems such as: poor organization, not matching the emergency management work, and poor navigation.

4 Evaluation of the Artifact

The REaCH project team partnered with an OFD firefighter squad "Engine 33" to define the requirements and evaluate REaCH. The members of Engine 33 consisted of the Battalion Chief, Station Captain, Incident Commander, several Firefighters, and Special Operations personnel. The research team consisted of HCI experts, Emergency Response Management researchers, Computer Scientists, a Medical Doctor, and graduate students with cross-expertise in the specialties. After the use case scenarios were verified, the research team began creating a UI design using Protoshare (a Wireframe tool). The research team met weekly for nine months including monthly iteration cycles wherein ICs interacted with a low fidelity UI to provide additional in-depth feedback.

Based on these series of meetings, minimum design criteria were proposed and iterated upon. The criteria are human centric, and concentrate on the required criteria from seven perspectives – Team Leaders, SEMS Operator, System Administrators, Users, FRs, the REaCH System, and ancillary Devices (Table 1). In particular, the evaluation focused on making the elements work together in way that is not (more) cognitively taxing to support ICs and FRs when HAZMAT scenarios are taking place.

We address the data integration problems by displaying all of the bio-health and environment indicators on one screen as shown in Fig. 3. Our system is designed using well established design principles, including heuristic evaluation, to overcome data integration problems and outdated technology. The user interface was designed to overcome IC cognitive overload and usability issues of current user interfaces that were also identified through focus groups. We are conducting evaluations on the dashboard visualizations that will validate the IC's current cognitive load compared to the cognitive load involved in utilizing the REaCH system. As future work, we plan a predictive algorithm to determine when a FR should be removed from a scene based on their health biosensor parameters. This will be determined by data rather than the FR realizing s/he does not feel good or IC directive.

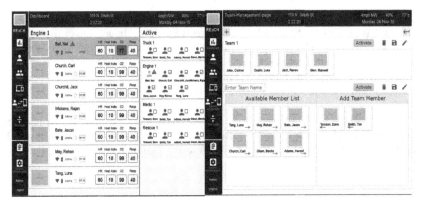

Fig. 3. Sample views from REaCH dashboard for first responder management.

5 Artefact Implementation

REaCH is a working interactive prototype that being tested by OFD using various usability evaluation methods such as cognitive walkthroughs, focus groups and an incident simulation lab. After the improvements from these usability evaluations are incorporated into the UI design for a high fidelity prototype will be developed for field testing at a large first responder and firefighter training sight using scenario based-testing and live sensor data from wearable devices. The technology will be made available to professional emergency management organizations at the conclusion of the project.

Acknowledgements. This research is funded by the Mid-America Transportation Center via a grant from the U.S. Department of Transportation's University Transportation Centers Program [USDOT UTC grant number for MATC: 69A3551747107], and this support is gratefully acknowledged. The contents reflect the views of the authors, who are responsible for the facts and the accuracy of the information presented herein and are not necessarily representative of the sponsoring agencies.

References

1. Lasisi, A., Bai, L., Sun, Z.: An empirical study on risk mitigation in transporting hazardous material. In: 62nd IIE Annual Conference and Expo 2012, pp. 2715–2724 (2012)
2. Peffers, K., Tuunanen, T., Rothenberger, M., Chatterjee, S.: A design science research methodology for information systems research. J. Manag. Inf. Syst. **24**(3), 45–77 (2007)
3. Peffers, K., Rothenberger, M., Tuunanen, T., Vaezi, R.: Design science research evaluation. In: Peffers, K., Rothenberger, M., Kuechler, B. (eds.) DESRIST 2012. LNCS, vol. 7286, pp. 398–410. Springer, Heidelberg (2012). https://doi.org/10.1007/978-3-642-29863-9_29
4. Palen, L., Anderson, K.M.: Crisis informatics—New data for extraordinary times. Science (80-.) **353**(6296), 224–225 (2016)
5. Thoring, K., Mueller, R.M., Badke-Schaub, P.: Workshops as a research method: guidelines for designing and evaluating artifacts through workshops. In: Proceedings of the 53rd HICSS, pp. 5036–5045 (2020)

6. Fahy, R.F., Molis, J.L.: Firefighter Fatalities in the US - 2018 (2019)
7. Campbell, R., Evarts, B., Molis, J.L.: United States Firefighter Injury Report 2018 (2019)
8. Smith, D.L., DeBlois, J.P., Kales, S.N., Horn, G.P.: Cardiovascular strain of firefighting and the risk of sudden cardiac events. Exerc. Sport Sci. Rev. **44**(3), 90–97 (2016)
9. Petruzzello, S.J., Gapin, J.I., Snook, E., Smith, D.L.: Perceptual and physiological heat strain: examination in firefighters in laboratory-and field-based studies. Ergonomics **52**(6), 747–754 (2009)
10. Medcalf, S., Hale, M.L., Achutan, C., Yoder, A., Shearer, S., Fruhling, A.: Requirements Gathering Through Focus Groups for A Real-Time Emergency Communication System For Hazmat Incidents (REaCH). Transportation Research Board Annual Meeting, Jan 12–16, Washington D.C. (2020)

Designing Digital Community Service Platforms for Crowd-Based Services in Urban Areas

Christian Bartelheimer[(✉)], Verena Wolf, Nico Langhorst, and Florian Seegers

Paderborn University, Warburger Str. 100, 33098 Paderborn, Germany
{christian.bartelheimer,verena.wolf,nico.langhorst,
florian.seegers}@uni-paderborn.de

Abstract. Digital technology facilitates the interaction among different groups of actors, including those that would not engage with each other in the real-world. Thus, digital technology can foster the emergence and development of (virtual) communities. IS research provides a rich but siloed knowledge base on physical and virtual communities. Our study is the first that integrates both views by prescribing a nascent design theory for *Digital Community Service Platforms*. In addition, we ground the artifact's design on knowledge about the co-creation of service, and crowd-sourcing. As a preliminary result, we present a prototype of the platform for the domain of high street retail that exemplifies the artifact's form and function, and we abstract a nascent design theory for this class of IT artifacts. Practitioners can instantiate the platform pursuing the principles of implementation, prescribed in the design theory. In future work, we will empirically evaluate the artifact in a naturalistic real-world study to examine the artifact's impact on the urban community.

Keywords: Community · Crowd-sourcing · Co-creation of value · Prototype · Digital platform · Design science research

1 Introduction

City centers are important destinations for both residents and visitors to go shopping, get information, and meet with other people. As a city's flagship, its center does constitute a city's public image and shape its residents' common identity, which is described in the scientific literature as *sense of community* [1]. One of the most important factors for a city center's attractiveness is its high street and in particular, the local retail stores. Current trends like digitalization and globalization challenge and transform people's habits around the globe (e.g., towards online shopping) and put high street retail under increasing pressure [2].

To reverse the trend of decaying city centers, we develop, implement, and evaluate a *Digital Community Service Platform* as a new class of IT artifacts. Existing crowd-sourcing platforms inspired the platform's design. Consequently, the designed platform provides crowd-based services by enabling different groups

© Springer Nature Switzerland AG 2020
S. Hofmann et al. (Eds.): DESRIST 2020, LNCS 12388, pp. 35–41, 2020.
https://doi.org/10.1007/978-3-030-64823-7_4

of actors (i.e., sourcers and workers) to post and complete tasks such as running errands for a third-party. Thereby, we pursue the twofold goal of simultaneously strengthening both the sense of virtual community [3] via interactions with digital technology affiliated to the platform as well as strengthening the sense of (physical) community [4] by matching sourcers and workers in the real-world. Ultimately, we aim at upholding and enhancing a city center's attractiveness by increasing the participation in a community and thus, the interaction among different groups of actors in an urban area [5].

2   Design of the Artifact

2.1   The Digital Community Service Platform Prototype

To address the decline of revenue in high street retail and the decreasing sense of community in urban areas, we present a prototype of the IT artifact to outline the form and function of *Digital Community Service Platforms*. We chose high street retail as application domain since prior research identified it as a suitable environment for implementing digital community platforms [6]. Based on the premises of the service-dominant logic [7] and available design knowledge on digital platforms (e.g., [6,8]), we took a service-oriented approach for the platform's architecture. It composes of multiple loosely-coupled modules (i.e., front-end services) that are affiliated with a stable core (i.e., back-end services). We used *Firebase*[1] to host micro-services (e.g., user management, push messaging) that constitute the server-side business logic of our prototype's back-end (Fig. 1).

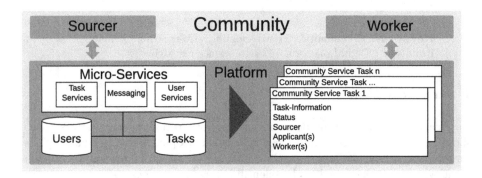

Fig. 1. Abstract architecture of the IT artifact.

The prototype offers three distinct functionalities: a delivery service, a temporary storage service, and a shopping buddy service. The delivery service is

---

[1] https://firebase.google.com/.

analog to a traditional delivery service (for local deliveries), while the temporary storage enables users to store luggage or purchases at a third-party retail store, or residents' homes. The shopping buddy service matches the sourcer (e.g., a shopper) with a dedicated resident or one with high local knowledge, helping him or her with questions or guiding around the city. For example, the buddy can help to find stores that match the sourcer's interests and tastes.

We employed the *Flutter Framework*—a framework for designing GUI applications for multiple operating systems—to develop the affiliated front-end applications (i.e., a hybrid mobile application for Android and iOS). To reduce the complexity of the application and enable the artifact's mutability, we applied the guidelines of the Business Logic Component (BLoC) pattern[2]—an architectural best practice pattern proposed by Google LLC. BLoC provides platform-independent data streams/sinks for input and output. Any complex UI component passes the input-data into a BLoC component without any data preprocessing. Vice versa, after data processing, the BLoC component passes a singular output back to the UI component.

The front-end applications consist of multiple views: a *home screen* with an individualized dashboard listing personal information and statistics, a *tasks board*, announcing currently available tasks, and a screen for *personal tasks*, which provides an overview about available, active, and accomplished tasks. The *settings* enable modifying the user's profile and setting preferences for messaging (Fig. 2).

Fig. 2. Views of the prototype's mobile front-end.

2.2 A Design Theory for Digital Community Service Platforms

Abstracting the knowledge gained through the design and evaluation of the prototype, we propose eight components of a nascent design theory [9] for *Digital Community Service Platforms* as a new class of IT artifacts.

---

[2] https://github.com/topics/bloc.

1. **Purpose and Scope:** Digital Community Service Platforms for high street retail shall strengthen the Sense of Community (SOC) in urban areas. The class of IT artifacts enables retailers to publish tasks, which can be picked and fulfilled by locals, offering additional customer service.
2. **Constructs:** Service co-creation, virtual/physical community, multi-sided (digital) platform, sense of (virtual) community, crowd-sourcing.
3. **Principles of Form and Function:** The IT artifact serves as intermediary between groups of actors in urban communities. The artifact enables sourcers (e.g., retailers, other stakeholders) to create, publish, and delete tasks, while workers (e.g., residents, visitors) can complete these tasks for the benefit of the community and/or adequate monetary compensation.
4. **Artifact Mutability:** The IT artifact can be adapted to various application domains, considering context-specific requirements. The multi-sided digital platform's design enables the mutable integration and exclusion of additional functionalities, services, and stakeholders. The content is built during run time and, therefore, differs in each instantiation.
5. **Testable Propositions:** The artifact can serve for refining or extending the kernel theories that informed its design: (1) Fostering interactions among different groups of actors (i.e., engage in service co-creation) in urban areas via digital and physical channels strengthens both the sense of physical and virtual community; (2) Crowd-sourcing that aims at offering services as value propositions for third-parties can enhance customer experience; (3) Instantiating Digital Community Service Platforms positively impacts maintaining and strengthening urban communities, increasing a city's attractiveness.
6. **Justificatory Knowledge:** Kernel theories that informed the design of the artifact include the foundational premises of service-dominant logic, knowledge about physical/virtual (sense of) communities, and crowd-sourcing.
7. **Principles of Implementation:** The platform can be instantiated in any urban community in four steps: (1) Identify and determine the stakeholders for whom the platform is relevant (platform provider, retailers and/or neighborhood organizations); (2) Customize and adapt the platform to the specific local environment; (3) Sourcers (e.g., retailers) publish tasks to be fulfilled by other community members (e.g., residents); (4) The mobile app is distributed to potential sourcers.
8. **Expository Instantiation:** We developed a prototype that offers basic functionality of the Digital Community Service Platform. A screencast demonstrates its form and function (https://youtu.be/0XRx6xZKx78).

3   Implications for Research

We contribute to research on communities by outlining how digital platforms can facilitate both physical and digital interactions to strengthen communities in urban areas. The sense of (digital) community is a conventional construct for describing the quality of life and relationships in urban neighborhoods [1], which is measured by the extent and quality of interaction through communication [4]. While qualitative and quantitative research on communities dominates the IS discipline, recent studies on communities do foremost investigate either virtual communities (e.g., [3,10]) or physical communities in the real world (e.g., [11,12]). Our study is the first that integrates these two research streams since the physical and virtual world are complementary (e.g., searching products online while strolling around the high street). Further, we present design knowledge to prescribe the implementation of *Digital Community Service Platforms* as crowd-sourcing platforms for urban areas. Our approach is the first that combines both physical touchpoints for enhancing the sense of community and digital touch-points for enhancing the sense of digital community. This enables strengthening the sense of community in urban areas as a whole.

4   Implications for Practice

Local high street retail continuously loses market share to online retail due to shifting customer expectations towards digital channels [13]. Services like home delivery, availability check, or 24/7 availability reinforce this development. We developed a prototype of a crowd-sourcing platform and provide a corresponding design theory for *Digital Community Service Platforms* for urban areas. Prac-titioners (e.g., retailers, city managers) can instantiate the design theory for the class of IT artifacts following our proposed principals of implementation. Thereby, they support high street retail, encouraging and technically enabling retailers and other stakeholders to provide similar services as known from online retail (e.g., delivery service) as well as additional services (e.g., temporary stor-age, matching with a buddy) without the need for building digital capabilities. Ultimately, continuously connecting different groups of stakeholders that are affiliated with the digital platform might positively impact the community and consequently, enables a city's successful long-term development.

5   Evaluation of the Artifact

We will conduct a three-phase evaluation. Each phase pursues different goals for the evaluation. In the first phase, we iterate between design and evaluation to ensure the proper form and function of the prototype. Currently, the prototype does explicitly cover the predefined requirements and could already be instan-tiated. However, the prototype might still require improvements regarding an user-friendly design of the interfaces, IT security issues, and scalability to ensure its utility for subsequent evaluation steps. In the second phase, we will concep-tually evaluate our artifact against rival artifacts to demonstrate our artifact's uniqueness, following a *quick & simple* evaluation strategy [14]. A first analysis reveals that there might be related artifacts, but none of them explicitly builds on knowledge about both virtual and physical communities. Furthermore, studies that developed IT artifacts (i.e., digital platforms) do not generalize their results to obtain prescriptive design knowledge. Naturally, our development process and thus, the form and function of the prototype was inspired by instantiations in the real-world (e.g., postmates.com, helpling.com). However, such a platform has not been scientifically developed and analyzed, yet. In the third phase, we aim at instantiating the artifact in a real-world context and conduct an extensive evaluation for *human risk & effectiveness* [14]. Such evaluation strategies serve best for situations in which it is essential to test an artifact's usefulness and efficiency. Thus, it enables us to examine if our artifact does support our assumptions, delineating a positive impact on maintaining and strengthening urban communities. In particular, we will test the propositions that stem from the kernel theories that informed the design of the artifact. This final evaluation step intends to confirm or reject the testable propositions (see Sect. 2.2, page 3f.) to refine the kernel theories.

References

1. Jeffres, L.W., Bracken, C.C., Jian, G., Casey, M.F.: The impact of third places on community quality of life. ARQOL **4**(4), 333–345 (2009)
2. Betzing, J.H., et al.: HMD Praxis der Wirtschaftsinformatik **54**(5), 659–671 (2017). https://doi.org/10.1365/s40702-017-0343-0
3. Martínez-López, F.J., Anaya-Sánchez, R., Aguilar-Illescas, R., Molinillo, S.: Types of virtual communities and virtual brand communities. In: Online Brand Communities, PI, pp. 125–140. Springer, Cham (2016). https://doi.org/10.1007/978-3-319-24826-4_8
4. Doolittle, R.J., MacDonald, D.: Communication and a sense of community in a metropolitan neighborhood: a factor analytic examination. Commun. Q. **26**(3), 2–7 (1978)
5. Chavis, D.M., Wandersman, A.: Sense of community in the urban environment: a catalyst for participation and community development. In: A Quarter Century of Community Psychology: Readings from the American Journal of Community Psychology, pp. 265–292. Springer, Boston (2002)
6. Bartelheimer, C., Betzing, J.H., Berendes, C. I., Beverungen, D.: Designing multisided community platforms for local high street retail. In: ECIS2018, Paper 140, Portsmouth (2018)
7. Vargo, S.L., Lusch, R.F.: Institutions and axioms: an extension and update of service-dominant logic. J. Acad. Market. Sci. **44**(1), 5–23 (2016)
8. Tura, N., Kutvonen, A., Ritala, P.: Platform design framework: conceptualisation and application. Technol. Anal. Strateg. Manage. **30**, 1–14 (2017)
9. Gregor, S., Jones, D.: The anatomy of a design theory. J. Assoc. Inf. Syst. **8**(5), 312–335 (2007)
10. Nikitina, B., Korsun, M., Sarbaeva, I., Zvonovsky, V.: Development of the practice of sharing economy in the communicative information environment of modern urban communities. In: Ashmarina, S., Mesquita, A., Vochozka, M. (eds.) Digital Transformation of the Economy: Challenges, Trends and New Opportunities. AISC, vol. 908, pp. 376–394. Springer, Cham (2020). https://doi.org/10.1007/978-3-030-11367-4_37
11. Kalkbrenner, B.J., Roosen, J.: Citizens' willingness to participate in local renewable energy projects: the role of community and trust in Germany. Energy Res. Soc. Sci. **13**, 60–70 (2016)
12. Ross, A., Searle, M.: Conceptual model of leisure time physical activity, neighborhood environment, and sense of community. Environ. Behav. **51**(6), 749–781 (2019)

13. Bollweg, L., Lackes, R., Siepermann, M., Sutaj, A., Weber, P.: Digitalization of local owner operated retail outlets: the role of the perception of competition and customer expectations. In: PACIS 2016 Proceedings, Paper 348 (2016)
14. Venable, J., Pries-Heje, J., Baskerville, R.: FEDS: a framework for evaluation in design science research. Eur. J. Inf. Syst. **25**(1), 77–89 (2016)

Designing for Digital Government Innovation in Resource Constrained Countries: The Case of Woredas in Ethiopia

Debas Senshaw[1,2]([envelope]) [iD] and Hossana Twinomurinzi[1,3] [iD]

[1] Sudan University of Science and Technology, Khartoum, Sudan
debassenshaw@gmail.com, twinoh@gmail.com
[2] Bahir Dar Institute of Technology, Bahir Dar University, Bahir Dar, Ethiopia
[3] Department of Applied Information Systems, University
of Johannesburg, Johannesburg, South Africa

Abstract. This paper was aimed at developing a design artefact to identify opportunities for digital innovation based on the adaptive capabilities of government organizations in resource constrained low-income countries. The study was guided by the recent elaborated action design research method. Adaptive capability themes that were elicited from Woredas (government districts) in Ethiopia were used as the requirements to create a web-based application (app). UTAUT was used to evaluate the potential adoption and acceptance of the app (n = 270) using structural equation modeling (SEM). The results reveal that social influence significantly influences the behavioral intention to use the app, which finding reveals how social factors have a stronger influence on digital government innovations in resource constrained low-income countries. The design principle elicited in the paper can guide future digital government innovation efforts in resource constrained low-income countries. The study contributes to design science research in revealing the utility of the elaborated action design research method.

Keywords: Digital government · Woredas · WoredaNet · Adaptive capability · Design science · Elaborated action design research · UTAUT

1 Introduction

Governments are increasingly giving significant attention to digital technology investments as a means to make public services more efficient and effective [1, 2]. Nonetheless, the rapid rate of advancements in digital technology and the changing global, regional and local environments and the consequent political, structural and financial pressures that governments face call for continuous innovation [3, 4].

Many low-income countries, notwithstanding the resource constraints and the pressure of international donors and a global community, have made considerable investments in digital technology infrastructure. Despite the investment, they continue to experience low digital government adoption [5, 6]. This paper argues for more efforts to

© Springer Nature Switzerland AG 2020
S. Hofmann et al. (Eds.): DESRIST 2020, LNCS 12388, pp. 42–55, 2020.
https://doi.org/10.1007/978-3-030-64823-7_5

be placed on contextual innovation in the digital government of low-income countries through the dynamic capabilities framework [7–9].

Dynamic capabilities are strategic organizational routines through which an organization reconfigures its internal resources in order to adapt to continually changing environments [10–12]. Wang & Ahmed [13] identify three main types of dynamic capabilities; adaptive – the ability to identify opportunities from changes in the environment, absorptive – the ability to exploit the opportunities and, innovative – the ability to rearrange internal resources in order to take advantage of the changes and opportunity through new products/services. The choice of the dynamic capability theory is mainly because of its focus on resourcefulness and not resources, which resources are a constraint in low-income countries, and the theory is inclusive of the role of ICT as an important organizational resource [14, 15].

Particularly, this paper focused on the adaptive capability for its emphasis on identifying opportunity based on context [16, 17]. Digital innovations in low-income countries that are based on the local context such as m-pesa [18] have been shown to enjoy rapid adoption compared to innovations that have been adopted from other contexts. The paper, therefore, sought to answer the research question: *How can opportunities for digital government innovation be identified in the context of resource-constrained low-income countries?*

The paper used Woredas (districts) of Ethiopia and the digital government platform, the WoredaNet, as the case study.

The remainder of the paper is structured as follows: The next section presents the literature review of dynamic capabilities and digital government. It is followed by the research methodology. The discussion of findings is then presented followed by the conclusion.

2   Literature Review

2.1   Dynamic Capabilities

The dynamic capabilities framework (DCF) emerged from the Resource Based View (RBV) perspective of strategic management [19] and has fast been gaining attention as a result of the rapid changes in digital technology and society [10]. The most important concern in the DCF is the usage of resources, including digital technologies, not the possession of resources [20]. Wang & Ahmed [21] identify three categories of dynamic capabilities; adaptive capabilities are the ability to identify opportunity from changes in the external environment, absorptive capabilities enable those opportunities to be exploited through a reorganization of internal resources, and innovative capabilities where new products and/or services are created to take advantage of the identified opportunity.

Recently, public sector organizations have also begun to consider the DCF as a means to create new public services driven by digital technology [22–26]. While the functions and structures between the public sector and private organizations differ, the organizational features such as resources, routines, and capabilities are similar [23, 25, 27]. Senshaw & Twinomurinzi [24] particularly found that most low-income countries did not begin by identifying the changes in their context before creating new digital government innovations. Rather, most simply adopted digital artefacts that had worked elsewhere. This paper therefore argues for a digital artefact that would enable public sector organizations in low-income countries to first identify the opportunity within the local context.

2.2 Digital Government

Digital government is broadly defined as the exploitation of digital technologies to assist government to be more effective and efficient [28, 29]. The improvements can be through better access to information and improved services, and even ensuring that the government is more answerable to its citizens. Digital government is not only about implementing new technologies, but more about effective and efficient public service delivery, for example by increasing transparency and accountability [30, 31].

The next section describes the research method to conduct the study.

3 Research Method- Elaborated Action Design Research

The paper adopted the recent Elaborated Action Design Research (EADR) approach of Mullarkey & Hevner [32]. The approach was considered easy to follow especially in resource-constrained environments where the context has not been well articulated. The EADR uses four iterative stages: diagnose, design, implement and evolve.

3.1 Diagnosis

The diagnosis stage is where the problem or opportunity to be solved is detailed, which in this study was to identify opportunity for digital government innovation in low-income countries. The study was conducted in the content of government administrative regions (called Woredas) in Ethiopia using the WoredaNet digital platform.

The WoredaNet is a digital government platform using fiber and satellite infrastructure across Ethiopia to provide government services to Woredas. The name WoredaNet comes from "Woreda" which is Amharic for an administrative region with a population of about 100,000. It has the equivalent meaning of a district. The WoredaNet provides various digital government services to different arms of the government in Woredas. Among the services provided are video-conferencing, internet, electronic messaging and voice over IP between federal, regional and Woreda sites.

There are 1,050 Woredas in Ethiopia, 976 (93%) of which have access to the WoredaNet. Despite the access, only a few Woredas actively use the WoredaNet [33]. This study therefore sought to create a digital artefact based on the adaptive capabilities of those Woredas that actively use the WoredaNet, which digital artefact can be used by other Woredas to similarly understand their contexts and identify opportunities for digital innovation.

3.2 Design

Design is the stage where the problem domain is turned into digital solution classes. The ICT management of the Amhara Regional State Science, Technology, Information and Communication Commission recommended three different public agencies, namely, Judiciary (court) office, Human Resources (HR) office and the Finance office from each of the three Woredas for their active usage of the WoredaNet. The task was to identify the adaptive capabilities of the three Woredas and then to create a digital artefact based on the adaptive capabilities. The digital artefact could be used by other Woredas to similarly identify opportunities for digital innovation and use the WoredaNet as well.

A qualitative-interpretive approach was used to identify the adaptive capabilities of the innovative Woredas. The interview data (based on Appendix A) were transcribed into text, and thematic analysis using process coding in Atlas.ti8^{TM} was adopted to elicit codes and themes [34]. The identified codes and themes were then presented back to the ICT management for further discussion. It took two iterations to reach consensus on the final themes. Some capabilities were eliminated due to their insignificance and the unique codes were arranged and grouped based on their underlying meaning. Eventually, 8 themes (adaptive capabilities) and 20 unique codes (capability manifestations) were

Table 1. Adaptive Capabilities of Woredas that innovatively use the WoredaNet

Adaptive capability themes	Adaptive capability codes	Frequency
Using feedback of reports as well as learning and growth programmes (26)	Using the feedback of reports	15
	Using learning and growth programmes	8
	Performing regular supervision	3
Using the internet and following social media (23)	Using the internet	12
	Following mainstream media	2
	Following social media	9
Learning from experience sharing and analyzing best practices (19)	Analyzing best practices	9
	Learning from experience sharing	10
Using SMS and email exchange (16)	Using email exchange	12
	Using SMS	4
Participating in video conferencing and using voice-over IP telephone (12)	Using intranet communication	1
	Participating in video conferencing	10
	Using voice-over IP telephone	1
Creating industry-university linkages and consulting IT firms (9)	Consulting IT firms	2
	Creating industry-university linkages	7
Visiting ICT trade fairs and workshops (8)	Visiting ICT festivity	1
	Visiting ICT trade fairs	2
	Visiting workshops	5
Using websites and web-based apps (7)	Using web-based applications	2
	Using websites	5
Total		120

elicited with a total count of 120 (Table 1). The column frequency in the table indicates how often the capability manifested in those Woredas.

The identified adaptive capabilities suggest that Woredas that actively use the WoredaNet use their access to constantly understand their context both locally and globally. They also actively create partnerships and attend external events as an extra means to understand their context. The Woredas are, therefore, easily able to identify opportunity from their contexts for digital innovation.

3.3 Implementation Stage

The adaptive capability themes and codes that were created in the design stage were used as the functional requirements to develop a web-based app, the digital artefact (Fig. 1). The reason for developing a web-based app is because a web-based app is usually easier to implement and test for efficacy, especially for Woredas that are not actively using the WoredaNet [35].

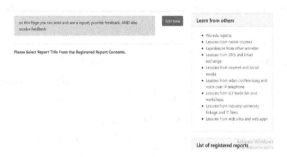

Fig. 1. Digital government adaptive capability app

3.4 Evolution

Evolution is an ongoing process where opportunities for app improvements can be identified. The app was evaluated for its fit among different Woredas using the Unified Theory of Acceptance and Use of Technology (UTAUT) [36, 37]. UTAUT is a popular Information Systems theory that assesses the intention to use a technological artefact and to adopt the artefact later.

Effort Expectancy (EE) in UTAUT is the perceived ease with using the artefact [32]. EE is particularly important during the first period of usage but becomes insignificant with continued usage [38–40]. The following hypothesis was therefore tested:

H1: Effort expectancy positively influences the behavioral intentions of government employees to use the app.

Performance Expectancy refers to the extent to which an individual trusts the technology to help with enhancing job performance [41]. The following hypothesis was tested:

H2: Performance expectancy positively influences behavioral intentions of government employees to use the app.

Social Influence is the degree to which an individual perceived that the boss or colleague considers his or her using the new technology [38]. The following hypothesis was tested:

H3: Social Influence positively impacts the behavioral intentions of government employees to use the app.

Facilitating Conditions are the users' awareness of facilities to use the technology [32]. In conditions of unpredictable support or facilities, pressure on the intention to use will be low [41], whereas when the support is predictable, facilitating conditions positively influence use behavior [41]. The following hypotheses were tested:

H4: Facilitating Conditions positively influence government employee's use behavior of the app.
H5: Behavioral Intentions positively influence government employee's use behavior of the app.

A non-probability sampling technique was applied to select ten Woredas that have access to the WoredaNet, including the three innovative Woredas that participated in the diagnostic qualitative study to elicit the adaptive capabilities. The Woredas were selected by the same ICT management who included Woredas that have access to the WoredaNet but do not actively use it. A similar respondent sample space was used consisting of process owners (those who manage similar tasks or processes in government organizations), ICT support staff, Woreda administrators and representatives.

Following the suggestions by Owoseni and Twinomurinzi [42] 20 question items were modified from literature to ensure scale validity (Appendix B). The second type was related to demographic questions. Of the 400 questionnaires distributed, 270 were completed in 25 days.

SPSS 25 and AMOS 25 were used for analysis [42–44]. The normality of the data, skewness and kurtosis of the constructs (for each item) were checked. Most of the items were within the acceptable range of -2 and $+2$ [45, 46], except a few whose kurtosis was greater than 2.0. As a whole, the result showed acceptable skewness and kurtosis values. Table 2 below presents the respondent demographics.

Table 2. Respondents' demographic data

	Variable	Frequency	Percent
Gender	Male	185	68.5
	Female	85	31.5
Job experience	5years and below	29	10.7
	6–10years	123	45.6
	11–15	101	37.4
	16–20	17	6.3
Age	30 and below	43	16
	31–35	121	44.8
	36–40	86	31.9
	41 and above	20	7.3
Education	Diploma	35	13
	Bachelor	186	68.9
	Masters	49	18.1

Confirmatory Factor Analysis confirmed the model was reliable and valid ($\chi 2 = 234.850$, df $= 154$, p-value $= 0.000$) and had fit indices: $\chi 2/df = 1.530$, GFI $= 0.920$, TLI $= 0.956$, CFI $= 0.964$, NFI $= 0.904$, RMSEA $= 0.044$.

Maximum likelihood estimation was used to measure the structural model giving acceptable fit indices ($\chi 2/df = 1.848$, GFI $= 0.902$, TLI $= 0.928$, CFI $= 0.940$, NFI $= 0.880$, RMSEA $= 0.056$). Results of regression weights as indicated in the structural model are represented in Appendix C. The structural model with chi-square ($\chi 2$) value of 293.786, df value of 159 and p-value of 0.000 was displayed. This revealed that the model fitted the data adequately. As a result, it is possible to conclude the fitness of the structural model (Fig. 2).

The numbers next to the UTAUT constructs in the SEM indicate the question items in each construct. For example, PE1 represents the first question item under the Performance Expectancy (PE) construct.

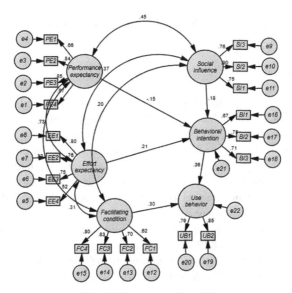

Fig. 2. The structural model

The results indicate that social influence has a considerable positive impact on the intention to use the app ($\beta = 0.184$, p < 0.05).This means that when employee's leaders or colleagues support them to use the app, the intention to use it will be increased. Moreover, the behavioral intention ($\beta = 0.36$, p < 0.05) demonstrates a considerable positive impact on the use behavior of government employees. This shows that when government employees have more intention of using the app, they use it more frequently. Facilitating conditions ($\beta = 0.301$, p < 0.05) indicates the importance of having the means to use the app. In other words, when government employees obtain more resources to use the app, they frequently use it. However, the performance expectancy ($\beta = -0.151$,

Table 3. Summarized outcomes of the hypotheses tests

	Hypothesis	Result
H1	Effort expectancy positively influences the behavioral intentions of government employees to use the app	Rejected
H2	Performance expectancy positively influences the behavioral intentions of government employees to use the app	Rejected
H3	Social Influence positively impacts the behavioral intentions of government employees to use the digital government adaptive capability web-based app	Accepted
H4	Facilitating conditions positively influence government employee's use behavior of the app	Accepted
H5	Behavioral intentions positively influence government employee's usage behavior of the app	Accepted

p > 0.05) and effort expectancy with ($\beta = 0.213$, p > 0.05) do not influence the intention to use the app (Table 3).

4 Discussion

The design stage revealed that the Woredas that actively use the WoredaNet exhibit clear adaptive capabilities which enable them to understand any changes in the environment, and as such easily identify any opportunities for digital innovation.

The evaluation of the app created in the design stage from the adaptive capability however reveals that despite the artefact not being easy to use (high effort expectancy) and also not making work any easier (low performance expectancy), the government employees still expressed an intention to use the app because of the social influence and the availability of accompanying resources to use it.

It is important to note that the majority of the respondents are highly qualified with Bachelor and Master degrees (87%) and are in the prime of their working career (the age group of above 31 is 84%) having spent more than 6 years in the Woredas (89.3%).

The paper therefore proposed the following design principle:

- Creating digital artefacts to identify opportunity for digital government innovation in resource-constrained low-income countries requires more effort in the social aspect compared with the technical.

5 Conclusion

The study investigated the design of digital artefacts in governments of resource-constrained low-income countries to identify opportunities for digital innovation based on the adaptive dynamic capability. The study argued the importance of adaptive capabilities in low-income countries as it allows for contextual and innovative design rather than the tradition of satisficing with digital artefacts designed from other contexts. Using the WoredaNet of Ethiopia, a digital artefact (app) was created following the new Elaborated Action Design Research (EADR) process and statistically evaluated for its acceptance and possible adoption.

The digital artefact was shown to have efficacy for potential use and that Woredas (government administration districts in Ethiopia) are able to learn to digitally innovate using the digital artefact according to their environment. Nonetheless, the intention to use the app was mainly based on social influences compared with the task aspects. The study concludes that in as much as digital government innovation occurs in resource constrained low-income countries, the greater effort is needed on the social aspects compared with the technical aspects.

This paper contributes to Information Systems theory further identifying the importance of social aspects in creating digital government innovations especially in governments of low-income countries. The paper also identifies this as a design principle that is required in creating digital artefacts for government in such countries.

The study was limited in creating an app mainly based on the adaptive capabilities. It was also limited in its numbers of evolution iterations to update the app to take into account the important social influences. Further design research is required for this.

Appendices

See Tables 4, 5 and 6.

Table 4. Appendix A: Interview questions

Sub-research question	Interview questions		
	Process owner	ICT support	Woreda (district) administrator (or a representative)
SR1: What are the adaptive capabilities of Woredas that innovatively use the WoredaNet?	1. From your experience, how do you use WoredaNet to identify opportunities in the environment? 2. From your experience, how do you use WoredaNet to identify threats in the environment? 3. From your experience, how does WoredaNet help to manage problems created due to external factors such as recurrent policy and political impositions? 4. From your experience, how do you use WoredaNet to align internal resources with environmental demands?	1. From your experience, how do you use ICT to support admin processes to identify opportunities on the WoredaNet? 2. From your experience, how is WoredaNet used to support admin processes to identify threats in the environment? 3. From your experience, how is WoredaNet used to support admin processes to manage problems created due to external factors such as recurrent policy and political impositions? 4. From your experience, how is WoredaNet used to support admin processes to align internal resources with environmental demands?	1. From your experience, how do you use WoredaNet to manage ways to identify best practices from other neighbouring Woredas? 2. From your experience, how do you use WoredaNet to support government agencies in the Woreda to identify threats in the environment? 3. From your experience, how is WoredaNet used to help government agencies in the Woreda to manage problems created due to external factors such as recurrent policy and political impositions? 4. From your experience, how is WoredaNet used to support government agencies in the Woreda to align internal resources with environmental demands?

Table 5. Appendix B: Question items of the survey adapted from [47]

Construct	Question items	
PE	PE1	I find the web-based app useful to learn about what others are doing
	PE2	Using the web-based app increases my chances of getting important information
	PE3	Using the web-based app helps me obtain important information more quickly
	PE4	Using the web-based app increases my productivity at work
EE	EE1	Learning how to use the web-based app is easy for me
	EE2	My interaction with the web-based app is clear and understandable
	EE3	I find the web-based app easy to use
	EE4	It is easy for me to become skilful at using the web-based app
SI	SI1	People who are important to me think that I should use the web-based app
	SI2	People who influence my behavior think that I should use the web-based app
	SI3	People whose opinions that I value prefer that I use the web-based app
FC	FC1	I have the resources necessary to use the web-based app
	FC2	I have the knowledge necessary to use the web-based app
	FC3	The web-based app is compatible with other technologies I use
	FC4	I can get help from others when I have difficulties using the web-based app
BI	BI1	I intend to continue using the web-based app in the future
	BI2	I will always try to use the web-based app in my daily life
	BI3	I plan to continue to use the web-based app frequently
UB	UB1	I have ever used a web-based app
	UB2	I often use web-based apps

Note: PE = performance expectancy, EE = effort expectancy, SI = social influence, FC = facilitating condition, BI = behavioral intention, UB = use behavior

Table 6. Appendix C: Regression weights

Independent variable	Relations	Dependent variable	Estimate (β-values)	P-value
Performance expectancy	→	Behavioral intention	−0.151	0.256
Social influence	→	Behavioral intention	0.184	0.033
Effort expectancy	→	Behavioral intention	0.213	0.105
Behavioral intention	→	Use behavior	0.360	0.000
Facilitating condition	→	Use behavior	0.301	0.000

References

1. Wang, H.-J., Lo, J.: Adoption of open government data among government agencies. Gov. Inf. Q. **33**, 80–88 (2016)
2. Alzadjali, K., Elbanna, A.: Smart institutional intervention in the adoption of digital infrastructure: the case of government cloud computing in Oman. Inf. Syst. Front. **22**, 365–380 (2019)
3. Gottschalk, P.: Maturity levels for interoperability in digital government. Gov. Inf. Q. **26**, 75–81 (2009)
4. Allen, B.A., Juillet, L., Paquet, G., Roy, J.: E-governance & government on-line in Canada : partnerships, people & prospects. Gov. Inf. Q. **18**, 93–104 (2001)
5. Zhenmin, L.: United Nations e-grovernment survey 2018 (2018)
6. Hussen, K.H.: E-Government implementation in public service organizations of developing economies. J. Public Policy Adm. (JPPA) **2**, 19–36 (2017)
7. Helfat, C., et al.: Dynamic Capabilities: Understanding Strategic Change In Organisations. Blackwell Publishing, Hoboken (2007)
8. Pisano, G.P.: Toward a prescriptive theory of dynamic capabilities : connecting strategic choice, learning, and competition. Ind. Corp. Chang. **26**, 747–762 (2017)
9. Coulon, T., Templier, M., Bourdeau, S., Pascal, A., Vieru, D.: Open innovation in the public sector: a dynamic capabilities perspective and the role of information technology. In: Proceedings of the 53rd Hawaii International Conference on System Sciences. pp. 5942–5951, Hawaii (2020)
10. Eisenhardt, K.M., Martin, J.A.: Dynamic capabilities : what are they? Strateg. Manag. J. **21**, 1105–1121 (2000)
11. Collis, D.J.: Research note : how valuable are organizational capabilities ? Strateg. Manag. J. **15**, 143–152 (1994)
12. Augier, M., Teece, D.J. (eds.): The Palgrave Encyclopedia of Strategic Management. Palgrave Macmillan UK, London (2018). https://doi.org/10.1057/978-1-137-00772-8
13. Wang, C.L., Ahmed, P.: Dynamic capabilities : a review and research agenda. Int. J. Manag. Rev. **9**, 31–51 (2007)
14. Tolani, A., Owoseni, A., Twinomurinzi, H.: Exploring the effect of mobile apps on SMEs in Nigeria: a critical realist study. IFIP Adv. Inf. Commun. Technol. **551**, 606–618 (2019)
15. Piening, E.P.: Dynamic Capabilities in Public Organizations. Public Manag. Rev. 9037, (2013)
16. Davison, R.M., Martinsons, M.G.: Context is king! considering particularism in research design and reporting. J. Inf. Technol. **31**, 241–249 (2016)
17. Twinomurinzi, H., Schofield, A., Hagen, L., Ditsoane-Molefe, S., Tshidzumba, N.A.: Towards a shared worldview on e-skills: A discourse between government, industry and academia on the ICT skills paradox. S. Afr. Comput. J. **29**(3), 215–237 (2017)
18. Kim, M., Zoo, H., Lee, H., Kang, J.: Mobile, financial inclusion and development: a critical review of academic literature. In: 10th Annual Pre-ICIS SIG Global Development Workshop, p. 28. Association for Information Systems eLibrary, Seoul (2017)
19. Lin, Y., Wu, L.Y.: Exploring the role of dynamic capabilities in firm performance under the resource-based view framework. J. Bus. Res. **67**, 407–413 (2014)
20. Rauch, A., Wiklund, J., Lumpkin, G.T., Frese, M.: Entrepreneurial orientation and business performance: An assessment of past research and suggestions for the future. Entrep. Theor. Pract. **33**(3), 761–787 (2009)
21. Wang, C.L., Ahmed, P.K.: Dynamic capabilities: A review and research agenda. Int. J. Manag. Rev. **9**, 31–51 (2007)
22. Cheol, L., Moldogaziev, T.T.: Public sector corruption in the U.S. local debt finance : do local governments pay a corruption premium ? SSRN Electron. J. pp. 25–48 (2015)

23. Vries, H.D.E., Bekkers, V., Tummers, L.: Innovation in the public sector : a systematic review and future research Agenda. Public Adm. **94**, 146–166 (2016)
24. Senshaw, D., Twinomurinzi, H.: Reflecting on the role of dynamic capabilities in digital government with a focus on developing countries. In: Proceedings of the 11th Annual Pre-ICIS SIG GlobDev Workshop, p. 5. AIS eLibrary, San Francisco, USA (2018)
25. Klein, P.G., Mahoney, J.T., Mcgahan, A.M., Pitelis, C.N.: Capabilities and strategic entrepreneurship in public organizations. Strateg. Entrep. J. **7**, 70–91 (2013)
26. Mcnulty, T., Ferlie, E.: Process transformation : limitations to radical organizational change within public service organizations. Organ. Stud. **25**(8), 1389–1412 (2004)
27. Pablo, A.L., Reay, T., Dewald, J.R., Casebeer, A.L.: Identifying, enabling and managing dynamic capabilities in the public sector *. J. Manag. Stud. **44**, 687–708 (2007)
28. Misuraca, G., Pasi, G.: Landscaping digital social innovation in the EU : structuring the evidence and nurturing the science and policy debate towards a renewed agenda for social change. Gov. Inf. Q. 592–600 (2019)
29. Norris, D.F., Reddick, C.G.: Local E-government in the United States: transformation or incremental change? Public Adm. Rev. **73**, 165–175 (2013)
30. Janowski, T.: Digital government evolution : from transformation to contextualization. Gov. Inf. Q. **32**, 221–236 (2015)
31. Khamallag, M.M., Kamala, M., Tassabehji, R.: Digital government Implementation in chaotic environment - case study of Libya. In: Proceedings of the British Academy of Management Annual Conference, pp. 6–8., Newcastle, UK (2016)
32. Mullarkey, M.T., Hevner, A.R.: An elaborated action design research process model. Eur. J. Inf. Syst. 1–15 (2018)
33. Miruts, G., Asfaw, M.: The implementation of civil service reforms in Ethiopia: the Woreda-Net as a sole promoter to implement civil service reform of Tigray National Regional State. Civ. Environ. Res. 6 2014)
34. Braun, V., Clarke, V.: Thematic analysis. In: Cooper, H., Camic, P.M., Long, D.L., Panter, A.T., Rindskopf, D., Sher, K.J. (eds.) APA Handbooks in Psychology®. APA Handbook of Research Methods in Psychology, vol. 2. Research Designs: Quantitative, Qualitative, Neuropsychological, and Biological, pp. 57–71. American Psychological Association (2012)
35. Teece, D.J.: Explicating dynamic capabilities: The nature and microfoundations of (sustainable) enterprise performance. Strateg. Manag. J. **28**, 1319–1350 (2007)
36. Raman, A., Don, Y., Khalid, R., Hussin, F., Omar, M.S., Ghani, M.: Technology acceptance on smart board among teachers in terengganu using UTAUT model. Asian Soc. Sci. **10**, 84 (2014)
37. Tai, Y., Ku, Y.-C.: Will stock investors use mobile stock trading? a benefit-risk assessment based on a modified UTAUT model. J. Electron. Commer. Res. **14**, 67–84 (2013)
38. Venkatesh, V., Morris, M.G., Davis, G.B., Davis, F.D.: User acceptance of information technology: toward a unified view. MIS Q. **27**, 425–478 (2003)
39. Davis, F.D., Bagozzi, R.P., Warshaw, P.R.: User acceptance of computer technology : a comparison of two theoretical models. Manag. Sci. **35**, 982 (1989)
40. Lim, W.M., Su, C., Phang, C.: Toward a conceptual framework for social media adoption by non-urban communities for non-profit activities : insights from an integration of grand theories of technology acceptance. Australas. J. Inf. Syst. **23**, 1–11 (2019)
41. Attuquayefio, S.N.: Using the UTAUT model to analyze students' ICT adoption. Int. J. Educ. Dev. Inf. Commun. Technol. **10**, 75–86 (2014)
42. Owoseni, A., Twinomurinzi, H.: Mobile apps usage and dynamic capabilities : A structural equation model of SMEs in Lagos. Nigeria. Telemat. Inform. **35**, 2067–2081 (2018)
43. Fan, Y., et al.: Applications of structural equation modeling (SEM) in ecological studies : an updated review. Ecol. Process. **5**, 19 (2016)

44. Adil, M.S., Owais, M., Qamar, A.: Impact of occupational stress, interpersonal trust, and organizational commitment on valence, OCB and job satisfaction: a variance-based SEM analysis. J. Manag. Sci. **5**(1), 38–61 (2018)
45. Abdullah, N.A., Chong, M., Widjaja, W., Shahrill, M.: Utilizing lesson study in improving year 12 students' learning and performance in mathematics. Math. Educ. Trends Res. **2017**, 24–31 (2017)
46. DeLemos, J.L.: Development of risk maps to minimize uranium exposures in the Navajo Churchrock mining district. Environ. Heal. **8**, 1–15 (2009)
47. Tan, P.J.B.: Applying the UTAUT to understand factors affecting the use of English E-learning websites in Taiwan, pp. 1–12 (2013)

Designing Transport Supporting Services Together with Users with Intellectual Disabilities

Sofie Wass[1]([⊠]) [iD], Lise Amy Hansen[2], and Chris Safari[1]

[1] University of Agder, Grimstad, Norway
sofie.wass@uia.no
[2] The Oslo School of Architecture and Design, Oslo, Norway

Abstract. Transportation is an important yet challenging aspect in terms of mobility for persons with intellectual disabilities (ID). Despite positive implications of designing services with users, persons with ID are rarely given the opportunity to be involved in such design processes. In this action design research (ADR) study we involve persons with ID in the design through observations, photovoice interviews and in a staged, yet naturalistic user enactments on a bus. Our research contributes with design insights on transport supporting services and insights on user involvement of persons with ID in ADR. The three ADR cycles showed that people with ID is a heterogenous group of users and as such emphasizes the need for customizable solutions that support cognitive functions such as conceptual understanding of time and location, language and communication abilities, and alerts and notifications. There is more work to be done on addressing how the IT artifact is shaped by the situational context and vice versa for issues such as stress management and autonomy. User involvement is time-consuming, especially in settings where participants are asked to independently follow instruction such as in photovoice, and during naturalistic evaluations with several uncontrolled variables, such as prototype testing on a bus. Our work shows that this is vital for gaining insights into the worlds and needs of persons with ID to inform design.

Keywords: Action design research · User involvement · Intellectual disability · Transport

1 Introduction

In our project we focus on transport supporting services for cognitive disabled groups in society. One important aspect of our approach with action design research (ADR) is the inclusion of practitioners and end-users in the research process [1]. In line with action research, this is characterized by a participatory approach with user involvement to understand and intervene in social systems [2]. Previous studies stress the need to involve persons with special needs, such as intellectual disability (ID), in design processes [3, 4]. However, this is still an emerging area and most studies report on experiences and benefits of involving proxies or children with special needs in the design process [5–7]. There is a need for more studies that allow individuals with ID to contribute to the

© Springer Nature Switzerland AG 2020
S. Hofmann et al. (Eds.): DESRIST 2020, LNCS 12388, pp. 56–67, 2020.
https://doi.org/10.1007/978-3-030-64823-7_6

design of digital services [6]. Our study contributes with insights on user involvement of marginalized groups by designing services together with youngsters and adults with ID.

Transportation is an important element in terms of mobility and a vital component for independent living [8]. Public transportation, such as busses, trains and subways, is an important resource for those who cannot or do not have access to a car. However, public transportation presents challenges for persons with cognitive disabilities since the independent use of transportation requires skills related to memory, attention, time management, literacy, multitasking and problem-solving [9, 10]. Digital services have the potential to ease and enable transportation for persons with cognitive disabilities. For instance, it can provide prompts for independent travel [11] such as support for identification and orientation during travels [12]. Despite the existing services, transportation remains a challenge and there is a need for more research on how to contribute to independent transportation [10]. In addition, few existing studies seem to involve persons with ID in the design of transport supporting services and in ADR.

In this paper, we describe the design of a prototype for transport supporting services and reflect on our user involvement practices for persons with ID in this design process. The paper makes two main contributions: (a) design insights on transport supporting services and (b) insights on user involvement of persons with ID in ADR.

2   Related Work

In the following sections we introduce intellectual disability and user involvement.

2.1   Intellectual Disability

ID is a cluster term for different syndromes and disorders. The health conditions defined as "intellectual disability" are the conditions, often lifelong, that are manifested during the developmental years. They are characterized by below-average general intellectual function and limitations in adaptive functioning and skills [13–15]. ID is typically operationalized as scoring more than two standard deviations below the population mean on an intelligence test [16, 17]. The World Health Organization's International Classification of Diseases (ICD-11) defines ID as *"a group of developmental conditions characterized by significant impairment of cognitive functions, which are associated with limitations of learning, adaptive behavior and skills"* [13, 15]. The ICD classifies ID into four main clinical subcategories; mild, moderate, severe and profound ID [15].

ID is often characterized as a marked impairment of core, cognitive functions necessary for development of knowledge, reasoning and communication skills. Other main descriptors of ID are difficulties with memory and managing behavior and emotions. In addition, individuals with ID have difficulties meeting the demands of daily life. These difficulties are often related to limitations in social and practical skills [13]. Mental health difficulties like anxiety, depression, attention deficit disorder and attention deficit hyperactivity disorder are also associated with ID [6]. One potential barrier is that individuals with ID experience communicative challenges in terms of production of words and symbols and understanding complex grammatical structures and abstract concepts

[18]. Diagnostically a set of requirements may reflect a disability such as cognitive impairment, yet the way to address each requirement may vary greatly - whether to the individual or in a changing social context.

As a concept, disability has changed in the recent past which have had implications on the perception of what a disability is and how individuals with disabilities are addressed. The medical and social models of disability are the two most prominent models of disability [6]. The medical model of disability views disability as a direct consequence of an impairment. According to Anderberg [19] this perception of disability places the problem with the individual. The impairment or disability is viewed as a condition that must be treated or rehabilitated as far as possible, framing disability as a technical problem as opposed to a social one [20]. In contrast, the social model of disability places the problem with the society. This model, often adopted by individuals with disabilities, calls for social and structural change to enable full participation for individuals with disabilities [6, 20, 21]. The Gap model or the Scandinavian model views disability as a mismatch between the demands from the society and the individual's abilities. Disabilities can therefore be reduced or removed by changing the environment or by strengthening the individual, or both [21]. For technology, Holmes [22] describes such mismatches as *'building blocks of exclusion'*.

2.2 Involving Users with Intellectual Disabilities

User involvement can be understood from various perspectives. It has been described as a term denoting direct contact with users, ranging from an active role in design activities to providing information or being observed [23]. Main approaches include for instance participatory design, user-centered design, ethnography and contextual design. User involvement has a long tradition and the involvement of users in the design process is proven to have positive implications on aspects like user satisfaction, system performance and system quality [24, 25]. It has also been recognized that user involvement can empower participants, change business processes and contribute to social equity [26]. User involvement has been described along a continuum of providing information, commenting on design solutions and/or actively participating in decisions-making [27].

However, the involvement of users is a challenging activity [23, 24] and our user group (individuals with ID) exemplifies and magnifies the challenges with user involvement for design development. Although individuals with ID often vary in their communicative abilities, there are still some shared difficulties which those with ID are likely to encounter. For instance, cognitively loaded skills and communicative difficulties may pose challenges. It is therefore important to reflect and consider how the concept of disability is positioned in a design process and how adjustments can be made to facilitate user involvement [6]. Taking these cognitive disabilities into consideration, we shortly present the visual approach of photovoice and experiential prototyping.

Participation and Engagements. Photovoice aims to capture the reality of people's lives and can provide means of accessing other peoples' worlds and making those worlds accessible to others [28, 29]. In photovoice, the participants take photographs documenting aspects of their lives which are later used to encourage self-initiated reflections on feelings and experiences [30]. It can facilitate the inclusion of persons with ID in design processes as it does not require the ability to read and write nor verbal fluency [28–30]. Whereas methods for including individuals with ID in participatory research has tend to be limited to interviews [28, 31], photovoice offers a means of concretizing in a manner that corresponds more closely to the reasoning of these participants.

Prototypes and Scenarios. Prototyping is a central part of gaining understanding by enabling insight and involvement and ownership alike [32]. It enables designers and developers to understand existing experiences and contexts. It allows users and other stakeholders to explore and evaluate incomplete design ideas [33]. Prototypes and scenarios may enable people to influence the functions and fit of the technology development in authentic settings since: *"users possess the needed practical understanding but lack insight into new technical possibilities"* [34]. Experiential prototypes and scenarios allow the participants to *"experience it "themselves" rather than witnessing a demonstration or someone else's experience"* [33].

3 First and Second ADR Cycles on Problem Diagnosis

The research project follows the guidelines of ADR and the cycles of (a) problem formulation, (b) building, intervention and evaluation, (c) reflection and learning and (d) formalization of learning as described by Sein et al. [1] and elaborated upon by Mullarkey and Hevner [35]. During the early phases of an ADR process, a practice-inspired problem space is explored and formulated, supported by existing theories. This is followed by a design process which includes three principles: reciprocal shaping, mutually influential roles and concurrent evaluation. These principles stress the inseparability of the IT artifact and the context, mutual learning among the participants of the project and the importance of continuous and naturalistic evaluation [1]. The research in this paper includes three ADR cycles to design a prototype for transport supporting service. In line with the recommendation of ADR, we frame transport supporting services as a class of problems [1] which allows us to approach insights and individual evaluations towards systemic development.

3.1 Problem Diagnosis Using Interviews and Observations

In the first cycle we conducted a triangulation of data, consisting of focus group interviews, individual interviews and participant observations. The participants in the focus group interviews included representatives that work closely in practice with persons with ID (i.e. the Norwegian Labour and Welfare Administration, community-based housing, secondary school, day-care centres, work-training centres, public employers and parents). In total, 27 persons participated in the seven focus group interviews (average attendance four persons). Six additional employers participated in individual interviews. All focus group interviews, and the individual interviews focused on work participation and the transition into working life, current barriers and enablers, and the use of technology.

In addition, seven adolescents with ID were observed during a whole day, focusing on school or work activities. The participants included five males and two women who all lived at the same community-based housing and either attended secondary school or had recently started working. Six of them also took part in a focus group interview. The focus groups interviews and individual interviews were recorded and later transcribed. This was combined with the field notes from the observations. The material was analyzed by inductive analysis [36], focusing on challenges and opportunities for work inclusion and the use of technology.

Design Insights from the First Cycle. The first cycle resulted in several insights that described a complex problem space of work inclusion of persons with ID. One of the emergent themes focused on the importance but also challenges of using public transportation in the context of work inclusion for persons with ID. One quote from the focus group with parents: *"In fact, I think a lot of their biggest problem is actually about transport and it's not just the work itself, but the transport [...] So that's part of the entire picture. Because it can ruin the whole day. It [work and transport] is really closely connected.".* The first cycle showed that the transport aspect included several challenges and design insights (see Table 1).

Table 1. Design insights from the first ADR-cycle.

Design insights	Description of requirements
Identifying the correct bus	Assisting in identifying the correct bus for users with vision impairment or limited literacy
Time management	Assisting with time management and reduce the time spent waiting or the need for personal assistance
Reminders	Supporting reminders of when to exit the bus
Changing buses	Supporting change from one bus to another
Social interaction	Supporting in navigating social situations such as handling lack of seating, initiating or avoiding conversations
Sense of direction	Supporting an understanding of orientation, in case of unforeseen events
Stress management	Lessening stress to avoid ruining concentration at work

3.2   Problem Diagnosis Using Photovoice

To gain a deeper understanding of the problem space and to get direct insights from persons with ID about their experiences of transport, we decided to carry out another cycle of problem diagnosis using photovoice interviews. The participants were recruited through purposive sampling in agreement with employers in two regions in Norway. In total, nine adults with ID participated from three different workplaces (one day-care center and two adjusted workplaces). The employers nominated participants based on their ability to (1) give consent, (2) take photos on their own or with the assistance of a researcher, (3) describe and reflect verbally on photos taken, and (4) that they either walk, go by buss, taxi or other means of transportation to work. The participants included seven men and two women, three of them were adults while the remaining were adolescents. Two participants usually travelled by maxitaxi, three participants by bus, one participant by taxi, two participants combined subway and bus, and one participant combined taxi and bus. All participants were initially informed about the study by their manager and a second time repeated by the researchers. During the preparation session, we talked about ethics in regards to taking photos.

The participants used their own smartphones to take photos on their way home and to work. The following day we carried out interviews with the participants in their workplaces. The participants could also invite a colleague or assistant to accompany them during the interview. We started the interview by asking them to tell us about their experience of transportation. They were then asked to show us the photos that they had taken. In connection to each photo we talked about why they had taken the photo, if it represented something that was important or difficult or made them feel a certain way. We discussed the possibilities of using other means of transport and if they would have liked to take other photos. The interviews were transcribed, and the photos were inserted into the interview transcripts to connect them to the reflections made by the participants. The transcribed material was analyzed using thematic analysis [37]. During the analysis we focused on two types of insights: transport and user involvement using photovoice.

Design Insights from the Second Cycle. The second cycle confirmed that the user experiences and needs of persons with ID are heterogenous. For instance, some participants struggled with social interaction and anxiety while others preferred social settings. The photovoice study showed us that both positive and negative experiences of transport are related to routines and the handling of unpredictable situations. Daily transport is less challenging compared to embarking on new routes, or when unpredictable events are experienced as stressful and challenging (See Table 2).

Table 2. Design insights from the second ADR-cycle.

Design insights	Description of requirements
Cognitive load	Customizable and simple instructions
Predictability	Supporting predictability in order to feel safe
Social interaction	Social interaction can be stressful for some and a resource for others
Communication support	Supporting communication with predefined persons in case of unforeseen events
Stigma	Avoiding stigmatizing features
Self-regulation	Making use of existing stress management strategies such as music and drinking soda
Autonomy and the ability to influence	Supporting autonomy and the ability to express preferences for instance to the driver

4   Third ADR Cycle on Design Conceptualization

The design insights from the first two cycles were presented to our advisory board of practitioners in line with the principle of mutual influential roles [1]. They confirmed the practical relevance of the problem space and we discussed the connection to current work practices. During an ideation session they also identified existing digital services that could be relevant and contribute to the solution space. As a parallel process we reviewed literature on intellectual disability and transport to structure the problem and to guide the design towards a theory-ingrained artifact. Based on these, two researchers and a UX-designer started to design the first prototype using Adobe Xd (see Fig. 1). The prototype was then tested in a staged, yet naturalistic user observation [33]. In line with the ADR principle of authentic and concurrent evaluation [1], we rented a bus from the local public transport company - complete with a bus driver - who per our instructions created the necessary scenarios to gain further insights. This gave us the opportunity to understand how the environment influenced the use of our prototype.

Fig. 1. Screenshots of the prototype showing a reminder and different modes of communication during unforeseen events (including a prewritten SMS).

4.1   Design Insights Using Prototypes and Scenarios

Three participants from the photovoice sessions took part in the third cycle. In addition, nine new participants were recruited to cover the diversity of the user group. These were recruited through purposive sampling in agreement with the same employer and with a secondary school in the same region. Eight researchers participated in the observation, four as facilitators and four as observers. The participants included six men and six women, five working in an adjusted setting and seven attending secondary school. All had prior experience of taking the bus but only four of those working in an adjusted setting did it regularly and independently. The scenarios on the bus were carried out in three iterations during the same day: each iteration with three to five participants.

The participants were given a smartphone with the first prototype. The scenarios were structured according to the different themes of the prototype i.e. identifying the correct bus, time management, managing unforeseen events and communication and after which the users were asked to reflect on their experience. Each participant was guided by a researcher and observed by a second research who took notes (See Fig. 2). The field notes from the observation were summarized individually by all researchers directly after the workshop. The notes were then discussed in pairs to cover potentially missing elements. Finally, all notes were combined and analyzed by two of the involved researchers, using thematic analysis [37].

Fig. 2. Photo from the testing of the prototype during the bus transport scenarios.

Design Insight from the Third Cycle. The third cycle confirmed the relevance of the prototype for persons with ID. The design insights centered on the need for a customizable solution that is part of a larger system of assistance (See Table 3).

Table 3. Design insights from the third ADR-cycle.

Design insights	Description of requirements
Practice or daily transport	Supporting users training towards taking the bus as well as users who need support on daily basis
Time visualization	Supporting alternative understandings of time
Font size	Supporting adjustment of font size for users with vision impairment
Text-to-speech	Supporting text-to-speech for users with limited literacy
Customized reminders	Supporting choice of visualization, frequency and kind of reminders during the journey
Mode of communication	Supporting preferences (SMS, voice call or prewritten SMS) during unforeseen events in order to contact predefined people
Part of a larger system	Complementing existing services such as signage, screens and voice information on buses

5 Future Work and Reflections

In the following section we reflect on future work on the design of transport supporting services and the involvement of users with ID in design processes.

5.1 Design of Transport Supporting Services

The contribution and generalization of ADR outcomes can focus on problem and solution outcomes, and design principles [1]. In this paper we contribute with generalization of the problem and solutions instances for transport supporting services for persons with ID. We find that transport supporting services, including public transportation such as buses, metro and community supported taxi travels need to support cognitive functions such as conceptual understanding of time and location. In addition, there is a need to support individual adjustments according to language and communication abilities, such as the use of symbols or photography and prewritten messages that can alert your contacts. There is also a need to customize both the kind and frequency of alerts and notifications. In line with previous studies, we find that digital services could enable independent travel by supporting time management, literacy, problem-solving and memory [9, 18].

There is more work to be done on addressing how transport supporting services sits as part of a larger system, and how the IT artifact is shaped by the situational context and vice versa [1]. For instance, transport supporting services need to make use of already existing signage system such as screens and sound notifications on buses [33]. It is also possible to assist in handling the social scenarios of transport, whether to protect from or to engage in social interactions and to support stress management and autonomy. One could envision the possibility to message the driver for assistance during stressful scenarios. There also scope to include prompts for self-regulation as part of stress management. Future work will focus on redesign of the prototype and formulating design principles for the solution.

5.2 Reflections on User Involvement

Our study shows that user involvement of persons with ID in ADR is time-consuming. Being invited into a design process may be immensely daunting due to the new roles, requests and the potentially long timeline in such developments [38]. There is a need to spend significant time on building trust as well as understanding between the participants and the researchers, especially in settings where the participants are asked to independently follow instruction such as in photovoice, and during naturalistic evaluations with several uncontrolled variables, such as prototype testing on a bus. Involving several groups of participants with ID can therefore be challenging but also important to understand diverse user needs. We see that the *"exclusion shifts toward inclusion when more people can openly participate as designers"* [22] by which we mean contribute visual elements and alter and adapt to the process of shaping the IT artifact. Photovoice proved to be a useful source and a facilitation during the design process as the photographs provide visual support towards a shared design conceptualization. Our study shows that photovoice can provide design insights that otherwise would have been excluded. Naturalistic user observations to get authentic and concurrent evaluation demonstrate context-dependent insights and a step towards reciprocal shaping of the IT artifact and the context. During this cycle, it proved to be important to have one-on-one facilitators and observers to assist and to gather design insights (e.g. Fig. 2).

As mentioned in Sect. 2.1, disability has two prominent models which has implications for how change is introduced: the medical 'deficit' model which focuses on the individual and the social model of disability which places an onus on the social fabric [19–21]. We have found that when designing digital services for persons with ID we need to take both into account: *"people's experiences with products and systems are a complex integration of personal and circumstantial factors"* [33]. 'True' participatory research includes collaboration in every aspects of research: problem definition, methods, data collection, analysis, publication, and dissemination [39] - for this paper we have focused on the processes shaping the design. Our participants have so far had an informative and consultative role in the design process [27].

6 Conclusion

This paper contributes with (a) design insights on transport supporting services and (b) insights on user involvement of persons with ID in ADR. The three ADR cycles showed that people with ID is a heterogenous group of users and as such emphasizes the need for customizable solutions that support cognitive impairment in different social contexts. Our work suggests that the presented outcomes are generalizable to other solution instances that focus on marginalized groups such as users with dementia, stroke or temporary loss of cognitive abilities. While user involvement can be time-consuming it is essential for gaining insights into the worlds and needs of persons with ID. These insights are relevant for other situations where user needs and experiences of marginalized groups are central for innovation and design of services. Understanding, exploring and communicating the experiential aspects of design insights are vital activities [33]. The use of visual support such as photovoice and naturalistic evaluations should be emphasized when designing with people with ID. The study shows the need of user involvement across different modes of engagements in order to gain insights that are individual and context dependent.

Acknowledgements. We thank all the involved participants, research colleagues and project partners. The project is financed by The Research Council of Norway.

References

1. Sein, M., Henfridsson, O., Purao, S., Rossi, M., Lindgren, R.: Action design research. Manag. Inf. Syst. Q. **35**(1), 37–56 (2011)
2. Baskerville, R.L.: Investigating information systems with action research. Commun. Assoc. Inf. Syst. **2**(1), 19 (1999)
3. Rogers, Y., Marsden, G.: Does he take sugar? moving beyond the rhetoric of compassion. Interactions **20**(4), 48–57 (2013)

4. Hook, J., Verbaan, S., Durrant, A., Olivier, P., Wright, P.: A study of the challenges related to DIY assistive technology in the context of children with disabilities. In: Proceedings of the 2014 Conference on Designing Interactive Systems, pp. 597–606. Association for Computing Machinery, New York, NY (2014)
5. Millen, L., Cobb, S., Patel, H.: A method for involving children with autism in design. In Proceedings of the 10th International Conference on Interaction Design and Children, pp. 185–188, Association for Computing Machinery, New York, NY (2011)
6. Benton, L., Johnson, H.: Widening participation in technology design: a review of the involvement of children with special educational needs and disabilities. Int. J. Child-Comput. Interact. **3**, 23–40 (2015)
7. Bossavit, B., Parsons, S. Designing an educational game for and with teenagers with high functioning autism. In: Proceedings of the 14th Participatory Design Conference, pp. 11–20, Association for Computing Machinery, New York, NY (2016)
8. Rosenkvist, J., Risser, R., Iwarsson, S., Wendel, K., Ståhl, A.: The challenge of using public transport: descriptions by people with cognitive functional limitations. J. Transp. Land Use **2**(1), 65–80 (2009)
9. Davies, D.K., Stock, S.E., Holloway, S., Wehmeyer, M.L.: Evaluating a GPS-based transportation device to support independent bus travel by people with intellectual disability. Intellect. Dev. Disabil. **48**(6), 454–463 (2010)
10. Price, R., Marsh, A.J., Fisher, M.H.: Teaching young adults with intellectual and developmental disabilities community-based navigation skills to take public transportation. Behav. Anal. Pract. **11**(1), 46–50 (2018)
11. Mechling, L.C., Seid, N.H.: Educ. Training Autism Dev. Disabil. **46**(2), 220–237 (2011)
12. Mechling, L.C., Seid, N.H.: Use of a hand-held personal digital assistant (PDA) to self-prompt pedestrian travel by young adults with moderate intellectual disabilities. Educ. Training Autism Dev. Disabil. **46**(2), 220–237 (2011)
13. Carulla, L.S., et al.: Intellectual developmental disorders: towards a new name, definition and framework for "mental retardation/intellectual disability" in ICD-11. World Psychiatry **10**(3), 175–180 (2011)
14. McKenzie, K., Taggart, L., Coates, V., McAloon, T., Hassiotis, A.: Systematic review of the prevalence and incidence of intellectual disabilities: current trends and issues. Curr. Dev. Disord. Rep. **3**(2), 104–115 (2016)
15. Mulhall, P., Taggart, L., Coates, V., McAloon, T., Hassiotis, A.: A systematic review of the methodological and practical challenges of undertaking randomised-controlled trials with cognitive disability populations. Social Science and Medicine **200**, 114–128 (2018)
16. Rutter, M.J., et al.: Rutter's Child and Adolescent Psychiatry. Wiley, Chichester (2011)
17. Emerson, E., Hatton, C., Baines, S., Robsertson, J.: The physical health of British adults with intellectual disability: cross sectional study. Int. J. Equity Health **15**(1), 11 (2016)
18. Finlay, W.M.L., Antaki, C.: How staff pursue questions to adults with intellectual disabilities. Journal of Intellectual Disability Research **56**(4), 361–370 (2012)
19. Anderberg, P.: Making both ends meet. Disabil. Stud. Q. 25(3) (2005)
20. McKenzie, J.: Models of intellectual disability: Towards a perspective of (poss) ability. Journal of Intellectual Disability Research **57**(4), 370–379 (2013)
21. Shakespeare, T.: Social models of disability and other life strategies. Scand. J. Disabil. Res. **6**(1), 8–21 (2004)
22. Holmes, K.: Mismatch: How Inclusion Shapes Design. MIT Press, Cambridge (2018)
23. Kujala, S.: User involvement: a review of the benefits and challenges. Behav. Inf. Technol. **22**(1), 1–16 (2003)
24. Baroudi, J.J., Olson, M.H., Ives, B.: An empirical study of the impact of user involvement on system usage and information satisfaction. Communications of the ACM **29**(3), 232–238 (1986)

25. Bano, M., Zowghi, D.: A systematic review on the relationship between user involvement and system success. Information and Software Technology **58**, 148–169 (2015)
26. Keay-Bright, W.: The reactive colours project: demonstrating participatory and collaborative design methods for the creation of software for autistic children. Des. Principles Pract. Int. J. **1**(2), 7–15 (2007)
27. Damodaran, L.: User involvement in the systems design process - a practical guide for users. Behav. Inf. Technol. **15**(6), 363–377 (1996)
28. Povee, K., Bishop, B.J., Roberts, L.D.: The use of photovoice with people with intellectual disabilities: Reflections, challenges and opportunities. Disabil. Soc. **29**(6), 893–907 (2014)
29. Booth, T., Booth, W.: In the frame: Photovoice and mothers with learning difficulties. Disabil. Soc. **18**(4), 431–442 (2003)
30. Wang, C., Burris, M.A.: Photovoice: Concept, methodology, and use for participatory needs assessment. Health Educ. Behav. **24**(3), 369–387 (1997)
31. Jurkowski, J.M.: Photovoice as participatory action research tool for engaging people with intellectual disabilities in research and program development. Intellect. Dev. Disabil. **46**(1), 1–11 (2008)
32. Boehner, K., DePaula, R., Dourish, P., Sengers, P.: Affect: from information to interaction. In: Proceedings of the 4th Decennial Conference on Critical Computing: Between Sense and Sensibility, pp. 59–68 (2005)
33. Buchenau, M., Suri, J.F.: Experience prototyping. In: Proceedings of the 3rd Conference on Designing Interactive Systems: Processes, Practices, Methods, and Techniques, pp. 424–433. ACM (2000)
34. Ehn, P.: Scandinavian design: on participation and skill. In: Adler, P., Winograd, T. (eds.) Usability: Turning Technologies into Tools. Oxford University Press, Oxford (1992)
35. Mullarkey, M.T., Hevner, A.R.: An elaborated action design research process model. Eur. J. Inf. Syst. **28**(1), 6–20 (2019)
36. Graneheim, U.H., Lundman, B.: Qualitative content analysis in nursing research: concepts, procedures and measures to achieve trustworthiness. Nurse Educ. Today **24**(2), 105–112 (2004)
37. Clark, V., Braun, V.: Thematic analysis. In: Michalos, A.C. (ed.) Encyclopaedia of Quality of Life and Well-Being Research. Springer, Dordrecht, Netherlands (2014)
38. Frauenberger, C., Good, J., Alcorn, A., Pain, H.: Supporting the design contributions of children with autism spectrum conditions. In: Proceedings of the 11th International Conference on Interaction Design and Children, pp. 134–143 (2012)
39. Balcazar, F.E., Keys, C.B., Kaplan, D.L., Suarez-Balcazar, Y.: Participatory action research and people with disabilities: Principles and challenges. Can. J. Rehabil. **12**, 105–112 (1998)

Intrinsic Motivation to Share Health Information: Design Guidelines and Features for Patient Sharing Platforms

Lina Bouayad[1,2]([✉]), Monica Chiarini Tremblay[3], Hemant Jain[4], and Carmelo Gaudioso[5]

[1] Florida International University, Miami, FL 33199, USA
lbouayad@fiu.edu
[2] James A. Haley Veterans Hospital, Tampa, FL 33612, USA
[3] College of William and Mary, Williamsburg, VA 23185, USA
Monica.Tremblay@mason.wm.edu
[4] The University of Tennessee at Chattanooga, Chattanooga, TN 37403, USA
Hemant-jain@utc.edu
[5] Roswell Park Comprehensive Cancer Center, Buffalo, NY 14203, USA
carmelo.gaudioso@roswellpark.org

Abstract. Health-related social media platforms, such as PatientsLikeMe, have enabled patients to share information with other patients with similar conditions and more advanced in their health care continuum (i.e., survivors). These platforms have demonstrated the value of patient to patient communication; such as learning more about new treatment options, outcomes, and quality of life. Yet, evidence suggests that most health applications have low usage rates by physicians and patients. Data sharing platforms where patients share their medical information will not succeed unless security and confidentiality are assured, and enough patients are motivated to participate. Drawing on the theories of motivation, we developed design guidelines and features for a platform that encourages long-term participation. The proposed design guidelines and features are anticipated to increase users' intrinsic motivation through feelings of competence and autonomy; which in turn will increase information sharing. In collaboration with an oncologist and a non-profit cancer survivor organization, we design an experimental study to test our design guidelines and features.

Keywords: Platform design · Motivation theory · Intrinsic motivation · Personal health record

1 Introduction

A recent New York Times article reported that Electronic Health Record (EHR) vendors that impede data-sharing—a practice called information blocking—could be fined up to $1 million per violation. Additionally, doctors accused of information blocking could be subject to a federal investigation [1]. New regulations by the Department of Health and

© Springer Nature Switzerland AG 2020
S. Hofmann et al. (Eds.): DESRIST 2020, LNCS 12388, pp. 68–74, 2020.
https://doi.org/10.1007/978-3-030-64823-7_7

Human Services (HHS) and the Centers for Medicare and Medicaid Services (CMS) aim at empowering patients through the access of their health information. These new regulations will result in the proliferation of data sharing platforms and applications which utilize EHR to improve health outcomes and reduce costs.

However, data sharing platforms will not be sustainable unless enough patients agree to participate. Research on sharing health information for medical research indicates that patient's willingness to share information depends on anonymity, intended use, the trust of the intermediary, transparency around personally controlled health records' access and use, and payment. The decision to share sensitive health information on these platforms depends on the perceived benefits versus the perceived privacy risk. Current efforts to design sustainable online platforms; mostly focus on enhancing the extrinsic motivations to share information such as reputation and respect by others in the online community. Yet, to our knowledge, no study has looked at the design of platform for sharing health information that encourages a patient to share their health information by deliberately designing features that increase intrinsic motivation of the user.

Drawing on the theories of motivation, we develop design guidelines and identify features for a platform that encourages long-term use by participants. Design guidelines include a method to match with relevant patients and feedback mechanisms that map to the various forms of intrinsic motivations. In our instantiation, we focus on the sharing of information related to cancer survivorship skills such as management of side effects, toxicity, complications, and treatment costs. We study the impact of design features that enhance the feeling of competence and autonomy of the participants. In collaboration with an oncologist and non-profit cancer survivor organization, we design an experimental study to test our design guidelines. The rest of this paper is organized as follows. Section 2 includes background and related work. Section 3 describes the design framework and design features. Section 4 presents evaluation guidelines using a breast cancer use case. Section 5 lists concluding remarks and future work.

2 Related Work

Most patient healthcare records today have been digitized through the implementation of the EHR. This digitation has enabled the creation and storage of massive health datasets. Mirroring the provision of care in the United States, there is significant fragmentation of digital patient information among various healthcare facilities, insurance providers, and patient's personal records. Each of these entities has access to a local but incomplete copy of the patient's health record. Fragmented patient records negatively affect the effective and efficient treatment of a patient's conditions.

Recently, health-related social media websites, such as PatientLikeMe that are designed to support patient's sharing of their health information with other patients with similar condition are becoming popular. These sites have demonstrated the value of patient to patient communication; such as learning about new treatment options and informing disease self-management [2]. Unfortunately, these efforts are entirely separate from patient medical records, which may result in participants potentially sharing incomplete, inaccurate, and unvalidated information on these websites. Studies have suggested positive associations between better health and using the internet to gather health information. Others suggest that a substantial portion of medical information on the Internet is false or misleading, causing significant difficulties for providers and patients alike.

There have been attempts to address patient information fragmentation through the development of the health information exchanges (HIEs). HIEs enable the electronic sharing of clinical information across different health care organizations to improve the efficiency, cost-effectiveness, quality, and safety of health care delivery. HIEs have enabled providers to collaborate resulting in a reduction in duplication of medical procedures [3, 4]. Real-time access to interinstitutional healthcare data has therefore shown to be very effective at improving patient health outcomes, reducing costs [4] and reducing readmissions [5]. Unfortunately, HIEs have been suffering from sustainability issues [6], and the full impact of HIE is inadequately studied [7]. Frameworks for sustainable HIEs is still lacking [8].

These platforms should be designed and dA potential approach to address the completeness and veracity of information shared on health-related social media websites is to create information management platforms that allow integration of the Patient Health Record (PHR) and patient-reported outcomes [9]. Reviews of the literature reported a positive impact on efficiency, healthcare disparities, patient-centeredness, patient satisfaction, and safety. Conversely, the lack of incorporating EHR (sharing EHR with patients) would lessen these reported benefits [10, 11].

Prior research lists several explanations for participating in online communities from reputation and joy to helping others to reciprocity and commitment [11, 12]. These studies investigate the link between different motivators and system use. In our work, we develop design guidelines and identify features that can significantly impact the long-term use of sharing platforms.

eployed in ways that motivate patients to participate and share information. There is no shortage of literature extolling the potential of technologies to improve patient care, yet evidence suggests that most applications have low usage rates by physicians and patients [13]. Using prior knowledge on user motivators to share information, we design new features for patient-to-patient sharing platforms. The objective of this research is to study the impact of the above design features on sharing of health information among patients.

3   Framework and Design Features

Prior studies have relied on motivation theories to understand the information sharing behavior on online platforms [14,15]. Widely adopted in education, the Self-Determination Theory (SDT) proposed by Deci and Ryan [16, 17], is used to understand the motivations that guide human behavior. The theory emphasizes the importance of inner motivation for personality development and self-regulation. As opposed to extrinsic motivation, where external outcomes guide actions, intrinsically motivated behavior is interesting and/or enjoyable. The central concept of intrinsic motivation is divided into three primitives, namely: intrinsic motivation to experience stimulation (IS), intrinsic motivation to know (IM), and intrinsic motivation to accomplish things (IA) [17]. Extensive research shows that intrinsic motivation leads to a higher quality outcome and a better personal experience. Cognitive Evaluation Theory (CET) is an extension of SDT that looks at factors that diminish and enhance intrinsic motivation [16]. As per the theory, two main aspects of intrinsic motivation are *feeling of competence* and *feeling of autonomy*. Grounded in (SDT) and (CET), we develop design guidelines and identify features to enhance the three types of intrinsic motivation (IS, IM, and IA) to share health information.

3.1 Design Framework and Features

In our framework, cancer patients will have the ability to share information with other cancer patients. While other factors such as system trust may impact participation on sharing platforms, those have been studied extensively in prior literature and are outside the scope of this study. Based on our kernel theories, we focus on designing features that will encourage patients to share EHR and patient-reported data as follows:

Feeling of Autonomy Features (choice): Using criteria such as disease type, severity and prognosis, patient matching is personalized to fit the preferences of the participants. Additionally, patient has complete freedom to decide what information to share and with which other patients.

Feeling of Competence Features (impact and outcomes): The participant (cancer survivor) that has shared their information with another patient (cancer patient) will have

Table 1. Components of the proposed design framework (adapted from [15])

Meta-requirements	Support the participants' intrinsic motivation to 1) experience stimulation, 2) to know, and 3) to accomplish things through enhanced feelings of competence and autonomy
Meta-design	The development of features that will support the various types of intrinsic motivation as follows: – Choice of users to support based on the demographic information, type and severity of the case (feeling of autonomy) – Choice of information to share based on need and privacy concerns (feeling of autonomy). – Access to information on impact of health data sharing following recommendation (feeling of competence) – Access to impact of information and experience shared on patient decision (Feeling of Competence)
Kernel theories	Self-Determination Theory (SDT), Cognitive Evaluation Theory (CET)
Testable design product hypotheses	Using an instantiation of the system design, test the following hypotheses: – Positive effect of the choice features on the continued participation in the sharing platform – Positive effect of the impact and outcome features on the continued participation in the sharing platform

the ability to see the impact (such as improvements in quality of care, quality of life, and treatment costs) of the information they have shared has had on the other patient.

To enhance the privacy of patients, health information shared on the platform will be de-identified (Table 1).

4 Design Guidelines Evaluation: The Case of Breast Cancer Survivors

To evaluate and refine our design guidelines, we plan to conduct a focus group followed by an experiment involving breast cancer survivors in the US. We have partnered with a non-profit organization BreastConnect[1], which will provide us with participants. We will recruit patients that were previously diagnosed with breast cancer and completed at least one type of treatment (surgery, radiotherapy, or chemotherapy), regardless of cancer stage or clinical outcomes. We will utilize focus groups of breast cancer survivors to 1) identify the current barriers to participation in online sharing platforms, and 2) determine the level of privacy to be supported by the design, and 3) pilot our experiment instrument. Results from these exploratory focus groups will allow us to refine the instrument of our experiment as needed.

4.1 Controlled Experiment

Experimental Design
A between-subjects design will be used to evaluate the impact of platform design features on the survivor's intention to respond in the long term. Each participant will be presented with fictional patient scenarios and asked to select the most appropriate one to respond to. Participants will be randomly placed into four different groups with varying feeling of competence and autonomy levels.

Experiment Procedures
Participants will have to certify that they were breast cancer survivors on Qualtrics before accessing the experiment questionnaire. In order to prevent learning effects, participants will also be required to certify completing the experiment once only.

First, participants will be presented with an informed consent agreement page describing the purpose of the study, the study procedures, alternatives to participation, compensation and contact information. Participants' identity will remain anonymous.

Next, each participant will be presented with fictional patient cases. The cases used in the experiment were created in collaboration with an oncologist. Each case includes the patient's demographics, diagnosis and treatment information in a post format. The response section will be intentionally left out since the participant's task will be to determine the response to the post. The participants will be prompted to respond. Last, participants will have to indicate whether they would like to share part or all of their (fictional) PHR data.

---

[1] https://www.breastconnect.org/.

Participants will be randomly placed into different groups. Depending on their group assignment, practitioners will either be 1) presented with the feeling of competence features, or 2) not presented with the feeling of competence features and will either 1) be given the option to select the patient they are willing to share with, or 2) not given that option. Follow-up survey questions will be presented for manipulation checks. Results from the experiment will be presented at the conference.

5   Conclusions

In this study, we investigate the effect of platform design features that are grounded on motivations theories, on the willingness to share PHR data and patient-reported outcomes on a data sharing platform. The proposed design guidelines describe design features that are anticipated to increase users' feelings of competence and autonomy. Using a focus group and a controlled experiment with cancer patients, we evaluate the effectiveness of our proposed design guidelines. Results from this study extend the design science literature by informing the design of online platforms for sensitive information sharing. In practice, the proposed design guidelines can help design systems that facilitate the level, scale, and liquidity of data sharing. For cancer patients, sharing of health records and patient-reported outcomes would 1) enable cancer survivors to contribute to the decision making and healing newly diagnose patients, and 2) raise awareness about under-studied treatment outcomes.

References

1. Singer, N.: When apps get your medical data, your privacy may go with it. The New York Times, 03-Sep-2019
2. Frost, J.H., Massagli, M.P.: Social uses of personal health information within PatientsLikeMe, an Online patient community: what can happen when patients have access to one another's data. J. Med. Internet. Res. **10**(3), e15 (2008)
3. Bardhan, I., Ayabakan, S., Zheng, E., Kirksey, K.: Value of health information sharing in reducing healthcare waste: an analysis of duplicate testing across hospitals. ICIS 2014 Proceedings (2014)
4. Saef, S.H., Melvin, C.L., Carr, C.M.: Impact of a health information exchange on resource use and medicare-allowable reimbursements at 11 emergency departments in a Midsized City. West J Emerg. Med. **15**(7), 777–785 (2014). https://doi.org/10.5811/westjem.2014.9.21311
5. Vest, J.R., Kern, L.M., Silver, M.D., Kaushal, R.: The potential for community-based health information exchange systems to reduce hospital readmissions. J. Am. Med. Inform. Assoc. **22**(2), 435–442 (2015). https://doi.org/10.1136/amiajnl-2014-002760
6. Kruse, C.S., Regier, V., Rheinboldt, K.T.: Barriers over time to full implementation of health information exchange in the United States. JMIR Med. Inform. **2**(2) (2014). https://doi.org/10.2196/medinform.3625
7. Hersh, W., et al.: Health Information Exchange. Agency for Healthcare Research and Quality (US) (2015)
8. Adler-Milstein, J., Lin, S.C., Jha, A.K.: The number of health information exchange efforts is declining, leaving the viability of broad clinical data exchange uncertain. Health Aff. **35**(7), 1278–1285 (2016). https://doi.org/10.1377/hlthaff.2015.1439

9. Bouayad, L., Ialynytchev, A., Padmanabhan, B.: Patient health record systems scope and functionalities: literature review and future directions. J. Med. Internet Res. **19**(11), e388 (2017). https://doi.org/10.2196/jmir.8073

10. Wasko, M.M., Faraj, S.: Why should i share? examining social capital and knowledge contribution in electronic networks of practice. MIS Q. **29**, 35–57 (2005)

11. Otte-Trojel, T., de Bont, A., Rundall, T. G., van de Klundert, J.: How outcomes are achieved through patient portals: a realist review. J. Am. Med. Inf. Assoc. **21**(4), 751–757 (2014). https://doi.org/10.1136/amiajnl-2013-002501

12. Bateman, P. J., Gray, P. H., Butler, B. S.: Research note—the impact of community commitment on participation in online communities. Inf. Syst. Res. **22**(4), 841–854 (2010). https://doi.org/10.1287/isre.1090.0265

13. Tarricone, R., et al.: Mobile health divide between clinicians and patients in cancer care: results from a cross-sectional international survey. JMIR mHealth and uHealth, **7**(9), e13584 (2019). https://doi.org/10.2196/13584

14. Oh, S.: The characteristics and motivations of health answerers for sharing information, knowledge, and experiences in online environments. J. Am. Soc. Inf. Sci. Tech. **63**(3), 543–557 (2012). https://doi.org/10.1002/asi.21676

15. Zhang, X., Liu, S., Chen, X., (Yale) Gong, Y.: Social capital, motivations, and knowledge sharing intention in health Q&A communities. Manage. Decis. **55**(7), 1536–1557 (2017). https://doi.org/10.1108/MD-10-2016-0739

16. Deci, R., Ryan, E. L.: Self-determination and intrinsic motivation in human behavior. EL Deci, RM Ryan (1985)

17. Ryan R. M., Deci, E. L.: Intrinsic and extrinsic motivations: classic definitions and new directions. Contemp. Educ. Psychol. **25**(1), 54–67 (2000). https://doi.org/10.1006/ceps.1999.1020

Technology Personalization in Health Applications for Patients with Autism Spectrum Disorder: Artifact Design and a Controlled Experiment

Lina Bouayad[1,2]([✉]), Anol Bhattacherjee[3], Mavara Agrawal[1], Spurthy Dharanikota[1], and Polina Durneva[1]

[1] Florida International University, Miami, FL 33199, USA
{lbouayad,mmirzaag,sdhar006,pdurn001}@fiu.edu
[2] James A. Haley Veterans Hospital, Tampa, FL 33612, USA
[3] University of South Florida, Tampa, FL 33199, USA
abhatt@usf.edu

Abstract. This study will examine the design of speech conversion techniques to create a personalized voice alert system to improve user compliance and reduce wandering among individuals with autistic spectrum disorder (ASD). Using a controlled experiment with ASD patients, we will evaluate our proposed design feature under different conditions of technological familiarity and disease severity.

Keywords: Health application design · Speech conversion · Familiarity · Personalization · Generalized learning disability · Autism spectrum disorder

1 Introduction

Personalization of technology, an effective means for accommodating individual differences [1], is associated with a series of cognitive, social, and emotional effects [2]. Personalization of user interfaces is a desired feature among users of personal computers and smartphone applications [2], In the context of recommender systems, personalization has been shown to enhance system trust and adoption [3]. Personalized recommendations also improve productivity, efficiency, and decision effectiveness [4], and provide a more enjoyable user experience [1].

While the general benefits of personalization are well known, less known are its application and utilization by users with special needs. In the special needs context, the focus of technological interventions is often not to improve productivity, efficiency, or effectiveness, but to minimize serious risks like inadvertently wandering off outside a shelter home. User safety is a primary goal in such settings and user compliance with system notifications is expected to improve user safety. The use of technologies among special needs population is not only an understudied topic in the information systems literature, but to the best of our knowledge, the use of technologies to enhance user safety has also not been explored previously. In addition, voice systems in use today

S. Hofmann et al. (Eds.): DESRIST 2020, LNCS 12388, pp. 75–80, 2020.
https://doi.org/10.1007/978-3-030-64823-7_8

generate alerts and notifications, are not personalized to the specific needs of the target population. In this study, we aim at filling the above gaps in the literature by designing a new customized voice feature connected with the geolocation of special need users that can alert them if they are stepping outside of a safe zone, like a shelter zone, and investigate the effect of this personalization feature on compliance behaviors and safety outcomes among people with Autism Spectrum Disorder (ASD) using a controlled experiment.

According to CDC, ASD affects 1 in 59 children in the United States and has seen increasing prevalence in recent years. Individuals with ASD have higher rates of comorbidity and mortality compared to age-matched peers (Croen et al. 2015; Krahn, Hammond, and Turner 2006), and worse health outcomes due to behaviors such as wandering and elopement [5, 6, 7]. Wandering poses safety and security risks for ASD patients as well as significant challenges for their caregivers. For example, 23-year old ASD patient Arnaldo Rios Soto wandered out of his group home in North Miami, Florida on July 18, 2016, and was shot at by police officers for failing to respond to officers' orders; the shot injuring his therapist Charles Kinsley who was trying to retrieve his patient from the street [8].

Monitoring devices that generate alerts in case of wandering and tracking/locating devices help mitigate wandering [9] and reduce time to discovery [10] among dementia patients. However, in the ASD population, social and communication impairments limit the chances that ASD patients may respond to technological alerts such as text messages, Individuals with ASD lack the ability to relate new stimuli to past experiences and are therefore often unable to respond to new or unexpected circumstances in a safe and consistent manner [11, 12]. Furthermore, ASD patients tend to exhibit response to familiar voices such as that of therapists or caregivers with whom they have established rapport, but not with unfamiliar others. Alerts would therefore need to be converted to a recognizable (personalized) voice to work with ASD patients. Our plan is to design a voice conversion layer that will be incorporated with monitoring devices in intended to improve ASD patients' compliance with automated alerts. Lack of familiarity with technology is often described as a factor limiting the acceptance and use of new technology [13]. Personalization may help ASD patients compensate for unfamiliar technologies or in unexpected circumstances, such as an alert in a familiar voice warning autistic patients when they are stepping out of a group home. Yet, the joint effects of personalization and familiarity on technology acceptance is yet to be studied, to the best of our knowledge, and more so, among specialized user populations.

In this study, we investigate the effects of technology personalization and user familiarity with technological interventions on ASD users' compliance with voice alerts under varying conditions of disability severity. Personalization is manipulated using a voice recognizable by the user, such as the voice of their therapist or caregiver. Using an experimental study, we will evaluate the efficacy of this artifact in improving patient compliance and safety in various scenarios of familiarity and disease severity. In doing so, we hope to contribute toward building a theory of technology compliance behavior for special needs users, which is currently missing from the literature.

2 Theoretical Background

Prior research on personalized content, such as those obtained from recommendation agents, has typically focused on their adoption and use in utilitarian personal or work settings in order to improve user productivity, efficiency, or effectiveness in volitional choice behavior. In these contexts, three theoretical perspectives has helped explain user behavior: information overload, uses and gratification, and user involvement [14]. The information overload perspective suggests that increased fit between recommended content and user interests, as a result of personalization, reduces information overload, and thereby improves work outcomes and user satisfaction. The use and gratifications perspective suggest that users will adopt personalized content if they find it useful or enjoyable. The user involvement perspective implies that explicit involvement in the personalization process secures users' buy-in into the technology and consequently drive their preference for personalized content. However, these theories are less applicable in the unique context of our study, where users are not making a conscious choice to use technology personalization based on their productivity, efficiency, or efficiency benefits, but rather instinctively reacting to a recognized voice, without concern about potential outcomes. Furthermore, behavioral outcomes such as improve patient safety is observable by other observers, but not the intended user.

Personalization research has previously explored multiple dimensions of implementation choices, such as the object of personalization (e.g. what is personalized - interface, content, etc.), subject of personalization (e.g. for whom technology is personalized – individuals, groups, or organizations), and means of personalization (i.e. who/what does personalization) [15]. Based on these dimensions, prior literature has identified four major types of personalization: architectural, relational, instrumental, and commercial [15]. Architectural personalization focuses on improving user experience by constructing pleasant user space through arrangement of digital artifacts. Relational personalization refers to the mediation of interpersonal relationships by providing a convenient platform for interactions. Then, instrumental personalization primarily focuses on the functionality of technology and aims to provide user-friendly tools to meet users' needs. Finally, commercial personalization aims to differentiate products and services to tailor to the needs of specific segments of customers. The voice personalization artifact designed in our study is a form of instrumental and relational personalization in that we provide a technology that meets the specific instrumental needs of individuals with ASD, and that this technology embeds relationships between ASD patients and their caregivers though the use of familiar voices.

Prior literature emphasizes the distinction between personalization, customization and adaptation, often used interchangeably in common parlance [15], [16]. Customization refers to user-initiated actions towards creating personalization and relies primarily on data provided by the user [15]. Then, adaptation refers to the properties of a system to adjust its behavior and interactions to fit users' needs. Overall, customization and adaptation can be considered components of personalization.

A related stream of information systems research suggests that lack of familiarity with new technologies is often a significant factor limiting the acceptance and use of those technologies [13]. Familiarity is the result of repeated exposure to certain people, tools, or circumstances that allow people to respond in a programmatic manner though experience or unconscious priming, rather than through a process of deliberate and conscious thinking [17]. In our ASD study context, familiarity may be viewed at two levels: (1) familiarity with the technology and (2) familiarity with the voice embedded in that technology. Through repeated use, users with ASD will become more familiar with the device. However, the use of a non-recognizable (a non-personalized) voice may limit the technology's efficacy in improving patient compliance with system notifications to avoid wandering to dangerous areas; which in turn improves patient safety. This second familiarity dimension is referred to as personalization (of voice) in this study (Table 1).

Higher condition severity may also increase the need for familiarity (with voice). Prior research has shown that severity of an illness could have direct consequences on a patient's behaviors such as medication adherence [18, 19] and treatment compliance [20, 21]. In the context of autism, Ekas et al. examined the development of compliance in toddlers with and without ASD and found that high-risk children's ASD symptom severity was associated with decreased compliance [22]. Severity of autism further aggravates a patient's social, communication and behavior impairments such as noncompliance to unfamiliar voices or situations. Autism patients' compliance with new system (voice alert system) recommendations can therefore be problematic owing to their impairments and may vary with the severity of the condition.

3   Design Framework and Features

Using deep autoencoders for voice conversion [23], we intend to design a feature that enables the customization of existing tracking devices to fit the needs of users with ASD. The supervised learning method uses voice segments from the target user (the

Table 1. Components of the proposed design framework (adapted from [24])

Meta-requirements	Improve participants' response to and compliance with automated alerts at different levels of disease severity
Meta-design	The development of a personalization feature that *converts automated alerts to a recognizable voice*. This will support the need for familiarity among this user population
Kernel theories	Personalization concepts
Testable design product hypotheses	Using an instantiation of the system design, test the following hypotheses: – Compared to prompts in a *generic voice*, prompts in a *recognizable voice* is more likely to generate a compliance behavior among users with ASD – The relationship between voice conversion and compliance will be stronger among users with higher *disease severity* – The relationship between voice conversion and compliance will be stronger among users with lower *system familiarity*

patient's caregiver in this case), to learn speaker features. The voice conversion layer to be incorporated with tracking devices. The speaker features will be used to convert all wandering related notifications into recognizable voices for each ASD patient. We then evaluate the effectiveness our newly developed feature at improving the compliance with system notifications to avoid wandering to dangerous areas.

4 Design Evaluation: Controlled Experiment

Using an experiment involving young adults with ASD, we intend to assess the effectiveness of the newly developed voice conversion feature at enhancing subject compliance with the system notifications. An initial convenience sample of 50 young adults with ASD and their parents or caregivers will be selected at the Health Care Network Faculty Group Practice in Miami, Florida. Our goal is to expand this study to other locations where adults and/or families of individuals with autism attend activities to obtain a final sample of 160 subjects or above.

4.1 Preliminary Survey of Caregivers

Before running our controlled experiment, we will conduct a cross-sectional survey with the participants' caregivers to assess the participants' disease prevalence, and prior prevalence of response to directions and notifications. After signing an informed consent, the participants will complete a survey investigating wandering or elopement behaviors of adults with autism. The survey will be administered by a trained research assistant in person on the FIU campus or other respective location.

4.2 Controlled Experiment

Experimental Design
A 2 × 2 × 2 between-subject factorial design will be used to evaluate the effectiveness of our proposed personalization feature on the response to notification among adults on the Autism Spectrum (Table 2).

Table 2. Experimental design

| | | Disease Severity | | | |
| | | Low Severity | | High Severity | |
		Familiarity Low	Familiarity High	Familiarity Low	Familiarity High
Personalization (Voice Conversion Feature)	*Not Present*	Group 1	Group 2	Group 5	Group 6
	Present	Group 3	Group 4	Group 7	Group 8

Participants will be first screened for disease severity. We will try to recruit a balanced sample of low and high severity participants. Participants within each severity group will then be randomly divided into four experimental treatment groups of high/low personalization or high/low familiarity.

Experiment Procedures

First, the participants' caregivers will be asked to read a sample text of 10 sentences. The voice of the caregivers will be recorded and used for the voice conversion. Each participant will then be presented with a scenario of wandering. The participants will be left to wander from one room to another. As they are walking within the facility, they will be prompted to turn left or right.

Depending on their treatment group, participants will hear a generic voice, or a voice converted by the software to resemble the one of their caregivers. Participants in the low familiarity group will only go through the task once, whereas participants in the high familiarity group will perform the same task three consecutive times.

A research assistant will observe the participants' response to the system notifications and record their compliance behavior. Results from the experiment will be presented at the conference.

5 Conclusions

This study investigates the role of personalization in technology solutions for a marginalized population. Our study is expected to inform how personalization and familiarity can enhance compliance with system notifications. If proven effective, the proposed artifact can increase the compliance with system notifications to avoid wandering to dangerous areas; which in turn will improve the safety of special need users. In addition, this study also represents an initial step to build a design theory that links personalization and familiarity with instinctive use (compliance) behaviors toward safety outcomes, which diverge from traditional theories that focus on informed or reasoned use in personal or organizational settings.

References

1. Arazy, O., Nov, O., Kumar, N.: Personalityzation: UI personalization, theoretical grounding in HCI and design research. AIS Trans. Hum. Comput. Interact. **7**(2), 43–69 (2015)
2. Blom, J.O., Monk, A.F.: Theory of personalization of appearance: why users personalize their PCs and mobile phones. Hum. Comput. Interact. **18**(3), 193–228 (2003). https://doi.org/10.1207/s15327051hci1803_1
3. Komiak, S.Y.X., Benbasat, I.: The effects of personalization and familiarity on trust and adoption of recommendation agents. MIS Q. **30**(4), 941–960 (2006). https://doi.org/10.2307/25148760
4. Li, T., Unger, T.: Willing to pay for quality personalization? trade-off between quality and privacy. Eur. J. Inf. Syst. **21**(6), 621–642 (2012). https://doi.org/10.1057/ejis.2012.13
5. Guan, J., Li, G.: Injury mortality in individuals with Autism. Am. J. Public Health **107**(5), 791–793 (2017). https://doi.org/10.2105/AJPH.2017.303696
6. Bilder, D., et al.: Excess mortality and causes of death in Autism spectrum disorders: a follow up of the 1980s Utah/UCLA Autism epidemiologic study. J. Autism Dev. Disord. **43**(5), 1196–1204 (2013)

The Suggestion of Design Theory Artefacts for e-Government in South Africa

Romi Vidmar[1]([✉]) [iD], Eduan Kotzé[2] [iD], and Thomas M. van der Merwe[1] [iD]

[1] University of South Africa, Johannesburg, Republic of South Africa
romividmar@gmail.com

[2] University of the Free State, Bloemfontein, Republic of South Africa

Abstract. DSR is growing in acceptance as a research methodology in information systems for the design of innovative artefacts including design theory artefacts. Practical application of DSR can prove challenging when design theory artefacts are suggested for the first time originating from the field of practice. Within the described research context, this paper focuses on explaining how design theory artefacts were conceived as a consequence of the researcher's immersion as a government chief information officer in South Africa. Using DSR methodology enabled the rigorous design and evaluation of a tentative theory of e-Government from an information systems perspective, comprised of a framework of twelve component design theory artefacts which may enhance the progress of e-Government in South Africa and which may have a broader application internationally.

Keywords: e-Government · Enterprise architecture · DSR · TOGAF · e-Government theory · e-Government reference architecture · Theory of practice

1 Introduction

Research in e-Government dates to the 1990s and is seen as a multidisciplinary field of study. The two primary fields contributing to e-Government are public administration (PA) and information systems (IS). Both these fields are considered to be lacking strong native theories, which are descriptive, predictive and testable. The researcher identified the lack of e-Government theory from an IS perspective as a distinct and recognized knowledge gap and a barrier to its possible future recognition as a branch of information systems (Bannister and Connolly 2015; Goldkuhl 2016; Paulin 2017). Enterprise architecture, applied in this work is also a young and formative field of theory and practice requiring more research (van der Raadt 2011; Boucharas et al. 2010). Lack of theory to guide e-Government implementation can produce detrimental effects of poor system implementation and bring into question the viability of e-Government as a possible future discrete field of IS research (Anthopoulos et al. 2010; Bannister and Connolly 2015; Paulin 2017; GITOC 2009). Some researchers observed that South Africa is not progressing well in e-Government noting a regression in its achievements (Cloete 2012).

e-Government refers to the use of ICTs to reengineer the government organisation using the possibilities offered by advancing ICTs to enable government to become more

© Springer Nature Switzerland AG 2020
S. Hofmann et al. (Eds.): DESRIST 2020, LNCS 12388, pp. 81–92, 2020.
https://doi.org/10.1007/978-3-030-64823-7_9

efficient and cost effective as a complex organisation, and enabling citizens and government to have a simplified single view of each other (DPSA 2006). Enterprise architecture (EA) is a widely followed business practice that uses standardised IT architecture frameworks to align the strategy of a business enterprise with IT enabled capabilities. The use of EA has moved to government organisations, and there is a growing realisation now in academic circles that e-Government cannot be effectively implemented without the use of EA (Mentz et al. 2014; Anthopoulos et al. 2010). This research found in the first empirical cycle of evaluation that e-Government cannot be effectively implemented from an IS perspective without a theory to provide understanding and guidance to the implementers. Although the South African Government Wide Enterprise Architecture framework (GWEA) makes provision for inclusion of a reference architecture, such a reference architecture is currently not a part of GWEA and therefore one can deduce that this objective of designing effective e-Government solutions may then not be achieved (GITOC 2009; Mentz et al. 2014).

This work offers a tentative solution to the two knowledge gaps of absence of e-Government theory and absence of a reference architecture for GWEA. This may effectively resolve the detrimental effects of undertaking e-Government implementation without underpinning architectures and without the understanding and direction provided to the stakeholders by the proposed e-Government theory (Baskerville et al. 2018; Bourdieu 1990; Krauss 2013, Vidmar et al. 2020).The research appears unique in that the theory artefacts were evaluated empirically and analytically with the suggested final result that they provide a useful and valid theoretical and practical orientation to e-Government practitioners in South Africa and possibly further afield within the limits of this study (Baskerville et al. 2018; Kotze et al. 2015, Vidmar et al. 2020).

Having identified the research problem, the researcher encountered the task of designing a suitable research methodology (Vidmar et al. 2019). It is currently an accepted principle of scientific research that a theory cannot be proven correct. One can only formulate and utilise a theory and hold it to be true, while no experimental evidence exists to disprove it (Popper 1976). Based on the researcher's study into accepted approaches to studies in information systems, it was determined that a qualitative approach using the Design Science Research (DSR) methodology would be the best suited to the needs of this study. However, there is still reported resistance to the use of DSR in general and in the context of theory construction (Kotze et al. 2015, Timmermans and Tavory 2012, Peffers et al. 2018). Recent work by Paulin (2017) gives credence, and presents a theoretical context, for the use of DSR in the area of e-Government theory development although DSR has been used in information systems research for some time (Kotze et al. 2015).

Research articles have been accumulated through automated alert facility of the Scopus database since the research project began in 2014, using the broadest search terms; e-Government and Enterprise Architecture. The purpose of the literature review is to contribute to the essential knowledge base for this study as depicted in Fig. 1.

2 Application of DSR

This section briefly illustrates how the researcher elected to apply the selected DSR framework in this study which is that of Vaishnavi and Kuechler (2016) due to its clear

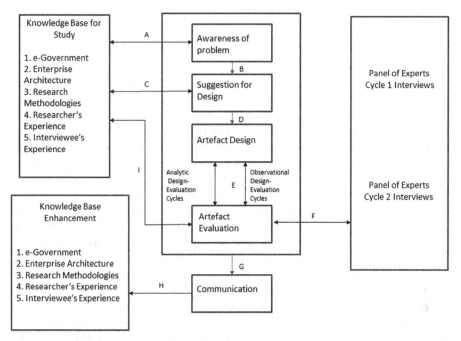

Fig. 1. Researcher's DSR process followed in this study (Vidmar, 2019)

exposition and wide acceptance in doctoral information systems research and because of inclusion of criteria for design theory (Kotze et al. 2015; Kotzé and Goede, 2016, Vidmar et al. 2019).

The labels A to I in Fig. 1 show the interactions that take place between the various components of the process model. The following two sections reference the process steps depicted in the figure.

3   Suggestion for Design Theory Artefact Design for e-Government

This section, which is focus of this paper, reveals how the DSR process step of suggestion resulted in the proposed set of design theory artefacts. The researcher initially engaged in a process of reflection which brought about the recollection of the researcher's experience as Government CIO (GCIO) for almost three years with responsibility for e-Government leadership in South Africa. This led to the inference that some or all of the conceptual artefacts conceived during that period of practice might prove useful as a starting point. They had undergone extensive consultation in government under the researcher's leadership, and the researcher was curious to see if they might have some theoretical utility and validity (Farelo 2005; DPSA 2006). This process of thought is reflected in the process of abduction conceptualised by Peirce (1997: 181), and quoted in Timmermans and Tavory (2012). As noted by Peirce insights should be viewed as fallible. The contribution of DSR methodology in social sciences is to provide the context wherein the artefacts that result from such insights can be evaluated as having some potential of solving the identified research problem. DSR supports the contribution of theory in IS in the form of innovative design theory artefacts. This is a recognized arte-fact in IS literature for expressing a design theory (Gregor and Hevner 2013; Vaishnavi and Kuechler 2016; Kotze et al. 2015).

The step of suggestion requires the researcher to creatively conceive ideas and initial artefacts that address the solution to the research problem. The precise manner of doing this, however, is not made clear in the literature and some discussions continue regard-ing the creative role of design in IS (Purgathofer 2006). Vaishnavi and Kuechler (2016) state that "Suggestion is an essentially creative step wherein new functionality is envi-sioned based on a novel configuration of either existing or new and existing elements. The step has been criticized as introducing non-repeatability into the design science research method since human creativity is still a poorly understood cognitive process. However, the creative step has necessary analogues in all research methods; for example, in positivist research creativity is inherent in the leap from curiosity about an organiza-tional phenomenon to the development of appropriate constructs that operationalize the phenomena and an appropriate research design for their measurement."

Gregor and Hevner (2013) allude to the necessary use of kernel theories in the design of artefacts. In this context, and as discussed by Krauss (2013), there is acknowledgement amongst researchers in social sciences, drawing on the Theory of Practice of Bourdieu (1990), that any theory that seeks to influence a cultural environment should be influenced by the immersion of the researcher in such a cultural environment and that theory and practice should inform each other. Bourdieu (1990) shows in his work how human nature requires the effective interplay of knowledge and the practical use of that knowledge. The researcher was immersed as a practitioner in the cultural work of e-Government in South Africa for nearly three years. It was in the course of learning and socialising with fellow e-Government practitioners that the researcher conceived the initial eight of the twelve artefacts discussed below that were intended to enable the exercise of practical leadership and implementation support for an envisaged e-Government program in the future. These artefacts were socialized and appeared useful and valid during an extensive period of consultation in government involving senior managers and enterprise architects from government departments and agencies closely related to e-Government and formal endorsements were obtained from the State IT Agency (SITA) and the Government Officers Council (GITOC). Evidently the artefacts were never practically implemented possibly because of frequent change of leadership in the public service and consequent loss of knowledge (Farelo 2005; DPSA 2006). The proposed novel artefacts therefore have a provable grounding in the practical experience of e-Government in South Africa and possibly internationally as official visits by the researcher to India and Brazil during his tenure showed many similarities with South Africa (Gregor and Hevner 2013). Three of the twelve artefacts deal with the GWEA reference architecture and were invented by the researcher during the course of research in the step of suggestion from the current general experience as an enterprise architect working for a government entity.

When initially conceiving the design artefacts it is recommended to engage in a process of logical evaluation. Vaishnavi and Kuechler (2016) state that "In a sense eval-uation takes place continuously in a design process (research or otherwise) since a large number of "micro-evaluations" take place at every design detail decision. Each decision is followed by a "thought experiment" in which that part of the design is mentally exercised by the designer." Some of the questions posed by the researcher were as follows. Is it important for e-Government participants to understand the current information systems challenges in government and how could this be done? Is it important to depict the end-goal or aspirational state of the future e-Government, as espoused by the South African government (DPS 2001), and how could this be done? Is it important to establish e-Government upon a legal foundation and informed by policy, strategy and architecture, and an appropriate public service ethic? Is governance, coordination, planning, accountability, authority and consultation, important to operate an e-Government programme? Is it important to leverage existing government structures, such as the State IT Agency (SITA) and the Government IT Officers Council (GITOC) that are already mandated to participate in e-Government from a coordinating and implementation and support perspective? Given that e-Government is a complex undertaking, with an enduring nature, should its implementation be attempted in one big project or in a measured evolutionary way, taking into account international experience and prior research such as that of Layne and Lee (2001) and local studies of e-Government challenges (PRC 1998; Cloete 2012)? Is it important to show to the various stakeholders how e-Government is progressing and contributing to their interest on an on-going basis?

The process of reflection on the documented problems of e-Government in South Africa described above finally resulted in the initial design of eleven design theory artefacts by the researcher (Vidmar and Kotzé 2015a). Three of the eleven artefacts relate to a reference architecture for GWEA, from a business architecture domain perspective. A twelfth artefact was added later from the result of the first cycle of evaluation. The twelve design theory artefacts, in the form of architecture models with associated descriptions were submitted to further four design-evaluation cycles, which terminated in a composite design theory framework artefact comprised of twelve component artefacts, termed the e-Government Framework.

Each of the framework component artefacts designed by the researcher is listed and described briefly below. In the study each artefact is also illustrated in the form of an architectural model and these have been described in Vidmar (2019). The purpose of these artefacts is to provide understanding and instruction to enterprise architects in the implementation of e-Government.

As-Is View of Government Information Systems. This As-Is component artefact acts as a baseline description of the current structure of information systems in government, revealing the nature of the major problems that e-Government is designed to solve. This includes multiple access channels to government and extensive system, process and data duplication and lack of system integration across government information systems making government service delivery problematic.

The To-Be View of e-Government in South Africa. This component reveals the essential features and properties of the broad e-Government information systems solution and acts as a representation of the goals to be achieved by enterprise architects and e-Government decision makers. This includes integration and consolidation of systems, establishment and reuse of authoritative sources of data throughout government, the use of shared processes to support reengineered e-Government services and a single access point to government with government having a single view of any legal entity, such as citizen, business, etc. Similarly, citizens and businesses may gain a more simple and holistic view of government. These goals are implemented through the use of the reference architecture artefacts described below.

Conceptual e-Government Progamme Architecture. This component shows how the proposed e-Government programme can be established on a solid foundation building up from the core ideals of a developmental state and informed by policy, strategy, architecture and the government's public service ethic.

e-Government Governance Framework. This component shows how the governance for the proposed government-wide e-Government programme can be achieved with assigned authority and accountability and providing for stakeholder participation in the context of South African government.

SITA Business Model in Support of e-Government. This component shows that as the mandated and established entity SITA may play its designated role as an e-Government implementation agency, not in isolation, but as part of the overall e-Government programme.

Model of Supporting GITOC Structures for e-Government. This component shows the vital coordinating and consultative role played by GITOC in the e-Government programme to ensure government-wide endorsement and alignment with the e-Government programme amongst the ICT leaders in government.

Phased Implementation Approach to e-Government. This component promotes a step-wise application implementation approach for e-Government with progressive sophistication and investment in e-Government information systems solutions consistent with international practice. This artefact is based on what appears as the only existing class of theoretical e-Government IS concept, proposed by Layne and Lee (2001), Bannister and Connolly (2015).

e-Government Project Portfolio. This component promotes the summary view of e-Government applications as they mature through the designated steps of development in support of the recognised e-Government stakeholder classes, including the public service itself.

Departmental Level Business Reference Architecture. This component is the proposed high level business reference architecture at the business level which is intended to guide e-Government enterprise architects in the design of e-Government systems in a way that promotes the reuse of authoritative sources of data, reusable business processes across government departments and interfaced with standardised and well managed interface channels for service delivery.

Solution Architecture View – Controlling Node. This component is provided as an example of how the reference architecture can be translated into a technology-based solution in the case of a controlling node in the networked departments forming part of e-Government as a whole.

Solution Architecture View – Departmental Level Node. This component is provided as an example of how the reference architecture can be translated into a technology-based solution in the case of a government department node in the network of government departments forming part of e-Government as a whole and not performing any controlling node function.

e-Government Capability Map. This component is included to provide a higher-level perspective of the proposed e-Government capabilities than just the reference architecture artefact, making it more suitable for non-technical e-Government stakeholders to understand e-Government while also supporting enterprise architects in their e-Government implementation role.

4 Artefact Evaluation

Following the initial artefact design the first research objective was to investigate empirically if the e-Government artefacts meet the requirements of an explanatory and a design theory, within the limits of this research and if such a theory was needed. Since the artefacts are designed to guide the implementation of e-Government systems and enterprise architects are mandated with this responsibility, it was determined that one rigorous approach to evaluate artefacts for utility and validity in the context of DSR as applied in this study, is to gather the expert opinions of qualified, experienced and practicing enterprise architects who have worked in various South African national government departments, provinces and local government on information systems projects. Hevner et al. (2004) describe five different methods of artefact evaluation which may be appropriate according to the nature of the design artefact. Use was made in this study of three sets of theoretical criteria, as explained below (Bannister and Connolly 2015; Vaishnavi and Kuechler 2016; Kotze et al. 2015; Mentz et al. 2014). In total five design-evaluation cycles were found to be necessary to obtain a rigorous evaluation of the design artefacts in this research work both from an empirical and analytical evaluation perspective (Kotze et al. 2015).

The interviewees selected for the observational portion of this study covered in the first two design-evaluation cycles include people skilled in the practice and management of enterprise architecture and e-Government projects within the South African government as well as Gauteng province, local government and those in the private sector who support government in setting standards and adopting best practices (DPSA 2003).

The first design-evaluation cycle is based on the observational evaluation method using a semi-structured interview of nine expert participants. The qualitative data analysis result using the thematic approach indicated that e-Government in South Africa had an absence of theory and GWEA was not in effective practice, largely confirming prior South African research findings (Cloete 2012). There was evident general support for the theory framework demonstrated to the participants consisting of the initial eleven artefacts, with the suggestion of including an additional design theory artefact.

After designing and adding a twelfth component artefact called the e-Government Capability Map to the theory framework, the second observational design-evaluation cycle was done approximately two years later based on a semi-structured interview of six experts. This cycle focused entirely on evaluating the validity and utility of the twelve component artefacts using the seven components of a design theory as described by Vaishnavi and Kuechler (2016). These components are purpose and scope, constructs, knowledge of form and function, abstraction and generalization, evaluation and validation propositions, justificatory knowledge and principles of implementation. As these are theoretical artefacts, not yet in operation, other artefact criteria such as quality and efficacy, could not be evaluated (Gregor and Hevner, 2013). The subsequent qualitative data analysis result showed support for the validity and utility of the expanded framework of artefacts with no further need for design changes but some changes were made to descriptive text to emphasise certain attributes of the artefacts mentioned by the interviewees.

In the third cycle of evaluation the same core components of criteria for an effective DSR design theory are evaluated logically by the researcher in alignment with the research design of this work. From the analytical review of the artefacts there is found to be broad agreement with all the seven components of a design theory.

In the fourth cycle of DSR design-evaluation the researcher, using logic, evaluated the proposed e-Government theory component artefacts according to the eight features or virtues of a good theory for information systems, proposed in Bannister and Connolly (2015) and agreement was found between the proposed e-Government theory with all the virtues of a good theory within the limits of the research work. The eight virtues encompass uniqueness, conservatism, generalisability, fecundity, parsimony, internal consistency, empirical riskiness, and abstraction this cycle required no artefact changes.

An additional method of analytical evaluation of architecture analysis is performed in the fifth design-evaluation cycle as the proposed artefacts are designed for use by enterprise architects and as indicated by Hevner et al. (2004) they should fit into technical IT architecture. The only theory that appears relevant as a basis for such analysis currently is the set of six enterprise architecture propositions of Mentz et al. (2014). The first proposition states that enterprise architecture is a description of the structure of the systems of an enterprise in terms of components and their relationships. The second asserts that the current view of the enterprise is captured in an as-is model and the third that the future view of the enterprise is captured in a to-be model. The fourth sees enterprise architecture translate the values/strategy of the enterprise into operational information systems. The fifth states that enterprise architecture relates the actions and or behaviour that relates to the information technology and information systems management and implementation of the enterprise. The final sixth proposition states that enterprise architecture captures a representation of the enterprise in the form of a model or set of models. The evaluation found that the proposed e-Government theory effectively utilises enterprise architecture as a vehicle for e-Government implementation as the set of proposed artefacts agree with the stated propositions and hence no artefact design adaptations are required. This evaluation terminated the design-evaluation cycle allowing the communication of the research findings.

5   Discussion

Theory is a recognized form of knowledge contribution in IS and the proposed framework is an example of a level 2 DSR contribution, referred to as nascent design theory by Gregor and Hevner (2013). Using the typology suggested by Gregor (2006) for information systems theory the proposed e-Government theory may be seen as a broad native theory in e-Government information systems including all classes of theory in an interrelated fashion as may be deduced from the brief description of the component artefacts given in Sect. 3. The theory is falsifiable and includes Type IV and Type V theory as it explains, predicts and is oriented towards design and action in the field of e-Government implementation (Baskerville et al. 2018; Vidmar and Kotzé 2015). The overall contribution of this study is to have applied Design Science Research methodology in a new and complex research area of information systems, spanning e-Government and enterprise architecture. An important and innovative aspect of the study discussed here is to show how rigour may be introduced to initially suggest theory artefacts based on ideas conceived originally in the field of practice (Baskerville et al. 2018; Krauss 2013). Measures such as perceived validity and utility by knowledge domain experts and analytical analysis against accepted theory criteria were found relevant for the e-Government theory evaluation as was the logical form of abduction (Vaishnavi and Kuechler 2016; Paulin 2017; Timmermans and Tavory 2012).

This research appears to be the first to use The Theory of Practice (Bourdieu 1990) as the theoretical basis that underpins and gives credence to the initial suggestion of the e-Government design theory artefacts as a direct consequence of the researcher's deep immersion in the practice of e-Government in South Africa (Farelo 2005). Some of the resistance to the use of DSR reported by doctoral students (Kotze et al, 2015) may have come from the non-repeatability aspect of human creativity mentioned by Vaishnavi and Kuechler (2016). Following the recommendation for rigorous theory construction by Timmermans and Tavory (2012) the researcher developed the following abductive statement to further test the reasonableness of the proposed theory. Evidence of support for the researcher's proposed theoretical framework for e-Government has been observed.

But if a e-Government theory acceptable to practitioners has been demonstrated by the researcher; Evidence of support for the researcher's proposed theoretical framework for e-Government is observable, would be a matter of course. Therefore, there is reason to suspect the truth of; e-Government theory, thought to be useful to e-Government practitioners, was demonstrated.

In alluding to the relatively poor acceptance of DSR research by top tier journals and social scientists steeped in tradition, Peffers et al. (2018) describe five prototype genres that DSR research may fall into. It appears to the researcher that the applicable DSR genre for this study is IS design theory. Importantly it is stated that a design instantiation is not obligatory to support a design theory. Lack of instantiation of the proposed theory is a limitation due to practical constraints of this research.

6 Conclusion

The scientific study of e-Government is recognised as being relatively new and important by the research community. Analysis of local and international literature by the researcher revealed a gap in the area of e-Government theory and reference architecture from an IS perspective. This paper shows that DSR is equipped to enable the rigorous design and evaluation of e-Government design theory artefacts which are reported here. This paper reveals an instance of how design theory artefacts can come into existence from the knowledge base related to the field of e-Government practice using the Theory of Practice (Bourdieu 1990) as the kernel theory in IS, in the DSR step of suggestion. The initial eleven design theory artefacts emerged from the researcher as concepts from the field of practice and were then designed with functional attributes and evaluated empirically in two cycles separated in time by two years, using a cohort of qualified and experienced e-Government enterprise architects, managers and consultants. This resulted in a modification of the functional attributes of several artefacts as well as the addition of a twelfth artefact. The framework of twelve artefacts was then evaluated analytically in three further cycles against three sets of applicable theoretical criteria published by researchers in the course of research. An appeal to abduction was also used as a test of reasonableness. It is suggested that the high level of rigour reported here is necessary to thoroughly evaluate the utility and validity of artefacts to instruct and guide system architects in the work of e-Government implementation. A limitation of the research is that as yet the artefacts lack any practical implementation experience as they have not yet been implemented as part of South Africa's e-Government endeavours. This paper shows how the practice of e-Government can inform the formulation of theory in IS and how the product of theory design using DSR might influence the field of e-Government practice as envisaged by Bourdieu (1990). Another practical research limitation is the constrained cohort of qualified and experienced enterprise architects and e-Government managers. Future research could repeat the study with a larger and more varied cohort of participants from other provinces in South Africa or be performed internationally and might be directed at suitable practical instantiations of one or more artefacts (Peffers et al. 2018).

References

Anthopoulos, L.G., Gerogiannis, V., Fitsilis, P.: The impact of enterprise architecture's absence in e-government development: the Greek case, pp. 122–127 (2010)

Bannister, F., Connolly, R.: The great theory hunt: does e-government really have a problem? Gov. Inf. Q. **32**(1), 1–11 (2015)

Baskerville, R., Baiyere, A., Gregor, S., Hevner, A., Rossi, M.: Design science research contributions: finding a balance between artifact and theory. J. Assoc. Inf. Syst.ms **19**(5), 358–376 (2018)

Boucharas, V., van Steenbergen, M., Jansen, S., Brinkkemper, S.: The contribution of enterprise architecture to the achievement of organizational goals: a review of the evidence. In: Proper, E., Lankhorst, M.M., Schönherr, M., Barjis, J., Overbeek, S. (eds.) TEAR 2010. LNBIP, vol. 70, pp. 1–15. Springer, Heidelberg (2010). https://doi.org/10.1007/978-3-642-16819-2_1

Bourdieu, P.: The Logic of Practice (Trans. by, R. Nice). Polity, Cambridge (1990)

Cloete, F.: e-Government lessons from south africa 2001–2011: institutions. State Prog. Meas. **12**, 128–142 (2012)

DPSA: Electronic Government The Digital Future: A Public Service IT Policy Framework (2001)

DPSA: The Machinery of Government, pp. 1–106, May 2003

DPSA: DPSA e-Government Update Portfolio Committee August 2006, Cape Town (2006)

Farelo, M.: The e-government consultative progress. Serv. Deliv. Rev. **4**(1), 37–39 (2005). http://www.dpsa.gov.za/dpsa2g/documents/service_delivery_review

GITOC: Government-Wide Enterprise Architecture (GWEA) Framework, Pretoria (2009)

Goldkuhl, G.: E-government design research: towards the policy-ingrained IT artifact. Gov. Inf. Q. **33**, 1–9 (2016)

Gregor, S., Hevner, A.R.: Positioning and presenting design science research for maximum impact. MIS Q. **37**(2), 337–355 (2013). https://doi.org/10.2753/MIS0742-1222240302

Hevner, A.R., March, S.T., Park, J., Ram, S.: Design science in information systems research. MIS Q. **28**(1), 75–105 (2004)

Kotze, P., van der Merwe, A., Gerber, A.: Design science research as research approach in doctoral studies. In: Proceedings of the 21st Americas Conference on Information Systems (AMCIS 2015), pp. 1–14 (2015)

Kotzé, E., Goede, R.: Preparing postgraduate students for industry without neglecting scholarly development: using project-based learning and design science research to develop a software artefact. In: 7th Annual International Conference on Computer Science Education: Innovation & Technology (CSEIT 2016), vol. 6(Cseit), pp. 57–64 (2016)

Krauss, K.E.M.: Practice-driven theory: using Bourdieu's critical lineage in ICT4D work. In: 7th International Development Informatics Association Conference, November 2013, pp. 126–151 (2013)

Layne, K., Lee, J.: Developing fully functional e-government: a four stage model. Gov. Inf. Q. **18**(2), 122–136 (2001)

Mentz, J., Kotzé, P., Van Der Merwe, A.: Propositions that describe the intended meaning of enterprise architecture. In: Proceedings of the Southern African Institute for Computer Scientist and Information Technologists Annual Conference 2014 on SAICSIT 2014 Empowered by Technology, pp. 304–313 (2014)

Paulin, A.: e-Gov theory and the role of design science in transforming public governance. In: Proceedings of the 18th Annual International Conference on Digital Government Research, pp. 541–545 (2017)

Peffers, K., Tuunanen, T., Niehaves, B.: Design science research genres: introduction to the special issue on exemplars and criteria for applicable design science research. Eur. J. Inf. Syst. **27**(2) (2018). https://doi.org/10.1080/0960085X.2018.1458066

Peirce, C.S.: Pragmatism as a Principle and Method of Right Thinking: The 1903 Harvard Lecture Notes on Pragmatism. SUNY Press, Albany (1997)

Popper, K.: The myth of the framework. In: Pitt, J.C., Pera, M. (eds.) Rational Changes in Science: Boston Studies in the Philosophy of Science, vol. 98. Springer, Dordrecht (1976). https://doi.org/10.1007/978-94-009-3779-6_2

PRC: Towards a culture of good governance. Report of the Presidential Commission on the Reform and Transformation of the Public Service in South Africa. PRC, Pretoria (1998). http://www.polity.org.za/polity/govdocs/reports/presreview/index.html

Purgathofer, P.: Is informatics a design discipline? Poiesis Prax. **4**(4), 303–314 (2006). https://doi.org/10.1007/s10202-006-0029-0

Timmermans, S., Tavory, I.: Theory construction in qualitative research: from grounded theory to abductive analysis. Sociol. Theory **30**(3), 167–186 (2012)

Vaishnavi, V., Kuechler, B.: Des. Sci. Res. Inf. Syst. (2016). https://doi.org/10.1007/978-1-4419-5653-8

Vidmar, R: Towards the development of an e-government theory and reference architecture for South Africa. Ph.D. thesis UNISA EA Forum, South Africa, 26–27 June 2019 (2019). http://opengroup.co.za/presentations

Vidmar, R., Kotzé, E.: Proposing a descriptive theory to support South Africa's e-government efforts. In: SAICSIT 2015, Stellenbosch, South Africa (2015)

Vidmar, R., Kotzé, E: An investigation into the challenges and shortcomings faced by the implementers of the government wide enterprise architecture: national government and Gauteng Province. In: 2015 Annual UNISA Student Research and Innovation Showcase, Pretoria, South Africa (2015a)

Vidmar, R., Kotzé, E., van der Merwe, M., Mentz, J.: An approach to design and evaluation of e-government theory for South Africa. In: Proceedings of the 12th Annual Pre-ICIS SIG GlobDev Workshop, Munich, Germany, Sunday, 15 December 2019. AIS E-Library (2019). ISBN 978-0-9976176-9-6

Vidmar, R., Kotzé, E., van der Merwe, M., Mentz, J.: Proposed theory of e-government for South Africa. Paper presented at 11th International Development Informatics Association (IDIA2020) Conference, Macau SAR, China (2020)

van der Raadt, B.: Enterprise architecture coming of age. Informatica Manag. (2011). https://www.cs.vu.nl/en/Images/B-van-der-Raadt-25-02-2011_tcm75-259632.pdf

Tutorbot: A Chatbot for Higher Education Practice

Jonas Sjöström[(✉)] and Maritha Dahlin

Uppsala University, Campus Gotland, 62167 Visby, Sweden
`jonas.sjostrom@im.uu.se`

Abstract. In this paper, we present the design of Tutorbot – a chatbot software to support learning and teaching in higher education. We account for the implementation of the design as a proof-of-concept and share reflections from experiences in the design and implementation process expressed as design considerations for the design of chatbots in a higher education setting.

Keywords: Chatbot · Design · Architecture · Higher education · Practice · Design science research

1 Introduction

While chatbot technology has matured over time, there is still need for research on how to appropriately add value to human practice through the use of chatbot technology, including challenges to design effective dialogue between humans and bot technologies [3, 11, 14, 17].

In this work, we focus on chatbots in higher education (HE) practice. Potentially, the use of chatbots may influence educational flow to be more interactive and dynamic [1, 6]. A potential advantage of using a chatbot in an educational setting is the facilitation of instant retrieval of information for the learners [4]. Chatbots have also been proposed as a means to estimate learning styles [10, 20], and to stimulate student feedback in e-learning environments [12]. Chatbots may be part of the motivation for continued communication for educational purposes [3]. However, there is a need to factor in expectations from teachers and other stakeholders when designing bot technology in an education setting [18].

While there is a lot of research on chatbots in education, there is little or no research adopting a broader educational practice perspective [16]. A practice approach entails that we take into account multiple stakeholders in the learning situation, and investigate the emergence of social practices and stakeholder interactions given the introduction of chatbot technology. In this paper, we present Tutorbot – a software based on a theoretically and empirically grounded conceptual design for chatbots in HE practice. We provide a set of design reflections for chatbots in HE practice based on our experiences from the design process.

© Springer Nature Switzerland AG 2020
S. Hofmann et al. (Eds.): DESRIST 2020, LNCS 12388, pp. 93–98, 2020.
https://doi.org/10.1007/978-3-030-64823-7_10

2   The Tutorbot Software and Its Rationale

We searched in the web of science core collection for publications where either the topic or the title contained the word "chatbot" or the word "conversational agent", rendering 374 hits. A refined search within the search result where the title or topic contained the word "education" or "learning" rendered 99 results. We read through each abstract to further narrow down our search. After the reading of abstracts, we ended up with 50 articles that were considered relevant. In addition to those articles, we identified another 13 articles while reading or from suggestions by peers. In total, 63 articles from the years 2001–2017 were identified – informing the rigor cycle both with foundations and contextually relevant methodologies. Also, we factored in literature on general design topics including software architecture [2, 15] and communication as shown below. Also, repeated group discussions with teachers informed the design process.

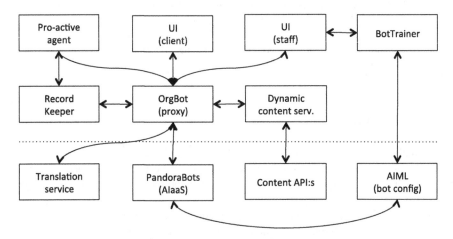

Fig. 1. The Tutorbot architecture.

Figure 1 shows a conceptual architecture for chatbots in higher education, drawing from the literature review as well as from interviews with a teacher group. The core of the architecture is the *OrgBot*, acting as a proxy with built-in logic for every interaction in the system. The OrgBot receives a question from learner through the *client UI* and passes it on to the AI as a service (AIaaS). The AIaaS reads the AIML configuration to find a suitable response for the question. If there is no response, a 'fallback' feature is activated, asking the learner if the question should be sent to the teacher. If yes, the OrgBot forwards the question to the *staff UI*. All the steps in the process are recorded by the *RecordKeeper* component, which logs data for future analysis (e.g., for research or education improvement purposes).

The OrgBot and its interaction with the AIaaS correspond to the basic idea of chatbots: Responding to questions. The teacher interviews showed that the chatbot should be able to answer common questions from students, e.g., regarding course content, prerequisites and requirements for a course, and information regarding exams deadlines. From a student point of view, the chatbot may simplify access to important information.

From a teacher point of view, the chatbot's ability to answer such questions could reduce administrative overhead. That is; we view the bot as support and supplement, rather than a substitute for the learner-teacher or peer. The fallback function makes the bot act as a doorway to the teacher when needed. While many studies of bots focus on the interaction between a learner and a bot, we are interested in the bot as an integral part of learning practice. A lack of such a perspective creates a risk that bots decrease interaction between students and teachers, which may cause negative feelings and consequently affect learning negatively.

Sometimes, the AIaaS returns control codes to the OrgBot. If a return message includes such a control code, it is passed along to the dynamic content service, which fetches data using external content API:s, and injects them into the response message. The mechanism allows for control codes in the AIML definitions that translate into dynamic content at run-time. The design supports fetching data about the syllabus, schedule, assignments, et cetera. By providing such content dynamically, the AIML definitions remain useful over time.

The *BotTrainer* subsystem allows teachers to provide answers to questions from the 'fallback' scenario above, while at the same time allowing for supervised training of the chatbot. The chatbot needs to evolve under the supervision of humans, to align its behavior with institutional norms, and to promote the quality of responses. Even though it is technologically feasible to automatically train bots [e.g., 7], we believe that it is risky to do so in higher education. In the Swedish context, bot actions in a University context are a form of agency, likely comparable to exercising public authority.

The *pro-active agent* subsystem contains the logic to initiate conversations, e.g., quizzes, course evaluations, or reminders to log on to the course Intranet. The main idea is to facilitate a mechanism to promote student activity, in keeping with the idea of supportive accountability in eHealth [13]. Conceptually, the subsystem exists in the conceptual architecture to allow for chatbot features beyond question-answers, i.e., design for mutability as suggested by Gregor and Jones [5]. Continued research may, for instance, include designs where data analytics methods are employed to identify when and how to trigger conversations with learners based on quiz results, inactivity, et cetera.

Finally, the idea of a *translation service* is still in its infancy, but it may prove very powerful to integrate a cloud translation service to facilitate interaction with international students, and provide them with an automatic translation of essential course information into their native language.

3   Proof-of-Concept Evaluation

The architecture discussed above was implemented into software both (1) as a proof-of-concept and (2) in preparation for continued evaluation in a Java course. The architecture consists of a set of interacting subsystems, which resonates well with the design of a microservices architecture [2, 15], i.e., small, loosely coupled components that interact over the Internet via the REST lightweight protocol. A microservices architecture and its loose coupling allows different subsystems to be implemented using different programming languages, and in different server environments.

We used PandoraBots as an AIaaS, due to two reasons. It allows us to define bot behavior using AIML, a 'de facto' standard that is reasonably convenient and works well with supervised learning. Also, it was available as a cloud service via a REST API, making it seamless to integrate into the architecture.

We implemented the software to operate in communication channels that the students already use, to make it easily accessible and to avoid the risk of non-use. We justify this idea by drawing on design thinking [9] – thinking of Tutorbot as part of an ecology of artifacts as experienced by the learners. The principle is also supported by the teacher feedback, which clearly shows the importance of bot accessibility, both from a student and from a teacher point of view. Following a survey among the students, we decided to implement the Tutorbot UI in the Facebook Messenger environment.

The other services in the architecture were all quite trivial to implement. The dynamic content service and the pro-active agent are only stubs at his point, but they are integrated into the architecture and ready to develop further when needed.

One lesson learned from the implementation work is the need to address privacy issues at an early point. Not only is it necessary *per se* when we use educational technology for education and research, but it was also needed in this case due to requirements from the Facebook Messenger API. Facebook requires us to upload a privacy policy to open up the chatbot for other users than invited testers. Also, requirements from the cloud services in use demand encrypted communication channels. The privacy issue may prove problematic in a scenario where this technology is used in a larger scale, still running in a cloud setting. While legislation differs between different parts of the world, we suspect that student questions may sometimes be rather sensitive in nature, thus not always suitable for cloud storage. Privacy issues needs to be thoroughly factored in to the design work, from the very inception of the process.

4   Concluding Discussion

In this paper, we have presented a conceptual architecture for chatbots in higher education. The architecture has been implemented into a chatbot software accessed via Facebook Messenger. Through the design process, we have identified a set of tentative design considerations: (i) A recommendation to deliver HE chatbot functionality within the existing *student ecosystem* of applications to promote use – useful to promote the use of the chatbot. (ii) A call to build HE chatbot technology that *promotes human interaction* in the learning context – rather than considering it a substitute to human interaction. (iii) An argument for *supervised learning* – due to the demand for quality controlled responses from the chatbot, and a potential role of the chatbot as an agent exercising public authority. (iv) A reflection about the *multitude of privacy norms* that govern design – in this case both educational norms, research ethics, and regulations to comply with third party cloud services regulations.

Future work includes the process of defining chatbot behavior for a particular course. The behavior will be defined through the creation of AIML documents drawing from both literature and an analysis of student questions from previous instances of the course. Clearly, the behavior of the chatbot is an essential part of design. Previous research, insofar as feasible, will be factored in to the AIML design process, such as the concept of academically productive talk [e.g., 19]. During the course, we promote students to the Tutorbot as a first resort when asking questions. Chatbot log data will be used to produce descriptive statistics of the use of the chatbot. In addition, we will conduct interviews with students and teachers to obtain qualitative (and possibly quantitative) data about their experience of using the chatbot.

We see an interesting future field of research in combining the practice-oriented approach suggested here with collaborative learning environments based on multiple interacting agents [8]. In such a setting, various agents with different roles would intervene in discussions among learners and teachers. Great challenges lies ahead for social science research to understand how to design and employ conversational agents to facilitate an education practice effectively supporting students' learning.

References

1. AbuShawar, B., Atwell, E.: ALICE chatbot: trials and outputs. Comput. Sist. **19**(4), 625–632 (2015)
2. Dragoni, N., et al.: Microservices: yesterday, today, and tomorrow. In: Mazzara, M., Meyer, B. (eds.) Present and Ulterior Software Engineering, pp. 195–216. Springer, Cham (2017). https://doi.org/10.1007/978-3-319-67425-4_12
3. Fryer, L.K., et al.: Stimulating and sustaining interest in a language course: an experimental comparison of chatbot and human task partners. Comput. Hum. Behav. **75**, 461–468 (2017)
4. Ghose, S., Barua, J.J.: Toward the implementation of a topic specific dialogue based natural language chatbot as an undergraduate advisor. In: 2013 International Conference on Informatics, Electronics and Vision (ICIEV), pp. 1–5 (2013)
5. Gregor, S., Jones, D.: The anatomy of a design theory. J. Assoc. Inf. Syst. **8**(5), 312–335 (2007)
6. Griol, D., Molina, J.M., de Miguel, A.S.: The *Geranium* system: multimodal conversational agents for e-learning. In: Omatu, S., Bersini, H., Corchado, J.M., Rodríguez, S., Pawlewski, P., Bucciarelli, E. (eds.) Distributed Computing and Artificial Intelligence, 11th International Conference. AISC, vol. 290, pp. 219–226. Springer, Cham (2014). https://doi.org/10.1007/978-3-319-07593-8_26
7. Hassani, K., et al.: Architectural design and implementation of intelligent embodied conversational agents using fuzzy knowledge base. J. Intell. Fuzzy Syst. **25**(3), 811–823 (2013)
8. Hayashi, Y.: Togetherness: multiple pedagogical conversational agents as companions in collaborative learning. In: Trausan-Matu, S., Boyer, K.E., Crosby, M., Panourgia, K. (eds.) ITS 2014. LNCS, vol. 8474, pp. 114–123. Springer, Cham (2014). https://doi.org/10.1007/978-3-319-07221-0_14
9. Krippendorff, K.: The Semantic Turn - A new Foundation for Design. CRC Press, Boca Raton (2006)
10. Latham, A.M., et al.: Oscar: an intelligent conversational agent tutor to estimate learning styles. In: 2010 IEEE International Conference on Fuzzy Systems (FUZZ-IEEE 2010). IEEE, New York (2010)
11. Leonhardt, M.D., et al.: Using chatbots for network management training through problem-based oriented education. In: Spector, J.M., et al. (eds.) 7th IEEE International Conference on Advanced Learning Technologies, p. 845. IEEE Computer Society, Los Alamitos (2007)
12. Lundqvist, K.O., Pursey, G., Williams, S.: Design and implementation of conversational agents for harvesting feedback in elearning systems. In: Hernández-Leo, D., Ley, T., Klamma, R., Harrer, A. (eds.) EC-TEL 2013. LNCS, vol. 8095, pp. 617–618. Springer, Heidelberg (2013). https://doi.org/10.1007/978-3-642-40814-4_79

13. Mohr, D.C., et al.: Supportive accountability: a model for providing human support to enhance adherence to eHealth interventions. J. Med. Internet Res. **13**, 1 (2011)
14. Neves, A.M.M., et al.: IAIML: a mechanism to treat intentionality in AIML chatterbots. In: Proceedings - International Conference on Tools with Artificial Intelligence, ICTAI, pp. 225–231 (2006)
15. Newman, S.: Building Microservices: Designing Fine-Grained Systems. O'Reilly Media Inc, Newton (2015)
16. Orlikowski, W.J.: Sociomaterial practices: exploring technology at work. Organ. Stud. **28**(9), 1435–1448 (2007)
17. Picard, R.W., et al.: Affective learning—a manifesto. BT Technol. J. **22**(4), 253–269 (2004)
18. Tamayo-Moreno, S., Perez-Marin, D.: Adapting the design and the use methodology of a pedagogical conversational agent of secondary education to childhood education. In: Garci-aPenalvo, F.J., Mendes, A. (eds.) 2016 International Symposium on Computers in Education (SIIE). IEEE, New York (2016)
19. Tegos, S., Demetriadis, S., Papadopoulos, P.M., Weinberger, A.: Conversational agents for academically productive talk: a comparison of directed and undirected agent interventions. Int. J. Comput.-Supported Collab. Learn. **11**(4), 417–440 (2016). https://doi.org/10.1007/s11 412-016-9246-2
20. Yun, E.K., Cho, S.B.: Learning classifier system for generating various types of dialogues in conversational agent. In: Liu, J., Cheung, Y.M., Yin, H. (eds.) IDEAL 2003. LNCS, vol. 2690, pp. 84–88. Springer, Berlin (2003). https://doi.org/10.1007/978-3-540-45080-1_11

Data Science

An OOV-Aware Curation Process for Psycholinguistic Analysis of Social Media Text - A Hybrid Approach

Kun Liu[✉] and Yan Li

Claremont Graduate University, Claremont, USA
{kun.liu,yan.li}@cgu.edu

Abstract. Massive user generated social media text posits new opportunities as well as challenges for psycholinguistic analysis to understand individual differences such as personality. Traditional off-the-shelf NLP (Natural Language Processing) tools perform poorly when analyzing text from social media because of the frequent out-of-vocabulary (OOV) words usage. Existing dictionary-based, closed-vocabulary approach and data-driven, open-vocabulary approach are both limited in handling OOV words. This research designs an OOV-aware curation process with a specific focus on OOV words. Following a design science research process model, the curation process is designed through four design cycles. The curation process includes a hybrid approach that integrates closed-vocabulary dictionary with expanded OOV categories and open-vocabulary approach with normalized OOV words. The curation process would enable psycholinguistic researchers and practitioners to exploit more psycholinguistic cues for tasks similar to personality predictions using social media text.

Keywords: Social media text · Out-of-vocabulary · OOV · Psycholinguistic · Personality

1 Introduction

The field of psycholinguistics is the study of the interrelation between linguistic patterns and psychological facets [1, 2] to extend our understanding of the affection, behaviors, and cognition of individuals in the social situation [3]. It is based on the hypothesis that individuals' everyday language encodes their differences that are socially relevant. Linguistic data can be used to not only gain insight about individuals and the community they socially interact with, but also to assess their personalities. The personality assessment results can be further used to predict various life-outcomes such as political attitude and mental health state [4, 5].

Social media platforms, such as Facebook, Twitter, and Youtube, have become a common place for Internet users to share their opinions and to interact with their networks through posting of messages in texts, audios, images and videos. These platforms host an unprecedented amount of user-generated contents (UGCs). This research specifically focuses on the UGCs in the text form. Through Natural Language Processing (NLP)

© Springer Nature Switzerland AG 2020
S. Hofmann et al. (Eds.): DESRIST 2020, LNCS 12388, pp. 101–113, 2020.
https://doi.org/10.1007/978-3-030-64823-7_11

of social media text (SMT), complex lexical and linguistic patterns about individual users can be discovered to understand user online behaviors as well as individuals' characteristics such as personality [6]. Thus, SMT has become a valuable data source for psycholinguistic analysis.

Psycholinguistic analysis of social media texts can be summarized into two camps: expert-driven closed-vocabulary approach and data-driven open-vocabulary approach. Closed-vocabulary approach uses predefined psycholinguistic tools such as Linguistic Inquiry and Word Count (LIWC) to map and count word usage to predefined categories. Closed-vocabulary approach predominated in early 2000s because its dictionaries are experts validated and have shown consistent predictive power of individual character-istics [7, 8]. However, these predefined repositories are mostly trained to analyze text from sources like newspaper articles and law documents that follows syntactic and grammatical rules of formal writing [9]. SMT are often written in casual and informal style. Thus, SMT exhibit lexical variants from formal writing, such as misspelled words, abbreviations, and emoticons. Hence, closed-vocabulary approach fails short to uncover these lexical variants in SMT, especially with regards to the out-of-vocabulary (OOV) words. OOV words are as a non-standard English word collection of frequent typo-graphic errors/misspellings, nonstandard abbreviations, colloquial language, phonetic substitutions, ungrammatical structures, and emoticons [10].

This leads to the rising popularity of open-vocabulary approach towards SMT anal-ysis that inductively discovers language patterns from text that are not predefined. It has outperformed closed-vocabulary approaches in many recent studies [11, 12]. However, open-vocabulary models are usually based on text distribution and thus, are often biased towards high frequency words and phrases. Mostly sparsely distributed, individual OOV word is often ignored by open-vocabulary models. Additionally, open-vocabulary app-roach either replaces OOV words with labelled OOV tags or normalize them into respec-tive in-vocabulary words. Intentionally used OOV words, such as irregular capitalization, elongated characters or punctuation, are also ignored.

We hypothesize that hidden linguistic patterns in OOV word usage might reflect individual characteristics [13, 14]. The objective of this research is to design an OOV-aware curation process for psycholinguistic analysis of SMT. More specifically, this research seeks to address aforementioned limitations of existing approaches towards psycholinguistic analysis of SMT.

The rest of the paper is organized as follows: Sect. 2 presents background of existing psycholinguistic analysis approaches, with a specific focus on OOV words usage in SMT. Section 3 describes the research methodology and proposed research design. Section 4 presents artifact design, development, and evaluation in four design cycles and Sect. 5 highlights research contributions and describes future research.

2   Background

2.1   OOV Words in SMT

SMT analysis is different from traditional text analysis in different ways. First, SMT are 'noisier'. They often contain spelling errors and unorthodox capitalization, make fre-quent use of emoticons, abbreviations and hashtags, and they tend to be less grammatical

[15]. Second, certain word patterns are SMT-exclusive such as @user or #topic. Third, SMT often includes URLs or email addresses that contain multiple special characters which could cause tokenization errors using traditional NLP tools. Because of these characteristics, analyzing social media text requires specific considerations [10]. There is a need for design tools that curated specially for social media text to capture language features at different granularity.

There are three main approaches towards analyzing OOV words in SMT [13]. First approach simply ignores OOV word usage patterns [16–18], some of which could be potentially meaningful. Second approach replaces OOV words into a set of pre-defined OOV labels. However, such a rule-based replacement achieves limited performance improvements for SMT prediction tasks [19]. The third approach uses lexical normalization to replace non-standard OOV words with context-appropriate in-vocabulary (IV) words [20, 21].

There are three issues that the OOV normalization approach have not addressed sufficiently. First, SMT-exclusive OOV words are ignored because they do not have matching IV word [18]. Second, users would often express their emotions through intentionally using OOV words, such as irregular capitalization, elongated words, or elongated punctuations. Existing approaches do not capture emotions embedded in those OOV words. Third, existing approaches treat each OOV word uniquely without considering their semantic similarities. For example, elongated words "heeeello" and "hellooooo" are derived from the same word, and should be considered as the same.

2.2 Psycholinguistic Analysis

Psycholinguistic analysis techniques can be summarized into two major camps range from expert-driven closed vocabulary to more data-driven open-vocabulary [22]. Closed-vocabulary approach maps and counts relative word frequency to a pre-compiled word dictionary using tools like LIWC. Open-vocabulary approach relies on more inductive ways of establishing the pattern of word use. Instead of relying on predefined word dictionaries, it discovers patterns emerges from the given corpus, and find most frequent occurred words, phrases and topics as predictive features [4].

Many early psycholinguistic studies [7, 8, 23] used closed-vocabulary (such as LIWC) approaches to analyze language usages. LIWC was carefully developed to capture multiple psychological dimensions with high internal reliability [2]. It contains over 2,300 word stems that are categorized into over 90 psycholinguistic dimensions by experts. Although LIWC itself does not address OOV words, it represents state-of-art psycholinguistic analysis knowledge. Table 1 compares the limitations of existing closed- and open-vocabulary approaches towards processing different OOV features that this research attempts to address.

Recent studies showed that open-vocabulary approaches have outperformed closed-vocabulary approaches in personality prediction using SMT [24–26]. This is expected because the open-vocabulary approach is more representative of SMT than closed-vocabulary approach. However, psycholinguistic features extracted through the open-vocabulary approach are often sparsely distributed, which makes it harder to aggregate and interpret discovered patterns.

Table 1. Closed- and open-vocabulary approaches towards OOV words

OOV feature	Closed-vocabulary	Open-vocabulary
Interjection words	Missed	Omitted as "stopwords"
Slang words	Mapped limited slang collection	Not able to normalize
Punctuation	Mapped limited emoticon collection	Cannot aggregate repeated punctuations '??!!!!' and '?!'
Elongated words	Only if the last character is used repeatedly such as 'soooooo'	Cannot aggregate similar words 'soo' and 'sooo'
Mis-spells	Missed	Not able to normalize

3   Research Methodology

Design science research is problem-solving focused framework through the creation of artifacts and contribute new knowledge to the field. Design science research process model (DSRPM) [27] is used to guide our design (Fig. 1). The DSRPM includes five iterative process steps, where each iteration is a design cycle (DC) with a specific focus and research outputs. The five process steps and their outputs are: (1) an awareness of problem step with a formal or informal research proposal; (2) a suggestion step to propose a tentative design; (3) a development step where the proposed artifact is developed and implemented iteratively to meet design objectives; (4) an evaluation step that evaluates artifact performance rigorously; and (5) a conclusion step when results are consolidated and knowledge gained through the research is summarized.

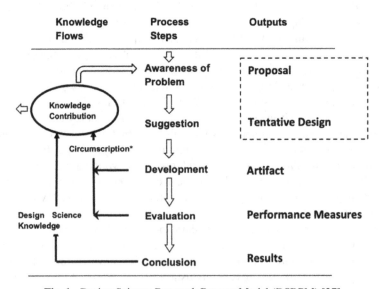

Fig. 1. Design Science Research Process Model (DSRPM) [27]

This research aims to design an OOV-aware curation process for psycholinguistic analysis of SMT. One of the most studied areas in psycholinguistic analysis is the inference of personality traits through language. Personality is "individual characteristic pattern of thought, emotion, and behavior, together with the psychological mechanisms hidden or not behind those patterns" (p40) [29]. The "Big Five" personality model [30] is the most widely accepted and used framework that scores people's personality traits on five dimensions: Openness, Conscientiousness, Extraversion, Agreeableness and Neuroticism.

In this research, we use the myPersonality dataset [28] to develop and test the proposed OOV-aware curation process for personality prediction. The myPersonality[1] was a Facebook application that allowed users to take a personality test of their Big Five personality trait scores. In return, users opted to share their scores and Facebook profile data for research purposes. The personality dataset contains over 6 million users and over

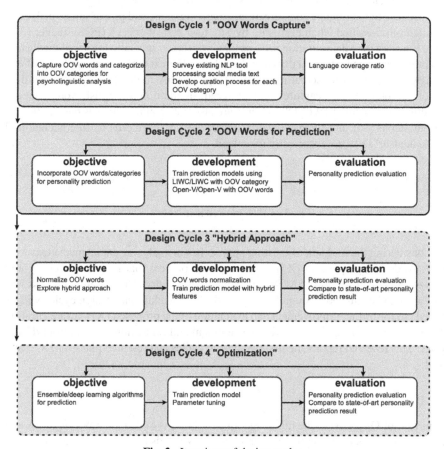

Fig. 2. Iterations of design cycles

---

[1] http://mypersonality.org/.

20 million status updates represents the largest study by order of magnitude of language and personality.

Our research starts with definitions of the problem and objectives of tentative design. Then, we went through two design cycles and identified two additional design cycles that would be further implemented (Fig. 2). Each DC includes the following steps: definition of objectives, artifact design and implementation, and evaluation.

4   Artifact Design, Development and Evaluation

As discussed earlier, social media texts exhibit new challenges to conventional text analytics because of the frequent OOV words usage such as emoticons, misspells, and etc. Thus, traditional off-the-shelf NLP tools perform poorly when analyzing social media text. Many NLP repositories are trained using formal sources like news articles and other official documents. These repositories have performed poorly on Twitter data [34]. because the unreliable capitalization, common nouns, and proper nouns in Tweets are often misclassified when evaluated by Stanford part-of-speech (POS) Tagger [35]. There is a need for a data curation process that is designed specially for social media text to capture language features at different granularity. For example, when applying LIWC to analyze the following social media text (Fig. 3), only highlighted words (less than half of the total text) are captured and analyzed. In addition to English words that are not defined in existing LIWC, OOV words are also not captured, such as punctuation (!, !!!), emoticons (:-)), and elongated words (heeeeeeeello). Furthermore, Internet featured text such as url links are incorrectly tokenized.

Goodbye Cambridge. Heeeeeeeeeeello White Mountains! EARTHQUAKE!!! Wait...what?! Go Bears! :-) GO BEARS! http://www.theinsider.com/news/2300431__Man_vs_Wild_Saves_Life_of_9_Year_Old_Boy American Clean Energy

Fig. 3. LIWC colored text analysis

Considering the problem of existing approaches in analyzing social media text with OOV words, we propose an OOV-aware curation process that is able to identify and analyze OOV words used in SMT for personality prediction. The curation process was developed and evaluated through DC 1 and DC 2. Two additional design cycles will be carried out for further improvement and evaluation of the proposed OOV-aware curation process. Figure 3 presents objectives, development and evaluation plans for four design cycles. This research reports the first two design cycles and research plans for DC 3 and DC 4.

4.1   Design Cycle 1

Definition of Objective. The main objective for DC 1 is to define OOV categories and create an NLP process to capture and annotate OOV words for each OOV category. The proposed OOV categorization and tokenization process should not only offer similar word coverage like the open-vocabulary approach, but also be able to capture intentional linguistic behaviors in OOV words using categorization mechanism similar to the closed-vocabulary approach.

Development. The development starts with surveying existing literature and tools used to analyze SMT with a special emphasis in capturing OOV words. We observed common issues raised using off-the-shelf NLP tools for SMT analysis, such as tokenization errors with the use of emoticons, emails, or URL links that have period ('.') as part of the word, and the separation of SMT exclusive features like @user or #topic. We have reviewed and selected three tokenizers[2] as they work well with SMT.

Instead of using the full dataset, we stratified sampled 1,352 users to classify their openness trait using mean score plus minus standard deviation as cutoff to determine high or low in openness. This user cohort contains 243,724 status updates with total of 4,113,493 words. On average each user posted 180 status updates and around 18 words per post. We then tokenized the sample data and labeled OOV words by comparing each token with a standard English dictionary. Then, based on popular OOV categories from literature, we developed a set of regular expressions to classify OOV words into OOV categories (e.g., elongated words, irregular capitalization, irregular punctuation) based on the morphology. For OOV categories such as emoticons and internet slangs, we developed custom dictionaries from related literature. A total of 4,113,493 tokens were created that included 100,983 unique words. Within these tokens, 431,712 OOV words were captured and annotated with 70,148 unique OOV words, which accounted for roughly 10% of the total tokens and 69% unique words in our dataset. Table 2 lists the curation process for capturing OOV words.

Table 2. Curation process for capturing OOV words

OOV category	Curation	Examples
Elongated words	regex pattern	*goooood yayyyy*
Irregular punctuation	regex pattern	*?!?!?!*
Irregular capitalization	regex pattern	*YEAH Horray*
Emoticon	custom dictionary lookup	*:-) 8D*
Abbreviation/Slang	custom dictionary lookup	*lol omg*

Evaluation. Evaluation in this DC focuses on the effectiveness of OOV words captured by comparing word coverage using our curated OOV word discovery process with LIWC-based closed-vocabulary approach and open-vocabulary approach. The result (see Table 3) shows that our OOV word discovery process are able to capture much more OOV words in different OOV categories. For example, none of the existing approaches are able to capture irregular capitalization. LIWC-based closed- vocabulary approach is able to capture an elongated word if the repeated character is the last one of its IV word (e.g. sooo, sooooo).

---

[2] spaCy https://spacy.io/; happierfuntokenizing https://github.com/dlatk/happierfuntokenizing; ekphrasis https://github.com/cbaziotis/ekphrasis [35].

Table 3. Captured OOV results

OOV words category	Closed-vocabulary	Open-vocabulary	Proposed approach
Elongated words	6,309	12,223	17,166
Emoticon	10,809	33,079	33,079
Abbreviation/Slang	61,129	90,617	108,617
Irregular capitalization	0	0	172,396
Internet Features	0	1,188	1,567

4.2 Design Cycle 2

Definition of Objective. After OOV words are discovered and categorized OOV words from DC 1, we observed that the usage of some OOV categories are higher than regular LIWC categories. This indicates that OOV categories may be potentially used as additional features to existing LIWC categories. The objective of DC 2 is to test the hypothesis that incorporating OOV words and categories will improve the predictive performance of existing closed-vocabulary and open-vocabulary approaches.

Development. Using LIWC as the baseline for closed-vocabulary approach, we prepared a feature set that expanding LIWC features with OOV categories. Using top 200 in-vocabulary words as the baseline for open-vocabulary approach, we added OOV words as additional feature. Using the sample data, we trained logistic regression model to classify the Openness personality trait using the experiment feature sets as shown in Table 4.

Table 4. Experiment feature sets

Feature set	Description
LIWC 2015	LIWC features
LIWC with OOV words	LIWC 2015 with relative frequency of top OOV categories
Top English Words	Top word features include stopwords and punctuation (English words only)
Top English and OOV Words	Top word features include stopwords and punctuation (English + OOV words)

Evaluation. We conducted the experiment utilizing Python's scikit-learn library and trained classification models using support vector machine and logistic regression techniques. We trained and evaluated personality classification models with different features sets using five-fold cross validation and compared the predictive power of different feature sets (see Table 5). The result shows that open-vocabulary models outperformed the closed-vocabulary models. This confirms with prior research. Additional, expanded

LIWC model improve upon the baseline LIWC model. This confirms our hypothesis that OOV categories contribute to explain personality trait. However, adding OOV words to the open-vocabulary approach did not improve the performance. This finding suggests that OOV words cannot be simply treated as open-vocabulary features. It might because many OOV words that have the same semantic meaning but are in different of forms (e.g. soooo, sooooooo, SOOOOO).

Table 5. Comparison of personality predictive results

Model name	Number of features	Approach	Accuracy
LIWC 2015	93	Closed-V	54.8%
LIWC with OOV words	101	Closed-V	60.0%
Top English Words	200	Open-V	65.3%
Top English and OOV Words	400	Open-V	60.4%

4.3 Design Cycle 3

Definition of Objective. While we believe that open-vocabulary approach offers better language coverage to process OOV words, we also believe that LIWC categories are valuable in personality prediction because they are expert validated. Thus, a new design objective arises to create a hybrid approach that combines the advantages of open-vocabulary and closed-vocabulary approaches while mitigates their limitations. Such a hybrid approach has demonstrated its effectiveness in the field of machine translation [31, 32]. Thus, there is a strong empirical foundation for a proposed hybrid-approach. Additionally, we want to address the different forms of the same OOV word. Thus, the objective of DC 3 is to test if a hybrid approach with OOV words normalization would improve personality prediction performance.

Development. Frist, we propose OOV word normalization that is similar to these used in open-vocabulary approach. However, instead of replacing normalized OOV word with IV word, we will save each OOV word into a tuple of (*OOV word, Normalized IV word, OOV category*). This would be a key feature in the proposed hybrid approach design. There are two reasons of why we propose such a design. First, normalized IV word would not only increase mapped words using closed-vocabulary dictionaries such as LIWC, but also boost the signal of frequently used words/phrases in open-vocabulary approach. Second, OOV category adds useful features to existing LIWC categories as shown in DC 2. Both classification models (treating each personality category as a Boolean outcome High or Low) and regression models (treating each personality score as a continuous variable). If the evaluation results show that the hybrid approach improves the predictive modeling performance, we would propose an OOV-aware curation process for psycholinguistic analysis using SMT as shown in Fig. 4.

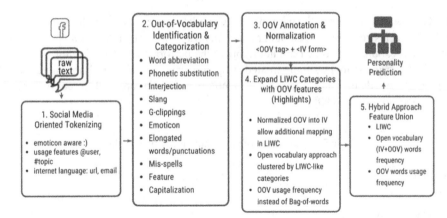

Fig. 4. Curation process for social media text

Evaluation. The full dataset will be processed for the development of hybrid approach and optimization in DC 3. We will continue evaluate our predictive models using common performance measures. More specifically, we will use accuracy to measure classification model performance and root-mean-square error to measure regression model performance.

4.4 Design Cycle 4

Definition of Objective. In this DC, we will focus on creating an optimized prediction model to compete against the state-of-art results of existing personality prediction studies using SMT.

Development. We will develop different prediction models using different modeling techniques, including ensemble learning and deep learning. We will experiment different hyper-parameter tuning to create models with best predictive performance.

Evaluation. We will compare the performance metrics of our best model with previous design cycles to assess the area of improvement. We will also compare the result with published state-of-art personality prediction results [12, 14, 23].

5 Conclusion and Future Research

In this research, we trained and evaluated classification models to predict personality by incorporating OOV features extracted from the proposed OOV-aware curation process. For future research, we would experiment the proposed hybrid approach using the full dataset for all Big 5 personality dimensions. Additionally, we would experiment different predictive modeling techniques, including ensemble learning and deep learning to create the best model for personality prediction. An improved performance would demonstrate the value of our proposed OOV-aware curation process for analyzing SMT.

This research makes the following contributions. First, it contributes to the knowledge base of psycholinguistic analysis by expanding LIWC categories with additional OOV-related dimensions. Second, it proposes a novel hybrid approach for psycholinguistic analysis. Although such an approach has been widely used in other NLP fields such as machine translation, this research is the first to demonstrate its effectiveness in analyzing SMT for personality prediction. Third, this research designs an OOV-aware curation process that other psycholinguistic researchers and practitioners can adopt to incorporate OOV words when analyzing SMT. The OVV-aware curation process gives social scientists a key to unlock the great potential of SMT. It allows them to discover and extract more relevant and meaningful linguistic features in SMT than existing NLP tools. These features can be then used to improve common psycholinguistic analysis tasks such as personality prediction. This research not only contributes to the current psychologic analysis of SMT, but will also provide new directions for NLP psycholinguistic knowledge in analyzing unstructured texts.

References

1. John, O.P., Angleitner, A., Ostendorf, F.: The lexical approach to personality: a historical review of trait taxonomic research. Eur. J. Pers. **2**, 171–203 (1988). https://doi.org/10.1002/per.2410020302
2. Pennebaker, J.W., King, L.A.: Linguistic styles: language use as an individual difference. J. Pers. Soc. Psychol. **77**, 1296–1312 (1999). https://doi.org/10.1037/0022-3514.77.6.1296
3. Krippendorff, K.: Content Analysis. https://us.sagepub.com/en-us/nam/content-analysis/book258450. Accessed 01 Dec 2019
4. Kern, M.L., et al.: Gaining insights from social media language: Methodologies and challenges. Psychol. Methods **21**, 507–525 (2016). https://doi.org/10.1037/met0000091
5. Youyou, W., Kosinski, M., Stillwell, D.: Computer-based personality judgments are more accurate than those made by humans. PNAS **112**, 1036–1040 (2015). https://doi.org/10.1073/pnas.1418680112
6. Lambiotte, R., Kosinski, M.: Tracking the digital footprints of personality. Proc. IEEE **102**, 1934–1939 (2014). https://doi.org/10.1109/JPROC.2014.2359054
7. Mairesse, F., Walker, M.A., Mehl, M.R., Moore, R.K.: Using linguistic cues for the automatic recognition of personality in conversation and text. J. Artif. Int. Res. **30**, 457–500 (2007)
8. Golbeck, J., Robles, C., Turner, K.: Predicting personality with social media. In: Extended Abstracts on Human Factors in Computing Systems, CHI 2011, pp. 253–262. ACM, New York (2011). https://doi.org/10.1145/1979742.1979614
9. Fast, E., Chen, B., Bernstein, M.S.: Empath: understanding topic signals in large-scale text. In: Proceedings of the 2016 CHI Conference on Human Factors in Computing Systems, pp. 4647–4657. ACM, New York (2016). https://doi.org/10.1145/2858036.2858535
10. Sarker, A.: A customizable pipeline for social media text normalization. Soc. Netw. Anal. Min. **7**(1), 1–13 (2017). https://doi.org/10.1007/s13278-017-0464-z
11. Yarkoni, T.: Personality in 100,000 words: a large-scale analysis of personality and word use among bloggers. J. Res. Pers. **44**, 363–373 (2010). https://doi.org/10.1016/j.jrp.2010.04.001
12. Schwartz, H.A., et al.: Personality, gender, and age in the language of social media: the open-vocabulary approach. PLoS ONE **8**, e73791 (2013). https://doi.org/10.1371/journal.pone.0073791
13. Han, B., Cook, P., Baldwin, T.: Lexical normalization for social media text. ACM Trans. Intell. Syst. Technol. **4**, 5:1–5:27 (2013). https://doi.org/10.1145/2414425.2414430

14. Azucar, D., Marengo, D., Settanni, M.: Predicting the Big 5 personality traits from digital footprints on social media: a meta-analysis. Pers. Individ. Differ. **124**, 150–159 (2018). https://doi.org/10.1016/j.paid.2017.12.018
15. Bontcheva, K., Derczynski, L., Funk, A., Greenwood, M.A., Maynard, D., Aswani, N.: TwitIE: an open-source information extraction pipeline for microblog text. In: RANLP (2013)
16. Kramer, A.D.I., Rodden, K.: Word usage and posting behaviors: modeling blogs with unobtrusive data collection methods. In: Proceedings of the SIGCHI Conference on Human Factors in Computing Systems, pp. 1125–1128. ACM, New York (2008). https://doi.org/10.1145/1357054.1357230
17. Han, B., Baldwin, T.: Lexical normalisation of short text messages: makn sens a #twitter. Presented at the Proceedings of the 49th Annual Meeting of the Association for Computational Linguistics: Human Language Technologies June (2011)
18. Arnoux, P.-H., Xu, A., Boyette, N., Mahmud, J., Akkiraju, R., Sinha, V.: 25 Tweets to Know You: A New Model to Predict Personality with Social Media. arXiv:1704.05513 [cs] (2017)
19. Oberlander, J., Nowson, S.: Whose thumb is it anyway? Classifying author personality from weblog text. In: Proceedings of the COLING/ACL on Main Conference Poster Sessions, pp. 627–634. Association for Computational Linguistics, Stroudsburg (2006)
20. Contractor, D., Faruquie, T.A., Subramaniam, L.V.: Unsupervised cleansing of noisy text. In: Proceedings of the 23rd International Conference on Computational Linguistics: Posters, pp. 189–196. Association for Computational Linguistics, Stroudsburg, PA, USA (2010)
21. Liu, F., Weng, F., Wang, B., Liu, Y.: Insertion, deletion, or substitution? Normalizing text messages without pre-categorization nor supervision. In: Proceedings of the 49th Annual Meeting of the Association for Computational Linguistics: Human Language Technologies: Short Papers, vol. 2, pp. 71–76. Association for Computational Linguistics (2011)
22. Schwartz, H.A., Ungar, L.H.: Data-driven content analysis of social media: a systematic overview of automated methods. Ann. Am. Acad. Polit. Soc. Sci. **659**, 78–94 (2015). https://doi.org/10.1177/0002716215569197
23. Farnadi, G., et al.: Computational personality recognition in social media. User Model. User-Adap. Interact. **26**, 109–142 (2016). https://doi.org/10.1007/s11257-016-9171-0
24. Settanni, M., Marengo, D.: Sharing feelings online: studying emotional well-being via automated text analysis of Facebook posts. Front. Psychol. **6** (2015). https://doi.org/10.3389/fpsyg.2015.01045
25. Iacobelli, F., Gill, A.J., Nowson, S., Oberlander, J.: Large scale personality classification of bloggers. In: D'Mello, S., Graesser, A., Schuller, B., Martin, J.-C. (eds.) ACII 2011. LNCS, vol. 6975, pp. 568–577. Springer, Heidelberg (2011). https://doi.org/10.1007/978-3-642-24571-8_71
26. Schwartz, H.A., et al.: Toward personality insights from language exploration in social media. In: 2013 AAAI Spring Symposium Series (2013)
27. Vaishnavi, V.K., Kuechler Jr., W.: Design Science Research Methods and Patterns: Innovating Information and Communication Technology. Auerbach Publications, USA (2007)
28. Funder, D.C.: Accurate personality judgment. Curr. Dir. Psychol. Sci. **21**, 177–182 (2012). https://doi.org/10.1177/0963721412445309
29. Goldberg, L.R.: An alternative "description of personality": The Big-Five factor structure. J. Pers. Soc. Psychol. **59**, 1216–1229 (1990). https://doi.org/10.1037/0022-3514.59.6.1216
30. Kosinski, M., Stillwell, D., Graepel, T.: Private traits and attributes are predictable from digital records of human behavior. PNAS **110**, 5802–5805 (2013). https://doi.org/10.1073/pnas.1218772110
31. Finin, T., Murnane, W., Karandikar, A., Keller, N., Martineau, J., Dredze, M.: Annotating named entities in Twitter data with crowdsourcing. In: Proceedings of the NAACL HLT 2010 Workshop on Creating Speech and Language Data with Amazon's Mechanical Turk, pp. 80–88. Association for Computational Linguistics, Los Angeles (2010)

32. Ritter, A., Clark, S., Mausam, Etzioni, O.: Named entity recognition in tweets: an experimental study. In: Proceedings of the 2011 Conference on Empirical Methods in Natural Language Processing, pp. 1524–1534. Association for Computational Linguistics, Edinburgh (2011)
33. España-Bonet, C., Costa-jussà, M.R.: Hybrid machine translation overview. In: Costa-jussà, M.R.R., Rapp, R., Lambert, P., Eberle, K., Banchs, R.E.E., Babych, B. (eds.) Hybrid Approaches to Machine Translation. TANLP, pp. 1–24. Springer, Cham (2016). https://doi.org/10.1007/978-3-319-21311-8_1
34. Eisele, A., Federmann, C., Saint-Amand, H., Jellinghaus, M., Herrmann, T., Chen, Y.: Using moses to integrate multiple rule-based machine translation engines into a hybrid system. In: Proceedings of the Third Workshop on Statistical Machine Translation (2008). https://doi.org/10.3115/1626394.1626422
35. Baziotis, C., Pelekis, N., Doulkeridis, C.: DataStories at SemEval-2017 task 4: deep LSTM with attention for message-level and topic-based sentiment analysis. In: Proceedings of the 11th International Workshop on Semantic Evaluation (SemEval-2017), pp. 747–754. Association for Computational Linguistics, Vancouver (2017). https://doi.org/10.18653/v1/S17-2126

Codifying Interdisciplinary Design Knowledge Through Patterns – The Case of Smart Personal Assistants

Ernestine Dickhaut[1]([⊠]), Andreas Janson[2], and Jan Marco Leimeister[1,2]

[1] University of Kassel, Kassel, Germany
{ernestine.dickhaut,leimeister}@uni-kassel.de
[2] University of St.Gallen, St.Gallen, Switzerland
{andreas.janson,janmarco.leimeister}@unisg.ch

Abstract. Smart personal assistants (SPAs) are proliferating into our daily lives and are a ubiquitous platform for providing digital services. However, when designing such innovative IT artifacts, interdisciplinary domain knowledge is often needed. For example, SPAs utilize a plethora of sensors and cloud-based computation of data to deliver high-quality services, but those services, for example, may conflict with current regulations of law, e.g., with the Data Protection Regulation (GDPR) in Europe. In that sense, approaches are needed to overcome the limited domain knowledge of developers. Thus, we propose in our study a pattern-based approach to codify interdisciplinary design knowledge. For this purpose, we derive theory-motivated requirements, develop design principles for patterns, and evaluate the utility of the patterns. Our results from a 2 × 2 fully randomized field study show that the provision of patterns for SPA development supports interdisciplinary design through better consideration of both service quality and law compatibility. Thus, we provide design contributions concerning how we effectively codify and communicate design knowledge and provide practical guidance for supporting interdisciplinary IS development.

Keywords: Smart personal assistants · Legal compatibility · Design knowledge

1 Introduction

Smart personal assistants (SPAs) such as Amazon Alexa are more popular than ever before. One key success factor of SPAs is the adaptability to the user, which offers new support in everyday life. Nonetheless, this is only possible by collecting and evaluating personal user data. Conversely, the protection of one's own data and legal aspects is becoming increasingly important when considering recent privacy scandals. Higher legal standards increase the pressure on developers of IT artifacts. However, developers often lack the necessary domain expertise to develop a legally compatible IT artifact such as SPAs. They do not correctly understand the contents of legal requirements and cannot take them into account satisfactorily in the development.

© Springer Nature Switzerland AG 2020
S. Hofmann et al. (Eds.): DESRIST 2020, LNCS 12388, pp. 114–125, 2020.
https://doi.org/10.1007/978-3-030-64823-7_12

Therefore, we present a pattern-based approach for system development to improve the legal compatibility of an SPA while also considering the quality aspects of these IT artifacts. We provide a way that enables developers to, on the one hand, gain knowledge from other disciplines and, on the other hand, present concrete solution approaches during the development process. In this context, we also pay attention to the cognitive processes of the pattern user, i.e., the system designer. To achieve this goal, we map elements of cognitive load theory to the development and design of our design patterns. Based on relevant literature, we identify requirements for the codification of knowledge and derive design principles for the development of patterns considering cognitive load theory. Finally, our patterns are a manageable way to support developers in designing legally compatible SPAs but also to acquire expertise and use it for other purposes. The goal of our paper is to present a theory-driven design approach to provide a set of design principles for building design patterns that, ultimately, support designing legally compatible SPAs and are based on the following two research questions (RQ):

RQ: How should we codify interdisciplinary design knowledge in patterns to support SPA developers, and what are the effects of those patterns on IS development?

To answer our research question, we evaluate our developed patterns in an experimental user study. We pay particular attention to two aspects. On the one hand, we examine the extent to which a legally compatible SPA can be developed with the help of our patterns. On the other hand, we focus on the usefulness, comprehensibility, and cognitive processing of each design pattern.

2 Related Work

2.1 Smart Personal Assistants

SPAs can support everyday life in many ways, such as on smartphones, in cars, in service encounters, in smart home environments, or as support for elderly or impaired people [1]. According to Knote et al., SPAs can be further differentiated into five archetypes: Adaptive Voice (Vision) Assistants, Chatbot Assistants, Embodied Virtual Assistants, Passive Pervasive Assistant, and Natural Conversation Assistants [1].

To develop SPAs, we have to pay more and more attention to the requirements of various disciplines. Key aspects of SPAs relate, for example, to their usability and user experience, which we can sum up as the overall service quality. Service quality is frequently being paid much attention during the development process. However, there is also growing skepticism and concern that these systems, for example, "listen" without being activated by a wake word [2], thus showing that quality perceptions are difficult to achieve with these devices. More importantly, legal requirements are often only addressed to a minimum extent in order to be compliant with the minimal requirements of law [3]. However, the protection of one's data is also becoming important, especially when taking new legal regulations and user fears into account. In this context, system developers often lack the necessary domain expertise to be able to implement legal requirements for developing a legally compatible SPA. Furthermore, there is a lack of and great uncertainties in research on how to support developers in their design process of user assistance systems such as SPAs [4].

2.2 Codification of Design Knowledge

During the development process, requirements from unfamiliar disciplines are often addressed sparsely by system developers, e.g., ethical or legal requirements. One possible reason for this is the lack of expertise related to those domains [5]. Nonetheless, we know that humans need familiarity, even in system development processes. However, this familiarity is often not provided by other domains, e.g., legal regulations. Therefore, design knowledge and solution approaches for system development problems should be codified in a way that supports system developers. By reusing knowledge, effectiveness and efficiency can also be achieved, especially related to the knowledge transfer of solutions to new use cases [6].

The codification of design knowledge is gaining importance in the DSR field, also enabling transferability of design knowledge to other fields [6]. Design knowledge is used in DSR projects for various purposes. Gamma et al. [7] found that most knowledge is used for designing artifacts. Therefore, it is crucial to have the right design knowledge in the most helpful presentation form for the specific application. Different approaches, such as wikis and documentations [8], are already used to capture knowledge. These approaches do not offer a solution to the problem of codifying knowledge in a way that is understandable for disciplines outside the field. Facts such as missing structure, using technical terms, and incompleteness lead to low usage of these tools. It needs to be guaranteed that the design knowledge is formulated in clear, unambiguous, accessible language, without inconsistencies and contradictions [9].

In this context, requirement and design patterns are a solution to solve recurring problems and challenges [10]. In addition to the previously used application areas, they can now be used to enable a broad understanding of periphery disciplines. Patterns contain templates to describe information in tabular form [11] and represent established instruments to make complex knowledge accessible and applicable for system developers [12]. A pattern thus defines the basic structure of a solution for a specific problem but does not yet describe a complete solution to the problem. This approach supports the developer in solving the interdisciplinary problem but does not restrict their creativity by abstracting the pattern [12]. The use of patterns has been established in many different disciplines and has become an integral part of the basic education of a software developer.

3 Designing Patterns for Smart Personal Assistants' Design

3.1 Design Science Process and Methodological Considerations

We use the Design Science Research (DSR) process by Peffers et al. [13] for designing and evaluating our design patterns (see Fig. 1). In specific, we follow a problem-centered approach that centers around the lack of interdisciplinary design knowledge to develop a legally compatible SPA.

Therefore, we derive design requirements from the literature based on which we create design principles for patterns. The patterns should support developers to design a legally compatible SPA because there are a lot of law elements that must be taken into account when designing a legally compatible SPA, such as the protection of personal data and the transparency of data storage. To develop a satisfactory system for the user, our patterns also take quality into account [6].

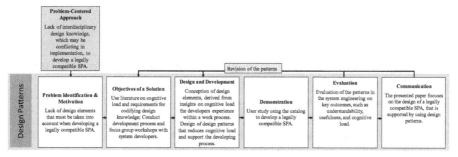

Fig. 1. Design Science Research Approach (adapted from [13])

3.2 Kernel Theories for Scaffolding Requirements Derivation

Design patterns are intended to support the user in the development of the specific system. We do not want the users to have the patterns at hand again and again during the implementation, but rather we want them to learn and expand their knowledge by using them. To derive our requirements for codifying design knowledge in design patterns, we draw on theories related to conceptualizing design knowledge, the representation of design knowledge, and refer in this paper especially to cognitive load theory (CLT). With its origins in educational psychology [14], CLT provides a theoretical framework for studying how individuals process information during learning and problem-solving processes while at the same providing guidance on how to structure information for better learning results [15]. We argue that using design patterns in interdisciplinary IS development is also a problem-solving process, where developers acquire design knowledge and apply it to complex problems, i.e., when conflicts occur that arise from conflicting requirements. Since it is important that patterns have a long-term learning effect on the users, we use CLT as the kernel theory.

Since the cognitive resources of an individual are limited, it is essential to manage cognitive load related to the pattern presentation when taking design advice offered by design patterns into account [16]. We derive in the following theory-based requirements to codify design knowledge in design patterns. The patterns are built on CLT as a kernel theory but also involve other concepts, such as research on codifying design knowledge.

3.3 Derivation of Theory-Driven Requirements

To ensure that our patterns have the highest possible added value for the user – in our specific case, SPA developers – we first conducted a literature research including various literature dealing with the codification and representation of design knowledge (see Table 1). By this means, we derive requirements from theory for codifying design knowledge to develop SPAs from an interdisciplinary perspective, thus addressing the first part of the objectives of the solution phase of the design science approach by Peffers et al. [13].

In addition to requirements for the structure and design of the patterns, the content is particularly important when creating the patterns. It is important to not only deal with the content of the interdisciplinary knowledge in the patterns but also to consider the

Table 1. Theory-driven Design Requirements

	Design requirements	Source
R1	A pattern should provide implementation guidance but should not restrict the pattern users in their creativity	[18]
R2	A pattern should present relationships between the involved disciplines and any necessary explanations and adjustments	[19]
R3	A pattern should contain a description of why it is useful to use the pattern to illustrate the importance and the added value of the pattern	[20, 21]
R4	The core content of the pattern should enable knowledge transfer, document knowledge, and provide good repositories for knowledge dissemination	[22]
R5	A pattern should provide additional domain-specific information and knowledge to support the implementation	[22]
R6	A pattern should account for different knowledge levels when considering domain-specific knowledge needed for SPA design	[22]
R7	The procedural steps of a pattern should be adjusted by a clear subdivision of the content to reduce the extraneous load	[22]
R8	The content of the pattern should be presented in a compact and clear way without inducing unnecessary extraneous load, i.e., by avoiding split-attention effects	[17]

structure of the patterns. Both factors are essential for the success of the patterns in practice. There are various requirements for elements, which must be presented and offered in any case in order to offer a practical use for the users of the patterns. That is why the patterns should contain not only a problem solution but also details about an introduction in the problem-solving context, information about actions, and concrete implementation examples. Doing so refers especially to the process of scaffolding problem-solving processes that lower the cognitive load by pointing out important aspects relevant to the task.

In order to guarantee general validity, the patterns should have general applicability. Chandra et al. assume that design knowledge is codified for the purpose of reuse, and even though reusing is sometimes associated with repetition, reuse has been observed in contexts that strive toward innovation and customization [17].

However, for the success of the patterns, not only the content and its preparation are important but also the presentation form. A clear presentation form increases the quality and usefulness of the patterns for the users. Chandra et al. highlight the importance that the design knowledge presented should be as compact and clear as possible [17]. Less extraneous load through a clear presentation form facilitates the work with the patterns [22]. Although the information is often codified in written form, the long continuous text makes the application of patterns more difficult. As such, there is a lack of an overview and the possibility to get the information you are looking for as quickly as possible. Therefore, the design knowledge presented should be supplemented by graphic representations [17].

3.4   Design Principles for Design Patterns

We identified in Sect. 3.2 requirements by analyzing literature to extract design-relevant knowledge from previous work, which helped us to address design principles for our case, the development of design patterns for the implementation of a legally compatible SPA (see Fig. 2). In addition, we also ground our design principles in literature concerned with scaffolding problem-solving, which has also proven to manage cognitive load [23]. To ground our artifact in practical relevance, we conducted a focus group workshop (n = 8) to justify the design principles derived from the literature. The participants in the workshop had both expertise in software engineering and knowledge of legal compatibility to assess the efficiency of the derived principles to solve the practical problem. In the workshop, requirements for patterns for the special field of application, the development of a legally compatible SPA, were jointly sought, and then possible approaches for solving conflicts between service quality and legal compatibility were elaborated.

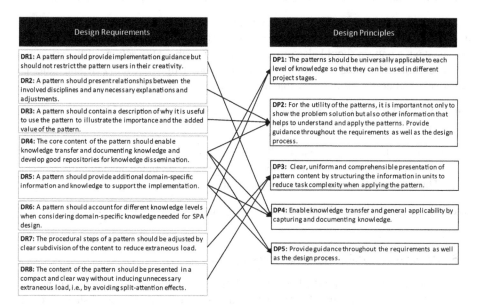

Fig. 2.   Design Requirements and Design Principles for Interdisciplinary Design Patterns

To make sure our design patterns bring the highest possible added value for many different users, special attention must be paid to the different levels of knowledge that developers have. The design incorporates both technical knowledge and artistry and occurs as a reflective conversation between designers, their actions, and their situations [22]. Thus, we suggest our first design principle:

DP1:   The patterns should be universally applicable to each level of knowledge so that they are reusable and applicable.

To support the user in solving the problem, a concrete example for the implementation is necessary [21]. The solution approach should include requirements, the relationship between constructs and domain objects, explanation, and justification [19]. By adding further content and information, not only the comprehensibility of the problem and the possible solution are improved but also the expertise of the user is increased to solve related problems and engage to work on domain knowledge shortcomings [23]. This results in our second design principle:

DP2: For the utility of the patterns, it is important not only to show the problem solution but also other information that helps to understand and apply the patterns.

The content is not only of great importance for the applicability and added value of the pattern but also for the way the design knowledge is presented. For this purpose, a clear presentation method should be used in order to keep the cognitive process to a minimum [21, 24]. Thus, we suggest our third design principle:

DP3: A clear, uniform, and comprehensible presentation of pattern content by structuring the information in units to reduce task complexity when applying the pattern.

In addition to the actual problem-solving, information should be provided that allows the user to understand the context of the problem [21] and critical task aspects [25]. In this context, a pattern should also provide information about the actions of the artifacts, and according to boundary conditions, to enable knowledge transfer [21]. The patterns must be as generally valid as possible to be generally applicable. Hence, we propose:

DP4: Enable knowledge transfer and general applicability by capturing and documenting knowledge.

In order to have the greatest possible impact on the learning effect of the patterns from a cognitive point of view, they should be used throughout the development process [22]. Thus, we suggest our fifth design principle:

DP5: Provide guidance throughout the requirements as well as the design process.

3.5 Patterns for Designing Smart Personal Assistants

We developed patterns with the help of our design principles. For the development, we have decided on a procedure that consists of different methods, like workshops, expert interviews, and literature research.

First, we created requirement patterns as a prerequisite for design patterns by conducting a literature search and identified higher-level goals related to achieving service quality and legal compatibility (**DP5**). In the next step, we compared the goals of legal compatibility and service quality in order to identify possible connections and conflicts. The requirement patterns do not yet solve any concrete implementation problems in the development process but initially serve as support for the specification of legal and service quality requirements. Therefore, we need patterns to support the development process, namely design patterns (see Fig. 3 for an example design pattern). Based on **DP2**, our patterns start with an introduction, including links to relevant background information in the problem-solving context. That is why each pattern starts with its individual goal and, as with the requirement pattern, represents the best possible final state for the developed system. As the design patterns are based on the already presented requirement patterns and their high-level goals, the influences on the respective patterns are presented in each design pattern.

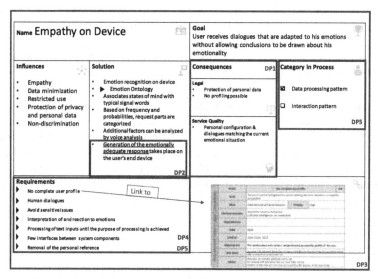

Fig. 3. Realization of the Design Principles in the Design Patterns

Thus, legal influences and service quality influences, as well as their priorities, are considered in the patterns (**DP4**). At the core of the pattern are possible solution approaches. They demonstrate concrete, reusable solutions and explain their positive and negative consequences (**DP1**). We have taken great care to ensure that all patterns follow the same structure to guarantee the highest possible added value through use (**DP3**). Because we have already paid special attention to cognitive load theory when creating the design principles, our design patterns also consider cognitive processing.

4 Evaluation

With the following evaluation, we address the phases of demonstration and evaluation as depicted in the design science cycle [13] by evaluating the patterns and their utility to scaffold interdisciplinary IS development projects. For our evaluation, we drew on the framework for evaluating DSR [26] and chose a formative ex-post evaluation approach [26, 27] that will help us to form the design of our method early in the development process.

4.1 Methodological Aspects

The data collection took place in the university course "Business and Information Systems Engineering" in a Western European university and was embedded in a fully randomized between-subject experiment. The patterns were applied by students, who were trained in requirements engineering as well as systems design; thus, they are a suitable sample for evaluating the utility of our artifact. Overall, the task was to prototypically design a chatbot application. In total, 22 groups of two persons each, who all studied in business with a major in information systems, participated in the voluntary task that was incentivized with three extra credits for the final exam. To ensure the seriousness of participation, extra credit could only be obtained when individuals followed the tasks as described.

The subjects were provided with a mockup and received information regarding the case, such as interview documents of the clients and customers. In addition, they pursued the overall task of developing a chatbot prototype of an SPA for higher education that supports teaching. In order to meet the requirements of university teaching and the latest data protection regulations, it was necessary to make the SPA as legally compatible as possible but still ensure high service quality. The participants were completely randomly divided into two groups. Concerning the experimental evaluation, we designed a 2×2 experiment with two experimental manipulations that correspond to the provision of (1) requirement patterns (n = 6), (2) design patterns (n = 6), and (3) requirement patterns as well as design patterns (n = 6). In that sense, the experiment also included a control group (n = 4) without the support of patterns during the development process of the prototype (see Fig. 4).

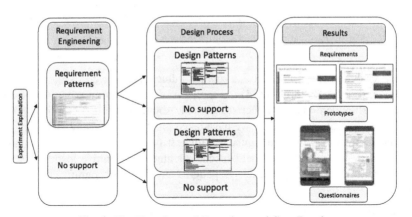

Fig. 4. The Experimental Procedure and Core Results

We used the developed prototypes for a rating and evaluation procedure by five subject matter experts experienced in digital service design as well as the legally compatible design of IT artifacts concerning the two outcome variables of interest, service quality and legal compatibility. The selected experts did not know the used patterns. All experts have scientific publications either in the field of service quality (n = 3) or legal compatibility (n = 2).

4.2   Results

The experiment was conducted in groups of two persons each. The control group (CG) counted four groups. The treatment groups (TG) consisted of 18 groups in total, of which six groups were subject to a different treatment. All subjects were about the same age, with a range from 21 to 26 ($\bar{x} = 24.34$). We conducted the field experiment with two goals in mind: first, we investigate how the design principles provide the benefits and added value. Second, we examine how interdisciplinary knowledge through patterns is used by system designers. Both aspects are evaluated by the expert panel assessment of the developed prototypes. The results of the expert evaluation are presented in the table below. The results (see Table 2) show that the subjects who have used both the requirement and design patterns have also had significantly better ratings in service quality and legal compatibility in the expert evaluation. In the groups that used the pattern, more attention was paid to the implementation of legal criteria.

Table 2. Comparison between Control and Treatment Groups' Prototypes

Legal Compatibility & Service Quality	Group	Support	Groups N	Rating (1-5) Mean (SD)	Post hoc tests RP	DP	RPDP
	CG	No Support	4	2.63 (.95)	.88	.45	.02*
	TG 1	Requirement patterns (RP)	6	2.66 (1.07)		.36	.01*
	TG 2	Design patterns (DP)	6	2.38 (1.03)			<.05*
	TG 3	Requirement and Design patterns (RPDP)	6	3.16 (1.05)			

In addition to the expert evaluation, we have conducted further surveys, in the form of questionnaires, concerning the use of the patterns. The questionnaires contained, on the one hand, the content and, on the other hand, the form of presentation of the used patterns. We used the already proven questionnaire for evaluating requirement patterns from [28], which we adapted to our evaluations. An exemplary item examined the degree of abstraction and the concreteness of the content associated with it. Items that deal with the structure and presentation of the patterns achieve particularly good results. The clarity of the content is particularly well received.

Both evaluations show that the form of presentation and the content of the interdisciplinary expertise in the patterns lead precisely to the desired goal: namely, the design of an SPA that is both legally compatible and still includes high service quality, which in practice often leads to conflicts during development.

5   Discussion and Implications

To support developers to design a legally compatible SPA, we derived requirements based on the literature on codifying design knowledge [17–22]. With the help of the requirements, we were able to generate design principles that are applied to generate requirements and design patterns for interdisciplinary knowledge [11]. We followed the design science research approach of Peffers et al. to extract our design principles [13] for designing patterns.

We hypothesized that interdisciplinary patterns in the development process better support SPA developers. Therefore, especially for interdisciplinary projects, there often arise conflicts between different requirements, which led us to consider the codification of knowledge first. Our results confirm that the codification of knowledge in requirement and design patterns leads to better results regarding the legal compatibility and service of SPAs.

Our design principles for patterns are not without limitations that, at the same time, present avenues for future research. Moreover, we had the design principles tested by potential users to rely on these insights to improve the patterns further. Regarding our pattern design, our next steps will be to improve the patterns by integrating the feedback of the study subjects. Based on this feedback, we can revise and improve our design principles for pattern design. In addition to the preparation and the presentation of the content, a particular focus is given to the ability to learn through the patterns in the following improvement. In this context, the findings of cognitive load theory play a key role and need to be further integrated. An overall goal of the patterns is the extraction of interdisciplinary knowledge through the use of our patterns. Future research could also validate if improving the learning processes of information system developers leads to an improvement of knowledge transfer to other development projects. This would enable us to capture the utility of patterns beyond single development projects. The method was evaluated partially with students. We remark that professional IS developers would have potentially applied the method differently, which would lead to different results. Especially the evaluation of the patterns could be more comprehensive to show the implications of practical software development and the learning from patterns. We evaluated the patterns and the developed prototypes but not directly our design principles. Nevertheless, by evaluating the patterns, conclusions can be made about the quality of the design principles.

To answer our RQ, we would like to summarize: first, we provide insights into the understanding and difficulties of design knowledge codification in interdisciplinary projects, which, in practice, is particularly difficult to implement. Second, our patterns contribute to the ongoing discussion in design science research on providing real guidance for how to design IT artifacts [29] and how to accumulate design knowledge.

Acknowledgements. This paper presents research that was conducted in context of the project "AnEkA" (project number:348084924), funded by the German Research Foundation (DFG).

References

1. Knote, R., Janson, A., Söllner, M., Leimeister, J.M.: Classifying smart personal assistants: an empirical cluster analysis. In: Proceedings of the 52nd HICSS (2019)
2. https://www.wired.com/2016/12/alexa-and-google-record-your-voice/
3. Hoffmann, A., Schulz, T., Zirfas, J., Hoffmann, H., Roßnagel, A., Leimeister, J.M.: Legal compatibility as a characteristic of sociotechnical systems. Bus. Inf. Syst. Eng. **57**(2), 103–113 (2015). https://doi.org/10.1007/s12599-015-0373-5
4. Maedche, A., Morana, S., Schacht, S., Werth, D., Krumeich, J.: Advanced user assistance systems. BISE **58**, 367–370 (2016)
5. Knote, R., Söllner, M., Leimeister, J.M.: Towards a pattern language for smart personal assistants. In: PLoP 2018 (2018)

6. vom Brocke, J., Winter, R., Hevner, A., Maedche, A.: Accumulation and evolution of design knowledge in design science research–a journey through time and space. JAIS (2019)
7. Sturm, B., Sunyaev, A.: A good beginning makes a good ending: incipient sources of knowledge in design science research. In: ICIS 2019 Proceedings (2019)
8. Phuwanartnurak, A.J.: Interdisciplinary Collaboration through Wikis in Software Development. IEEE, Piscataway (2009)
9. Lukyanenko, R., Parsons, J.: Design theory indeterminacy: what is it, how can it be reduced, and why did the polar bear drown? J. Assoc. Inf. Syst. (JAIS) 1–59 (2020)
10. Alexander, C.: A Pattern Language: Towns, Buildings, Construction. Oxford (1977)
11. Knote, R., Baraki, H., Söllner, M., Geihs, K., Leimeister, J.M.: From requirement to design patterns for ubiquitous computing applications. In: EuroPlop 2016, pp. 1–11 (2016)
12. Thies, L., Knote, R., Jandt, S., Söllner, M., Roßnagel, A., Leimeister, J.M.: Anforderungs- und Entwurfsmuster als Instrumente des Privacy by Design. Springer (2018)
13. Peffers, K., Tuunanen, T., Rothenberger, M.A., Chatterjee, S.: A design science research methodology for information systems research. JMIS **24**, 45–77 (2007)
14. Miller, G.A.: The magical number seven, plus or minus two: some limits on our capacity for processing information. Psychol. Rev. **63**, 81–97 (1956)
15. Sweller, J.: Cognitive load during problem solving: effects on learning. Cogn. Sci. **12**, 257–285 (1988)
16. Kirschner, P.A., Ayres, P., Chandler, P.: Contemporary cognitive load theory research. The good, the bad and the ugly. Comput. Hum. Behav. **27**, 99–105 (2011)
17. Chandra Kruse, L., Nickerson, J.: Portraying Design Essence (2018)
18. Ahrens, J., Sankar, C.: Tailoring database training for end users. MIS Q. **17**(4), 419–439 (1993)
19. Heinrich, P., Schwabe, G.: Communicating nascent design theories on innovative information systems through multi-grounded design principles. In: Tremblay, M.C., VanderMeer, D., Rothenberger, M., Gupta, A., Yoon, V. (eds.) DESRIST 2014. LNCS, vol. 8463, pp. 148–163. Springer, Cham (2014). https://doi.org/10.1007/978-3-319-06701-8_10
20. Garud, R.: On the distinction between know-how, know-what, and know-why (1997)
21. Chandra, L., Seidel, S., Gregor, S.: Prescriptive knowledge in IS research: conceptualizing design principles in terms of materiality, action, and boundary conditions. In: HICSS, pp. 4039–4048 (2014)
22. Chandra Kruse, L., Seidel, S.: Tensions in design principle formulation, pp. 180–188 (2017)
23. Janson, A., Söllner, M., Leimeister, J.M.: Ladders for learning: is scaffolding the key to teaching problem solving in technology-mediated learning contexts? AMLE (2019)
24. Doering, A., Veletsianos, G.: Multi-scaffolding environment: an analysis of scaffolding and its impact on cognitive load and problem-solving ability. JECR **37**, 107–129 (2007)
25. Reiser, B.J.: Scaffolding complex learning: the mechanisms of structuring and problematizing student work. J. Learn. Sci. **13**, 273–304 (2004)
26. Venable, J., Pries-Heje, J., Baskerville, R.: FEDS: a framework for evaluation in design science research. Eur. J. Inf. Syst. **25**, 77–89 (2016)
27. Sonnenberg, C., vom Brocke, J.: Evaluation patterns for design science research artefacts. In: Helfert, M., Donnellan, B. (eds.) EDSS 2011. CCIS, vol. 286, pp. 71–83. Springer, Heidelberg (2012). https://doi.org/10.1007/978-3-642-33681-2_7
28. Janzen, A., Hoffmann, A., Hoffmann, H.: Anforderungsmuster im Requirements Engineering. Information Systems, Kassel University (2013)
29. Gregor, S.: The nature of theory in information systems. MIS Q. **30**(3), 611–642 (2006)

Exploring Design Principles for Enterprise Chatbots: An Analytic Hierarchy Process Study

Jasper Feine[1]([⊠]), Martin Adam[2], Ivo Benke[1], Alexander Maedche[1], and Alexander Benlian[2]

[1] Institute of Information Systems and Marketing (IISM), Karlsruhe Institute of Technology (KIT), Karlsruhe, Germany
{jasper.feine,ivo.benke,alexander.maedche}@kit.edu
[2] Institute of Information Systems and Electronic Services, Technical University of Darmstadt, Darmstadt, Germany
{adam,benlian}@ise.tu-darmstadt.de

Abstract. Chatbots have attracted tremendous interest in recent years and are increasingly employed in form of enterprise chatbots (ECBs) (i.e., chatbots used in the explicit context of enterprise systems). Although ECBs substantially differ in their design requirements from, for example, more common and widely deployed customer service chatbots, only few studies exist that specifically investigate and provide guidance for the design of ECBs. To address this emerging gap, we accumulated existing design knowledge from previous studies and created a list of 26 design features (DFs) which we integrated into 6 design principles (DPs). Subsequently, 36 practitioners from an IT consulting company which are experienced in using ECBs evaluated the importance of the DPs and DFs following the Analytic Hierarchy Process method. Our results provide evidence that DPs and DFs promoting usability and flexibility are ranked more important than DPs and DFs promoting socialness and human likeness. These findings provide valuable insights, as they are partially contrary to some existing studies investigating the importance of social cues of chatbots in other domains. Overall, the identified lists of DPs and DFs and their importance rankings provide guidance for the design of ECBs and can serve as a basis for future research projects.

Keywords: Chatbot · Enterprise system · AHP · Design principle · Design feature

1 Introduction

Chatbots (i.e., text-based conversational agents) are currently popular and widely spread technologies that communicate via text messages in an automated manner [13]. They offer many benefits to their users in contrast to traditional alternatives such as 24/7 IT helpdesk availability [19, 49]. While mostly known for and applied in customer service contexts [1, 17], chatbots are increasingly used in enterprise systems [49]. Thereby, chatbots offer great potential to support workers with routine and complex

© Springer Nature Switzerland AG 2020
S. Hofmann et al. (Eds.): DESRIST 2020, LNCS 12388, pp. 126–141, 2020.
https://doi.org/10.1007/978-3-030-64823-7_13

tasks, shaping the future of work [30, 39]. Advancing from traditional definition, recent enterprise systems evolve from *"comprehensive software solutions integrating the complete range of a business' processes"* [27, p. 357] towards enterprise systems that *"cover all organizational-wide IS as well as associated platforms"* [48, p. 5]. To facilitate their usage, different types of enterprise systems, such as collaboration systems (e.g. Microsoft Teams, Slack) and ERP & CRM systems (e.g. SAP Conversational AI, Salesforce Einstein Bot), are offering natural language interfaces with chatbots. As a consequence, we refer to this specific kind of chatbots as *enterprise chatbots* (ECB).

Prior research on ECB has focused predominantly on basic task support, like cost reductions and computer-based support for decision making [49]. In a recent study, Stoeckli et al. [44] have further investigated potential affordances of ECBs, revealing perceptual differences and potentials through balancing capabilities of ECBs and traditional enterprise systems. In addition, Lechler et al. [26] analyzed over 100 feedback-ECBs and distilled six archetypes covering the roles in facilitating feedback exchange on performance, culture, and ideas. Concrete instantiations of ECBs are the chatbot Tilda which facilitates tagging and summarization in groups [50], Mila which reschedules meetings for employees [49], or Searchbot which supports collaborative search [4]. In practice, ECBs have primarily focused on rather simple task executions and less intelligent work flows [44]. A well-known example for an early ECB is Microsoft's *"Clippy"*, which was perceived as intrusive and disturbing and quickly disappeared [32]. Overall, we see that ECBs have big potential to improve the usage of enterprise systems. Nevertheless, their design and implications are still understudied and prior research contributions on this topic are limited [24, 35]. Therefore, this paper seeks to overcome this challenge by investigating potential design knowledge for ECBs. Hence, we investigate the following research question (RQ):

RQ: Which design principles should guide the development of enterprise chatbots?

To answer this research question, we review research studies that investigate chatbots at work and combine their design knowledge into a list of design features (DFs) and design principles (DPs). Subsequently, we evaluate the importance of these DFs and DPs with practitioners from an IT consulting company that are experienced in using ECBs (e.g., ECBs to make appointments). We follow the Analytic Hierarchy Process (AHP) method in order to create importance rankings of the identified DPs and DFs. Overall, the identified lists of DPs and DFs and their importance rankings provide guidance for the design of ECBs and serve as a basis for future design science [37] and action design research projects [42].

2   Related Work

Chatbots are software-based systems designed to communicate with humans via natural language [13]. Although Weizenbaum introduced the first chatbot ELIZA a few decades ago, organizations have recently identified chatbots as a key interface to enhance user experience and introduced several chatbots in organizations [13, 49]. Major advantages of ECBs are their intuitive and easy-to-use natural language human-computer interface [35] as well as their ability to function as one central interface for several enterprise systems [49]. Therefore, ECBs can provide workers with decision-support and information while workers use collaboration systems (e.g., Slack) or CRM systems (e.g., Salesforce) [49]. Consequently, ECBs can support workers in *"scheduling and prioritizing tasks, switching tasks, providing break reminders, dealing with social media distractions and reflection on tasks accomplished"* [24, p. 337].

Besides their increasing popularity, the design of ECBs has received little attention in order to appropriately add value to human practices [2, 24, 43]. Besides general advice and high-level suggestions for functional aspects such as *"make interactions simpler"* and social aspects such as *"don't sound like a robot"* [33, p. 46], there are no precise design guidelines existing [16, 24, 35]. However, some recent studies argue that chatbot designers should not only carefully consider the functional aspect of an ECB but should account for their social aspects [15, 39]. In this context, previous research has shown that chatbots need more than just sophisticated technical capabilities to succeed [14]. Chatbots should act socially and should display believable and expressive behaviors [14]. This is important because studies have shown that users apply gender stereotypes towards a chatbot based on its appearance [18], react socially to the chatbot's response time [20], or predict a chatbot's personality based on its language strength, interaction order, and expressed confidence level [14]. To describe these phenomena, Nass and colleagues have introduced the Computer are Social Actors (CASA) paradigm which states that human-computer interaction is fundamentally social [36]. Social reactions are always triggered whenever the computer exhibits a certain amount of social cues that can be associated with interpersonal communication (e.g., use of natural language, small talk) [36]. Consequently, it seems crucial to pay attention to social cues to design successful ECBs as they, for example, can affect user satisfaction [20], working alliances [8], and perceived social presence [14]. However, studies investigating the importance of social cues of ECBs are still at an early stage.

3   Research Method

To answer our research question, we apply the AHP method to evaluate the importance of existing design knowledge for ECBs. In the remainder of this section, we first illustrate the AHP method in general and then outline how we retrieved and aggregated existing design knowledge from research studies investigating the design of chatbots at a workplace. Subsequently, we provide details on the participants and their evaluation task.

3.1   Analytical Hierarchy Process Method

To evaluate existing chatbot design knowledge for the design of ECBs, we follow Venable et al. [47] who *"emphasizes formative evaluations early in the process, possibly with artificial, formative evaluations"* [47]. To select such an evaluation method, we follow the work of Karlsson et al. [23] who evaluate several methods for prioritizing items according to their performance, design, and adaptation. The results of their comparisons with other well-established methods indicated that the AHP method is the most promising method. The AHP method can be defined as a *"decision-making support method for selecting a solution from alternatives based on a number of evaluation criteria"* [41, p. 1]. The AHP method has been frequently used in IS research for such application areas [7] and has the ability to provide reliable results in an industrial context, promote knowledge transfer and, most importantly, create census among participants [23].

Using AHP to prioritize items involves pairwise comparison of all items in order *"to determine which of the two is of higher priority, and to what extent"* [23, p. 940]. Thus, this leads to $n \cdot (n - 1)/2$ pairwise comparisons. To reduce evaluation effort, the items can be aggregated into hierarchies. Participants compare items on each hierarchy level and do the same at each subsequent level to propagate the priorities down the hierarchy. Although AHP is quite demanding, this approach leads to very trustworthy results since the big amount of redundancy in the pairwise comparisons makes the process fairly insensitive to judgmental errors [23].

3.2 Identification of Existing Design Knowledge for ECBs

According to Gregor and Hevner [21] and Baskerville et al. [6] several types of design knowledge contributions exist. One of the most important vehicles to convey prescriptive design knowledge are design principles (DPs) [5, 6]. Following Chandra et al. [11] a DP is *"a statement that prescribes what and how to build an artifact in order to achieve a predefined design goal"* [11, p. 4040]. While DPs abstract from technical specifics, Meth et al. [34] further argue that design features (DFs) close the last step of conceptualization. They define DFs as *"specific ways to implement a design principle in an actual artifact"* [34, p. 807]. To identify and evaluate the importance of meaningful design knowledge for ECBs, we followed a bottom up approach. First, we reviewed studies that investigate the design of chatbots at a workplace and extracted their investigated DFs. Second, we reviewed them and aggregated the DFs into a list of higher-level DPs.

To extract DFs and DPs, we first had to select relevant research studies. Our selection strategy was to collect a range of different DFs from studies with several research foci. The collected studies in consequence helped us to look at the design of the ECB from different perspectives and, above all, to compare which types of DFs seem to be most important for the design of ECBs. Therefore, we selected design-oriented publications that investigate chatbots at work, but with different facets in regards to different user groups (i.e., first time [22] and experienced users [28]), different research methods (i.e., field study [45] and conceptual study [19]), different communication contexts (i.e., one-to-one [28] and team communication [45]). The selected studies and their research foci represent meaningful application scenarios of chatbots at a workplace. However, they are not exhaustive. The selected papers are described in more detail in Table 1.

Table 1. Studies investigating chatbots in workplace contexts.

Ref.	Scenario	Description
[28]	Information management	Paper investigates the individual preferences for engaging in human-like social interactions with a personal agent that supports employees to find work-related information
[22]	First time users	Paper investigates chatbot interactions of first-time users. Based on these findings, the paper provides several design implications
[19]	Social customer service	Paper investigates the design of cooperative and social chatbots for customer service. By drawing on social response theory, the paper provides several design implications
[45]	Task management of teams	Paper investigates a chatbot for team communication that helps team members to formulate, discuss, refine, assign, and track the progress of their collaborative tasks

Subsequently, we reviewed all publications in order to extract a list of DFs. Therefore, we defined the structure and the knowledge pieces that must be included in the DFs. This ensures a comparability of the to-be-evaluated DFs at a later stage. To do so, we followed the design template for the description of design requirements proposed by Rupp [40]. Rupp argues that design requirement statements should contain a description of the system or subsystem (e.g., ECB), a legal obligation (e.g., shall: legally binding, should: not legally binding, will: future requirements), the activity (e.g., independent system activity, user interaction, interface requirement), and the final object of interest. For example, an ECB (i.e., system) should (i.e., legal obligation) be able to access (i.e., interface requirement) sales data for customers (i.e., object). Next, we reviewed all studies and mapped their articulated design knowledge into our predefined framework in order to articulate DFs. We articulated all requirements with the legal obligation *should* in order to account for the fact that in specific situations the design features can be modified to adapt to a specific situation [40]. In total, we extracted a list of 37 DFs. Next, we sorted out duplicates and merged DRs with the same intentions to create a list of 26 mutually exclusive DFs which are listed in Table 2.

Table 2. List of design features.

DFs	Description	Ref.
DF1	The ECB should be able to communicate either person-oriented or fact-oriented based on the user's preference	[28]
DF2	The ECB should develop a user model that stores the user's preferred communication style	[28]
DF3	The ECB should exhibit social cues that can be adjusted by the users	[28]
DF4	The ECB should adapt its degree of human likeness in its communication style based on the user's preferences	[28]
DF5	The ECB should be able to change the number of proactive messages based on the user's preferences	[19]
DF6	The ECB should have access to business data that is necessary to answer related requests	[19]
DF7	The ECB should be able to retrieve stored knowledge from previous conversations	[22]
DF8	The ECB should be able to change the length and segmentation of a message based on the situational context	[19]
DF9	The ECB should be able to use clarification and confirmation messages	[19, 45]
DF10	The ECB should be able to present its functionalities at the beginning and during a conversation	[22]
DF11	The ECB should be able to display the current conversation context and its capabilities	[22]
DF12	The ECB should be able to explain its functions to the user in a tutorial	[22]
DF13	The ECB should use social cues (e.g., appearance or language style) that are appropriate to the context and do not over- or underplay its abilities	[19]
DF14	The ECB should not pretend to be a real human being	[45]
DF15	The ECB should be able to explain its functions and capabilities as well as answer questions about them	[28]
DF16	The ECB should communicate in a human-like interaction style	[19, 22]
DF17	The ECB should engage in one-to-one communication as well as team communication	[45]
DF18	The ECB should provide functionalities required by employees of different hierarchy levels	[45]
DF19	The ECB should be able to communicate with the user about several topics at the same time while understanding to which active conversation the user input belongs to	[45]
DF20	The ECB should be able to provide visual input and output elements like buttons or maps	[22]
DF21	The ECB should animate users to use the correct syntax for mentioning others in a team chat or should have the ability to understand this automatically	[45]
DF22	The ECB should be able to adjust the frequency and type of interruption with a proactive message to avoid disturbing the user	[28]

(*continued*)

Table 2. (*continued*)

DFs	Description	Ref.
DF23	The ECB should be able to reduce proactive messages based on decreasing user responses or based on the user status in a collaboration tool	[28]
DF24	The ECB should be able to clarify requests that it did not recognize	[19, 22]
DF25	The ECB should be able to fail gracefully and apply mitigation strategies when an error occurs	[45]
DF26	The ECB should be able to save and categorize errors for future improvement	[45]

To further aggregate the identified list of DFs into higher-order DPs, we first defined the structure and the knowledge pieces that are relevant to articulate purposeful DPs. Therefore, we followed the work of Chandra et al. [11] who review prescriptive knowledge frameworks. They argue that purposeful DFs should contain three knowledge pieces (KP): (KP1) an information about a property making an action possible, (KP2) boundary conditions for when it will work, and (KP3) the actions made possible through the property. Subsequently, we labelled all KPs in the list of DFs and systematically differentiated, partitioned, and integrated these in several iterative adjustment cycles into DPs. By following this approach and by solving all disagreements, we were able to group the 26 DFs into 6 higher-order DPs. The six DPs are sociability (5 assigned DFs), flexibility (4), transparency (6), usability (6), proactive communication (3), and fault tolerance (3) (see more details in Table 3).

Table 3. List of design principles.

DP	Definition	DFs
DP1: Sociability	Provide the ECB with the ability to adapt its conversation style in order to communicate in the user's preferred way	DF1-5
DP2: Flexibility	Provide the ECB with conversational flexibility in order to react to changing contexts, tasks, and data requests	DF6-9
DP3: Transparency	Provide the ECB with functional transparency so that users can understand its functions and decisions	DF10-15
DP4: Usability	Provide the ECB with user-friendly interactive capabilities in order to create an effective, efficient, and satisfying communication experience	DF16-21
DP5: Proactive Communication	Provide the ECB with the ability to use proactive messages in order automatically notify users about changes	DF22-23;5
DP6: Error handling	Provide the ECB with the ability to handle errors of any kind and to save them for future improvements	DF24-26

3.3   Participants

To evaluate the relative importance of the 26 identified DFs and the 6 DPs for the design of ECBs, we followed the AHP method and performed it with relevant stakeholders of an ECB [31]. We selected participants of an IT consulting company that has over 400 employees and operates mostly in Europe. The selected participants are suitable candidates because of two reasons. First, the company already uses two ECBs internally in order to support their employees to conduct basic tasks (e.g., organize meetings). Consequently, the experience with ECBs is relatively high among the employees. Second, all participants deploy enterprise systems at other companies or develop it as software engineers and therefore are using different types of enterprise systems on a daily basis (e.g., ECBs to make appointments).

Overall, we invited 39 employees to evaluate all items on both hierarchy levels, namely the collected DPs and their respective DFs. From these 39 employees 36 finished the AHP evaluation task. From these 36 employees, 12 are technology consultants, 11 are general consultants, 4 software engineers, 4 working students and 2 senior consultants. 29 of the participants were males, 3 females, and 2 diverse. The mean age was 30.14 (SD = 4.42). The experience of using as well as developing ECBs was measured on a five-point Likert scale ranging from 1 (no experience) to 5 (very high experience). The average experience of using an ECB was 3.39 (SD = 0.75) and the average experience to develop an ECB was 1.89 (SD = 1.20). Consequently, the experience of using ECBs is relatively high which may be explained by the two ECBs that the company uses internally.

3.4   Evaluation Task

We started the evaluation task by sharing a survey link with the employees of the IT consulting company. In the introduction, the survey states that users should imagine using a chatbot implemented in an enterprise system. We defined scenario rather broad in order to receive a more general perception of the identified DFs in an ECB context and to avoid receiving results which are only applicable for one specific chatbot task (e.g., check the source code of a program). Subsequently, they pairwise compare the importance of the identified DPs following the AHP method which we rephrased to fit to the survey format. Therefore, two DPs were displayed on the screen and the participants had to evaluate them on a ratio scale ranging from 0 (both DPs are equivalent important) to 9 (one DP is extremely more important). This resulted in a total of 15 pairwise DP comparisons. Subsequently, all participants did the same for each DF down the hierarchy which were also rephrased to fit the survey format. This means that they had to pairwise evaluate all 5 DFs assigned to DP1, all 4 DFs assigned to DP2 and so on which resulted in a total of 52 pairwise DF comparisons. Thus, the participants executed 67 pairwise comparisons which were in a fully randomized order. Before conducting the main evaluation, we conducted a pretest with some employees of the company to ensure that participants understand the task and the meaning of the DPs and DFs. Based on the pretest feedback, we adjusted and modified the evaluation design and rephrased some DPs and DFs in order to make them better understandable.

4 Results

In the first step, we accumulated all scores that the participants awarded to each DP in order to calculate their arithmetic means. Thus, the mean score of each DP ranges between 0 and 9, whereas 0 means not important and 9 means very important compared to the other DPs. The results are shown in Table 4 which is sorted in a descending order.

Table 4. Ranking of DPs.

Rank	DP	Mean value
1.	DP4: Usability	7.297
2.	DP2: Flexibility	6.216
3.	DP1: Sociability	3.838
4.	DP3: Transparency	3.676
5.	DP6: Error handling	3.568
6.	DP5: Proactive Communication	3.162

When analyzing the results, it becomes apparent that the DPs usability (DP4) and flexibility (DP2) were evaluated to be more important than the other four DPs. As a consequence, DPs that support employees to effectively and efficiently fulfill their tasks seem to be highly important for employees of an IT consulting company. In addition, the results show that an ECB should react flexibly to varying user requests (DP2). This accounts for the constantly changing working environment that employees may experience during a task. An ECB that only follows predefined conversation flows and that does not react to changing contextual information limits its applicability in an enterprise system. Interestingly, a high degree of the ECB's socialness (DP1), the transparency regarding its functionalities (DP3), its error handling capabilities (DP6), as well as the usage of proactive messages (DP5) were rated to be less important in an enterprise context.

The pairwise comparison of the DFs for each DP category further provided insights into the importance of specific DFs for ECBs. The scores and their rankings are listed in Tables 5, 6, 7, 8, 9 and 10. In the sociability category, it becomes visible that DF2 is ranked as being the most important DF for designing an ECB. DF2 states that ECBs should use a user model that stores the user's preferred communication style. Since every human uses a different form of natural language, the participants seem to expect that an ECB should adapt its language capabilities to the user. Similar features are required in DF1, DF4, and DF5 that require the ECB to ask the user for their preferred language style. These results are in line with the similarity attraction theory. The similar attraction theory states that humans are more likely to feel attracted to those similar to themselves [9]. This means that users have a better attitude toward ECBs which exhibit a language similar to their own [10]. As a consequence, adapting the language style of an ECB can be a powerful DF to increase the user experience and boost adoption in an enterprise context. Interestingly, the participants did not believe that social cues (e.g., gender and age of an ECBs avatar) are very important in an enterprise system (DF3). They might see these as optional addons which are not directly related to the productivity benefits of using an ECB.

Table 5. Sociability DFs.

Ranking	DF	Mean
1.	DF2	4.784
2.	DF1	3.757
3.	DF4	3.649
4.	DF5	3.054
5.	DF3	2.297

Table 6. Flexibility DFs.

Ranking	DF	Mean
1.	DF6	6.378
2.	DF7	2.811
3.	DF9	2.351
4.	DF8	0.838

Table 7. Transparency DFs.

Ranking	DF	Mean
1.	DF15	6.135
2.	DF10	5.027
3.	DF14	4.432
4.	DF11	3.595
5.	DF12	3.324
6.	DF13	3.270

Table 8. Usability DFs.

Ranking	DF	Mean
1.	DF19	7.432
2.	DF20	6.973
3.	DF17	4.351
4.	DF18	3.811
5.	DF21	3.027
6.	DF16	2.703

Table 9. Proactive communication DFs.

Ranking	DF	Mean
1.	DF22	1.946
1.	DF23	1.946
2.	DF5	1.595

Table 10. Error handling DFs.

Ranking	DF	Mean
1.	DF24	2.568
2.	DF26	1.459
3.	DF25	1.378

In the flexibility category, we found that the most important DF is DF6. Since DF6 states that it is important that an ECB has access to business data in order to answer business related requests, it is not surprising that the mean value DF6 differs strongly from the other DFs. This underlines the fact that the employees appreciate ECBs that support them in their daily work routines like accessing relevant data sources. The participants did not rank the other DFs of an ECB as being more important in this category. For example, the DF that an ECB should use confirmation messages (DF7), should retrieve stored knowledge from previous conversations (DF9), or should change the length and segmentation of a message related to the context (DF8). As a consequence, productivity related DFs were higher valued than DFs that structure the interaction styles between the user and the ECB.

In the transparency category, the results show that the employees appreciate ECBs that explain their functionalities before and during a conversation (DF15 and DF10). This seems important because being aware of potential functionalities of an ECB is a requirement to use them effectively in a workplace context. In addition, the participants do not appreciate ECBs that imitate the behavior of a real human-being (DF14).

Similarly, the capability of a chatbot to use social cues was not rated to be important for ECBs (DF13).

In the usability category, we found that an ECB's capability to communicate about multiple topics with a user and map the user inputs to the right topic is highly important (DF19). Such a DF supports multitasking which can be valuable for employees of an IT consulting company because they usually do not follow a linear and strongly hierarchical development process. In addition, the participants ranked the use of visual elements like buttons or menus (DF20) quite important. As a consequence, special attention should be given to their application during implementation. Interestingly, the capability to communicate in a human-like interaction style was ranked as being least important for an ECB's usability (DF16).

In the proactive communication and error handling categories, the employees did not find that the three proactive communication and error handling features have very different importance. However, participants slightly preferred that an ECB should be able to fail gracefully and apply mitigation strategies when an error occurs (DF24). As a consequence, chatbot designers may implement troubleshooting strategies for not understanding or giving wrong answers. Therefore, several repair strategies could be applied [3]. Most promising approaches seem to be to provide options and explanations because they manifest initiative from the chatbot and are actionable to recover from breakdowns [3].

5   Discussion

In this paper, we investigated which DPs should guide the development of ECBs. To answer our research question, we reviewed studies investigating chatbots at work and extracted respective DFs and DPs. Subsequently, we evaluated the importance of 26 DFs and 6 DPs following the AHP method with 36 chatbot experienced practitioners from an IT consulting company which already uses two ECBs internally. Our results provide evidence that DPs and DFs promoting usability and flexibility are ranked more important than DPs and DFs promoting socialness and human likeness.

Our overall results are interesting because previous studies on chatbots have shown that chatbots using social cues (e.g., small talk, jokes, human avatar) increase the perceived social presence [14] and thus the trusting beliefs, perceived enjoyment, perceived usefulness, and finally the intention to use a chatbot [38]. In addition, a recent survey among practitioners revealed that not only functional but also social cues are influencing the perceived usefulness of chatbots in collaboration systems [39]. Consequently, the interesting question remains why practitioners did not rank these DFs as similar important in an enterprise system context in order to confirm existing knowledge from a practitioner perspective.

A reason that might explain the documented results is the fact that the participants in our study had a high experience with ECBs because the IT consulting company already uses two of them internally. Similarly, other studies have shown that users with different levels of task experience also prefer different language styles of a chatbot [12]. Because our evaluation was influenced by their personal experience, it must be noted that our findings might not be generalizable to unexperienced employees which might prefer more social ECBs. However, the results reflect real-world experiences of IT consultants in what they literally found important during the usage of ECBs. Therefore, these findings contribute to existing literature on how experienced IT consultants perceive and use ECBs in their daily work routine.

These ECB experiences of the IT consultants could have been similar as stated in the Uncanny Valley which explains that it is not desirable to let chatbots appear very human-like because this can trigger negative reactions by their users. Moreover, many of the experimental studies that argue to use an extensive amount of social cues often investigated chatbots in specific domains such as online shopping or customer service [25]. These findings might differ from real-world enterprise scenarios in which *"user needs may be different and avoiding disrupting work and improving efficiency are important"* [25, p. 882].

Moreover, it must also be noted that the preferences for specific designs of an ECB might further differ depending on the task in which an ECB supports the user, the department in which the ECB is applied, and the type of company in general. Because we did not define a specific task in the evaluation phase in order to receive a more general evaluation for the identified DPs and DFs for ECBs, there may be some other tasks and environments in which a specific DP and DF might be preferable although the results of this study show something different.

Consequently, future research should further investigate the importance of the identified DPs and DFs with other practitioners with less chatbot experience and further investigate their effects in other contexts than at an IT consultancy. Moreover, future ECB research should further shift the *"attention to the gap between user interactions in the lab and those in the wild"* [29, p. 1]. This can be done by investigating whether users of enterprise system will have the same design preferences in a naturalistic field experiments. This is importance because the practitioners in our evaluation did not use an ECB. Consequence, the study results are driven by the practitioner's conscious evaluation of the benefits for an application context and not by real-world reactions towards these DFs. To do so, future research can further follow the principles of Sein et al. [42] for generating prescriptive design knowledge through building and evaluating artifacts (i.e., development of ECBs) in organizational settings (e.g., IT consulting company). This could help to establish the utility of ECBs in field use [42, 46]. Therefore, the identified list of existing DPs and DFs and their importance ranking provide initial guidance for the design and future research of ECBs.

6 Conclusion

In this paper, we investigate which design principles should guide the development of ECBs. Therefore. we conducted a literature search and identified 26 DFs which we further aggregated into 6 higher-level DPs. Subsequently, we evaluated the identified DPs with 36 chatbot experienced employees of an IT consulting company following the AHP method. Our results reveal that practitioners with much chatbot experience ranked DPs and DFs promoting usability and flexibility more important than DPS and DFs promoting the socialness and human likeness of an ECB. This finding is partially contrary to existing studies investigating social cues of chatbots in other domains. We critically discuss these findings and provide avenues for future research.

Acknowledgement. We want to thank Florian S. for his support in conducting the study as well as the associate editor and the anonymous reviewers for their valuable input to further improve the quality of the paper.

References

1. Adam, M., Wessel, M., Benlian, A.: AI-based chatbots in customer service and their effects on user compliance. Electron. Mark. **9**(2), 204 (2020). https://doi.org/10.1007/s12525-020-00414-7
2. André, E., et al.: Humane anthropomorphic agents: the quest for the outcome measure; position paper. In: AIS SIGPrag, Munich, 15–18 December 2019, 2019 pre-ICIS Workshop Proceedings "Values and Ethics in the Digital Age", Munich, 14 December 2019 (2019)
3. Ashktorab, Z., Jain, M., Liao, Q.V., Weisz, J.D.: Resilient chatbots. repair strategy preferences for conversational breakdowns. In: Proceedings of the 2019 CHI Conference on Human Factors in Computing Systems, CHI 2019, pp. 1–12. ACM Press, New York (2019)
4. Avula, S., Chadwick, G., Arguello, J., Capra, R.: SearchBots. In: Shah, C., Belkin, N.J., Byström, K., Huang, J., Scholer, F. (eds.) Proceedings of the 2018 Conference on Human Information Interaction & Retrieval - CHIIR 2018. The 2018 Conference, New Brunswick, NJ, USA, 11–15 March 2018, pp. 52–61. ACM Press, New York (2018). https://doi.org/10.1145/3176349.3176380
5. Baskerville, R., Pries-Heje, J.: Design theory projectability. IS&O 2014. IAICT, vol. 446, pp. 219–232. Springer, Heidelberg (2014). https://doi.org/10.1007/978-3-662-45708-5_14
6. Baskerville, R., Baiyere, A., Gregor, S., Hevner, A., Rossi, M.: Design science research contributions: finding a balance between artifact and theory. J. Assoc. Inf. Syst. **19**(5), 358–376 (2018)
7. Benlian, A.: Is traditional, open-source, or on-demand first choice? Developing an AHP-based framework for the comparison of different software models in office suites selection. Eur. J. Inf. Syst. **20**(5), 542–559 (2011). https://doi.org/10.1057/ejis.2011.14
8. Bickmore, T.W., Picard, R.W.: Establishing and maintaining long-term human-computer relationships. ACM Trans. Comput.-Hum. Interact. **12**(2), 293–327 (2005)
9. Byrne, D.E.: The Attraction Paradigm. Academic Press, New York (1971)
10. Callejas, Z., López-Cózar, R., Abalos, N., Griol, D.: Affective conversational agents: the role of personality and emotion in spoken interactions. In: Conversational Agents and Natural Language Interaction: Techniques and Effective Practices, pp. 203–222 (2011). https://doi.org/10.4018/978-1-60960-617-6.ch009
11. Chandra, L., Seidel, S., Gregor, S.: Prescriptive knowledge in IS research: conceptualizing design principles in terms of materiality, action, and boundary conditions. In: 48th Hawaii International Conference on System Sciences, pp. 4039–4048 (2015)
12. Chattaraman, V., Kwon, W.-S., Gilbert, J.E., Ross, K.: Should AI-based, conversational digital assistants employ social- or task-oriented interaction style? A task-competency and reciprocity perspective for older adults. Comput. Hum. Behav. **90**, 315–330 (2019). https://doi.org/10.1016/j.chb.2018.08.048
13. Dale, R.: The return of the chatbots. Nat. Lang. Eng. **22**(5), 811–817 (2016). https://doi.org/10.1017/S1351324916000243

14. Feine, J., Gnewuch, U., Morana, S., Maedche, A.: A taxonomy of social cues for conversational agents. Int. J. Hum.-Comput. Stud. **132**, 138–161 (2019). https://doi.org/10.1016/j.ijhcs.2019.07.009

15. Feine, J., Morana, S., Maedche, A.: Designing a chatbot social cue configuration system. In: Proceedings of the 40th International Conference on Information Systems (ICIS), AISel, Munich (2019)

16. Feine, J., Morana, S., Maedche, A.: Leveraging machine-executable descriptive knowledge in design science research – the case of designing socially-adaptive chatbots. In: Tulu, B., Djamasbi, S., Leroy, G. (eds.) DESRIST 2019. LNCS, vol. 11491, pp. 76–91. Springer, Cham (2019). https://doi.org/10.1007/978-3-030-19504-5_6

17. Feine, J., Morana, S., Gnewuch, U.: Measuring service encounter satisfaction with customer service chatbots using sentiment analysis. In: 14. Internationale Tagung Wirtschaftsinformatik (WI2019) (2019)

18. Feine, J., Gnewuch, U., Morana, S., Maedche, A.: Gender bias in chatbot design. In: Følstad, A., et al. (eds.) CONVERSATIONS 2019. LNCS, vol. 11970, pp. 79–93. Springer, Cham (2020). https://doi.org/10.1007/978-3-030-39540-7_6

19. Gnewuch, U., Morana, S., Maedche, A.: Towards designing cooperative and social conversational agents for customer service. In: Proceedings of the 38th International Conference on Information Systems (ICIS), AISel, Seoul (2017)

20. Gnewuch, U., Morana, S., Adam, M., Maedche, A.: Faster is not always better: understanding the effect of dynamic response delays in human-chatbot interaction. In: Proceedings of the 26th European Conference on Information Systems (ECIS), Portsmouth, United Kingdom, 23–28 June (2018)

21. Gregor, S., Hevner, A.R.: Positioning and presenting design science research for maximum impact. MIS Q. **37**(2), 337–355 (2013)

22. Jain, M., Kumar, P., Kota, R., Patel, S.N.: Evaluating and informing the design of chatbots. In: Koskinen, I., Lim, Y.-K., Cerratto-Pargman, T., Chow, K., Odom, W. (eds.) Proceedings of the 2018 Conference on Designing Interactive Systems, DIS 2018, Hong Kong, 9–13 June 2018, The 2018, Hong Kong, China, 9–13 June 2018, pp. 895–906. Association for Computing Machinery, New York (2018). https://doi.org/10.1145/3196709.3196735

23. Karlsson, J., Wohlin, C., Regnell, B.: An evaluation of methods for prioritizing software requirements. Inf. Softw. Technol. **39**(14–15), 939–947 (1998). https://doi.org/10.1016/S0950-5849(97)00053-0

24. Kimani, E., Rowan, K., McDuff, D., Czerwinski, M., Mark, G.: A conversational agent in support of productivity and wellbeing at work. In: 2019 8th International Conference on Affective Computing and Intelligent Interaction (ACII), pp. 1–7 (2019)

25. Kocielnik, R., Avrahami, D., Marlow, J., Lu, D., Hsieh, G.: Designing for workplace reflection: a chat and voice-based conversational agent. In: Proceedings of the 2018 Designing Interactive Systems Conference (DIS 2018), pp. 881–894. ACM (2018)

26. Lechler, R., Stöckli, E., Rietsche, R., Uebernickel, F.: Looking beneath the tip of the iceberg: the two-sided nature of Chatbots and their roles for digital feedback exchange. In: Proceedings of the 27th European Conference on Information Systems (ECIS), Stockholm & Uppsala, Sweden (2019)

27. Lee, J.C., Myers, M.D.: Dominant actors, political agendas, and strategic shifts over time: a critical ethnography of an enterprise systems implementation. J. Strateg. Inf. Syst. **13**(4), 355–374 (2004). https://doi.org/10.1016/j.jsis.2004.11.005

28. Liao, Q.V., Davis, M., Geyer, W., Muller, M., Shami, N.S.: What can you do? Studying social-agent orientation and agent proactive interactions with an agent for employees. In: Proceedings of the 2016 ACM Conference on Designing Interactive Systems, pp. 264–275. ACM, New York (2016). https://doi.org/10.1145/2901790.2901842

29. Liao, Q.V., et al.: All work and no play? In: Mandryk, R., Hancock, M., Perry, M., Cox, A. (eds.) Proceedings of the 2018 CHI Conference on Human Factors in Computing Systems - CHI 2018, 21–26 April 2018, pp. 1–13. ACM Press, New York (2018). https://doi.org/10.1145/3173574.3173577

30. Maedche, A., et al.: AI-based digital assistants. Bus. Inf. Syst. Eng. **61**(4), 535–544 (2019). https://doi.org/10.1007/s12599-019-00600-8

31. Maedche, A., Gregor, S., Morana, S., Feine, J.: Conceptualization of the problem space in design science research. In: Tulu, B., Djamasbi, S., Leroy, G. (eds.) DESRIST 2019. LNCS, vol. 11491, pp. 18–31. Springer, Cham (2019). https://doi.org/10.1007/978-3-030-19504-5_2

32. McGregor, M., Tang, J.C.: More to meetings: challenges in using speech-based technology to support meetings. In: Proceedings of the 2017 ACM Conference on Computer Supported Cooperative Work and Social Computing, pp. 2208–2220 (2017)

33. McTear, M.F.: The rise of the conversational interface: a new kid on the block? In: Quesada, J.F., Martín Mateos, F.J., López-Soto, T. (eds.) FETLT 2016. LNCS (LNAI), vol. 10341, pp. 38–49. Springer, Cham (2017). https://doi.org/10.1007/978-3-319-69365-1_3

34. Meth, H., Mueller, B., Maedche, A.: Designing a requirement mining system. J. Assoc. Inf. Syst. **16**(9), 799 (2015)

35. Meyer von Wolff, R., Hobert, S., Schumann, M.: How may I help you? - state of the art and open research questions for chatbots at the digital workplace. In: Proceedings of the 52nd Hawaii International Conference on System Sciences, pp. 95–104 (2019)

36. Nass, C., Moon, Y.: Machines and mindlessness. Social responses to computers. J. Soc. Issues **56**(1), 81–103 (2000). https://doi.org/10.1111/0022-4537.00153

37. Peffers, K., Tuunanen, T., Rothenberger, M.A., Chatterjee, S.: A design science research methodology for information systems research. J. Manag. Inf. Syst. **24**(3), 45–77 (2007). https://doi.org/10.2753/MIS0742-1222240302

38. Qiu, L., Benbasat, I.: Evaluating anthropomorphic product recommendation agents. A social relationship perspective to designing information systems. J. Manag. Inf. Syst. **25**(4), 145–181 (2009)

39. Rietz, T., Benke, I., Maedche, A.: The impact of anthropomorphic and functional chatbot design features in enterprise collaboration systems on user acceptance. In: 14. International Conference on Wirtschaftsinformatik (WI2019) (2019)

40. Rupp, C.: Requirements-Engineering und -Management, 5th edn. Hanser, Munich (2014)

41. Saaty, T.L.: The Analytic Hierarchy Process. McGraw-Hill, New York (1980)

42. Sein, M., Henfridsson, O., Purao, S., Rossi, M., Lindgren, R.: Action design research. MIS Q. **35**, 37–56 (2011). https://doi.org/10.2307/23043488

43. Sjöström, J., Aghaee, N., Dahlin, M., Ågerfalk, P.: Designing chatbots for higher education practice. In: International Conference on Information Systems Education and Research, AISel, San Francisco, CA, USA (2018)

44. Stoeckli, E., Dremel, C., Uebernickel, F., Brenner, W.: How affordances of chatbots cross the chasm between social and traditional enterprise systems. Electron. Mark. **30**(2), 369–403 (2019). https://doi.org/10.1007/s12525-019-00359-6

45. Toxtli, C., Monroy-Hernández, A., Cranshaw, J.: Understanding chatbot-mediated task management. In: Mandryk, R., Hancock, M., Perry, M., Cox, A. (eds.) Proceedings of the 2018 CHI Conference on Human Factors in Computing Systems, CHI 2018, 21–26 April 2018, pp. 1–6. ACM Press, New York (2018)

46. Tremblay, M.C., Berndt, D.J.: Focus groups for artifact refinement and evaluation in design research. Commun. Assoc. Inf. Syst. **26** (2010). https://doi.org/10.17705/1cais.02627

47. Venable, J., Pries-Heje, J., Baskerville, R.: FEDS: a framework for evaluation in design science research. Eur. J. Inf. Syst. **25**(1), 77–89 (2016). https://doi.org/10.1057/ejis.2014.36

48. vom Brocke, J., Maaß, W., Buxmann, P., Maedche, A., Leimeister, J.M., Pecht, G.: Future work and enterprise systems. Bus. Inf. Syst. Eng. **60**(4), 357–366 (2018). https://doi.org/10.1007/s12599-018-0544-2
49. Watson, H.J.: Preparing for the cognitive generation of decision support. MIS Q. Exec. **16** (3), 153–169 (2017)
50. Zhang, A.X., Cranshaw, J.: Making sense of group chat through collaborative tagging and summarization. Proc. ACM Hum.-Comput. Interact. **2**(CSCW), 1–27 (2018)

Knowledge Visualization for Sensemaking: Applying an Elaborated Action Design Research Process in Incident Management Systems

Quintus van Wyk(iD), Judy van Biljon(✉)(iD), and Marthie Schoeman(iD)

School of Computing, University of South Africa, Johannesburg, South Africa
vbiljja@unisa.ac.za

Abstract. Incident management systems are designed to support sensemaking of emergency incidents and their immediate environment with the use of digital technology. The usability of the user interface is critical in supporting knowledge transfer for sensemaking. Visualization has been used to improve the usability of interactive systems, but evidence-based criteria are lacking. This paper follows an elaborated Action Design Research process in the design, development and evaluation of a prototype of an incident management system utilizing the principles of knowledge visualization to support usability and ultimately sensemaking. The context is that of emergency incidents (fire, medical, environmental, etc.) where the system is used to manage responses to the incidents. The novel contribution of this paper is the triangulation between the usability evaluation results of the two artefacts, i.e. the knowledge visualization criteria and the system's interface as a basis for proposing validated knowledge visualization criteria for incident management systems that employ visualization for sensemaking.

Keywords: Incident management systems · Sensemaking · Knowledge visualization · Action design research

1 Introduction

Incidents of a critical nature may lead to the damaging of property and infrastructure in the environs of the incident and may result in injuries to individuals involved in the incident and even fatalities [1, 2]. To minimise these consequences the response to such incidents should be effective, efficient and resourceful [3]. Managing an incident comprises directing the various components of the incident, including the responders, communication and allocated resources [4–6]. Incident management systems are designed to support human endeavors in providing an optimal response to incidents by the timeous, optimal use of the resources available [7]. The relevance, accuracy, completeness and presentation format of the incident and context related information provided by the incident management system (IMS) assist the responders in their sensemaking processes, thus leading to more informed decisions [8]. This relationship between the technology design and sensemaking has motivated research into the design of the visual artefacts in interactive systems [9]. Previous work involving visualization and sensemaking relate to

© Springer Nature Switzerland AG 2020
S. Hofmann et al. (Eds.): DESRIST 2020, LNCS 12388, pp. 142–153, 2020.
https://doi.org/10.1007/978-3-030-64823-7_14

information visualization in sensemaking across collections of textual reports [10]; the use of visualization for sensemaking of processes and challenges [11] and reducing the perceived complexity of software through information visualization [12]. However, no evidence-based visualization design criteria to support sensemaking in IMSs could be found in the extant literature and therefore the purpose is to present knowledge visualization (KV) criteria that satisfy both the domain experts and the usability experts. The essential philosophy of Design Science Research (DSR), is to build adequate, efficient information technology artefacts that address or solve real world problems while producing research outcomes that contribute to the academic body of Information Systems knowledge [13–15]. Therefore, DSR is appropriate for this study that encompassed the elicitation of the KV criteria from literature, the design and development of the IMS where the interface design was guided by said KV criteria and the usability evaluation of the interface and the criteria towards proposing knowledge visualization principles for IMSs. The eADR (elaborated action design research process model) [15] was employed as method with DSR as paradigm and pragmatism as philosophy.

2 Theoretical Basis

2.1 Incident Management Systems and Sensemaking

There are various definitions of what an *incident management system* is. According to Kim, Sharman, Rao and Upadhyaya [16: 236], "a critical incident management system (CIMS) is a system that utilises people, processes, and technologies for managing critical incidents". The resources, personnel and technological infrastructure used in the efficient and effective management of an incident constitute the components that make up an incident management system (IMS).

Sensemaking is an ongoing accomplishment originating from the efforts to create order and make retrospective sense of what has occurred. Sensemaking occurs as a series of components iterating in the following order: creation, interpretation and enactment [9]. If executed correctly the outcomes of sensemaking may lead to restored sense and restorative action; the absence of sensemaking may lead to a response that lacks integration and cohesion often with dire consequences. Sensemaking has been investigated in connection with concept-driven visual analytics but current visualization tools do not provide interactions to scaffold this expectation-guided analysis [17]. Sensemaking is a vital element of knowledge work where critical patterns in the amorphous situation (the ambiguous event) are found by means of refined representations in relation to which information is tailored in service of the task(s) at hand [18]. This process may be augmented by means of support systems which have been found to stem from visualization techniques [19]. These systems involve different technologies. *Technology* is one of the growing influences in the sensemaking perspective where information and communication technologies (ICT) have been found to influence sensemaking in indisputable ways [9, 19, 20]. A well-designed Knowledge Management System (KMS) may promote a timely response in disaster situations by bringing together experts with prior knowledge and experience and crisis specific knowledge when making decisions with regard to the response [21]. The sharing of information and knowledge between all the actors involved in an incident may minimise both the risk and fatalities by mobilising and facilitating a fast and effective response [22]. However, the proviso is that the knowledge is presented in a format that supports and facilitates knowledge transfer and ultimately sensemaking.

2.2 Knowledge Visualization

Knowledge visualization refers to the use of visual representations to improve the creation of knowledge and the transfer of knowledge between at least two people [23, 24]. The existing literature on Information Visualization and KV presents multiple criteria for improving visualization, notably KV focuses on knowledge transfer between humans via an artefact. Adopting *why, whom* and *how* as meta-criteria for structing KV criteria (as advocated by Renaud and van Biljon [24]), we identified, verified and published a list of 11 criteria namely *Clarity; Consistency; Discrimination; Semantic Transparency; Complexity; Management; Dual Coding; Legend; Layout (Shape); Context; User* and *Intention* which are most relevant to IMS's. Those criteria were extracted from literature and validated by domain experts [25] in part one of this study.

3   Research Approach

Design science outputs are produced by two main complementary activities namely, *building and evaluation* [26]. Action Design Research (ADR) provide a structured process model for combining the activities of action research and design science research [27] where ADR conceptualizes the research process as containing the inseparable and interwoven activities of building, intervention and evaluation. Mullarkey and Hevner [15] introduce the eADR (elaborated action design research) method and distinguish between DSR as a research paradigm and eADR as one method for conducting DSR. Alternatively, eADR is considered a DSR project that involves an action intervention that moves through the DSR design stages, i.e. *diagnosis, design, implementation* and *evolution* with the abstraction of artefacts in each eADR cycle within the stages [15]. eADR is appropriate for this study due to the rapid iterations of problem formulation, artefact creation, evaluation, reflection, and learning activities in each eADR cycle where an artefact is developed. Using an objective-centred entry point, this paper focuses on the evaluation of the KV criteria (Artefact1) from the diagnosis stage and the usability evaluation of the IMS interface (Artefact2) from design stage towards presenting validated KV criteria. It is imperative that the utility of the criteria be proved by materializing the design criteria and evaluating the result [28]. Evaluating the system and the criteria at the same time involves trade-offs between the value of in situ evaluation and the possibility of masking effects. However, DSR projects are known to have overarching objectives beyond the development of an artefact [29] and revealing latent issues by iterative design and testing. The four cycle view of DSR [29] (see Fig. 1) depicts the main components of DSR as the *External Environment*, the *Internal Environment*, the *Build Design Artefacts and Processes* and the *Foundations* and the underlying cycles of *change and impact, relevance, design and* rigor supporting the processes.

3.1   Socio-technical System Context and Immediate Application Context

The practical need for an IMS originated in the socio-technical context of emergency incident management where a digital system was required to manage responses to fire,

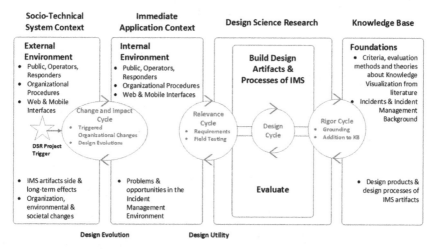

Fig. 1. DSR cycle adapted from Drechsler and Hevner [29]

medical, environmental and other incidents in the Gauteng province of South Africa. The management commissioned an IMS with specific requirements. The emphasis on the end-users' (responders) ability to make sense of the system triggered the usability focus and the investigation into visualization for sensemaking.

3.2 Knowledge Base Encompassing Knowledge Visualization Principles

As indicated in Fig. 1, there are continuous interactions between the [**Knowledge Base**] and the [**Design Science Research**] cycles to ensure rigor. A list of KV criteria from the interaction between the [**Knowledge Base** (Literature)] and the [**Design Science Research** (Build Design Artefacts & Process of IMS)] (Fig. 1) was proposed as a point of departure in designing the IMS. Given the importance of context in IMS and sense-making, the criteria had to be implemented before they could be evaluated. After the evaluation with domain experts, the list of 11 validated criteria were published [25]. It is not feasible to include all the possibly important but sometimes also conflicting criteria, so prioritization is required. Therefore, these 11 criteria are proposed as a point of departure for this study while acknowledging that further iterative refinement cycles within the eADR research method is advisable. Henceforth, visualization and knowledge visualization will be used interchangeably in this paper.

3.3 Application Context and Artefact Development

A cloud-based IMS was developed to provide the infrastructure required. This 3-tier system has a public interface, an operator interface, and a responder interface as depicted in Fig. 2 where the Activator (public interface) is the initiation point of an incident in the system. The Operator receives the incident detail, confirms the validity of the incident and compiles additional details regarding the incident. The Responder receives the compiled information that the operator captured. The responder level consists of users identified as responders, and they have the role of responding to an incident in a predefined capacity.

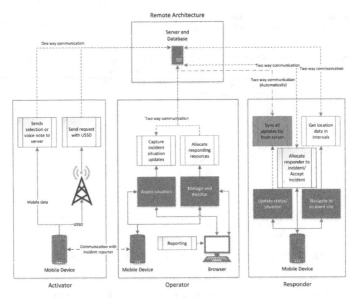

Fig. 2. IMS Infrastructure Layout

The process flow of an incident in this system is as follows:

1. A member of the public (activator) activates an alert via a public application. The activation appears on the system as a new incident and informs an operator about this by means of a notification on the browser interface of the system.
2. The operator contacts the activator and confirms the validity and type of incident. Additional information regarding the incident is then captured.
3. Once the incident has been verified, the operator pushes the incident detail to a group of predefined responders. The incident detail shows on the responder devices by means of a mobile notification, and once opened displays the information of the incident.
4. The responder decides whether he or she can respond to the incident.
5. If the responder accepts the incident the mobile interface opens additional functionality to interact with all responders to the incident. Should the responder decline the incident is removed from the responder's device.

This study is done on the mobile interface of the third level, the responder tier. The incident types were divided into three representative categories: SOS, Enforcement, and Ecological (or Hazmat) as presented in the next section.

4   Usability Evaluation

The KV criteria needs to be evaluated in context, i.e. after being implemented in an IMS. Furthermore, the implications of the responder's actions can be critical; hence it is necessary to ensure a minimum level of usability before the system is deployed. The focus of the usability evaluation was two-fold: to evaluate the KV criteria (Artefact1), to evaluate the IMS interface (Artefact2) and then to evaluate the latter against the KV criteria (Artefact1). The findings from the KV criteria evaluation by domain experts with contextual knowledge on the South African Fire Service were published in 2019 [25]. That first part of the study used questionnaire driven interviews as research method to evaluate the importance of the KV criteria. This second part of the study presents the findings from the evaluation by usability experts (usability testing with eye-tracking and the standardized System Usability Scale (SUS) post-test questionnaire), their evaluation of the importance of the KV criteria and the triangulation between the findings from both evaluations.

Eye-tracking is the process of capturing participants' gaze points and eye movement (while they are doing specific, predefined tasks) to provide information about the sequence, timing and nature of the cognitive procedures that took place [30]. The basic metrics are fixations and saccades, a fixation is the accretion of all the gaze points captured from viewing an interface and a saccade is the quick movement between fixations [30]. Fixations are used to generate a gaze plot or a heatmap of the interface, the heatmap indicates where the participants' viewed the interface and how intensely they viewed it. We used both gaze plots and heat maps in this study.

4.1 Data Collection

Participants were required to complete a task on each of the three incident categories. Usability metrics like performance time, ability to complete the task without assistance and the participants' eye movements were captured. Thereafter, they were requested to complete the SUS post-test questionnaire. Finally, having been exposed to the system's interface the participants were requested to evaluate the importance of the KV criteria on a scale of 1 to 5. Eight usability experts were involved in the study. Eye-tracking is resource intensive, generally, 5 participants are considered an acceptably large number. The participants had a minimum of an honours degree with experience in teaching human computer interaction. Their ages ranged from 35 to 61.

Usability with Eye-Tracking: A Tobii 1750 eye-tracker was used to record participant eye movements while they performed usability tasks on the IMS. The participants were introduced to the research purpose and requested to sign a consent form. The participant was briefed on how the usability tasks would be presented and the actions that would be required on his/her part. The eye-tracking system was then calibrated according to the participant's eye movement. Once the calibration had been completed the participants were presented with the first task. The usability tasks (together with the eye-tracking) constituted one of two components of the data collection process which was carried out on a computer with the other being the SUS questionnaire. The tasks were completed, while eye-tracking was being done. The participants had to evaluate the request and decide whether the interface provided enough information to make an informed response regarding the incident represented. Participants were interviewed individually.

Interviews: The KV criteria identified from literature were used as the questionnaire items in the interviews where the usability experts rated the importance on a Likert scale of 1-5. The average scores for the three tasks are presented in Table 2.

4.2 Results of the Usability Tasks

Table 1 presents the usability evaluation results containing the participants' indexing, the time it took to complete each usability task and users' satisfaction according to the SUS questionnaire results. The last row of the table represents the average of the time (in seconds) to complete the tasks of all the participants. There was a notable decrease in the time required to complete a task from the first task to the third task, thus indicating that the participants were learning how to use the system. The average of the SUS questionnaire ratings resulted in an overall degree of acceptable usability.

Table 1. Usability tasks tming & usability evaluation results

Participant number	Time (seconds)			User satisfaction (SUS) results
	SOS	ENFORCEMENT	HAZMAT	
1	26	31	24	77.5
2	51	41	28	60.0
3	230	180	107	62.5
4	247	32	14	82.5
5	21	32	Incomplete	85.0
6	12	22	10	67.5
7	35	23	11	100.0
8	99	131	124	52.5
Average	90	62	45	73.44

The processing (completing) of the three usability tasks are discussed below.

Task 1: The aim was to test whether the participants would be able to understand what to do by merely reading the task and using the interface for the first time. As the result in Table 1 indicates the first task (SOS) took the most time since the participants had to figure out how to navigate and interact with the system. Most of the participants required assistance.

Task 2: Once the users had familiarized themselves with this task, they were quicker in selecting the associated incident and were then able to analyze the interface of the incident detail far more quickly before indicating whether there was enough information. Very little assistance was required.

Task 3: At this point the participants' confidence in relation to the system was at its highest and it took them a few seconds only to read the task and select the associated incident. Inspection of the incident detail and selecting the result took the least time of all the tasks. Notably, the SOS screen (task 2 not shown here) had a maximum of 61 fixations while the HAZMAT required only 35. This indicates that the responder mobile application interfaces were learnable. The majority of the 8 participants felt that the interfaces displayed enough information to make an informed decision with regards to the incident type, for task 1 (87.5%); task 2 (75%) and task 3 (87.5%). Suggestions included that more detail be provided about the visual elements utilized for additional content and that the additional detail should be displayed for integration with other systems (e.g. global positioning coordinates). The gaze plots and heat maps highlighted only one additional usability problem, namely the positioning of additional information on the left of the screen gave it unintended importance. The SOS images interface in Fig. 3 indicate that the *incident location* was the primary focus.

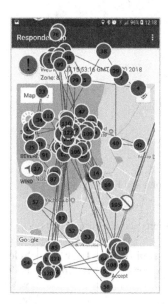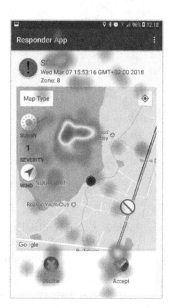

Fig. 3. SOS Gazeplot & Heatmap

In the ENFORCEMENT heat map for participant 6 (Fig. 4) the incident location received some attention, but the focus was on additional information. The results (Table 1) show that most participants believed they would have been able to make an informed decision about the incident by considering the interface (visual elements in the IMS). Importantly, this revealed that the IMS interface achieved adequate *knowledge transfer* for sensemaking based on the visualization of the incident related information.

Results from the interviews with the domain experts [25] and the usability experts are depicted in Table 2. Criteria with scores above 3 out of 5 were considered as the basis for the design principles and confirmed by observations from user testing.

The knowledge visualization criteria (KVC) were selected as one of the validated criteria if one of the values were above 4. *Dual Coding* was included for security implications and representing *Discrimination*. Layout's relevance was confirmed by eye-tracking. This resulted in the following, updated KV criteria:

D1: Clarity - The meaning of the symbols should be clear, exact and unambiguous.

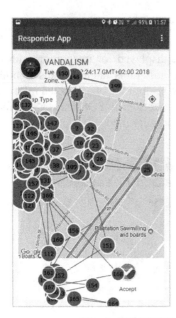 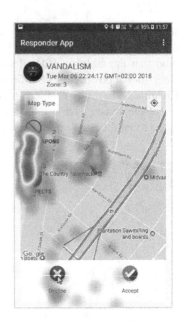

Fig. 4. ENFORCEMENT Gazeplot and Heatmap

Table 2. Criteria evaluation Domain experts and Usability experts

Criteria	Domain experts	Usability experts	User testing	Selected KVC
Clarity	4.4	3.8	√	Yes
Consistency	4.5	4.1	√	Yes
Discrimination	3.9	3.6		No
Semantic Transparency	4.2	3.9	√	Yes
Complexity Management	4.4	3.5	√	Yes
Dual Coding	3.6	3.6	√	Yes
Legend	3.4	3.2		No
Context	4.7	4.1	√	Yes
User	3.5	3.7		No
Intention	4.5	4.2	√	Yes
Layout (Shape)	2.9	3.9	√	Yes

D2: Consistency - The visual components should be used consistently, i.e. the same symbol should represent the same concept throughout.
D3: Semantic Transparency - The mapping between symbols and their meaning should be clear.
D4: Complexity Management - There should not be any redundant visual elements.
D5: Dual Coding – Visualization should be represented by both text and graphics.

D6: Context - The visual artefact should be adequate for the situation, conditions, situation and environment.

D7: Intention - The visual artefact is aimed at realizing a specific goal.

D8: Layout - The layout should follow design conventions and strive for a symmetrical (balanced) shape.

Based on the feedback from the domain experts, the *User* criteria, i.e. matching the symbols and notation with the end user's mental model was removed as the target audience was heterogeneous. The legend requirement was removed as it is covered by *Dual Coding*. The Layout principle was retained despite the result (both below 4) and modified to include design layout conventions. This is based on eye-tracking evidence confirming the preference for scanning from left to right (following convention).

5 Discussion and Conclusion

In this paper, we report on the first three stages of an eADR process namely *diagnosis*, *design* and *implementation* where we developed KV criteria for the interface design of an IMS and focused on the evaluation of the criteria. The criteria were evaluated by interviews with domain experts in the incident response environment (part 1 of this study) as well as with usability experts (part two of this study as reported here). The IMS system was evaluated by user testing with eye-tracking and a post-test questionnaire. Based on the triangulation of the results of part 1 and part 2 of this study, 8 KV criteria for sensemaking in IMSs are proposed for the design of digital visualization artefacts. Due to the high-risk environment the evaluation involved domain experts and usability experts, not the actual responders. The KV criteria for IMS's proposed are not new or counterintuitive; the value lies in those criteria having been selected from scientific literature, implemented and validated. Future research is needed to evaluate the impact of knowledge visualization on usability and sensemaking by first responders in the IMS environment, in situ. The inevitable changes to the artefact in response to the changes in the problem environment as described by the fourth (*evolution*) stage of the eADR process is still ongoing and not discussed here. The knowledge visualization criteria were evaluated in only one case and the findings could be biased by contextual and design factors. Therefore, future research should complete the evolutionary processes of reformulation, technology advancements and design improvements including considerations of how the solution (including the knowledge visualization criteria and the IMS) can be generalized to solve similar problems in other contexts.

References

1. Hällgren, M., Rouleau, L., de Rond, M.: A matter of life or death: how extreme context research matters for management and organization studies. Acad. Manag. Ann. **12**, 111–153 (2018)
2. Spiekermann, R., Kienberger, S., Norton, J., Briones, F., Weichselgartner, J.: The disaster-knowledge matrix - reframing and evaluating the knowledge challenges in disaster risk reduction. Int. J. Disaster Risk Reduct. **13**, 96–108 (2015)

3. Luokkala, P., Virrantaus, K.: Developing information systems to support situational awareness and interaction in time-pressuring crisis situations. Saf. Sci. **63**, 191–203 (2014)
4. Perry, R.W.: Incident management systems in disaster management. Disaster Prev. Manag. Int. J. **12**, 405–412 (2003)
5. Hossain, L., Kuti, M.: Disaster response preparedness coordination through social networks. Disasters **34**, 755–786 (2010)
6. Anderson, A.I., Compton, D., Mason, T.: Managing in a dangerous world - the national incident management system. Eng. Manag. J. **16**, 3–9 (2004)
7. Galindo, G., Batta, R.: Review of recent developments in OR/MS research in disaster operations management. Eur. J. Oper. Res. **230**, 201–211 (2013)
8. Bai, X., White, D., Sundaram, D.: Contextual adaptive knowledge visualization environments. Electron. J. Knowl. Manag. **10**, 1–14 (2012)
9. Sandberg, J., Tsoukas, H.: Making sense of the sensemaking perspective: its constituents, limitations, and opportunities for further development. J. Organ. Behav. **36**, 6–32 (2015)
10. Stasko, J., Görg, C., Liu, Z.: Jigsaw: supporting investigative analysis through interactive visualization. Inf. Vis. **7**, 118–132 (2016)
11. Attfield, S., Hara, S., Wong, B.L.W.: Sensemaking in visual analytics: processes and challenges. In: 1st European Symposium on Visual Analytics Science and Technology, Bordeaux, France (2010)
12. Bartens, Y., et al.: A visualization approach for reducing the perceived complexity of COBIT 5. In: Tremblay, M.C., VanderMeer, D., Rothenberger, M., Gupta, A., Yoon, V. (eds.) DESRIST 2014. LNCS, vol. 8463, pp. 403–407. Springer, Cham (2014). https://doi.org/10.1007/978-3-319-06701-8_34
13. Venable, J.R.: The role of theory and theorising in design science research. In: DESRIST 2006, Claremont, CA, pp. 1–18. Springer (2006)
14. Haj-Bolouri, A.: Design principles for E-learning that support integration work: a case of action design research. In: Tulu, B., Djamasbi, S., Leroy, G. (eds.) DESRIST 2019. LNCS, vol. 11491, pp. 300–316. Springer, Cham (2019). https://doi.org/10.1007/978-3-030-19504-5_20
15. Mullarkey, M.T., Hevner, A.R.: An elaborated action design research process model an elaborated action design research process model. Eur. J. Inf. Syst. **28**, 6–20 (2019)
16. Kim, J.K., Sharman, R., Rao, H.R., Upadhyaya, S.: Efficiency of critical incident management systems: Instrument development and validation. Decis. Support Syst. **44**, 235–250 (2007)
17. Choi, I.K., Mishra, S., Childers, T., Harris, K., Raveendranath, N.K., Reda, K.: Concept-driven visual analytics: an exploratory study of model - and hypothesis-based reasoning with visualizations. In: Proceedings of the 2019 CHI Conference on Human Factors in Computing Systems, pp. 1–14 (2019)
18. Wu, A., Convertino, G., Ganoe, C., Carroll, J.M., Zhang, X.L.: Supporting collaborative sensemaking in emergency management through geo-visualization. Int. J. Hum Comput Stud. **71**, 4–23 (2013)
19. Seidel, S., Chandra Kruse, L., Székely, N., Gau, M., Stieger, D.: Design principles for sensemaking support systems in environmental sustainability transformations. Eur. J. Inf. Syst. **27**, 221–247 (2018)
20. Berthod, O., Müller-Seitz, G.: Making sense in pitch darkness: an exploration of the sociomateriality of sensemaking in crises. J. Manag. Inquiry **27**, 52–68 (2018)
21. Dorasamy, M., Raman, M., Kaliannan, M.: Knowledge management systems in support of disasters management: a two decade review. Technol. Forecast. Soc. Chang. **80**, 1834–1853 (2013)
22. Balfour, R.E.: An emergency information sharing (EIS) framework for effective shared situational awareness (SSA). In: 2014 IEEE Island Systems, Application and Technology Conference, LISAT 2014 (2014)

23. Burkhard, R.A.: Towards a framework and a model for knowledge visualization: synergies between information and knowledge visualization. In: Tergan, S.-O., Keller, T. (eds.) Knowledge and Information Visualization. LNCS, vol. 3426, pp. 238–255. Springer, Heidelberg (2005). https://doi.org/10.1007/11510154_13

24. Renaud, K., van Biljon, J.: Charting the path towards effective knowledge visualisations. In: Proceedings of the Southern African Institute of Computer Scientists and Information Technologists (SAICSIT), pp. 1–10. ACM (2017)

25. van Wyk, Q., van Biljon, J., Schoeman, M.: Visualization criteria: supporting knowledge transfer in incident management systems. In: Conference on Information Communications Technology and Society, pp. 1–6. IEEE (2019)

26. Hevner, A.R., March, S.T., Park, J., Ram, S.: Design science in information systems research. MIS Q. **28**, 75–105 (2004)

27. Sein, M.K., Henfridsson, O., Purao, S., Rossi, M., Rossi, M.: Action design research. MIS Q. **35**, 37–56 (2011)

28. Rudmark, D., Lind, M.: Design science research demonstrators for punctuation – the establishment of a service ecosystem. In: Jain, H., Sinha, A.P., Vitharana, P. (eds.) DESRIST 2011. LNCS, vol. 6629, pp. 153–165. Springer, Heidelberg (2011). https://doi.org/10.1007/978-3-642-20633-7_11

29. Drechsler, A., Hevner, A.: A four-cycle model of IS design science research: capturing the dynamic nature of IS artifact design. In: Breakthroughs and Emerging Insights from Outgoing Design Science Projects, DESRIST 2016, St. John, Canada (2016)

30. Tullis, T., Albert, B.: Measuring the User Experience: Collecting, Analysing and Presenting Usability Metrics. Morgan Kaufmann, Amsterdam (2013)

Multi-interest User Profiling in Short Text Microblogs

Herman Wandabwa[1]([✉]), M. Asif Naeem[1,2], Farhaan Mirza[1], Russel Pears[1], and Andy Nguyen[3]

[1] Auckland University of Technology, Auckland, New Zealand
{herman.wandabwa,muhammad.asif.naeem,farhaan.mirza,
russel.pears}@aut.ac.nz
[2] National University of Computer and Emerging Sciences, Islamabad, Pakistan
[3] University of Oulu, Oulu, Finland
andy.nguyen@oulu.fi

Abstract. Discourse on short text platforms like Twitter shapes the design of underlying knowledge-based recommendation engines. The resulting recommendations are powered by user connections as *social network nodes* as well as with shared interests. Twitter as a platform provides a complex mesh of users' interest levels where some users tend to consume certain topical content to a lesser or greater extent. This consumption of content is usually considered a defining factor in curation of their online identity. Our aim in this paper is to quantify the multi-interests of users based on the tweets they disseminate. We do this by *(i) representing all tweets as vectors for computations (ii) generating cluster centroids representative of the topics of interest. (iii) computing a responsibility matrix to depict their interest levels in the topics (iv) aggregating intra-user interest levels to define the user's multi-topic affinities.* We use a Twitter dataset geolocated to Kenya to validate users' intra-topical interests. Our experimental results demonstrate the effectiveness of our approach in terms of capturing their multi-interests and in turn generate their multi-topic interest profiles.

Keywords: Information retrieval · Taste profiling · Social web · Neural networks

1 Introduction

Microblogs such as Twitter proliferate fast digital data due to their constant streaming nature [22]. This makes them ideal in data dissemination, especially from a journalism perspective. The diversity in the nature of disseminated content presents an arduous algorithmic task in deciphering the extent of topical interests in the streaming data. Tweeters – people who disseminate content on Twitter – in essence share photos, videos, hyperlinks and locations to members in their networks. In addition, intra-user interactions in form of *"likes"*, *"mentions"*

© Springer Nature Switzerland AG 2020
S. Hofmann et al. (Eds.): DESRIST 2020, LNCS 12388, pp. 154–168, 2020.
https://doi.org/10.1007/978-3-030-64823-7_15

and *"retweets"* compound the algorithmic learning and representation challenges in such short text microblogs. Cumulatively, the disseminated content to a large extent should define the true identity of such users.

Tweeters for example extrinsically declare their interests at sign up. Changes to these original interests are still user driven which is not always the case for many short text microblog users. Such changes are in the form of new friendships or *"hashtag"* suggestions which do not overly represent the true identities of such online users. Diversity in the disseminated content makes it difficult to align interests of one user to those they declared at sign up. For instance, a tweeter may continuously disseminate political related content during electioneering times, but also occasionally tweet about his favourite football team yet his extrinsic profile leans towards car racing. Capturing the diverse nature of interests in this respect for better presentation of third-party recommendations e.g. for personalised marketing, is important. Without capturing the context, keywords are insufficient in most cases as they may be used in negation. For example, a tweet such as *"I don't like KFC"* depicts someone with lack of interest in KFC. However, keyword search by the word "KFC" might just present this as a potential entity of interest, yet is not. This is one of the reasons, we looked at the contextual understanding of the entire sentence over the dataset via embeddings. This is more relevant compared to keywords. Therefore, this presents an interesting research problem in the deduction of user-interest levels in streaming texts to formulate short text microblogs user profiles. This formulation process raises the below questions that depict the need for this research:-

- Is it possible to extract diverse but user-representative topics of interests in streaming short text microblogs?
- Are user representative interests deducible in short text microblogs based solely on disseminated content?
- Is it possible to quantify a user's level of interest in various topics based on his/her disseminated content?

In this work, we present a framework that extracts diverse topics of interest and computes user's interests based on the disseminated content. We acknowledge that users on such platforms present a divergent space in terms of topical interests. We compute a responsibility matrix depicting users and their levels of interest in the varied topics which ultimately defines their profiles. To validate the framework performance, we consider a generic Twitter dataset geolocated to Kenya over a period of one year. Kenyan Twitterspace is considered based on the authors knowledge of tweeting patterns and language in the country as well as the diversity in topics over the time period.

This work is a build up to our initial work in computation of the Degree of Interest in Sports Betting [28]. The current framework differs from our earlier work in the responsibility matrix aspect as well as the approach used in the deduction of diverse topics of interest in the definition of user profiles. Scientifically, our contributions are as below:-

1. We design a user profiling framework that considers most definitive aspect of online users in true extrinsic identity deduction i.e. the disseminated content.
2. We develop a soft computation approach that assigns an interest responsibility level per topic to each user. This ultimately generates more succinct profiles.
3. We test our framework using known Twitter users in the Kenyan Twitterspace. We also validated the output in the formulation of true user identities of such short text microblog users.
4. In the design science aspect, this work encompasses the definition of the research problem and development of artefacts [12,16]. In our case this is done through modelling via neural networks approaches. The output in the form of word embeddings is the input to the Gaussian Mixture Model (GMM) with Expectation Maximization (EM). EM builds soft clusters to compute the degree of interest that users have in certain topics in the dataset. We are able to detail the processes to the quantifiable outputs and validation by human evaluators to make sure that the model works and objectives are met.

The rest of the paper is organized as follows. Section 2 summarizes the background and related literature of our study. Our approach is described in Sect. 3. The experimental framework is presented in Sect. 4 while the results of our approach are shown in Sect. 5. Conclusions and future work are summarized in Sect. 6.

2   Related Works

Short text microblog users consume content on the platforms based on their interest levels in certain topical content. Interest in the content may either be self-driven or given by recommender engines. This defines their user interest profile. Table 1 highlights some approaches by various authors in User Interest Profiling (UIP).

Table 1. Related literature in User Interest Profiling

Reference	Year	Contribution
[2]	2009	Statistically modeled for the discovery and distribution of user interests for categories such as "games," "food" and "movies." in tweets spanning 10 cities wordwide for four weeks using keywords
[3]	2013	A temporal and social probabilistic matrix factorization model was constructed to predict potential user interests in micro-blogging
[10]	2013	Constructed a user profiling model based on topical categorization of URLs in tweets. A mean profile prediction accuracy of 0.73 for 32 users over 18 coarse-grained interest categories was achieved
[14]	2014	Used hierarchical semantics of concepts from tweets to infer richer user interests expressed as a hierarchical interest graph
[15]	2015	Proposed a Named Entity Recognition (NER) model for Twitter user interests based on user profile modeling
[13]	2015	Developed a framework for identifying user interest changes over time on Twitter. External knowledge sources (Topic Hierarchy Tree) was constructed to infer the interests better in a hierarchical form
[23]	2017	Used soft ratings to model subjective, qualitative, and imperfect information about user preferences. The same was used for a more realistic and flexible means for users to express their preferences on products and services
[30]	2018	Proposed a framework for profiling users based on their posting activities. This was particularly in their posting frequency and temporal patterns
[11]	2018	Used semantic relatedness for tag clustering to construct a strong user interest profile (UIP). Other tags for inferring user interest, such as comments and reviews, were neglected in this work
[9]	2018	Proposed a Wiki-MID for extraction of user preferences in multi-lingual tweets with mappings to Wikipedia. The authors used popular services e.g. Spotify to reliably extract users' preferences
[18]	2018	Proposed the use of embeddings to jointly model users and their representative content in the same semantic space. The essence was to measure semantic similarity between users and words in inferring user representations
[7]	2019	Considered individual interactions to construct an evolving Bayesian non-parametric framework, called Dirichlet Process Mixture Model to model user interests. The model showed superiority in prediction of user behaviour and effectiveness in preference modelling
[33]	2019	Modeled a user interest graph represented by a hierarchical tree structure covering 167 nodes on three levels. The study also considered decay over time
[32]	2019	Developed a hierarchical interest overlapping community (HIOC) detection method by studying similar relationships between user profiles, and further presented a personalized recommendation model

Our work differs from the above with respect to the state-of-the-art in short text interest-based responsibility user profiling. We made use of vector representations to learn short and often misspelled words in the disseminated content. Classifications for extraction of interest responsibilities for each user are computed based via a Gaussian Mixture Model (GMM) with Expectation Maximization (EM).

3   Our Approach

As the aim of this study is to develop a model for extracting topics from microblogs and quantifying the level of user interests, we adopt the design science research by Peffers et al. [24]. Our study centres on the creation and evaluation of the proposed framework as a research artefact that seeks to deliver both theoretical and practical contributions. We elicit the core profiling processes in the proposed framework. The framework encompasses processes related to *modeling and representation of short texts*, *clustering* and *user interest-based responsibility matrix computation*. Therefore, for the design and development of the model, we adopted several neural network approaches in the representation of tweets. This assumption is based on the success of other neural network approaches in short texts as demonstrated in [17,21,31]. We followed the below processes in computing the responsibilities that users have towards topics (clusters in this case) in the dataset.

1. **Modeling of Short Texts** - Several neural network based models of tweets are trained to achieve this. They are based on *FastText* [6], *WordVec* [20] and *Glove* [25] technologies. The output is low vector representation of words in the corpus [6].
2. **Clustering and Extraction of Centroids** - Tweets depicting higher similarity are grouped together via K-Means++. K-Means++ optimizes the selection of cluster centres [1]. Similarity of tweets to a certain cluster is computed by averaging their pairwise distances to the respective cluster centroid. In our approach, both centroids and individual tweets are represented as vectors.
3. **Responsibility Matrix Computation** - We made use of the Expectation Maximization algorithm [8] to define soft clusters over test tweets.
4. **Multi-interest user Profiling** - The responsibility matrix above represents individual users and their level of interest in the generated topics. Multi-interest user profiles are generated by aggregating individual interest levels in the responsibility matrix. Based on a user defined inter-topic threshold, users surpassing the value are then profiled based on the interest levels in that topic.

To evaluate the proposed model, we applied an additional dataset of users drawn from the same population, the Kenyan twitter space. Then we conduct human validation with 3 evaluators. The evaluators have knowledge in the domain topics as well as the language of use.

3.1   Modelling Short Texts

We based the modeling process on *Word2Vec* neural algorithm based on its classification performance over other neural network approaches as depicted in

Fig. 1. The model outputs word embeddings that typically reconstruct linguistic contexts of words. Each word is assigned a vector space in such a way that contextually close words are located close to one another in the dimensional space [20]. For vector representations, parameter specifications across the models were attributed the same way as in [28]. Unspecified parameters assumed the default values specific to each modeling technique.

3.2 Clustering and Initialization of Centroids

The intuition behind the clustering process in our case is that semantically close tweets are usually grouped together. To define clusters, manual inspection of underlying keywords in each cluster are observed. These keywords ideally are representative topics for each of the clusters. *K-Means++* was the algorithm of choice in clustering and extraction of initial centroids[1]. As mentioned by authors in [28], the algorithm initially spreads out the set of cluster centroids thus optimizing the choice of initial cluster centers. This guarantees an $O(\log k)$ solution for convergence.

The choice of the number of clusters was based on two factors. First, we determined the optimal set of topics in the dataset using the conventional Latent Dirichlet Allocation (LDA) [5]. Owing to the weaknesses of modelling topics with LDA on short and sparse texts, we further opted to manually seed the extracted topics using MELDA [29]. Therefore, topics that were semantically close were merged. The final topics provided a better indication of the expected cluster numbers as ideally semantic closeness is key in both topic modelling and clustering. Secondly, we used a heterogeneity measure [4] to determine the optimal cluster numbers in the dataset which ideally should be as close as possible to the optimal number of topics. The well known Elbow method [4] was applied in determining this. With this method, several tests were run considering different k values representing the number of clusters.

3.3 Responsibility Matrix Computation

Expectation-Maximization algorithm [8] was applied in identification of the responsibility levels in terms of topical alienation and by extension cluster affiliation as described in Sect. 3.2. We followed the below steps in the Expectation Maximization (EM) computation:-

1. Chose the initial values for estimations. Instead of randomizing the starting values, we chose the initial set of cluster centroids extracted for the chosen K, number of topics. The cluster centroids are in the form of vectors and were extracted from the Word2Vec model. This is because EM is sensitive to the initial means therefore a bad choice of means can lead to overlapping points [26].
2. Secondly, the conditional expectations are fulfilled by initializing each cluster weight based on the number of tweets in individual clusters assigned by K-means++. The process is then followed by maximization of the log-likelihood

with respect to the cluster weights assignment where missing data points are replaced by the conditional expectation.

3. Lastly, the initial co-variance matrix is computed as convergence is assessed.

EM in this case defines the extent to which topics (clusters) have influence over tweets. The resultant output after convergence is a matrix of topics and their respective responsibilities over the individual tweets. The summation of shared topical responsibilities over each tweet should add up to 1. The formulation of the above steps is in Sect. 3.4.

3.4   Multi-interest User Profiles

Input in the computation of multi-interest user profiles is the responsibility matrix computed in Sect. 3.3. To define a *userx* profile, *rows of individual modeled tweetsv* corresponding to the user Y_x, are selected from *test dataset matrix* Y. Therefore, $Y_x \in Y$. The *user-interest representative model* is derived by averaging user interest vectors per topic. The output is representative of individual topical interests $Z_w = \sum_{i=0}^{|Y_x|-1} w_{xb}$.

To represent the above, let w be the *count of modeled tweets per user* x. For $b \in [0, K-1]$, the user-representative interest model is computed as the average of Z_w and $E = \sum_{b=0}^{K-1} Z_w$. This is representative of the *sum of vector values* b. The Multi-interest User Profile ($MiUP$) is thus computed as $(Z_w/E) * 100$. Therefore, b values are simply the *interest values* to each of the 10 topics averaged per user.

Its essential to define users in homogeneous groups in profiling. Therefore, a threshold value n is introduced as definitive least interest value to be included in grouping users with a certain level of interests. The value is determined based on the inter-topic interest median. For example, if the test user's median value is 0.4, then 0.4 will be set as the threshold for that topic across all users.

4   Experimental Framework and Setup

Processes to validate our proposed approach are outlined in Sect. 3. For validation of our results, *Glove*, *Word2Vec* and *FastText* models are trained on the same dataset with different dimensions. A description of the source and nature of the dataset is in Sect. 4.1.

4.1   Datasets and Settings

Our corpus comprised of 650,055 unique tweets geo-localized to Kenya. They were collected in JSON format for a period of a year starting 17/10/2018. Each tweet entry contained associated metadata such as hashtags, mentions etc. We filtered out all retweets from the collection. The tweeting language was majorly English and Swahili, Kenya's national languages. Just like in [28], the choice of Kenya's Twitterspace was largely influenced by the author's familiarity with Kenyan's tweeting patterns, diversity in topics as well as the availability of some domain specific data that augmented our dataset.

Dataset Augmentation. Regarding domain specificity and validation of our approach, we augmented the dataset with 50639 sports betting related tweets geolocalized to Kenya. We needed this known set for validation of our methodology. To be specific, the betting related tweets were queried and collected from Twitter handles specified in Sect. 4.1 of [28]. Therefore, the entire training set comprised of 700, 694 unique tweets all geolocalized to Kenya.

Sample of Users for Evaluation. To evaluate our methodology, we made use of two known but diverse datasets. We considered 1000 tweets associated with sports betting Twitter handles labelled *Sports Betting Related*. In addition, we considered 1000 politics related tweets generated on 8th August 2017 during the last general election in Kenya. These two divergent but geographically relevant sets of data provided a mechanism for testing our modeling approach before the profiling process. In essence, the best modelling approach should be able to separate the two sets in almost equal segments.

The 2000 tweets were pre-processed and duplicates removed. All tweets with less than 25 characters were also removed from the set. The pre-processing steps are described in detail in our previous work [28]. At the end, 784 sports betting related and 769 politically related tweets were validated.

4.2   Model Training and Evaluation

We followed the short text modeling process described in Sect. 3.1 to train the models. Our trained models were based on *FastText* [6], *Word2Vec*[20] and *Glove*[25] neural network modelling techniques. The output of the modelling process is a vector representation of a word(s) based on the context within which the word is commonly used. However, for *FastText*, word modelling is independent of the language of expression and vocabulary size as its based on a sliding window of characters instead of comparing the whole words.

Model Training. Five neural network based models *Word2vec-SkipGram (100 dimensions), Word2vec-CBOW (200 dimensions), FastText-SkipGram (100 dimensions), Glove (300 dimensions) and FastText-CBOW (100 dimensions)* were trained for evaluation and consistency purposes. The choice of the above models with their respective parameters was based on their success in our earlier work [28]. A preprocessed and tokenized corpus of tweets was the input in the model's training framework. Ideally, the models learn character or word patterns by mapping words in the corpus to a vector space. In general, the models predicted the next word based on the surrounding words contextually. FastText models further learnt word contexts by averaging windows of character representations. These models therefore dealt better with out vocabulary or misspelled words compared to say Word2Vec or Glove based models. The models to a large extent contextually learnt Swahili and English terms well. The below parameters were specified before training *Word2Vec* and *FastText* models:

– *size* or the number of dimensions, *min_count* or least count of a word in the corpus for it to be factored in the training set;
– The *window* parameter. This is the maximum distance between the current and predicted word in a tweet;
– *sg* for training a Continuous Bag of Words (CBOW) if $sg = 0$ or undefined and skip-gram model if $sg = 1$.
– *word n_grams* to enrich word vectors with subword(n_grams) information if specified as 1; and *iter* or iterations which was the number of iterations (epochs) over the corpus.
– Number of *epochs* i.e. one full cycle in training was defined for the *Glove* model as well as the *learning rate(lr)*.

The model outputs were vectors of each word in the cleaned corpus. An in-depth view of the word representation process in the three modeling techniques is explained in Sect. 3 of [28] under model training.

Model Evaluation. There was need for evaluating each of the state-of-the-art modeling techniques in order to select the most relevant one for multi-interest user profiling approach. In this instance, each of the models is subjected to a labeled set of test data. Based on the heterogeneity results in Fig. 2, the dataset had approximately 22 topics. Out of the 22, we had ground truth tweets for two topics i.e. **Sports Betting** and **Politics**. The tweets were extracted from timelines of betting companies and politicians in Kenya respectively which were then aggregated with the training data. Each tweet was annotated as *political* or *sports betting* related based on the disseminating Twitter handle. The heterogeneity measurement is computed via *K-means++* as illustrated in Sect. 5.

Topical Classifications. The topical classifications of tweets under the 22 topics via *K-means++* depicted some overlap across the dataset. However, hashtagged tweets provided better generalizations, especially with the smaller topics. Hashtags such as *#uhuru-mustgonow, #Istandwith-NdindiNyoro, #Punguza-MizigoBill2019* were label-led as **Political Discourse**. On the other hand, hashtags such as *#mensfinal, #USOpen,*

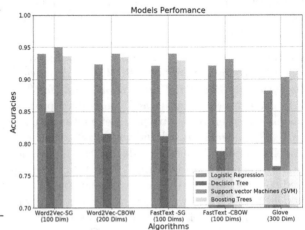

Fig. 1. Models classification results

#Nadal define the **Sports** topic. Tweets classified under **Newspaper Dailies** were specific to major dailies in Kenya. *#Natiomedia, #thestarkenya* are some examples in this category. **News & Emerging issues** characterized breaking news, that could still be related to topics such as sports, politics etc. However, the idea was to generate very specific interest profiles for users. Some users for example may be interested in emerging news and sports and not politics thus categorizing them as news, may not be very specific to their taste profiles. The resultant topical classifications after merging of smaller topics were 10 as shown in Table 2.

A subset of 2000 out of 5320 randomized tweets from the two categories were selected for labelling and subjected to the five neural-network based models for classification. Adjustable parameters were replicated in the classification algorithms for consistency. *Support Vector Machines (SVM), Boosting Tree, Decision Tree* and *Logistic Regression* algorithms were selected for the classification purpose. The idea was to select the best performing modelling framework whose embeddings could be subjected to Expectation Maximization (EM) to generate soft topic assignments.

From the results in Fig. 1, *Word2Vec-SkipGram* with 100 dimensions consistently outperformed the other algorithms. Therefore, *Word2Vec-SkipGram (100 dimensions)* was selected as the modelling technique of choice for further EM experiments. Technically, soft cluster assignments from the rest of the algorithms was not very meaningful at this stage as *Word2Vec-SkipGram (100 dimensions)* generated the best set of embeddings for soft cluster assignments in this setup.

5 Results

The *Word2Vec-SkipGram* model in Sect. 4.2 was trained with the following parameter specifications. **Size = 100**, **min_count = 3** and **window = 10**. Default *Word2Vec* values were assumed for the rest of the parameters. The output of the modelling process was a vectorized dictionary of 140252 words.

The optimal number of clusters in tweets for EM were computed following the Elbow heuristic [4] measure. To compute this, several K values representing probable number of clusters were factored. For each value of K, *K-means++* was applied to calculate

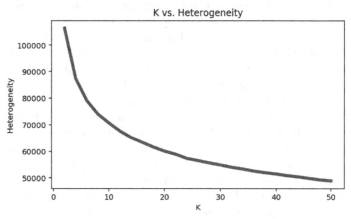

Fig. 2. Elbow heuristic results

Table 2. EM topical classifications

Usernames	Life and Well-being	Development Projects	Sports	Counties	Swahili Chatter	Newspaper Dailies	Political Discourse	Elections	News & Emerging Issues	Condolences
xxxnchxxxixxx	14.650000	0.000000	0.000000	0.000000	27.344231	1.865385	49.434615	1.911538	0.015385	4.776923
xxxxs_xxxi	2.732292	0.000000	0.000000	0.000000	3.599479	0.203646	92.355729	0.000000	0.000000	1.109896
hxxxenxxx	8.312000	0.000000	0.000000	0.335000	14.804000	1.003000	72.578000	0.000000	0.000000	2.968000
xxxengmuxxx	12.070186	0.000000	0.588199	0.030435	28.661491	2.173913	53.783851	0.439130	0.168944	2.080745
xxxkxxxdo	21.471809	0.000000	0.108511	0.000000	0.063298	3.369149	57.862766	5.003191	0.946809	11.169681
xxxuingixxx	18.790526	0.000000	0.420526	0.000000	4.048421	5.322105	64.768947	0.000526	0.557895	6.089474
xxxojaxxxon	5.366327	0.000000	0.000000	0.000000	13.888265	1.035714	78.695408	0.000000	0.000000	1.011224
xxxte_kexxx	9.029592	0.510204	0.497959	0.080102	10.478061	1.841837	73.866837	0.000000	0.000000	3.692857
xxxcentxxxnga	18.246875	0.520833	0.000521	0.000000	11.870833	0.958333	63.434375	0.001042	0.000000	4.965625
mpxxxkahaxxx	18.752717	0.000000	0.000000	0.000000	2.834783	6.498913	65.819022	0.525543	0.002174	5.561413

heterogeneity. Heterogeneity is a measure of compactness in the clustering process. Ideally, the optimal cluster numbers should be as close as possible to the number of topics identified in Sect. 4.2. Results shown in Fig. 2 depicts K to be a value between 20 an 30 which corresponds to the 22 topics representative of the dataset as derived in Sect. 4.2. However, overlapping cluster centroids for 12 topical classifications were merged with the rest of topics as they were contextually similar by manual observation leaving 10 topics. The resultant centroids were then extracted and used as initial means for EM.

5.1 Methodology Validation

To further validate the methodology and results of the EM process, we used a validation dataset of 282 users drawn from the Kenyan twitter space. 82 of the users are current politicians thus the assumption is that their interests are largely political. Its worth acknowledging that politicians do not just disseminate political content. They would often tweet about current affairs in the country, development projects they undertake etc. However, with EM, we are only looking at quantifying the interest in specific topics. Therefore, if the interest that a user labelled as politician has in the **politics** topical cluster is higher/close to the highest classification value, then it is enough proof that the user actually is a politician. We acknowledge that this may not be the same for a few of them. Output of this validation process is a responsibility matrix depicting soft cluster assignments for the users in question. For each, user, average interest vectors per topic were computed representing the users profile as described in Sect. 3.4. For example, user *kithurekindiki*, a senator tweeted only 4 times in the course of our data collection process. Averaging the user's interest in the extracted topics, his interest was 100% in *Political Discourse*. On the other hand, a user such as *mutuamuluvi*, though with very few tweets, the diversity in topics was evident with 42.9% of his tweets being profiled as *Political Discourse*, 7.7% in *Life and Well-being*, and 8.6% *Condolences* among others. A subset of the entire output is shown in the Table 2. Usernames in the table have been anonymized for privacy reasons. The same output in Fig. 3 shows that on average, **67.259955%** of content disseminated by the politicians is political. This affirms that our framework largely classifies correctly. Results in such a modelling process can be applicable in follower - followee recommendations, dealing with cold-start recommendations and third-party content propagation in short text microblogs.

5.2 Human Validation

To validate, the results obtained in Sect. 5, we made use of 3 human evaluators. The evaluators were selected based on their knowledge of the English and Swahili languages i.e in deciphering content and assignment to a probable topic as well as their familiarity with specific domains e.g. sports betting. General knowledge about Kenya was also a requirement as some tweets needed someone well versed with Kenya to discern their true contextual representation. We presented them with 20 tweets from 10 random tweeters, in the test set for validation. The evaluators were also presented with a curated list of topics in the test set outputs as in Table 2. They were expected to classify each tweet based on the presented subset of the identified topics. For consistency purposes, the extent i.e. percentage of influence the topic had on the validation tweet was not considered. The evaluators were to just identify whether a tweet was relevant to the presented topics in line with the soft clustering approach. The results were presented the same way as in [28] where $X1$ to $X3$ represented the evaluators. x_{1u} to x_{3u} are the individual soft topic classifications as per evaluators. $M_{1u}..M_{3u}$ represents the model's topical assignments for the same tweet. The Kappa score is then computed representing the agreement between classifications in the model and human evaluators [19]. k_{1u} to k_{3u} represented the Kappa score across the topics. Therefore, Kappa score k is computed as $k = p_o - p_e / 1 - p_e$ where p_e is the hypothetical probability of chance agreement. On the other hand, p_o is the relative observed agreement between the model's and evaluators' observations.

Table 3 shows the classification agreements between evaluators and the model in our proposed approach. From the table, the agreement between the model's and evaluators' classifications were 59.2% depicting a *moderate* to *substantial* agreement in the classifications as per the Kappa statistic scale [27]. This is a very strong indicator of profile consistency based on the fact that only 20 tweets were considered for each user. A larger number of tweets would have likely resulted in a better Kappa score.

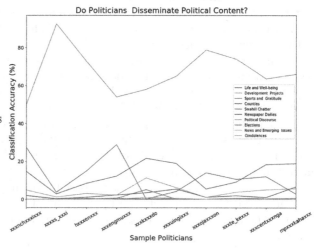

Fig. 3. Politicians EM classifications and relevance to political content

Table 3. Kappa Scores K depicting rating agreement between the model and human evaluators

| | X_1 | | | X_2 | | | X_3 | | |
	X_{1u}	M_{1u}	K_{1u}	X_{2u}	M_{2u}	K_{2u}	X_{3u}	M_{3u}	K_{3u}
Life & Well-being	4/20	3/20	**0.828**	3/20	3/20	**0.608**	4/20	3/20	**0.483**
Development Projects	2/20	1/20	**0.643**	1/20	1/20	**1.0**	1/20	1/20	**1.0**
Sports	6/20	6/20	**0.762**	6/20	6/20	**0.524**	6/20	6/20	**0.524**
Counties	3/20	4/20	**0.483**	4/20	4/20	**0.688**	4/20	4/20	**0.688**
Swahili Chatter	1/20	1/20	**1.0**	1/20	1/20	**1.0**	0/20	1/20	**0.0**
Newspaper Dailies	5/20	6/20	**0.625**	5/20	6/20	**0.625**	5/20	6/20	**0.875**
Political Discourse	14/20	12/20	**0.783**	13/20	12/20	**0.681**	10/20	12/20	**0.4**
Elections	0/20	2/20	**0.0**	2/20	2/20	**0.44**	2/20	2/20	**0.44**
News & Emerging Issues	9/20	7/20	**0.588**	6/20	7/20	**0.659**	5/20	7/20	**0.529**
Condolences	0/20	1/20	**0.0**	0/20	1/20	**0.0**	0/20	1/20	**0.0**

6   Conclusion and Future Work

Short text micro-blogging platforms are definitive in profiling user's long and short term interests based on their disseminated content. The propagated content will depict certain topical preferences to a large or lesser extent. We proposed a framework that optimizes vector representations in classifying tweets as soft clusters via Expectation Maximization. For computation of a user's multi-interest profile, we aggregated individual topical classifications. We validated the outputs of our approach by assigning random tweets belonging to a few tweeters for manual topical classifications. This validation showed strong agreement (**0.592** Kappa Score) between model and evaluator's classification.

Our study provides an enhanced model for user interest profiling as well as sheds light on the design knowledge of such models. For instance, we demonstrate that the use of vector representations to learn short and often misspelled words in the disseminated content will potentially enhance the effectiveness of user interest profiling. Furthermore, the combination of the state-of-the-art techniques shows promising results.

We are inclined towards time-stamp based profiling in short text microblogs in future for better and timely third party content recommendations. An evaluation of the approach against other graph-based approaches will be integral in future.

References

1. Arthur, D., Vassilvitskii, S.: k-means++: the advantages of careful seeding. In: Proceedings of the Eighteenth Annual ACM-SIAM Symposium on Discrete Algorithms, pp. 1027–1035. Society for Industrial and Applied Mathematics (2007)
2. Banerjee, N., et al.: User interests in social media sites: an exploration with microblogs. In: Proceedings of the 18th ACM Conference on Information and Knowledge Management, pp. 1823–1826 (2009)
3. Bao, H., Li, Q., Liao, S.S., Song, S., Gao, H.: A new temporal and social PMF-based method to predict users' interests in micro-blogging. Decis. Support Syst. **55**(3), 698–709 (2013)
4. Bholowalia, P., Kumar, A.: EBK-means: a clustering technique based on elbow method and k-means in WSN. Int. J. Comput. Appl. **105**(9), 17–24 (2014)
5. Blei, D.M., Ng, A.Y., Jordan, M.I.: Latent Dirichlet allocation. J. Mach. Learn. Res. **3**(Jan), 993–1022 (2003)
6. Bojanowski, P., Grave, E., Joulin, A., Mikolov, T.: Enriching word vectors with subword information. Trans. Assoc. Comput. Linguist. **5**, 135–146 (2017)
7. Cami, B.R., Hassanpour, H., Mashayekhi, H.: User preferences modeling using Dirichlet process mixture model for a content-based recommender system. Knowl.-Based Syst. **163**, 644–655 (2019)
8. Dempster, A.P., Laird, N.M., Rubin, D.B.: Maximum likelihood from incomplete data via the EM algorithm. J. Roy. Stat. Soc.: Ser. B (Methodol.) **39**(1), 1–22 (1977)
9. Di Tommaso, G., Faralli, S., Stilo, G., Velardi, P.: Wiki-MID: a very large multi-domain interests dataset of Twitter users with mappings to wikipedia. In: Vrandečić, D., Bontcheva, K., Suárez-Figueroa, M.C., Presutti, V., Celino, I., Sabou, M., Kaffee, L.-A., Simperl, E. (eds.) ISWC 2018. LNCS, vol. 11137, pp. 36–52. Springer, Cham (2018). https://doi.org/10.1007/978-3-030-00668-6_3
10. Garcia Esparza, S., O'Mahony, M.P., Smyth, B.: CatStream: categorising tweets for user profiling and stream filtering. In: Proceedings of the 2013 International Conference on Intelligent User Interfaces, pp. 25–36 (2013)
11. Goel, S., Kumar, R.: Folksonomy-based user profile enrichment using clustering and community recommended tags in multiple levels. Neurocomputing **315**, 425–438 (2018)
12. Grenha Teixeira, J., Patrício, L., Huang, K.H., Fisk, R.P., Nóbrega, L., Constantine, L.: The minds method: integrating management and interaction design perspectives for service design. J, Serv. Res. **20**(3), 240–258 (2017)
13. Jiang, B., Sha, Y.: Modeling temporal dynamics of user interests in online social networks. Procedia Comput. Sci. **51**, 503–512 (2015)
14. Kapanipathi, P., Jain, P., Venkataramani, C., Sheth, A.: Hierarchical interest graph from tweets. In: Proceedings of the 23rd International Conference on World Wide Web, pp. 311–312 (2014)
15. Karatay, D., Karagoz, P.: User interest modeling in twitter with named entity recognition. In: 5th Workshop on Making Sense of Microposts (2015)
16. Lapão, L.V., Da Silva, M.M., Gregório, J.: Implementing an online pharmaceutical service using design science research. BMC Med. Inform. Decis. Mak. **17**(1), 31 (2017)
17. Li, J., Xu, H., He, X., Deng, J., Sun, X.: Tweet modeling with LSTM recurrent neural networks for hashtag recommendation. In: 2016 International Joint Conference on Neural Networks (IJCNN), pp. 1570–1577. IEEE (2016)

18. Liang, S., Zhang, X., Ren, Z., Kanoulas, E.: Dynamic embeddings for user profiling in twitter. In: Proceedings of the 24th ACM SIGKDD International Conference on Knowledge Discovery and#38; Data Mining, pp. 1764–1773. KDD '18, ACM, New York, NY, USA (2018). https://doi.org/10.1145/3219819.3220043
19. McHugh, M.L.: Interrater reliability: the kappa statistic. Biochem. Medica **22**(3), 276–282 (2012)
20. Mikolov, T., Sutskever, I., Chen, K., Corrado, G.S., Dean, J.: Distributed representations of words and phrases and their compositionality. In: Advances in Neural Information Processing Systems, pp. 3111–3119 (2013)
21. Mishra, S., Rizoiu, M.A., Xie, L.: Modeling popularity in asynchronous social media streams with recurrent neural networks. In: Twelfth International AAAI Conference on Web and Social Media (2018)
22. Morstatter, F., Pfeffer, J., Liu, H., Carley, K.M.: Is the sample good enough? comparing data from twitter's streaming API with Twitter's firehose. In: Seventh International AAAI Conference on Weblogs and Social Media (2013)
23. Nguyen, V.D., Sriboonchitta, S., Huynh, V.N.: Using community preference for overcoming sparsity and cold-start problems in collaborative filtering system offering soft ratings. Electron. Commer. Res. Appl. **26**, 101–108 (2017)
24. Peffers, K., Tuunanen, T., Rothenberger, M.A., Chatterjee, S.: A design science research methodology for information systems research. J. Manag. Inf. Syst. **24**(3), 45–77 (2007)
25. Pennington, J., Socher, R., Manning, C.: Glove: global vectors for word representation. In: Proceedings of the 2014 Conference on Empirical Methods in Natural Language Processing (EMNLP), pp. 1532–1543 (2014)
26. Recalde, L., Baeza-Yates, R.: What kind of content are you prone to tweet? multi-topic preference model for tweeters. arXiv preprint arXiv:1807.07162 (2018)
27. Viera, A.J., Garrett, J.M., et al.: Understanding interobserver agreement: the kappa statistic. Fam. Med. **37**(5), 360–363 (2005)
28. Wandabwa, H., Naeem, M.A., Mirza, F., Pears, R.: Follow-back recommendations for sports bettors: a Twitter-based approach. In: Proceedings of the 53rd Hawaii International Conference on System Sciences (2020)
29. Wandabwa, H., Naeem, M.A., Pears, R., Mirza, F.: A metamodel enabled approach for discovery of coherent topics in short text microblogs. IEEE Access **6**, 65582–65593 (2018)
30. Ying, Q.F., Chiu, D.M., Venkatramanan, S., Zhang, X.: User modeling and usage profiling based on temporal posting behavior in OSNs. Online Soc. Netw. Media **8**, 32–41 (2018)
31. Zhang, Z., Robinson, D., Tepper, J.: Detecting hate speech on Twitter using a convolution-GRU based deep neural network. In: Gangemi, A., Navigli, R., Vidal, M.-E., Hitzler, P., Troncy, R., Hollink, L., Tordai, A., Alam, M. (eds.) ESWC 2018. LNCS, vol. 10843, pp. 745–760. Springer, Cham (2018). https://doi.org/10.1007/978-3-319-93417-4_48
32. Zheng, J., Wang, S., Li, D., Zhang, B.: Personalized recommendation based on hierarchical interest overlapping community. Inf. Sci. **479**, 55–75 (2019)
33. Zhu, Z., Zhou, Y., Deng, X., Wang, X.: A graph-oriented model for hierarchical user interest in precision social marketing. Electron. Commer. Res. Appl. **35**, 100845 (2019)

Design Principles

Design Principles Exposition: A Framework for Problematizing Knowledge and Practice in DSR

Magnus Rotvit Perlt Hansen[1(✉)] and Amir Haj-Bolouri[2]

[1] Department of People and Technology, Roskilde University, Roskilde, Denmark
magnuha@ruc.dk
[2] University West, Informatics, Trollhättan, Sweden
amir.haj-bolouri@hv.se

Abstract. Design principles (DPs) have been recognized as a central contribution in Design Science Research and the research community has begun acknowledging their importance. Much of this work implicitly assumes that design principles are natural components of contributions that can easily be derived by researchers without a need for criteria for their proposal, application or evaluation. In this paper we infer a framework for how to expose the conceptual structure of DPs as both components and sole contributions. We find a danger in assuming that design principles alone are contributions as they are very broadly used to propose utility yet the specific target audience or the explicit use of them as components of design theory occur less frequent. Furthermore, by applying our framework to a set of DPs, we offer four parts of their conceptual structure that can be used to convey the nature of design principle contributions and further identify potential areas for improvement or further research. We derive 8 questions that offer a guiding hand to researchers who attempt to embed DPs as components of their contribution either to research or to practice.

Keywords: Design principles · Practical knowledge · Technological rules · Design theory components

1 Introduction

Allow us to preface the initial sentence of this introduction with a bold and, perhaps provocative, statement: *"The current state of design science research on design principles has a serious utilization problem"*. Why? Because the conceptualization of Design Principles (DPs) as a highly attainable DSR contribution is in a weird spot.

15 years ago, van Aken [1] wrote that *"Academic management research has a serious utilization problem."* [1, p. 219] in a call for more prescriptive research to *"open up the incestuous, closed loop of the Academy's conferences"* [1, p. 219]. The main point of the paper was to include prescriptive, research-oriented 'technological rules' to close the researcher-practitioner gap that had kept widening. While we do not dare call the state of DPs in DSR 'incestuous', we see several fundamental issues with how the field has

S. Hofmann et al. (Eds.): DESRIST 2020, LNCS 12388, pp. 171–182, 2020.
https://doi.org/10.1007/978-3-030-64823-7_16

evolved, specifically the continuous publication of *"design principles"* as prescriptive DSR contributions.

Design principles are considered to be an essential and guiding part of design theories [2–4]. The concept of "design principles" was initially proposed as a way to 1) close the gap between researchers and practitioners" and 2) provide more theoretical prescriptive research to the field of management of information systems. Seminal models and methods of DSR position design principles as a prominent set of outcomes [5, 6]. Chandra Kruse et al. [7] characterize DPs as *"knowledge about the creation of other instances of artifacts belonging to the same class"* (p. 39). Design principles should have their value assessed based on both practical and theoretical value, much in line with "principles of form and function", and "principles of implementation" as proposed by Gregor and Jones [8]. Often design principles are framed in a logical order from theoretical and/or empirical grounding but can also be elicited post-hoc from after an instantiation has been built or evaluated [4]. Recently, the area has garnered attention in terms of the meaning and usefulness to practice and guidelines on how to formulate DPs [7, 9], making it difficult to assess their usefulness to either practice or theory based on their current formulation.

The conundrum of where to place and how to propose design principles infer a thorough investigation into the different conceptual structures of design principles. As such, the paper proposes the following research question: *How to expose design principles so that their potential can be revealed on a practical and theoretical level?*

We have structured the paper the following way. First, we present the seminal works that conceptualize design principles or similar and consolidate the differences and commonalities on a conceptual level. Second, we infer a framework that can be used to expose the structure of DPs and apply this framework to a range of recent DSR journal publications that contribute with DPs and expose their underlying structure, origin and implications. We suggest a series of central questions that include the potential for future design-related work based on the DPs. Finally, we discuss the impact of having different knowledge contribution spaces as well as aims and criteria that can indicate how and why design principles can be viewed as both true and effective, as well as the potential for further research on an ontological and epistemological level.

2 The Conceptual Space of Design Principles

The origin of 'design principles' as a concept is somewhat difficult to historically pinpoint. In 'The Sciences of the Artificial', Simon [10] makes little to no mention of such a thing as design principles, and even the works of Hevner et al. [11] also do not mention the concept. Conceptually, *principles* have been defined as being a central part of 'Design Theory' [8] and are both *prescriptive* in nature and considered as new *generalized* or *abstract knowledge* through either *improvement* (applying new design solutions to old problems) or *exaptation* (applying old design knowledge to new problems) [4]. Despite rigorous ontologies for DSR concepts and being epistemologically rooted in *realism* [4, 8], the ontological definitions of DPs have not shared a similar inception.

In the following we present a dissemination of the conceptual space of the seminal works that have proposed structures of the DP concept in one form or another. The seminal works that are drawn on are the results of those papers that have been cited as DP origins by newer DSR DP papers (identified after the 'selection' phase of the literature review methodology on page 5).

2.1 Different Application Levels

Design principles can be viewed on three different levels of application; technology, domain and formal level. The term is primarily defined as a matter of abstraction, from a concrete product and artefact-focused level (class of artefacts, systems or methods) to more general areas and contexts up to the highest level and spanning various technologies and domains (see Table 1).

Table 1. Seminal works supporting the different application levels of design principles

		Bunge [16]	van Aken [1]	Walls et al. [2]	Gregor and Jones [8]
Application level	**Formal**	Laws Rules	"Organization theory"	Process and product kernel theories	Justificatory knowledge as kernel theories
	Domain	Technological rules	"Management theory"	Meta-requirements	–
	Technology	–	Design exemplar	Meta-design	Expository instantiation

Formal Level: As early as 1966, Bunge [12] proposed prescriptive statements as normative rules that can be derived from laws. On the formal level, laws are defined as overall explanations of world phenomena that science will uncover and rules of conduct or action, utilized in practice are then (often) inferred from these laws. Distinct from laws. Van Aken [1] exemplified this distinction as *organization theory* that consists of describing, understanding and predicting phenomena.

Walls et al. [2] pioneered the notion of *product and process kernel theories* (used as seminal works of the foundation of DSR [8, 11]); various theories used to explain phenomena of the world used to derive and test prescriptive statements.

One example is that of the design features of relational databases [13] that over time has been applied to so many domains and technologies that the principles behind can be argued to be on the formal level. Another example is the Gestalt Principles from Psychology [14], also widely adopted and taught in other domains, including interaction design [15], all of which have been referenced, utilized, applied and evaluated so thoroughly that they can be considered "laws" of organization.

Domain Level: On the domain level resides technological rules. These type of rules are directly inferred from laws and tested out in practice to both evaluate their usefulness but also to provide more knowledge about the existing laws from where they were derived

[12, 16]. Bunge and van Aken provide the following example of a technological rule: *if wanting to provide outcome X, in context Z, then something like Y can help.*

Van Aken [1] proposes this level as *management theory* that provides prescriptive technological rules to guide practitioners in solving problems that can be applied to *classes* of domains. The level is can be considered similar to that of Walls et al. [2] and Gregor and Jones [8] who identify *meta-requirements* as: "[…] the class of goals to which the theory applies." (Walls et al. [2], p. 43).

Technological Level: This level has a concrete focus on a specific, tangible technology or class of technologies to which prescriptive statements are applied. As domain level is not always specific enough, an application instance that can show the result of the application has been denoted a *design exemplar* [1], *expository instantiation* [8, 11] or the *meta-design* [2].

2.2 Types of Design Principles

We identify DPs into two types; **concrete attribute principles** (CAPs) of a type of design that is needed to attain a certain goal, and **process action principles** (PAPs) that explicates how designers, developers or other actors should perform actions to attain the design or its use (see Table 2). The CAPs have been proposed as *algorithms* [1] (specific and concrete specifications that are required), *meta-design* [2] (defined as a generalized artefact that should correspond to the requirements), and principles of form and function [8] (the essence of an artefact; its *causa formalis*).

Table 2. Seminal works supporting the design principle types

		Bunge [16]	van Aken [1]	Walls et al. [2]	Gregor and Jones [8]
Principle types	**Concrete attributes**	–	Algorithmic	Meta design	Of form and function
	Process actions	–	Heuristics	Design method	Of implementation

On the other side are the PAPs, proposed as *heuristics* [1] (qualitative and interpretative), the *design method* [2] (actions needed to attain the finalized design), or as *principles of implementation* [8] (*causa efficients*; producing or using the material artefact).

2.3 Utility Interest

We also find that DPs have a proposed utility in terms of the final recipient, either as **abstract knowledge** in which researchers would have an interest, or as **practical action** in which practitioners could benefit from applying the principles (see Table 3).

Table 3. Seminal works supporting varieties of utility interest

		Bunge [16]	van Aken [1]	Walls et al. [2]	Gregor and Jones [8]
Utility interest	**Abstract knowledge**	Solution fit to domains, testing laws	Solution fit to domains	Prescriptive design theory	Prescriptive design theory
	Practical action	Practical, general solutions	Practical, managerial solutions	–	–

Bunge [16] and Van Aken [1] explicitly note that technological rules are used to solve practical problems and hence utilized by either practitioners and managers respectively. Hence, it is not necessary practitioners to know the underlying laws behind the rules as long as they use them effectively. Walls et al. [2] and Gregor and Jones [8] see focus more on components of prescriptive design theory with a stronger focus on the abstract knowledge.

2.4 Criteria for Evaluation and Aim

The final part of our framework is that of *criteria*, including the **evaluation** of the principles, or at very least the proposed design (which is considered an important activity in DSR [11]) as well as the **aim** of the DPs, defined as the overall motivation. Note the potential overlap between utility interest and aim, though distinguished in terms of the onset (aim) and the end product (utility) (see Table 4).

Table 4. Seminal works supporting criteria of design principles

		Bunge [16]	van Aken [1]	Walls et al. [2]	Gregor and Jones [8]
Criteria	**Evaluating**	Empirical	Beta testing (empirically)	Testable hypotheses	Testable propositions
	Aim	Domain fit	Transferability	–	Design theory components

Evaluation: As the technological rules are being utilized by researchers to either learn more of existing laws or about the effectiveness of the rules, Bunge [16] suggests thorough *empirical* testing. Van Aken denotes this *beta testing* [1]. Interestingly enough, neither Walls et al. [2] or Gregor and Jones [8] mention that the components of principles should be tested but rather the whole prescriptive design theory where principles take part should be evaluated through either *testable hypotheses* [2] or *testable propositions* [8] (note the difference in nomenclature as a silent acknowledgment that not all design theories reside in the objective domain where hypotheses are possible).

Aim: Bunge [16] proposes the importance of technological rules being used to test the fit to domains as well as the laws they were derived from. Van Aken [1] acknowledges that technological rules can be motivated by producing *practice-oriented, middle-range theories* through *transferability* between domains. On the other hand, Gregor and Jones [8] both see aim of principles as the components of producing prescriptive design theory (adopted from Walls et al. [2] who do not use the term *principles*).

3   Methodology

In order to fulfil the research purpose of this study and to answer the proposed research question, we performed a literature review of past and present knowledge about design principles in DSR. Our performed literature review was undertaken through an 'author-centric' approach [17] in order to present a summary of the relevant literature on a topic. Consequently, the review process into three distinct steps: (i) search and identification of literature (e.g. journal articles, conference papers), (ii) selecting relevant literature, and (iii) analyzing the selected literature. We explain each of the steps as follows.

Identification: The first step of the review process emphasized a search and find activity. Here, we performed an initial search via Ebscohost, looking for papers that included design principles as their main contribution. Consequently, we used the concatenated search queries for papers proposing design principles as part of their abstract: 'ab "design principles" AND ("Information Systems" OR "Information Technology")'. The search returned 122 hits and included CAIS, JMIS, MISQ, ISJ, JAIS, ISR, EJIS and JIS. A similar query was made on JIT (journal's own library) and SIS (using Science Direct) with 25 hits and 12 hits respectively, making a total of 159 hits. Finally, we also drew on references from previous papers on design principles [e.g. 6, 8, 16] that already focused on finding design principles papers.

Selection: The second step of the review process focused a selection of 14 papers. We systematically emphasized papers that explicitly focused and mentioned design principles as their main research contribution. As a consequence, we excluded meta-papers, theoretical papers, papers about design guidelines, or papers that used design principles without contributing to design theory, DSR, or evaluation of artifacts.

Analysis: The third and final step of the review process included an analysis of the 13 selected papers. Here, we divided the analysis process between the two authors by coding a number of crucial aspects such as: explicating the design principles of each paper and highlighting how the authors of each paper propose the utility of their design principles (e.g. principles for practice, theory), deriving the abstraction level of the principles (e.g. principles for technology, domain), and more.

Throughout the analysis process, we specifically noted where conflicts of interpretation were present and used the conflicts as areas of problematization for the results. We are thus aware that some may prefer to resolve conflicts, whereas for this specific paper, we addressed conflicts as essential elements of the results. The criteria for each illustration of our framework in the findings were a weighting based on whether the conflicts were unique to each finding or general for several of them.

4 Results

No papers contributed with DPs on the formal level (strange but not entirely surprising), though 3 papers contributed to DPs on both domain level and technology level. 4 papers drew on both CAPs and PAPs, and one of the papers introduced the notion that the two types of DPs were interdependent. 2 papers were found to be potentially utilized by both researchers and practitioners. Of most interest was the concept of criteria as this contained the most papers that fell into more than one category. As a result, we had to distinguish between evaluating through theoretical grounding; 9 papers where DPs were derived from justificatory theory and discussed through the same, and evaluating through empirical grounding; also 9 papers that derived DPs from practice and/or evaluated them through practice. Another distinction of criteria was the aim. Here, 5 papers were found to have an explicit theoretical aim (contribution of DPs as components of a design theory), and 9 papers were found to have an explicit practical aim (contributing to practical knowledge or middle-range theory). Table 5 illustrates these findings. In the following sections, we reveal our findings of the analysis through a set of *propositions*.

Table 5. Using the framework to expose the DPs of articles into different streams

		References
Application level	**To domain**	[19–23]
	To technology	[24–29]
	To technology and domain	[30–32]
Principle types	**Concrete attributes**	[20, 21, 24, 26–28]
	Process actions	[19, 22, 23, 25]
	Interdependent	[29–32]
Utility	**To Research knowledge**	[21, 29]
	To Practical action	[19, 20, 22–24, 26–28, 30, 31]
	To Knowledge and action	[25, 32]
Criteria	**Evaluating through grounding**	[20–23, 25–27, 29, 31, 32]
	Evaluating empirically	[20, 24–28, 30–32]
	Theoretical Aim	[25–27, 29, 32]
	Practical Aim	[20–25, 28, 30–32]

4.1 Application Level Combination as Knowledge Potential

We found a rough, even split between domain (5 papers) and technology (6 papers) application, while 3 papers focused on both technology and domain. No principles were found to be applied to the formal level (most likely because of the contemporariness of the identified papers, since formal level design principles need to be utilized in many domains and through many technologies). The principles that focused specifically on the technology application levels were written as requirement specifications with close to testable hypothesis connected to it. One paper [28] had so specific requirements of the principles that they could be read almost down to an interaction scenario level:

"DP1: The user interface should provide a mechanism for customizing the vocabulary of terms used by the system in its communication to the user, the composition of business transactions, and the content of the system's informational output to match the practices of the organization." ([28], p. 195)

The detailed nature of the principle above reveals a highly detailed specification of how the artefact should act and what criteria should be evaluated against, and thus implicitly aids any designer or developer in developing the artefact. For example, Hustad and Olsen [19] propose 8 DPs that can be applied to teaching users about systems, in this context enterprise systems. Yet the application domain remains within user teaching as the DPs are so abstract that they could also be tested on other technologies and across domains. The wording of the principles shows how sticking to a single application level, and also abstracting principles, can reveal a high potential in further knowledge potential either across domains or to other specific technologies. Yang et al. [28] who propose 5 design principles for designing an integrated information platform for an emergency response system and hence focus on both applying principles from technology (integrated information platforms) and applying these to the domain of emergency response through both CAPs and PAPs. The principles reveal a large potential for further knowledge creation by further coupling the two application levels: how well can the CAPs integrate into other emergency response domains, and into which other technologies can PAPs be applied to?

4.2 Phrasing of Design Principles Influence the Design Principle Type

While the principle of DPs might seem straightforward, many areas remain unclear. Areas such as the specific phrasing of a principle based on which type of knowledge one wants to convey, the context of the principle as well as the application level. For the papers analyzed, this was represented through a somewhat unclear distinction between CAPs and PAPs (also mentioned previously).

Some principles were clearly CAPs and others were clearly PAPs but other principles could be interpreted in a way that either included or excluded actual actors, or actors acting on a system and somewhat implying a certain functionality. In other cases, such as the one we mentioned in the previous section in regards to [30], we found a huge potential for further inquiry that could lead to even more design principles to be named, somewhat hinting that the list of relevant DPs is still incomplete.

The finding can be condensed into two main areas: (i) the dialectically causal nature between certain kinds of CAPs and PAPs, and (ii) the inclusion of implicit or explicit actors. The first finding implied that certain PAPs had to be performed prior or after other CAPs, or that certain CAPs were a baseline for PAPs to even occur. The second finding implied that to categorize a DP one should look into whether the actor was the artefact or product itself or actions taken by or on human actors. Examples include Gregor et al. [22] who contribute a list of PAPs for finding sweet spot change strategies, yet implicitly focused on actions that some actor needs to or should perform:

"Principle 1: Identify and act on the sweet spot(s) - Undertake a thorough analysis to identify the primary underlying inhibitor(s) for a desired outcome and target the initial intervention activity to address and overcome the primary inhibitor(s)" ([22], p. 664).

The implicitly phrased DPs thus hold a high potential in identifying specific actors that, in finding a challenge in identifying change strategies, could work together or act on the problem.

Another example included the potential to identify further CAPs from PAPs by Markus et al. [25] who contribute with 5 DPs for designing systems that support emergent knowledge process. DP2 through DP5 are all explained as actions that should lead to specific functionality of the final system. In this sense, designers' actions precede the functionality of the system but in such and open way that the DPs can still not be used as either requirements, use cases or as actual testable propositions.

4.3 Knowledge Contribution Through Instantiation and Evaluation

The findings of the papers revealed that it is not always easy to explicitly identify a knowledge contribution of the principles themselves. Many of the papers showed that certain aspects of the principles were not entirely new, though the knowledge contribution came from the unique context that the principles resided in. Classical papers revealed how DPs were identified from literature, applied to an instantiation of an artefact and then evaluated and/or refined, showing the contribution as knowledge to practical application [22, 24, 26–30]. Other papers revealed a more theoretical proposal for DPs [19–21, 25].

For the latter referenced papers, DPs were identified or created based on meta-requirements, and then evaluated or inferred through literature. The following two vignettes illustrate the two mentioned issues further:

Two papers explicitly mentioned an intended *audience* for the DPs [22, 28] and greatly helped identify to *whom* the DPs can be targeted at. Identifying the target audience was not trivial, however, and heavily relied on interpreting the current state of the contribution. For example, Lee et al. [24] present 5 design principles (CAPs) proposed to be fundamental to achieve "Bright Internet", meaning the potential for a more secure and privacy-oriented use of the internet. The principles are derived from other theories across the formal domain of "internet security". The contribution is theoretical but could have the potential to be tested and evaluated through an artifact that supports the proposed "Bright Internet", hence showing evidence for the usefulness in practice and then grounded on the technological application level.

5 Concluding Remarks

In this paper, we contribute to DSR in IS with a framework for design principles that expose where potential and further design knowledge can be uncovered. We extend existing research on the matter by proposing a higher level framework than e.g. Cronholm and Göbel [9] (who primarily focused on structural aspects of the phrasings of DPs) that can be used to identify potential application levels that can be used to further the knowledge contribution and explain how to end up on DPs on a formal level. Similar to Chandra Kruse et al. [7], we also identified similar issues in regards to who the recipient of

DPs are. One additional contribution of our framework included the fact that the utility and criteria can sometimes be confused but can be important to distinguish; simply because a DP is meant for practical action does not mean that the aim of the DP in itself is a theoretical one. If a principle is purely evaluated through theory with no instantiation, the DP might still be useful for practice though can certainly have the potential to add to a theoretical knowledge base. We also have to acknowledge the essentiality of design principles as the factor that spans application domains, either in existing research or future research. It is interesting that design principles that reach the formal level will be easier applicable to practice through formal education (e.g. Gestalt Psychology that can be considered a cookbook within many design-oriented fields) than more nascently oriented DPs that still cling to their specificity of either domain or technology application level.

Our results also include criticism toward the content of principles as being a valid form of DSR contributions. However, our work delineates from establishing a heavy-handed criticism and instead withholds a central trademark of science and research in general, namely to question the current state of what the concept of design principles really means for making a theoretical and practical contribution to DSR. Through the development of the framework, we can identify a certain theoretical fuzziness initially that should be solved as theoretical problem areas.

For example, if one ontologically assumes that 'principles' as a term, is more abstract and spans different technologies or domains than for instance, 'guidelines', which implicitly infers a choice (e.g. a guideline is only valid after testing it to reality), then the implications for evaluating principles would be that principles should be evaluated 'upwards' (e.g. towards a universal claim or high-level theory), whereas a specific instantiation of guidelines should be evaluated 'downwards' (e.g. toward a practice by testing the guideline). In light of such line of argumentation, together with our findings, it can be necessary to suggest the following distinction: the target audience of design principles are first and foremost academics and researchers as the level of abstraction and general utility is oriented towards a higher type of contribution (e.g. design theory), whereas the target audience of design guidelines are first and foremost practitioners because practitioners follow guidelines that other practitioners create and propose based on a cumulative process of utility and evaluation of in situ artifacts that are created by professional designers and developers, not researchers.

The above is only one example of fleshing out entangled views on the concept of design principles, whereas in reality, we could problematize other aspects that concern the differentiation between principles and 'laws', 'procedures', and/or 'rules'. Finally, we argue that the DSR community would benefit from critical inquiries that questions the distinction between such interrelated concepts and differentiates their meaning by encompassing how they differ, what role or function do they have in a larger DSR project, and why principles are usually accepted as great outputs of rigorous DSR projects. Hence, we identify a need for further research on DPs and how they can be derived in the DSR process. As a help, we also propose that researchers should consider carefully the following questions when DPs are derived from the research process:

- *Q1: Which design principles have been used from other application levels?*
- *Q2: To which application level are the set of design principles applied?*

- **Q3:** *Wherein lies the potential if the set of design principles are applied to another application level?*
- **Q4:** *Assuming the principles belong to a single type; what would the complementary corresponding CAP or PAP be for each design principle proposed?*
- **Q5:** *Which actors will specifically have to perform the corresponding PAPs?*
- **Q6:** *How can design principles that are derived purely from theory be concretely instantiated into an artifact (e.g. with attributes or actions proposed by the principles)?*
- **Q7:** *How can design principles derived from an instantiated artefact be validated (e.g. to solve a similar specific or class of problems) by a 3rd party?*
- **Q8:** *How unique are the principles in isolation and how unique is the total set of principles?*

We also consider the formulated questions above as questions for further discussion and research, which could contribute to a genre theory as a possible solution area. As a genre, loosely structured design principle contributions could find both an ontological and epistemological linkage that assist practitioners and academics in producing and consuming DSR publications.

References

1. Van Aken, J.E.: Management research based on the paradigm of the design sciences: the quest for field-tested and grounded technological rules. J. Manag. Stud. **41**, 219–246 (2004)
2. Walls, J.G., Widmeyer, G.R., El Sawy, O.A.: Building an information system design theory for vigilant EIS. Inf. Syst. Res. **3**, 36–59 (1992)
3. Gregor, S.: The nature of theory in information systems of theory in information systems. MIS Q. **30**, 611–642 (2006)
4. Gregor, S., Hevner, A.R.: Positioning and presenting design science research for maximum impact. MIS Q. **37**, 337–355 (2013)
5. Sein, M.K., Henfridsson, O., Purao, S., Rossi, M., Lindgren, R.: Action design research. MIS Q. **35**, 37 (2011)
6. Peffers, K., Tuunanen, T., Rothenberger, M.A., Chatterjee, S.: A design science research methodology for information systems research. J. Manag. Inf. Syst. **24**, 45–77 (2007)
7. Chandra Kruse, L., Seidel, S., Purao, S.: Making *use* of design principles. In: Parsons, J., Tuunanen, T., Venable, J., Donnellan, B., Helfert, M., Kenneally, J. (eds.) DESRIST 2016. LNCS, vol. 9661, pp. 37–51. Springer, Cham (2016). https://doi.org/10.1007/978-3-319-39294-3_3
8. Gregor, S., Jones, D.: The anatomy of a design theory. J. Assoc. Inf. Syst. **8**, 312–335 (2007)
9. Cronholm, S., Göbel, H.: Guidelines supporting the formulation of design principles. In: 29th Australasian Conference on Information Systems, vol. 1, 1–11 (2018)
10. Simon, H.A., Herbert, A.: The Sciences of the Artificial. MIT Press (1969)
11. Hevner, A.R., March, S.T., Park, J., Ram, S.: Design science in information systems research. MIS Q. **28**, 75–105 (2004)
12. Bunge, M.: Technology as applied science. Technol. Cult. **7**, 329–347 (1966)
13. Codd, E.F.: A relational model of data for large shared data banks. Commun. ACM **13**, 377–387 (1970)
14. Wertheimer, M.: Untersuchungen zur Lehre von der Gestalt. Gestalt Theory. **39**, 79–89 (2017)
15. Ben, S., Catherine, P.: Designing the User Interface : Strategies for Effective Human-computer-Interaction. Addison Wesley, Longman (1998)

16. Bunge, M.: Scientific Research II - The Search for Truth. Springer, Heidelberg (1967). https://doi.org/10.1007/978-3-642-48138-3
17. Webster, J., Watson, R.T.: Analyzing the past to prepare for the future: writing a literature review. MIS Q. **26**, xiii–xxiii (2002)
18. Iivari, J., Hansen, M.R.P., Haj-Bolouri, A.: A framework for light reusability evaluation of design principles in design science research. In: 13th International Conference on Design Science Research and Information Systems and Technology: Designing for a Digital and Globalized World, pp. 1–15 (2018)
19. Hustad, E., Olsen, D.H.: Educating reflective enterprise systems practitioners: a design research study of the iterative building of a teaching framework. Inf. Syst. J. **24**, 445–473 (2014)
20. Kolkowska, E., Karlsson, F., Hedström, K.: Towards analysing the rationale of information security non-compliance: devising a value-based compliance analysis method. J. Strateg. Inf. Syst. **26**, 39–57 (2017)
21. Lee, J.K., Cho, D., Lim, G.G.: Design and validation of the bright internet. J. Assoc. Inf. Syst. **19**, 63–85 (2018)
22. Gregor, S., Imran, A., Turner, T.: A "sweet spot" change strategy for a least developed country: Leveraging e-Government in Bangladesh. Eur. J. Inf. Syst. **23**, 655–671 (2014)
23. Hanseth, O., Lyytinen, K.: Design theory for dynamic complexity in information infrastructures: the case of building internet. J. Inf. Technol. **25**, 1–19 (2010)
24. Lindgren, R., Henfridsson, O., Schultze, U.: Design principles for competence management systems: a synthesis of an action research study. MIS Q. **28**, 435–472 (2004)
25. Markus, M.L., Majchrzak, A., Gasser, L.: A design theory for systems that support emergent knowledge processes. MIS Q. **26**, 179–212 (2002)
26. Meth, H., Mueller, B., Maedche, A.: Designing a requirement mining system. J. Assoc. Inf. Syst. **16**, 799–837 (2015)
27. Germonprez, M., Hovorka, D., Collopy, F.: A theory of tailorable technology design. J. Assoc. Inf. Syst. **8**, 351–367 (2007)
28. Babaian, T., Xu, J., Lucas, W.: ERP prototype with built-in task and process support. Eur. J. Inf. Syst. **27**(2), 1–19 (2017)
29. Chaturvedi, A.R., Dolk, D.R., Drnevich, P.L.: Design principles for virtual worlds. MIS Q. Manag. Inf. Syst. **35**, 673–684 (2011)
30. Yang, L., Su, G., Yuan, H.: Design principles of integrated information platform for emergency responses: the case of 2008 Beijing olympic design principles of integrated information platform for emergency responses: the case of 2008 Beijing olympic games. Inf. Syst. Res. **23**, 761–786 (2012)
31. Spagnoletti, P., Resca, A., Sæbø, Ø.: Design for social media engagement: Insights from elderly care assistance. J. Strateg. Inf. Syst. **24**, 128–145 (2015)
32. Giessmann, A., Legner, C.: Designing business models for cloud platforms. Inf. Syst. J. **26**, 551–579 (2016)

The Origins of Design Principles: Where do… they all come from?

Sandeep Purao[1(✉)], Leona Chandra Kruse[2], and Alexander Maedche[3]

[1] Bentley University, Waltham, USA
spurao@bentley.edu
[2] University of Liechtenstein, Vaduz, Liechtenstein
leona.chandra@uni.li
[3] Karlsruhe Institute of Technology (KIT), Karlsruhe, Germany
alexander.maedche@kit.edu

Abstract. This essay reports the results of a reflective study to explore the question: *where do… design principles come from*? While a consensus is slowly emerging about the structure and content of design principles, the origins of design principles remain open to scholarly explorations and debates. Scholars have suggested, and speculated about several paths to identifying design principles, such as reflecting on the design efforts, looking to source theories, and even examining prior design products in an archaeological manner. We bring together these threads to develop a framework that consists of four dimensions, each an unsettled concern: (a) what can and should be the key influences on design principles, (b) when can and should design principles be generated, (c) who can and should identify design principles, and (d) how can and should design principles be documented? Two illustrative examples demonstrate how these dimensions may be used to identify, elaborate and defend the design principles as knowledge outcomes. We conclude by outlining some next steps for deeper, thoughtful investigations of the origins of design principles.

Keywords: Design principles · Origins · Design science research · Framework

1 Motivation

As scholars have continued to engage in design science research (DSR) [12], they have implicitly embraced the spirit of pragmatism [20], and accepted design principles as the predominant way to capture prescriptive knowledge about the design of information systems artifacts [28]. Following their status as a customary and *de facto* norm for documenting and sharing knowledge from a DSR effort, there is an emerging consensus about the content and structure of design principles [4, 15, 27]. Scholars have suggested that such 'design principles' [2] contain wisdom "…about creating other instances of artefacts that belong to the same class" [28]. However, some fundamental questions (about the nature and origins of knowledge in design principles) have remained. We explore one such question in this essay: *design principles: where do… they all come from?*

S. Hofmann et al. (Eds.): DESRIST 2020, LNCS 12388, pp. 183–194, 2020.
https://doi.org/10.1007/978-3-030-64823-7_17

Our question reflects deeper concerns about generating [6] and accumulating prescriptive design knowledge [4] from DSR efforts. These concerns have been the undercurrent of much scholarly work. Consider the following received schemas and wisdom about what constitutes design principles. Sein et al. [28] propose formalization of learning into design principles as part of an action design research approach, suggesting that they should be 'theory-ingrained.' Gregor et al. [16] borrow and extend ideas from the field of architecture to suggest that design principles can and should reflect form and function of the designed artifacts. In [13] design principles are suggested as a way to formalize knowledge gained from DSR efforts.

Precursors to these conceptualizations are ideas that have originated outside the DSR community. Bunge [5] describes technical knowledge and technological rules, and classifies design knowledge into substantive and operative theories. A substantive theory provides knowledge about objects, whereas an operative theory prescribes action. Van Aken [30] suggests a different term for these outcomes: technological rules to characterize products in management research that prescribe courses of action. Gibbons et al. [32] set forth another perspective on this mode of knowledge production, calling it Mode 2 knowledge, and point to the possibilities about how this recognition may reform established practices of scholars. They describe Mode 2 knowledge as problem-based trans-disciplinary knowledge that is heterogeneous, hierarchical, transient, more socially accountable, and reflexive (in contrast to Mode 1 knowledge, which represents traditional scientific knowledge inspired by the Newtonian model). These ideas emphasize how scholars beyond the DSR community have grappled with understanding and representing this new knowledge form that the DSR community calls design principles.

The clearest exposition may be attributed to [27] who mapped design research as ideal-typical mode of research and further developed the idea of knowledge outcomes. They succinctly describe these as design propositions: "in Situation S, to achieve Outcome O, perform Action A." Prior work [10] has built on these precursors to summarize different types of outcomes and knowledge contributions that DSR scholars emphasize. In spite of such efforts, that acknowledge the importance of clarifying such knowledge outcomes, it remains difficult to understand "how to get there." Broad methodological mandates (e.g. [28]) rarely go beyond suggesting reflection, and scholarly debates, while they describe what the design principles may contain [15], do not clearly identify the space of possibilities for discovering and articulating the design principles. Without such guidance, we describe the challenge for DSR scholars in the words of two master songwriters: "*where do … they all come from?*" We hope to provide a first approximation of the key dimensions that define the space of possibilities for discovering design principles, drawing on and extending much prior research.

We proceed as follows. In Sect. 2, we develop a framework defined by four key interrogatives. Section 3 showcases illustrative examples to show how the framework may be used by researchers to make decisions about, and reflect on their decisions to discover design principles. Section 4 provides concluding remarks and points to next steps to guide the investigation.

2   Key Dimensions

To explore the question – *where do ... they all come from* – we followed a reflective research approach, treating the design principles as an abstract artifact produced by the DSR scholars. The inputs to our reflective research approach included: (a) a review of work that we have briefly summarized above, (b) an examination of research results published in recent proceedings of the DESRIST conference, and (c) ongoing conversations with scholars within the DSR community who described what we realized may be seen as potentially incompatible approaches to the generation of design principles. Therefore, we do not claim that our effort is driven by a singular or overarching theoretical perspective that may allow us to "derive" the different dimensions. Instead, it is the outcome of reflections that combine knowledge gleaned from the multiple sources we point to above. For example, the review of prior work (source 'a' above) clearly pointed to possibilities for different influences on discovering design principles; the examination of work in proceedings of the design science conference (source 'b' above) revealed clear differences in how different researchers viewed the role of design principles in designs science efforts; and the conversations with scholars in the design science community (source 'c' above) provided insights into how it may be necessary to acknowledge and integrate multiple paths to discovery of design principles. We describe the four dimensions that define our framework as key interrogatives that can define the space for the discovery and generation of design principles. The interrogatives are intended to be inclusive of the set of possibilities. However, we do not yet claim to be comprehensive, i.e., the interrogatives we suggest may not be all-encompassing. With this description and caveats, we turn to the four dimensions. Each is described as an interrogative, and elaborated by drawing on the sources above.

Dimension 1: Influences

- We begin with the first dimension, expressed as the interrogative: *what can and should be the key influences on design principles?*

   This interrogative is not about the content of design principles. Instead, it asks us to think about what a DSR scholar may and should consider as inspiration for and/or inputs to the discovery and generation of design principles.

- One source of influence is prior theories (described elsewhere as kernel theories [31]), and acknowledged by DSR scholars as necessary with the phrase "theory-inspired design principles" [28]. These are necessary also because they can provide the justificatory grounding [14, 23].
- Another source that can provide inspiration for the discovery of design principles would be the design effort by the research team, acknowledged in prior work as the need for reflection and formalizing [28]. In essence, engaging in the design effort allows the research team to capture not only what worked, but also what did not work (the so-called blind alleys in a design process).
- A third, somewhat obvious, influence would be the outcome of the design efforts, such as an instantiated artifact [25], along with the features and capabilities of the artifact.

The newly designed IT artifact (and any associated work practices) would be tangible results that future designers may seek. The design researchers may, therefore, look to these as inspiration for the discovery of design principles.

- A final, sometimes overlooked input is likely to be results from formative and summative evaluation as discussed by [4] as essential for design science research. The design researchers may use these results to emphasize those elements from the research effort that have produced the desired outcomes.

It is tempting to categorize these influences (e.g. internal vs. external, or theory-based vs. design-based or in some other manner, for example, following the genres suggested by [1]). We have, instead, favored the enumeration strategy because it allows a more specific examination of the pros and cons for each of these influences, and allows room for dialog. For example, if the research team were to consider only prior theories as the influences on design principles (e.g. [22]), it is possible that they may risk the criticism that the design efforts are merely application of prior research (and therefore, akin to consulting). If the research team argues that only design efforts should be considered as the influence on the design principles, then they face the risk that the work will be described as atheoretical tinkering. On the other hand, if the research team does not consider the influence of research efforts, the design principles may adequately acknowledge or convey the difficulties in moving from the problem space to the solution space. Next, if the research team does not consider evaluation results as part of the effort to formulate the design principles, then their proposals for design principles may be perceived as a version of "trust me" [33]. However, if the research team only describes and relies on practitioner and user inputs to justify the design principles, then they may be criticized for "not asking the why question." This brief contemplation points to the overwhelming sense that these influences and inspirations should not be seen as mutually exclusive. Instead, they represent a multiplicity of opportunities to discover the design principles, which may require iterations to explore each source individually and with one another.

Dimension 2: Temporality

- The second dimension can be expressed as the interrogative: *when can and should design principles be generated?*

This interrogative encourages the research team to consider several alternatives, some that may be closer to the norms that are part of the contemporary practice for conducting design science research, and others that may challenge these norms.

- First, we note that some methodological prescriptions for DSR [33] and action design research (ADR) [28] suggest that the research team should engage in the discovery of design principles as part of their design-evaluate iterations [33] and build-intervene-evaluate (BIE) cycles [28].
- Next, methodological guidance also points to a separate learning and reflection stage [28] that emphasizes the need for considerable refinement and formalization of design principles during this separate stage. The methodological prescriptions do not preclude

both – the derivation of tentative design principles throughout the design research process, and then, the refinement during the final reflection stage with the advantage of hindsight.

- A third possibility as illustrated in [9] and [29] is to formulate the design principles before implementing the artifact. This approach corresponds to what Iivari calls Strategy 1 in DSR [19]. We note the likely overlap between this possibility and the reliance on only one of the many sources (prior theories) we identified as part of the previous dimension.

- A fourth, potentially interesting position may be to consider discovery of design principles after deployment of the artifact. This may be a possibility in projects that follow the ADR [28] approach because of the pre-established working relationship with industry partners.

- A final possibility is one that is put forward by [8], who go beyond the tight coupling between the time for conducting the DSR effort, and the generation of design principles. They suggest returning to influential and/or successful IT artifacts from the past (whether or not they were part of a DSR project) for the purpose of generating design principles (see, e.g. [17]).

The alternatives enumerated above can be examined for appropriateness and effectiveness in a variety of ways. For example, some scholars may argue that reserving the effort needed to generate design principles for the end of the research process would provide the research team the time necessary for careful reflection. Others may argue that doing so only at end of research cycle will mean that the researchers will miss the opportunity for refinement. Researchers engaged in DSR efforts may agree that the design efforts often tend to be time and effort-intensive, and careful reflection may need to wait. However, if the design principles are not outlined (at least in a rudimentary form) during the design-evaluate or BIE cycles, the opportunities to iterate and refine, and incorporate practitioner viewpoints may be missed (see, e.g. [24]). The option to reflect and generate the design principles 'post-deployment' may not be available for all research projects. However, if available, exercising this option may provide the DSR scholars with new ideas about what the deployment effort may reveal, beyond a proof-of-concept. The final alternative aimed at generating design principles from past influential and/or successful IT artifacts following an archaeological approach may present valuable opportunities for design science because it may allow them to build a body of knowledge from these successful efforts [17]. However, this option may be critiqued because it will limit the ability to capture the design principles during the design effort and instead, force the researchers to rely only on the artifact and its use. In the absence of a window into the underlying design processes, the effort to capture design principles may face the iceberg effect [18], where only the tip of the efforts and features may be visible to the researchers who visit the artifact, with significant details and efforts hidden from the view.

Dimension 3: Actors

- This dimension can be expressed as the interrogative that asks the researchers to carefully consider: *who can and should identify design principles?*

This interrogative is aimed at considering the different actors who may be involved in the generation of design principles. These may be different actors involved in the DSR efforts, with the word 'artiste' indicating the need to consider the unstructured, craft component necessary in this effort.

- One straightforward response to this interrogative may be that it is the researchers engaged in the DSR effort who would be responsible for and in the best position for identifying and articulating design principles. Methodological prescriptions [28] implicitly grant this role to the DSR team.
- However, such a response may negate the possibility for incorporating inputs from users or practitioners who may provide valuable insights. Consider, for example, an IT artifact that addresses a concern related to healthcare delivery [35] or one that is related to sustainability and climate change [29]. In such cases, it may be critical to collaborate with relevant stakeholders (e.g., physicians, nurses, and employees involved in a sustainability initiative) for the discovery of design principles, to ensure that they acknowledge the domain knowledge.
- A third possibility may be to either expand the research team to include new academic partners, or even hand over the responsibility for articulating the design principles to an entirely new team of scholars.

The accepted norm within the DSR community suggests that the specific task of generating design principles is often taken on by the DSR team [3], sometimes, with the addition of new actors added to the research team [24]. The clear advantage for the research team itself to engage in the derivation of design principles is that members of the team are intimately familiar with the research, and therefore, in the best position to discover the design principles. On the other hand, it may be argued the research team may be 'too close to the effort,' and therefore, may not be best placed to engage in the reflection necessary for identifying design principles. The addition of new partners to the research team (new DSR scholars and/or domain experts) may help with this concern. The addition of new scholars familiar with prior theories may be of value in the task of generating design principles. A logical extreme for this position (handing over this responsibility to a new research team) may, however, present some difficulties. It is likely that such hand-over will promote greater reflection. However, the lack of context and not having access to lessons learned during the DSR effort may result in design principles that may be more rigorously connected to prior theory but less grounded in the design effort. These opportunities and concerns may also apply if an archaeological approach is used to generating design principles from past IT artifacts (owing to the iceberg effect mentioned earlier), even though the approach also advocates collecting hindsights from the designers who built the artifacts [7].

Dimension 4: Content

- The final dimension can be expressed as the interrogative: *how can and should design principles be documented?*

This concern has been the topic of much exploration within the DSR community as well as in other disciplines, perhaps because it deals with ideas of content and structure and therefore, more stable (as a result, more directly amenable to scientific inquiry). The content of design principles reflects "what should be articulated in a design principle," and the container refers to "how it should be packaged."

- One dominant alternative here is the formulation by [27] that we have described earlier, copied here for ease of reference: "in [situation] S, to achieve [outcome] O, perform [Action] A."
- Another possibility is to follow the distinction that is suggested in [13]: form vs. function. Here, it is described how the content of design principles may focus on either the structure (form) of the artifact or the capabilities (function) of the artifact.
- We note that a more common format of design principles has, however, been simple assertions, where the DSR team provides a simple articulation without placing these design principles in different categories.
- Elsewhere, more elaborate structures have been proposed for different kinds of design principles [6] such as materiality-oriented and action-oriented design principles.
- A more recent work includes a schema that captures the anatomy of a design principle [15]. It suggests: "For Implementer I to achieve or allow Aim A for User U in Context C employ Mechanisms M1, M2, M3.... involving Enactors E1, E2, E3,... because of Rationale R".

These options may orient a DSR team to consider different possibilities for articulating design principles. It is possible that a simple and straightforward criterion for the DSR team may be easier to follow. A more nuanced and detailed representation of design principles would require greater effort from the DSR team. It may also add a level of specificity that makes the actual use of design principles more challenging for practitioners. On the other hand, it may provide the DSR community a more precise articulation of knowledge gleaned from the DSR effort, and therefore, greater opportunities for accumulation of knowledge across projects. This may explain why a number of DSR projects still continue to articulate the design principles as a simple set of assertions without any of the structures that have been suggested by [6, 13, 27] or others. Figure 1 summarizes the four dimensions.

We emphasize that these four dimensions are not intended to be comprehensive. As described earlier, our work has followed a reflective research approach drawing on (a) prior work related to design science research, (b) outcomes from design science research published in design science conferences, and (c) ongoing conversations with scholars in the design science community. We add that the dimensions may not be seen as independent. A decision along one of the dimensions may suggest appropriate possibilities or constraints for another dimension. As an example, the decision to expand the research team by adding new researchers for the purpose of identifying design principles *may* lead to acknowledging a greater influence of prior theories on the generation of design principles. We turn next to two illustrations.

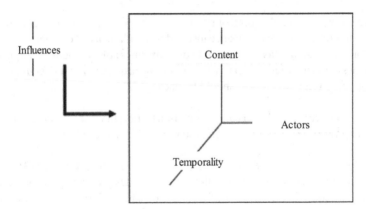

Fig. 1. The four dimensions

3   Illustrative Examples

To illustrate the potential of the dimensions proposed, we refer to two recently published papers in the Design Science conference that describe DSR projects, and present design principles derived from the DSR efforts.

The first describes a DSR project to design conversational agents for energy feedback [11]. The starting point for the effort was prior empirical studies that have shown that providing feedback can encourage consumers to use energy more sustainably. With this starting point, the DSR effort investigated how conversational agents (such as chatbots) can be designed for energy feedback with a natural and intuitive interface. The paper presented design principles based on existing literature, instantiated these in a text-based conversational agent and evaluated in a focus group session with industry experts (Table 1).

Table 1.   Example 1 - energy feedback with conversational agents

Category	Description
Project	Design energy feedback with conversational agents
Artifact	Conversational Agent
Evaluation	Focus group evaluation with practitioners
Prior Theories	Feedback theory
Stakeholders	Consumers, Utility service provider

The second illustration highlights a DSR study that was aimed at supporting organizational sensemaking as part of sustainability transformation [29]. The researchers did so by developing design principles for a sensemaking support platform and refining them in three iteration rounds. Table 2 summarizes the general information about this study.

Table 2. Example 2 – supporting sensemaking for organizational transformation

Category	Description
Project	Supporting organizational sensemaking in sustainability transformation
Artifact	A sensemaking support systems
Evaluation	Focus group evaluation with stakeholders, analyzing log data
Prior Theories	Sensemaking, the role of IS in sensemaking, affordance,
Stakeholders	Every organization member

Table 3. Using the dimensions for example 1

Dimension	Application
Influences	The design principles *followed tenets of feedback theory*, and how these could be used for the specific domain: feedback about energy use
Temporality	Initial, tentative versions of design principles were formulated *before design*, they guided the design and research activities, and were *revised*
Actors	Junior researchers within *the research team* formulated initial versions, which were then refined by more experienced researchers. Final versions were *tested with representatives from an industry partner*
Content	*The format* proposed by [Chandra et al. 2015] was used as a skeleton to articulate the design principles. The design principles were subjected to informal evaluation via focus groups with the stakeholders

Table 4. Using the dimensions for example 2

Dimension	Application
Influences	Initial design principles were formulated based on *kernel theories* of sensemaking process. The final versions were influenced through *iteration* and evaluation
Temporality	Initial design principles *before design and implementation*. The DSR team kept *refining* those principles during design, implementation, and evaluation
Actors	*The research team* formulated the initial design principles. The final set of design principles resulted from several evaluations and iterations that *involved stakeholders*
Content	*A specific format* [Chandra et al. 2015] was followed to describe both user activities and the key functionalities of the sensemaking support platform

We explore how each interrogative dimension can be used to understand how the research team identified design principles from the DSR efforts (Tables 3 and 4).

The examples illustrate how the dimensions we have outlined may be used to understand and appreciate the choices that the research team would make for identification of design principles.

4 Next Steps

The question we have explored in this paper is a difficult one – partly because most of us may believe we already know the answer, and partly because it is difficult to peel back the layers of uncertainty that researchers face. Although some prior work such as [15] has tackled design principles in depth, and others have identified different genres (e.g. [1]), it has been difficult to chart out the terrain in a pragmatic manner so that the alternatives that design science researchers face can be laid bare. The emerging consensus is providing some guidance about the structure of design principles [15], but empirical studies about the use of design principles continue to point to new puzzles [7]. An exercise to explore the origins of design principles cannot, therefore, be merely driven from a theoretical perspective. It must respond to the challenges that design science researchers face as they engage in DSR efforts. What makes these challenges especially complex is that the concerns are often resolved by the researchers within the specific research context, but the researchers find it difficult to articulate a general version of the concerns. This is precisely our effort with the dimensions and the interrogatives. Our effort is, therefore, to consciously avoid starting with concepts such as affordances or materiality (see discussion in [6]) and map these towards possible operationalizations. Instead, we have attempted an approach that starts with the simple interrogatives, the questions that the design science researchers face, in a bottom-up approach that respects the pragmatic starting points that the DSR community has adopted. When a DSR team engages in a design science project, the immediate challenges are rarely about generating design principles (see, e.g. [21]). Although the team acknowledges the need to extract and articulate design principles as a way of generating knowledge, the immediate challenges are often about choice of technology layers, dealing with external stakeholders, obtaining and managing the resources needed for research conduct. As the research team addresses these challenges, it is important to be aware of dimensions that they should consider so that the eventual knowledge outcomes – design principles – can be discovered, captured, articulated and defended. The interrogatives we have suggested can provide these starting points.

Our effort has been to explore the origins of design principles. To paraphrase the words of two master songwriters[1], we have posed the question: "all the lonely Design Principles – where do they all come from? all the lonely Design Principles – where do they all belong?" This, in turn, has allowed us follow a reflective research approach and identify four dimensions that define key decisions that the research team may make to obtain these answers. The dimensions we have identified point to several configurations. We note that these dimensions are meant as a guideline and should not be followed blindly so as to restrict future work. The paper identifies and describes these four dimensions, which a DSR team may use to reflect on possible configurations. By examining these,

---

[1] These are lines from the song Eleanor Rigby, in the Album Revolver, lyricists: John Lennon and Paul McCartney.

a DSR team would then be able to identify and/or evaluate the options for discovery of design principles. There are considerations that the design science researcher may use, such as the maturity of the project [13], progression towards a meso-level theory [34], whether the project fits a particular quadrant (e.g. exaptation) suggested by [13], and others. Exploring these possibilities remains on our future agenda.

References

1. Baskerville, R.L., Myers, M.D.: Design ethnography in information systems. Inf. Syst. J. **25**, 23–46 (2015)
2. Baskerville, R., Pries-Heje, J.: Explanatory design theory. Bus. Inf. Syst. Eng. **5**, 271–282 (2010)
3. Blaschke, M., Riss, U., Haki, K., Aier, S.: Design principles for digital value co-creation networks: a service-dominant logic perspective. Electron. Markets **29**(3), 443–472 (2019). https://doi.org/10.1007/s12525-019-00356-9
4. vom Brocke, J., Winter, R., Hevner, A., Maedche, A.: Accumulation and evolution of design knowledge in design science research – a journey through time and space. Assoc. Inf. Syst. (2020)
5. Bunge, M.: Scientific Research II: The Search for Truth. Studies in the Foundations Methodology and Philosophy of Science. vol. 3/II. Springer, New York (1967)
6. Chandra, L., Seidel, S., Gregor, S.: Prescriptive knowledge in IS research: conceptualizing design principles in terms of materiality, action, and boundary conditions. In: 48th Hawaii International Conference on System Sciences, pp. 4039–4048 (2015)
7. Chandra Kruse, L., Seidel, S., Purao, S.: Making *Use* of Design Principles. In: Parsons, J., Tuunanen, T., Venable, J., Donnellan, B., Helfert, M., Kenneally, J. (eds.) DESRIST 2016. LNCS, vol. 9661, pp. 37–51. Springer, Cham (2016). https://doi.org/10.1007/978-3-319-392 94-3_3
8. Chandra Kruse, L., Seidel, S., vom Brocke, J.: Design archaeology: generating design knowledge from real-world artifact design. In: Tulu, B., Djamasbi, S., Leroy, G. (eds.) DESRIST 2019. LNCS, vol. 11491, pp. 32–45. Springer, Cham (2019). https://doi.org/10.1007/978-3-030-19504-5_3
9. Chanson, M., Bogner, A., Bilgeri, D., Fleisch, E., Wortmann, F.: Blockchain for the IoT: privacy-preserving protection of sensor data. J. Assoc. Inf. Syst. **20**(9), 1274–1309 (2019)
10. Dwivedi, N., Purao, S., Straub, Detmar W.: Knowledge contributions in design science research: a meta-analysis. In: Tremblay, M.C., VanderMeer, D., Rothenberger, M., Gupta, A., Yoon, V. (eds.) DESRIST 2014. LNCS, vol. 8463, pp. 115–131. Springer, Cham (2014). https://doi.org/10.1007/978-3-319-06701-8_8
11. Gnewuch, U., Morana, S., Heckmann, C., Maedche, A.: Designing conversational agents for energy feedback. In: Chatterjee, S., Dutta, K., Sundarraj, Rangaraja P. (eds.) DESRIST 2018. LNCS, vol. 10844, pp. 18–33. Springer, Cham (2018). https://doi.org/10.1007/978-3-319-91800-6_2
12. Goes, P.B.: Design science research in top information systems journals. MIS Q. **38**(1), iii–viii (2014)
13. Gregor, S., Hevner, A.R.: Positioning and presenting design science research for maximum impact. MIS Q. **37**, 337–355 (2013)
14. Gregor, S., Jones, D.: The anatomy of a design theory. J. Assoc. Inf. Syst. **8**, 313–335 (2007)
15. Gregor, S., Chandra Kruse, L., Seidel, S.: The anatomy of a design principle. J. Assoc. Inf. Syst. (2020)

16. Gregor, S., Müller, O., Seidel, S.: Reflection, abstraction and theorizing in design and development research. In: Proceedings of the European Conference on Information Systems, Milan (2013)
17. Hanseth, O., Lyytinen, K.: Design theory for dynamic complexity in information infrastructures: the case of building internet. J. Inf. Tech. **25**(1), 1–19 (2010)
18. Herskovic, V., Ochoa, S.F., Pino, J.A., Neyem, H.A.: The iceberg effect: behind the user interface of mobile collaborative systems. J. UCS **17**(2), 183–201 (2011)
19. Iivari, J.: Distinguishing and contrasting two strategies for design science research. Eur. J. Inf. Syst. **24**(1), 107–115 (2015)
20. James, W.: Pragmatism: a new name for some old ways of thinking (1907). https://en.wikisource.org/wiki/Pragmatism:_A_New_Name_for_Some_Old_Ways_of_Thinking
21. Janiesch, C., Rosenkranz, C., Scholten, U.: An information systems design theory for service network effects. J. Assoc. Inf. Syst. (2019)
22. Johnson, J.: Designing with the Mind in Mind: Simple Guide to Understanding User Interface Design Guidelines. Elsevier, Boston (2013)
23. Lidwell, W., Holden, K., Butler, J.: Universal principles of design, revised and updated: 125 ways to enhance usability, influence perception, increase appeal, make better design decisions, and teach through design. Rockport Pub. (2010)
24. Lukyanenko, R., Parsons, J., Wiersma, Y., Wachinger, G., Huber, B., Meldt, R.: Representing crowd knowledge: guidelines for conceptual modeling of user-generated content. J. Assoc. Inf. Syst. **18**(4), 2 (2017)
25. March, S.T., Smith, G.F.: Design and natural science research on information technology. DSS **15**, 251–266 (1995)
26. Peffers, K., Tuunanen, T., Rothenberger, M., Chatterjee, S.: A design science research methodology for information systems research. J. Manage. Inf. Syst. **24**(3), 45–77 (2008)
27. Romme, A.G.L., Endenburg, G.: Construction principles and design rules in the case of circular design. Org. Sc. **17**, 287–297 (2006)
28. Sein, M.K., Henfridsson, O., Purao, S., Rossi, M., Lindgren, R.: Action design research. MIS Q. **35**, 37–56 (2011)
29. Seidel, S., Chandra Kruse, L., Székely, N., Gau, M., Stieger, D.: Design principles for sensemaking support systems in environmental sustainability transformations. Eur. J. Inf. Syst. **27**(2), 221–247 (2018)
30. Van Aken, J.E.V.: Management research based on the paradigm of the design sciences: the quest for field-tested and grounded technological rules. J. M. Stud. **41**(2), 219–246 (2004)
31. Walls, J.G., Widmeyer, G.R., El Sawy, O.A.: Building an information system design theory for vigilant EIS. Inf. Syst. Res. **3**, 36–59 (1992)
32. Gibbons, M., Limoges, C., Nowotny, H., Schwartzman, S., Scott, P., Trow, M. The new production of knowledge: The dynamics of science and research in contemporary societies. Sage Publications, Inc. (1994)
33. Hevner, A.R., March, S.T., Park, J., Ram, S.: Design science in information systems research. MIS Q. **28**(1), 75–106 (2004)
34. Kuechler, B., Vaishnavi, V.: On theory development in design science research: anatomy of a research project. Eur. J. Inf. Syst. **17**(5), 489–504 (2008)
35. Gaudioso, C., Jain, H., Purao, S.: A patient-centered CDSS for cancer treatment decisions. Paper presented at the Pre-ICIS Workshop on Information Technologies and Systems, Dublin (2016)

Developing Design Principles for Digital Platforms: An Agent-Based Modeling Approach
Research-in-Progress

Marius Schmid[(✉)], Kazem Haki, Stephan Aier, and Robert Winter

Institute of Information Management, University of St. Gallen, St. Gallen, Switzerland
{marius.schmid,kazem.haki,stephan.aier,robert.winter}@unisg.ch

Abstract. In the context of digital platforms, platform owners strive to maximize both their platform's stability and generativity. This is complicated by the paradoxical relationship of generativity and stability, as well as associated tensions. To aid B2B platform owners in their design decisions, we aim to derive specific design principles that address the inherent tensions such that generativity and stability are maximized simultaneously. This requires a better understanding of when and to which extent a platform's generativity and stability are paradoxical, and under which circumstances they can be maximized simultaneously. Thus, we first develop an agent-based simulation model to analyze the effects of an exemplary design decision regarding a tension (i.e. control vs. openness) on a platform's generativity and stability. The developed simulation model enables predictive analyses of varying degrees of control and openness and their effect on generativity and stability. The simulation model must be further refined and applied to other tensions to thoroughly understand the impact of design decisions on a platform's generativity and stability, and ultimately derive design principles.

Keywords: Digital platforms · Complex adaptive systems · Agent-based modeling · Design principles

1 Introduction

Despite an increasing research focus on digital platforms, the understanding of reasons for success versus failure remains limited [1]. It is clear, however, that digital platforms must ensure both generativity and stability to survive and prosper [2]. We consider generativity as leveraging external resources to satisfy evolving end-user demands [3], and stability as the ability to yield long-term returns to be financially viable [2]. Attaining both outcomes simultaneously is challenging as they are paradoxical [2], resulting from numerous underlying tensions, like aligning individual and collective incentives [2, 4]. Optimizing generativity and stability thus primarily requires handling such tensions [2]. We aim to support platform owners in the B2B context by deriving design principles [5] to manage tensions in a way that optimizes a digital platform's stability and generativity. Following the first steps of the design science research (DSR) method [6], we present an agent-based simulation model as a preliminary artifact with which we can investigate

© Springer Nature Switzerland AG 2020
S. Hofmann et al. (Eds.): DESRIST 2020, LNCS 12388, pp. 195–201, 2020.
https://doi.org/10.1007/978-3-030-64823-7_18

platform-related tensions and their effects on a platform's generativity and stability. This allows us to better understand how to optimize both outcome variables and thereby paves the way for deriving design principles.

2 Research Background

2.1 Digital Platforms

We consider digital platforms as the central building block that provides the technological foundation for other firms to engage and develop complements [4]. Value creation expands across the boundaries of a single firm, as platform owners, partners, and end users form an ecosystem of loosely coupled actors [3]. The platform itself then evolves as a result of interactions between these heterogenous actors with unforeseen outcomes [2, 7]. Ultimately, it must generate sufficient external innovation to satisfy evolving end-user needs [3, 8], whilst remaining financially sustainable and economically viable, so achieve a balance of generativity and stability [2]. Attaining this requires an alignment of individual and platform-wide incentives and objectives [2, 4], so yields tensions [9], as every actor in the ecosystem primarily pursues their own interests [2].

A central tension for platform owners is that of control vs. openness [9–11]. In the B2B context for example, where owners, partners, and end users are firms, a platform owner like SAP must decide how much of its core resources to share with partners and how much freedom partners have to collaborate and develop solutions for customers [12]. Essentially, owners decide how far to ease "restrictions on the use, development, and commercialization of platform technologies" [10] (p. 1851), so define the degree of openness. Literature in the B2C context suggests that more openness can foster platform innovation [10], but also increases vulnerability [11]. Boudreau [10], even finds an inverted-U relationship between openness and the development rates of complements. We argue that the degree of openness is not only decisive for a platform's generativity, but also its financial stability. Thus, we extend existing research [10] by considering both generativity *and* stability of digital platforms, as well as the B2B context. For this analysis, we employ complex adaptive systems (CAS) theory as a kernel theory that enables us to capture the components and mechanisms of complex systems.

2.2 Complex Adaptive Systems

CAS are open, non-linear dynamic systems that adapt and evolve in the process of interacting with their environment [13]. Effectively, actors in such complex systems adapt their behavior through interactions with one another and the environment, bringing about the emergent properties of the system as a whole that impedes accurate predictions regarding the outcomes of said interactions [13, 14]. Interactions at the local level thus create a system with non-linear characteristics at the global level [14]. More precisely, CAS comprise agents (as representatives of a system's actors), interactions, and the environment [15]. Agents attempt to survive in their environment by converting the information obtained into action that will improve their chances of survival, depending on both their own attributes and the defined behavioral rules [14, 15].

In the context of digital platforms, heterogenous actors like partners join and produce unforeseen outcomes as a result of their interactions [2, 7] in an increasingly complex environment [1]. As is indicative of CAS, interactions among a platform's actors (at the local level) shape the development and delineate the properties of the platform as a whole (at the global level), producing unpredictable outcomes. Chains and cycles of digital platform-related tensions [9] reveal interdependencies and nonlinearity that are also symptomatic of CAS [13, 15]. In this study, we posit that anticipating the emergent outcomes of digital platforms as complex adaptive systems may be feasible with the assistance of a theoretically grounded simulation model as it enables us catering predictive analyses [14]. Thus, we opt for simulation to develop an agent-based simulation model as a foundational artifact that enables an analysis of design decisions' implications and thereby create a basis for deriving design principles for digital platforms.

3 Methodology

To generate this foundational model, we adhere to design science research (DSR) as a research method (see Table 1). DSR has an established history in the context of IS research and revolves around creating IT-related artifacts [16], but also knowledge in the form of design principles [17, 18]. It suits our context because the study ultimately centers around generating such design principles for digital platforms to maximize their stability and generativity, and thus utility [16]. Currently, we are at the first step of designing a simulation model for an exemplary tension.

Table 1. Methodology for developing digital platform design principles

Activity [6]	Implementation
Problem: "Define the specific research problem and justify the value of a solution" (p. 52)	Digital platform owners must deal with several design decisions to balance the interests of a plethora of actors (i.e. tensions) to reach the desired generativity and stability in their platforms
Requirements: "Infer objectives of a solution and knowledge of what is possible and feasible" (p. 55)	The requirements for the design principles are specified based on [5] and the insights into the relation between stability and generativity
Design: "Create the artifact" (p. 55)	The derived design principles shall be presented in the structure proposed by [5]
Demonstration: "Demonstrate the use of the artifact to solve one or more instances of the problem" (p. 55)	The derived design principles shall be compared to success and failure cases using the case survey method [19] to demonstrate their utility
Evaluation: "Observe and measure how well the artifact supports a solution to the problem" (p. 56)	The derived design principles shall be evaluated based on the results of the case survey

4 Development of the Simulation Model

Informed by CAS theory and proven simulation models [14, 20], the agent-based model of a B2B platform ecosystem is developed (using NetLogo software). In such ecosystems, core actors are the platform's owner, partners, and end users [21], which thus are considered as agents of the CAS with attributes and behavioral rules (see Table 2).

After creating the simulation model of a digital platform ecosystem, it was internally validated and verified following [14, 22] and employed to analyze the effects of varying degrees of openness (from entirely open to entirely closed as a proxy of tension) on a platform's stability and generativity. The output variable generativity is operationalized as the ratio of executed opportunities vs. all opportunities this digital platform was exposed to [14], to account for the necessity to satisfy evolving end-user needs [2, 3, 8]. Stability is calculated as the sum of payoffs received by partners in the ecosystem divided by the sum of costs incurred from building and maintaining digital services [14], representing a digital platform's economic viability [2]. Leaning on a proven model [20], 50 simulation runs were conducted for every level (550 runs in total), each comprising

Table 2. Simulation model design

Conceptual design	Operational design	Literature reference
Partners combine their heterogenous resources with those of the owner to develop complements, i.e. digital services; the owner thus leverages a community of partners that develop unforeseeable outcomes and defines the degree of openness	Digital services are feature sets with 20-element vectors of 0s, 1s, and ?s (e.g. [0 1 0 0 1 ? 1 0 0 1 ? ? 1 1 0 0 1 1 1 0]), where the first 10 digits represent a partner's resources, the second 10 digits represent the technological codebase provided by the owner, and ?s represent the freedom to improvise (realized as either 1 or 0 with equal probability) or the degree of openness	[4, 7, 10, 12, 14, 15, 20, 21]
End users are represented by their demands in form of opportunities that arise in the environment of the ecosystem	Opportunities are represented by patches in the environment that have feature sets with 20-element vectors and are updated continuously	[1, 3, 20]
Partners interact amongst each other and with their digital services to share information; some partners have more connections than others	Partners can access each other's feature sets to communicate; the number of initial and maximum partner-partner connections are defined by respective parameters	[3, 12, 14]
As learning and utility-based agents, partners execute opportunities by using or building digital services to receive payoffs and maximize their utility; they can use their own or connected partners' digital services	If there are enough matches between a digital service and an opportunity, partners will execute the opportunity and receive the associated payoff; if no matching service is available in the network, partners will build a new digital service if most of their past opportunities could have been executed with a service that has the exact features of the current opportunity	[2, 8, 14, 15]
Building digital services extends the technological core resources of the digital platform, reflecting an adaptation to evolving end-user needs	The initial feature set of the platform owner is augmented by the first 10 digits of any newly built digital service	[2, 3, 8]

(continued)

Table 2. (*continued*)

Conceptual design	Operational design	Literature reference
Partners' survival is contingent on receiving more payoffs than the accumulated costs from building and maintaining their digital services	Partners constantly calculate their profitability (payoffs – cost); every x time steps, they check if a participation is profitable and will leave the ecosystem if it is not (x is defined by an adjustable parameter)	[14, 15]
New partners enter the ecosystem to account for low barriers of entry	Every y time steps, a new partner enters the ecosystem (y is defined by an adjustable parameter)	[2]
The dynamic environment is defined by four dimensions of environmental dynamism	Each dimension (velocity, ambiguity, unpredictability, complexity) is realized as an adjustable parameter	[14, 20]

1,000 time steps. Figure 1 illustrates exemplary results of varying degrees of openness, i.e. different manners of handling the control vs. openness tension, on a digital platform's generativity and stability in more and less dynamic environments.

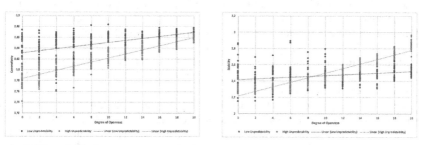

Fig. 1. Effect of varying degrees of openness on generativity (left) and stability (right) in environments with low and high unpredictability

5   Discussion and Outlook

The exemplary illustrations present clear effects of the degree of openness and environment on generativity and stability, but the simulation model evidently requires further elaboration to better capture digital platforms as non-linear CAS. This paper's main contribution is thus a theory-informed simulation model as an extendible instrument to enable predictive analyses of the impact of design decisions on a B2B platform's generativity and stability in different environments. The immediate next step is to further refine the model and extend the investigation to other relevant tensions, like standardization vs. differentiation, or quality vs. variety [9], to analyze the impacts of associated design decisions on the platform's generativity and stability. This enables us to derive concrete design principles that include materiality, action, and boundary conditions [5], for the effective management of tensions. In the B2B context, platform owners may address the control vs. openness tension by decreasing the control of partners in their development of digital services to optimize generativity in a highly unpredictable environment, for example. After deriving the design principles, we plan to demonstrate and evaluate them by employing a case survey method [19]. For researchers, this would enrich both the extant descriptive knowledge on digital platforms and their governance, as well as CAS on how to harness the unpredictable evolution of complex systems. For B2B platform managers, it would yield concrete actionable advice for different environments.

References

1. de Reuver, M., Sørensen, C., Basole, R.C.: The digital platform: a research agenda. J. Inf. Technol. **33**(2), 124–135 (2018)
2. Wareham, J., Fox, P.B., Giner, J.L.C.: Technology ecosystem governance. Organ. Sci. **25**(4), 1195–1215 (2014)
3. Blaschke, M., Haki, K., Aier, S., Winter, R.: Capabilities for digital platform survival: insights from a business-to-business digital platform. In: 39th International Conference on Information Systems (ICIS2018), pp. 1–17, Association for Information Systems, San Francisco (2018)
4. Gawer, A.: Bridging differing perspectives on technological platforms: toward an integrative framework. Res. Policy **43**(7), 1239–1249 (2014)
5. Chandra, L., Seidel, S., Gregor, S.: Prescriptive knowledge in IS research: conceptualizing design principles in terms of materiality, action, and boundary conditions. In: 2015 48th Hawaii International Conference on System Sciences, pp. 4039–4048. IEEE (2015)
6. Peffers, K., Tuunanen, T., Rothenberger, M., Chatterjee, S.: A design science research methodology for information systems research. J. Manag. Inf. Syst. **24**(3), 45–77 (2007)
7. Tiwana, A.: Platform Ecosystems: Aligning Architecture, Governance, and Strategy. Morgan Kaufmann, Amsterdam (2014)
8. Ghazawneh, A., Henfridsson, O.: Balancing platform control and external contribution in third-party development: the boundary resources model. Inf. Syst. J. **23**(2), 173–192 (2013)
9. Mini, T., Widjaja, T.: Tensions in digital platform business models: a literature review. In: Proceedings of the 40th International Conference on Information Systems (ICIS 2019), Munich (2019)
10. Boudreau, K.: Open platform strategies and innovation: granting access versus devolving control. Manag. Sci. **56**(10), 1849–1872 (2010)
11. Karhu, K., Gustafsson, R., Lyytinen, K.: Exploiting and defending open digital platforms with boundary resources: android's five platform forks. Inf. Syst. Res. **29**(2), 479–497 (2018)
12. Huber, T.L., Kude, T., Dibbern, J.: Governance practices in platform ecosystems: navigating tensions between cocreated value and governance costs. Inf. Syst. Res. **28**(3), 563–584 (2017)
13. Merali, Y.: Complexity and information systems: the emergent domain. J. Inf. Technol. **21**(4), 216–228 (2006)
14. Haki, K., Beese, J., Aier, S., Winter, R.: The evolution of information systems architecture: an agent-based simulation model. MIS Q. **44**(1), 155–184 (2020)
15. Nan, N., Tanriverdi, H.: Unifying the role of IT in hyperturbulence and competitive advantage via a multilevel perspective of IS strategy. MIS Q. **41**(3), 937–958 (2017)
16. Winter, R.: Design science research in Europe. Eur. J. Inf. Syst. **17**(5), 470–475 (2008)
17. Hevner, A.R., March, S.T., Park, J., Ram, S.: Design science in information systems research. MIS Q. **28**(1), 75–105 (2004)
18. Gregor, S., Hevner, A.R.: Positioning and presenting design science research for maximum impact. MIS Q. **37**(2), 337–355 (2013)
19. Larsson, R.: Case survey methodology: quantitative analysis of patterns across case studies. Acad. Manag. J. **36**(6), 1515–1546 (1993)

20. Davis, J.P., Eisenhardt, K.M., Bingham, C.B.: Optimal structure, market dynamism, and the strategy of simple rules. Adm. Sci. Q. **54**, 413–452 (2009)
21. Blaschke, M., Haki, K., Aier, S., Winter, R.: Taxonomy of digital platforms: a platform architecture perspective. In: 14th International Conference on Wirtschaftsinformatik (WI2019), Association for Information Systems: Siegen (2019)
22. Beese, J., Haki, M.K., Aier, S., Winter, R.: Simulation-based research in information systems: epistemic implications and a review of the status quo. Bus. Inf. Syst. Eng. **61**(4), 503–521 (2019)

Knowledge Creation - A Perspective on the Development of Design Principles

Sofie Wass$^{(\boxtimes)}$ (iD) and Carl Erik Moe

University of Agder, Grimstad, Norway
`sofie.wass@uia.no`

Abstract. In this paper we reflect on and conceptualize on the development of design principles in a design process. We use the concept of *ba* to describe how design principles can be created when involving users, domain experts, designers and researchers in the design process. The study applies action design research (ADR) to design and develop a self-reflective career support tool for persons with intellectual disabilities (ID). We have applied processes of knowledge creation and their corresponding *ba*, the originating *ba*, the interacting *ba*, the systemizing *ba* and the exercising *ba* to conceptualize the development of design principles. Preliminary findings imply that a structured process of knowledge creation and sharing, applying the concept of *ba*, can support the development of design principles when users, domain experts, designers and researchers work together to design and develop theory-ingrained artifacts for a class of systems.

Keywords: Knowledge creation · Design principles · Action design research

1 Introduction

Action design research (ADR) has been applied in information systems development in a number of contexts and is a powerful research method for generating prescriptive design knowledge, for developing theory-ingrained artifacts. With the aim to solve practical problems and at the same time generating prescriptive knowledge, ADR involves users, domain experts, and designers in the design and development of artifacts [1]. As a part of this, researchers and designers need to share their knowledge but also access the knowledge of users and domain experts, including their tacit knowledge. Eventually, the sharing and combination of knowledge is instantiated in the design of artifacts and in generalizing design principles for a class of systems [1]. The formulation of design principles is an important form of knowledge abstraction in the design process [2] and have been used to share research findings [3] and are reported to be consciously incorporated in the design process by designers [2]. Even if knowledge creation is an important element in the design process, it is an emerging part of ADR [4].

In defining knowledge, a distinction between data, information and knowledge is instrumental. On a continuum, data represents facts, information represents processed data and knowledge represents know-how and understanding of information [5]. Alavi and Leidner [6] describe the human mind as the key difference when distinguishing

© Springer Nature Switzerland AG 2020
S. Hofmann et al. (Eds.): DESRIST 2020, LNCS 12388, pp. 202–207, 2020.
https://doi.org/10.1007/978-3-030-64823-7_19

knowledge from information. Information becomes knowledge when it is processed by the human mind and knowledge is turned into information when it is presented in for instance words, text, graphics, images etc. This implies that knowledge is personal and needs to be shared in ways which makes it useful and interpretable by others [6].

Knowledge is also viewed as tacit or explicit. Tacit knowledge includes cognitive understandings and is connected to senses, movement, physical experiences and intuition and know-how of specific contexts [7]. Explicit knowledge includes knowledge that is communicated in language or symbolic forms [8]. Knowledge conversion is used to describe the transformation of tacit and explicit knowledge [7]. In order to act, one needs to make use of explicit and tacit elements of knowledge [8]. Knowledge creation is described as a creative process, including the individual's internalization of explicit knowledge, externalization or codification of tacit knowledge, socialization around tacit knowledge, and combination of explicit knowledge [7–9]. We believe that this knowledge creation process could help to better understand the development of design principles in a design process.

According to Nonaka and Konno [9], knowledge creation takes place through interaction in physical, mental and virtual *ba*. The Japanese expression *ba* can be explained as a space were the involved actors share knowledge and turn knowledge into action. Knowledge creation has previously been frequently used to study knowledge management in firms, while few studies seem to focus on design processes. We believe *ba* could form the base for development of design principles and contribute to an understanding of how tacit knowledge from users, domain experts and designers is made explicit, shared and turned into action in a design process. In this paper, we apply the concept of *ba* to conceptualize the development of design principles in a design process and to contribute to a better understanding of the development of design principles in ADR [e.g. 2, 4].

2   Research Approach and Context

The case focuses on an ADR project in which we design and develop a self-reflective career tool for youngsters with ID, a user group with challenges in terms of cognitive functioning. The overall goal of the project is to improve work inclusion of this group. The project follows the steps and guidelines of ADR, with problem formulation, building intervention and evaluation, and reflection and learning [1]. We have collected data from observations of seven youngsters with ID and a focus group interview with six of the youngsters. We also arranged focus group interviews with 27 domain experts, and six individual interviews, one ideation workshop and one concept workshop with both users and domain experts before starting to develop the actual artifact. The artifact is a self-reflective career tool, that can support youngsters with ID to identify and reflect on their preferences, skills and abilities needed for the job they are planning towards. The project is on-going, and currently in the design and development phases, hence this is a research-in-progress paper.

3   Background – the Concept of *ba*

In this section we introduce knowledge creation and the concept of *ba* as described by Nonaka et al. [7–9]. *Ba* is a Japanese concept which Nonaka describes as a contextual space and a foundation where knowledge and relationships can be created, shared and interpreted. The space of *ba* can be of three different forms: physical, mental and virtual [9]. Examples of the physical ba can be a conference room or a lunch area, a mental ba can be shared ideas and experiences and the virtual *ba* can be different kinds of information systems such as e-mails and social media. When an individual participates in the *ba*, his or her perspective can be extended beyond the individual perspective. *Ba* is closely connected to the knowledge creation processes of socialization, externalization, combination and internalization. These four processes are a representation of knowledge creation through sharing, use and conversion of knowledge between individuals, in a group or across organisations. Every process has a corresponding type of *ba*, a space or platform, in which knowledge is created. The knowledge creation is described along two dimensions, type of interaction (individual or collective) and type of media (face-to-face or virtual media) [9].

The originating *ba* is where the knowledge creation starts through socialization and sharing of tacit knowledge between people. Direct contact among people and face-to-face meetings are crucial to transfer feelings, emotions, experiences and mental models during this process. The interacting (also called dialoguing) *ba* entails dialogue and converting mental models and skills into common concepts and terms. During this process, knowledge is shared with others through dialogue and reflection by making knowledge more explicit. Dialogue is the key as individuals also reflect their own mental models and knowledge. This *ba* is more conscious, in the sense that individuals with the right knowledge has to be included in the process. The systemizing (also called the cyber) *ba*, is a space for sharing and combining existing explicit knowledge with new information and new knowledge. An important element in this process is the use of 'virtual worlds' i.e. information systems to support systematization and interaction among individuals. The exercising *ba* focuses on internalization and the use of explicit knowledge in real life settings or simulated settings to make it tacit. During this process, individuals use the explicit knowledge and turn it into action and reflect through action [9].

4   Preliminary Findings

The following paragraphs describe the process and the attempt to develop and make use of design principles together with users, domain experts and designers. We apply the different types of *ba* and their role during this process to structure and describe the lessons learned.

The originating *ba* is characterized by socialization and direct contact between people to share feelings, emotions and experiences [9]. Our knowledge creation process started as we conducted focus group interviews with domain experts involved in the problem space. They were employees in the Norwegian Labour and Welfare Administration, community-based housing, secondary school and day-care centers, work training centers, private and public employers and parents of youngsters with ID. They shared their experiences in both writing (using post-its, paper and pen) and through direct discussion where they reflected on their emotions and experiences. To learn more about the end user, persons with ID, we visited a community-based housing to introduce ourselves and socialize. Two researchers stayed for pizza and soda and had a focus group interview around employment. The following day, we carried out participant observations to learn about their daily activities and the context of their experiences. This gave us an initial understanding of their tacit and explicit knowledge. The experiences were codified in field notes and transcribed interview material which were analyzed and summarized into different problem areas. One of the problem areas focused on mapping of needs and abilities of persons with ID.

The interacting *ba* focuses on dialogue, to make knowledge explicit and to establish common concepts and terms among individuals [9]. To convert the tacit knowledge into explicit knowledge we arranged ideation and concept workshops to discuss possible solutions to the identified problems. A heterogenous group of users and domain experts were invited to share their knowledge through dialogues with each other, designers and researchers. To facilitate the discussions, we provided prompts and presented previous findings. The suggestions that emerged from the workshops and knowledge on user needs were circulated through various dialogues to other users and domain experts such as practitioner conferences. The knowledge was externalized in the form of a concept describing the main affordances and requirements of the IT artifact. *"An information space that provides a coherent mapping of the youths' skills and abilities. The artifact follows the students and his/her development towards working life. In education it is used as a support to promote self-perception and self-representation."* Based on the gathered experiences we explored theory on self-determination [10], consulted domain experts (i.e. researchers and practitioners in the disability field) and attended conferences on disability research. This dialogue resulted in the first formulation of the design principles, including the terms self-assessment based on input from the workshops and goal setting based on the theory of self-determination. These were presented to the designers who initiated a workshop to discuss the deeper meaning of the design principles and to establish a shared understanding of the design principles. As a result, the design principles were rephrased into what the designers described as 'human speak' in their native language and with a shorter guiding version described as the user activity (one example of a design principle is presented in Table 1).

Table 1. Example of the first version of one of the design principles and the 'user activity'.

Design principle	User activity
Provide features for self-assessment and goal setting so that the system supports cognitive impaired users to make conscious and autonomous employment decision	Who am I and what would I like to become?

The systemizing *ba* is a space to systematize, share and combine gathered explicit knowledge with new information and new knowledge [9]. As the project developed, we realized that we needed a flexible space to share ideas among the project members, regardless of location and time. The insights built from dialogues and face-to-face meetings needed to be collected and systemized. To enable the combination of both explicit knowledge and existing information (the cyber *ba*), one designer suggested the use of 'Miro'. The application supported the use of text, visuals and sound and real-time interaction between researchers, designers and developers (screenshot provided in Fig. 1).

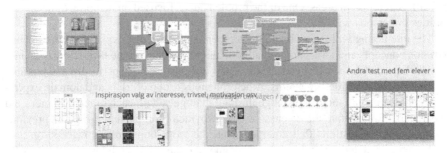

Fig. 1. Gathered knowledge, suggestions on inspirations and visualization of design principles.

The exercising *ba* includes internalization and use of explicit knowledge that is turned into action [9]. The gathered and combined explicit knowledge (preliminary design principles and user needs) were turned into action and instantiated in a first paper prototype. Using the prototype, the designers and researchers tested out the knowledge created together with students with ID in school settings. The ADR mindset of contentious evaluation together with users in real settings [1] supported that knowledge was turned into action and tested.

5   Discussion and Further Work

The artefact will be further developed and documented in later publications, however, it is outside the scope of this paper. Our focus is on how the concept of *ba* can contribute to a better understanding of the development of design principles in ADR. From the perspective of knowledge creation, the originating *ba* established an environment of trust between researchers and most importantly participants with ID. Observations, listening and doing contributed to a better understanding of tacit knowledge and the experiences and worlds of users with limited cognitive abilities. During the interacting *ba* knowledge was made more explicit and a service concept was used to support a shared mental understanding of the problem space. Findings from this project, indicate that it is crucial to spend time on dialogues. Theories that could inform the design were discussed among the researchers early in the process, but this proved to be less useful as a shared mental understanding of the problem was needed first. A collaborative and iterative approach with both domain experts, designers and users was important, as it confirmed the relevance of the theory for a class of systems but also how it could be combined with other concepts. A dialogue among research and designers on how to externalize the suggested design principles was fruitful for both parties as they became more explicit. In the systemizing *ba*, Miro, supported creative sharing of ideas but also grouping of knowledge and information between designers and researchers. It allowed us to work simultaneously in a shared space and systemize the ideas in relation to the design principles. Finally, in the exercising *ba*, a first version of the design principles could be explicitly presented in the prototype and we observed the use of it in action. These triggered new cycles of knowledge creation and development of design principles.

Our preliminary findings imply that applying and making use of the concept of *ba* can support the development of design principles. The different aspects of originating, interacting, systemizing and exercising *ba* can contribute to a more structured knowledge creation process that can be communicated to users, domain experts, designers and researchers who work together to design and develop theory-ingrained artifacts for a class of systems. We are currently interviewing designers and developers to learn how they view the process of developing design principles together with researcher and their view on the knowledge creation process. This will further inform our preliminary findings on knowledge creation, the concept of *ba* and the development of design principles.

References

1. Sein, M., Henfridsson, O., Purao, S., Rossi, M., Lindgren, R.: Action design research. MIS Q. **35**(1), 37–56 (2011)
2. Chandra Kruse, L., Seidel, S., Purao, S.: Making *use* of design principles. In: Parsons, J., Tuunanen, T., Venable, J., Donnellan, B., Helfert, M., Kenneally, J. (eds.) DESRIST 2016. LNCS, vol. 9661, pp. 37–51. Springer, Cham (2016). https://doi.org/10.1007/978-3-319-392 94-3_3
3. Seidel, S., Chandra Kruse, L., Székely, N., Gau, M., Stieger, D.: Design principles for sense-making support systems in environmental sustainability transformations. Eur. J. Inf. Syst. **27**(2), 221–247 (2018)
4. Otto, B., Osterle, H.: Principles for knowledge creation in collaborative design science research. In: 33rd International Conference on Information Systems (2012)
5. Davenport, T.H., Prusak, L.: Working Knowledge: How Organizations Manage What They Know. Harvard Business Press, Boston (1998)
6. Alavi, M., Leidner, D.E.: Knowledge management and knowledge management systems: conceptual foundations and research issues. MIS Q. **25**(1), 107–136 (2001)
7. Nonaka, I., von Krogh, G.: Perspective—tacit knowledge and knowledge conversion: controversy and advancement in organizational knowledge creation theory. Organ. Sci. **20**(3), 635–652 (2009). https://doi.org/10.1287/orsc.1080.0412
8. Nonaka, I.: A dynamic theory of organizational knowledge creation. Organ. Sci. **5**(1), 14–37 (1994)
9. Nonaka, I., Konno, N.: The concept of "Ba": Building a foundation for knowledge creation. Calif. Manag. Rev. **40**(3), 40–54 (1998)
10. Shogren, K.A., Wehmeyer, M.L., Palmer, S.B., Forber-Pratt, A., Little, T.J., Lopez, S.J.: Causal agency theory: reconceptualizing a functional model of self-determination. Educ. Train. Autism Dev. Disabil. **50**(3), 251–263 (2015)

Towards a Method for Design Principle Development in Information Systems

Frederik Möller[1,2(✉)], Tobias Moritz Guggenberger[1,2], and Boris Otto[1,2]

[1] TU Dortmund University, Dortmund, Germany
{Frederik.Moeller,Tobias.Guggenberger,Boris.Otto}@tu-dortmund.de
[2] Fraunhofer ISST, Dortmund, Germany

Abstract. A central goal of doing research is to make findings available to the academic and practitioner community in order to extend the current knowledge base. The notion of how to generalize, abstract, and codify knowledge gained in design endeavors is a vital issue in design science, especially in the strand of design theory. Design principles provide a medium to make such design knowledge available to others and to make it transferable from a single application onto more scenarios that are subject to similar boundary conditions. The study proposes a preliminary method for the development of design principles based on a structured literature review and the inductive derivation of methodological components from it. The purpose of the method is to give researchers and practitioners executable steps to generate design principles.

Keywords: Design principles · Method · Design theory · Taxonomy

1 Introduction

Researchers and practitioners that *design* are concerned with the creation of meaningful artifacts that solve an organizational problem [1]. Quintessentially, the act of designing anything may be understood as the iterative transformation of an undesirable problem-state (*problem space*) to a more desirable solution state (*solution space*) through the use of artifacts [1–4]. Artifacts, generally, differ from natural objects, as they come into existence by design, i.e., with intended functionalities, with one or multiple authors, and, ultimately, to serve some human purpose [5–7]. In that, it is the process of analysis and understanding of how the constituent components of an artifact come into being that shapes the act of *designing* [8]. During that process, the designer generates *design knowledge*, which requires codification in a conceptual shell in order to be made useful for a broader user base and to contribute to the persistent knowledge base [9]. *Design knowledge* is knowledge about the artifacts, how they are constituted, and how they come into existence [10]. A central goal of *Design Science* is to accumulate design knowledge [11] and to make it available [12] so that it can be reused in multiple instances and to elevate knowledge gained about a singular solution to a more generally applicable level [13, 14]. The common purpose of design principles is to codify design knowledge and, given the consideration of respective boundaries, enable its reuse [15]. Additionally,

© Springer Nature Switzerland AG 2020
S. Hofmann et al. (Eds.): DESRIST 2020, LNCS 12388, pp. 208–220, 2020.
https://doi.org/10.1007/978-3-030-64823-7_20

design principles (as a part of design theory) should assist the designer in bringing about an artifact that has a set of specific functionalities and result in the expected effects [16]. Research on design principles and, more generally, design theories is beneficial as they enable the "(…) progression from an abstract level of situated implementation to a more generic and applicable level" [17 p. 4], and, subsequently, they "(…) would be a significant enhancement or addition to the existing scientific body of knowledge" [18 p. 5]. The medium of *design principles* is useful to codify *design knowledge* and to make it available as prescriptive guidelines that support design both as a *process* and a *product* [19]. [20 p. 227] defines *prescriptiveness* as "(…) if you want to achieve Y in situation Z, then perform action X."

As of now, there are a plethora of ways to develop design principles with studies varying vastly in their development approach. For example, some studies employ Action Design Research (ADR) and follow the notion of eliciting design principles reflectively from a design process or finished artifact [4, 13]. Other studies derive design principles in Qualitative Studies, Case Studies, or using Design Science Research (DSR) methods (e.g., [21]), with some employing the concept of *meta-requirements* (requirements addressing a class of artifacts [22]) and some skipping them. As of now, studies propose conceptual guidelines and frameworks to develop (nascent) design theory, of which design principles are an integral component (e.g., see [18, 23, 24]), yet, however, there is lack of an operationalizable set of steps to develop them. Thus, we see a need for a standard set of steps summarized in a method to assist design principle development according to both best practices established in the literature and epistemological foundations provided by the core literature on design theory. The present article proposes, firstly, a taxonomy of design principle development approaches generated from a structured literature review and, secondly, derives from it a method with specific steps representing the key tasks for their design. Because of the above, the research question of the present article is:

Research Question (RQ): Which steps need to be followed to develop design principles successfully?

The paper is structured as follows. Firstly, after the introduction, we illustrate the conceptual foundations of design principles. Section 3 describes the approach to identifying relevant literature and the research design in general. Subsequently, Sect. 4 starts with taxonomizing the inductively gained insights from the literature review and proceeds to derive a method from them. Lastly, in Sect. 5, we discuss our findings, explicate the contributions, and define the limitations of our work.

2 Design Principles

The term "design principles", as a linguistic composition, consists of two parts, namely *design* and *principle*. First, *design* (as a verb) can be defined as "(…) the process in which the designer progresses from a description of requirements to a model of an IS artifact (…)" [2 p. 2]. A principle, on the other hand, can be defined as "A fundamental rule or law, derived inductively from extensive experience and/or empirical evidence, which provides design process guidance to increase the chance of reaching a successful solution." [25 p. 2]. Subsequently, we can establish the understanding of design principles, linguistically, as fundamental propositions that aid designers in achieving a successful transfer of requirements to design. That notion is widely supported by authors from the field, from which Table 1 shows selected definitions.

Table 1. Selected definitions of the term "design principle".

Definition
"As a definition, consider a design principle as a 'recommendation or suggestion for a course of action to help solve a design issue'" [26 p. 357]
"Design Principles (in so far they are considered a form of design knowledge) represent knowledge that is codified, explicit knowledge, readily accessible as prescriptive statements" [15 p. 39]
"The design principles capture the knowledge gained about the process of building solutions for a given domain, and encompass knowledge, about creating instances that belong to this class (…)" [13 p. 45]
"(…) are design decisions and design knowledge that are intended to be manifested or encapsulated in an artifact, method, process, or system" [27 p. 17]

Even though it is their purpose, design principles, per se, cannot directly be transferred onto any given application context, but rather are constrained by boundary conditions set both by the environment that they are supposed to be used in an by the experience of the user [11, 28].

The objective of design principles is supporting the design of artifacts, design principles as such are at a higher, "meta" level. However, design principles themselves often are the product of a DSR endeavor themselves [29, 30]. That makes them an artifact in the traditional, philosophical sense, i.e., an artificially designed (conceptual) object, which is different from natural objects that come into existence to fulfill some human purpose with specific functionalities [7]. To position design principles in the sphere of artifacts but at the same time demarcate them from *material* artifacts (usually, methods, models, constructs, and instantiations [5]) [30], one might employ, e.g., the *termini meta-artifact* [31], or *abstract artifact* [30].

Following the duality of the term design, as both a verb and a noun, design principles may both address the process of designing an artifact (i.e., the *development process* [32]), as well as its functionalities (i.e., the *system features* [32]) [22]. The literature provides various ways to further classify design principles in detail, e.g., through their inclusion as parts of design theories, as principles of form, principles of function, or principles of implementation [33].

3   Research Design

Our research approach is a structured literature review, as proposed by [34–36]. As it is our goal to construct a method for design principle development based on findings in the literature, we set the scope of our search strategy to only include those papers that explicitly deal with the development of design principles, i.e., have, in our view, identifiable methodological components [37]. Next, the scope of our study delimits the methodological frame onto design science and the domain of Information Systems (IS).

To construct a nexus of literature that is as relevant as possible to the study, we search explicitly for the occurrence of the term "design principle" or "design principles" in the *titles* and *abstracts,* respectively, in the AISeL[1] database. The literature core is extended, on the one hand, through backward search [36] and reduced, on the other, through eliminating doubles and papers that are out of scope. The search was restricted to AISeL, as, during the search process, it became clear that the theoretical saturation has been achieved and that, most likely, no new information could be gained by incorporating additional databases and also extensive backward searches [36, 38]. Subsequently, the study does not claim completeness but instead builds upon a representative, methodical subset [37]. We started with 251 papers, of which, after both reduction and extension, 97 remained for more in-depth analysis.

We focused on papers presenting completed research studies on design principles (in terms of design theory), yet, if the method used to develop design principles was sufficiently recognizable, we also included Research-in-Progress papers.

4   A Method for Design Principle Development

4.1   Taxonomizing Features of Design Principle Development

Based on the literature review outlined in Sect. 3, we chose an inductive approach, in that we taxonomize different approaches to design principle development in the literature. Using a taxonomical approach is especially suitable, as it enables us to give structure to the field of design principle development and to identify central dimensions and characteristics [39], which we, later on, transfer into methodological components. We have identified seven dimensions and corresponding characteristics (see Table 2) that are suitable to map the development process according to our literature search [39].

Table 2. Taxonomy of development approaches. EX = Exclusivity, ME = Mutually Exclusive, NE = Not Mutually Exclusive. Unknown or Unspecified characteristics have been omitted.

Dimension (D_n)	Characteristics (C_{nm})					EX
Perspective	Supportive		Reflective			NE
Research Design	DSR	A(D)R	Qualitative	Case Study		NE
MR Source	Literature	Theory	Interviews	Workshops/ Focus groups	None	NE
DP Design	Derived		Extracted		Responsive	NE
Iterations	Single		Multiple			ME
Evaluation	Expert/User Feedback		Instantiation/ Field Testing		Argumentation	NE
Formulation	Free		Based on Template			ME

---

[1] https://aisel.aisnet.org/do/search/.

The *Perspective* (D_1) dichotomously classifies the design principles alongside two characteristics. First, *Supportive* (C_{11}) design principles assist the design of an artifact *ex-ante*, i.e., before the design process has started and thus justify future design decisions [40, 41]. On the other hand, *Reflective* (C_{12}) design principles emerge after or during the design iterations of the artifact. The dimension is not mutually exclusive as, naturally, the designer may produce design principles before the actual designing of an artifact, but may, at any point in the design process, refine them or add new ones.

Each design principle has some *Research Design* (D_2), either as the central artifact (or *meta-artifact* [31]) to be developed or as part of a more extensive design process. Most prominently, design principles emerge alongside *Design Science Research (e.g.,* [21]), (C_{21}), *Action (Design) Research* [13] (C_{22}), *Qualitative Studies* (C_{23}), or *Case Studies* (C_{24}).

Next, studies differ in their approach to *Meta-Requirement elicitation* (D_3). Meta-Requirements are derived from one or multiple sources, such as *Literature Reviews* (C_{31}), derived from *Kernel Theories* (i.e., Service-Dominant Logic) (C_{32}), *Interviews* (C_{33}), or *Workshops* (C_{34}). However, not all studies employ the concept of meta-requirements (C_{35}). For example, studies using *ADR* to derive reflective design principles usually do not derive meta-requirements before design principle development, as they are extracted rather than developed *a priori*.

Our findings show that design principles are *generated* (D_4) in three ways. Firstly, by *deriving* (C_{41}) them directly (without meta-requirements) from a suitable knowledge base (e.g., Literature, Theory, or Case Studies), by *extracting* them from an on-going or finished design process (C_{42}), or by formulating them as a *response* to meta-requirements (even though, some authors use different terminology, e.g., *design requirements* [42]) (C_{43}).

Design principle generation can be iterative (D_5), which is why we distinguish between *Single* (C_{51}), and *Multiple* (C_{52}) iterations.

We see three evaluation strategies that are usually used in studies developing design principles (D_6). Researchers may employ the assistance of experts (e.g., in interviews or workshops) (C_{61}), provide illustrative documentation *via* instantiation or field testing of the corresponding artifact (C_{62}), or, lastly, give argumentative reasons, e.g., by constructing a scenario, about the quality of the design principles (C_{63}).

Lastly, scholars, either formulate (D_7) *freely*, with the restriction being that the design principle is formulated prescriptively (C_{71}) or based on a *linguistic template* (C_{72}).

4.2   Method-Elements

The following section explains the **Method Components (MC)** derived based on the taxonomy shown in Table 2 and the findings of the structured literature review. The focus lies on the strand considering supportive design principles, both because of spacing limitations, as well as the intuitive and self-explanatory nature of the reflective approach. Furthermore, our literature review shows that the supportive approach is characterized by methodological heterogeneity rather than the reflective approach, which predominantly utilizes ADR or methods of DSR. Figure 1 visualizes both approaches as a procedural model. Additionally, the method represents and overarching framework, which, hopefully, spurs creativity in designers by conducting the individual steps necessary for design principle development, yet, leaves the instantiation of each activity flexible. Thus, we provide typical best practices that we have derived from the literature review (e.g., visualizing the relationship between design principles and meta-requirements or using a template for their formulation).

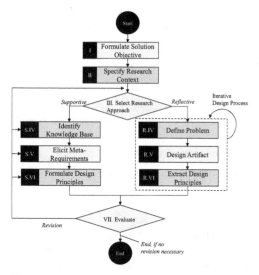

Fig. 1. Method for Design Principle Development.

ME I - Formulate the Solution Objective (SO): The first step in developing design principles is to formulate their purpose. Their purpose, generally, is to support the design of an artifact successfully. That objective can be called *Solution Objective*, i.e., the formulation of the specific task the artifact should, at some point, be able to fulfill [23] (see Table 3). The goal of **ME 1** is to present the purpose of the design principles concisely and precisely.

Table 3. Exemplary Solution Objectives formulated in design principle development.

Exemplary Solution Objectives
"What are appropriate design principles for tools that allow for reflecting sustainability in business models?" [43 p. 2]
"Which data-specific design principles can be used to assess business model representations regarding their applicability for data-driven business models?" [44 p. 2]

ME II - Specify Research Context: Once the general direction of the research endeavor is set, the researcher must select an adequate research method. Design principles may both be the part of a more comprehensive research endeavor and come into existence during that process, or they might be the artifact themselves. For example, if the study includes close interaction with practitioners and collaborative design of an artifact, the choice could fall on ADR (e.g., see [45]). However, if the design principles were to be designed *ex-ante*, e.g., from interviews, one might opt to conduct a qualitative study to develop them (e.g., see [46]). Table 4 gives three examples of design principles and their corresponding methodological research context. Design principle development may span multiple studies and experience refinements in subsequent research projects.

Table 4. Examples of different research contexts for design principle development.

Design principles	Research context
DP to asses business model representations for data-driven business models [44]	Qualitative Study
Multiple DP for Blended Learning Services [48]	ADR [13]
DP for attention aware BI & Analytics dashboards [49]	DSR [50]

ME III - Select Research Approach: We propose a dichotomous decision between, firstly, a *Supportive* approach and, secondly, a *Reflective* approach. The primary difference between both approaches is the point of artifact design and the logic of generating design principles. In the *supportive* approach, the goal of design principles is the provision of design knowledge in advance to support the design of an artifact before the design process takes place. These design principles are derived in advance from the literature, kernel theories, case studies, expert interviews, or comparable, suitable sources for design knowledge. Contrarily, the *Reflective* approach means that a design action has been taken, and "(…) reflecting on what has been done is required (…) and design principles need to be abstracted" [47 p. 7]. Design principles can be reflected in one's own design processes or those carried out by others [4, 10, 33]. Thus, we follow the terminology of [4] and name that approach *Reflective*. Generally, this distinction is in alignment with the inductive and deductive understanding in the epistemological loop of *relevance* and *rigor* in DSR outlined in [18].

ME SIV/S.V - Identity Knowledge Base/Elicit Meta-requirements:
Meta-Requirements, as proposed by [22], refer to requirements addressing a class of artifacts. In that, these requirements need to be abstract and general to be valid for more-than-one instances [51] (see Table 5). While the origin of meta-requirements lies in the construction of a *design theory* and their derivation relied on using kernel theories, today, multiple studies show various possible backgrounds. These include, exclusively or in combination, the derivation from theory, literature, interviews, or similar suitable data sources. Suitable data are all data that assist the researcher in extracting design knowledge (e.g., [52] argue for using user-review from an online software comparison portal to derive design principles). No matter their origin, meta-requirements need to be tied directly to the solution objective to ensure the continuity of the red path throughout design principle development [23].

Table 5. Examples of *meta-requirements* and *design principles* from the literature corpus.

Exemplified Meta-requirement	Source
"Full accessibility to project insight database for all organization members" [53 p. 12]	Interviews
"**MR1:** Record user's eye-movement data with an eye-tracking device while processing visualized information." [49 p. 5]	Literature
Exemplified Design Principle	Template
"Provide the collaboration system with **communication medium** that have at least **one high** and one **low level** of **synchronicity** (…) to build consensus for efficient collaboration among them." [54 p. 7–8]	[28]
"Frame the ill-structured problem by developing an ontology in which the main components of the problem and their relationships are modeled." [55 p. 403]	None

Our literature review has shown that only a few studies employ the concept meta-requirements while extracting design principles from a designed artifact, e.g., in the context of an ADR-Study (an example would be [53]). Usually, meta-requirements are derived from the literature in developing supportive design principles *a priori* to any instantiation of an artifact.

Even though not all studies employ meta-requirements, we include this step in the method (for supportive design principles), as we agree with the concept of *Value Grounding* explained by [24], which proposes a close link between design theory and the corresponding goal that it intends to achieve (i.e., the *causa finalis* [33]). Correspondingly, supportive design principles mandatorily should address at least one or multiple *meta-requirements* (which may be aggregated to *key requirements*) [18, 23].

ME S.VI - Formulate Design Principles: Design principles are formulated twofold. Firstly, they must include specific, prescriptive instruction for an artifact design (content), that addresses meta-requirements [23]. A precise tool to visually illustrate that correlation is the mapping diagram (see Fig. 2) that shows which design principles address which requirement. Thus, we recommend visualizing the connection and derivation logic between design principles and meta-requirements as a mapping diagram mandatorily to giver ready, easy, a visual aid to understand the connections. One step further, some authors extend another layer and append, e.g., design features that result from design principles. Second, when formulating design principles, the researcher can draw from established templates. In [19], the authors identify six formulation templates, namely

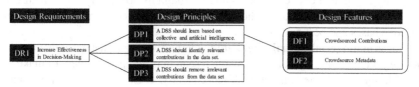

Fig. 2. Example of mapping diagrams. The excerpt is taken from [42 p. 2662].

[20, 22–24, 28, 56], and provide enhanced guidelines themselves. For examples of design principle formulation, see Table 5.

ME VII - Evaluate: The literature on *design theories* and *design principles* offers multiple underlying conditions that design principles need to fulfill. Our literature review has shown ways to evaluate design principles (see Table 2), such as *Expert Feedback* (Interviews, Workshops), *Instantiation,* or *Argumentation.* To support a goal-oriented evaluation of design principles, we provide two categories of evaluation criteria.

First, design principles should be correct in form. Meaning that there are some necessary conditions, let us call them the smallest common denominator, that design principles need to fulfill in order to be called so. Thus, design principles need to prescribe, precisely, a specific action, a prescription to bringing an artifact into existence through the codification of design knowledge (**Prescriptiveness**) [9, 13, 26, 27, 57]. Next, the design principle should be adequately general in order to address a class of artifacts, rather than one specific instance (**Abstractedness**) [13, 28, 32, 33, 58].

Arguably the most crucial purpose of design principles is to make design knowledge reusable in different application scenarios as if that is not so, their very meaning and purpose, i.e., their "(…) practical ethos (…)" is lost [59 p. 1]. Thus, we draw from [59], who propose a framework for light reusability evaluation of design principles, which can be used as tools for argumentative justification or evaluation. The framework consists of five criteria, namely *Accessibility, Importance, Novelty & Insightfulness, Actability & Guidance,* and *Effectiveness.*

5 Contributions, Limitations, and Outlook

The present study develops a method for design principle development based on the taxonomized results of a structured literature review. Thus, our **scientific contributions** lie in assisting researchers in developing design principles in a research setting that is not as clear cut as, e.g., design principle elicitation in ADR. We outline a way to generate design principles in alignment with epistemological underpinnings based on different types of knowledge bases. Additionally, we collect, contextualize, and synthesize approaches to design principle evaluation and propose essential properties that design principles need to have. Thus, our work assists in extending the scientific body of knowledge by providing a method that makes design principle development more structured, applicable, and goal-oriented. Through generating more design principles, the paper, indirectly, contributes to extending the body of design knowledge [18 p. 5]. Lastly, while there have been some studies providing guidelines in generating design principles (e.g., [13, 18, 41]), we argue, that ours contributes merit through its operationalizable nature and, through the conjoint utilization of the taxonomy, gives advice on possible, underlying knowledge bases and best practices.

As far as **managerial contributions** are concerned, we argue that through the support of design principle development, we enable researchers and practitioners to make their attained design knowledge available and, subsequently, assist their users in implementing them in their new design endeavors. Ultimately, through providing well-founded design principles, our method helps the generation of excellent designs, which "(…) can go far beyond a single success story." [11 p. 186].

Lastly, our work is subject to **limitations**. As the data on design principle development stems from AISeL, we restrict our view only on Information Systems, which leaves the potential for further research in additional databases. Also, using only the keywords "design principle" and "design principles" excludes, at this point, synonyms, which need to be investigated further. Thus, it is likely that not all papers developing design principles were found and that broader inclusion of databases and publications covering design science, in future work, is necessary. Also, the method only builds on publications purely developing design principles. Naturally, as they are part of design theory, the next step could be to extend the literature review and include methods for developing comprehensive design theories. For example, [60] give a detailed overview of publications thematizing design science. The method is yet a preliminary version and thus requires continuous testing and improvement, but is, as of now, an initial approach to operationalize design principle development and establish a best practice (in conjunction with the taxonomy given in Table 2. Future evaluation strategies could include conducting focus groups, checking the method for applicability (e.g., by using the framework of [61]), or instantiating it in a real-world design project. Currently, we plan to evaluate further and develop the method in both the academic research setting of universities, but also in applied research institutes. Additionally, the method could profit from a more structured underlying design framework, such as Method-Engineering, to enhance formalization and to zoom in on the activities even further.

Acknowledgment. This research was supported by the Excellence Center for Logistics and IT funded by the Fraunhofer Gesellschaft and the Ministry of Culture and Science of the German State of North Rhine-Westphalia.

References

1. Simon, H.A.: The Sciences of the Artificial. MIT Press, Cambridge (1996)
2. Purao, S., Bush, A., Rossi, M.: Problem and design spaces during object-oriented design: an exploratory study. In: Proceedings of the 34th HICSS (2001)
3. Dorst, K., Cross, N.: Creativity in the design process: co-evolution of problem-solution. Des. Stud. **22**, 425–437 (2001)
4. Gregor, S., Müller, O., Seidel, S.: Reflection, abstraction, and theorizing in design and development research. In: Proceedings of the 21st ECIS (2013)
5. March, S.T., Smith, G.F.: Design and natural science research on information technology. Decis. Support Syst. **15**, 251–266 (1995)
6. Hilpinen, R.: Belief systems as artifacts. Monist **78**, 136–155 (1995)
7. Baker, L.R.: The shrinking difference between artifacts and natural objects. American Philosophical Association Newsletter on Philosophy and Computers (2008)
8. Simon, H.A.: Problem forming, problem finding and problem solving in design. In: Design & Systems, pp. 245–257 (1995)
9. Seidel, S., Chandra Kruse, L., Székely, N., Gau, M., Stieger, D.: Design principles for sensemaking support systems in environmental sustainability transformations. EJIS **27**, 221–247 (2017)

10. Cross, N.: Designerly ways of knowing: design discipline versus design science. Des. Issues **17**, 49–55 (2001)
11. Chandra Kruse, L., Seidel, S.: Tensions in design principle formulation and reuse. In: Proceedings of the 12th International Conference on DESRIST (2017)
12. Cross, N.: Design research: a disciplined conversation. Des. Issues **15**, 5–10 (1999)
13. Sein, M.K., Henfridsson, O., Purao, S., Rossi, M., Lindgren, R.: Action design research. MIS Q. **35**, 37–56 (2011)
14. Cronholm, S., Göbel, H.: Design science research constructs: a conceptual model. In: Proceedings of the 23rd PACIS (2019)
15. Chandra Kruse, L., Seidel, S., Purao, S.: Making use of design principles. In: Proceedings of the 11th International Conference on DESRIST (2016)
16. Lukyanenko, R., Parsons, J.: Research perspectives: design theory indeterminacy: what is it, how can it be reduced, and why did the polar bear drown? JAIS **21**(5) (2020). https://doi.org/10.17705/1jais.00639. Article 1
17. Hansen, M.R.P., Pries-Heje, J.: Value creation in knowledge networks: five design principles. SJIS **29**, 61–79 (2017)
18. Koppenhagen, N., Gaß, O., Müller, B.: Design science research in action - anatomy of success critical activities for rigor and relevance. In: Proceedings of the 20th ECIS (2012)
19. Cronholm, S., Göbel, H.: Guidelines supporting the formulation of design principles. In: Proceedings of the 29th ACIS (2018)
20. van Aken, J.E.: Management research based on the paradigm of the design sciences: the quest for field-tested and grounded technological rules. JMS **41**, 219–246 (2004)
21. Peffers, K., Tuunanen, T., Rothenberger, M.A., Chatterjee, S.: A design science research methodology for information systems research. JMIS **24**, 45–77 (2007)
22. Walls, J.G., Widmeyer, R.G., Sawy, O.A.: Building an information system design theory for vigilant EIS. ISR **3**, 36–59 (1992)
23. Heinrich, P., Schwabe, G.: Communicating nascent design theories on innovative information systems through multi-grounded design principles. In: Tremblay, M.C., VanderMeer, D., Rothenberger, M., Gupta, A., Yoon, V. (eds.) DESRIST 2014. LNCS, vol. 8463, pp. 148–163. Springer, Cham (2014). https://doi.org/10.1007/978-3-319-06701-8_10
24. Goldkuhl, G.: Design theories in information systems-a need for multi-grounding. JITTA **6**, 59–72 (2004)
25. Fu, K.K., Yang, M.C., Wood, K.L.: Design principles: the foundation of design. In: Proceedings of the ASME Design Engineering Technical Conference, p. 7 (2015)
26. McAdams, D.A.: Identification and codification of principles for functional tolerance design. J. Eng. Des. **14**, 355–375 (2003)
27. Gregor, S.: Design theory in information systems. AJIS **10**(1) (2002)
28. Chandra Kruse, L., Seidel, S., Gregor, S.: Prescriptive knowledge in is research: conceptualizing design principles in terms of materiality, action, and boundary conditions. In: Proceedings of the 48th HICSS (2015)
29. Gregor, S., Hevner, A.R.: Positioning and presenting design science research for maximum impact. MIS Q. **37**, 337–355 (2013)
30. Vaishnavi, V., Kuechler, W., Petter, S.: Design science research in information systems. http://www.desrist.org/design-research-in-information-systems/
31. Iivari, J.: Towards information systems as a science of meta-artifacts. CAIS **12**, 568–581 (2003)
32. Markus, M.L., Majchrzak, A., Gasser, L.: A design theory for systems that support emergent knowledge processes. MIS Q. **26**, 179–212 (2002)
33. Gregor, S., Jones, D.: The anatomy of a design theory. JAIS **8**, 312–335 (2007)
34. Vom Brocke, J., et al.: Reconstructing the giant: on the importance of rigour in documenting the literature search process. In: Proceedings of the 17th ECIS (2009)

35. Vom Brocke, J., Simons, A., Riemer, K., Niehaves, B., Plattfaut, R., Cleven, A.: Standing on the shoulders of giants: challenges and recommendations of literature search in information systems research. CAIS **37**, 205–224 (2015)
36. Webster, J., Watson, R.T.: Analyzing the past to prepare for the future: writing a literature review. MIS Q.: Manag. Inf. Syst. **26**, xiii–xxiii (2002)
37. Cooper, H.M.: Organizing knowledge syntheses: a taxonomy of literature reviews. Knowl. Soc. **1**, 104 (1988)
38. Leedy, P.D., Ormrod, J.E.: Practical Research: Planning and Design. Pearson, London (2014)
39. Nickerson, R.C., Varshney, U., Muntermann, J.: A method for taxonomy development and its application in information systems. EJIS **22**, 336–359 (2013)
40. Schermann, M., Gehlert, A., Krcmar, H., Pohl, K.: Justifying design decisions with theory-based design principles. In: Proceedings of the 17th ECIS (2009)
41. Nunamaker, J.F., Chen, M., Purdin, T.D.M.: Systems development in information systems research. JMIS **7**, 89–106 (1990)
42. Rhyn, M., Blohm, I.: Combining collective and artificial intelligence: towards a design theory for decision support in crowdsourcing. In: Proceedings of the 25th ECIS (2017)
43. Schoormann, T., Behrens, D., Knackstedt, R.: Design principles for leveraging sustainability in business modelling tools. In: Proceedings of the 26th ECIS (2018)
44. Kühne, B., Zolnowski, A., Bornholt, J., Böhmann, T.: Making data tangible for data-driven innovations in a business model context. In: Proceedings of the 25th AMCIS (2019)
45. Sun, D., Ying, W., Zhang, X., Feng, L.: Developing a blockchain-based loyalty programs system to hybridize business and charity: an action design research. In: Proceedings of the 40th ICIS (2019)
46. Kühne, B., Böhmann, T.: Data-driven business models - building the bridge between data and value. In: Proceedings of the 27th ECIS (2019)
47. Gregor, S.: Building theory in the sciences of the artificial. In: Proceedings of the 4th International Conference on DESRIST (2009)
48. Bitzer, P., Söllner, M., Leimeister, J.M.: Design principles for high-performance blended learning services delivery. Bus. Inf. Syst. Eng. **58**(2), 135–149 (2015). https://doi.org/10.1007/s12599-015-0403-3
49. Toreini, P., Langner, M., Maedche, A.: Designing attention-aware business intelligence and analytics dashboards to support task resumption. In: Proceedings of the 26th ECIS (2018)
50. Kuechler, B., Vaishnavi, V.: On theory development in design science research: anatomy of a research project. EJIS **17**, 489–504 (2008)
51. Lee, A.S., Baskerville, R.L.: Generalizing generalizability in information systems research. ISR **14**, 221–243+315 (2003)
52. Möller, F., Guggenberger, T., Otto, B.: Design principles for route-optimization business models: a grounded theory study of user feedback. In: Proceedings of the 15th WI (2020)
53. Schacht, S., Morana, S., Maedche, A.: The evolution of design principles enabling knowledge reuse for projects: an action design research project. JITTA **16**, 5–36 (2015)
54. Tavanapour, N., Bittner, E.A.C., Brügger, M.: Theory-driven-design for open digital human collaboration systems. In: Proceedings of the 25th AMCIS (2019)
55. Avdiji, H., Elikan, D.A., Missonier, S., Pigneur, Y.: Designing tools for collectively solving ill-structured problems. In: Proceedings of the 51st HICSS (2018)
56. van den Akker, J.: Principles and methods of development research. In: Design Approaches and Tools in Education and Training, pp. 1–14. Kluwer Academic Publishers (1999)
57. Kuechler, W., Vaishnavi, V.: A framework for theory development in design science research: multiple perspectives. JAIS **13**, 395–423 (2012)
58. Schermann, M., Böhmann, T., Krcmar, H.: Explicating design theories with conceptual models: towards a theoretical role of reference models. In: Wissenschaftstheorie und gestaltungsorientierte Wirtschaftsinformatik, pp. 175–194 (2009)

59. Iivari, J., Hansen, M.R.P., Haj-Bolouri, A.: A framework for light reusability evaluation of design principles in design science research. In: Proceedings of the 13th International Conference on DESRIST (2018)
60. Tremblay, M., Vander Meer, D., Beck, R.: The effects of the quantification of faculty productivity: perspectives from the design science research community. CAIS **43**, 625–661 (2018)
61. Rosemann, M., Vessey, I.: Toward improving the relevance of information systems research to practice: the role of applicability checks. MIS Q. **32**, 1–22 (2008)

Methodology

Considering Context in Design Science Research: A Systematic Literature Review

Philipp zur Heiden[✉]

Paderborn University, Paderborn, Germany
philipp.zur.heiden@uni-paderborn.de

Abstract. The question of whether a particularist or a universalist stance to Information Systems (IS) research is more important has long divided the IS research community. Particularism acknowledges the context of research, whereas universalism aims to abstract theories to higher levels, neglecting the role played by context. This dilemma is especially relevant to Design Science Research (DSR) because the designed artifact and its context are inextricably connected. However, do design science researchers sufficiently consider and adequately specify context and, on this basis, do they generalize the knowledge generated through designing artifacts? Using a systematic literature review I analyze the specification of context and design implications in DSR papers from leading IS journals. The results show that both are generally underspecified. Although DSR, by its nature, seems to be particularistic and rarely generalizes findings, I help researchers conduct more context-aware DSR by providing guidelines for optimizing the consideration of context. Thus, this paper seeks to optimize the potential for generalizing findings in DSR and, thereby, to enhance theory building in the discipline.

Keywords: Design science research · Context · Particularism · Universalism · Literature review

1 Introduction

In IS, two research approaches are hotly debated: particularism and universalism. Particularist research draws on theory, or investigates phenomena explicitly acknowledging their contexts. It thus takes environmental differences into account [10]. In contrast, when adopting a universalist design, researchers generalize contextual details to discover novel theories with universal applicability [3]. Social science theories and research are inevitably highly context-dependent, often adopting a particularist research design and struggling with generalization. Some research misleadingly claims to be universalist by obfuscating contextual details in a particularist research design, because particularism has limited research relevance. They view particularism as only a small step towards generalizability which is deemed the ultimate goal of scientific research. This

© Springer Nature Switzerland AG 2020
S. Hofmann et al. (Eds.): DESRIST 2020, LNCS 12388, pp. 223–234, 2020.
https://doi.org/10.1007/978-3-030-64823-7_21

increasingly applies to the IS discipline, as researchers adopt a wide range of opinions and strategies on this issue [9,10,13,37]. Davison and Martinsons [10], for example, argue for a pluralistic approach to increase specification of context. Previous studies confirm the general lack of context specification, on the basis of which unfounded claims are made for universal generalization [24].

Design science research (DSR) is a design-oriented stream in IS research which focuses on the development, evaluation, and improvement of IT artifacts [44]. However, considering context in DSR is particularly important for two reasons. First, context plays an essential part in executing DSR, as the design requires the interplay between artifact and context to deliver useful solutions. The context inevitably sets boundaries and requirements for IT artifacts because the artifact can only be useful when fitting its context. Second, unlike general knowledge about context in IS [10,24], there is no quantitative research on the specification and consideration of context in DSR. Lee [23] states that DSR studies are focusing on technology and on organizational aspects, without combining either as part of context.

The purpose of this paper is to take a meta-theoretical view on the consideration and specification of context in DSR papers published in leading IS journals. To answer my research question of *how leading IS researchers view context in their DSR studies*, I undertake a systematic literature review [47], reviewing 115 high-quality publications in IS that apply DSR methods in different contexts. By critically discussing current considerations of context in DSR, my aim is to support researchers to optimize future DSR through greater awareness of the context surrounding the IT artifact they design. It currently is common practice, however, to leave out contextual characteristics, hoping this might be viewed more favorably by reviewers. I aim to improve future DSR practice in IS by analyzing the past and providing guidelines for more effective embedding of context in research design. The guidelines will help researchers adapt their DSR processes to improve and investigate contextual influences on the design of their IT artifacts.

The remainder of his paper is structured as follows. Section 2 present an overview of the related literature. Section 3 presents and justifies the literature review as the research method used. In Sect. 4, I display the results from the literature review, before discussing and proposing guidelines for context-aware DSR in Sect. 5. Section 6 concludes the paper.

2   Related Work

2.1   Context in Universalism and Particularism

Weighing up universalism and particularism is a hotly debated topic in IS literature, usually revolving around the role played by context. Context is a multi-dimensional [37] and obscure construct [1,37], causing discussion in management and IS literature. Johns [21] defines context in organizational behavior research as "situational opportunities and constraints that affect the occurrence and meaning of organizational behavior as well as functional relationships between variables" [21, p. 386]. Stressing the importance of context in research, he laments the lack of attention context is given in existing research, arguing that a change of context significantly changes the nature of theories that can be derived from it [21]. In the early years of IS, context in evaluation is separated from content and process [42]. Whereas context represents the 'why' in evaluation, content represents the 'what', and process the 'how' of evaluation [42]. Context is said to be a limiting factor in theories of social sciences, as it restricts the universal applicability and relevance of research [10].

Concerning IS, theory has long been viewed as the pinnacle of research. The generation of universal knowledge around IT has been a key focus since the early days of IS [3]. In the past, authors have—and continue to this day to experience—difficulties in publishing research that is lacking in theoretical contribution. To counteract this IS trend, papers call to focus less on theory and more on other contributions, e.g., arguments, facts, and patterns [4]. Considering that researchers understand generalization as knowledge claims expected to hold true outside of the evaluated setting [39], generalization in IS research may be achieved through successfully applying theories in contexts for which they were not initially developed. In other words, for theory to be valid it has to hold true in multiple contexts [22]. This universal approach—also described as universalism—is common in IS research and often announced as its ultimate goal [9].

Davison and Martinsons [10], however, criticize universalism and specifically researchers' lack of awareness when making universalist claims because certain results cannot be generalized to other contexts. Hence, particularism and universalism are opposed to each other. In particularistic research, researchers explicitly acknowledge the environment—the context—of their research [10] by considering characteristics, e.g., race or gender, which universalist research deems to be functionally irrelevant [25]. Applying a universalistic approach, however, would ignore these characteristics and generalize the findings.

For theory development, both universalism and particularism are needed. To balance the application of universalism and particularism, Davison and Martinsons [10] recommend that researchers make conscious decisions on the appropriate research context based on the goals of the research. They advise researchers to explicitly consider context in their research: "The research design is not complete without clear specifications of the context in which the research will be conducted and the contexts for which the findings may reasonably be useful." [10, p. 247] Other researchers support this call for a better specification of context in IS [19, 37, 43], especially given the interdisciplinary nature of IS [9]. Nevertheless, they underline the importance of generalizability as the ultimate goal of scientific research [9, 43]. Hence, applying a pluralistic approach that considers both universalism and particularism [35] would allow to avoid limitations inherent in taking an extreme position.

2.2   Design Science Research in Information Systems

In general, researchers differentiate between natural and artificial things. Human designers synthesize artifacts to serve specific goals and functions, imitating appearances in common natural things [41]. In this sense, artifacts lie at the interface between their surroundings and their inner environment (the substance of the artifact itself) [41], and, as such, are boundary objects between the two. In research, artifacts will contribute to the knowledge base if they prove to be useful to their users and solve a problem with an approach superior to preexisting artifacts [18,26]. IT artifacts discussed in IS are entities, objects, or a combination of both, designed to benefit people and their goals in a certain context [29,49]. IT artifacts can be constructs, models, methods, or instantiations [26].

Researchers characterize design as the act of creating innovative artifacts for the purpose of resolving problems. Simon [41, p. 111] acknowledges that "design is the core of all professional training" and that design is not focused on finding out how things are, but prescriptively deals with how they ought to be in order to work properly [41]. The use of design as research to investigate theories for design and action [15], is called design science. To scientifically create artifacts, DSR pursues a dual mission [40]: contributing to theoretical knowledge, and solving current problems. Therefore, DSR aims to both design IT artifacts and evaluate them with a view to building IS design theories [17].

From a philosophical point of view, the knowledge scope of DSR is both nomothetic, abstracting general and universal knowledge, and idiographic, focusing on situated artifacts and particular instantiations [6]. The reason for this is the duality of DSR consisting of design (build and evaluate) and science (justify and theorize) [6], thus, combining particularism and universalism. DSR contributions can vary in the level of abstraction [34]. Whereas high-level abstractions (design theories) tend to a more nomothetic knowledge scope, instantiations as a contribution show a stronger idiographic knowledge scope [16].

2.3   Context in Design Science Research

In pioneering fashion Alexander [1] determines form as the ultimate object of design, as every design problem begins with trying to achieve a fit between form and context: "When we speak of design, the real object of discussion is not form alone, but the ensemble comprising the form and its context." [1, p. 16]. He defines context as the problem itself, putting demands on the form, whereas form is the solution to the problem. The form is the only part of the world which designers have control over and which they can change through design, therefore reflecting all known facts relevant to the design of an artifact. To measure the criterion of fit, Alexander recommends putting a designed prototype (form) into its intended context and checking if it fulfills the requirements [1]. However, as these requirements are derived from an obscure context, there is a potentially endless list of them. Therefore, the criterion of fit can only be measured by the absence of the most obvious misfits [1].

The work of Alexander [1] has influenced the very foundations of DSR [17,31]. In DSR, the IT artifact as a representation of the form is seen as surrounded by and embedded into its context [27]. Therefore, context in DSR describes the differences in which DSR studies are executed [20]. From a designer's perspective, context is also obscure and immutable so that changes can only be applied to the IT artifact and not to the context itself.

Hevner et al. [18], amongst others [13], agree to the dependence of an IT artifact on its context and further clarify and categorize the different aspects that define context: people (roles, skills, characteristics), organizations (strategies, structure, culture, processes), and technology (infrastructure, applications, communications architecture, development skills) [18]. This context view is often used to frame the context of an IT artifact, e.g., as the organizational (sociotechnical) context [27]. While other researchers may name these categories differently or assign different attributes to them [2,11], they, nevertheless, tend to describe similar aspects. Concerning organizational context in previous research, Pettigrew [32] distinguishes between inner context, consisting of the structure of organizations, and outer context, consisting of the social, economic, political and competitive environment.

IT artifacts—the results of DSR—should not and cannot be built to solve the corresponding design problem, but have to be evaluated in the context for which they were designed [2]. As with the abstraction of a design problem to a class of problems, the IT artifact also has to be regarded in an abstracted view. Therefore, to generalize the findings of DSR and generate robust theories, an IT artifact has to be evaluated in different contexts [17].

3   Methodology

Up to now, there is no IS research quantitatively analyzing existing DSR publications in terms of their consideration of context. Only Schuster et al. [38] analyze design theories and the context they were evaluated in qualitatively. To investigate the emphasis placed on context in DSR, I conduct a literature review synthesizing and extending existing research in design science. I follow guidelines for literature reviews in IS [47], which offer a rigorous and traceable way to collect and review the existing literature [45]. I choose a narrow scope of publications to only include high-quality publications in IS because the aim is to portray context consideration in leading DSR publications, trading off quality against quantity. Therefore, the literature search is restricted to the senior scholars' basket of journals [28], including the eight most influential journals of the IS discipline. Instead by limiting the review to a specific time frame I analyze the complete body of literature in IS' leading journals.

First, I conducted an electronic search for the keywords "design science" and "design research" in the selected journals. With these keywords, I was able to identify applications of the different procedures and guidelines of DSR, including, for example, Action Design Research [40]. This initial search yielded a total of 528 hits across the selected databases, with the same result after using backward and forward searches. As the analysis focuses on the application of DSR in a scientific context, all meta-theoretical DSR papers, which do not apply DSR to design IT artifacts, were excluded, as well as those that only obliquely mention DSR. Therefore, after checking the research methods used in these 528 papers, in a second step over 78% of the initial set of identified papers were excluded, resulting in 115 papers being considered for further analysis. The detailed results are displayed in Table 1. In contrast to Prat et al. [33] I only consider studies explicitly calling their methodology according to my keywords.

Table 1. Journals analyzed and papers included in the review

Journal	Initial hits	Papers applying DSR
European Journal of Information Systems	94	19
Information Systems Journal	40	7
Information Systems Research	44	9
Journal of AIS	83	21
Journal of Information Technology	37	2
Journal of MIS	71	28
Journal of Strategic Information Systems	22	3
MIS Quarterly	137	26
Total	528	115

In a third step, I categorize the literature based on predefined concepts [47]. As I want to find out if and how existing papers consider and describe the context that DSR is applied to, I first scan the papers for a description of the context. I focus on the characteristics of context by Hevner et al. [18]: people (roles, skills, characteristics), organizations (strategies, structure, culture, processes), and technology (infrastructure, applications, communications architecture, development skills). This serves as a set of coherent macro-concepts [36]. Next, I investigate whether the authors explain the implications the context has had on the designed IT artifact. This allows me to clarify the use of DSR, i.e. whether it is for solving design problems or solely for representing and communicating findings with or without proper context specification [10]. Again, I consider the three dimensions of context. Next, I look at how the authors generalize their findings, whether the designed IT artifacts were evaluated in their original or in other contexts [17], e.g., by presenting a design theory as the highest level of contribution abstraction in DSR [16]. This research process is in line with recommended prescriptions by Davison and Martinsons for ensuring the appropriate communication of both context and scope of validity [10].

4   Results

The results enable a conclusive answer to the research question. Having analyzed all 115 papers it shows that 60 papers (52%) describe people-specific aspects of context, 74 (64%) the organizational context, and 60 (52%) the technological context. Many papers focus on minor characteristics mentioned throughout the design or evaluation phase of the paper, whereas others extensively discuss certain dimensions. The papers display a holistic view, which focuses on each contextual dimension of context in only 20 out of 115 papers (17%). In contrast, 15 (13%) papers did not mention any contextual aspects at all. The combined results of the context description are portrayed in Table 2.

Table 2. Papers showing design implications of context dimensions (Papers can appear several times in Table 2. For example, a paper describing people-specific and technological context characteristics counts for 'People', 'Technology', and 'People and Technology'. Thus, percentages add up to more than 100%.)

Context dimension	A: Number of papers describing context dimension	Percentage (of all 115 analyzed papers)	B: Number of papers outlining design implications of context dimension	Percentage (of all 115 analyzed papers)	Percentage (B/A)
People	60	52%	41	36%	68%
Organization	74	64%	33	29%	45%
Technology	60	52%	41	36%	68%
People and Organization	44	38%	18	16%	41%
People and Technology	31	27%	13	11%	42%
Organization and Technology	39	34%	16	14%	41%
People, Organization, and Technology	20	17%	8	7%	40%
No context description	15	13%	39	34%	–

If authors want to show the design implications of their IT artifact, they have to justify these design decisions based on contextual or decision-based factors. Therefore, the context drawn upon has to be at least described beforehand. As seen in Table 2, the number of papers showing the design implication of their respective contexts is even lower than the number of papers describing contextual dimensions. Although possible in theory, there was no paper showing the design implications of a contextual dimension without also providing a description.

Out of the 115 papers analyzed, 41 (36%) show design implications of people-specific characteristics of context, 33 (29%) show design implications of the organizational context, and 41 (36%) show implications of the technological context. The organizational context dimension is the most often described dimension, while its design implications are shown the least often. Only about 40% of papers describing multiple context dimensions also feature resulting design implications. While only 8 papers describe the context and show the design implications across all three dimensions, 39 papers fail to mention the influence the context has on the design of the IT artifact as the focus of their DSR endeavor.

Concerning generalization, 28 out of 115 analyzed papers generalized their DSR findings by abstracting their results to a class of problems [17] or presenting a design theory [16]. Out of 58 papers published before 2015, 7 generalized their results, in contrast to 21 out of 57 papers from 2015 onwards. Apart from this, the results do not vary significantly between the years of publication.

5   Discussion

Based on the results derived from the systematic literature review, I propose three guidelines that researchers ought to consider when conducting DSR studies. These guidelines serve as recommendations for context-aware DSR studies and do not invalidate existing DSR guidelines [16,18], but rather complement them. Furthermore, some DSR studies already apply some of these guidelines, whereas others could be improved using the following guidelines.

As the results show, there are different approaches to DSR. Some studies are technology-driven and introduce technological innovation (e.g., [48]) or transfer technological innovation to other domains, for example, IoT-based sensors being used to assist diabetes patients in healthcare [8]. Others use a people-focused approach or base their DSR contribution in an organizational context. This is in line with different approaches to DSR [23]. Furthermore, some authors refrain from describing (some) context dimensions as drivers for DSR because the context cannot be specified inherently. For example, Famideh et al. [12] develop a generic process model for cloud migration, but fail to make explicit roles or agents as examples of people-specific characteristics of context. The analysis shows that DSR studies differ in the extent to which they accord any importance to context dimensions. Nevertheless, context consists of a potentially endless list of requirements [1], which researchers cannot describe entirely. Context and IT artifacts are mutually constitutive. Therefore, I recommend to define the particular characteristics of the DSR-specific context and to include design implications deriving from contextual characteristics, as their omission can compromise the scientific validity of findings. As the context dimensions are described similarly frequent, this applies to the three dimensions of context. Analyzing all DSR papers, the context description is often placed in an introductory section or a dedicated problem description, whereas design implications from context characteristics are integrated into the IT artifact's design section. Researchers should place the context description and design implications into these research sections, refraining from adding new context-specific or even context-dimension-specific sections, because context and its dimensions are an essential part of DSR. To provide a positive example, Chatterjee et al. [8] provide excellent context descriptions and design implications resulting from context characteristics. I therefore propose the following:

Guideline 1. *Authors of DSR should describe the three context dimensions of their IT artifact designed in the problem description and explain the design implications resulting from the context dimensions in the IT artifact's design section.*

Another aspect that was discovered by analyzing 115 DSR papers from IS journals is the effective relationship between the IT artifact and its context.

IT artifacts are designed within a specific context [18]. Hence, not only does the context affect the design of the IT artifact, but, vice versa, the IT artifact and its design affect the context. Few of the papers, however, analyzed the anticipated shifts in the different context dimensions, which can also be seen in similar studies [38]. Therefore, I propose the second guideline:

Guideline 2. *Authors of DSR should specify the anticipated changes of context resulting from the IT artifact and its design.*

Concerning the generalization of results, the majority of the analyzed DSR papers lack an abstraction to a class of problems, as advised for plausible DSR studies by Gregor and Jones [17]. Some papers generalize their results superficially, refraining from abstracting the essential design insights to a broader class of problems (e.g., [14]). The overall results show the particularistic approach that DSR is subject to. Additionally, the time-based analysis shows a change towards more universalistic DSR because current papers more often generalize their findings, thus aiming for the ultimate goal of scientific research. In line with Davison and Martinsons [10], I propose the third guideline:

Guideline 3. *Authors of DSR should generalize their findings and their IT artifacts to an abstract class of problems.*

With these guidelines the aim is to lay the foundation for future DSR in IS with a pluralistic approach that considers both universalism and particularism, which is often requested [35]. The guidelines require a further description of the context in which the researchers initiate their IT artifact, as described in Guideline 1. Abstracting the findings and the knowledge generated to general knowledge, as Guideline 3 suggests, meets the challenges of universalism. Thus, DSR according to these guidelines covers both an idiographic and a nomothetic knowledge scope [6]. Nevertheless, researchers should follow approved guidelines and frameworks for DSR, which is common practice. The papers analyzed mostly focus on Hevner et al. [18], Peffers et al. [31], and Gregor & Jones [17]. This aligns with findings of another meta-analysis of DSR studies [7].

6 Conclusion

Context is an important construct in IS, especially in DSR. The analysis of the whole body of DSR studies in leading IS journals shows that context seems to be much neglected, although DSR studies feature particularistic research approaches. Despite providing yet another meta-theoretical view on DSR in IS, my paper contributes and communicates clear guidelines with a view to improving future DSR or related research in IS and related disciplines. The research presents the current status of DSR in IS and the consideration of context according to its three dimensions (people, organization, technology). I also introduce guidelines for context-aware DSR, complementing popular DSR frameworks and models. The guidelines can be used by researchers and practitioners to conduct DSR studies and extend their focus to the context of their research subjects.

Limitations include the selection of papers for the literature review, because I only include influential journals of IS, dismissing related disciplines, other IS journals and conferences. The potential bias of editorial policies in these leading IS journals is often discussed [5, 30, 46] and can lead design science researchers to submit their research to design-related journals or conferences, fearing rejection in leading IS journals. Furthermore, I do not analyze the papers based on the quality of their context consideration, but use a binary approach for their classification. Both limitations can be avoided in future research, which can sharpen the proposed guidelines by qualitatively investigating context in DSR studies.

Future research should aim to validate the proposed guidelines by applying them to DSR studies. Additionally, the research conducted in this paper could be extended both to other disciplines and to more practice-oriented publications or applications of specific DSR (e.g., Action Design Research [40]) to test the validity of the proposed guidelines and merge them with existing DSR guidelines.

Acknowledgements. I acknowledge the feedback provided by my supervisor, Daniel Beverungen, who pointed me to the need to investigate the nature of context in design science research. This paper was developed in the research project FLEMING, which is funded by the German Federal Ministry for Economic Affairs and Energy (BMWi), promotion sign 03E16012F.

References

1. Alexander, C.: Notes on the Synthesis of Form. Harvard University Press, Cambridge (1964)
2. Alturki, A., Gable, G.G., Bandara, W.: A design science research roadmap. In: Jain, H., Sinha, A.P., Vitharana, P. (eds.) DESRIST 2011. LNCS, vol. 6629, pp. 107–123. Springer, Heidelberg (2011). https://doi.org/10.1007/978-3-642-20633-7_8
3. Avgerou, C.: The significance of context in information systems and organizational change. Inf. Syst. J. **11**(1), 43–63 (2001)
4. Avison, D., Malaurent, J.: Is theory king?: questioning the theory fetish in information systems. In: Willcocks, L.P., Sauer, C., Lacity, M.C. (eds.) Formulating Research Methods for Information Systems, pp. 213–237. Palgrave Macmillan, London (2015). https://doi.org/10.1057/9781137509857_9
5. Baskerville, R., Lyytinen, K., Sambamurthy, V., Straub, D.: A response to the design-oriented information systems research memorandum. Eur. J. Inf. Syst. **20**(1), 11–15 (2011)
6. Baskerville, R.L., Kaul, M., Storey, V.C.: Genres of inquiry in design-science research: justification and evaluation of knowledge production. MIS Q. **39**(3), 541–564 (2015)
7. Cater-Steel, A., Toleman, M., Rajaeian, M.M.: Design science research in doctoral projects: an analysis of Australian theses. J. Assoc. Inf. Syst. **20**(12), 3 (2019)
8. Chatterjee, S., Byun, J., Dutta, K., Pedersen, R., Pottathil, A., Xie, H.: Designing an internet-of-things (IoT) and sensor-based in-home monitoring system for assisting diabetes patients: iterative learning from two case studies. Eur. J. Inf. Syst. **27**, 1–16 (2018)

9. Cheng, Z., Dimoka, A., Pavlou, P.A.: Context may be king, but generalizability is the emperor!. J. Inf. Technol. **31**(3), 257–264 (2016)

10. Davison, R.M., Martinsons, M.G.: Context is king! considering particularism in research design and reporting. J. Inf. Technol. **31**(3), 241–249 (2016)

11. Dresch, A., Lacerda, D.P., Antunes Júnior, J.A.: Design Science Research: A Method for Science and Technology Advancement. Springer, Cham (2015). https://doi.org/10.1007/978-3-319-07374-3

12. Fahmideh, M., Daneshgar, F., Rabhi, F., Beydoun, G.: A generic cloud migration process model. Eur. J. Inf. Syst. **28**(3), 233–255 (2019)

13. Fernández, W.D.: Commentary on Davison and Martinsons' 'context is king! considering particularism in research design and reporting'. J. Inf. Technol. **31**(3), 265–266 (2016). https://doi.org/10.1057/s41265-016-0004-8

14. Giesbrecht, T., Schwabe, G., Schenk, B.: Service encounter thinklets: how to empower service agents to put value co-creation into practice. ISJ **27**, 171–196 (2016)

15. Gregor, S.: The nature of theory in information systems. MIS Q. **30**(3), 611–642 (2006)

16. Gregor, S., Hevner, A.R.: Positioning and presenting design science research for maximum impact. MIS Q. **37**(2), 337–355 (2013)

17. Gregor, S., Jones, D., et al.: The anatomy of a design theory. J. Assoc. Inf. Syst. **8**(5), 312–335 (2007)

18. Hevner, A., March, S., Park, J., Ram, S.: Design science in information systems research. MIS Q. **28**(1), 75–105 (2004)

19. Hong, W., Chan, F.K.Y., Thong, J.Y.L., Chasalow, L.C., Dhillon, G.: A framework and guidelines for context-specific theorizing in information systems research. Inf. Syst. Res. **25**(1), 111–136 (2014)

20. Iivari, J.: Distinguishing and contrasting two strategies for design science research. Eur. J. Inf. Syst. **24**(1), 107–115 (2015)

21. Johns, G.: The essential impact of context on organizational behavior. Acad. Manag. Rev. **31**(2), 386–408 (2006)

22. Lee, B.: Conceptualizing generalizability: new contributions and a reply. MIS Q. **36**(3), 749 (2012)

23. Lee, A.S.: Retrospect and prospect: information systems research in the last and next 25 years. In: Willcocks, L.P., Sauer, C., Lacity, M.C. (eds.) Formulating Research Methods for Information Systems, vol. 1, pp. 19–47. Palgrave Macmillan UK, London (2015). https://doi.org/10.1057/9781137509857_2

24. Li, L., Gao, P., Mao, J.Y.: Research on it in China: a call for greater contextualization. J. Inf. Technol. **29**(3), 208–222 (2014)

25. Long, J.S., Fox, M.F.: Scientific careers: universalism and particularism. Ann. Rev. Sociol. **21**(1), 45–71 (1995)

26. March, S.T., Smith, G.F.: Design and natural science research on information technology. Decis. Supp. Syst. **15**(4), 251–266 (1995)

27. McKay, J., Marshall, P., Hirschheim, R.: The design construct in information systems design science. J. Inf. Technol. **27**(2), 125–139 (2012). https://doi.org/10.1057/jit.2012.5

28. Members of the College of Senior Scholars: Senior scholars' basket of journals (2011). https://aisnet.org/page/SeniorScholarBasket

29. Orlikowski, W.J., Iacono, S.: Research commentary: desperately seeking the IT in IT research - a call to theorizing the it artifact. Inf. Syst. Res. **12**, 121–134 (2001)

30. Österle, H., et al.: Memorandum on design-oriented information systems research. Eur. J. Inf. Syst. **20**(1), 7–10 (2011)

31. Peffers, K., Tuunanen, T., Rothenberger, M.A., Chatterjee, S.: A design science research methodology for information systems research. J. Manag. Inf. Syst. **24**(3), 45–77 (2007)
32. Pettigrew, A.M.: The Awakening Giant: Continuity and Change in Imperial Chemical Industries. Blackwell, Oxford (1985)
33. Prat, N., Comyn-Wattiau, I., Akoka, J.: A taxonomy of evaluation methods for information systems artifacts. J. Manag. Inf. Syst. **32**(3), 229–267 (2015)
34. Purao, S.: Design research in the technology of information systems: truth or dare. GSU Department of CIS Working Paper 34 (2002)
35. Ravitch, D.: Diversity and democracy: multicultural education in America. Am. Educ.: Prof. J. Am. Feder. Teach. **14**(1), 16–20 (1990)
36. Rowe, F.: Toward a richer diversity of genres in information systems research: new categorization and guidelines. Eur. J. Inf. Syst. **21**(5), 469–478 (2012)
37. Sarker, S.: Building on Davison and Martinsons' concerns: a call for balance between contextual specificity and generality in is research. J. IT **31**(3), 250–253 (2016). https://doi.org/10.1057/s41265-016-0003-9
38. Schuster, R., Wagner, G., Schryen, G.: Information systems design science research and cumulative knowledge development: an exploratory study. In: Proceedings of the ICIS 2018 (2018)
39. Seddon, P.B., Scheepers, R.: Generalization in is research: a critique of the conflicting positions of lee & Baskerville and Tsang & Williams. In: Willcocks, L., Sauer, C., Lacity, M.C. (eds.) Formulating Research Methods for Information Systems, vol. 31, pp. 179–209. Palgrave Macmillan, New York (2015)
40. Sein, M.K., Henfridsson, O., Purao, S., Rossi, M., Lindgren, R.: Action design research. MIS Q. **35**(1), 37 (2011)
41. Simon, H.A.: The Sciences of the Artificial, 3rd edn. MIT Press, Cambridge (1996)
42. Symons, V.J.: A review of information systems evaluation: content, context and process. Eur. J. Inf. Syst. **1**(3), 205–212 (1991)
43. Urquhart, C.: Response to Davison and Martinsons: context is king! yes and no - it's still all about theory (building). J. Inf. Technol. **31**(3), 254–256 (2016). https://doi.org/10.1057/s41265-016-0002-x
44. Vaishnavi, V.K., Kuechler, W.: Design Science Research Methods and Patterns: Innovating Information and Communication Technology, 2nd edn. CRC Press, Hoboken (2015)
45. vom Brocke, J., Simons, A., Riemer, K., Niehaves, B., Plattfaut, R., Cleven, A.: Standing on the shoulders of giants: challenges and recommendations of literature search in information systems research. Commun. Associ. Inf. Syst. **37**, 9 (2015)
46. Walsham, G.: Are we making a better world with ICTs? Reflections on a future agenda for the is field. J. Inf. Technol. **27**(2), 87–93 (2012)
47. Webster, J., Watson, R.T.: Analyzing the past to prepare for the future: writing a literature review. MIS Q. **26**(2), xiii–xxiii (2002)
48. Zahedi, F.M., Walia, N., Jain, H.: Augmented virtual doctor office: theory-based design and assessment. J. Manag. Inf. Syst. **33**(3), 776–808 (2016)
49. Zhang, P., Scialdone, M.J., Ku, M.C.: IT artifacts and the state of is research. In: Proceedings of the ICIS 2011 (2011)

Having a Positive Impact with Design Science Research – Learning from Effective Altruism

Alexander Herwix[1]([✉]) [iD] and Amir Haj-Bolouri[2] [iD]

[1] Cologne Institute for Information Systems (CIIS), University of Cologne, Cologne, Germany
herwix@wiso.uni-koeln.de
[2] Department of Informatics, University West, Trollhättan, Sweden
amir.haj-bolouri@hv.se

Abstract. How to increase the chances of overall positive, rather than negative, impacts from new technology developments is expected to be a key challenge for the future of design-oriented research. In this context, we argue that a thorough understanding of the ethical dimension of research and technology is needed so that researchers can make an informed assessment of the expected impact of their work and carry it out more effectively. Myers and Venable [1] took a first step towards investigating the role of ethics in design science research (DSR) and proposed a tentative set of principles that aim to help researchers achieve outcomes that are good from an ethical perspective. We extend this stream of research and present an ethics-aware DSR framework, which describes how values and ethics are fundamentally related to DSR and how we measure its impact. Most importantly, the framework can act as an actionable guideline for how to maximize the expected positive impact of DSR projects. Moreover, the framework can also be used to discuss the structure, direction and expected positive impact of DSR.

Keywords: Ethics · DSR · Effective altruism · Theoretical framework

1 Introduction

Design science research (DSR) is a research paradigm focused on the creation of useful knowledge through the development of novel solutions to relevant problems [2, 3]. Thus, DSR has the implicit goal of *having a positive impact on the world*, either directly via solution artifacts or indirectly via useful knowledge [1–3]. This positions DSR well in times where important stakeholders of research (e.g., government agencies, foundations, etc.) are starting to evaluate (and fund) research projects based on (expected) outcomes and societal impact [4, 5].

However, so far, research on DSR has mainly been focused on a means-end oriented perspective to DSR that neglects a critical questioning of the ends of research [5–7]. This is a problem because our world and technologies are now so complex that it is increasingly difficult to ensure that even well intentioned ICT projects have an overall positive impact on the world [5, 8]. How to increase the chances of overall positive, rather than negative, impacts from new technology developments is expected to be a key challenge for the future of design-oriented research [5].

© Springer Nature Switzerland AG 2020
S. Hofmann et al. (Eds.): DESRIST 2020, LNCS 12388, pp. 235–246, 2020.
https://doi.org/10.1007/978-3-030-64823-7_22

We argue that a thorough understanding of the ethical dimension of research and technology is needed so that DSR scholars can make an informed assessment of the expected impact of their work and carry it out more effectively. Pragmatically, researchers would want to, on the one hand, minimize the negative impact (i.e., outcomes that make the world worse) and, on the other hand, maximize the positive impact (i.e., outcomes that make the world better).

Myers and Venable [1] took a first step toward investigating the role of ethics in DSR and proposed a tentative set of ethical principles that could guide researchers in the planning and reflection of their own work. They argue that it requires careful deliberation and standards of inquiry to make sure that actions and designed artifacts actually have a positive impact on the world and do not create unintended harm. Thus, they generally tackle the question of how to minimize the negative impact of DSR. However, their tentative principles are not well suited to help with the maximization of the positive impact of DSR projects. We aim to resolve this gap and focus on the question of: *How can ethical considerations be integrated in the context of DSR to maximize the expected positive impact of the research done?*

Toward this goal, we turn to the effective altruism (EA) movement [9, 10], a key reference field on the topic of applied ethics and specifically the question of how to maximize the positive impact of the resources that are available. Informed by a reflection of the authors multiple-year experience engaging in DSR in IS and EA as well as an informed review of the literature, we extend Hevner's et al. [11] seminal framework into an ethics-aware perspective of DSR. We also demonstrate how to use the framework for the maximization of the expected positive impact of DSR projects. Next to actionable advice, our work provides vocabulary that can help the DSR community in discussing the structure, direction and expected positive impact of its work.

The rest of the paper is structured as follows. First, we present the theoretical background for our framework development by reviewing the literature on ethics in DSR and providing a summary of key considerations emanating from the effective altruism movement. Second, we present and explain our framework. Third, we apply the framework in a short example. Fourth, we conclude our paper with a discussion of contributions as well as limitations and outline next steps for future research.

2 Theoretical Background

2.1 Design Science Research and Ethics

The entry point towards recognizing a need for ethical discussions in DSR origins from identifying a gap within contemporary guidelines and methods of DSR. For example, Myers and Venable [1] highlight that DSR so far has tended to look at efficiency and effectiveness as the main values of the field and neglected important ethical considerations regarding whether the developed outcomes actually improved the world for the public at large. For instance, recent research on the dark side of IT use [8] raises concerns that highly effective and efficient IT solutions can still lead to adverse and often unforeseen consequences.

As a first attempt to address the gap of ethical discussions in the DSR literature, Myers and Venable [1] suggest a set of tentative ethical principles for DSR (p. 6):

1. **The public interest**. Design science researchers should explicitly identify all stake-holders who may be affected by the artifacts once placed into use and critically consider what benefit or harm may result for/to such stakeholders.
2. **Informed consent.** All design science researchers in IS should obtain informed consent from any person who is in some way involved with the research project.
3. **Privacy.** All design science researchers in IS should ensure that there are adequate safeguards in place to protect privacy.
4. **Honesty and accuracy.** Design science researchers should not plagiarize ideas but should acknowledge inspiration from other sources.
5. **Property.** All design science researchers in IS should ensure that there is an agreement about ownership of the IP at the beginning of the project.
6. **Quality of artifact.** Every attempt should be made to ensure the quality of the artifact(s).

The proposed principles by Myers and Venable [1] addresses ethical issues by high-lighting critical questions regarding each of the guidelines. They call for DSR researchers to start taking ethical questions seriously and to explicitly discuss how ethical guide-lines have been addressed in DSR projects. While Myers's and Venable's [1] work is certainly a welcome step toward more ethical awareness in DSR, their tentative principles are generally focused on the minimization of negative impacts through DSR projects. Considerations for how to maximize the positive impact of DSR projects are barely discussed and remain an important gap in the DSR literature.

Going beyond Myers and Venable [1] other studies have mentioned the importance of the ethical dimension in DSR in IS but few have presented ethical considerations in an actionable way. For instance, in a paradigmatic analysis of DSR, Ivari [7] proposes three different perspectives on DSR relating to the ethical dimension of DSR (sic., means-end oriented, interpretative, critical), which, however, remain descriptive in nature. The framework for evaluation in DSR (FEDS) [12] mentions ethics as a goal to take into consideration for evaluations but, e.g., does not go into detail what that would entail. In light of this background, we will advance the discussion around DSR and ethics by looking at how ethics (and in particular considerations for how to maximize the positive impact of projects) can be incorporated into the paradigm of DSR.

2.2   Ethics and Effective Altruism

According to Singer [13], "ethics, also called moral philosophy, [is] the discipline con-cerned with what is morally good and bad and morally right and wrong." At its core, ethics aims to address questions such as those outlined by Myers and Venable [1] and also proposes ways for resolving them. Effective Altruism (EA) is an emerging move-ment grounded in the discipline of ethics that is deliberately trying to take insights from ethics and apply them in practice to have the greatest positive impact possible, given the resources that are available. More specifically, Will MacAskill [9], a leader in the EA movement, defines EA as two interlinked projects:

1. a research program into how to maximize the good with a given unit of resources, tentatively understanding 'the good' in impartial 'welfarist' terms.

2. the use of insights generated by (1) to try to improve the world.

MacAskill [9] highlights that this definition of EA is:

- *Non-normative.* Effective altruism consists of two projects, rather than a set of normative claims.
- *Maximizing.* The point of these projects is to do as much good as possible with the resources that are dedicated towards it.
- *Science-aligned.* The best means to figuring out how to do the most good is the scientific method, broadly construed to include reliance on careful rigorous argument and theoretical models as well as data.
- *Tentatively impartial and welfarist.* As a tentative hypothesis or a first approximation, doing good is about promoting well-being, with everyone's well-being counting equally. [This working hypothesis may change if convincing evidence should become available that promoting non-welfarist goods is a better way to do good.]

In sum, EA advocates for an open, scientific mindset when considering ethical questions [14]. As such it is consistent with many moral views as it does not imply a normative claim as to how to act, but rather focuses on informing the broad range of moral views that are at least partially interested in improving the positive impact of actions by benefiting others well-being from an impartial perspective [9]. In particular, EA empathizes with a consequentialist perspective [15] (i.e., the results of actions determine their moral value) but also advocates for moral uncertainty [16] (i.e., we are not certain that any one moral theory is completely right) such that most religions (e.g., Christianity, Islam, Buddhism, etc.) and moral theories (e.g., virtue ethics, deontology, utilitarianism) can be informed by insights from EA. Thus, EA can be considered as a key field of reference for a scientifically grounded approach to ethics and specifically practical ethical decision-making with the purpose of maximizing the positive impact of a given set of resources. In the following, we follow the EA Concepts website [10] and outline key considerations for practical ethical decision-making.

Practical Ethical Decision-Making. In practical ethical decision-making, decisions in EA are generally structured in terms of *problems, interventions,* and *focus areas* [10]. A problem is something true about the world, which, if it stopped being true, would improve the world [10]. For example, "people dying from malaria" would be a problem. Interventions are attempts to solve or make progress on problems [10]. For example, "distribution of bed nets" would be an intervention aimed at solving "people dying from malaria". A focus area is a bundle of (inter)related problems that make up a broad field of inquiry [10]. For example, "global health" would be a focus area, which would include the problem "people dying from malaria" but also other related problems such as "people suffering from neglected tropical diseases".

The benefit of distinguishing between problems, interventions, and focus areas is that it allows for a structured approach to identify the *best* opportunities for doing good. Given the vast range of opportunities out there and the limited amount of resources available, it is necessary to engage in some form of triage or prioritization [17]. Assessing the relevance of focus areas allows for a rough mapping of the overall problem space in terms of likelihood of containing the best opportunities for doing good, which, in turn, allows for the prioritization of more in-depth investigations and engagement. Importantly, EA advocates for impartiality and being open to focus on any focus area as long as it is likely to lead to best ways to improve the world [17, 18].

To facilitate this assessment of focus areas, the *importance, tractability, neglectedness (ITN) framework* [10] has emerged as a useful tool within the EA movement. The ITN framework holds that a focus area is more likely to contain great opportunities for doing good the more *important* (the more important the problem, the higher the payoff), *tractable* (the more tractable the problem, the less resources need to be invested), and *neglected* (the more neglected the problem, the higher is the expected marginal utility of additional resources) it is. These factors can then be assessed either qualitatively or quantitatively, which allows for a very rough estimation of the expected value of directing additional resources into a focus area [19].

Given the recognition of marginal utility [20], assessments of focus areas are highly context specific and may change over time. At the moment, mainstream thinking in EA generally recognizes three major focus areas that the movement as a whole should focus on, namely, *global poverty and health, animal welfare*, and *improving the long-term future* [21]. However, personal fit and other contextual considerations may rightfully push individuals or subgroups to engage in and explore other focus areas [19]. For example, the Global Priorities Institute at the University of Oxford explicitly focuses on the identification of relevant focus areas which have yet to be identified [22].

On the level of specific interventions, practical ethical decision-making is generally built around cost-effectiveness or cost-benefit estimates. When faced with resource constraints investing resources cost-effectively is the most responsible thing to do [17]. A challenging topic in cost-effectiveness analyses is the inherent uncertainty but possibly overwhelming importance of long-term consequences [23]. Within EA there is currently no consensus on how to solve this challenge. Thus, informed judgments become an important factor in choosing the most promising interventions to work on [19].

3   Research Approach

This project follows other methodological contributions in the DSR field [3] in applying a DSR approach to framework development with iterative design and evaluate cycles [11]. To develop our framework, we constantly moved back and forth between the literature and our personal experience from the field until we converged on a coherent framework. We assessed the framework by applying it in the context of this research project as well as discussing it at the 2019 pre-ICIS SIGPrag workshop and at a research seminar at the University of Cologne. We used the valuable feedback to further refine our work. An online appendix details this design process in more depth [24].

In terms of the literature search, we conducted an informed narrative literature review [25] covering the domains of ethics in DSR and EA with the goal of synthesizing a common perspective that is grounded in both traditions. We argue that this is an appropriate approach because a systematic literature would have been limiting in terms of sources that could be considered and identified [26]. This is due to the creative element of our research question, the pragmatic nature of EA (i.e., sources are strewn across several websites and not systematically searchable), and the state of discourse on ethics in DSR (i.e., ethics is generally only tangentially mentioned). Thus, we had to build on the in-depth engagement of the researchers in both fields[1] to structure and guide the literature review and conceptual development presented in this paper.

4   An Ethics-Aware Perspective on Design Science Research

We have synthesized an ethics-aware perspective on DSR to provide researchers with a tool that can help them understand and maximize the positive impact of their work. Figure 1 presents our framework as an extension of Hevner's [11] seminal three cycle view of DSR. More specifically, we build on Hevner's [11] framework to conceptualize that DSR projects are:

- initiated by *relevance cycles* which localize the project in the *environment* and define project requirements as well as acceptance criteria,
- carried out through *design cycles* where design and evaluate activities take place,
- informed by *rigor cycles* that integrate the project with related *knowledge bases*.

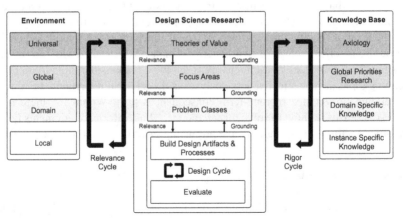

Fig. 1. Our ethics-aware DSR framework extends Hevner's [11] framework with four perspectives to be considered in the optimization of the positive impact of DSR.

Going beyond Hevner [11], we highlight that it is useful to stratify this basic framework according to the *scope* of the environment that is considered. The different perspectives introduced by the scopes allow for a systematic approach to the optimization of the expected positive impact of DSR projects. In the following we describe each of the four scopes that we propose in turn.

Starting from the bottom, the *local* scope concerns the immediate environment that is directly investigated and impacted by the activities of the design cycle of a DSR project.

---

[1] The authors have a combined experience of over 15 years in DSR and more than 3 years in the EA movement.

We propose that activities in the local scope are the ultimate arbiter of the impact of design artifacts as they *ground* knowledge, theories as well as moral considerations in actual experience. Specifically, rigorous observation can lead to the generation of *instance specific knowledge* that directly relates to the effects and outcomes of instantiated artifacts in a particular local environment. However, as one of the main goals of DSR is to generate design artifacts and knowledge that are *relevant* and projectable across different local contexts [2, 3], it is also important to look beyond the local scope.

The *domain* scope concerns a set of local environments and contexts that are aggregated based on shared characteristics. For example, the IS research community is interested in the domain of information systems and IT artifacts. As such the domain scope leads to a perspective where multiple design artifacts can be compared and benchmarked in relation to their *problem classes* (i.e., generalized problems that exists in multiple local contexts). These types of activities can lead to the generation of *domain specific knowledge* that relates to the effects and outcomes of instantiated artifacts across local environments. Importantly, on the one hand, the domain scope helps to assess the *relevance* of the impact of the work done in the local scope (e.g., its novelty or efficacy). On the other hand, the local scope helps to ground the knowledge in the domain scope.

The *global* scope transcends particular domain scopes and emphasizes a holistic perspective on the relationships and trade-offs between global problems or *focus areas*. We define a focus area as a cluster of entangled problem classes that are strongly interrelated without necessarily belonging to the same domain. Because there are not enough resources to address all focus areas to the full extent, priorities for global action need to be identified, set, and evaluated [17, 22]. Traditionally, the global scope has been firmly in the hands of politicians and policy makers without a systematic consideration of ethical concerns. However, recently the emerging field of "*Global Priorities Research*" (GPR) has started to systematically investigate how ethical concerns should influence the global policy arena [22]. One of the main insights of this research stream is that prioritization in the global scope is needed to maximize the expected value that is generated by the resources available [22]. Thus, the global scope is emerging as an important perspective to consider in the optimization of the positive impact of DSR projects. Specifically, it helps to assess the relevance of specific domains and problem classes, which, in turn, provide grounding for work done in the global scope.

The *universal* scope is concerned with foundational questions around the nature of the "goodness", "badness" or "value" of actions and their outcomes. In this perspective, *theories of value* [27] articulate the final measures for assessing the impact of all work done. For example, welfarist theories of value hold that increasing the well-being of sentient beings is the final yardstick by which to measure the positive impact of actions but other theories of value exist [15]. Thus, defining a fixed set of evaluative criteria for design artifacts is challenging as different theories of value may argue for different criteria. Considerations in this scope are generally studied in *axiology* (i.e., the study of values which encompasses the fields of *ethics* and *aesthetics*) which provides a contested but comprehensive body of knowledge. Believes held in the universal scope, on the one hand, determine the *relevance* that is ascribed to actions on the lower levels and, on the other hand, are *grounded* in the actual experiences from the lower levels.

In summary, our ethics-aware perspective argues that the impact of DSR programs and projects gains its relevance from supporting or addressing the universal theories of value that one holds (e.g., increasing the well-being of sentient beings, doing no harm, enabling autonomy, etc.). In turn, theories of value are ultimately grounded in the experiences and outcomes of local actions. Our framework explicates this relationship via four interdependent scopes and perspectives.

5   Application of the Framework

Table 1 details how to optimize the expected positive impact of a research project using our framework with a 3-step procedure that considers all of the perspectives of the framework moving from the universal scope to the local scope. We highlight that this top-down procedure is not the only way to apply the framework but useful to illustrate the general utility of the framework. We use a still ongoing research project by one of the authors as an example [28].

Table 1.   Application of the framework

Step 1: Select a theory of value and terminal target metrics (Universal)

One of the main motivations for engaging in a research project is to have the biggest possible positive impact given the resources that are available to the researchers. However, to optimize for having the biggest positive impact, it is necessary to clarify what is actually meant by "having a positive impact" in the first place. Thus, a clear theory of value and associated terminal target metrics (i.e., metrics which measure the final goals one aims to achieve) need to be identified For the example research project, a welfarist and inclusive theory of value [27] with a pluralist view on values [29] was settled on:

In the universal scope, they *value* the well-being of all sentient beings with consideration for average happiness and equality [29]. Thus, the terminal target metric they optimized for is the number of worthwhile lives under consideration of average happiness and equality. This theory of value was chosen to be deliberately broad and focused on *terminal* rather than *instrumental* values to allow for the impartial assessment of a broad range of focus areas and not restrict the search space prematurely

Step 2: Investigate possible focus areas and select a relevant problem class to work on (Global & Domain)

Given a theory of value and terminal target metrics, the rational goal is to find the problem with the highest expected value to work on. This is a quite challenging endeavor due to the huge size of the problem space. Thus, EA has developed useful heuristics that can help to break down this complex problem into more manageable chunks. For example, it makes sense to scan the global problem space for focus areas that are likely to contain the greatest opportunities for having a positive impact. The main justification for doing this, are the estimated differences in positive impact that focus areas are likely to have [10, 19]. The goal of this heuristic is to narrow down the problem space to the most relevant opportunities that need to be considered

The ITN-framework [10, 19] provides a pragmatic lens to identify focus areas, which has been extensively applied in EA. Thus, there is already a range of focus areas which have been identified as very promising – given one aligns with an impartial and welfarist theory of value as advocated for in EA, which the researchers in the example project did. Consequently, the exploration process proceeded by considering established focus areas in combination with the talents, interests, and resources of the researchers and looking for a good personal fit [30]. This unfolded iteratively by looking at relevant problem classes within the focus areas and assessing the expected value that the researchers could contribute towards addressing them. Activities within this step would generally include making resource assessment for the researchers and rough cost-benefit estimates for working on a specific problem class, etc. [30]. The result for the example project was the following focus area and problem class:

In the global scope, the research project aims to contribute to the focus area of *improving institutional decision making* by investigating and contributing to the problem class of *digital platform initiatives that support bottom-up learning from practitioner initiatives* [28] in the domain scope of ICT4D. The focus area has a capacity building function that can help raise humanities ability to deal with large scale challenges and, thus, potentially affect large numbers of people. The problem class is relevant to this focus area in that such digital platform initiatives can not only support decision making in practitioner initiatives directly but also inform policy making on local, national, and global levels [28]. The project expects to make a meaningful contribution toward solving the problem class because research on the topic is still nascent and, contrasted with its potential impact, neglected [28]

(*continued*)

Table 1. (*continued*)

Step 3: Contribute toward solving the selected problem class (Local & Domain)
Given a relevant problem class with high expected value, the next step is to fully engage in the more established phases of the research process. For example, identify concrete research questions and iterate toward design artifacts and evaluated contributions. For the example research project, this meant: The research project so far resulted in an exploratory case study of the global learning partnership "PANORAMA – Solutions for a Healthy Planet" [28]. PANORAMA is a unique and revelatory case because it developed its own reflection-based method for facilitating knowledge capture in a well-structured format. The research question investigated was: *"How can the developmental potential of digital platforms that facilitate bottom-up learning from practitioner initiatives (such as PANORAMA) be released?"* The work contributes to the theoretical development of the ICT4D research stream by demonstrating a theoretical framework for the study of such platform initiatives and positioning this as a relevant problem class. The analysis of PANORAMA illustrates a reference instance of the problem class and can guide further investigations into related platforms. Moreover, empirical insights into how the developmental potential of such digital platforms can be leveraged is presented, which can inform their design and future development

6   Concluding Remarks

With this paper, we aim for three major contributions. First, we present a framework that integrates ethics with DSR into an *ethics-aware DSR framework*. Our framework explicates four different scopes of considerations regarding DSR projects that are otherwise only implicitly addressed. In particular, it describes a holistic perspective of DSR projects with a coherent link from universal consideration about theories of value and axiological (i.e., moral and aesthetic) considerations to the implementation of a specific local project. While most of the scopes have been individually discussed in prior IS research [1, 2, 4] this framework is the first to structure them into a holistic perspective that is useful to guide action along all scopes. This work has been influenced by research in the field of EA [31], which has articulated a related framework to improve coordination between actors. Similar to our work, the extant framework proposes a chain from (high-level) values to (lower-level) actions and illustrates a way for optimizing the translation between those. Our work goes beyond those efforts in that we present a cohesive integration of core EA concepts into a seminal DSR framework.

Second, we answer our research question and demonstrate the utility of the framework by describing a *procedure for the maximization of the positive impact of research projects*. In summary, our procedure advocates for a deliberate and systematic engagement with a) the theories of value that are motivating specific DSR projects and b) the consideration of focus areas with global relevance, before engaging in the established DSR process. Although this procedure will likely entail many personal (and maybe controversial) judgments [19], it provides a clear, ethically grounded and reproducible way to optimize the positive impact of a project given a theory of value as an entry point. However, this approach does not alleviate researchers from the general challenge of defining relevant and impactful research questions and carrying out rigorous work. Nevertheless, it supports them in finding the best possible starting points for their efforts.

Third, we propose that the framework provides a clear *vocabulary to discuss the prioritization, justification and positioning of research*. By introducing the global scope and the associated concept of focus area, considerations about the global state of affairs in the world can be explicitly integrated into the DSR discourse. Specifically for a field that is trying to have an impact, having a vocabulary and associated concepts to discuss, assess, and prioritize opportunities for doing so is important [4]. The ITN framework provides a useful scaffolding for such discussions. In particular, we argue that it supports useful interdisciplinary discussions of priorities within the DSR community as well as with external stakeholders, as demonstrated by the EA movement. Importantly, a discussion about the most promising focus areas for DSR could help to justify engagement in DSR outside of the traditional business setting (e.g., in the context of ICT4D) and, thus, help create novel research opportunities with high expected positive impact (e.g., IS that help to increase pandemic preparedness or IS that help to improve institutional decision making [30]).

Considering the prior work by Myers and Venable [1], our work mostly relates to principle 1 (i.e., the public interest) and presents a procedure to maximize the expected positive impact of research. Looking at principles 2 to 6 by Myers and Venable (2014), we would argue that they are different in character to principle 1. Whereas principle 1 has the character of a terminal value (i.e., work derives value from supporting public interest), principles 2 to 6 seem to be of more instrumental character (i.e., adhering to the principles generally helps to support public interest). Thus, principles 2 to 6 act as guideposts that can help with the implementation of ethical behavior. While we believe that such principles can be useful (especially for inexperienced scholars), we would argue that they can sometimes stand in conflict (e.g., privacy and quality of the artefact). Here, our framework can be helpful by highlighting the need to clarify a coherent theory of value and recommending to turn to research on axiology for guidance (e.g., [29]).

In terms of limitations, we submit that we did not have enough page space to demonstrate the application of the framework in its entirety. For example, in addition to the top-down starting point illustrated in the example research project, many researchers who are engaged in existing projects already might be wondering how to apply the framework to their case. Given such constraints, the application of the framework could be similar but have the goal of identifying additional opportunities for contribution or new projects that might not have been considered before.

Moreover, we acknowledge that our framework has not extensively been tested with other DSR scholars. While we have presented it on various occasions and iterated based on the feedback we received [24], we cannot present a summative evaluation at this point. However, this does not automatically limit the general validity or applicability of the framework as we have demonstrated in the preceding section. Future research should, in a first step, evaluate the framework through in-depth application in a variety of contexts and reflective assessments by the involved researchers. In a second step, more quantitative assessment of the results of applying the framework would be desirable. To generate the required data, we encourage future research to, both, critique our work as well as make deliberate use of the framework and our proposed vocabulary to prioritize and present their work.

References

1. Myers, M.D., Venable, J.R.: A set of ethical principles for design science research in information systems. Inf. Manag. **51**, 801–809 (2014)
2. Hevner, A.R., March, S.T., Park, J., Ram, S.: Design science in information systems research. MIS Q. **28**, 75–105 (2004)

3. Gregor, S., Hevner, A.R.: Positioning and presenting design science research for maximum impact. MIS Q. **32**, 337–355 (2013)
4. Winter, S.J., Butler, B.S.: Creating bigger problems: grand challenges as boundary objects and the legitimacy of the information systems field. J. Inf. Technol. **26**, 99–108 (2011)
5. Jirotka, M., Grimpe, B., Stahl, B., Eden, G., Hartswood, M.: Responsible research and innovation in the digital age. Commun. ACM **60**, 62–68 (2017)
6. Constantinides, P., Chiasson, M.W., Introna, L.D.: The ends of information systems research: a pragmatic framework. MIS Q. **36**, 1–19 (2012)
7. Iivari, J.: A paradigmatic analysis of information systems as a design science. Scand. J. Inf. Syst. **19** (2007)
8. Tarafdar, M., Gupta, A., Turel, O.: The dark side of information technology use. Inf. Syst. J. **23**, 269–275 (2013)
9. MacAskill, W.: The definition of effective altruism. In: Greaves, H., Pummer, T. (eds.) Effective Altruism – Philosophical Issues. Oxford University Press, Oxford (2019)
10. Centre for Effective Altruism: Effective altruism concepts. https://concepts.effectivealtruism. com/. Accessed 01 Dec 2018
11. Hevner, A.R.: A three cycle view of design science research. Scand. J. Inf. Syst. **19**, 4 (2007)
12. Venable, J., Pries-Heje, J., Baskerville, R.: FEDS: a framework for evaluation in design science research. Eur. J. Inf. Syst. **25**(1), 77–89 (2014). https://doi.org/10.1057/ejis.2014.36
13. Singer, P.: Ethics (2019). https://www.britannica.com/topic/ethics-philosophy
14. Centre for Effective Altruism: CEA's guiding principles. https://www.centreforeffectivealt ruism.org/ceas-guiding-principles/. Accessed 01 Dec 2018
15. Sinnott-Armstrong, W.: Consequentialism. In: Zalta, E.N. (ed.) The Stanford Encyclopedia of Philosophy. Metaphysics Research Lab, Stanford University (2019)
16. MacAskill, W.: Normative uncertainty (2014)
17. Ord, T.: The moral imperative toward cost-effectiveness in global health (2013)
18. Jollimore, T.: Impartiality. In: Zalta, E.N. (ed.) The Stanford Encyclopedia of Philosophy. Metaphysics Research Lab, Stanford University (2018)
19. Wiblin, R.: How to compare different global problems in terms of impact? https://80000h ours.org/articles/problem-framework/. Accessed 04 Dec 2018
20. The Library of Economics and Liberty: Margins and thinking at the margin. https://www.eco nlib.org/library/Topics/College/margins.html. Accessed 04 Dec 2018
21. Centre for Effective Altruism: Introduction to effective altruism. https://www.effectivealt ruism.org/articles/introduction-to-effective-altruism/. Accessed 04 Dec 2018
22. Greaves, H., MacAskill, W., O'Keeffe-O'Donovan, R., Trammell, P.: A research agenda for the global priorities institute (2019)
23. Beckstead, N.: On the overwhelming importance of shaping the far future (2013)
24. Herwix, A., Haj-Bolouri, A.: Having a Positive Impact with Design Science Research – Learning from Effective Altruism (Online Appendix) (2020). https://osf.io/pcv3e/
25. Paré, G., Trudel, M.-C., Jaana, M., Kitsiou, S.: Synthesizing information systems knowledge: a typology of literature reviews. Inf. Manag. **52**, 183–199 (2015)
26. Boell, S.K., Cecez-Kecmanovic, D.: On being 'systematic' in literature reviews in IS. J. Inf. Technol. **30**, 161–173 (2014). https://doi.org/10.1057/jit.2014.26
27. Schroeder, M.: Value theory. In: Zalta, E.N. (ed.) The Stanford Encyclopedia of Philosophy. Metaphysics Research Lab, Stanford University (2016)
28. Herwix, A.: Towards a panorama of sustainable solutions: exploring a global learning partnership for sustainable development. In: Proceedings of the Twenty-Eighth European Conference on Information Systems (ECIS 2020), Marrakesh, Morroco (2020)

29. Carter, A.: A plurality of values (2013)
30. Todd, B., 80,000 Hours team: Our new guide to doing good with your career. https://80000h ours.org/key-ideas/. Accessed 19 Mar 2020
31. Ellen, R.: The values-to-actions decision chain: a lens for improving coordination. https://forum.effectivealtruism.org/posts/Ekzvat8FbHRiPLn9Z/the-values-to-actions-decision-chain-a-lens-for-improving. Accessed 03 Oct 2019

Integrating CCM4DSR into ADR to Improve Problem Formulation

Coquessa Jones[(✉)] and John R. Venable

Curtin University, Perth, WA 6845, Australia
{coquessa.jones,j.venable}@curtin.edu.au

Abstract. Action Design Research (ADR) is a commonly used methodology for conducting Design Science Research (DSR). The first activity in ADR is Problem Formulation, which defines the scope of the research and establishes the working relationships between the researcher(s) and the client(s). However, while tasks and principles are defined for Problem Formulation in ADR, specific ways of performing those tasks to achieve ADR's principle of "theory-ingrained artifact" are lacking in the methodology description. This paper proposes combining Coloured Cognitive Mapping for Design Science Research (CCM4DSR) with ADR to support problem formulation. The combination is demonstrated and evaluated using the case study of an ADR project aiming to develop a purposeful artefact to support melanoma survivors in diligently performing effective skin check behaviours. The paper presents example coloured cognitive maps (CCMs) drawn from the case study and discusses how combining CCM4DSR with ADR contributes to ADR's problem formulation activities, as well as subsequent ADR activities.

Keywords: Action Design Research (ADR) · Coloured Cognitive Mapping for Design Science Research (CCM4DSR) · Design Science Research (DSR) · Problem formulation · Kernel theory · Design theory

1 Introduction

The research presented in this paper was conducted in the context of a larger Action Design Research (ADR) research project, which seeks to determine whether and how a "theory-ingrained artifact" (Sein et al. 2011), in the form of a mobile app, can effect behaviour change in survivors, in the form of increased vigilance i.e. more frequent skin self-examination (SSE) or clinical based monitoring.

Within that context, the project sought to formulate the problem and come up with ideas for such a theory-ingrained artefact. Problem formulation is a key activity/phase within ADR and other DSR methodologies as well. While a key ADR principle (#2) is to develop a theory-ingrained artefact, it is not readily apparent how one can go about doing so. ADR provides principles and activities in its problem formulation phase to support this, but lacks specifics about how to base an artefact design on extant theory. This issue raised our research question.

"How can one operationalise ADR principle #2: Theory-Ingrained Artefact?"

© Springer Nature Switzerland AG 2020
S. Hofmann et al. (Eds.): DESRIST 2020, LNCS 12388, pp. 247–258, 2020.
https://doi.org/10.1007/978-3-030-64823-7_23

To develop ideas for a theory-ingrained artefact, firmly grounded in extant kernel theories, the project combined Coloured Cognitive Mapping for Design Science Research (CCM4DSR) (Venable 2019; Venable 2014) with ADR. This paper presents a case study demonstration and evaluation of how the combination of CCM4DSR and ADR was able to assist in (1) distilling the vast amounts of information obtained through a review of the associated literature and (2) formulating the initial ideas for a viable artefact. Additionally, it illustrates how CCM4DSR will be used to facilitate the development of a strong researcher-client relationship in the next phase of the project.

The next section reviews literature relevant to the problem and its solution. Section 3 then presents the research methodology and research design. Sections 4 and 5 present evidence from the ADR project case study, demonstrating the combination of CCM4DSR with ADR and its benefits for problem formulation in ADR. Section 6 then discusses those findings, their limitations, and potential directions for further research.

2   Theoretical Background/Literature Review

This section gives brief overviews of (1) the overall DSR methodology used in the project (ADR), (2) the methodology that the research reported in this paper investigated for injecting (kernel) theory into the problem formulation (CCM4DSR), and (3) the relationship between kernel theory and design theory.

2.1   Action Design Research (ADR)

ADR is comprised of four stages: 1. Problem Formulation, 2. Building Intervention and Evaluation, 3. Reflection and Learning and 4. Formalisation of Learning (Sein et al. 2011). Each stage has principles associated with it. The research reported in this paper is concerned with how to operationalise ADR's first stage (Problem Formulation) and its second principle (Theory-Ingrained Artefact). ADR principle 2 ensures that ADR-developed artefacts are underpinned by a theoretical construct (or kernel theory) and can be employed at various areas of the research such as "to structure the problem, to identify solution possibilities and to guide design" (Sein et al. 2011).

There are six tasks in the Problem Formulation stage in ADR. Effective problem formulation is essential in DSR as it sets the scope and conceptualisation of the research project for all subsequent activity.

2.2   Coloured Cognitive Mapping for Design Science Research (CCM4DSR)

Venable (2014) proposed that Coloured Cognitive Mapping (CCM) could be used to fill several gaps in the DSR literature including lack of direction on "how to (1) formulate and define problems, (2) transform a problem definition into solution requirements, (3) creatively reason about potential solutions, (4) formulate design theories with constructs and relationships between them at an appropriate level of detail and precision, and (5) collaborate and communicate with multiple stakeholders to reach agreement when conducting the above activities."

Since his 2014 paper, Venable has designed CCM4DSR (Venable 2019) as a methodology supporting virtually all stages of DSR, including problem formulation, solution ideation, evaluation, and design theorising.

Coloured Cognitive Maps (CCMs) are a simple network of nodes and arrows connecting them. The arrows represent some degree of causality; the node at the tail of the arrow causes (contributes to, increases, enables, etc.) the node at the head of the arrow. Each node contains text giving its meaning. Following Eden and Ackermann (2001), the text is divided into two parts: the primary pole, which gives the intended meaning, and the secondary pole, which provides a contrasting opposite and enhances understanding of the meaning. The use of CCMs is preferable to other concept mapping tools as it allows the illustration of causality.

The CCM methodology also conceives two forms or emphases in CCMs. (1) A CCM can be of a "problem as difficulties", which focuses on the problem "as is" and in which most of the nodes have something undesirable as their primary pole. (2) A CCM can be of a "problem as opportunities", which focuses instead on what "ought to be", a vision for a transformation to a desirable future, in which most of the nodes have a change to something desirable as their primary pole. The CCM methodology further proposes a straightforward transformation from a "problem as difficulties" to a "problem as opportunities", i.e. a vision of a better future state.

CCM4DSR adapts CCM to include a procedure with five activities. (1) Problem Diagnosis, Formulation, and Shared Understanding involves mapping and agreeing upon a CCM of the problem as difficulties. (2) General Requirements Derivation converts the CCM of the problem as difficulties into a CCM of the problem as opportunities, envisioning the desired (or required) future state. (3) General Design Ideation identifies candidate purposeful artefacts or components, each of which could cause achieving one or more parts of the problem as opportunities, adds them to the CCM of the problem as difficulties. Based on this augmented CCM, the researchers (and clients) decide the actual scope of the DSR project. (4) Artefact and Design Theory Evaluation uses the CCM to determine which outcomes and/or artefact characteristics to evaluate. (5) Design Theory Formulation makes use of the nodes representing artefact components and the nodes representing desired goals (or purpose) to formulate a design theory.

The focus in this paper is primarily on activities 1–3, as these are the CCM4DSR activities relevant to Problem Formulation in ADR.

3   Research Design: A Case Study Using CCM4DSR in ADR

The research reported in this paper was conducted in the context of a larger Action Design Research (ADR) (Sein et al 2011) project. The first phase of ADR is Problem Formulation, a key principle of which is "Theory-ingrained artefact". This study, potentially like many ADR studies, requires some means to investigate relevant kernel theory and incorporate it into both the formulation of the problem (What is the problem? What are its characteristics?), as well as the design for the artefact (What sort of purposeful artefact might work to solve the problem? What should/could the artefact components and characteristics be, informed by theory about the problem or its solution?).

To investigate the suitability of combining CCM4DSR with ADR, the authors applied it to problem formulation during an ADR project. The ADR project serves as a case study demonstration and evaluation of the combination of CCM4DSR with ADR.

3.1 Case Description

The DSR project that serves as our case study is a PhD-level DSR project investigating how IT can be used to improve upon the problem that many melanoma (skin cancer) survivors do not undertake sufficient preventative measures to reduce recurrence of the cancer and do not undertake frequent enough follow-up checks of their skin health to identify recurrences in a timely fashion. The research is being conducted in collaboration with melanoma clinicians and survivors. The initial idea is to develop an app that helps to increase preventative and monitoring behaviours in melanoma survivors.

Extensive theory exists concerning causes of sub-optimal behaviours as well as some potential remedies. However, at the start of the research project, it was unclear how disparate theory could be integrated and inform features in the app design.

The authors integrated CCM4DSR into the ADR problem formulation stage to gain a rich understanding of the problem and extant (inadequate) solutions, to develop ideas for what artefact requirements and features could address those problems, and also to communicate with potential collaborators on the research project, in order to form a strong agreement for collaboration as well as a rationale for the artefact design.

4 Kernel Theories Informing the Theory-Ingrained Artefact in the Case Study

4.1 The Health Belief Model

The Health Belief Model (HBM) is the main theoretical underpinning of the artefact. The Health Belief Model (HBM) is an individually focused model (Glanz et al. 2008) that originated in America's Public Health Service during the 1950's (Rosenstock 1974). Since its inception it has evolved to include 6 constructs: perceived susceptibility, perceived severity, perceived benefits, perceived barriers, cue to action and self-efficacy (Glanz et al. 2008).

Indeed, medical practitioners already instruct melanoma survivors about appropriate health behaviours (self-skin examination (SSE) and clinical-based monitoring), but we also know that there are still insufficiently high rates of such behaviour. So, the remaining question is, "How can we inform and teach in a way that increases belief and overcomes problems in learning and belief?" To address this problem, we need to understand what causes low belief or other causes of inadequate health behaviours.

4.2 Barriers and Problems with Melanoma Survivor Health Behaviours

Research assessing the HBM has identified perceived barriers and perceived susceptibility as the most predominant constructs (Janz and Becker 1984). The HBM has been used in research to explore early detection and prevention of skin cancer in various age categories from adolescents to aged (Carmel et al. 1994; Lamanna 2004) as well as gender and occupation (Friedman et al. 1995; Jackson and Aiken 2000). Below is a summary of some of the research that can be used as kernel theory to develop a refined understanding and inform the artefact design and further the theory-ingrained result.

Female melanoma patients suffer more adverse psychological effects and report higher levels of distress, anxiety and depression (Tesio et al. 2017). Research has shown that women's anxiety levels nearly double that of men's (Missiha et al. 2003). Female survivors, along with youth, suffer the most from fear of cancer recurrence (FCR) (Tesio et al. 2017).

In general, men have been found to undertake unhealthy behavior that underscores perceived societal gender expectations (Courtenay 2000), leading to poorer health outcomes (Courtenay 2000). This behavior is consistent with male melanoma survivors, leading to significantly higher mortality rates (Australian Institute of Health and Welfare 2018a).

Patients from a lower socio-economic background, ethnic minority, are uneducated or living with an intellectual or physical disability suffer from poorer health outcomes (Bernat et al. 2016). They also have a challenging time obtaining, comprehending and acting on information relevant to their health condition (Bernat et al. 2016).

Health outcomes for regional and remote patients are generally poorer than for the urban population, due in part to difficulties accessing healthcare services (Kim et al. 2017). For melanoma patients, this translates to a greater frequency of the disease and higher mortality rates, as the primary lesion is less likely to be picked up, or a healthcare visit is deferred because it is inconvenient (Inc. 2014). This is most prevalent in males over the age of 65 (Inc. 2014). Rural melanoma sufferers also have an increased need for psychological support (Stamataki et al. 2014).

Older cancer patients share many similar characteristics with the previously mentioned vulnerable patients, in that their comprehension of information is lower than average (Passalacqua et al. 2012; Ramanadhan and Viswanath 2006). The aged do not actively seek information about their condition and treatment options but rely mostly on clinicians, health professionals, family and friends for guidance (Chaudhuri et al. 2013; Eheman et al. 2009; Ramanadhan and Viswanath 2006). This may be in part due to some elderly people having an aversion to technology and reluctance to access the internet (Hanna et al. 2018).

The melanoma survivors most engaged in information seeking are younger, female, have a high socio-economic background and are more educated (Bernat et al. 2016).

The next section demonstrates and evaluates the integration of CCM4DSR into ADR using the problem formulation stage of the larger research project as a case study.

5 Demonstration of Integrating CCM4DSR into ADR for Problem Formulation in the Case Study

This section describes how CCM4DSR was combined with ADR in the problem formulation stage of the case study.

5.1   Problem Diagnosis, Formulation, and Shared Understanding

The first step of CCM4DSR is Problem Diagnosis, Formulation, and Shared Understanding. The step develops a CCM of the problem as difficulties (i.e. the undesirable "as is") and seeks agreement among researchers and stakeholders about the nature, structure, and scope of the problem to be solved. The work reported in this paper presents an initial, literature-based conceptualisation, which can be used a starting point for discussion and seeking agreement with ADR clients. We divide the outcomes of the analysis of the problem as difficulties into two figures (Fig. 1 and 2). Figure 1 outlines the consequences of melanoma survivors failing to adopt good health behaviours, while Fig. 2 shows (some of) the causes.

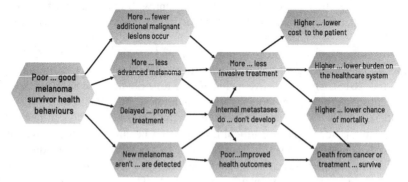

Fig. 1. CCM of consequences of the problem as difficulties (as is)

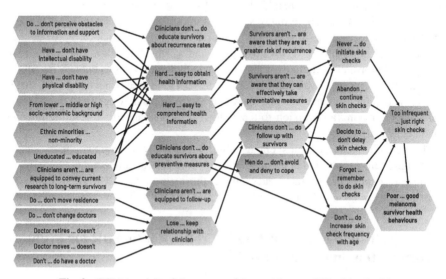

Fig. 2. CCM (partial) of the causes of the problem as difficulties (as is)

In cognitive maps, the elipses ("…") are read as "as opposed to". Thus, the main problem node (on the left) is read as "Poor, as opposed to good, melanoma survivor health behaviours". This node, which is a statement of the core of the problem, is repeated in both Figs. 1 and 2 and forms the link between the two parts of the map.

CCM nodes are coloured to indicate desirability or undesirability. The nodes in Fig. 1 and 2 are all undesirable, so they are coloured red, but also shaped as hexagons since some people are colourblind or the figure might be displayed in black and white. The outcomes shown include outcomes both for individual survivors and for society at large. Further outcomes from death and other aspects, such as prolonged illness and consequences for friends and relatives, are not shown, but are fairly obvious.

Figure 2 shows the causes of the problem. Figure 2 identifies five primary causes (e.g. not initiating skin checks), but also shows causes of the causes, causes of the causes of the causes, etc. Due to space limitations, Fig. 2 excludes some of the causes of three of the primary causes (delaying, forgetting, and not increasing frequency with age).

5.2   General Requirements Derivation

The second step of CCM4DSR is General Requirements Derivation. In this step, the CCMs in Fig. 1 and 2 (problem as difficulties) are inverted to focus on opportunities for solutions (problem as opportunities, including candidates for areas of scope to be research in the DSR project). To do so, each node in Fig. 1 and 2 was converted from an undesirable state to an action to reach a desirable state and the nodes recoloured green (and redundantly shaped as ovals) to indicate desirability. Exceptions are made to that process for nodes that are not inherently undesirable, outside the scope of the project, and/or cannot be changed (e.g., a survivor belongs to a minority). Figure 3 and 4 convey the outcomes of that process, based on Fig. 1 and 2 respectively.

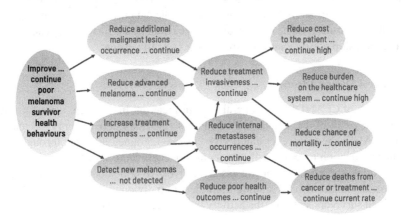

Fig. 3. CCM of the desired outcomes of solving the problem (problem as solutions)

Figure 3 shows what the benefits would be of solving or improving upon the problem. Each of the undesirable nodes from Fig. 1 have been reversed to a desirable outcome and rephrased as an imperative verb phrase indicating action to achieve change.

As shown in Fig. 4, reversing the nodes in Fig. 2 from causes of the problem identifies potential ways to eliminate or reduce the causes of the problem. As in Fig. 3, the text for

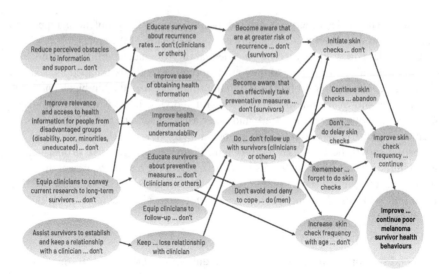

Fig. 4. CCM of actions to reduce causes of the problem (problem as solutions)

each node is placed in the imperative/action tense to indicate action to achieve change. Each node is then a candidate requirement for the DSR artefact to be developed. Not all of the nodes would have to be addressed in a particular DSR project; the researcher(s) and client(s) instead agree on some subset to pursue.

Importantly, some nodes from Fig. 2 cannot actually be changed (e.g., people moving, doctors retiring, or belonging to some disadvantaged group). In those cases, we consider what actions are relevant to overcoming the extant conditions (which are neither desirable nor undesirable). For example, we could assist survivors to establish and keep a relationship, despite various circumstances or life events.

5.3   General Design Ideation

The third step of CCM4DSR is General Design Ideation. In this step, ideas for how to achieve some or all of the actions identified in the previous step, i.e. in Fig. 3 and 4. In support of ADR, the researcher can derive "theory-ingrained artefact" through design thinking and ideation together with the client. For each node, we consider the question "How?" For example, "How can we assist survivors to remember to do skin checks?" Various means might include sending reminders to individuals, placing advertisements to remind all survivors, entering the activity into diaries, and so on. Each idea for "how" is then a candidate feature or aspect of the artefact to be designed in the DSR project. Importantly, some "how" ideas apply to more than one requirement, leading to serendipitous design outcomes. The ideation can be done individually or in a group environment (e.g. brainstorming). The CCM of the problem as solutions provides a way to guide and focus discussion, but considering how the different candidate requirements might be met.

It is beyond the scope of this paper (and the space available) to discuss specifics of what is being done and what "how" candidates/alternatives are raised for the artefact in our ADR project. To summarise though, the project's main vision is to develop an app to serve both practitioners and survivors. By integrating CCM4DSR into ADR to model and synthesise current research into the problem, the improvement of consequences through meeting a selection of requirements is being driven by the literature and will grow and evolve to include feedback and input gathered from key stakeholders.

6   Discussion

6.1   Evaluation of Integration of CCM4DSR with ADR Problem Formulation: Benefits for the Case Study DSR Project

Integrating CCM4DSR into ADR fills a gap in ADR Problem Formulation by taking behavioural or natural science theories about a problem and transforming them into design theories of solving/improving a problem.

After reviewing over 200 publications, we confirmed that there are numerous issues faced by melanoma patients and that survivorship is a point in the disease timeline requiring some form of support, which isn't readily available. Moreover, we identified a large set of problems that were hard to connect and distil into a workable problem formulation that could be progressed into an ADR research direction.

Undertaking the CCM process aided in narrowing the research focus. It provided structure to numerous problem parts (see Fig. 1 and 2) and then forced an inversion of thought from problem structuring to solution ideation and visioning (see Fig. 3 and 4), forming the beginnings of a solution framework.

The process provided key insights that will lead to a more comprehensive and relevant artefact. Instead of developing an artefact that meets general user requirements, we determined the need for a solution that can be tailored towards distinctly different user groups (males, females, disadvantaged, etc.). The necessity for educating survivors wasn't an apparent requirement before using CCM. It had been identified that there is a lack of knowledge around risks (Chen et al. 2016), but until the problem inversion took place there hadn't been a solution considered for this issue. Additionally, until the exercise was conducted, only low and high frequency of skin checks were considered. The CCM process led us to consider several other possible parameters including; not initiating skin checks, abandoning skin checks and forgetting to have skin checks.

Addressing the difficulty of 'men using avoidance and denial as a coping mechanism' (Tesio et al. 2017) and the 'higher male melanoma mortality rates' (Australian Institute of Health and Welfare 2018b) led to further exploration of men's health theory. This uncovered a segment of psychological/health theory centred on the relationship between masculinity and poor health outcomes in men (Courtenay 2000).

6.2   Discussion of Weaknesses of ADR in the Absence of CCM4DSR

Problem Formulation is the foundation upon which the remainder of an ADR project is based. Sein et al. (2011) states that "the problem serves as inspiration for research efforts" (Sein et al. 2011). ADR delivers a framework broken down into stages and principles (Sein et al. 2011) to guide the process but stops short of providing a way to comprehensively explore problem formulation. Without a robust process, there is a possibility that the problem will not be fully understood and that aspects of it will remain hidden to researchers. Failure to perform this step and progress through the ADR stages could then result in an artefact that, on the extreme end, fails to solve the problem as it does not address the nuanced complexities. Researchers can be left with an unsuccessful project and the stakeholders with an artefact that doesn't meet their needs.

Incorporating CCM4DSR into ADR aids ADR researchers to explore the problem and possible improvements/solutions in a constructive manner that promotes well-rounded contemplation of the subject and leads to insights that can be conveyed into realised features and functionality of the artefacts.

A CCM can also serve as a "socially recognisable" (Sein et al. 2011) construct that facilitates the "critical element" of "securing long-term commitment from the participating organization(s) beyond this stage" (Sein et al. 2011). A CCM can be presented to potential participants, help them understand and comprehend the breadth of the problem landscape, and show them that the researchers understand details of the problem and its theoretical and literature context. It also allows space to critique and/or augment existing theoretical knowledge with knowledge obtained from practitioners.

6.3   Theoretical Significance

In this paper, the authors have proposed ideas that form the core of a design theory. The purposeful artefact proposed is one that combines the constructs of CCM4DSR with the ADR methodology, in particular ADR's Problem Formulation stage. It augments CCM4DSR by using it to model theory concerning the causes of a problem. The application of this combination of CCM4DSR with ADR is asserted to have utility for solving the problem of a lack of guidance for problem formulation in ADR, particularly for achieving the ADR guideline of a "theory-ingrained artefact". The paper has provided a demonstration of the artefact as well as evidence (through the power of the results of the case study) of the utility of the approach for generating a theory-ingrained artefact.

The paper has further argued that the purposeful artefact combining CCM4DSR and ADR has utility for securing commitment from clients to participate in an ADR project.

Combining CCM4DSR with ADR yields benefits for the research beyond those anticipated for CCM4DSR. The exaptation of CCM4DSR into the ADR context results in a better theory-ingrained artefact and better client recruitment and engagement.

7   Future Research and Conclusion

The authors plan to further empirically evaluate the integration of CCM4DSR into ADR through the remainder of the main ADR project. The utility of using CCMs to help "secure long-term commitment" (Sein et al. 2011) from stakeholders, including clinicians, melanoma nurses, psychologists, and support groups will be evaluate through using them in dialog with stakeholders. We expect that these interactions will augment, shape, and change the current CCM to better encapsulate the problem/solution landscape, including the specific needs and issues raised by clients/decision makers.

We plan to further demonstrate and evaluate the utility of integration CCM4DSR into ADR's Stage 2: Building, Intervention, and Evaluation and Stage 3: Reflection and Learning (Sein et al. 2011). We anticipate that new knowledge can be integrated into the CCMs as they grow based on outcomes of the BIE cycles and learning about the problem(s) as they are encountered.

References

Australian Institute of Health and Welfare: Melanoma of the skin statistics I Melanoma of the skin. https://melanoma.canceraustralia.gov.au/statistics

Australian Institute of Health and Welfare: Australia's Health 2018 - 3.4 Cancer (2018 b)

Bernat, J.K., Skolarus, T.A., Hawley, S.T., Haggstrom, D.A., Darwish-Yassine, M., Wittmann, D.A.: Negative information-seeking experiences of long-term prostate cancer survivors. J. Cancer Survivorship **10**(6), 1089–1095 (2016). https://doi.org/10.1007/s11764-016-0552-5

Carmel, S., Shani, E., Rosenberg, L.: The role of age and an expanded Health Belief Model in predicting skin cancer protective behavior. Health Educ. Res. **9**, 433–447 (1994). https://doi.org/10.1093/her/9.4.433

Chaudhuri, S., Le, T., White, C., Thompson, H., Demiris, G.: Examining health information-seeking behaviors of older adults. Comput. Inform. Nurs. **31**, 547–553 (2013). https://doi.org/10.1097/01.NCN.0000432131.92020.42

Chen, J., Shih, J., Tran, A.: Gender-based differences and barriers in skin protection behaviors in melanoma survivors. J. Skin Cancer **2016**, 4 (2016)

Courtenay, W.H.: Constructions of masculinity and their influence on men's well-being: a theory of gender and health. Soc. Sci. Med. **50**, 1385–1401 (2000). https://doi.org/10.1016/S0277-9536(99)00390-1

Eden, C., Ackermann, F.: SODA - The Principles. In: Rational Analysis for a Problematic World Revisited (2001)

Eheman, C.R., Berkowitz, Z., Lee, J., Mohile, S., Purnell, J., Marie Rodriguez, E., Roscoe, J., Johnson, D., Kirshner, J., Morrow, G.: Information-seeking styles among cancer patients before and after treatment by demographics and use of information sources. J. Health Commun. **14**, 487–502 (2009). https://doi.org/10.1080/10810730903032945

Friedman, L.C., Webb, J.A., Bruce, S., Weinberg, A.D., Cooper, H.P.: Skin cancer prevention and early detection intentions and behavior. Am. J. Prev. Med. **11**, 59–65 (1995). https://doi.org/10.1016/s0749-3797(18)30502-6

Glanz, K., Rimer, B.K., Viswanath, K. (Kasisomayajula), Orleans, C.T.: Health Behavior and Health Education: Theory, Research, and Practice. Jossey-Bass (2008)

Hanna, L., et al.: Effect of early and intensive nutrition care, delivered via telephone or mobile application, on quality of life in people with upper gastrointestinal cancer: study protocol of a randomised controlled trial. BMC Cancer **18**, 707 (2018). https://doi.org/10.1186/s12885-018-4595-z

Hoyt, M.A.: Masculinity and Cancer: Emotional Approach Coping Processes in Men with Cancer (2007)

Inc., N.R.H.A.: Submission to House of Representatives Standing Committee on Health - Skin Cancer in Australia: awareness, early diagnosis and management, Deakin (2014)

Jackson, K.M., Aiken, L.S.: A psychosocial model of sun protection and sunbathing in young women: the impact of health beliefs, attitudes, norms, and self-efficacy for sun protection. Heal. Psychol. **19**, 469–478 (2000). https://doi.org/10.1037/0278-6133.19.5.469

Janz, N.K., Becker, M.H.: The health belief model: a decade later. Health Educ. Q. **11**, 1–47 (1984). https://doi.org/10.1177/109019818401100101

Kim, H., Goldsmith, J.V., Sengupta, S., Mahmood, A., Powell, M.P., Bhatt, J., Chang, C.F., Bhuyan, S.S.: Mobile health application and e-Health literacy: opportunities and concerns for cancer patients and caregivers. J. Cancer Educ. **34**(1), 3–8 (2017). https://doi.org/10.1007/s13187-017-1293-5

Lamanna, L.M.: College students' knowledge and attitudes about cancer and perceived risks of developing skin cancer - proquest. Dermatology Nurs. **16**, 161–164 (2004)

Missiha, S.B., Solish, N., From, L.: Characterizing anxiety in melanoma patients. J. Cutan. Med. Surg. **7**, 443–448 (2003). https://doi.org/10.1177/120347540300700602

Passalacqua, S., et al.: Information needs of patients with melanoma. Clin. J. Oncol. Nurs. **16**, 625–632 (2012). https://doi.org/10.1188/12.CJON.625-632

Ramanadhan, S., Viswanath, K.: Health and the information nonseeker: a profile. Health Commun. **20**, 131–139 (2006). https://doi.org/10.1207/s15327027hc2002_4

Rosenstock, I.M.: Historical origins of the health belief model. Health Educ. Monogr. **2**, 328–335 (1974). https://doi.org/10.1177/109019817400200403

Sein, M.K., Henfridsson, O., Purao, S., Rossi, M., Lindgren, R.: Action design research. MIS Q. **35**, 1–20 (2011)

Stamataki, Z., Brunton, L., Lorigan, P., Green, A.C., Newton-Bishop, J., Molassiotis, A.: Assessing the impact of diagnosis and the related supportive care needs in patients with cutaneous melanoma. Supportive Care Cancer **23**(3), 779–789 (2014). https://doi.org/10.1007/s00520-014-2414-x

Tesio, V., et al.: Psychological characteristics of early-stage melanoma patients: a cross-sectional study on 204 patients. Melanoma Res. **27**, 277–280 (2017). https://doi.org/10.1097/CMR.000 0000000000348

Venable, J.R.: Using coloured cognitive mapping (CCM) for design science research. In: Tremblay, M.C., VanderMeer, D., Rothenberger, M., Gupta, A., Yoon, V. (eds.) DESRIST 2014. LNCS, vol. 8463, pp. 345–359. Springer, Cham (2014). https://doi.org/10.1007/978-3-319-06701-8_25

Venable, J.R.: Coloured Cognitive Mapping for Design Science Research (CCM4DSR) (2019). Unpublished tutorial slides available from the author

Problematizing in IS Design Research

Peter Axel Nielsen$^{(\boxtimes)}$ (iD)

Human-Centred Computing, Department of Computer Science, Aalborg University, Aalborg,
Denmark
pan@cs.aau.dk

Abstract. This paper is based on the interest to see how problems are addressed in
information systems design research. Problems addressed by design research are
often implicit, sometimes open, and sometimes even underdeveloped. Problem-
solving processes, action research and in a broader sense, engaged scholarship
all encompass the explicit addressing of problems and investigation problem situations. Such a problem-orientation is to a lesser degree part of design research.
In this paper, we will investigate how we can provide a better understanding of
problematizing in design research; and in particular what we may learn from other
approaches with a stronger problem-orientation.

Keywords: Problematization · Problem formulation · Problem analysis · Action
research · Design research · Engaged scholarship

1 Introduction

With this paper, we seek to understand problematization in information systems design
science research and how and why problematization may be improved. There is a
sequence in the argument:

1. Problematization is already known within inquiry and design. In research it is well-
   known in engaged scholarship and in action research.
2. Design science research methodologies mention problems, but they do not seem to
   play a vital role.
3. Compared to other problem-oriented approaches, what is missing in design science
   research is:

   a. an explication of problematization,
   b. viewing the process as problem-setting rather than problem-solving, and
   c. empirical grounding of problematization in addition to theoretical grounding.

We do this by first looking at the role of problematization in inquiry and design
in general through the works by Checkland [1] and Schön [2]. Then we turn attention
towards how problematization is a crucial activity of engaged scholarship as explained
by Van der Ven [3] and key in information systems action research as explained by

© Springer Nature Switzerland AG 2020
S. Hofmann et al. (Eds.): DESRIST 2020, LNCS 12388, pp. 259–271, 2020.
https://doi.org/10.1007/978-3-030-64823-7_24

McKay and Marshall [4], in canonical action research by Davidson et al. [5] as well as collaborative practice research by Iversen et al. [6].

Based on a broad understanding of problematization we analyze its role and methods in information systems design science research (DSR) through Hevner et al.'s original exposition of the ideas [7], and DSR methodologies such as Peffers et al. [8] together with central examples of published DSR. There are exceptions [e.g., Venable 9, 10], but problematization does not play a key role in how design science research gets reported.

In summary, we intend to argue that problematization in design science research can be informed by what is already known about problem-solving and problem-setting. That is, we should concern ourselves with what we can learn from problem-solving and research approaches engaging in problem situations. From this, we can discuss how an empirical process for problem formulation can be understood and supported, and thereby contribute to the grounding of problematization in DSR studies.

2   Problematizing in Inquiry and Design

A problem is not just given as though it exists objectively. A problem situation may be open to different ideas or interpretations. This has been referred to as 'unstructured problem situation' by Checkland [1, 11], as 'problem setting' by Lanzara [12], and as 'reflection-in-action' by Schön [2]. It is key to a modern understanding of inquiry and design that it takes effort to arrive at an understanding and formulation of what the problem may be taken to be. We will refer to this effort as 'problematization.'

2.1   Soft Systems Methodology

Checkland's Soft Systems Methodology (SSM) is a process for organizational change and problem-solving [1, 11]. It is suggested in SSM that every problematic situation is unique. In SSM, the problematization process is based on several techniques including analysis of problem owners and intervention, analysis of the political system, and analysis of the system [13]. The problem situation is expressed in rich pictures. The problem analysis can be elaborate, but in all cases, the reason for performing the problem analysis is to lead to the solving of problems (or in Checkland's terms the alleviation of problems). It prepares the ground for achieving better results, it is an empirical process that links the more formal thinking to the problem situation at hand, and it is also suggesting which changes may be feasible in the present problem situation [13]. Following Checkland on problem analysis, we should take care in analyzing problem situations empirically to such a degree that it prepares the ground for evaluating and accepting solutions the better they match the understanding of the problem situation. The process of moving back and forth between understanding the problem situation and the solutions is genuinely iterative.

2.2   Problem Setting in Design

There are many accounts of what problem-solving is or perhaps more rightly, what problem-setting should be taken to be. For information systems design, Lanzara argues that there are three distinctly different ways of looking at it: functional analysis, problem-solving, and problem setting [12]. Few will take functional analysis to be a design process, but it nevertheless gets practiced. Problem-solving, on the other hand, is ascribed to Simon and his work on bounded rationality and satisficing behaviour. A problem is taken as given and design is the search for a solution. The emphasis is on the search and not on what the problem is taken to be. Lanzara argues that Simon's theory of design processes is limited and that it provides a poor understanding of design practice. He emphasizes that design is "a process of collective inquiry" "among several actors in cooperation or competition, or with mixed interests over the problem at hand" [12, p. 33]. He then argues that we need to embrace design processes as problem-setting as done by Schön. His argument is compelling as it emphasizes how a problem is a particular framing of a situation and that there are many possible framings that all make sense.

Schön is a key innovator in turning design as problem-solving into design as problem-setting [2]. Schön's empirical studies of design processes reveal a critique and a new theory of design as reflection-in-action. First, in his critique he argues strongly against what he calls 'technical rationality' in which problems, as addressed by professional practitioners, fall into scientific categories each pointing to solutions through instrumental problem-solving, and "with this emphasis on problem-solving, we ignore problem setting" [2, p. 40]. Problem setting, to Schön, is a "process in which, interactively, we name the things to which we will attend and frame the context in which we will attend to them" [2, p. 40]. Situations rarely fall into scientific categories as situation are unique, thus escaping an idealized image of professional knowledge.

Second, Schön's theory of design as reflection-in-action is an understanding of design where every situation is unique [2]. Following Schön, we shall need to see problems as embedded in a unique situation and requiring their own unique problem setting based on how we frame the situation. Key aspects are [2]:

- *Experimental problem setting* in which situations are complex, uncertain and problematic and means and ends are mutually dependent. Problem setting is seen as a series of experiments to reframe the situation (p. 132). The understanding of what constitutes an experiment is broad, and it may be as loose as asking 'what-if?', on the spot experiments, and exploratory experiments, and it may be as formal as hypothesis-testing experiments (pp. 145–147).
- *Repertoire* is the utilization of past experience in terms of "examples, images, understandings, and actions" (p. 138). The designer makes sense of a unique situation by seeing it "as something already present in [her/]his repertoire" (p. 138) to see the unfamiliar and potentially transcend it. This is not to succumb to existing theories, concepts, or rules. Seeing-as is rather an experimentation and thinking with metaphors, i.e., seeing it as something it is not (p. 184).
- *Stance towards inquiry* is about how the designer is not an observer or a spectator. The designer is an agent in "reflective conversation with a situation that [s]he treats as unique and uncertain" (p. 163). The designer imposes a framing and listens to the situation's backtalk and must entertain new confusion in the process of inquiry.

Schön's theory is concerned with many forms of professional knowledge and work, but his position on design is a significant part of it. In addition to seeing all situations a unique and requiring framing to set the problem, his research has also led to understanding design as an activity that is much more complex than search for a solution to a given problem.

It is also important to understand the implication of Schön's theory that problem setting includes problem solving. Problem setting does not preclude problem solving as there is an intricate not to say intrinsic relationship between the framed problem and the design outcome.

3   Problematizing in Research

Problematizing is a common aspect of much research. This is particularly the case in Van de Ven's approach to engaged scholarship and in all explanations of action research of which we give a few examples by McKay & Marshall and by Davidson et al.'s model of canonical action research for IS.

3.1   Engaged Scholarship

Engaged scholarship by Van der Ven is concerned with the relationship between research and practice, and it covers both action research and design research [3, 14]. One of the four key activities in engaged scholarship is problem formulation. It is understood as playing "a key role in grounding the subject or problem in reality" [3, p. 71]. Van de Ven discusses several challenges and suggests several perspectives that must be applied to problem formulation. These include [3, pp. 72–84]:

- Understanding the problem situation, its focus and timespan, organisational level, and scope.
- Gathering information to ground an understanding of the problem in its situational context is basically asking: who?, where?, what?, when?, why?, and how?
- Diagnosing its symptoms and characteristics, e.g., breakdown, clarifying observations, using heuristics to match problem and solution.

Van de Ven goes on to provide guidelines for conducting problem formulation and "situate, ground, diagnose and infer the problem up close and from afar" [3, p. 10]. At a detailed level the guidelines include problem diagnosis as an empirical process to classify phenomena into categories – existing or emergent. Part of the manifestation of problem formulation is also a research question that singles out the particular knowledge interest and as such it resembles Schön's framing through reflection-in-action. At an even more detailed level, Van de Ven employs two techniques to bring the diagnosis forward and surface the problems: cognitive mapping and group process technique.

3.2 Action Research

The need to address problems is clear from the definitions of action research [15, 16]. Action research aims to "contribute both to the practical concerns of the people in an immediate problem situation" and to research [16]. McKay and Marshall [4] explain what they call the dual imperative of action research, i.e., that is the problem-solving process and the research process. They explain

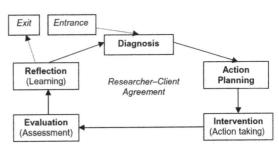

Fig. 1. Action research cycle [17]

this with a clear emphasis on the differences in the processes, but also with a clear focus on how, when and why they relate. The problem-solving interest has in particular two activities 'problem identification' and 'reconnaissance about the problem', the latter including "where the action researcher endeavours to find out about the nature of the problem and the problem context, who the problem owners are, key stakeholders in the problem-solving process, historical, cultural, and political components of relevance, and so on" [4, p. 50].

Action research comes in different forms, e.g., canonical action research [17] (Fig. 1) and collective practice research [6, 18]. Problem analysis is key in both forms. In canonical action research there is an explicit activity in the circular, iterative research process through which problems are addressed, e.g., diagnosis in canonical action research [5, 17], followed iteratively by a planned intervention to handle these identified problems. This is supported by two criteria claiming that the action researchers should conduct an independent diagnosis of the organizational situation and not only take the clients' problems at face value to understand the nature of the problems and determine their causes (criteria 2b) and whether the planned intervention was explicitly based on the diagnosis (criteria 2c). An exemplary use of canonical action research is found in [19]. In their diagnosis "researchers and practitioners jointly formulate a working hypothesis of the research phenomenon" [19, p. 441] from which they identify several problems and ended with a problem-solving hypothesis. In their second iteration, the problem-solving hypothesis focused more on the prototyping results, in which ways the initial problems had been solved, and in which ways new problems had arisen.

There are several examples of elaborate problem analysis in collaborative practice research [18, 20]. Further illustration of an empirical problematization in collaborative practice research is found in [6]. Their appreciation of the problem situation was based on months of joint meetings between the practitioners and researchers, qualitative interviews with key actors, and process assessments. The collaboration went on for three years, and when different problems were teased out, they were addressed iteratively and with their intervention planning. The problem situation was eventually framed as one of poor understanding of the risks faced by change initiatives and equally poor understanding of what to do about these risks. This appreciation of the problem situation did not come immediately and was not easily achieved.

4 Problematizing in Design Science Research

Design science research has with the account by Hevner et al. [7] gained increasing momentum in IS research. DSR methodologies are often used, and there is by now a body of knowledge on DSR [21] as well as very diverse applications of the research approach.

4.1 IS DSR

Design research as it is outlined by Hevner et al. is fundamentally problem-solving [7]. In their version of design science research, they emphasise a problem-orientation in stating "design science [...] creates and evaluates IT artefacts intended to solve identified orga-

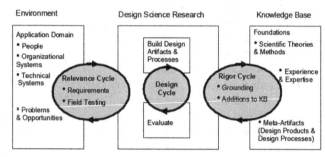

Fig. 2. Three cycles of design science research [23]

nizational problems" [7]. They also recommend seven guidelines of which one is 'problem relevance' as an objective to develop solutions to important and relevant business problems. The detailed guidelines are however more concerned with the relevance of research with little recommendation on how to address what the problem is or should be taken to be. There is much allegiance to a Simonian theory of problem-solving. This is emphasised in [22] where the relevance cycle translates the environment (of which the problem situation is part) to requirements, see Fig. 2.

The design theory of emergent knowledge processes was developed through action research [23], and that has later been taken as design science research [7]. There seems to be much consensus that this solid piece of research is exemplary of design science research. While there is a problem stated [23] there is no problem analysis on which the research focus has been grounded. From the standpoint of problematizing, there are two issues missing. First, it would have been very interesting to see what the specific problems were, how they were experienced by the practitioners, and how 'wicked' they were. Second, the research involved four companies, and we are not informed about how they saw the problem situation, how the researchers got to know about their problem situations and their differences.

4.2 IS DSR Methodology

DSR methodologies emphasise 'awareness of problem' [24] and 'problem identification and motivation' [8]. The problem identification in DSRM suggests to define a research problem, justify the value of a solution to this problem and underpin the researchers' reasoning about the problem [8]. The recommended activity is not further elaborated, cf. [10], and the illustrative cases are sparse on how the problem identification can be conducted.

Design science research published in a recent special issue of the European Journal of Information Systems reveals that problem analysis and problem presentation is often very brief and sometimes even missing completely. For example, one exemplary article provides a design theory as a response to a theoretically defined research problem [25]. Another exemplar provides a design theory where the research was driven by research objectives identified from the literature [26]. A third exemplar develops a fuller utilization of DSRM in which they identify and formulate the problem and objectives to which the response is a set of design principles [27]; yet the problematization is theoretical and not grounded in an empirical understanding of problem situations.

Not all design science research downplays the importance of problematizing. In [24] there is a strong emphasis on theory development through DSR, but there is also an exposition of 'awareness of the problem' in which they first elaborate on the research problem to be addressed and then define it through a research question. The elaboration though is more theoretical than grounded in an empirical understanding of a wicket problem situation.

There had been recent interest in the problem-orientation of DSR. In a literature review of 72 DSR articles of which 41 were empirical they classified the different types of problems addressed into [28]: business problems, technology problems, and systems development problems. They do, however, not review how the problematization led to the types of problems. Current research suggests that despite the importance of problem-orientation in DSR research that it lacks a conceptualization of what a problem space is [29]. Their conceptualization of problem space consists of three distinctly different parts: needs, goals, and requirements; and that these three parts relate to stakeholders. This conceptualization was derived theoretically and then shown on two examples that needs and stakeholders are (sometimes or often) missing in the explanation of the problem space. The conceptualization does not per se suggest how to problematize, but do suggest that the four concepts should be covered in the results of a problematization process.

A different direction was taken in a current literature review of how research questions get asked in DSR studies [30]. How research questions are formed is as important as a broader conceptualization of the problem space. They distinguish between a problem statement and a research question where the problem statement leads to the research question. The review leads to an elaborated set of options for formulating a research question in DSR. It does not per se suggest how to problematize.

The limited role of problematization and the differences between exemplars of DSR may occur because of different article genres [31]. They may also occur because most are following what Iivari has labelled Strategy 1 where there is no client, no situation, and no specific problem to be solved [32]. This seems not to the case, and it seems more likely that problematization in design science research has been downplayed over time. It is not that design science research is less supportive of problem-orientation [33] it is more that reporting on the problematization does not play a role.

There are exceptions to the mainstream DSR literature that emphasizes the importance of problematization [10]. Venable analyses the mainstream literature and reach the conclusion that there is "little to no guidance on how to understand, represent, and define the problem to be solved" [10, p. 347]. From this he suggests techniques to be used in the problematization process including fishbone diagrams, problematiques, and in particular coloured cognitive mapping. Coloured cognitive mapping is explained and evaluated in detail, and the emphasis is on the elaborate understanding and grounding of the problem situation.

4.3 Action Design Research

Action design research has come about as an attempt to cross-fertilise between action research and design research [34]. When "defining a problem as an instance of a class of problems" it places itself with design research in the sense that it purports to deal with several cases at the same time. The debate on whether action research and design science research are similar or distinctly different [35] has not been reconciled as they remain attached to what Iivari has termed Strategy 1 and 2 [32], but action design research is a serious attempt that creates much interest.

In action design research, there is through three problem-oriented tasks [34, p. 41] a stronger concern for the problem situation than in design research as suggested above. It is not clear, however, what is meant by a 'class of problems' in action design research or how these can be investigated, and it does not help much when a task of the learning stage is to abstract the learning into concepts for a class of field problems. It is then much easier to follow the exemplary action research because that has already been cast as action research in [19] in which the problematizing was empirically grounded as we have discussed above.

It is not only in action design research that we find the notion of 'class of problems'. It is also found in much DSR research, e.g., [9, 36–38]. The 'class of problems' seems to be a construct that is more needed for purposes of theorizing, for example, as can be seen in "the design is incomplete because it describes a class of design problems, not a single specific design problem" in the exposition of explanatory design theory [38]. It is more connected to a range of designs, i.e., a class of designs rather than a class of problems.

Designs that cater for a class of problem could perhaps be better understood as what Alexander refers to as 'patterns' [38], where a pattern acts as 'a partial solution looking for a problem' [39]. The patterns known from object-oriented modelling and programming are fine-tuned to suggest design opportunities to practitioners, and they encapsulate much knowledge of relationships between problems and solutions.

5 What's Missing?

In engaged scholarship, there is a clear distinction between action research and design research, namely that action research is conducted inside an organisation, attached, and where the researcher examines the problem domain as an internal participant [3]. Design research, on the other hand, is conducted as an external observer, detached from the organisation. The argument is that design research often requires evaluation across several cases [3]. This distinction has been utilised in an analysis of Scandinavian information systems research [14], but for information systems, in general, this distinction is not clear from the main bulk of design science research methodologies. Design science research does not take a clear stance on the inside-outside issue. For action design research, it is not clear whether it is based on an insider view of the problem situation, or it is an outsider view of a class of problems. The case in action design research [19, 34] stem clearly from action research and is viewed from the inside.

The outside view may be inherent in design research. It may be inherited from the origins of design research, from Simon, from walls et al. [36], or from Markus et al. [23]. In the case of [23], there is no grounding in problems inside an organization but across four organisations. With a design theory as the contribution, it is easy to see the design science research in it – also with the distinction from engaged scholarship. In early design research, there is the idea of 'meta-requirements' "rather than simply requirements because a design theory does not address a single problem but a class of problems" [36]. This initial understanding of what a problem is (or may be taken to be) is then transformed into requirements for the solution. It seems that while the problems are present in the research, they are not necessarily based on an empirical understanding. There is little reporting of empirical data being gathered and analysed.

While design science research at one level seems to be based on problem-solving, we can now see that much problematizing in design research is searching for research gaps in the literature and with less concern for an empirical grounding. We suggest that problematizing should not merely be gap-closing theory, and it should not take problems as given.

If we want to maintain that design research is genuinely problem-solving, we must pay attention to what the problem is taken to be. We may as much design research stay with a Simonian view of problem-solving and take problems as given, or we can take the view of pragmatism on problem-setting as Schön. The latter view on problematizing is so far underrepresented in information systems design research, and it is underdeveloped conceptually and methodologically. This raises the question: How can we improve on problematizing?

We need three things. First, we will need to take the consequences for problematizing of a modern stance towards problem-solving and problem-setting. This should include what we can learn from Schön, Checkland, and others on problem analysis as presented above. It should also include what we can learn from action research regarding problem diagnosis and from engaged scholarship regarding problem formulation. Borrowing from action research will not take care of the issue of whether we are inside an organisation solving problems for a client or we are outside working across cases. The problem formulation in engaged scholarship does not choose a side on this issue and can be applied irrespective of the inside-outside issue.

Second, we will need to figure out how the problematizing can become an empirical activity. The reported experiences are scattered, Nielsen & Persson [40] reports from a problem formulation activity inspired by engaged scholarship. From this experience they suggest three principles: (1) problem dialogue between practitioners and researchers including assessing assumptions underlying the problem situation; (2) problem deliberation involving practitioners in assessing relevance and priorities; and (3) problem flexibility to allow for an open problem space and re-visit the problem formulation. In their problem formulation, they employed qualitative interviewing in several organisations, a survey of all relevant organisations, and joint workshops with selected organisations. They also show one way to transition from a solution that worked for one organisation (as in Van de Ven's inside view) to evaluating how well it worked for several organisations (as in the outside view). They pursue empirical problematization further in [41].

Table 1 summarises a few techniques which can likely be transferred from problem-solving and design and from action research. Two concerns exist:

Table 1. A repertoire of problem analysis techniques

Problem analysis technique	References, e.g.,
Drawing rich pictures	[13, 49]
Grounded action research	[50]
Problem diagnosis based on qualitative interviewing	[20]
Coloured cognitive mapping	[10]
Analysis of the intervention, the social systems, and the political system	[13]
Problem formulation including cognitive mapping and group process technique	[3]
Engaged problematizing: survey, qualitative interviewing, and workshops	[40]
Qualitative interviewing	[42]
Participant observation	[42]
Prototyping	[51]
Research diaries and reflection	[43, 44]
Diagnostic mapping	[52]

- What is the stance towards collecting data as an observer or as an involved actor? The observer and the participant-observer are the more common, but the engaged scholar and the action researcher are usually much more involved and sometimes even proactive. The former calls for data collection techniques such as observation and interviewing, e.g., [42], while the latter utilises more reflective techniques, e.g., [43, 44], and requires researchers with problem-solving competences.
- What is the stance towards the analysis of the data? The information systems literature is already filled with much background and discussion of this issue from a positivist stance, over an interpretive stance, to a critical, or a pragmatist stance, e.g., [45–48].

Third, we need criteria by which we can evaluate the problematizing. It is interesting to observe a historical difference between action research and design research. Action research struggled early on with clarifying how theory comes into action, and all criteria now emphasise the need for a theory or framework in the research design. This came into action research through [53] and into information systems action research with the MIS

Quarterly special issue and some key exemplars in which the criteria were elaborated [6, 19, 54, 55]. IS design science research has, from the very beginning been driven towards theory and design theory [7, 23, 36]. There has from the beginning been a focus on evaluating the design theories through empirical evaluation of the designed artefacts. What is now missing is a stronger empirical grounding of problems against which the artefacts (hence design theories) can be evaluated. It may be too early to suggest what the criteria should be, but with a starting point in criteria from action research, we can transfer and extend these. As an ending note:

- The problematizing should be empirically grounded and include transparent data collection and analysis
- The problematizing should be summarised and presented as an analysis of the empirical data and justify when the analysis is based on a theoretical framework.

6 Conclusion

In this paper, we started with the simple observation that information systems design research was lacking a clear and strong component covering problem analysis. This is somewhat surprising as the design research literature claims a strong allegiance to a problem-solving paradigm. We have therefore investigated this by first outlining how it has been done in problem-solving processes based on Schön and Checkland then we have outlined it as it occurs in action research and the broader social research thinking behind engaged scholarship. From this, we have suggested that design research is missing this very important component of problematizing.

We can do better. The three things that can contribute to this are: (1) the stance towards problematizing should be based on problem-setting; (2) problematizing needs to become an empirical activity; and (3) problematizing requires new and elaborated criteria to be evaluated properly.

References

1. Checkland, P.: Systems Thinking, Systems Practice. Wiley, Chichester (1981)
2. Schön, D.: The Reflective Practitioner: How Professionals Think in Action. Basic Books (1983)
3. Van de Ven, A.H.: Engaged Scholarship: A Guide for Organizational and Social Research. Oxford University Press, Oxford (2007)
4. Mckay, J., Marshall, P.: The dual imperatives of action research. IT People 14, 46–59 (2001)
5. Davison, R.M., Martinsons, M.G., Ou, C.X.J.: The roles of theory in canonical action research. MIS Q. 36, 763–786 (2012)
6. Iversen, J., Mathiassen, L., Nielsen, P.A.: Managing risk in software process improvement: an action research approach. MIS Q. 28, 395–411 (2004)
7. Hevner, A.R., March, S.T., Park, J., Ram, S.: Design science in information systems research. MIS Q. 28, 75–105 (2004)
8. Peffers, K., Tuunanen, T., Rothenberger, M.A., Chatterjee, S.: A design science research methodology for information systems research. J. Manag. Inf. Syst. 24, 45–77 (2007)

9. Venable, J.R.: The role of theory and theorising in design science research. DESRIST **2006**, 1–18 (2006)

10. Venable, J.R.: Using coloured cognitive mapping (CCM) for design science research. In: Tremblay, M.C., VanderMeer, D., Rothenberger, M., Gupta, A., Yoon, V. (eds.) DESRIST 2014. LNCS, vol. 8463, pp. 345–359. Springer, Cham (2014). https://doi.org/10.1007/978-3-319-06701-8_25

11. Checkland, P.: Soft systems methodology: a thirty year retrospective. Syst. Res. Behav. Adcience **17**, 11–58 (2000)

12. Lanzara, G.F.: The Design Process: Frames, Metaphors, and Games. Systems Design for, with and by the Users, pp. 29–40 (1983)

13. Checkland, P., Scholes, J.: Soft Systems Methodology in Action. Wiley, Chichester (1990)

14. Mathiassen, L., Nielsen, P.A.: Engaged scholarship in IS research. Scand. J. Inf. Syst. **20**, 3–20 (2008)

15. Avison, D.E., Lau, F., Myers, M.D., Nielsen, P.A.: Action research. Commun. ACM **42**, 94–97 (1999)

16. Rapoport, R.N.: Three dilemmas in action research: with special reference to the tavistock experience. Hum. Relations **23**, 499–513 (1970)

17. Davison, R.M., Martinsons, M.G., Kock, N.: Principles of canonical action research. Inf. Syst. J. **14**, 65–86 (2004)

18. Mathiassen, L.: Collaborative practice research. Inf. Technol. People **15**, 321–345 (2002)

19. Lindgren, R., Henfridsson, O., Schultze, U.: Design principles for competence management systems: a synthesis. MIS Q. **28**, 435–472 (2004)

20. Iversen, J., Nielsen, P.A., Nørbjerg, J.: Situated assessment of problems in software development. Data Base Adv. Inf. Syst. **30** (1999)

21. Hevner, A., Chatterjee, S.: Design science research in information systems. In: Design Research in Information Systems, pp. 9–22. Springer, Boston (2010). https://www.springer.com/gp/book/9781441956521

22. Hevner, A.R.: A Three cycle view of design science research. Scand. J. Inf. Syst. **19**, 87–92 (2007)

23. Markus, M.L., Majchrzak, A., Gasser, L.: A design theory for systems that support emergent knowledge processes. MIS Q. **26**, 179–212 (2002)

24. Kuechler, B., Vaishnavi, V.: On theory development in design science research: Anatomy of a research project. Eur. J. Inf. Syst. **17**, 489–504 (2008)

25. Brandt, T., Feuerriegel, S., Neumann, D.: Modeling interferences in information systems design for cyberphysical systems: Insights from a smart grid application. Eur. J. Inf. Syst. **27**, 207–220 (2018)

26. Coenen, T., Coertjens, L., Vlerick, P., Lesterhuis, M., Mortier, A.V., Donche, V., Ballon, P., De Maeyer, S.: An information system design theory for the comparative judgement of competences. Eur. J. Inf. Syst. **27**, 248–261 (2018)

27. Seidel, S., Chandra Kruse, L., Székely, N., Gau, M., Stieger, D.: Design principles for sensemaking support systems in environmental sustainability transformations. Eur. J. Inf. Syst. **27**, 221–247 (2018)

28. Amrollahi, A., Ghapanchi, A.H., Talaei-Khoei, A.: From artefact to theory : ten years of using design science in information systems research. In: Proceedings of the 13th European Conference on Research Methodology for Business and Management Studies (ECRM), pp. 383–393. Academic Conferences International Ltd (2014)

29. Maedche, A., Gregor, S., Morana, S., Feine, J.: Conceptualization of the problem space in design science research. In: Tulu, B., Djamasbi, S., Leroy, G. (eds.) DESRIST 2019. LNCS, vol. 11491, pp. 18–31. Springer, Cham (2019). https://doi.org/10.1007/978-3-030-19504-5_2

30. Thuan, N.H., Drechsler, A., Antunes, P.: Construction of design science research questions. Commun. Assoc. Inf. Syst. **44**, 332–363 (2019)

31. Peffers, K., Tuunanen, T., Niehaves, B.: Design science research genres: introduction to the special issue on exemplars and criteria for applicable design science research. Eur. J. Inf. Syst. **27**, 129–139 (2018)
32. Iivari, J.: Distinguishing and contrasting two strategies for design science research. Eur. J. Inf. Syst. **24**, 107–115 (2014)
33. Baskerville, R., Baiyere, A., Gregor, S., Hevner, A., Rossi, M.: Design science research contributions: Finding a balance between artifact and theory. J. Assoc. Inf. Syst. **19**, 358–376 (2018)
34. Sein, M.K., Henfridsson, O., Purao, S., Rossi, M., Lindgren, R.: Action design research. MIS Q. **35**, 37–56 (2011)
35. Iivari, J., Venable, J.: Action research and design science research - seemingly similar but decisively dissimilar. In: 17th European Conference on Information Systems (2009)
36. Walls, J., Widmeyer, G., El-Sawy, O.: Building an information system design theory for vigilant EIS. Inf. Syst. Res. **3**, 36–59 (1992)
37. Gregor, S., Jones, D.: The anatomy of a design theory. J. Assoc. Inf. Syst. **8**, 312–335 (2007)
38. Baskerville, R., Pries-Heje, J.: Explanatory design theory. Bus. Inf. Syst. Eng. **2**, 271–282 (2010)
39. Mathiassen, L., Munk-Madsen, A., Nielsen, P.A., Stage, J.: Object-Oriented Analysis & Design. Marko, Aalborg (2000)
40. Nielsen, P.A., Persson, J.S.: Engaged problem formulation in IS research. Commun. Assoc. Inf. Syst. **38** (2016)
41. Nielsen, P.A., Persson, J.S.: Useful business cases: value creation in IS projects. Eur. J. Inf. Syst. **26**, 66–83 (2017)
42. Patton, M.Q.: Qualitative Research and Evaluation Methods. Sage Publications (2001)
43. Engin, M., Ed, D.: Research diary: a tool for scaffolding. Int. J. Qual. Methods. **10**, 296–306 (2011)
44. Jepsen, L.O., Mathiassen, L., Nielsen, P.A.: Back to thinking mode: diaries for the management of information systems development projects. Behav. Inf. Technol. **8** (1989)
45. Miles, M.B., Huberman, A.M.: Qualitative Data Analysis: An Expanded Sourcebook. Sage Publications, Thousand Oaks (1994)
46. Klein, H.K., Myers, M.D.: A set of principles for conducting and evaluating interpretative field studies in information systems. MIS Q. **23**, 67–93 (1999)
47. Pozzebon, M.: Conducting and evaluating critical interpretive research: examining criteria as a key component in building a research tradition. In: Kaplan, B., Truex, D., Wastell, D., Wood-Harper, A.T., DeGross, J.I. (eds.) Information Systems Research, pp. 275–292. Springer, Boston, MA (2004)
48. Goldkuhl, G.: Pragmatism vs interpretivism in qualitative information systems research. Eur. J. Inf. Syst. **21**, 135–146 (2012)
49. Monk, A., Howard, S.: Methods & tools: the rich picture: a tool for reasoning about work context. Interactions **5**, 21–30 (1998)
50. Baskerville, R., Pries-Heje, J.: Grounded action research: a method for understanding IT in practice. Accounting Manag. Inf. Technol. **9**, 1–23 (1999)
51. Lim, Y.-K., Stolterman, E., Tenenberg, J.: The anatomy of prototypes. ACM Trans. Comput. Interact. **15**, 1–27 (2008)
52. Lanzara, G.F., Mathiassen, L.: Mapping situations within a system development project. Inf. Manag. **8**, 3–20 (1985)
53. Checkland, P., Holwell, S.: Action research: its nature and validity. Syst. Pract. Action Res. **11**, 9–21 (1998)
54. Baskerville, R., Myers, M.D.: Special issue on action research in information systems - making IS research relevant to practice - foreword. MIS Q. **28**, 329–335 (2004)
55. Nielsen, P.A.: IS action rsearch and its criteria. In: Kock, N. (ed.) Information Systems Action Research, pp. 355–375. Springer, Boston (2007)

Validity in Design Science Research

Kai R. Larsen[1]([✉]), Roman Lukyanenko[2], Roland M. Mueller[3], Veda C. Storey[4],
Debra VanderMeer[5], Jeffrey Parsons[6], and Dirk S. Hovorka[7]

[1] University of Colorado, Boulder, CO, USA
kai.larsen@colorado.edu
[2] HEC Montreal, Montreal, QC, Canada
roman.lukyanenko@hec.ca
[3] Berlin School of Economics and Law, Berlin, Germany
roland.mueller@hwr-berlin.de
[4] Georgia State University, Atlanta, GA, USA
vstorey@gsu.edu
[5] Florida International University, Miami, FL, USA
vanderd@fiu.edu
[6] Memorial University of Newfoundland, St. John's, NL, Canada
jeffreyp@mun.ca
[7] University of Sydney, Sydney, Australia
dirk.hovorka@sydney.edu.au

Abstract. Research in design science has always acknowledged the need for evaluating its knowledge outcomes, with particular emphasis on assessing the efficacy and utility of the artifacts produced. However, the need to demonstrate the validity of the research process and outcomes has not received as much attention. This research examines scientific approaches to validity and their applicability to, and use in, design science. To do so, we assembled an extensive data set of research validities articles from various disciplines, as well as design science articles. We then examined the use of validity concepts in these articles and how these concepts could be employed to describe what validity means for design science research. The result is a *design science research validity framework* to guide how validity can become an integral aspect of design science research.

Keywords: Design science research · Research validity · Design science research validity framework · Artifact · Evaluation · Design validity framework · Senior scholar's basket of eight

1 Introduction

Design science research (DSR) has become an important part of the information systems (IS) community over the past decade, as evidenced by the special issue of *MIS Quarterly* in 2008, the annual DESRIST conference, the CAIS department on "Digital Design,"

Authorship order beyond the first three authors was determined through a random draw.

© Springer Nature Switzerland AG 2020
S. Hofmann et al. (Eds.): DESRIST 2020, LNCS 12388, pp. 272–282, 2020.
https://doi.org/10.1007/978-3-030-64823-7_25

and editorials in leading journals on the scope and importance of DSR (e.g., [1–3]). As the range of published examples of DSR has increased, scholars have focused attention on the nature of DSR contributions and the DSR process [3–5]. The development of DSR as a research approach has led to increased attention on articulating and systematizing what DSR is and how it can and should be conducted. However, an important aspect of research conduct, research validity, has not received much attention in DSR. Research validity focuses on the quality of scientific research and the dependability of the research findings [6], and is a fundamental part of systematization efforts in the social sciences. Research validity is important in DSR because it provides procedural templates to collect and analyze evidence, as well as to justify the arguments and conclusions of a research study [7].

IS research in general looks to validity measures to strengthen research claims [8]. Many of these validities (e.g., concepts such as internal validity, external validity, and construct validity) have been used primarily in psychometric behavioral studies (e.g., [8, 9, 31]) and apply procedures for establishing validity from fields such as sociology, psychology, marketing, and statistics.

This paper seeks to answer the following questions: How does the concept of validity support the claims of DSR? What are DSR validities? Which validities among existing ones can be considered DSR validities? Which of the DSR validities have been used in published articles in IS? What research opportunities exist for further developing the validity tradition in DSR?

The contribution of this research is to identify and define validities in design science research. To carry out our research, we extract a set of validities from the information systems literature, which we use to describe what constitutes a design science validity. We then group these validities into higher-level categories and survey their use in research published in the AIS Senior Scholars Basket of journals. This analysis yields insights into the nature and gaps of design validities. From this, we propose a design science research validity framework, the purpose of which is to organize these validities so that researchers can identify the types that will be appropriate for their projects. By reporting these types of validity, researchers can better and more easily communicate the rigor of their research design and research outcomes.

2   Literature Review

An *implicit* form of validity is part of nearly every DSR study, in that research work is expected to justify its use of the method to build the artifact and evaluate the results. Well-known and well-cited examples of this include [10–12].

In recent years, a method-oriented stream of work has developed within the DSR literature, proposing approaches for how to perform DSR with greater rigor and relevance. Work in this area includes efforts to help DSR researchers build and design artifacts [13, 14], design appropriate evaluations [15–17], and communicate results and help researchers outside the DSR community read and interpret DSR studies [5].

Interestingly, in a study of DSR publication trends and their implications, Tremblay et al. [18] found that these method-oriented studies represent roughly 50% of DSR publications in the AIS Senior Scholars' Basket of Eight journals. This finding was replicated and confirmed by Engel et al. [19]. This clearly indicates a strong desire in the DSR community for developing a more formal sense for how to do "good" DSR work, as well as the difficulty in doing such work. While this is a robust marker of interest in DSR, these studies do not specifically consider the issue of research validity.

Taking the term validity in a narrower sense, there is a smaller set of work explicitly addressing research validities in DSR. Evaluation of validity in DSR is much less common than evaluation of efficacy or usefulness [16, p. 252]. Evaluation has traditionally focused on the utility and quality of the artifacts and design knowledge produced. Hevner et al. [4] argued that an artifact should be evaluated by considering "functionality, completeness, consistency, accuracy, performance, reliability, usability, fit with the organization and other relevant quality attributes" (p. 85). Baskerville et al. [7] focus on different forms of reliability in design science research.

However, prior work has recognized and argued that validity is both important and applicable to DSR [3], including arguing that some existing behavioral validities (e.g., internal, ecological) apply to DSR as well [7]. Additionally, one type of validity specific to DSR has been proposed; *instantiation validity* [20, 21] has been defined as the extent to which an artifact faithfully instantiates a theoretical construct or design principle. This validity has been used in multiple DSR studies (e.g., [22–24]), attesting to the potential value of DSR-specific validities.

However, there has been no systematic analysis of the nature of design science validities. Nor has there been a concerted and focused attempt to identify which design science validities exist, or to systematically track the use of different validity concepts in design science scholarship. Thus, there is clearly a need to demonstrate the importance of validity for DSR, understand the how and why it should be carried out, and propose systematic ways of showing validity in DSR studies.

3   Identifying and Classifying Design Science Validities

Design science validities apply to research involving the design, implementation or evaluation of artifacts, and to the contribution of research to a design knowledge base. To better understand the nature of design science validities, we begin by describing what they are and then positioning them within the broader space of research validities.

First, we assembled a data set of research validities. Next, we defined what it means to be a design science validity. This definition made it possible to categorize a subset of the validities from the general validity dataset as those applicable to DSR. We further abstracted the design validities into higher-order categories. This analysis yielded insights into the nature and use of design science validities.

3.1   Phase 1: Assembly of the Dataset of General Validities

First, we collected all validities we could find and their definitions. This was done over a three-year period by two of the authors. We started by *identifying the initial sources*. These were documents containing a generalizable sample of validities, such as the American Psychological Association, the American Educational Research Association, and the National Council on Measurement in Education's standards for educational and psychological testing [25].

The second step was to find definitions for the identified validities. For this, we relied primarily on scientific books and articles. For every source found, the section containing the validity was further examined to find more *candidate validities*. A candidate validity was some concept claimed by the author to be a validity or concepts not claimed as such, but listed with validities (e.g., mundane realism – a concept closely related to ecological validity). We did not question the authors' claims. On average, we examined at least 15 sources to find five definitions of each validity, and in each case, we also recorded new candidate validities. At the end of this step, 2,418 candidate validities emerged from approximately 7,500 manually examined sources. At this point, if a validity was not in common use and we failed to locate five definitions, a candidate validity was disqualified from further evaluation. During this step, 158 candidate validities were disqualified.

In the third step, two of the authors independently read the five definitions for each validity and selected one or two definitions that represented the full aspects of the validities expressed by the other definitions. During a meeting, the decisions were discussed; when disagreement existed, we resolved them by reaching agreement on one or two definitions to represent the validity. Because there were many cases where highly similar or even identical validities existed, inter-rater reliability evaluations did not make sense. During this step, candidate validities were eliminated from consideration if they met any of the following conditions:

- A candidate validity was somewhat common, but no clear agreement existed about its definition, leading to the individual cases failing due to our inability to find five definitions for each new validity candidate (6 candidates dropped);
- A candidate validity was a poorly defined version of an existing validity (1 candidate dropped);
- British-English vs. U.S.-English spelling of same validity candidate (1 candidate dropped);
- Validity candidates not about research, such as validities specific to the discipline of law (2 candidates dropped);
- Focus on construct rather than justification of research claims. In this case, *temporal stability,* seen by some as a validity, was found to address the stability of a construct over time (1 candidate dropped).

In the fourth step, we extracted validities from the information systems discipline. All articles published in the AIS Senior Scholars' Basket of Eight journals [26] from 1994 through 2017 were examined. While it is likely impossible to find all proposed validities, an extensive manual review process of 6,083 articles yielded only 23 additional validities for a total of 441 candidate validities, suggesting the original process had been quite thorough. Any new validity name discovered was put through the process starting at the second step above, which supported the validity detection process.

3.2 Phase 2: Identifying and Classifying Design Science Validities

Next, we used the general validities dataset constructed from the steps described above to extract those that can be classified as design science validities. To accomplish this, we first defined design science validity, starting with seminal definitions of design science [3, 4, 15, 27, 28]. For example, Hevner et al. define it [4, p. 77] as research that "creates and evaluates IT artifacts intended to solve identified organizational problems." This definition highlights the central and essential role of IT artifacts, as well as the recognized need for their evaluation. However, not all DSR is organizationally focused, we thus adopt a broader perspective, not insisting on organizational DSR only. Following the accumulated thinking on the nature of DSR, we define **design science validities** as: *formalized procedures for justifying arguments and conclusions of a research study involving the design, development and/or evaluation of IT artifacts to solve identified problems.*

Based on this definition, we coded the remaining validity concepts from the dataset. The task was carried out independently by two of the authors, with combined research experience in design science and research validities of 35 years. Each researcher has also published DSR in top journals. The task was to code each concept as either a design science validity concept or not. The coders reached an agreement of 90.4%, with a Cohen's Kappa of 0.79 [17]. The coders discussed the cases on which they initially disagreed and reached consensus on all cases. Almost all disagreements came for criterion validities (See Table 1) where one researcher employed a more inclusive definition than the other. In total, 79 validity concepts were coded as design science validities.

To better understand the nature and prevalence of different kinds of design validities, the researchers coded each as belonging to a larger group or cluster. The definitions were scrutinized and categorized into nine design validity groups. These were labeled: *congruence validities, criterion validities* (with its subtype *criterion measures*), *data input validities, internal design validities, linguistic validities, relative improvement validities, representational validities, requirements validities,* and *theoretical validities.* Table 1 defines each validity group based on the original validity definitions and insights from the coding exercise.

The validity types suggest a set of entities involved in validity evaluation: the requirements or expectations for the IT artifact, the IT artifact itself and its internal components, the artifact's inputs and outputs (the latter often evaluated against an external criterion), external referent IT artifacts against which an IT artifact is judged, the reality in which an IT artifact is expected to function, and finally, the language and design theory surrounding the IT artifact.

To understand how validities contribute to DSR knowledge, we assigned each to one or more prescriptive DSR knowledge types. March and Smith [28] define four types of design knowledge: *constructs* (which provide the vocabulary and symbols used to define and understand problems and solutions), *models* (designed representations of the problem and possible solutions), *methods* (algorithms, practices, and recipes for performing a task), and *instantiations* (physical realizations that act on the natural world). These, together with design theories (theories that prescribe design and action) [29, 30],

Table 1. Design validity types

Validity group	Definitions	Example validities
Congruence validities	The extent to which an IT artifact faithfully instantiates design principles or design theory	Instantiation validity
Criterion validities	The extent to which an output of an IT artifact agrees with a target referent	Criterion validity, predictive validity
Criterion measures	A specific way to measure the extent to which an output of an IT artifact agrees with a target referent	F1-score, true positive rate, recall
Data input validities	The extent to which the data used as input to an IT artifact are suitable for a particular use	Data validity, functional validity
Internal design validities	The extent to which the internal components of an IT artifact are consistent, transparent, and explainable	Algorithmic validity, Consistency
Linguistic validities	The extent to which language used in descriptions and components of IT artifacts is appropriate (e.g., accessible to target users)	Semantic validity, Consistency
Relative improvement validities	The extent to which an IT artifact outperforms a referent IT artifact	Procedural validity
Representational validities	The extent to which an artifact faithfully represents relevant aspects of reality	Pragmatical validity, contextual validity, structural validity
Requirements validities	The extent to which a particular IT artifact satisfies physical or functional needs	Application validity, model validity
Theoretical validities	The extent to which a design theory is well justified, theoretically grounded and formed	Theoretical validity

have been widely accepted in the DSR community as constituting the core types of DSR knowledge contributions [3, 5].

Because some validity definitions claimed to address multiple areas, they were coded as members of more than one class, resulting in 101 validity-class combinations. There was one construct validity, 83 model validities (validities and measures are counted separately), four method validities, 12 instantiation validities, and one design theory validity. Table 2 reports the results of this analysis. Inter-rater agreement was 100% for this exercise.

Table 2. Design validity clusters and knowledge categories

Validity types Prescriptive knowledge types	Construct	Model	Method	Instantiation	Design theory	Totals
Congruence validities		0	0	1		1
Criterion validities		33	1	2		36
Criterion measure		30	0	0		30
Data input validities		4	0	2		6
Internal design validities	0	3	1	1	0	5
Linguistic validities	1	1	0	0	0	2
Relative improvement validities	0	0	1	0	0	1
Representational validities	0	9	1	4	0	14
Requirements validities	0	3	0	2	0	5
Theoretical validities					1	1
Totals	**1**	**83**	**4**	**12**	**1**	**101**

In Table 2, empty cells indicate that a given validity cluster is not applicable for a given knowledge type whereas a zero indicates that a validity cluster is applicable for a given knowledge type, but no validities were found. Specifically, as congruence, criterion and data input validities deal with instantiated IT artifacts and their usage, they do not (directly) apply to construct or design theory knowledge categories, as validities related to these latter categories deal with form, justification and consistency of constructs and theories. Likewise, theoretical validities only apply to construct and design theory, as they explicitly deal with properties of design theories.

4   Tracking the Use of Design Validities

We performed two different analyses to track the usage of design validity efforts. We examined the number of validities used for each of the five knowledge categories. While not all validity types are appropriate for each knowledge category, the frequency of validities addressing a given knowledge category suggests where gaps exist in our ability to appropriately evaluate IT artifacts.

Then, we examined the extent to which the 79 validities have been used in DSR papers in the "basket-of-eight" in a 14-year window from April 2004 to December 2017. To identify these DSR papers, we used two sources. The first was a manual analysis of all 1,233 papers of the AIS basket-of-eight from the years 2014 to 2017. Eighty-eight papers were coded as DSR. Our coding followed the DSR inclusion schema of Prat et al. [14]. We manually analyzed the 1,233 papers from the years 2014 to 2017 by title, abstract and (if necessary) full text. We excluded editorials, book reviews, and comments. The first sufficient inclusion criterion was the explicit mentioning of DSR as the main research paradigm of the paper.

We used three exclusion criteria, any of which was sufficient to exclude a paper [14, p. 234]: (1) the main research paradigm is not DSR; (2) the main objective is descriptive or explanatory (e.g., economic models aiming to understand a phenomenon); and (3) the central contribution is not an IS artifact.

The second (implicit) inclusion criterion was that the IS artifact had to be the central contribution of the paper. For each paper, the inclusion or exclusion criteria were recorded. A second researcher cross-checked the resulting 88 papers manually and agreed that all the papers were to be classified as DSR (100% precision).

As the second source, we referred to the list from Prat et al. [14] of DSR papers in the AIS basket of eight from April 2004 to April 2014. Their list consisted of 121 DSR papers [14]. Two papers of their list were from 2014 and were also classified by our manual process as DSR papers. The remaining 119 papers from April 2004 to December 2013 were added to our final list. This resulted in a total of 207 DSR papers from April 2004 to December 2017.

Every sentence in these 207 papers was examined against our list of validities, and regular expressions at the word-level were combined to find instances of these validities in sentences. Table 3 lists the number of times a validity was used at least once within a paper, aggregated by year and validity type.

Table 3. DSR articles using specific validities aggregated by validity type

Validity Type	2004	2005	2006	2007	2008	2009	2010	2011	2012	2013	2014	2015	2016	2017	Total
Congruence validities	0	0	0	0	0	0	0	0	0	0	0	0	0	1	1
Criterion validities	1	0	1	4	0	1	3	2	2	3	2	4	4	1	28
Criterion measure	19	11	34	31	55	9	37	22	89	31	38	58	104	55	593
Data input validities	0	0	0	0	0	0	0	0	0	0	0	1	0	1	2
Internal design validities	5	2	4	8	4	3	4	3	8	2	3	6	9	8	69
Linguistic validities	0	0	0	0	0	0	0	0	0	0	0	0	0	0	0
Relative improvement validities	0	0	0	0	0	0	0	0	0	0	0	0	0	0	0
Representational validities	0	0	0	0	0	0	0	0	0	0	1	1	1	1	4
Requirements validities	1	0	0	0	1	0	0	0	0	0	0	0	0	0	2
Theoretical validities	0	0	0	0	0	0	0	0	0	1	0	0	1	0	2
Total by year	26	13	39	43	60	13	44	27	99	37	44	70	119	67	701

Table 3 shows that *criterion validities,* or more specifically its subset of *criterion measures* are indicative of criterion validities being the most frequently used validity types. The most commonly used validities included accuracy and recall. *Internal design validities* were the second most common type of validities, potentially reflecting the desire of authors to attest to the internal qualities of the artifact. The most common internal validity was consistency. The rest of the validities might as easily not have been in use at all with the maximum number of articles identified at four.

5   Discussion

This paper has examined how the concept of validity applies in design science research by identifying different forms of validity in a large body of research literature. From the analysis, we conclude that the use of validity concepts is narrow in DSR, largely focusing on criterion measures and internal design validities. Our analysis shows that validity has been underutilized to strengthen the claims of design science research. The most frequently occurring terms in our dataset involved accuracy and a range of terms around concepts such as precision, recall, specificity, true positive and false positive, as they relate to evaluating machine learning models. Although relevant and important, validities that measure the performance of a machine learning model do not reflect the full scope of DSR research.

Furthermore, the validities used in DSR have been adopted or adapted primarily from approaches used in other disciplines. Criterion measures originate in computer science. There was little evidence of proposed validities intended to meet the specific needs of DSR to support claims about the "utility" of artifacts and other DSR contributions. One exception is the notion of instantiation validity discussed earlier. Historically, the four major areas in which knowledge claims have been made in DSR have been justified through formalized validation procedures, resulting in specialized validities (Table 1). However, the *construct, method,* and, *design theory* knowledge types are woefully underrepresented.

An important direction for future research is to examine and propose, as needed, validities that apply specifically to DSR. To guide this thinking, Fig. 1 proposes a Design Science Research Validity Framework based on design antecedents, the development and use context of artifact, and design outcomes, each of which emerged from the analysis of the validity literature.

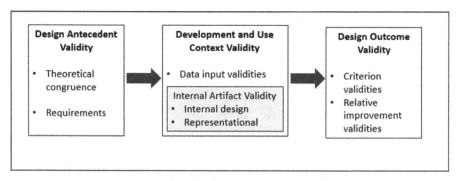

Fig. 1. Design science research validity framework

In the Design Science Research Validity Framework, validities for issues dealing with the quality and justification of the input to the design process are *Design Antecedents* and include theoretical congruence validities and requirements validities. The internal causal working of IT Artifacts (i.e., construct relations, functional models, methods, etc.), are the main focus of *Internal Artifact Validity*. Validities related to the artifact support claims about the internal composition of the artifact (e.g., internal design validities), as well as the relationship between the artifact's components and a referent in the broader environment (e.g., representational validities). The importance of situating the artifact is captured by its *Development and Use Context* (e.g., data input validities). The utility of the innovative design solution has always been a major focus of research in DSR, as evidenced by the number of related *Design Outcome* validities, (e.g. criterion validities (Tables 1 and 2) and their frequent occurrence (Table 3). The framework provides guidance to researchers in selecting and applying validities at various stages of the research process (as appropriate) to strengthen their arguments, designs, and evaluations. Depending on the project, some validities might be more germane than others.. Future work will develop detailed guidelines on how to determine when a particular validity is applicable to a project. We hope the framework could be used by reviewers/editors in evaluating the validity of knowledge claims, and by readers in evaluating published work.

6 Conclusions

This research has identified the need to study validity in design science research. An extensive literature review was conducted to identify concepts of validity from all branches of science and those that relate specifically to design science research. From the list of all validities, 79 were identified as design science validities and grouped into higher-level categories. We then conducted an extensive review of DSR to track usage of these validities and assign them to five types of knowledge contributions in DSR (i.e., *constructs, models, methods, instantiations,* and *design theories*). These categories can be useful to researchers as they position and present their research results to strengthen claims about evaluation and research rigor. A Design Science Research Validity Framework was proposed to guide the use of validities Future work will compare the validity classes to design science evaluation approaches in an expanded literature base and develop and provide templates and guidelines for applying the associated validity procedures. In addition, the framework will be expanded to capture the full range.

References

1. Goes, P.B.: Editor's comments: design science research in top information systems journals. MIS Q. **38**(1), iii–viii (2014)
2. Rai, A., et al.: Diversity of design science contributions. MIS Q. **41**(1), iii–xviii (2017)
3. vom Brocke, J., Winter, R., Hevner, A., Maedche, A.: Accumulation and evolution of design knowledge in design science research: a journey through time and space. J. Assoc. Inf. Syst. (2020)
4. Hevner, A., March, S., Park, J., Ram, S.: Design science in information systems research. MIS Q. **28**(1), 75–105 (2004)
5. Gregor, S., Hevner, A.R.: Positioning and presenting design science research for maximum impact. MIS Q. **37**(2), 337–355 (2013)
6. Lindzey, G., Gilbert, D., Fiske, S.T.: The Handbook of Social Psychology. Oxford University Press, Oxford (1998)
7. Baskerville, R., Kaul, M., Storey, V.C.: Genres of inquiry in design-science research: justification and evaluation of knowledge production. MIS Q. **39**(3), 541–564 (2015)
8. Boudreau, M.-C., Gefen, D., Straub, D.W.: Validation in information systems research: a state-of-the-art assessment. MIS Q. **25**(1), 1–16 (2001)
9. Straub, D., Boudreau, M.-C., Gefen, D.: Validation guidelines for IS positivist research. Commun. Assoc. Inf. Syst. **13**(24), 380–427 (2004)
10. Nunamaker Jr., J.F., Applegate, L.M., Konsynski, B.R.: Facilitating group creativity: experience with a group decision support system. J. Manag. Inf. Syst. **3**(4), 5–19 (1987)

11. Abbasi, A., Albrecht, C., Vance, A., Hansen, J.: Metafraud: a meta-learning framework for detecting financial fraud. Mis Q. 1293–1327 (2012)
12. Reinecke, K., Bernstein, A.: Knowing what a user likes: a design science approach to interfaces that automatically adapt to culture. Mis Q. 427–453 (2013)
13. Offermann, P., Blom, S., Schönherr, M., Bub, U.: Artifact types in information systems design science–a literature review. In: International Conference on Design Science Research in Information Systems, pp. 77–92 (2010)
14. Baskerville, R., Baiyere, A., Gregor, S., Hevner, A., Rossi, M.: Design science research contributions: finding a balance between artifact and theory. J. Assoc. Inf. Syst. 19(5), 358–376 (2018)
15. Venable, J., Pries-Heje, J., Baskerville, R.: FEDS: a framework for evaluation in design science research. Eur. J. Inf. Syst. 25(1), 77–89 (2016)
16. Prat, N., Comyn-Wattiau, I., Akoka, J.: A taxonomy of evaluation methods for information systems artifacts. J. Manag. Inf. Syst. 32(3), 229–267 (2015)
17. Cleven, A., Gubler, P., Hüner, K.M.: Design alternatives for the evaluation of design science research artifacts. In: International Conference on Design Science Research in Information Systems and Technology, pp. 1–8 (2009)
18. Tremblay, M., Vander Meer, D., Beck, R.: The effects of the quantification of faculty productivity: perspectives from the design science research community. Commun. Assoc. Inf. Syst. 43(1), 625–661 (2018). https://doi.org/10.17705/1cais.04334
19. Engel, C., Leicht, N., Ebel, P.: The imprint of design science in information systems research: an empirical analysis of the AIS senior scholars' basket. In: International Conference on Information Systems, Munich, Germany, pp. 1–10 (2019)
20. Lukyanenko, R., Evermann, J., Parsons, J.: Instantiation validity in IS design research. In: Tremblay, M.C., VanderMeer, D., Rothenberger, M., Gupta, A., Yoon, V. (eds.) DESRIST 2014. LNCS, vol. 8463, pp. 321–328. Springer, Cham (2014). https://doi.org/10.1007/978-3-319-06701-8_22
21. Lukyanenko, R., Parsons, J.: Design theory indeterminacy: what is it, how can it be reduced, and why did the polar bear drown?. J. Assoc. Inf. Syst. Forthcoming
22. Miah, S.J., Gammack, J.G., McKay, J.: A metadesign theory for tailorable decision support. J. Assoc. Inf. Syst. 20(5), 4 (2019)
23. Lukyanenko, R., Parsons, J., Samuel, B.M.: Representing instances: the case for reengineering conceptual modeling grammars. Eur. J. Inf. Syst. 28(1), 68–90 (2019). https://doi.org/10.1080/0960085X.2018.1488567
24. Recker, J.: Toward a design theory for green information systems. Presented at the 2016 49th Hawaii International Conference on System Sciences (HICSS), pp. 4474–4483 (2016)
25. American Educational Research Association, American Psychological Association, National Council on Measurement in Education, Joint Committee on Standards for Educational, and Psychological Testing (US), Standards for educational and psychological testing. Amer Educational Research Assn (2014)
26. Lowry, P.B., et al.: Evaluating journal quality and the association for information systems senior scholars' journal basket via bibliometric measures: do expert journal assessments add value? MIS Q. 993–1012 (2013)
27. Simon, H.A.: The Sciences of the Artificial. MIT Press, Mass (1996)
28. March, S.T., Smith, G.F.: Design and natural science research on information technology. Decis. Support Syst. 15(4), 251–266 (1995)
29. Gregor, S., Jones, D.: The anatomy of design theory. J. Assoc. Inf. Syst. 8(5), 312–335 (2007)
30. Markus, M.L., Majchrzak, A., Gasser, L.: A design theory for systems that support emergent knowledge processes. MIS Q. 179–212 (2002)
31. Schmitz, K., Veda C. S.: Empirical test guidelines for content validity: wash, rinse, and repeat until clean. Commun. Assoc. Inf. Syst. (2020)

Platforms and Networks

A Platform for Value Co-creation in SME Networks

Sarah Hönigsberg[(⊠)] [iD]

Chemnitz University of Technology, 09126 Chemnitz, Germany
sarah.hoenigsberg@wirtschaft.tu-chemnitz.de

Abstract. The design of digital value co-creation (VCC) platforms is an increasingly prominent research topic. The creation and introduction of these platforms are transforming the cooperation of entire company networks and ecosystems and is a challenging endeavor. In this paper, a multi-year action design research (ADR) study in a small and medium-sized enterprise (SME) network in the German textile industry is presented. As with many SME networks, the creation of value and innovation is hindered by discontinuous digitalization. This leads to major problems in the knowledge-intensive and complex development of technical textiles. A digital VCC platform mitigates production delays, interruptions, and errors under the competitive pressure of the textile industry, which is critical for the survival of such networks. For a lack of suitable solutions, a VCC platform is cyclically designed and evaluated in our network. Design principles and features are derived to address resource integration challenges in service innovation in SME networks.

Keywords: Value co-creation · Digital platform · Action design research

1 Introduction

The co-generating of value in company networks is being transformed by digital technologies, which can reshape business models and provide opportunities for growth and innovation in ecosystems [1]. The joint process of resource integration between different actors in these digitally enabled value networks is called value co-creation (VCC) [2, 3]. Ways are being sought to use digital technologies in the VCC to facilitate and transform this complex process of resource exchange between actors to create value [2]. In the design-oriented VCC discourse, the spectrum of studies ranges from the design of digital-enabled ecosystems [4], digital-enabled service and business models [5] to methods for designing service systems as a configuration of resources [6]. Lusch and Nambisan formulated a more technically oriented open research question in the context of VCC [3]: "How should the digital infrastructure be architected so as to facilitate the easy incorporation of a dynamic set of rules of service exchange among actors (e.g., business processes and standards)?". Regarding the digital enablement for VCC, it emerged that digital platform infrastructures represent an essential design paradigm [4, 5, 7, 8]. However, it turns out that design-oriented research on digital platforms, especially in connection with the surrounding ecosystem, is still scarcely conducted and many connections remain unexplored [8]. Furthermore, it is noticeable throughout the debate on

© Springer Nature Switzerland AG 2020
S. Hofmann et al. (Eds.): DESRIST 2020, LNCS 12388, pp. 285–296, 2020.
https://doi.org/10.1007/978-3-030-64823-7_26

digitalization efforts of VCC and platform strategies, that especially small and medium-sized enterprises (SMEs) are often overlooked [9]. SMEs are defined as enterprises with fewer than 250 employees and less than 50 million turnover or 43 million balance sheet total, which applies to 99.8% of European (non-financial sector) companies [10]. SMEs are characterized by being highly networked, limited in resources and being overpowered by bigger partners in the platform ecosystem [9, 10]. The resulting SME networks are not only the backbone of our economy, but also represent an enormous innovation potential, especially if the joint creation of value in those networks is enabled by digital technologies.

In this paper, we address the issue of digitally supporting the VCC in an SME network in our action design research (ADR) study [11] and focus on the design of a digital cross-company solution to support VCC and service innovation in the German textile industry. Our SME network focuses on new technical textiles development (i.e. service innovation) but faces problems with coordination, efficiency and information loss attributed to a lack of IT support across companies. The envisioned artifact is a network platform as a cross-organizational infrastructure consisting of processes and digital technologies owned by the network. We thus address the following class of problems: (inhibited) resource integration in service innovation (in our case textile development) in (SME) networks. For digital platforms, design-oriented research is an under-explored field [8] and previous solutions of VCC platforms focus on large powerful actors in the network [e.g. 4, 5] and are therefore inadequate for our case. However, we draw on the same formative influences for our research as a theoretical foundation that can be found in other designs of digital platforms for VCC: The service-dominant logic (SDL) [12] and the service innovation framework by Lusch and Nambisan [3]. Based on these foundations, we are designing a new artifact that specifically addresses the practical problems of our textile SME network. This leads to our research question: what design principles are appropriate for VCC platforms in SME networks to enable cross-organizational service innovation? We derive design principles for such platforms in our ADR study, addressing a highly relevant class of problems and approach a still open research gap on digital platforms for VCC in SME networks, which is of considerable importance for the economy.

The rest of this paper is organized as follows: after the foundations, the research method is presented before the ADR study with two building, intervention and evaluation (BIE) cycles, is presented. This is followed by a discussion and conclusion.

2   Foundations

We use SDL from marketing research as a theoretical foundation. This theoretical framework allows us to abstract from the tangibility or intangibility of exchanged resources in value creation (VC) [12]. The focus lies on the process of VC, not on the output of it, by defining all applications of competencies for the benefit of another as service [13]. In particular, we refer to the tripartite framework for service innovation of Lusch and Nambisan, which itself is based on the SDL. This framework is composed of a service ecosystem, a service platform, and VCC [3]. To emphasize the multilateral nature of the underlying process and activities of resource integration through the inclusion of different actors in the service ecosystem, this process is referred to as VCC [14]. While service is the use of resources for the benefit of another, service systems are dynamic configurations of resources that create value and can occur at various levels of actors such as people, organizations, cities or even countries [13]. The term actors in SDL abstracts from traditional roles such as producer and consumer [3] and imply equality of these [15]. Loose coupling of these service systems by common institutional logics creates a self-adapting system in which the VCC can take place, or in SDL terms, an actor-to-actor network (including the resource configurations that evolve around the actors) [3, 14]. According to Lusch and Nambisan, service platforms are defined as modular structures consisting of tangible and intangible components, for example, skills, knowledge and technological assets [3]. Such modular structure means that service platforms promote the interaction of actors and resources and provide the venue for VCC. IT can take on two important roles in this context, either as support for the service platform, e.g. by locating resources, or as digital components of the service platform itself and thus creating novel opportunities for resource integration [3].

Interpreting our case through this lens, the technical textile industry in Saxony, Germany can be seen as a local service ecosystem. In addition to textile companies, the ecosystem also includes e.g. business customers from other sectors (like airlines, hotel chains, hospitals, car manufacturers, etc.). The development of technical textiles as an industrial product is knowledge-intensive, which makes the knowledge about the production of textiles the most precious and operant resource in our case. These textiles must guarantee specific functions (e.g. fire or water protection for home textiles or cut and stab protection for protective clothing [16]) according to the customer's requirements. To achieve this, the requirements, but also the knowledge of all involved actors on how to produce this textile must be exchanged efficiently and effectively, demanding resource liquefaction and density to enable actors to integrate them [3].

In our case, we do not focus on the service ecosystem level but zoom in on a network of textile companies. The production networks for these technical textiles typically include yarn manufacturers, fabric manufacturers (such as weavers or knitters), finishers or coaters, and the production process typically results in ropes, cords, nets, threads, technical fabrics or wadding, but not tailored products [16]. Correspondingly, some partners in the network provide tangible (e.g. knitter) and others intangible (e.g. finisher) service. Each of the companies represents a service system as a configuration of skills, specialized knowledge, production machinery, and equipment. The VCC takes place in this loosely coupled actor-network by exchanging the service to create the new textile. Because the textile industry is a process industry (as opposed to discrete manufacturing), the modular service platform is in our case characterized by VC process steps as components (e.g. fabric inspection). Due to the joint knowledge-intensive cooperation in the network, we consider the development of the textile in our network as VCC. The lack of digitization of the cross-company innovation in our network is an impediment to network performance, and a digital VCC platform to support the network service platform is being sought as an artifact. This reflects the first role of IT, as it is not an integral part of the service platform. Previous design approaches address how digital VCC platforms should be designed around one or more focal providers [cf. 4, 5], which is guaranteed by the dominance of this actor in the network. This approach is not suitable for our case with textile SMEs. Those platforms strongly focus on digital service or components (e.g.

software) or discrete products [4], while we focus on the digital representation of VC steps and secondly, in those approaches SMEs are supposed to transfer their data and services to third-party platforms [9], which in our case is often contractually prohibited by customers.

3 Research Method

The findings presented here originate from an ongoing ADR study of several years, with four technical textile manufacturers from the German textile industry. The sampling was done in such a way that the case is a typical example for the technical textile chain (one weaver, one knitter, one finisher and one coater). These companies develop technical textiles together and have encountered resource integration challenges in service innovation due to a lack of digitalization. The companies all classify as SMEs. During the course of the study, both in the problem formulation and in the BIE cycles, various data collection activities were carried out (the exemplary quotes in this paper have been translated from German and the companies have been anonymized). We proceeded in an IT-dominant manner according to the four-stage model of ADR [11]: 1) problem formulation, 2) building, intervention and evaluation (BIE), 3) reflection and learning, and 4) formalization of learning. The targeted instance artifact is a digital VCC platform to improve the resource integration in the SME network and the formalized knowledge shall be captured in DPs. We decided to formulate the DPs in the form recommended by Chandra et al. and presented in the typical sequence from causa finales to causa materialis [17]. Our ADR team consists of researchers from three universities (including the author), representatives from a textile research institute and the four owners/leaders of the participating companies. The first ADR cycle took place mid-2017 to end-2018, the second started subsequently and is still ongoing (final evaluation). As this is a multi-year project, some results of the two ADR cycles have already been published (as ADR intends [18]), so we refer to three of our previous articles, but a paper about the platform has not yet been published. The presentation of this ADR study follows the example of Westin and Sein [19].

4 The PROFUND Project

4.1 Problem Formulation

Our research started in May 2017, inspired by practice, when the four company representatives in the first meeting told us that they had alignment problems, and coordination challenges in their collaboration on the new textile development. In questionnaires, the companies described their challenges as follows. Company A stated "inconsistencies in the network with necessary technical clarifications" as a current challenge. Company B saw "problems due to insufficient requirements communication" as the greatest challenge and Company D stated the general "coordination with network partners when developing new products" as the main challenge. Company C said the challenges lay in "new development and product optimization" and these challenges could be addressed with "electronic data exchange and automated data provision". During the problem analysis, it became clear that the issues were due to a lack of digitalization in the cross-company process and that IT support needed to be introduced. In the PROFUND project, a managerial procedure for the introduction of this IT solution in the network (based on classical strategy processes) was proposed and applied. The steps of the procedure are [20]: (I) define goal and formulate network vision, (II) record VCC process in the network, (III) define digitalization demand, (IV) identify digitalization potential, (V) synthesis and prioritization, and (VI) agile (IT) implementation and adaptation of network VCC. The following vision statement was agreed upon in the network: "IT support in the operative VCC process in the network. The IT support should be able to record the requirements of the network partners digitally, correctly, in detail and prioritized. The order requirements are to be bundled and passed on in the network […]. The IT support should enable a network-internal collaboration by shared access and customizable access management of the information with appropriate technical vocabulary". The process of developing textiles in the network was recorded in interviews and then modeled, and phases with high communication complexity were identified.

Our practice-oriented problem definition is, therefore: loss of information, incorrect specifications, inefficient communication as well as coordination during the development of new technical textiles in our network of textile companies. As a class of problems, we see: (inhibited) resource integration in service innovation in (SME) networks. Against the background of this class of problems, we can recognize that in the field of service innovation in actor networks it is agreed on that insufficient IT support in knowledge-intensive VCC processes leads to impediments, but that the design of IT support for such networks is still a research gap [3]. Current design proposals, such as [4], offer a significant contribution to closing this research gap, but, as mentioned above, are aimed at single big, focal actors. We position our desired solution diametrically in the same solution space on the side of smaller networked partners with (often) physical output and knowledge-intense work. In response to the question "What adaptations do actors need to make in their internal processes to facilitate value cocreation, and how do these processes/mechanisms interact with the digital infrastructure?" [3], we have previously developed four propositions to facilitate the VCC in SME networks drawing on the service innovation framework. These were incorporated as kernel theory into our artifact to ingrain it in theory.

4.2 BIE Cycle 1: Designing a Shared Platform for Network VCC

We use the four propositions to facilitate the network VCC (P1–4) as theoretical input for the first BIE cycle [15]: (P1) internal modular VC processes with clear interfaces, (P2) efficient standardized communication between the actors in the network, (P3) equalization of the actors in the network, and (P4) Cross-organizational IT support for the modular VC processes and the efficient communication between equal actors. The combination of the propositions with our digitalization demand analysis in our textile network resulted in the design requirements (DR) for the artifact.

Company B stated that: "We record specific configurations [of requirements] with machine settings and versioning [datasheet or sample order] so far with Excel or Word. Yes, a configuration tool would help us". In the evaluation of questionnaires, where the companies could weight desired functionalities for their IT solution, all four companies weighted functions to find and view process step information in the network and (re-)configuration of the network process as 'very relevant functions'. These insights in combination with (P1) led to (DR1): The system should enable the actor to (re-) configure internal VC processes with standardized interfaces.

Already in the first meeting in mid-2017, the companies articulated that 'data analysis in the network' would be helpful to improve the data and information supply. Thus, the research team also gathered the requirements for possible data analysis. With regard to challenges where data analysis might be helpful, company D stated the "selection of the most suitable materials/machines and network partners". Furthermore, all four companies stated that recommendations in the VCC process are important in the questionnaires. On average, data-driven optimizations in production, VCC process, and network were rated highest. Having (P2) in mind, this leads to (DR2): The system should provide the actor with decision-support when dealing with complex tasks.

In addition to the previously mentioned requests for more efficient information exchange, company C adds: "[…] Okay, the [order] is now with [company A], and an e-mail is sent out: It's now at [company A] […] This is then passed on to the end customer". And further: "Yes, but a login is also good […] And then [the customer] can see: Ah okay, that's now with the application technician or it's in the laboratory […]". This also makes the desired efficient flow of information and transparency across the core network boundaries apparent and along with (P2) we obtain (DR3): The system should enable the actor to efficiently exchange information and knowledge.

The close cooperation of the partners, which should be considered in the IT support of the VCC, is shown by the statement of company A: "What I also do […], if the article was with us and is then with [company C], I visit them and see how things are going. Especially when the articles are very complex. Not only does [company C] see how things are going here, […]. but I can also see where the challenges are at [company C]. […] or other customers - saying: Okay, when we process it, join us. […] That is thinking for others in the network". With our (P3) this leads to (DR4): The system should enable the actor to equally participate in network VCC.

In the digitalization demand analysis, we realized that the companies are already using various IT systems. We had the companies rate their digitization and standardization of the communication within the company, with customers and with partners. We saw that internal communication was satisfactory, but that the communication with customers and partners was hardly digitized or standardized [15]. This not only leads to discontinuous information flows but also causes re-digitization efforts if the non-digital information has to be digitally processed internally. Company A proposes a solution: "In the end, the system […] can quickly exchange information during new [product] development and also during the ongoing production process in case there are changes, so that we can always make adjustments during production […] with the knowledge of the other partners". (P4) and this leads to (DR5): The system should enable the actors and systems to interact with several IT solutions in an easy way.

These requirements were the basis for our artifact. The ADR team decided to build an online platform based on the JavaEE standard, with classic three-tier architecture and a simple SQL database in the persistence layer. Four design features (DF) as essential components could be identified, which are able to map the requirements and support the actor engagement in the VCC. These are [7]: (DF1) service configuration component, (DF2) analytics component, (DF3) centralized knowledge base, and finally (DF4) shared IT platform, as the host for all prior components. The ADR team developed and refined the first prototype with a lot of feedback and input from the company representatives in the team. Towards the end of 2018, a mature version of the prototype was evaluated in a workshop with all companies. The evaluation confirmed that an overarching system in the network, despite certain tradeoffs, is the desired goal. Company C: "You have to answer: what is the same for everyone [...] because otherwise everyone will have their own configurator, and we won't have anything [shared] along the chain". The general design with a multi-user platform with the possibility of jointly configuring new textile developments and then storing them in a central location was positively evaluated. The analysis function to find similar solutions was considered useful, but at this time it was realized in a separate tool. There were however some inconsistencies, e.g. what a 'maximum temperature' actually means (characteristic of the finished product or setting of the machine in production). In this context company C clarifies: "Hmm, first of all, the requirements together with the customer and secondly I have to say what requirements I have for the network or in my company". As company D explains: "That must actually dictate what we all do together. If the requirements for the product are there, he, she and I [pointing to network partners] know what we can or cannot do". Additionally, it was criticized that the production process of another company could be changed via the platform.

4.3 Reflection and Formalization from BIE Cycle 1

During the development and feedback loops with the company representatives, we were able to derive design principles (DP) that link the DR to the DF. Figure 1 shows both the theoretical input (P1–4) and the stronger practice related input (DR 1–5) that formed our artifact. We believe that the (DP 1–5) are valid for our class of problems. The anchoring in a theoretical world view of service innovation in conjunction with SDL abstracts from the generated company output and makes the solution valid for products and services of different industries. First, the shaping and evaluation of the artifact over time showed that the companies initially tried to design the platform from their perspective. But little by little this changed and a unified solution and the we-idea became predominant. This seems to be partly due to the used procedure, where a shared vision was formulated, which was then repeatedly used as a reference in the prioritization and agile implementation in the BIE. As a further formalization step beside the DPs, the managerial procedure was described as a method. Here, the procedural steps were embedded in a framework with several levels of initiatives and a three-phased usage cycle was described [cf. 7, 20].

4.4 Problem (Re-)Definition

Now that we had developed a basic version of our platform, we used the identified inconsistencies (cf. Sect. 4.2) as a starting point for the problem re-definition for the second BIE cycle. Problem A is called: Inappropriate access policy. The companies were dissatisfied that another company could change its input forms. Closing the input forms counteracts (P3/4) and associated DRs, but inter-organizational trust must be

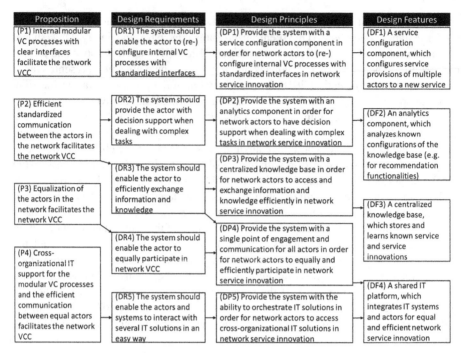

Proposition	Design Requirements	Design Principles	Design Features
(P1) Internal modular VC processes with clear interfaces facilitate the network VCC	(DR1) The system should enable the actor to (re-) configure internal VC processes with standardized interfaces	(DP1) Provide the system with a service configuration component in order for network actors to (re-) configure internal VC processes with standardized interfaces in network service innovation	(DF1) A service configuration component, which configures service provisions of multiple actors to a new service
(P2) Efficient standardized communication between the actors in the network facilitates the network VCC	(DR2) The system should provide the actor with decision support when dealing with complex tasks	(DP2) Provide the system with an analytics component in order for network actors to have decision support when dealing with complex tasks in network service innovation	(DF2) An analytics component, which analyzes known configurations of the knowledge base (e.g. for recommendation functionalities)
(P3) Equalization of the actors in the network facilitates the network VCC	(DR3) The system should enable the actor to efficiently exchange information and knowledge	(DP3) Provide the system with a centralized knowledge base in order for network actors to access and exchange information and knowledge efficiently in network service innovation	(DF3) A centralized knowledge base, which stores and learns known service and service innovations
(P4) Cross-organizational IT support for the modular VC processes and the efficient communication between equal actors facilitates the network VCC	(DR4) The system should enable the actor to equally participate in network VCC	(DP4) Provide the system with a single point of engagement and communication for all actors in order for network actors to equally and efficiently participate in network service innovation	(DF4) A shared IT platform, which integrates IT systems and actors for equal and efficient network service innovation
	(DR5) The system should enable the actors and systems to interact with several IT solutions in an easy way	(DP5) Provide the system with the ability to orchestrate IT solutions in order for network actors to access cross-organizational IT solutions in network service innovation	

Fig. 1. Derivation of the design principles

high for such an open design. Problem B is called: Mixing of configuration levels. Customer requirements for the textile and requirements for the production process should be separated. This in turn supports (P1) and related DRs.

4.5   BIE Cycle 2: Designing for More Effectiveness and Efficiency

With these new problems, a new version of the platform was built. The most important change is that the configuration is now shared on three levels in the system (requirement, network, internal process configuration, see Fig. 2).

The platform was now thoroughly tested with employees during the intervention phases and real customer orders were processed with it. With regard to access rights that were too loose, the evaluation rounds revealed that the now disabled input forms of partners were inconvenient and inefficient after all. However, in order to keep control in the own process, changes are now marked, a notification is triggered and changes must be accepted. In this evaluation round of our platform, the focus was placed on whether the platform actually facilitates service innovation and the VCC in the textile network. Company B stated about error prevention: "If this has been clarified in advance, I think it'll save time. And reduce errors […], which would not have been noticed before". Company A stresses the increased efficiency: "Well, I think it will definitely help us… [it] will never completely replace the phone, it's not supposed to. […] I think a lot of things: confirmations and maybe a follow-up question, […] we should put that in [the system] […] and then I can forget about it". And company D highlights how simple analyses

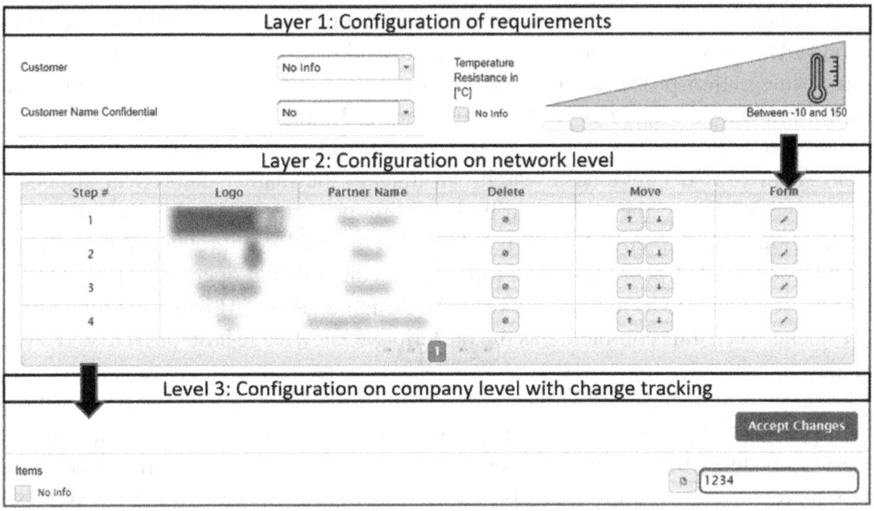

Fig. 2. Composition view of real platform - multi-layer configuration and tracking feature

help: "[…] Mostly saving time, that's the most important thing. You can simply react better and be more present". And in addition: "[…] It definitely broadens the spectrum. Because you are limited, for various reasons, you just don't think about something. The system doesn't do that [thinking] either, it just points you into a direction that you might not have thought about".

4.6 Reflection and Formalization from BIE Cycle 2

In this second BIE cycle, we have addressed two issues from the first cycle and shifted the focus from building the platform as a new artifact to actually designing a more efficient VCC for the network. We changed (changes in italics) (DP1) to: Provide the system with a service configuration component in order for network actors to *multi-layered* (re-)configure VC processes with standardized interfaces in network service innovation. As well as (DP4): Provide the system with a single point of engagement and communication for all actors in order for network actors to equally, efficiently and *transparently* participate in network service innovation. (DF1) and (DF4) have been modified accordingly. The method was likewise improved based on the case observations by the free choice of step order, the parallelism of method cycles and the role of external facilitators. During this BIE, it became clear that joint management, operation, and ownership of the platform in the network was desired.

5   Discussion

In our study, we developed a VCC platform for a textile network along the seven ADR principles [11]. Our work was inspired by our case but also influenced by service innovation and SDL theories [3, 21]. We were able to adhere to the principle of generalized output through our method to build and introduce a VCC platform in an SME network and our DPs. This generalization allowed us to address a class of problems, namely resource integration problems in service innovation in (SME) networks. As implications for practice, there are general propositions, DPs, and a method, but also for the concrete case a functioning VCC platform that positively influences their service innovation. Analogous to previous research, we transfer the mainly theoretical discourse on SDL and VCC into the real world by providing prescriptive knowledge and in our case designing and implementing a digital VCC platform. Recent related studies define design principles that position digital platforms as an essential operant IT resource for the VCC, for example as technology-oriented design element [4] or as an orchestrator hub [5]. Our work thus complements the prescriptive knowledge base on SDL and VCC with design principles for such digital VCC platforms as a class of solutions.

Looking at an instance of service innovation in the form of a textile development on our platform, the implications of the design decisions for the VCC in our network of service systems become evident (cf. Fig. 3). Via the shared IT platform arbitrary actors/service systems in the role of a customer can participate in the VCC process. A customized value proposition, which connects the service systems [13], for a textile development by the customer service system is requested via the requirement configuration. The service system acting as network architect [14] configures the other service systems to a network service system which is designed to match the formulated value proposition. This addresses the structural flexibility, free configuration of the network service system, but also structural integrity in that the actors are closely connected through the platform [3]. The interaction in the service system network is determined by the institutional logic [22] and our platform implements it to promote a common world view between different service systems. The implemented pattern is that new requests are compared with known solutions in the network, the most similar resource configurations are examined for optimization potentials and new (re-)configurations are learned. This pattern, previously practiced between the actors, has now manifested itself in the platform via the various components and thus also defines the architecture of participation [3]. In our example, the service platform of the service system network is characterized by defined modular VC process steps, which are digitally described in previously learned configurations and stored on the platform. The central knowledge base provides the modules in a liquified and dense way during the third configuration level. Through this liquefaction and density, the resource integration process of the VCC can be improved [3, 14] and thus the class of problems of resource integration in SME networks is addressed by the proposed platform design. As a contribution to the ADR method, we were able to demonstrate that in ADR projects DPs and a method for creating the artifact can be successfully developed simultaneously. By combining the real artifact (ingrained in theory for a clear purpose), the design method, and the DPs, a design theory is gradually emerging [23]. Our research contribution can be seen as an exaptation [23] since we transfer the known artifact type of VCC platforms into the still under-researched context of SME networks.

Nevertheless, our study has some limitations. We have considered a single case, which may entail problems of transferability of results. The platform is a stable version, but ongoing development by the companies is planned. This means that DRs, DPs, and

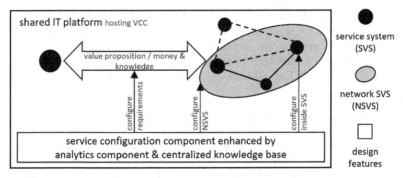

Fig. 3. Relationship of platform design and VCC in network service system [cf. Fig. 1 in 13]

DFs can evolve over time. There are also no long-term tests with the platform to monitor the impact on VCC and service innovation in the network over time.

6 Conclusion

In this paper, we presented a multi-year ADR study during which we designed a shared IT platform for a network of four textile SMEs. Our theoretical grounding lies in service innovation and SDL. We provided DPs and a method to help create a VCC platform in SME networks. Our work and related research open up new exciting future research opportunities. The generalized outcomes can be validated in other industries or developing countries as an interesting comparison to investigate whether the emerging design theory also holds in other socio-economic contexts. In the long-term, it is planned to investigate the impact on VCC and service innovation in our network. Likewise, shared ownership with a joint operating model and change management could be examined. We think we have laid a first foundation for the design of VCC platforms for SME networks and hope to have contributed to the knowledge base in this area.

Acknowledgements. PROFUND was supported by a grant from the German Ministry for Research and Education (BMBF), nr: 03ZZ0618C.

References

1. Pagani, M.: Digital business strategy and value creation: framing the dynamic cycle of control points. MIS Q. **37**, 617–632 (2013)
2. Breidbach, C.F., Maglio, P.P.: Technology-enabled value co-creation: an empirical analysis of actors, resources, and practices. Ind. Mark. Manag. **56**, 73–85 (2016)
3. Lusch, R.F., Nambisan, S.: Service innovation: a service-dominant logic perspective. MIS Q. **39**, 155–175 (2015)
4. Blaschke, Michael, Riss, Uwe, Haki, Kazem, Aier, Stephan: Design principles for digital value co-creation networks: a service-dominant logic perspective. Electron. Markets **29**(3), 443–472 (2019). https://doi.org/10.1007/s12525-019-00356-9

5. Kazan, E., Ghanbari, H., Tuunanen, T., Li, M., Tumbas, S.: Strategic design towards platform collaboration in the newspaper industry: a design science research study. In: 53rd Hawaii International Conference on System Sciences, pp. 5086–5095. Maui (2020)

6. Beverungen, Daniel, Lüttenberg, Hedda, Wolf, Verena: Recombinant service systems engineering. Bus. Inf. Syst. Eng. **60**(5), 377–391 (2018). https://doi.org/10.1007/s12599-018-0526-4

7. Hönigsberg, S., Dinter, B., Wache, H.: The impact of digital technology on network value co-creation. In: 53rd Hawaii International Conference on System Sciences, pp. 5233–5242. Maui (2020)

8. De Reuver, M., Sørensen, C., Basole, R.C.: The digital platform: a research agenda. J. Inf. Technol. **33**, 124–135 (2018)

9. Li, L., Su, F., Zhang, W., Mao, J.Y.: Digital transformation by SME entrepreneurs: a capability perspective. Inf. Syst. J. **28**, 1129–1157 (2018)

10. Muller, P., et al.: Annual Report on European SMEs 2018/2019 Research & Development and Innovation by SMEs, Brussels (2019)

11. Sein, M.K., Henfridsson, O., Purao, S., Rossi, M., Lindgren, R.: Action design research. MIS Q. **35**, 37–56 (2011)

12. Vargo, S.L., Lusch, R.F.: Evolving to a new dominant logic for marketing. J. Mark. **68**, 1–17 (2004)

13. Vargo, S.L., Maglio, P.P., Akaka, M.A.: On value and value co-creation: a service systems and service logic perspective. Eur. Manag. J. **26**, 145–152 (2008)

14. Lusch, R.F., Vargo, S.L., Wessels, G.: Toward a conceptual foundation for service science: contributions from service-dominant logic. IBM Syst. J. **47**, 5–14 (2008)

15. Hönigsberg, S., Dinter, B.: Network value co-creation goes digital – a case study. In: 25th Americas Conference on Information Systems, pp. 1–10. Cancun (2019)

16. McCarthy, B.J.: An overview of the technical textiles sector. In: Horrocks, A.R., Anand, S.C. (eds.) Handbook of Technical Textiles - Volume 1 – Technical Textiles Processes, pp. 1–20. Woodhead Publishing, Sawston (2016)

17. Chandra, L., Seidel, S., Gregor, S.: Prescriptive knowledge in IS research: conceptualizing design principles in terms of materiality, action, and boundary conditions. In: 48th Hawaii International Conference on System Sciences, pp. 4039–4048. Kauai (2015)

18. Sein, M.K., Rossi, M.: Elaborating ADR while drifting away from its essence: a commentary on Mullarkey and Hevner. Eur. J. Inf. Syst. **28**, 1–5 (2018)

19. Westin, S., Sein, M.K.: The design and emergence of a data/information quality system. Scand. J. Inf. Syst. **27**, 3–26 (2015)

20. Hönigsberg, S., Dinter, B.: Toward a method to foster the digital transformation in SME networks. In: 40th International Conference on Information Systems, pp. 1–8. Munich (2019)

21. Vargo, S.L., Akaka, M.A.: Value cocreation and service systems (re)formation: a service ecosystems view. Serv. Sci. **4**, 207–217 (2012)

22. Orlikowski, W.J., Barley, S.R.: Technology and institutions: what can research on information technology and research on organizations learn from each other? MIS Q. **25**, 145–165 (2001)

23. Gregor, S., Hevner, A.R.: Positioning and presenting design science research for maximum impact. MIS Q. **37**, 337–355 (2013)

A Typology of Digital Sharing Business Models: A Design Science Research Approach

Maria J. Pouri[1]([✉]) and Lorenz M. Hilty[1,2]

[1] Department of Informatics, University of Zurich, 8050 Zurich, Switzerland
pouri@ifi.uzh.ch
[2] Technology and Society Lab, Empa Materials Science and Technology,
8600 Dübendorf, Switzerland

Abstract. The digitally enabled sharing economy, also called the 'digital sharing economy' (DSE), has changed patterns of consumption by introducing new choices and channels for provision and receipt of services. The DSE encompasses sharing systems whose business models may vary distinctly from platform to platform. Although business models in the context of the sharing economy have been studied so far, we have observed that the current literature does not provide an approach that covers all the business models – in the broadest sense of the term – that potentially exist within the scope of the DSE. The present paper, therefore, aims to propose a typology of business models in the DSE that covers a wide space of models – even those which may not involve business in the commercial sense. This is achieved through an iterative process based on a design science research approach. The typology can assist in positioning the current and future sharing systems in the DSE by systematically classifying their business models. It is intended to serve as a guiding tool for the sustainability assessment of platforms from both resource and socio-economic perspectives. The present study can also enable researchers and practitioners to capture and systematically analyse digital sharing business models based on a structured, actionable approach.

Keywords: Digital sharing economy · Business models · Typology · Sharing platforms · Sharing systems · Design science research · Sustainability

1 Introduction

Since Lessig [1] has mentioned the term 'sharing economy' in his work, there has been a proliferation of studies proposing definitions for it (e.g. [2–5]). Several studies have reviewed these definitions (e.g. [6–8]). The present work is based on the approach taken by the authors in [9] in which the digitally enabled sharing economy, or the digital sharing economy (DSE), is conceptualized as a manifestation of the digital transition of society and defined as: *"A class of resource allocation systems based on sharing practices which are coordinated by digital online platforms and performed by individuals and possibly (non-) commercial organi-zations with the aim to provide access to material or immaterial resources. Digital sharing systems operate in the space between traditional sharing and the formal economy"* [9].

© Springer Nature Switzerland AG 2020
S. Hofmann et al. (Eds.): DESRIST 2020, LNCS 12388, pp. 297–308, 2020.
https://doi.org/10.1007/978-3-030-64823-7_27

The DSE has created a "new culture of sharing" [10, 11] whereby individuals collaborate in resource distribution in their peer networks rather than being purely dependent on services from the formal market [12]. Moreover, even in business-to-consumer models, it appears that sharing is becoming increasingly popular and even preferred to their conventional (non-sharing) counterparts.

Typically, sharing platforms offer a wide variety of services which are often more affordable, efficient, convenient, and accessible than their counterparts in the conventional market; hence more attractive in the eyes of consumers. The move towards sharing modes of consumption can be viewed as a shift of consumers' mindsets [13], expectations and values [14] on which sharing business models are based [15]. Business models support the provision of value to customers [16, 17]. From a business model perspective, it is therefore important to see how sharing platforms create value, and how this value is perceived and distributed across the sharing system [15].

Given that the DSE is an umbrella term for different sharing systems [18], its business models (BMs) can vary from platform to platform, targeting different mechanisms for value (co-)creation. Therefore, BMs in the DSE can substantially differ from one another.

We aim to design a typology for digital sharing BMs that can encompass the broad spectrum of sharing systems. In other words, our objective is to design a typology that looks at the BMs of sharing systems from a perspective that is open for various ways of practicing sharing and creating value. We think that such a typology can be useful to conceptualize and visualize the fundamental, common attributes of sharing systems and to systematically classify them by showing how they differ in the attribute values of their BM components. The result can particularly help platform providers to position themselves in the spectrum of market and non-market-based sharing models, and to tap into (new) practicable BM opportunities [19] in the area of the DSE. Another use case of our typology can be to apply it as a first step in systematic sustainability assessments of sharing platforms.

This paper proceeds as follows: Sect. 2 provides an overview of related work on the concept of BM in general, and on the study of sharing BMs in particular. Subsequent to Sect. 3, where we explain our research methodology, we describe the development of our proposed typology of sharing business models in Sect. 4. In Sect. 5, we discuss how the typology could be used to describe value in sharing and to direct the assessment of sustainability impacts of sharing from a structured BM approach. The paper closes with concluding remarks and an outlook for future work.

2 Related Work

Although mentions of the term 'business model' in scientific work dates back to late 50s (e.g. in [20] cited in [21]), it was during the mid-90s when the term turned into a buzzword in the business area, and in the late 90s when it particularly came to attention with the commercialization of the Internet [21]. As the literature on BMs is heterogeneous, there is no generally accepted definition of the BM concept yet [22–24]. Nevertheless, BM is a concept often used to describe how a firm works [25].

The BM concept is of practical and economic importance [21] and is considered an integral part of economic behaviors [26]. Although BMs have been usually studied in the context of commercial enterprises and conceived as a commercial logic of value capture and proposition [27], their concept can be applied also to non-commercial enterprises, governance models, and initiatives such as social innovation [15, 28] – wherein the DSE is known to have roots [29] – or in the context of actions for sustainability [30].

BMs have been discussed also in the context of the DSE (e.g. [31–34]). Some studies have researched the BM of one particular sharing platform (e.g. [35] for Airbnb and [36] for Uber), of a set of various platforms (e.g. [37]), or the BMs within a particular domain such as mobility (e.g. [31]). Others have come up with classifications for platforms in the DSE. For example, Barbu et al. [38] classify sharing business models into three main types: access-based, marketplace/platform economy, and on-demand service provider. Building on different configurations of initiatives (or platforms), contributors, peers, and users, Acquier et al. [15] propose a typology of four different BM configurations of sharing platforms. Their typology classifies platforms as commoners, mission-driven, shared infrastructure, and matchmakers. In the present paper, by including other BM components (such as basic types of sharable resources and sharing practices) and by differentiating between categories of participants, we intend to extend the typologies that already exist in the literature. For each component, we will identify its possible attribute values. The result is a typology of digital sharing BMs.

3   Method

3.1   Exploratory Study

For the present study, we used a list of platforms that are currently operating under the 'sharing economy' label. Due to space constraints, we cannot provide this full list which we have been using for other research purposes as well. Nevertheless, in Appendix A, we show a sample of platforms in the DSE taken from this list to illustrate the spectrum of encountered business models.

For the sake of completeness and transparency, we briefly explain the exploratory part of our research methodology. To prepare the initial comprehensive list of platforms, we followed a systematic search and collected any platform brand that is known as part of – or claimed to belong to – the sharing economy by searching for the term 'sharing economy' and related terms (e.g., 'collaborative consumption' [39], 'peer economy' [40], 'platform economy' [41], 'access-based consumption' [42], 'crowd-based capitalism' [43], 'gig economy' [44]). At this stage, our aim was to include as many platforms as possible in order to reach the most inclusive sample of platforms that are known to represent the phenomenon from literature or practice. This process of aggregating platforms was stopped when no further new types of sharing systems or patterns were found. At a second stage, we modified the list by eliminating the platforms that did not follow the principles of the DSE as conceptualized by the authors in [9]. For example, platforms whose services involve change of ownership, redistribution, or gifting/donating were removed. Appendix A shows an excerpt from this reduced list.

3.2   Design Science Research Approach

After the exploratory step described above, we followed a design science research (DSR) method to develop the artifact, i.e. the typology for sharing business models. DSR aims to add to knowledge of how things can be designed [45]. It is particularly useful and applicable for designing artifacts relevant to digital innovation [45, 46]. In addition, considering that the DSE could be primarily viewed as an innovation that leverages digitally enabled solutions [47] to develop innovative businesses [37], we found the DSR method most compatible and applicable to the focus of our study. Previous work has adopted this approach for developing business models as the targeted artifact in the context of digital innovation, e.g. for designing Internet of things (IoT) business models [19].

Throughout the design stage, we adhered to the DSR approach and guidelines as defined by Hevner [48] and followed his three-cycle view: the relevance cycle, the rigor cycle, and the design cycle. The relevance cycle of DSR initiates the research in a relevant application context in which the research problem takes place. The rigor cycle ensures a meaningful connection between the new research and past knowledge (i.e. the existing experiences, expertise, artifacts, processes, theories, etc.) and justifies the innovation and contribution of the research. The design cycle iterates between building the artifact and its evaluation – together with the subsequent feedbacks to refine the design – and keeps dependencies on the relevance and rigor cycles. In the following section, we will elaborate on how we implemented these cycles.

4   Artifact Development

4.1   Business Model Elements of the DSE

Here, we explain the results of the exploratory study of sharing platforms (as described in Sect. 3.1) by presenting a conceptualization of the DSE based on the classification of the following properties in the platforms under study:

- resource providers (*who* shares);
- resource receivers (*with whom* to share);
- sharable resources (*what* is shared);
- the socio-economic mechanism that allows the act of sharing to happen (*how* to share).

Resource providers can be: individuals, businesses (i.e. commercial enterprises), non-profit enterprises, and the public sector; the same applies for resource receivers.

We classify sharable resources in four broad categories: *durable material goods* (e.g., a car, tool), *consumable material goods* (e.g., food, fuel), *durable immaterial goods* (competence and durable information goods), and *consumable immaterial goods* (time and consumable information goods). Important sub-categories are *durable information goods* such as software [49] or timeless content that we distinguish (albeit not sharply) from *consumable information goods,* which lose their value over time. The latter is true for news or the information shared in community-based participatory sensing environments [50].

To differentiate between sharing practices, we use the concepts of reciprocity and compensation as the practical mechanisms for sharing [9]. All possible sharing practices in the DSE seem to belong to one of the following four classes:

1. Practices without reciprocity or compensation.
2. Practices with informal reciprocity or compensation: The receiver of a service is recommended (not enforced) to offer an equivalent service or a compensation to the provider or to the community at some point.
3. Practices with formal reciprocity or compensation: The receiver of a service is enforced to offer an equivalent service or a compensation to the provider or to the community at some point.
4. Practices with formal monetary compensation to the provider per service received.

This conceptualization addresses the basic elements required for designing a BM; the *what, who, with whom,* and *how* of sharing. These elements of sharing platforms could be mapped to the general archetypal business model approach by Gassmann et al. [51], in which the following elements are taken into consideration: targeted consumers (resource providers and receivers in the case of sharing platforms), what is offered to them (sharable resources), and practices that distribute the value (sharing practices).

4.2 Building the Typology

The rationale for pursuing the present research lies in the importance of the DSE from a sustainability perspective. Although it is often viewed or expected to be an enabler of positive changes towards mitigating the currently unsustainable consumption patterns, the DSE keeps raising concerns about the sustainability of the consumption modes as well as the socio-economic activities it promotes [3, 52–54][1]. Therefore, we seek to address the problem of assessing sustainability impacts of the DSE. This indicates that the intended application context of our artifact is the sustainability assessment of digital sharing systems (initiating relevance) [12].

Solutions produced by DSR should be generalizable, i.e. to be applicable to a same class of problems [60]. It is possible that both the problem (which here is assessing the sustainability impacts of the DSE) and the solution (here to model the DSE in a way that is helpful for the assessment of the sustainability impacts of its multifaceted manifestations) are general [61]. This is compatible with our partially inductive process of defining sharing types. The result, which is a general typology, would be then applicable to all manifestations of the DSE because it allows to classify sharing platforms in general.

To keep rigor, we have mainly depended on literature. An ample number of studies on the sharing economy were reviewed by the authors (to name a few [2–8, 55, 62–66]). Additionally, we are aware of the conceptual dissent and the theoretical disputes about the sharing economy (e.g. [67, 68]). The authors developed a conceptual framework for the DSE in [9], which was chosen here as a theoretical reference due to its inclusive DSE concept which integrates many of the existing categorizations of digital sharing systems.

Regarding the evaluation cycle, we examined each iteration of the design based on the criteria for the purpose of BMs ([69] cited in [21]) by checking if the types of platforms were still understandable as meaningful BMs. As a classification scheme, the primary function of a typology is to construct classes about which we make inductive

---

[1] For more studies on the relevance of the DSE for sustainability, see [12, 55–59].

generalizations [70]. We evaluated our proposed typology with Lambert's criteria for useful classification schemes [70, 71]: The typology reduced the complexity of the heterogeneity of digital sharing BMs by identifying the similarities and differences among them. It also created the possibility to compare different BMs through the presentation of the BM dimensions (or components) and their range of attribute values. Since it makes explicit the various aspects of DSE in a BM context, the typology demonstrates multifunctionality to suit multiple needs, in particular to help structuring the sustainability assessment of digital sharing BMs.

Each cycle of the artifact design iterated "between the core activities of building and evaluating the design artifacts and processes of the research." [48, p. 2], as foreseen in the DSR paradigm. Our design cycle was an iterative inductive and deductive process: inductive because we started from studying individual sharing systems, and deductive because we conceptualized sharing platforms based on a theoretical approach that we present in [9].

The results of the conceptualization of platforms in the DSE (as described in Sect. 4.1) were arranged, i.e. designed [45], through the DSR method in a 4-dimensional visual representation of the resource provider (*from*), resource receiver (*to*), shared resource (*what*) and sharing practice (*how*) aspects of sharing BMs in the DSE, as shown in Fig. 1.

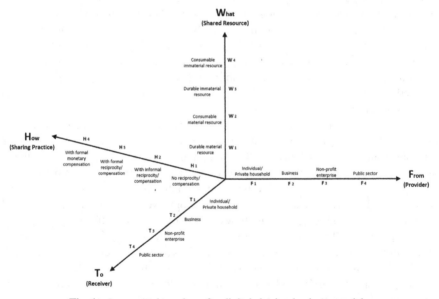

Fig. 1. A proposed typology for digital sharing business models.

We expect that any instance of the DSE can be represented in this 4D space and thus denoted by its "BM code", which is a vector in the "FTWH space". For example, the typical Uber riding service can be represented as follows:

BM Code of Uber: (F1, T1, W1, H4)

Appendix A includes the BM codes of additional examples of sharing platforms.

5 Discussion

The typology introduced above was built based on the required BM elements of sharing platforms from a holistic perspective of the DSE. The four dimensions do not include a *why* dimension because the reasons why participation in sharing takes place can be inferred from the other dimensions plus some assumptions about the value perceived by the participants that motivates them to use services [72, 73] offered by a sharing platform. Thus, the *why* question is located at a higher level of description. Recalling that BMs support the provision of value to customers [16, 17], we can describe with our typology what resource and what sharing practice combine to create a perceived value in the interaction between providers and receivers. What the perceived value actually is can then be inferred. To illustrate this, we resume the Uber example. In the case of Uber's typical riding service, a durable material resource (a car) is shared between an individual resource owner (the driver) and an individual resource receiver (the rider) for a certain fare for the riding service received (a formal monetary compensation). This can tell us about the motivation for users' participation, or the main value offered by the platform, which is normally to receive a less expensive riding service (compared to conventional taxi services) for the rider[2] and to earn an extra income for the driver. Therefore, the prime value for using this platform, and the similar ones, could be to benefit from the economic value of sharing [75]. It is notable that platforms do not necessarily create only one type of value for their consumers. Sharing via digital platforms may hold a combination of various value propositions, such as efficiency, convenience, enjoyment, reputation, a sense of community [76, 77] and others as well.

From a sustainability perspective, it is important to bear two aspects in mind [78]: 1) The implications of shared consumption of resources: For example, if the economic value of sharing decreases the unit price of the service for the user, this can trigger additional demand for the same service (direct rebound effect) or for other services (indirect rebound effect). Thus, the rebound effect may partially or completely balance out the favorable effects of shared consumption, which are usually referred to as optimization effects of sharing [79]. Such effects of digitalization can better be captured with dynamic modelling – as done in [80], an early study which however did not consider the DSE yet. 2) The implications of the specific sharing practices for the participants: For example, whether resource providers and receivers in the DSE are in a social position that is better or worse than before (e.g., regarding fair access to resources and markets, participation in cultural life, labor conditions) [12]. Sharing BMs can create issues related to consumer and labor protection [44, 52] and the promotion of tax avoidance [52]. With regard to underpayment and low wages, the DSE has been labeled as the "share-the-scraps economy" where most of the profits goes to the platform owners and the scraps go to the workers [81]. Apparently, the depth of the assessment in this aspect should go further in detail based on a particular sharing platform and the social and economic practices it promotes.

---

[2] Exceptions may be observed when dynamic pricing models become effective especially in peer-to-peer services. Dynamic pricing is already practiced in Uber's "Surge pricing" or in Lyft's "Prime Time", where a consumer faces prices ranging from a base price to multiples of that price [74], which in principle can exceed a conventional taxi fare.

This way, our typology of digital sharing BMs can work as an interface to tap into the possible opportunities for value creation in sharing systems and to direct the assessment of sustainability impacts of them.

6 Conclusion and Outlook

In the present work, we proposed a typology for classifying digital sharing platforms from a business model perspective. To develop this typology, we adopted a design science research approach. The artifact we designed – i.e. the typology for digital sharing business models – demonstrates descriptive power by creating a simple yet expressive language for differentiating $4^4 = 256$ theoretical types of digital sharing systems.

The relevance of this artifact comes from the insight that digital sharing systems operate in the space between traditional sharing and the formal economy and can generate non-monetary or monetary value for their participants. This not only opens a wide space for potential business models in the DSE, but also creates opportunities as well as risks when viewed from a sustainability perspective.

Our typology can provide guidance for entrepreneurs and also for established businesses that aim to implement potential business models in the DSE realm. It can also assist policymakers and public actors in regulating and supporting the implementation of digital sharing schemes that can envision sustainability scenarios in which organizations are able to operate in an environmentally compatible way that promotes life-enhancing social and economic activities. Future work may refine the proposed typology to make even finer-grained differentiations. We hope that this research will inspire the design of innovative business models that promote responsible, sustainable activities in the digital sharing economy.

Appendix A

A sample of digital sharing platforms and their business model codes based on the proposed typology of digital sharing platforms. Platforms may offer several types of service. In these cases, the table refers to the most resonating service type of the platform.

Platform	URL	Area of service	Business model code
Airbnb	https://www.airbnb.com	Lodging, hospitality	(F1, T1, W1, H4)
CouchSurfing	https://www.couchsurfing.com	Lodging, homestay	(F1, T1, W1, H2)
Fon	https://fon.com	Wi-Fi network	(F1, T1, W1, H3)
Too Good To Go	https://toogoodtogo.org	Avoiding food waste	(F2, T1, W2, H4)
TaskRabbit	https://www.taskrabbit.com	Personal service	(F1, T1, W3, H4)
hOurworld	https://hourworld.org	Time bank	(F1, T1, W3, H3)
Cohealo	https://cohealo.com	Healthcare	(F4, T4, W1, H4)
Zipcar	https://www.zipcar.com	Mobility- car sharing	(F2, T1, W1, H4)

References

1. Lessig, L.: Remix: Making Art and Commerce Thrive in the Hybrid Economy. Penguin, New York (2008)
2. Koopman, C., Mitchell, M., Thierer, A.: The sharing economy and consumer protection regulation: the case for policy change. J. Bus. Entrepreneursh. L **8**, 529 (2015)
3. Frenken, K., Schor, J.: Putting the sharing economy into perspective. Environ. Innov. Soc. Trans. **23**, 3–10 (2017)
4. Ranjbari, M., Morales-Alonso, G., Carrasco-Gallego, R.: Conceptualizing the sharing economy through presenting a comprehensive framework. Sustainability **10**(7), 2336 (2018)
5. Rachel Botsman: The sharing economy lacks a shared definition (2013). https://www.fastcompany.com/3022028/the-sharing-economy-lacks-a-shared-definition. Accessed 25 Apr 2020
6. Dillahunt, T.R., Wang, X., Wheeler, E., Cheng, H.F., Hecht, B., Zhu, H.: The sharing economy in computing: a systematic literature review. In: Proceedings of the ACM on Human-Computer Interaction, vol. 1, no. CSCW, pp. 1–26 (2017)
7. Oh, S., Moon, J.Y.: Calling for a shared understanding of the "sharing economy". In: Proceedings of the 18th Annual International Conference on Electronic Commerce: e-Commerce in Smart connected World, pp. 1–5 (2016)
8. Görög, G.: The definitions of sharing economy: a systematic literature review. Management (18544223) **13**(2), 175–189 (2018)
9. Pouri, M.J., Hilty, L.M.: The digital sharing economy: a confluence of technical and social sharing. Submitted for publication
10. Bucher, E., Fieseler, C., Lutz, C.: What's mine is yours (for a nominal fee)—exploring the spectrum of utilitarian to altruistic motives for internet-mediated sharing. Comput. Hum. Behav. **62**, 316–326 (2016)
11. Nadeem, W., Juntunen, M., Hajli, N., Tajvidi, M.: The role of ethical perceptions in consumers' participation and value co-creation on sharing economy platforms. J. Bus. Ethics 1–21 (2019)
12. Pouri, M.J., Hilty, L.M.: Conceptualizing the digital sharing economy in the context of sustainability. Sustainability **10**(12), 4453 (2018)
13. Barbu, C.M., Florea, D.L., Ogarcă, R.F., Barbu, M.C.: From ownership to access: how the sharing economy is changing the consumer behavior. Amfiteatru Econ. **20**(48), 373–387 (2018)
14. WEF: World Economic Forum (2018). https://www.weforum.org/agenda/2018/01/how-consumption-will-change-over-next-decade/. Accessed 25 Apr 2020
15. Acquier, A., Carbone, V., Massé, D.: How to create value(s) in the sharing economy: Business models, scalability, and sustainability. Technol. Innov. Manag. Rev. **9**(2) (2019)
16. Teece, D.J.: Business models, business strategy and innovation. Long Range Plan. **43**(2–3), 172–194 (2010)
17. Teece, D.J., Linden, G.: Business models, value capture, and the digital enterprise. J. Organ. Design **6**(1), 1–14 (2017). https://doi.org/10.1186/s41469-017-0018-x
18. Codagnone, C., Martens, B.: Scoping the sharing economy: origins, definitions, impact and regulatory issues. Cristiano Codagnone and Bertin Martens. Institute for Prospective Technological Studies Digital Economy Working Paper, 1 (2016)
19. Turber, S., Smiela, C.: A business model type for the internet of things (2014)
20. Bellman, R., Clark, C., Craft, C., Malcolm, D.G., Ricciardi, F.: On the construction of a multistage, multi-person business game. Oper. Res. **5**(4), 469–503 (1957)
21. Burkhart, T., Krumeich, J., Werth, D., Loos, P.: Analyzing the business model concept—a comprehensive classification of literature (2011)
22. Peric, M., Durkin, J., Vitezic, V.: The constructs of a business model redefined: a half-century journey. Sage Open **7**(3), 2158244017733516 (2017)

23. Novak, A.: Business model literature overview. Financial Reporting (2014)
24. Xu, L., Chen, J.: Technological rules based business models analysis: a design science approach. Int. J. Bus. Manage. **6**(9), 113 (2011)
25. Haggege, M., Collet, L.: Exploring new business models with a narrative perspective. In 18th International Product Development Management Conference. Delft, Netherlands Exploring New Business Models with a Narrative Perspective, vol. 18, June 2011
26. Cheah, S., Ho, Y.P.: Coworking and sustainable business model innovation in young firms. Sustainability **11**(10), 2959 (2019)
27. Laasch, O.: Beyond the purely commercial business model: organizational value logics and the heterogeneity of sustainability business models. Long Range Plan. **51**(1), 158–183 (2018)
28. Yunus, M., Moingeon, B., Lehmann-Ortega, L.: Building social business models: lessons from the grameen experience. Long Range Plan. **43**(2–3), 308–325 (2010)
29. Martin, C.J., Upham, P., Budd, L.: Commercial orientation in grassroots social innovation: Insights from the sharing economy. Ecol. Econ. **118**, 240–251 (2015)
30. Boons, F., Lüdeke-Freund, F.: Business models for sustainable innovation: state-of-the-art and steps towards a research agenda. J. Clean. Prod. **45**, 9–19 (2013)
31. Cohen, B., Kietzmann, J.: Ride on! Mobility business models for the sharing economy. Organ. Environ. **27**(3), 279–296 (2014)
32. Abhishek, V., Guajardo, J., Zhang, Z.: Business models in the sharing economy: manufacturing durable goods in the presence of peer-to-peer rental markets (2019). Available at SSRN 2891908
33. Ritter, M., Schanz, H.: The sharing economy: a comprehensive business model framework. J. Clean. Prod. **213**, 320–331 (2019)
34. Apte, U.M., Davis, M.M.: Sharing economy services: business model generation. Calif. Manag. Rev. **61**(2), 104–131 (2019)
35. Bashir, M., Verma, R.: Airbnb disruptive business model innovation: assessing the impact on hotel industry. Int. J. Appl. Bus. Econ. Res. **14**(4), 2595–2604 (2016)
36. Vargas-Hernández, J.G.: Uber's strategy as a competitive business model of sharing economy. In: Sharing Economy and the Impact of Collaborative Consumption, pp. 97–115. IGI Global (2020)
37. Richter, C., Kraus, S., Brem, A., Durst, S., Giselbrecht, C.: Digital entrepreneurship: innovative business models for the sharing economy. Creat. Innov. Manag. **26**(3), 300–310 (2017)
38. Barbu, C.M., Bratu, R.Ş., Sîrbu, E.M.: Business models of the sharing economy. Rev. Manag. Comparat Int. **19**(2), 154–166 (2018)
39. Botsman, R., Rogers, R.: What's Mine is Yours – The Rise of Collaborative Consumption. HarperCollins, New York (2010)
40. Witt, A., Suzor, N., Wikström, P.: Regulating ride-sharing in the peer economy. Commun. Res. Pract. **1**(2), 174–190 (2015)
41. Kenney, M., Zysman, J.: The rise of the platform economy. Issues Sci. Technol. **32**(3), 61 (2016)
42. Bardhi, F., Eckhardt, G.M.: Access-based consumption: the case of car sharing. J. Consum. Res. **39**(4), 881–898 (2012)
43. Sundararajan, A.: The Sharing Economy: The end of Employment and the Rise of Crowd-Based Capitalism. MIT Press, Cambridge (2016)
44. De Stefano, V.: The rise of the just-in-time workforce: On-demand work, crowdwork, and labor protection in the gig-economy. Comp. Lab. L. Pol'y J. **37**, 471 (2015)
45. Hevner, A., vom Brocke, J., Maedche, A.: Roles of digital innovation in design science research. Bus. Inf. Syst. Eng. **61**, 3–8 (2019)

46. Hjalmarsson, A., Rudmark, D.: Designing digital innovation contests. In: Peffers, K., Rothenberger, M., Kuechler, B. (eds.) DESRIST 2012. LNCS, vol. 7286, pp. 9–27. Springer, Heidelberg (2012). https://doi.org/10.1007/978-3-642-29863-9_2

47. Schwarten, G., Perini, F., Comolli, L.: The power of sharing: Exploring the digital sharing economy at the base of the pyramid. IDRC, Ottawa (2011)

48. Hevner, A.R.: A three cycle view of design science research. Scand. J. Inf. Syst. **19**(2), 4 (2007)

49. Linde, F.: Ökonomie der Information. Göttingen (2008). https://doi.org/10.17875/gup200 8-212

50. Whitney, M., Richter Lipford, H.: Participatory sensing for community building. In: CHI 2011 Extended Abstracts on Human Factors in Computing Systems, pp. 1321–1326 (2011)

51. Gassmann, O., Frankenberger, K., Csik, M.: Revolutionizing the business model. In: Gassmann, O., Schweitzer, F. (eds.) Management of the Fuzzy Front End of Innovation, pp. 89–97. Springer, Heidelberg (2014). https://doi.org/10.1007/978-3-319-01056-4_7

52. Martin, C.J.: The sharing economy: a pathway to sustainability or a nightmarish form of neoliberal capitalism? Ecol. Econ. **121**, 149–159 (2016)

53. Geissinger, A., Laurell, C., Öberg, C., Sandström, C.: How sustainable is the sharing economy? On the sustainability connotations of sharing economy platforms. J. Clean. Prod. **206**, 419–429 (2019)

54. Schor, J.: Debating the sharing economy. Great Transition Initiative, October 2014. http://www.greattransition.org/publication/debating-the-sharing-economy. Accessed 25 Apr 2020

55. Pouri, M.J., Hilty, L.M.: ICT-enabled sharing economy and environmental sustainability—a resource-oriented approach. In: Bungartz, H.-J., Kranzlmüller, D., Weinberg, V., Weismüller, J., Wohlgemuth, V. (eds.) Advances and New Trends in Environmental Informatics. PI, pp. 53–65. Springer, Cham (2018). https://doi.org/10.1007/978-3-319-99654-7_4

56. Pouri, M.J., Hilty, L.M.: Digitally enabled sharing and the circular economy: towards a framework for sustainability assessment. In: Schaldach, R., Simon, K.-H., Weismüller, J., Wohlgemuth, V. (eds.) Advances and New Trends in Environmental Informatics. PI, pp. 105–116. Springer, Cham (2020). https://doi.org/10.1007/978-3-030-30862-9_8

57. Plewnia, F., Guenther, E.: Mapping the sharing economy for sustainability research. Manag. Decis. **56**(3), 570–583 (2018)

58. Demailly, D., Novel, A.S.: The sharing economy: make it sustainable, vol. 3. IDDRI, Paris (2014)

59. Heinrichs, H.: Sharing economy: a potential new pathway to sustainability. Gaia **22**, 228–231 (2013)

60. Maedche, A., Gregor, S., Morana, S., Feine, J.: Conceptualization of the problem space in design science research. In: Tulu, B., Djamasbi, S., Leroy, G. (eds.) DESRIST 2019. LNCS, vol. 11491, pp. 18–31. Springer, Cham (2019). https://doi.org/10.1007/978-3-030-19504-5_2

61. Iivari, J.: Distinguishing and contrasting two strategies for design science research. Eur. J. Inf. Syst. **24**(1), 107–115 (2015)

62. Matzler, K., Veider, V., Kathan, W.: Adapting to the sharing economy. MIT Sloan Manag. Rev. **56**(2), 71 (2015)

63. Yaraghi, N., Ravi, S.: The current and future state of the sharing economy (2017). Available at SSRN 3041207

64. Piscicelli, L., Cooper, T., Fisher, T.: The role of values in collaborative consumption: insights from a product-service system for lending and borrowing in the UK. J. Clean. Prod. **97**, 21–29 (2015)

65. Gansky, L.: The Mesh: Why the Future of Business is Sharing. Penguin (2010)

66. Puschmann, T., Alt, R.: Sharing economy. Bus. Inf. Syst. Eng. **58**(1), 93–99 (2016)

67. Belk, R.: You are what you can access: sharing and collaborative consumption online. J. Bus. Res. **67**(8), 1595–1600 (2014)

68. Belk, R.: Sharing versus pseudo-sharing in web 2.0. Anthropologist **18**(1), 7–23 (2014)
69. Alt, R., Zimmermann, H.D.: Introduction to special section - business models. Electron. Mark. **11**(1), 3–9 (2001)
70. Lambert, S.: A business model research schema. In: BLED 2006 Proceedings, p. 43 (2006)
71. Bailey, K.D.: Typologies and Taxonomies: An Introduction to Classification Techniques. Sage Publications Inc., Los Angeles (1994)
72. Lan, J., Ma, Y., Zhu, D., Mangalagiu, D., Thornton, T.F.: Enabling value co-creation in the sharing economy: the case of mobike. Sustainability **9**(9), 1504 (2017)
73. Hamari, J., Hanner, N., Koivisto, J.: " Why pay premium in freemium services?" A study on perceived value, continued use and purchase intentions in free-to-play games. Int. J. Inf. Manage. **51**, 102040 (2020)
74. Newlands, G., Lutz, C., Fieseler, C.: Navigating peer-to-peer pricing in the sharing economy (2018). Available at SSRN 3116954
75. Zhang, T.C., Gu, H., Jahromi, M.F.: What makes the sharing economy successful? An empirical examination of competitive customer value propositions. Comput. Hum. Behav. **95**, 275–283 (2019)
76. Zhang, T.C., Jahromi, M.F., Kizildag, M.: Value co-creation in a sharing economy: the end of price wars? Int. J. Hospit. Manag. **71**, 51–58 (2018)
77. Hamari, J., Sjöklint, M., Ukkonen, A.: The sharing economy: why people participate in collaborative consumption. J. Assoc. Inf. Sci. Technol. **67**(9), 2047–2059 (2016)
78. Pouri, M.J., Hilty, L.M.: The relevance of digital sharing business models for sustainability. In: Proceedings of the 7th International Conference on ICT for Sustainability (ICT4S 2020), 11 p. ACM, New York (2020). https://doi.org/10.1145/3401335.3401344
79. Hilty, L.M., Aebischer, B.: ICT for sustainability: an emerging research field. In: Hilty, L.M., Aebischer, B. (eds.) ICT Innovations for Sustainability. AISC, vol. 310, pp. 3–36. Springer, Cham (2015). https://doi.org/10.1007/978-3-319-09228-7_1
80. Hilty, L.M., Wäger, P., Lehmann, M., Hischier, R., Ruddy, T., Binswanger, M.: The future impact of ICT on environmental sustainability. Fourth Interim Report – Refinement and quantification. Institute for Prospective Technological Studies (IPTS), Sevilla (2004)
81. Kim, K., Baek, C., Lee, J.D.: Creative destruction of the sharing economy in action: the case of Uber. Transp. Res. Part A: Policy Pract. **110**, 118–127 (2018)

Building Scalable Blockchain Applications - A Decision Process

Adrian Hofmann[(✉)]

Universität Würzburg, Sanderring 2, 97070 Würzburg, Germany
`adrian.hofmann@uni-wuerzburg.de`

Abstract. The blockchain technology faces many challenges before experiencing widespread adoption. One major challenge for many applications is the lack of scalability of the underlying architecture. While various technologies exist, that provide solutions to this issue, they are often overlooked when new applications are developed. To solve this problem we used a design science research approach to develop a decision process, that enables developers to choose the right technologies and ensure the scalability of their blockchain applications. The result is a four-step process, that helps to find the appropriate scalability solutions while still taking the business and technology environment into account. In addition the developed framework provides an overview of existing solutions and highlights gaps, where no solutions exist yet, providing a starting point for further research.

Keywords: Blockchain · Scalability · Decision process

1 The Need for Scalable Blockchain Applications

The blockchain technology is seen as one of the leading drivers of digitalization and decentralization. One of the fundamental limitations of blockchains for a variety of use-cases is scalability. Cryptocurrencies, the most well-known application for blockchains, suffer from several scalability issues that are often criticized. A popular example is the low transaction rate of 7 transactions per second for Bitcoin compared to centralized solutions like VISA[TM] reaching up 47,000 transactions per second [25]. Another point for criticism is high transaction latency of up to 41 hours, that occurred at especially high network loads in January 2018 [2]. Even though some experts state, that technical issues such as scalability and security are not an issue for the adaption and diffusion of blockchain technology [21], we argue that for some possible applications scalability is an essential factor. For example, blockchain is often seen as a device for trustless machine-to-machine transactions. CISCO[TM] predicts, that by 2020 about 50 billion devices will be connected to the internet [11] and even if only a fraction of these devices would communicate via a blockchain, the network load would be orders of magnitude higher than with current cryptocurrencies. While it is assumed by some researchers, that blockchain provides a scalable peer-to-peer

© Springer Nature Switzerland AG 2020
S. Hofmann et al. (Eds.): DESRIST 2020, LNCS 12388, pp. 309–320, 2020.
https://doi.org/10.1007/978-3-030-64823-7_28

communication protocol, this is not yet the case [16]. In contrast to peer-to-peer transactions in a trusted environment, the process of verifying transactions on a trustless distributed ledger is inherently inefficient. With the introduction of programmable smart contracts and distributed applications (DApps), that are executed and verified in the same manner, the problem of scalability became even more complex [5, 27].

There have been many contributions that developed solutions to those problems, however, it is hard for developers to find suitable solutions for their application. The goal of this paper is therefore to provide a standardized process for developing scalable blockchain applications, that developers can use as guidance. To do so, we propose the following research questions:

RQ1: Which technologies exist, that solve scalability issues in blockchain applications?

RQ2: What decisions have to be made to include these solutions in blockchain applications?

To answer these questions, we analyze the scalability problems that blockchains bring with them, accumulate existing solutions and develop a decision process that helps building scalable blockchain applications.

The following section gives an overview of the state of the art in scalability research, followed by the research process of this article. In Sect. 4 we provide an overview of existing solutions and introduce the decision process as the core of this article. The resulting artifact consists of a four-step process that guides developers while developing their applications. Section 5 explains our evaluation process, followed by the final section, that concludes this article by discussing the results.

2   Foundations and Related Work

Distributed ledger technology has a variety of scalability issues. The literature can be classified into five categories: transaction throughput, transaction latency, number of nodes, storage and computational complexity.

The majority of research focused on the *transaction rate*. This comes from the fact, that the most popular blockchain applications are cryptocurrencies (especially Bitcoin), whose transaction rate is often compared to the transaction rate of centralized transaction systems [17].

In addition to the overall throughput, the *latency of the transactions* was criticized by a majority of researchers. On the one hand, this problem was linked to the low throughput, by stating that a long transaction queue will delay transactions [8]. On the other hand, transactions are not considered secure until a few additional blocks have been mined. Therefore blockchains like Bitcoin with block times of approximately ten minutes do not enable instant transactions [8].

Four authors acknowledged, that some blockchains, in contrast to classical peer-to-peer systems, do not scale well with an increasing number of nodes. The reason for this is, that the scaling properties with the number of nodes in the network are heavily dependent on the consensus mechanism that is implemented. This is further discussed in Sect. 4.1. Independent from consensus mechanisms, the additional number of nodes are likely to contribute to a higher transaction count. This fact makes some blockchains, without special scaling solutions unsuitable for networks with many nodes, such as Internet-of-Things (IoT) applications.

For *storage and I/O* one common remark was, that the whole blockchain has to be stored on every node. This makes it hard to use especially for cheap devices with limited storage, like IoT devices. Another aspect is the manner in which storage is accessed in smart contracts. Blockchains like Ethereum or Hyperledger only support key-value based storage. This makes it difficult to efficiently store unstructured data such as images or database-like structures, that can easily be queried. Additionally, large data sets cannot be stored in single blocks due to limitations of the block size. While it has been shown, that arbitrary data can be stored and accessed in blockchains, it is often unfeasible to do so [24].

The *computational complexity* that comes with the decentralized calculation of smart contracts was directly acknowledged by only four authors. The problem of computational complexity and the cost of it have been shown to be two orders of magnitude higher for some applications, than in centralized systems [22]. Not only the global limitations of executing smart contracts but also the limits of single executions play a role when developing applications. Since smart contracts are executed on every mining node, the number of operations has to be limited [8]. This means, that some applications are not only impractical but also impossible to implement on certain blockchain architectures.

3   Research Design

To construct the decision framework we use a design science research process and follow the guidelines for design science research proposed by Hevner et al. [14]. It is stated, that IS research has to cater to business needs defined by the *environment* to assure the research relevance. We do not consider a specific business case, but the general need for scalability of blockchain applications. Additionally to achieve rigor, existing foundations from a broad *knowledge base* are to be applied to the research. With these side conditions, the actual *research* can be conducted through *building* and *evaluating* an artifact.

3.1   Ensuring Rigor

To get a better understanding of the current landscape of the most relevant scalability issues in IS research a literature review is conducted [26]. We conducted a literature review on articles from IS journals and conferences as well as literature from the fields of computer science and engineering. This allowed access to novel ideas and solutions, which is crucial in such a fast-evolving field as blockchain research. However, the literature was still focused on scholarly research and excluded white papers, blog entries or news stories, even though we acknowledge that they have been influential in the blockchain industry as well as in academia. The searched databases were: AIS Library, EBSCOHost, SpringerLink as well as Google Scholar. We limited the Google Scholar search to the first 200 articles, since there were overall over 14,000 results.

The search terms were dependent on the scalability issue they are supposed to solve. The search term was *"blockchain AND scalability AND ((transaction AND rate) OR (transaction AND throughput) OR latency OR bandwidth OR storage OR computation)"*. We filtered the papers by outlet, title and abstract, conducted a forward and backward search resulting in a set of 90 papers. The remaining literature was read and papers sorted for a final set of 48 papers.

3.2   Development and Evaluation

With the overview of existing solutions, we have a solid base to develop an artifact. In this step, the decision process is built on the foundation of the available solutions and evaluated with respect to the utility provided in solving scalability issues as well as the usability of the process. We examined all available solutions and in a first step categorized them. Since some solutions work in a very similar way and have the same advantages and disadvantages, we grouped them to avoid redundancies. We then examined further similarities, differences, dependencies and contradictions between the solutions to build the decision process. The development of the final process included multiple adjustments due to the dependencies and contradictions of some solutions.

The decision process falls in the category of *methods*, since it provides "guidance on how to solve problems" [14]. The evaluation of the artifact is carried out in a *descriptive* manner by testing it against multiple distinct scenarios to demonstrate its utility.

4   Building Scalable Blockchain Applications

In this section, we present the designed artifact in the form of a decision process that recommends suitable scalability solutions. In the first part, we give a short overview over the literature and the available solutions. In the second part, the final process is described.

4.1   Available Solutions

The solutions presented in the existing literature can be split into two main categories, depending on which aspect of the blockchain they target.

The first type of solution targets the *blockchain layer*, the second type the *application layer* [29]. In mainstream blockchain literature solutions targeting the blockchain layer, are referred to as layer 1 solutions, while solutions targeting the application layer are called layer 2 solutions [3] For the sake of brevity, we adhere to this naming convention. This distinction between the layers is important for building blockchain applications, since changing the blockchain infrastructure to implement layer 1 solutions is not trivial and requires a consensus among the network participants. Layer 2 solutions mostly provide scalability by interacting with the blockchain as little as possible and only using it as a final source of truth or as a settlement layer. Finally, all articles were grouped by the way the presented solutions work. We grouped the solutions further into six categories. Layer 1 solutions include the *consensus mechanism, architecture, sharding* and *parameters*, while layer 2 solutions can be categorized as *off-chain protocols* and *decentralized storage solutions*.

The effect of different *consensus mechanisms* especially on transaction throughput and latency has been discussed in 16 of the analyzed articles. Mostly Proof-of-Work (PoW), Proof-of-Stake (PoS), practical byzantine fault tolerance (PBFT) and Proof of Elapsed Time (PoET) were evaluated as mechanisms for the decision process. While we acknowledge, that there is a wider variety of consensus mechanisms, we focused on the most widespread to keep the decision process manageable.

This category *architectures* fits all solutions that do not use traditional blockchains to store the distributed ledger. Among those are articles proposing data structures other than a blockchain such as directed acyclic graphs (DAG), eg. a hashgraph or tangle [10]. Since these are not blockchains and have often had entirely different properties incompatible with other solutions we describe, they are excluded from the decision process. Other solutions such as sidechains and multichain architectures are too complex to fit into the scope of this paper but should be evaluated in future research.

Sharding is a process first introduced to distribute databases. The idea is to split the data into smaller data sets (shards) and spread them among multiple servers. For blockchains the principle is similar. The blockchain network is divided into smaller communities, that validate transactions with classical consensus mechanisms [12].

Adjusting the *blockchains parameters* is the most straightforward solution to increase the transaction rate or improve latency. However, it is only mentioned in six articles. It is stated, that latency, as well as transaction throughput, can be improved by decreasing the average time that is needed to confirm a block [6]. Additionally, an increased block size can improve the transaction throughput as well as the latency that comes from waiting queues at high network loads. This solution can also enable smart contracts, that rely on storing many variables.

The most discussed scalability solution is moving transactions to secure *off-chain* communication channels. Payment channels describe a class of techniques that enable users to conduct multiple transactions without committing single transactions to the blockchain. In the case of purely bidirectional transactions, state channels constitute bilateral agreements between two parties. Against this backdrop, multiple users can build networks, which allow unconnected users to conduct transactions by routing them over intermediaries [18]. A similar technique to offloading transactions from the blockchain, complex computations can also be done with minimal interaction with the blockchain itself. While in the current literature presented protocols do secure off-chain computation [19], they still impose some limitations. Newer solutions support efficient on-chain verification of off-chain computation results, which can solve some shortcomings. A downside of this procedure is that the verification contract has to be set up by every party that relies on the computation to be correct. However other less efficient solutions do not rely on a trusted setup process [13].

The means of *data storage* for blockchains is often limited to storing key-value pairs. While this is a good solution for a wide range of applications, it may be useful for the means to have the availability of mass storage for media files or to have a database structure that can be queried. Against this backdrop, several solutions have been introduced like the interplanetary file system (IPFS) [7] for decentralized trustless storage or decentralized cloud solutions based on smart contracts [30]. The choice of database solutions range to the scale of Hadoop based Big Data databases [23].

4.2   Decision Process

Before the decision process is started, it should be decided, whether a blockchain is needed to solve the problem at hand. The requirements to decide whether a decentralized trustless ledger is suitable for an application has already been researched [28], as well as whether a different architecture such as hashgraphs or tangles is suitable for an application [15].

To choose the right solutions for the desired applications, we derived a four-step process with an additional evaluation step.

In the first step, it should be decided whether to implement an own blockchain or to build the application on an existing one. While it is much easier to use an existing blockchain that is stable and trusted, it must be considered, that all applications running on this blockchain compete for the same limited resources of the blockchain. The second step is choosing the right consensus mechanism for the blockchain. Then the parametrization and layer 1 solutions for the blockchain have to be defined. If an existing blockchain is chosen, it should fit the desired parameters and layer 1 solutions as close as possible. In the fourth step, layer 2 solutions will be considered and chosen according to the scalability needs. Additionally, we recommend an evaluation as a final step. Here it should be checked, whether the chosen solutions are compatible with each other and if needed, adjust the decisions. Figure 1 provides an overview of the complete process.

Fig. 1. Overview of the decision process

Choosing a Consensus Mechanism. The choice of the consensus mechanism is independent from the choice of other layer 1 solutions and the choice of the consensus mechanism alone can result in a scalable solution for some use-cases. The decision tree to follow in order to choose the right mechanism is depicted in Fig. 2.

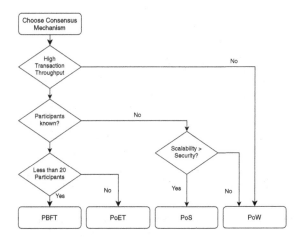

Fig. 2. Flowchart for choosing a suitable consensus mechanism

If the transaction throughput of the application is limited, the Proof-of-Work consensus is the most tested and stable consensus mechanism available. Typical PoW blockchains can handle around 25 transactions per second. If this limit is strongly exceeded by the application, another mechanism should be chosen.

If the participants of the blockchains (i.e. users of the application) are known, a permissioned blockchain can be utilized. Permissioned blockchains can utilize consensus mechanisms, that are more efficient, since they are resistant to Sybil attacks. If no permissioned blockchain can be utilized the PoS consensus mechanism should be considered, if the scalability is worth a security trade-off. If not, the PoW consensus should be chosen. Scalability can still be achieved with other solutions.

If a permissioned blockchain is suitable, it should be checked if the number of nodes is not too high for the PBFT. Studies showed, that in practical applications the protocol does not work efficiently if the number of nodes exceeds 20. If it does, the PoET consensus is recommended.

Choosing Layer 1 Solutions. After the consensus mechanism was considered, the parameters block-time and block-size have to be assigned, as well as if sharding and other architectural decisions are suitable and needed. In this step, multiple, or even all solutions can be chosen.

Often used functions of smart contracts or those that are expensive to execute such as cryptographic functions should be precompiled into machine language, so that they do not have to be executed with blockchain bytecode. Precompiling elliptic curve parings is a prerequisite for using efficient zkSNARK verification on blockchains (Fig. 3).

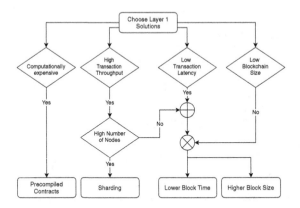

Fig. 3. Flowchart for choosing suitable layer 1 solutions

If a high transaction throughput is necessary, it should be checked whether the number of nodes is big enough to allow sharding. The transaction throughput scales linearly with sharding nodes, but too many nodes make the partial networks too small and in consequence not secure [4].

Therefore if the number of nodes does not allow this solution *or* a low latency is required, the block time should be minimized and the block size maximized. However, this is only possible, if the overall blockchain size is not of concern.

Choosing Layer 2 Solutions. The last step is to choose layer 2 solutions (Fig. 4).

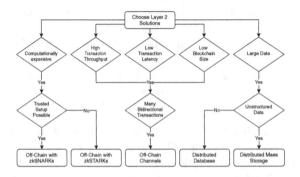

Fig. 4. Flowchart for choosing suitable layer 2 solutions

If the application is computationally expensive, off-chain computation with on-chain verification should be considered. Off-Chain computations that can be proven to be correct on-chain are only useful, if the verification of the proof is cheaper than the actual computation [13]. Verifying a zkSNARK on the Ethereum blockchain costs around 1.8 million gas [9]. Every function that requires less gas should not be considered for a off-chain computation. Additionally, the setup of the verification contract is not trivial and should include all parties that need to trust the verification process. If such a trusted setup is not possible, zkSTARKs should be considered for on-chain verification. However verification is computationally orders of magnitude more complex and therefore not the preferred option [1].

If either a high transaction throughput, low latency or a small blockchain size are required, it is recommended to offload most of the transactions off the blockchain into payment channels. Once a payment channel has been created, it offers instant payments as well as a high throughput. Since the transaction to open and close the channel underlies the same limitations as regular blockchain transactions these channels should only be used if it is likely that the parties involved will perform multiple bidirectional transactions. It should also be noted that, for security reasons, transactions with a high transaction value or with important data should be handled directly on the blockchain. The extension to a network of channels is only useful if the network is dense enough to provide a path between the parties involved.

If the application is reliant on data which is too big to fit into single blockchain blocks, the data must be stored in a different way. Here we have to differentiate between structured data that can be stored in a database and unstructured data, such as image or movie files, that requires mass storage. The usage of distributed databases is recommended, when the underlying blockchain architecture is insufficient for storing or querying the needed data sets. We do not differentiate between SQL-like databases or databases capable of processing big data, since the differences are well researched and discussed in other fields [25]. For unstructured data, solutions such as IPFS ensure data integrity as well as data availability among all participants.

5   Evaluation

To evaluate the framework designed here we utilized a scenario based evaluation [20]. We evaluated the process for its ease-of-use, reproducibility of the results and if it serves its purpose. We therefore supplied three fellow researchers with the decision process as well as the use-cases and let them chose the appropriate scalability solutions. They all chose the same scalability solutions and claimed, that the usage was straight forward. To test, whether the process served its purpose, we implemented the use-cases and tested them against implementations without scalability solutions. We hence tested it by implementing three use-cases, each with different challenges for scalability. The first scenario was a *distributed voting process*, that needs to handle a large burst of transactions in a short voting period. The second use-case was *tracing of goods in a supply network*. Here a few parties track a large number of items. The final use-case was a *blockchain-based chess game*. There have been several attempts to implement such a game without a trusted third party, most of which failed, because it is too computationally expensive to check whether moves are legal.

This example showed, that it was straightforward to chose the scalability options needed to implement the application. While the implementation itself was complex, the decision process in each scenario was simple and led to the desired results.

6   Conclusion and Future Work

Blockchain applications widely suffer from scalability issues that prevent them from reaching widespread popularity. While many solutions to those problems exist, there was no structured process to decide on how and when to apply them. We managed to extract those solutions for scalability limitations by reviewing state-of-the-art literature from IS, computer science and engineering, structured them and provided an overview, which answered our first research question. By building on this knowledge we answered our second research question and constructed a decision process, that helps developers, businesses and researchers to build scalable blockchain applications. The provided process is short enough to be executed before each development project and comprehensive enough to give developers an idea on which solutions to focus. The provided process is not without limitations. There is still a wide variety of scalability solutions, that had to be excluded from this work for complexity reasons. In future research, the process can be extended to give a more granular decision process. Additionally, the process can be evaluated in more practical scenarios. An evaluation and extension with domain experts are also possible. Another important consideration for every type of application is maturity and ease of use of the underlying technology. Many of the technologies presented here are new and not sufficiently tested in productive use. The quality of the documentation as well as the existence of a community, that can help develop the technology is also essential, especially if the developers of an application lack the resources needed to fix or improve immature software to use it in their projects. These issues became very clear when implementing some of the evaluation scenarios and the impact. We encourage, that the maturity of the presented technologies should be researched. The methodology used in this paper is also suitable to develop decision processes for objectives other than scalability such as privacy. Overall this paper opens up new ways for further research on decision processes and the development of blockchain applications.

Acknowledgement. This work has been developed in the project PIMKoWe. PIMKoWe (reference number: 02P17D160) is partly funded by the German ministry of education and research (BMBF) within the research programme "Industrie 4.0 – Kollaborationen in dynamischen Wertschöpfungsnetzwerken (InKoWe)" and managed by the Project Management Agency Karlsruhe (PTKA). The author is responsible for the content of this publication.

References

1. Ben-Sasson, E., Bentov, I., Horesh, Y., Riabzev, M.: Scalable zero knowledge with no trusted setup. In: Boldyreva, A., Micciancio, D. (eds.) CRYPTO 2019. LNCS, vol. 11694, pp. 701–732. Springer, Cham (2019). https://doi.org/10.1007/978-3-030-26954-8_23

2. bitinfocharts.com: Bitcoin block time historical chart (2019). https://bitinfocharts.com/comparison/bitcoin-confirmationtime.html

3. Buterin, V.: Ethereum scalability research and development subsidy programs (2018). https://blog.ethereum.org/2018/01/02/ethereum-scalability-research-development-subsidy-programs/

4. Cai, S., Yang, N., Ming, Z.: A decentralized sharding service network framework with scalability. In: Jin, H., Wang, Q., Zhang, L.-J. (eds.) ICWS 2018. LNCS, vol. 10966, pp. 151–165. Springer, Cham (2018). https://doi.org/10.1007/978-3-319-94289-6_10

5. Chauhan, A., Malviya, O.P., Verma, M., Mor, T.S.: Blockchain and scalability. In: 2018 IEEE International Conference on Software Quality, Reliability and Security Companion (QRS-C), pp. 122–128 (2018)

6. Croman, K., et al.: On Scaling Decentralized Blockchains. In: Clark, J., Meiklejohn, S., Ryan, P.Y.A., Wallach, D., Brenner, M., Rohloff, K. (eds.) FC 2016. LNCS, vol. 9604, pp. 106–125. Springer, Heidelberg (2016). https://doi.org/10.1007/978-3-662-53357-4_8

7. Cucurull, J., Rodríguez-Pérez, A., Finogina, T., Puiggalí, J.: Blockchain-based internet voting: systems' compliance with international standards. In: Abramowicz, W., Paschke, A. (eds.) BIS 2018. LNBIP, vol. 339, pp. 300–312. Springer, Cham (2019). https://doi.org/10.1007/978-3-030-04849-5_27

8. Dinh, T.T.A., Wang, J., Chen, G., Liu, R., Ooi, B.C., Tan, K.L.: Blockbench: a framework for analyzing private blockchains. In: Proceedings of the 2017 ACM International Conference on Management of Data, pp. 1085–1100. ACM (2017)

9. Eberhardt, J., Tai, S.: Zokrates-scalable privacy-preserving off-chain computations. In: IEEE International Conference on Blockchain. IEEE (2018)

10. El Ioini, N., Pahl, C.: A review of distributed ledger technologies. In: Panetto, H., Debruyne, C., Proper, H.A., Ardagna, C.A., Roman, D., Meersman, R. (eds.) OTM 2018. LNCS, vol. 11230, pp. 277–288. Springer, Cham (2018). https://doi.org/10.1007/978-3-030-02671-4_16

11. Evans, D.: The internet of things: how the next evolution of the internet is changing everything. CISCO White Paper 1(2011), 1–11 (2011)

12. Feng, X., Ma, J., Miao, Y., Meng, Q., Liu, X., Jiang, Q., Li, H.: Pruneable sharding-based blockchain protocol. Peer-to-Peer Netw. Appl. (2018). https://doi.org/10.1007/s12083-018-0685-6

13. Galal, H.S., Youssef, A.M.: Succinctly verifiable sealed-bid auction smart contract. In: Garcia-Alfaro, J., Herrera-Joancomartí, J., Livraga, G., Rios, R. (eds.) DPM/CBT -2018. LNCS, vol. 11025, pp. 3–19. Springer, Cham (2018). https://doi.org/10.1007/978-3-030-00305-0_1

14. Hevner, A.R., March, S.T., Park, J., Ram, S.: Design science in information systems research. Manag. Inf. Syst. Q. **28**(1), 6 (2008)

15. Koens, T., Poll, E.: What blockchain alternative do you need? In: Garcia-Alfaro, J., Herrera-Joancomartí, J., Livraga, G., Rios, R. (eds.) DPM/CBT -2018. LNCS, vol. 11025, pp. 113–129. Springer, Cham (2018). https://doi.org/10.1007/978-3-030-00305-0_9

16. Kouicem, D.E., Bouabdallah, A., Lakhlef, H.: Internet of things security: a top-down survey. Comput. Netw. **141**, 199–221 (2018). http://search.ebscohost.com/login.aspx?direct=true&db=buh&AN=130419466&site=ehost-live

17. Lacity, M.: Addressing key challenges to making enterprise blockchain applications a reality. MIS Q. Execut. **17**(3), 201–222 (2018)

18. McCorry, P., Möser, M., Shahandasti, S.F., Hao, F.: Towards bitcoin payment networks. In: Liu, J.K.K., Steinfeld, R. (eds.) ACISP 2016. LNCS, vol. 9722, pp. 57–76. Springer, Cham (2016). https://doi.org/10.1007/978-3-319-40253-6_4

19. Molina-Jimenez, C., Solaiman, E., Sfyrakis, I., Ng, I., Crowcroft, J.: On and off-blockchain enforcement of smart contracts. arXiv preprint arXiv:1805.00626 (2018)

20. Peffers, K., Rothenberger, M., Tuunanen, T., Vaezi, R.: Design science research evaluation. In: Peffers, K., Rothenberger, M., Kuechler, B. (eds.) DESRIST 2012. LNCS, vol. 7286, pp. 398–410. Springer, Heidelberg (2012). https://doi.org/10.1007/978-3-642-29863-9_29

21. Post, R., Smit, K., Zoet, M.: Identifying factors affecting blockchain technology diffusion. In: Twenty-fourth Americas Conference on Information Systems (2018)

22. Rimba, P., Tran, A.B., Weber, I., Staples, M., Ponomarev, A., Xu, X.: Quantifying the cost of distrust: comparing blockchain and cloud services for business process execution. Inf. Syst. Front. 1–19 (2018)

23. Sahoo, M.S., Baruah, P.K.: HBasechainDB – a scalable blockchain framework on hadoop ecosystem. In: Yokota, R., Wu, W. (eds.) SCFA 2018. LNCS, vol. 10776, pp. 18–29. Springer, Cham (2018). https://doi.org/10.1007/978-3-319-69953-0_2

24. Sleiman, M.D., Lauf, A.P., Yampolskiy, R.: Bitcoin message: data insertion on a proof-of-work cryptocurrency system. In: 2015 International Conference on Cyber-worlds (CW), pp. 332–336. IEEE (2015)

25. Trillo, M.: Stress test prepares visanet for the most wonderful time of the year. https://misc.visa.com/blogarchives/us/2013/10/10/stress-test-prepares-visanet-for-the-most-wonderful-time-of-the-year/index.html

26. Vom Brocke, J., et al.: Reconstructing the giant: On the importance of rigour in documenting the literature search process. In: Ecis, vol. 9, pp. 2206–2217 (2009)

27. Worley, C., Skjellum, A.: Blockchain tradeoffs and challenges for current and emerging applications: generalization, fragmentation, sidechains, and scalability. In: 2018 IEEE International Conference on Internet of Things (iThings) and IEEE Green Computing and Communications (GreenCom) and IEEE Cyber, Physical and Social Computing (CPSCom) and IEEE Smart Data (SmartData), pp. 1582–1587 (2018)

28. Wüst, K., Gervais, A.: Do you need a blockchain? In: 2018 Crypto Valley Conference on Blockchain Technology (CVCBT), pp. 45–54. IEEE (2018)

29. Xu, X., et al.: The blockchain as a software connector. In: 2016 13th Working IEEE/IFIP Conference on Software Architecture (WICSA), pp. 182–191. IEEE (2016)

30. Xue, J., Xu, C., Zhang, Y., Bai, L.: DStore: a distributed cloud storage system based on smart contracts and blockchain. In: Vaidya, J., Li, J. (eds.) ICA3PP 2018. LNCS, vol. 11336, pp. 385–401. Springer, Cham (2018). https://doi.org/10.1007/978-3-030-05057-3_30

Designing for Context Versus the Lock-in Effect of 'Free' Global Digital Platforms: A Case of SMEs from Nigeria

Adedamola Tolani[1]($\boxtimes$) ![ORCID], Adebowale Owoseni[2] ![ORCID], and Hossana Twinomurinzi[3] ![ORCID]

[1] School of Computing, University of South Africa, Pretoria, South Africa
damolat@gmail.com
[2] School of Computer Science and Informatics, De Montfort University, Leicester, UK
adebowale.owoseni@dmu.ac.uk
[3] Department of Applied Information Systems,
University of Johannesburg, Johannesburg, South Africa
twinoh@gmail.com

Abstract. This paper reports on the design and evaluation of an app that was designed using the newly created elaborated action design research method and critical realism to overcome the social and economic structural challenges that SMEs in Nigeria face. The results show that even though the app took into account the full range of SME dynamic capabilities and proved valuable, SMEs remained dependent on the affordances of the existing global digital platforms. The findings point to the lock-in effect of *'freely'* available digital platforms and that SMEs tend to default to their path dependency (and therefore the existing global digital platforms) rather than explore local digital innovations. The paper suggests that intentional efforts from powerful actors such as government might be necessary to overcome the path dependency and lock-in effect of *'freely'* available global digital platforms. The paper identifies the extra efforts required to sustain local digital innovation in the face of well-resourced global digital platforms. The paper further reveals the utility of the new elaborated action design research method for designing for context. Six (6) design principles for designing for SMEs in resource-constrained contexts were also elicited.

Keywords: Small and medium-sized enterprises (SMEs) · Digital platforms · Mobile app · Dynamic capabilities (DC) · Particularism · Context

1 Introduction

Digital technologies play an integral role in enhancing the dynamic capabilities (DCs) of Small and medium sized enterprises (SMEs) to make effective decisions and take planned and strategic decisions. DCs represent ways in which organisations reorganise

Electronic supplementary material The online version of this chapter (https://doi.org/10.1007/978-3-030-64823-7_29) contains supplementary material, which is available to authorized users.

© Springer Nature Switzerland AG 2020
S. Hofmann et al. (Eds.): DESRIST 2020, LNCS 12388, pp. 321–332, 2020.
https://doi.org/10.1007/978-3-030-64823-7_29

their internal resources and competences in response to evolving business environments [1]. For example, digital technologies influence product quality and services, resulting in the improvement of SME DCs [2]. SMEs also use mobile apps, particularly social media and e-commerce platforms [3–6], to serve their customers, maximize new business opportunities and achieve market advantage [5].

SMEs in Nigeria face structural challenges including lack of skilled human resources, limited training opportunities, poor policy implementation, inadequate infrastructure, lack of funding support and access to credit facilities, multiple tariffs and regulatory challenges (i.e. tax regulatory problems, delays in organisation and product registrations) compared to their counterparts in high-income countries [6–9].

This paper therefore sought to develop a context-suitable mobile app artefact that integrates the DCs of SMEs in Nigeria [7–9]. The paper posited the necessity of understanding the structural issues that influence SMEs in developing country contexts (Nigeria) from the critical realist philosophy. Critical Realism (CR) is a meta-theoretical philosophy by Bhaskar [11] that illustrates the significance of distinguishing knowledge from existence. CR allowed this study to identify the social and economic structural patterns that influence SMEs, and subsequently design a contextual mobile app for Nigeria SMEs [12–13]. Specifically, the study sought to: *design a mobile app artefact that allows SMEs in Nigeria to identify opportunity from a critical realist viewpoint.*

The remainder of the paper is structured as follows: The next section presents the related work. It is followed by the research approach and a section on the design of the digital artefact. The final section presents the conclusion and inferences.

2   Related Work

2.1   SMEs and Dynamic Capabilities (DCs)

SMEs in Nigeria are classified as businesses with a total cost of less than five hundred million (500,000,000) Naira ($1,383,040), excluding land, and fewer than two hundred (200) employees. Ninety six per cent of businesses in Nigeria are categorised as SMEs according to the Central Bank of Nigeria [14]. SMEs are valuable to Nigeria's economic growth. They provide entrepreneurial and leadership development of talents, the lack of which is often an impediment to economic development. The continuous development of these highly skilled entrepreneurial resources and competences drawing on DCs and digital technologies is important to the sensing and seizing of new business opportunities.

DCs are organisational and strategic routines that enable organisations to reorganise their internal resources and competencies continuously to create new sources of competitive advantage [1]. DCs involve the renewal of business processes, allocations of human resources, knowledge development and transfer, and decision-making in direct response to new business needs [15]. DCs are fundamental to SMEs as they reflect the ability to create, modify and renew business processes [16].

2.2   Mobile Apps and SMEs

Mobile apps are software programs that run on mobile devices and integrate specific digital platforms to accomplish specific tasks for individuals and organisations [17].

Mobile apps enable SMEs to take effective decisions and planned and strategic risks while carrying out their business processes seamlessly [18].

Owing to dynamic market needs, SMEs continually seek new approaches to differentiate their businesses using mobile apps [19]. The use of mobile apps is integral to SMEs as these apps assist SME owners in enhancing their ability to make effective decisions while developing, analysing, processing and transforming information. The adoption of mobile apps can also enable SMEs to increase their revenue growth and create more jobs faster than their competitors [20].

This paper reports on the design of a contextual mobile app from an ensembled viewpoint that sees ICTs as part of dynamic social networks that include people, their DCs and relationships, and artefacts [21].

2.3 Designing for Context

Context can be defined as the situation within which a phenomenon of study occurs in an organisation [22]. It also refers to the circumstances that produce the setting for an event that is well understood to capture clear constructs and specific implications [23, 24]. Context enables an in-depth understanding of the structural challenges and events that affect a phenomenon of interest. Takavarasha et al. [25] articulated the relevance of context to determine where and when ICTs are designed and used to conform with diverse cultures, capabilities, and social settings.

In the Nigerian context, SMEs are looking at new approaches to uniquely differentiate the products and services they offer because of dynamic market needs [5]. An approach largely considered by SMEs is the use of ICTs, such as mobile apps. ICTs are key enablers of SMEs in the development of products, market research and access to information [26, 27]. ICTs enhance the growth and development of SMEs in dynamic socio-economic environments, thereby enabling them to compete favourably in a fast-paced environment [20, 28]. The research reported here focused on creating and evaluating a digital artefact (mobile app) designed around contextual constructs developed from the DCs of SMEs in Nigeria using the elaborated action design research (EADR) [9].

2.4 Elaborated Action Design Research

EADR is a problem-driven approach that closely links activities that are specific to the design of an artefact while simultaneously evaluating it [29]. The EADR cycle follows the stages: diagnosis, design, implementation and evolution (Fig. 1).

Each stage of EADR includes the following activities: problem articulation, creation of artefact, artefact evaluation, new knowledge creation through reflection and learning formalisation [30]. These activities are carried out iteratively, as a sequence of specific tasks, based on certain principles to create new knowledge through learning formalisation. The EADR approach was further guided by the CR philosophy in the diagnosis phase to identify the underlying contextual mechanisms that exist in SMEs. This ensured that the design of the mobile app was based on rigorous theoretical and empirical evidence, and at the same time the relevance of the contextual mechanisms [31]. This study will use the EADR method to discuss the development and evaluation of the proposed ICT artefact.

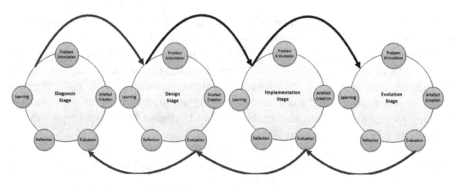

Fig. 1. Stages of EADR (Adapted from Mullarkey and Hevner [29])

3 Research Approach

The EADR method was adopted in the study to design and evaluate the artefact following the procedures depicted in Fig. 2.

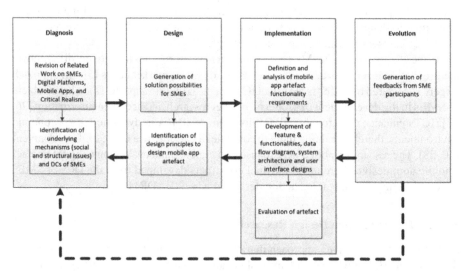

Fig. 2. Research process flow diagram

In this study, the researcher took the following steps as illustrated in the research process flow diagram:

1. Identifying underlying mechanisms to reveal social and structural issues experienced by SMEs in Nigeria.
2. Generating solution possibilities and design principles to address the issues experienced by SMEs.

3. Designing the artefact (including functionality requirements, a data flow diagram, the system architecture and user interfaces).
4. Evaluating the artefact to assess its efficacy in SMEs.

3.1 Identification of Underlying Mechanisms in Nigerian SMEs

Critical Realism Domains of SMEs in Nigeria

CR served as the philosophical lens to uncover the underlying mechanisms that influence SMEs, and served as the basis for the design and development of the mobile app artefact for SMEs in Nigeria. CR maintains a strong focus on ontology to illustrate that reality exists and that it is possible to create new knowledge about it [33]. According to Bhaskar [11], objective reality is identified and described in three hierarchical strata of reality: the real, the actual and the empirical.

The real includes social structures and mechanisms that exist independently of our perception of them; some of these are observable and others are not. Causal generative mechanisms emerge from the *social structures* in the real domain of CR [34]. These causal mechanisms describe the structural issues in Nigeria context [35], which this research sought to reveal. The actual domain consists of observable events that occur as a result of the interactions of causal mechanisms (i.e. the real) [35]. The empirical domain comprises events that occur through observations of experiences [33]; in this study these are the noticeable observations of the subjects being examined.

Previous research by Tolani et al. [36] identified the underlying mechanisms in the CR domain of SMEs, namely productivity, access to local market information, training and access to SME programmes that generate events (SME business processes and DCs). (See supplementary material). The identified mechanisms allowed this study to uncover the structural elements (i.e. problems) in SMEs. These structural elements or problems are discussed below.

SMEs use different freely available ICTs (i.e. digital platforms) with unique features that lack interoperability as a result of the loosely structured nature of their business. Also, the existing ICTs used by SMEs are globally oriented and lack the provision of local information services, which result in logistics, finance, human resources, taxation and regulatory issues. This problem affects SMEs' ability to access local market information and trends in Nigeria. In addition, SMEs lack continuous skills development owing to the inability of government agencies to convey information to SMEs or to deliver training via digital platforms. Finally, funds and capacity-building programmes set up by government agencies are inaccessible to SMEs as a result of inadequate dissemination of information and an ineffective organisational system.

The contextual mechanisms discussed above are the structural issues that exist in SMEs and provide an entry point to articulating the possible solutions and design principles to create the artefact.

Design Principles for Context

The paper adopted the contextual mechanisms as the requirements for the artefact to be developed [30]. The following are the five design principles that were identified: Digital artefacts for SMEs in resource constrained low-income countries should:

1. Incorporate the dynamic capability to identify local business opportunities.
2. Demonstrate the ability to do business in unstructured environments.
3. Gain easy access to SME government programmes and funding.
4. Provide access to entrepreneurship learning content.
5. Consider the local dialect and language.

3.2 Design of the Contextual Artefact

The mobile app artefact included the design principles based on the ensemble viewpoint to group SME owners, their relationships, existing ICTs, DCs and SME business processes in an organized way [37].

The design of the app, "MyBizAssistant" included features and functionalities, a data flow diagram, system architecture and user interface designs of the artefact (see supplementary material). The functionalities of the app and the DCs of SMEs in Nigeria are illustrated in Table 1.

Table 1. Functionalities of MyBizAssistant artefact and related DCs

Functionality	DCs of SMEs	Description
Productivity	Sales and marketing	The mobile app enables SMEs to carry out sales, marketing and branding activities, to manage expenditure, to interact and participate (i.e. communicate), and to do market research using existing digital platforms
	Market research	
	Interaction and participation	
	Product marketing and research	
	Review operations	
	Create new product ideas	
	Product branding	
	Expenditure management	
Access to local market information	Marketing strategy	The mobile app enables SMEs to overcome the organisational constraints and to get easy access to information tailored to the local market
	Access government SME programmes in Nigerian languages	
	Market research	
Training	Training and capacity development	This mobile app enables SMEs to access training easily for continuous skills development
Access to SME programmes	Marketing strategy	The mobile app enables the digital dissemination of information on SME programmes and funding
	Access government SME programmes	

3.3 Evaluation of the Artefact

The evaluation of the app was carried out with 20 SMEs using observational design evaluation methods through field studies [32]. The respondents provided five-point Likert-scale responses ranging from (1) "Not At All" to (5) "A Great Deal" to ten (10) questions as feedback on the app DC constructs (i.e. sales and marketing, strategic planning, expenditure management, trainings, communications, access to local market information, access to government programmes, market research and generate new product ideas) and app usage preference construct (i.e. preference to use MyBizAssistant over the freely available apps). The study conducted only one evaluation cycle due to time and logistical constraints.

Using descriptive statistics, the data fulfilled validity and normal distribution requirements: data points are within ± 3 standard deviation from the mean, and had kurtosis and skewness within an acceptable range of ± 2 and close variances [38]. Minitab 18 statistical software was used for the statistical tests.

4 Results

4.1 Evaluation: MyBizAssistant Mobile App Artefact

The SMEs in this study included 20 businesses that cut across 8 industries in Nigeria: agriculture, manufacturing, food, event planning, medical, information technology, gifts packaging, clothing. SME owners rated the app as an "effective tool" as follows: communication with customers (4.20); generating new product ideas (4.15); access to local market information (3.95); market research (3.90); attending entrepreneurial and leadership training (3.90); sales and marketing (3.85); expenditure management (3.75); strategic planning (3.65); access to government programmes (3.60); and prefer MyBizAssistant over existing global digital platforms (3.30). (See supplementary material). The app uses smartphone features (e.g. phone contacts and push notifications) and integrates existing digital platforms and government APIs to allow SME owners to maximize business opportunities. It gives SMEs easy access to information on the local market and SME programmes. The app also allows SMEs to interact in a Nigerian language (Yoruba, Ibo or Hausa), and to facilitate participation in training and collaboration. A comparison between MyBizAssistant and other digital platforms is described in Table 2.

The results suggest that the app has the potential to enhance SMEs' sales, marketing and strategic planning activities. In addition, the app can help SMEs to gain improved access to government programmes. However, a few SME owners indicated the need for deeper integration into government and market research content platforms to create seamless interaction with SME owners and to improve business insight. The evaluation confirms the usefulness of the app as a suitable tool for SME owners to enhance their DCs to identify opportunities. It also reveals functional issues and changes that could be made (as indicated by the respondents).

The functionalities of MyBizAssistant compared to the top 3 digital platforms used by Nigerian SMEs (Facebook, Instagram, WhatsApp) illustrated in Table 2 shows that the digital platforms *only* used by SMEs for sales and marketing, interaction and participation, product branding, and market research purposes; and are not suitable for access

Table 2. Functionalities and Related DCs of MyBizAssistant artefact compared with other digital platforms

Functionality	DCs of SMEs	MyBizAssistant	Facebook	Instagram	WhatsApp
Productivity	Sales and marketing	Yes	Yes	Yes	Yes
	Market research	Yes	Yes	Yes	No
	Interaction and participation	Yes	Yes	Yes	Yes
	Product marketing and research	Yes	No	Yes	No
	Review operations	Yes	No	No	No
	Create new product ideas	Yes	Yes	Yes	No
	Product branding	Yes	Yes	Yes	Yes
	Expenditure management	Yes	No	No	No
Access to local market information	Marketing strategy	Yes	Yes	Yes	No
	Access government SME programmesin Nigerian languages	Yes	No	No	No
	Market research	Yes	Yes	Yes	No
Training	Training and capacity development	Yes	No	No	No
Access to SME programmes	Marketing strategy	Yes	No	No	No
	Access government SME programmes	Yes	No	No	No

to localised information on market trends, government programs, funding, and training. Despite the availability of a better alternative "*MyBizAssistant*" that is based on the Nigerian context, SMEs still preferred the digital platforms because they are free, easily accessible, familiar and readily available to use; thus, creating a *lock-in effect*.

4.2   Discussion: Lock-in Effect of Digital Platforms on SMEs in Nigeria

The findings in this study showed that SMEs only moderately preferred the MyBizAssistant over *'freely'* available global digital platforms. This is a symptom of what is labelled a *"path dependency"* syndrome, which is seen not only in SMEs, but also in larger organisations. Path dependency refers to established organisational routines that endure despite evidence that the routines no longer provide any value [39, 40]. This result to the lock-in of SMEs as it pertains to the use of these digital platforms. This can be detrimental to the business as it often results in a reluctance to adapt to ICT evolution and/or reverse past decisions regarding ICT use.

The study therefore included one more design principle: Contextually designed apps for SMEs should engage with powerful actors especially government agencies in order to encourage adoption. MyBizAssistant app was integrated to government platforms to create a seamless interaction with SMEs and push contents that inform SMEs about product registration, tariffs, waivers, and funding opportunities.

5 Conclusions

The research focused on the design and evaluation of a contextual mobile app for SMEs in the resource constrained Nigerian context based on requirements that were elicited from critical realist mindset. The theoretical underpinnings of the business requirements were guided by the DC framework. The DC considers the dynamic nature of organisations and has at its centre innovativeness and resourcefulness of existing organisational resources. The research adopted the EADR to allow for the continuous diagnosis, design, implementation and evolution of the app.

Using CR the research the structural needs that affect SMEs' DCs were elicited, and these provided perspective which inform how SMEs use mobile apps in Nigeria. Subsequently, an app was created using EADR approach which enabled SMEs to improve their ability to maximize business opportunities. The app was evaluated to determine its relevance. The resultant design artefact was shown to be relevant for SMEs in allowing access to information and data about their business and operations, government SME programmes and cost-effective vendors. Particularly, the app could enhance sales, marketing, strategic planning, easy access to local market information and SME programmes. However, SMEs appears to be locked in to the freely available global platforms such as Facebook, Instagram and WhatsApp, revealing a strong *path-dependency* effect.

For SMEs to maximize the benefits of contextual-suitable apps, and improve DCs, the effects of path dependency, and the lock-in effect of these powerful, freely available global digital platforms [41], would require inputs from external and powerful actors such as government [42] to raise adoption among SMEs [43]. The awareness could begin with incremental steps in advocacy and incentivising usage of local digital platforms [44].

The paper was limited in the requirements space, the number of SMEs that evaluated the app and the time provided to test the app. Further research could be conducted on a longitudinal basis in a different context and country as adoption of digital technologies in society is often a gradual process.

References

1. Teece, D., Shuena, A., Pisano, G.: Dynamic capabilities and strategic management. Strategic Manage. J. **18**, 509–533 (1997)

2. Esselaar, S., Christoph, S., Ali, N., Deen-Swarray, M.: ICT usage and its impact on profitability of SMEs in 13 African countries. In: 2006 International Conference on Information and Communication Technologies and Development, pp. 40–47. IEEE (2006)

3. Constantinides, P., Henfridsson, O., Parker, G.: Platforms and infrastructures in the digital age (2018). https://doi.org/10.1287/isre.2018.0794

4. Asadullah, A., Faik, I., Kankanhalli, A.: Digital platforms: a review and future directions (2018)

5. O'Halloran, J.: SMEs get productivity from mobile applications. http://www.computerw eekly.com/news/2240088236/SMEs-get-productivity-from-mobile-applications. Accessed 20 June 2017

6. Nwagwu, I., Oni, T.: Lagos and its potentials for economic growth. https://ng.boell.org/2015/07/02/lagos-and-its-potentials-economic-growth. Accessed 30 Sept 2018

7. Muller, P., et al.: Annual report on European SMEs 2018/2019 (2019)

8. Urquhart, C.: Response to davison and martinsons: context is king! Yes and no - it's still all about theory (building). J. Inf. Technol. 31, 254–256 (2016). https://doi.org/10.1057/s41265-016-0002-x

9. Davison, R., Martinsons, M.: Context is king! Considering particularism in research design and reporting. J. Inf. Technol. 31, 241–249 (2016). https://doi.org/10.1057/jit.2015.19

10. Andoh-Baidoo, F.: Context-specific theorizing in ICT4D research. Inf. Technol. Dev. 23, 195–211 (2017). https://doi.org/10.1080/02681102.2017.1356036

11. Bhaskar, R.: A realist theory of science SE - radical thinkers. Verso (1975)

12. Heeks, R., Wall, P.J.: Critical realism and ICT4D research. In: Choudrie, J., Islam, M.S., Wahid, F., Bass, J.M., Priyatma, J.E. (eds.) ICT4D 2017. IAICT, vol. 504, pp. 159–170. Springer, Cham (2017). https://doi.org/10.1007/978-3-319-59111-7_14

13. Ng, E., Tan, B.: Achieving state-of-the-art ICT connectivity in developing countries: the Azerbaijan model of Technology Leapfrogging. Electron. J. Inf. Syst. Dev. Countr. 84, e12027 (2018). https://doi.org/10.1002/isd2.12027

14. Abdullahi, M., et al.: The nature of small and medium scale enterprises (SMEs): government and financial institutions support in Nigeria. Int. J. Acad. Res. Bus. Soc. Sci. 5, 527 (2015)

15. Easterby-Smith, M., Lyles, M.A., Peteraf, M.A.: Dynamic capabilities: current debates and future directions. Br. J. Manag. 20, S1–S8 (2009)

16. Mohamud, M., Sarpong, D.: Dynamic capabilities: towards an organizing framework. (2016). https://doi.org/10.1108/JSMA-11-2015-0088

17. Islam, D.M.D.R., Mazumder, T.: Mobile application and its global impact. Int. J. Eng. Technol. 10, 72–78 (2010)

18. Bula, H.: Evolution and theories of entrepreneurship: a critical review on the Kenyan perspective. Int. J. Bus. Commer. 1, 81–96 (2012)

19. Bălan, C.: The disruptive impact of future advanced ICTs on maritime transport: a systematic review (2018). https://doi.org/10.1108/SCM-03-2018-0133

20. Bezerra, J., et al.: The mobile revolution: how mobile technologies drive a trillion dollar impact. https://eliasgagas.files.wordpress.com/2015/03/the_mobile_revolution_jan_2015_tcm80-180510.pdf. Accessed 18 July 2017

21. Twinomurinzi, H., Schofield, A., Hagen, L., Ditsoane-Molefe, S., Tshidzumba, N.A.: Towards a shared worldview on e-skills: a discourse between government, industry and academia on the ICT skills paradox. South Afr. Comput. J. 29, 215–237 (2017). https://doi.org/10.18489/sacj.v29i3.408

22. Voss, C., Perks, H., Sousa, R., Witell, L., Wünderlich, N.: Reflections on context in service research. J. Serv. Manag. 27, 30–36 (2016). https://doi.org/10.1108/JOSM-04-2015-0115

23. Ayoung, A., Abbott, P., Kashefi, A.: The influence of intangible ('soft') constructs on the outcome of community ICT initiatives in ghana: a gap archetype analysis. Electron. J. Inf. Syst. Dev. Countr. 77, 1–22 (2016). https://doi.org/10.1002/j.1681-4835.2016.tb00562.x

24. Tennant, J.: Why 'context' is important for research. https://blog.scienceopen.com/2016/05/why-context-is-important-for-research/. Accessed 23 Oct 2019
25. Takavarasha Jr., S., Hapanyengwi, G., Kabanda, G.: Using livelihood profiles for assessing context in ICT4D resarch: a case study of zimbabwe's highveld prime communal. Electron. J. Inf. Syst. Dev. Countr. **79**, 1–22 (2017). https://doi.org/10.1002/j.1681-4835.2017.tb00582.x
26. Ongori, H.: Empowering small and medium enterprises (SMEs) with information communication technologies (ICTs): global perspective. EPRA Int. J. Econ. Bus. Rev. **4** (2016)
27. Siqueira, E., Souza, C., Barbosa, A., Senen, D., Meirelles, F.: Using a digital divide index among enterprises in the context of public policies in Brazil. Electron. J. Inf. Syst. Dev. Countr. **85**, e12088 (2019). https://doi.org/10.1002/isd2.12088
28. Dasuki, S., Quaye, A., Abubakar, N.: An evaluation of information systems students internship programs in Nigeria: a capability perspective. Electron. J. Inf. Syst. Dev. Countr. **83**, 1–19 (2017). https://doi.org/10.1002/j.1681-4835.2017.tb00614.x
29. Sein, M., Henfridsson, O., Purao, S., Rossi, M., Lindgren, R.: Action design research. MIS Q. **35**, 37 (2011). https://doi.org/10.2307/23043488
30. Mullarkey, M., Hevner, A.: An elaborated action design research process model (2018). https://doi.org/10.1080/0960085X.2018.1451811
31. McLaren, T., Buijs, P.: A Design science approach for developing information systems research instruments (2011)
32. Hevner, A., March, S., Park, J., Ram, S.: Design science in information systems research. MIS Q.: Manag. Inf. Syst. **28**, 75–105 (2006)
33. Jeppesen, S.: Critical realism as an approach to unfolding empirical findings: thoughts on fieldwork in South Africa on SMEs and environment. J. Transdisc. Environ. Stud. **4**, 9 (2005)
34. Elder-Vass, D.: Re-examining Bhaskar's three ontological domains: the lessons from emergence. In: Lawson, C., Spiro Latsis, J., and Martins, N. (eds.) Contributions to Social Ontology, pp. 160–176. Routledge Taylor & Francis Group (2013). https://doi.org/10.4324/9780203607473
35. Mingers, J.: Realizing information systems: critical realism as an underpinning philosophy for information systems. Inf. Organ. **14**, 87–103 (2004)
36. Tolani, A., Owoseni, A., Twinomurinzi, H.: Exploring the effect of mobile apps on SMEs in Nigeria: a critical realist study. In: Nielsen, P., Kimaro, H.C. (eds.) ICT4D 2019. IAICT, vol. 551, pp. 606–618. Springer, Cham (2019). https://doi.org/10.1007/978-3-030-18400-1_50
37. Owoseni, A., Twinomurinzi, H.: The use of mobile apps to enhance SMEs in conditions of uncertainty: A case study from Lagos, Nigeria. In: Proceedings of the 10th Annual Pre-ICIS SIG GlobDev Workshop, Seoul, South Korea (2017)
38. George, D., Mallery, P.: SPSS for Windows Step by Step : A Simple Guide and Reference 17.0 Update. Allyn & Bacon, Boston (2010)
39. Teece, D., Pisano, G., Shuen, A.: Dynamic capabilities and strategic management. Strateg. Manag. J. **18**, 509–533 (1997)
40. Modell, S., Jacobs, K., Wiesel, F.: A process (re) turn? Path dependencies, institutions and performance management in Swedish central government. Manag. Acc. Res. **18**, 453–475 (2007). https://doi.org/10.1016/j.mar.2006.12.001
41. Soyer, A., Onar, S.Ç., Sanchez, R.: Overcoming path dependency and "lock-in" in competence building and competence leveraging processes. Res. Compet.-Based Manage. **8**, 25–44 (2017). https://doi.org/10.1108/S1744-211720170000008002

42. HBS: WeChat: A winner in China but a loser abroad. https://digital.hbs.edu/platform-digit/submission/wechat-a-winner-in-china-but-a-loser-abroad/. Accessed 23 Oct 2019
43. Baierl, R., Grichnik, D., Herrmann, A.: Overcoming path-dependency with entrepreneurial self-efficacy (2013)
44. Djelic, M.-L., Quack, S.: Overcoming path dependency: path generation in open systems. Theory Soc. **36**, 161–186 (2007). https://doi.org/10.1007/s11186-007-9026-0

Making Cloud Service Selection Easy for SMEs: A Tool for Selecting SaaS Services

Raoul Hentschel[(⊠)], Marco Gercken, and Sebastian Leichsenring

Business Informatics, esp. IS in Trade and Industry, TU Dresden, Dresden, Germany
raoul.hentschel@tu-dresden.de,
{marco.gercken,sebastian.leichsenring}@mailbox.tu-dresden.de

Abstract. The selection and implementation of suitable cloud services that best fit customer requirements can be a complex, time-consuming and cost-intensive process, especially for small and medium-sized enterprises. In this paper, we propose a cloud brokering system that simplifies this process by implementing the (semi-)automated selection and recommendation of cloud services utilizing matchmaking and ranking technologies. The prototype includes the functionality to discover, rank and recommend cloud services from one or more decision components, which will allow consumers faster and easier selection guidance while considering individual sourcing preferences. Furthermore, the system provides interfaces for mutual interaction among other parties (e.g., cloud service providers, cloud integrators, etc.). The tool can be used to support in the selection and adoption phase of implementing cloud services and/or as part of a multicloud strategy.

Keywords: Cloud computing · Cloud brokering · Guidance support system · Multi-sided platform · Matchmaking platform

1 Introduction

Due to the recent proliferation of Cloud Computing (CC), the number of cloud services on the market is increasing rapidly. This makes it difficult to compare cloud services and select the option that best fits the requirements of a given company. Since there is no "one-fits-all" cloud service provider (CSP), companies face the challenge of selecting and combining services from different vendors to meet all their requirements. As a result, the selection process is a complex, time-consuming and cost-intensive ordeal that can prevent the adoption of CC, especially in small and medium-sized enterprises (SME) [1]. The reasons for this are manifold: a lack of universal definitions and standards for cloud services [2], the challenge of comparing the characteristics and performance metrics of cloud services over different maturity levels and quality standards, and different naming conventions for the same services. An understanding of which requires domain-specific knowledge [3]. To face these challenges, companies can engage consultants or brokers to assist them in selecting and implementing cloud services, but SMEs encounter several obstacles in this process. First, the in-house technical expertise is often limited

© Springer Nature Switzerland AG 2020
S. Hofmann et al. (Eds.): DESRIST 2020, LNCS 12388, pp. 333–338, 2020.
https://doi.org/10.1007/978-3-030-64823-7_30

within flatter organizational structures (e.g. a director may also be the owner/manager responsible for the IT investment), and in many cases, those who control the IT-sourcing projects do not have a strong IT background or the skills to assess the potential of CC [4]. Second, the process is performed manually, i.e. without the support of an information system (IS). It is important to note that an IS could be a cloud brokering system designed as a guidance support system [5], that is not only designed for large cloud implementation projects but is also better aligned with the nature of cloud services (e.g. flexible, automated) in terms of type and cost and, more importantly, as designed for SMEs. Since the selection and integration of new services is a very dynamic process, especially in the CC field, such an IS should be better integrated into daily business operations.

So far, multiple approaches have been suggested to support selection decisions for cloud services, but the majority are generic approaches that are not limited to a specific service model (IaaS, PaaS, etc.) [6]. Some effort has been made to generate decision-support for SaaS services [7], but the utility of these approaches is problematic for companies facing a concrete selection challenge. Therefore, we developed a prototype as part of a design science approach proposed by [8] and [9], that enables the (semi-)automated selection of cloud services as part of a recommendation system. The prototype allows consumers to query cloud services using an intuitive user interface that is easily understood even by consumers who have little technical understanding. It enables the user to discover, filter and recommend potential cloud service configurations in an intuitive way without requiring in-depth knowledge of specific cloud services.

The remainder of this paper is structured as follows. Next, we describe the design of the broker web application. Then, the applications' significance to research and practice is outlined. Finally, we present an evaluation of the new cloud broker application.

2   Design of the Artifact

In this section we will detail the design, potential uses, intended user groups and features of our prototype. In order to do so, different user stories were collected before the implementation of the application. User stories [10] were popularized by the agile software method Scrum [11]. In this case, there are four different stakeholders related to this platform: (1) *cloud service consumers* (CSC), (2) *cloud service providers* (CSP), (3) *experts* and (4) the *cloud platform owner* (CPO). The CSC is an enterprise searching for suitable cloud services. This includes information discovery, comparison and recommendation of the available SaaS services that best fulfill the needs of one or multiple use cases. The CSP can add service descriptions for existing cloud services using the backend access or a REST API. Since not every CSC is willing or able to sign a contract with a CSP immediately, the CSC can also evaluate cloud service options proposed by a neutral expert (i.e., consultants, integrators, etc.). Finally, the CPO is responsible for the management of the platform itself and undertakes the tasks of a cloud broker. In order to enable a two-sided perspective on the problem and ensure the practical relevance of the identified gap, we conducted a total of 27 exploratory interviews in previous studies with business experts from cloud service providers [12] and German SMEs that have already implemented cloud solutions [13]. As a whole, the interviews delivered a detailed overview of the problems that companies face when trying to adopt and implement cloud services. Supplemented by an extensive review of the academic literature, we identified design requirements (DR) from different stakeholder groups, representing the problem space, and derived design principles (DP) as solution spaces for the artifact development. Example: Users should be able to get concrete advice on how to use certain cloud services despite the lack of technological competence and/or IT experience often present with SMEs [13]. Therefore, we formulate the following design requirement: *The service discovery process should be supported by the framework to reduce requirements for intensive knowledge and cognitive efforts during service selection.* These DPs were applied in designing the *Virtual Broker as a Service Framework* [14], called *ViBROS* (see Fig. 1) as part of our design-oriented approach. The framework consists of the following main components, which are briefly described.

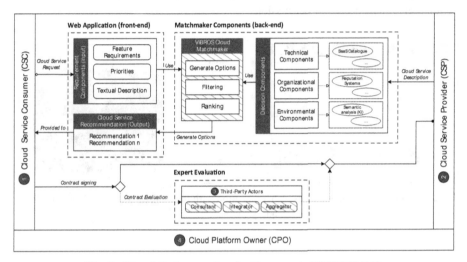

Fig. 1. Virtual Broker as a Service Framework (ViBROS) [14].

(1) *Requirement input component*—The CSC can enter requirements for the cloud service on the front-end using a multi-level input form. Since complex technologies can be hiding within the services, the query is conducted made in the form of questions about the desired use cases in order to simplify handling. Afterwards the requirements can be weighted to identify the CSC's priority requirements.

(2) *Decision components*—The decision components are defined by the CPO and can be dynamically added and/or removed. Each component can be addressed and enriched with information provided by CSPs. In our prototype, we implemented a SaaS catalog with features of cloud storage services (e.g. Encryption, Replication) and used feature service models [15] in order to discover and represent the commonalities of the services. This catalog is also available via API (RESTful Web services) for automated processing.

(3) *Matchmaker component*—Finally, the matchmaking component generates options determined by users' preferences through a pairwise comparison using the AHP [16] method with the previously defined weightings of every available cloud service

option. Then, the options are filtered, and those most suitable for the consumer are recommended. The result is a selection of suitable cloud services ordered and displayed according to the degree of fulfilment (see Fig. 2).

When implementing the prototype as an artifact of the ViBROS framework, we mapped the identified DRs to concrete design features that represent specific artifact capabilities addressing each of the DPs. Therefore, we created a web application[1] in Angular (https://angular.io/) with a state-of-the-art user experience. This application consists of a graphic user interface (GUI) that allows for interaction with and visualization of the platform among the different stakeholders. Furthermore, a multi-role authentication with JSON web tokens was implemented according to common best practices for implementing role-based permissions.

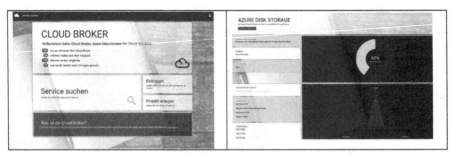

Fig. 2. Screenshots of the ViBROS web application with the landing page for cloud consumers (left) and results of an example service query (right).

3 Significance to Research and Practice

The *ViBROS* web application in this paper makes the following main contributions to research and practice. From the practice perspective, the implemented prototype provides a more reliable and cost-efficient (having no upfront investment costs) option for SMEs to discover and select appropriate cloud services. The application also allows non-technical business users to handle this complex selection process by filtering and ranking possible cloud service configurations. CSCs can use the web application in their daily work situations and benefit from its better aligned selection support for cloud services (e.g. flexible, automated) in terms of type and cost. Beyond the consumers' scope of application, CSPs can use the broker platform to increase visibility on the market and to establish relationships with potential customers. Additionally, vendors can better understand what type of service users are requesting for a particular use case and thus improve their own service profile. For researchers, the *ViBROS* framework and the implemented prototype represents a starting point for developing new broker platforms that simplify the traditional broker approaches by establishing it "as a service". Also, this approach

---

[1] A demo of the web application can be tested at https://vibros.isih.wiwi.tu-dresden.de.

makes it possible to extend the backend components according to individual preferences and thus continually improve the ranking algorithm. The prototypical implementation will be provided to the scientific community as an open source via GitHub[2]. In this way, we provides an opportunity to make artifacts more accessible for practical and scholarly use [17].

4 Evaluation

The evaluation of artifacts in design-oriented research can be performed in several ways [8]. As a first step, the proposed framework *ViBROS* was applied to develop the prototype artifact. Therefore, evaluated design requirements from this framework, which have been identified by a group of experts (cloud service consumers and cloud service providers), were chosen and mapped to concrete design features to build the innovative artifact and thus demonstrate a proof-of-concept [18], i.e. a piece of showing the feasibility of implementing the ideas into software.

As a second step, the Framework for Evaluation of Design Science Research (FEDS) [19] was applied to the created artifact using the 'Quick & Simple' evaluation strategy. Therefore, the properties of the prototype (e.g. usability, time-saving and comprehensibility) were evaluated by a group of four experts from IT service providers who have already assisted companies in cloud-sourcing decisions. The participants had to evaluate the selection process for cloud storage based on given criteria in contrast to a typical (manual) cloud service selection process. All participants expressed positive qualitative feedback and recognized the properties as being useful. One participant also remarked that the application should show more details about the ranking algorithm during the selection process. As a last step, we plan to conduct a focus group with users from SMEs where we will specifically assess the effectiveness of the *ViBROS* prototype. The results of the evaluation from the focus group will be used to further improve the usability and comprehensibility of the platform.

5 Conclusion and Outlook

In this paper, we instantiated a prototypical artifact from our proposed *ViBROS* framework that supports the discovery, selection and recommendation of cloud services with a service broker IS acting as a mediator. The broker web application simplifies the decision-making process for SMEs when selecting cloud services by recommending appropriate services through a matchmaking concept. Currently, our prototype supports only one cloud service category. In our further research, we plan to extend its support for additional cloud service categories such as online collaboration tools or customer relationship management software.

---

[2] Client: https://github.com/SebLeich/broker-client Backend: https://github.com/SebLeich/broker-backend-codefirst.

References

1. Yang, H., Tate, M.: A descriptive literature review and classification of cloud computing research. Commun. Assoc. Inf. Syst. **31**, 35–60 (2012). https://doi.org/10.17705/1CAIS. 03102
2. Höfer, C.N., Karagiannis, G.: Cloud computing services: taxonomy and comparison. J. Internet Serv. Appl. **2**, 81–94 (2011). https://doi.org/10.1007/s13174-011-0027-x
3. Slawik, M., Küpper, A.: A domain specific language and a pertinent business vocabulary for cloud service selection. In: Altmann, J., Vanmechelen, K., Rana, O.F. (eds.) GECON 2014. LNCS, vol. 8914, pp. 172–185. Springer, Cham (2014). https://doi.org/10.1007/978-3-319-14609-6_12
4. Harindranath, G., Dyerson, R., Barnes, D.: ICT adoption and use in UK SMEs: a failure of initiatives? Electron. J. Inf. Syst. Eval. **11**, 91–96 (2008)
5. Morana, S., Schacht, S., Scherp, A., Maedche, A.: A review of the nature and effects of guidance design features. Decis. Support Syst. **97**, 31–42 (2017)
6. Androcec, D., Vrcek, N., Seva, J.: Cloud computing ontologies: a systematic review. In: Proceedings of the Third International Conference on Models and Ontology-based Design of Protocols, Architectures and Services (2012)
7. Godse, M., Mulik, S.: An approach for selecting software-as-a-service (SaaS) product. In: 2009 IEEE International Conference on Cloud Computing, pp. 155–158. IEEE (2009)
8. Peffers, K., Tuunanen, T., Rothenberger, M.A., Chatterjee, S.: A design science research methodology for information systems research. J. Manag. Inf. Syst. **24**, 45–77 (2007)
9. Gregor, S., Jones, D.: The anatomy of a design theory. J. Assoc. Inf. Syst. **8**, 312–335 (2007)
10. Savolainen, J., Kuusela, J., Vilavaara, A.: Transition to agile development - rediscovery of important requirements engineering practices. In: Proceedings of 18th IEEE International Requirements Engineering Conference, pp. 289–294 (2010)
11. Rising, L., Janoff, N.S.: The scrum software development process for small teams. IEEE Softw. **17**, 26–32 (2000). https://doi.org/10.1109/52.854065
12. Hentschel, R., Leyh, C., Petznick, A.: Current cloud challenges in Germany: the perspective of cloud service providers. J. Cloud Comput. **7**(1), 1–12 (2018). https://doi.org/10.1186/s13677-018-0107-6
13. Hentschel, R., Leyh, C., Baumhauer, T.: Critical success factors for the implementation and adoption of cloud services in SMEs. In: Proceedings of the 52nd Hawaii International Conference on System Sciences (2019). https://doi.org/10.24251/hicss.2019.882
14. Hentschel, R., Strahringer, S.: A broker-based framework for the recommendation of cloud services: a research proposal. In: Hattingh, M., Matthee, M., Smuts, H., Pappas, I., Dwivedi, Y.K., Mäntymäki, M. (eds.) I3E 2020. LNCS, vol. 12066, pp. 409–415. Springer, Cham (2020). https://doi.org/10.1007/978-3-030-44999-5_34
15. Wittern, E., Zirpins, C.: On the use of feature models for service design: the case of value representation. In: Cezon, M., Wolfsthal, Y. (eds.) ServiceWave 2010. LNCS, vol. 6569, pp. 110–118. Springer, Heidelberg (2011). https://doi.org/10.1007/978-3-642-22760-8_12
16. Saaty, T.L.: How to make a decision: The analytic hierarchy process. Eur. J. Oper. Res. **48**, 9–26 (1990). https://doi.org/10.1016/0377-2217(90)90057-I
17. Doyle, C., Luczak-Roesch, M., Mittal, A.: We need the open artefact: design science as a pathway to open science in information systems research. In: Tulu, B., Djamasbi, S., Leroy, G. (eds.) DESRIST 2019. LNCS, vol. 11491, pp. 46–60. Springer, Cham (2019). https://doi.org/10.1007/978-3-030-19504-5_4
18. Nunamaker, J.F., Briggs, R.O.: Toward a broader vision for information systems. ACM Trans. Manag. Inf. Syst. **2**, 1–12 (2011). https://doi.org/10.1145/2070710.2070711
19. Venable, J., Pries-Heje, J., Baskerville, R.: FEDS: a framework for evaluation in design science research. Eur. J. Inf. Syst. **25**, 77–89 (2016). https://doi.org/10.1057/ejis.2014.36

Meta-requirements for Immersive Collaborative Spaces in Industrial Workplace Learning: Towards a Design Theory

Amir Haj-Bolouri[✉], Thomas Winman, and Lars Svensson

Department of Informatics, University West, Trollhättan, Sweden
{amir.haj-bolouri,thomas.winman,lars.svensson}@hv.se

Abstract. As the digital transformation of society accelerates, sophisticated Information Technologies (IT) emerge and are introduced into organizations and institutions of society. An example of such technologies is the Virtual Reality (VR) technology that has re-emerged and become a frequently used solution for supporting collaboration and workplace learning in immersive spaces. The deep sense of immersion in VR enables users to learn and develop working skills in an authentic virtual space, which facilitates an increased feeling of user presence and mapping with real world working scenarios. However, due to the emerging nature of using VR for collaboration and workplace learning, there are wide possibilities for Information Systems (IS) scholars to explore the prescriptive knowledge space of how to design and theorize VR technologies through Design Science Research (DSR). In this research in progress paper, we scrutinize the question of how to design immersive collaborative spaces for industrial workplace learning, and subsequently perform a preliminary round of literature review to address the question. Consequently, the findings of the review are reported as three meta-requirements, which we target as the contribution and input for further development of an information systems design theory.

Keywords: Meta-requirements · Virtual reality · Industrial workplace learning · Design science research · Presence

1 Introduction

The digital transformation of society is a multi-faceted phenomenon that provides people, social institutions, and organizations, access to the use of Information Technologies (IT) for success in various areas of everyday life (e.g. education, industry). In the field of Information Systems (IS), major initiatives have been undertaken and reported by IS scholars to study the challenges of digital transformation. The initiatives range from case to case and include a number of societal challenges such as: the effects of micro-work on crowd-workers and digital platform use training [1], infant mortality in rural areas and health information kiosks training [2], or social inclusion of refugees through access to online training via desktop computers and Internet access [3].

© Springer Nature Switzerland AG 2020
S. Hofmann et al. (Eds.): DESRIST 2020, LNCS 12388, pp. 339–346, 2020.
https://doi.org/10.1007/978-3-030-64823-7_31

As a consequence of the accelerated pace of digital transformation in general, the immense progress of immersive technologies has, within the last few years, manifested in the form of the release of high-end consumer-grade Virtual Reality (VR) hardware products such as the Oculus Rift and HTC Vive [4]. Organizations and workplaces in particular, have due to the re-emergence of VR technology use and needs of training organizational staff, been keen to adopt and employ VR for collaboration and workplace learning in the manufacturing industry [5]. In this paper, we address this phenomenon as 'industrial workplace learning' (IWPL), a phenomenon which emphasizes aspects such as: simulation of work processes through VR [6], the design of VR learning spaces for engineering [7], virtual prototyping during product development processes [8], or the design space of VR applications for assistive environments in manufacturing [9].

As the development of VR technologies have now reached a point where both hardware and software is powerful enough to allow sophisticated forms of collaboration and learning to take place in the industry [10, 11], scholars such as Cuendet et al. [12] point out that contemporary design research in AR and VR in general, still struggles to formalize and provide 'prescriptive design knowledge' [13] such as design principles [14] or design theories [15]. As a consequence, the design of VR applications for learning purposes become highly situated and less generalizable [16]. Subsequently, as a response to address this issue and to advance Design Science Research (DSR) in IS [17–19] around the topics of VR, collaboration, and learning in the manufacturing industry, we explore the following research question: *how to design immersive collaborative spaces for industrial workplace learning?*

We are fully aware of the fact that we cannot answer the research question in its entirety through a research in progress work. Instead, in order to address the research question, we will initiate the research process by identifying initial meta-requirements (MR) that we can use towards producing a design theory [15]. More specifically, our work emphasizes two main objectives: [i] reviewing literature on design of VR applications for collaboration and learning that are relevant for IWPL; and [ii] use early learning outcomes from related work and incorporate the knowledge into a set of meta-requirements. Consequently, we will follow Walls et al.'s process model [15, p. 44] for producing design theories, where meta-requirements are an essential component of informing the meta-design and producing a design theory. Additionally, proposing early DSR outputs that serve for further research, are justified as 'nascent' [20] outputs, meaning that the meta-requirements are proposed in a very early stage of our research to guide future DSR cycles.

The rest of the paper will be structured according to the identified meta-requirements: firstly, we propose an overview of the meta-requirements. After that, we go through the reviewed literature and show how and where we identified the proposed meta-requirements. Finally, we conclude the paper and shortly propose further research opportunities

2 Meta-requirements for Designing Immersive Collaborative Spaces for Industrial Workplace Learning

In this section, we identify and propose three meta-requirements for designing immersive collaborative spaces in IWPL. We do so in a narrative way by: (i) presenting and discussing a cross-section of a literature review relevant to VR, collaboration, and learning for IWPL, (ii) using the gathered knowledge from literature to identify and propose three meta-requirements. More specifically we condense our narrative and review as follows.

Firstly, we discuss relevant literature that describes and clarifies the meaning of *presence* in immersive spaces that are dedicated to *collaboration*; here, we demarcate our interest toward the concept of presence in VR because it is considered to be an essential element of an immersive space, which plays a vital role in design of new VR applications in general, and for collaboration and learning in particular [10, 11, 21–23].

Secondly, we discuss literature around the application of VR for IWPL in the manufacturing industry; more specifically, we emphasize helpful literature [5, 9, 24, 25] that report critical outcomes (e.g. challenges, lessons learned) of using VR applications for IWPL.

2.1 Presence in Immersive VR Spaces

VR is a technology that typically provides interaction and immerses the user's senses [26], which sets VR apart from other information technologies (e.g. traditional desktop computers, web applications). Research on VR [21–23] shows that a central phenomenon that is crucial to understand in order to design successful VR applications for collaboration and learning, is the phenomenon of *presence*.

As a concept, 'presence' is related to a wide field of research with a cluster of different applications that have been used in a wide range of literature including: computer-mediated presence [27], ontologies of presence [28], embodied presence in virtual environments [29], presence and cyber-sickness [30], presence and attitude change in VR [31], and more [32–34]. However, 'presence' as discussed in literature related to immersive VR in particular, is characterized by the concept of presence as transportation: people are usually considered 'present' in an immersive space when they report a sensation of being-in-the-virtual-world ('you are there') [30]. Moreover, the terms 'co-presence' and 'social presence' are reserved for the sense of being together in a VR space ('we are

Table 1. Type of presence in VR

Type	Definition
Personal presence	Refers to a measure of the extent to which the person feels like he or she is part of the VR space [32]
Social presence	Refers to the extent to which other beings (living or synthetic) also exist in the VR space [32–34]
Environmental presence	Refers to the extent to which the environment itself acknowledges and reacts to the person in the VR space [35]
Subjective presence	Refers to the likelihood that the person judges himself to be physically present in the remote or virtual space [29, 32]
Objective presence	Refers to the likelihood of successfully completing a task [32]

together'). Table 1 summarizes five essential types of presence that are frequently used in the VR literature [23], together with their definitions.

For the concept of presence to be useful and applicable to practical situations in a VR space, it is important to understand the implications of presence [29]. Here, we have reviewed the implications of presence for collaborative purposes in a VR space and identified four main implications that need to be taken into consideration in order to reinforce presence, and support collaboration successfully in an immersive collaborative VR space. The implications, their feature for supporting collaboration, and example references, are depicted in Table 2.

Table 2. Implications of presence for collaboration in VR

Implication	Feature
Embodiment	Features the mental representation of the immersive VR space in terms of patterns of possible actions, based on experienced presence (e.g. when actions include the perceived possibility to navigate and move the own body) [5, 29, 35]
Task performance	Features how successful a given set of tasks are performed through collaboration between multiple users of an immersive VR space. The degree of presence needs to be flexible for variation depending on the nature of tasks (e.g. easy tasks, abstract tasks) [23]
Social interaction	Features the possible forms of social interaction between multiple users in real time in the immersive VR space. A high degree of realism occurs when users are enabled to exercise their professional roles and behaviors through communicative and collaborative interactions [11]. Exchange of information and input responsiveness (e.g. tactile, audio immersion) are important factors that affect users' sense of presence
Technology awareness	Features Heidegger's [36] notion of technology awareness; when the user of an artifact (e.g. tool) moves his/her awareness from possessing a 'present-at-hand' awareness of his/her interaction with the artifact (e.g. a forced effort or representation), to a 'ready-to-hand' awareness where the user no longer is aware of the artifact itself but only the immediate presence and usefulness the artifact has in whatever task is performed [4, 31]

As a result of reviewing literature about presence, and its implications, for immersive collaborative spaces in VR, we identify and propose two meta-requirements as follows.

MR1: presence in VR is related to transportation and the feeling of being-in-the-virtual-world together with multiple users or alone in an immersive space. The immersive space and its constituting elements (e.g. environment, virtual objects, affordances) greatly influence users' feeling of presence. Hence, in order to mediate collaboration in an immersive VR space, the design needs to incorporate all five types of presence (shown in Table 1).

MR2: implications of incorporating all five types of presence in an immersive VR space, shall enable an embodied awareness of the immersive space, which provide users features for collaboration through social interaction and instant feedback on actions (e.g. task performance, communication) that are undertaken in the immersive space.

2.2 Virtual Reality for Industrial Workplace Learning

A prominent application domain of VR is connected to training of staff members and workplace learning in the manufacturing industry [4, 11], where sophisticated Head-Mounted Devices (HMD) are used by practitioners, such as engineers and operators, to collaborate with each other, execute common or individual goals, and develop new

Table 3. Positive characteristics

Characteristic	Description
Authentic interactivity	Authentic workplace learning experiences (e.g. training, collaboration) are possible to recreate in VR spaces; for example, a trainee mechanic assembling virtual car parts can hear squeaks if a mistake is made or the parts can push back, or even guide the trainee's hand to the correct assembly and offer audio feedback as an explanation [6, 10]
Flexibility	An immersive VR space is flexible, self-paced, and can be easily modified to suit the needs of individual learner situations; for example, an engineer might need VR features that engage his/her attention to assemble parts of a machine [5], whereas an operator needs other features that help him/her with maintenance issues
Wider availability	As VR widens the availability for workplace training in an organization, a great number of learners can take part in one and the same VR space; for example, the Cybersphere application [24] for manufacturing industries
Safe, customizable, low cost environments	VR applications for IWPL provide features for a controlled, simulated environment where the learner can accomplish tasks safely; for example, improved safety awareness within a workforce, multilingual functions, diverse range of training scenarios, safely simulate hazardous situations, and administrative functions for instructors so that they can easily identify problem areas for the learner and adjust the training program accordingly [24, 25]

working skills [9, 24, 25]. The pedagogical relevance of using VR for industrial workplace learning lies essentially in the valuable learning platform that constitutes a number of positive characteristics, shown in Table 3.

Despite all the positive features and characteristics, there are still a number of challenges that designers need to consider when designing VR applications for IWPL [24, 25]. Examples of such challenges vary in their complexity and include a number of different aspects: *assessment validation* (e.g. whether the knowledge gained in a VR space is transferable to comparable situations in other training tasks), *fear of technology* (e.g. fear of making mistakes in VR, fear of confusion or identity loss), *pre-training requirements* (e.g. training strategies that teach learners when to do what), and *trainer readiness* (e.g. technophobic instructors or instructors that are IT-illiterate).

Finally, to our knowledge, we could not find any research in the literature that proposes design principles or design theories for guidance of designing VR applications for IWPL. As a consequence, this gap makes it challenging for designers that want to re-use prescriptive knowledge and solve a class of problems and solutions [17], forcing them to design and implement solutions that are on a specific level of DSR outputs [15].

In light of the identified gap, and the gathered knowledge from this section's review, we identify and propose the third and final meta-requirement (**MR3**), as the domain which integrates **MR1** and **MR2,** as following: the immersive collaborative space needs to provide interactive freedom as the visualization of pedagogical means (e.g. instructor, module) become more detailed depending on the nature of learning purpose (e.g. instructions, training procedure). Moreover, for the immersive space to become sufficiently supportive for IWPL, the representation of tasks, training procedures, instructions, and modules, needs to be flexible for assessment validation and different levels of expertise (e.g. novice user, advanced user).

3   Concluding Remarks

In this research in progress paper, we have explored, identified, and proposed three meta-requirements for designing immersive collaborative spaces in VR for IWPL. The meta-requirements were identified and extracted from relevant literature on VR, collaboration, and learning, with a particular focus on the elements of presence and characteristics of supportive VR for IWPL. The contribution of this work is thus nascent and in progress, representing an initial understanding about how to proceed towards a future design theory for immersive collaborative spaces for IWPL.

References

1. Deng, X., Joshi, K.D., Galliers, R.D.: The quality of empowerment and marginalization in microtask crowdsourcing: giving voice to the less powerful through value sensitive design. MIS Q. **40**(2), 279–302 (2016)
2. Venkatesh, V., Rai, A., Sykes, T.A., Aljafari, R.: Combating infant mortality in rural India: evidence from a field study of eHealth Kiosk implementations. MIS Q. **40**(2), 353–380 (2016)
3. Díaz Andrade, A., Doolin, B.: Information and communication technology and the social inclusion of refugees. MIS Q. **40**(2), 405–416 (2016)

4. Anthes, C., Garcia-Hernandez, R.J., Wiedemann, M., Kranzlmuller, D.: State of the art of virtual reality technology. In: 2016 IEEE Aerospace Conference, pp. 1–19 (2016)
5. Choi, S., Jung, K., Do Noh, S.: Virtual reality applications in manufacturing industries: past research, present findings, and future directions. Concurr. Eng.: Res. Appl. **23**(1), 40–63 (2015)
6. Turner, C.J., Hutabarat, W., Oyekan, J., Tiwari, A.: Discrete event simulation and virtual reality use in industry: new opportunities and future trends. IEEE Trans. Hum.-Mach. Syst. **46**(6), 882–894 (2016)
7. Vergara, D., Rubio, M., Lorenzo, M.: On the design of virtual reality learning environments in engineering. Multimod. Technol. Interact. **1**(2), 11 (2017)
8. Aromaa, S.: Virtual prototyping in design reviews of industrial systems. In: Proceedings of the 21st International Academic Mindtrek Conference, pp. 110–119. ACM, September 2017
9. Büttner, S., et al.: The design space of augmented and virtual reality applications for assistive environments in manufacturing: a visual approach. In: Proceedings of the 10th International Conference on Pervasive Technologies Related to Assistive Environments, pp. 433–440. ACM, June 2017
10. Le, K.D., Fjeld, M., Alavi, A., Kunz, A.: Immersive environment for distributed creative collaboration. In: VRST 2017 (2017)
11. Greenwald, S., et al.: Technology and applications for collaborative learning in virtual reality (2017)
12. Cuendet, S., Bonnard, Q., Do-Lenth, S., Dillenbourg, P.: Designing augmented reality for the classroom. Comput. Educ. **68**, 557–569 (2013)
13. Gregor, S.: The nature of theory in information systems. MIS Q. **30**(3), 611–642 (2006)
14. Chandra, L., Seidel, S., Gregor, S.: Prescriptive knowledge in IS research: conceptualizing design principles in terms of materiality, action, and boundary conditions. In: 2015 48th Hawaii International Conference on System Sciences, pp. 4039–4048. IEEE, January 2015
15. Walls, J.G., Widmeyer, G.R., El Sawy, O.A.: Building an information system design theory for vigilant EIS. Inf. Syst. Res. **3**(1), 36–59 (1992)
16. Dawley, L., Dede, C.: Situated learning in virtual worlds and immersive simulations. In: Spector, J.Michael, Merrill, M.David, Elen, J., Bishop, M.J. (eds.) Handbook of Research on Educational Communications and Technology, pp. 723–734. Springer, New York (2014). https://doi.org/10.1007/978-1-4614-3185-5_58
17. Hevner, A., Chatterjee, S.: Design science research in information systems. In: Design Research in Information Systems, pp. 9–22. Springer, Boston (2010). https://doi.org/10.1007/978-1-4419-5653-8_2
18. Gregor, S., Hevner, A.R.: Positioning and presenting design science research for maximum impact. MIS Q. **37**, 337–355 (2013)
19. Baskerville, R., Baiyere, A., Gregor, S., Hevner, A., Rossi, M.: Design science research contributions: finding a balance between artifact and theory. J. Assoc. Inf. Syst. **19**(5), 358–376 (2018)
20. Heinrich, P., Schwabe, G.: Communicating nascent design theories on innovative information systems through multi-grounded design principles. In: Tremblay, M.C., VanderMeer, D., Rothenberger, M., Gupta, A., Yoon, V. (eds.) DESRIST 2014. LNCS, vol. 8463, pp. 148–163. Springer, Cham (2014). https://doi.org/10.1007/978-3-319-06701-8_10
21. Slater, M., Wilbur, S.: A framework for im- mersive virtual environments (FIVE): speculations on the role of presence in virtual environments. Presence: Teleoper. Virtual Environ. **6**, 603–616 (1997)
22. Sanchez-Vives, M.V., Slater, M.: From presence to consciousness through virtual reality. Nat. Rev. Neurosci. **6**(4), 332 (2005)
23. Schuemie, M.J., Van Der Straaten, P., Krijn, M., Van Der Mast, C.A.: Research on presence in virtual reality: a survey. CyberPsychol. Behav. **4**(2), 183–201 (2001)

24. Fernandes, K.J., Raja, V.H., Eyre, J.: Immersive learning system for manufacturing industries. Comput. Ind. **51**(1), 31–40 (2003)
25. Abidi, M.H., Al-Ahmari, A., Ahmad, A., Ameen, W., Alkhalefah, H.: Assessment of virtual reality-based manufacturing assembly training system. Int. J. Adv. Manuf. Technol. **105**(9), 3743–3759 (2019). https://doi.org/10.1007/s00170-019-03801-3
26. Steuer, J.: Defining virtual reality: dimensions determining telepresence. J. Commun. **42**(4), 72–93 (1992)
27. Lombard, M., Ditton, T.: At the heart of it all: the concept of presence. J. Comput. -Mediated Commun. **3**(2), JCMC321 (1997)
28. Sheridan, T.B.: Descartes, heidegger, gibson, and god: towards an eclectic ontology of presence. Presence **8**, 551–559 (1999)
29. Schubert, T.W., Friedman, F., Regenbrecht, H.T.: Embodied presence in virtual environments. In: Paton, R., Neilson, I. (eds.) Visual Representations and Interpretations, pp. 268–278. Springer-Verlag, London (1999). https://doi.org/10.1007/978-1-4471-0563-3_30
30. Weech, S., Kenny, S., Barnett-Cowan, M.: Presence and cybersickness in virtual reality are negatively related: a review. Front. Psychol. **10**, 158 (2019)
31. Tussyadiah, I.P., Wang, D., Jung, T.H., Tom Dieck, M.C.: Virtual reality, presence, and attitude change: empirical evidence from tourism. Tourism Manage. **66**, 140–154 (2018)
32. Lee, K.M.: Presence, explicated. Communication theory **14**(1), 27–50 (2004)
33. Zahorik, P., Jenison, R.L.: Presence as being- in-the-world. Presence **7**, 78–89 (1998)
34. Sadowski, W., Stanney, K.: Presence in virtual environments (2002)
35. Durlach, N., Slater, M.: Presence in shared virtual environments and virtual togetherness. Presence Teleoper. Virtual Environ. **9**(2), 214–217 (2000)
36. Heidegger, M.: Being and Time. HarperColl, San Francisco (1962). (Macquarie, J., Robinson, E. transl.)

Smart Factory – Requirements for Exchanging Machine Data

Chiara Freichel[(✉)], Anna Fuchs, and Peter Werner

Chair of Business Management and Information Systems, University of Wuerzburg,
Wuerzburg, Germany
{chiara.freichel,a.fuchs}@uni-wuerzburg.de,
peter.werner@stud-mail.uni-wuerzburg.de

Abstract. Trends and future concepts like *Smart Factory* contribute to the competitiveness of manufacturing companies by more flexible, automated and efficient processes. Smart Factories are defined by a complete integration of machines, processes and information flows based on advanced information and communication technology with a database containing information about capacities, delivery times or future demand. Essential for a complete integration is an automated machine data exchange. To achieve this goal and contribute to the competitiveness of producers, we seek to elaborate the technically necessary core components required for a Smart Factory. By using the *Design Science Research* approach, we aim to build a blueprint for implementing an integrated Smart Factory system by defining requirements for machine data exchange. Our results suggest that manufacturing environments must address various requirements, which can be grouped under the categories data acquisition, data storage and data transmission. A successful integration of these components provides the basis for Smart Factory scenarios.

Keywords: Smart factory · Manufacturing · Production machines · Machine data · Integrated data exchange

1 Introduction

In an environment shaped by the digital transformation with increasing customer demands, cost pressure and market dynamics, manufacturers are increasingly faced with trends like *Smart Factory, Internet of Things* (IoT) or *Sharing Economy*. Within challenging targets, the success of manufacturing companies is defined by factors like capacity load, delivery performance and time, flexibility during peaks as well as transparency of order processes while minimizing costs and capital expenditure. In particular, meeting delivery times and deadlines significantly affects overall customer satisfaction. A further challenge is to identify the optimum number of manufacturing machines to meet varying capacity demands, a high number of product variants and quantities.

© Springer Nature Switzerland AG 2020
S. Hofmann et al. (Eds.): DESRIST 2020, LNCS 12388, pp. 347–359, 2020.
https://doi.org/10.1007/978-3-030-64823-7_32

Smart Factory enables companies to optimize their production which contributes to their competitiveness. While manufacturing processes are usually supported and controlled by information and planning systems, most Industry 4.0 scenarios require a complete integration of machines, processes and information flows based on advanced information and communication technology. An integrated database contains information about manufacturing capacities, delivery times, and future demand [4]. Automated machine data exchange is essential for a complete integration ranging from shopfloor/machine level to the management and planning level. This includes the acquisition of relevant data in order to optimize production, e.g. by reducing down-times or achieving a higher degree of automation. Therefore, communication between machines and systems as well as data transfer between machines must be considered.

Against this backdrop, this study seeks to elaborate the technically necessary core components required for a transformation from a conventional to a *Smart Factory*, specifically for the exchange of machine data. Many approaches and sub-concepts of Smart Factory are already implemented in industry. We aim to take a holistic view on the concept and investigate how individual factors known and implemented in the industry should be linked and integrated. Thereby, differences on machine level as well as information system level are investigated, although there are many similarities. Finally, this catalog of requirements can be used to classify and compare different information systems regarding their ability to exchange machine data. Building on this, our research is guided by the following research questions (RQ):

1. How can we design machine data exchange as one dimension of an integrated Smart Factory system?
2. What are the requirements for machine data exchange within a Smart Factory?

To answer these RQ, we structure this study as follows: We present the applied *Design Science Research* (DSR) methodology in the subsequent section. Theoretical foundations on *Smart Factory* and *Machine Data* are summarized in Sect. 3. Afterwards, we identify design possibilities of machine data exchange and define requirements subdivided in different categories. Subsequently, we integrate our findings in Sect. 5. An evaluation is performed in Sect. 6. Ultimately, Sect. 7 concludes this work with a summary, limitations and possible future research.

2   Research Methodology

The structure of this work follows the process and guidelines of DSR. Design Science, as one area of research in the field of business information systems, pursues the goal of creating new and innovative artifacts and thus solving real human and organizational problems [8]. Artifacts are objects created by humans for a practical purpose [26]. We develop an innovative artifact by means of design requirements and principles for an integrated Smart Factory system regarding machine communication. For this reason, the paradigm of DSR is chosen as method and design concept for this paper.

Peffers et al. [19] describe the process of DSR in six steps. The first step is *Problem Identification and Motivation*, which we already discussed. The second step includes the *Objectives of a Solution*, which we define in Sect. 3. We identify design possibilities of machine data exchange and define corresponding requirements as one basis for the design of a Smart Factory for the third step *Development and Design* as core of this paper. We demonstrate the artifact in Sect. 5 by building an integrated machine data exchange concept as one dimension of Smart Factory. To evaluate our artifact, we chose a scenario-based *Evaluation* by analyzing companies fulfillment of requirements and their maturity for Smart Factory as the last step of this paper to verify the applicability and feasibility of our solution. If there is a need for improvements, we return to the step *Design* and repeat the process. If the artifact fulfills the requirements, Peffers et al. [19] propose the *Communication* of the results in scholarly or professional publications, which is the target of this work.

In order to ensure that the artifacts developed are of high value, seven guidelines for the application of the DSR have been established [8]. The conception of artifacts for already solved problems is not part of the DSR, therefore, we particularly consider the guideline of problem relevance [8]. The present work constructs an artifact that addresses problems in the context of Smart Factory. The evaluation of the artifact was an accompanying task during the development. An in-depth analysis of the result is a future task of research.

3   Theoretical Foundations

The ongoing trend of *Smart Factory* describes a multi-faceted and wide-ranging topic, which may be interpreted slightly differently depending on the particular point of view of industrial practitioners as well as of researchers. Therefore, there is no consistent definition [21, 24]. Terms such as *Ubiquitous Factory* [27], *Factory-of-Things* [15] or *Real-time Factory* [31] are used as synonyms for Smart Factory. Summarizing several definitions, a Smart Factory combines two perspectives to provide flexible, accurate and visualized production processes within a dynamic and rapidly changing manufacturing environment. Automation, as first perspective, combines software and hardware to optimize the use of resources. The second facet targets a dynamic organization through easy collaboration between actors within the production network [21]. In essence, a Smart Factory contains a preferably wireless networking of all components of the operative and managerial level in manufacturing. A continuous flow of information in real time conduces the support of all manufacturing processes [24, 28–30]. Developing a Smart Factory requires profound knowledge about machine data, data storage, exchange and integration.

The term *Machine Data* is subordinate to the term operational data. Operational data are primarily those data which arise or are obtained during production, such as lead times, material consumption or output in terms of production quantities [17]. These data are generated directly at the manufacturing machines [16]. Examples for machine data include the quantity of units produced by a particular machine, available capacities, temperature of components or downtimes. Furthermore, manufacturing factories generate so-called process data as well as quality data, which highlight the ability to be directly assigned to a process and by serving quality assurance [11,17]. In this study, we define machine data as a subset of the operational data which logically correspond to process data. All data generated at machines during the manufacturing process are to be considered.

4 Requirements for Exchanging Machine Data

To develop our artifact, we describe design possibilities of machine data exchange for implementing a Smart Factory and define resulting requirements. As core of this paper, this section answers RQ1 and RQ2. Our findings are divided in the sections *Machine Data Acquisition, Machine Data Storage and Management* and *Machine Data Transmission* as relevant elements of machine data exchange. When analyzing data acquisition, we focus on the operational data, instead of data concerning the business and management level.

4.1 Machine Data Acquisition

In order to exchange machine data and develop a Smart Factory, it is essential to ensure and automate data collection. Sensors are of central importance for the automated acquisition of machine data [11]. They can measure various variables, e.g. physical or chemical properties, and convert them into an electronic signal. Afterwards, they are transferred into a digital signal using appropriate software. The digital signal can be converted into a standardized format and used for further applications. Smart sensors are able to perform the measurement and conversion in the sensor itself. Examples of characteristics are shapes, surfaces, fabrics, or positions of objects [7]. In addition, information about the status and condition of the machine as well as environmental effects are relevant [11]. The machines, as first instance in the process, generate data, which are possibly used in many more instances. Therefore, a plausibility check and the assurance of data correctness are important during data acquisition [17]. Following these descriptions, we can define the first requirement.

Requirement 1. *For autonomous data acquisition, sensors are essential to provide comprehensive information on the characteristics, features and status of the machine and products to be manufactured.*

4.2 Machine Data Storage and Management

If data cannot be transferred directly, a possibility for storage is necessary. Cloud systems, which can be accessed from anywhere, serve as a solution for a modern data basis. Data storage can be achieved directly at *machine level* or by using *separate information systems.* Additionally, information systems serve to analyze and manage the data.

First, we analyze how the data is determined and stored directly at *machine level* when, at this level, there is no direct interaction with a separate system. A central role for developing Smart Factory concepts are Cyber-Physical Systems (CPS). They are characterized by the combination of physical and computer-aided capabilities [2]. While the physical capability is represented by the ability to connect to the physical world for data acquisition, e.g. by using sensors, the internal data management represents the contact point to the computer-based level [14]. CPS are based on micro-computers, the so-called embedded systems, which operate independently, provide high performance and finally turn into CPS by additional interconnection [10]. By extending the sensor technology, machine data can be acquired directly from the machines control system [11]. One example is the Programmable Logic Controller (PLC). A PLC consists of an own processor, a short-term main memory, a long-term data memory, input and output channels for interaction with actuators and sensors as well as the software programmed for the specific system. Thereby, it maintains relevant data in the own memory, which can be transferred from there. Another type of machine control, especially in the environment of Manufacturing Execution Systems (MES) or Enterprise Resource Planning (ERP) systems, is Computerized Numerical Control or Direct Numerical Control (CNC/DNC). Although CNC/DNC is a more complex control system with higher precision, it is more flexible and adaptable. It is usually equipped with a user interface and doesn't need a complete change and re-installation of the software [5]. Accordingly, there is an option to store it in the object's internal memory. In addition, the objects can also be equipped with other external storage media, for example Radio-Frequency Identification (RFID) chips.

In a next step, planning and control of *information systems*, which are relevant for production will be considered. The manufacturing process is influenced by many factors, such as batch size, sequence of production orders or lead times. These business-related data are maintained, analyzed and managed in information systems. In the past, manufacturing processes were usually supported by separate Production Planning and Control Systems (PPS). Today, production is supported by MES or ERP systems [30]. ERP systems integrate all data and information of a company for supporting and automating everyday business processes. One interface between machines and information systems are MES [11]. Vertical integration describes the complete connection of ERP systems with an underlying MES to machines [11]. A central database ensures data storage for the information systems. Figure 1 summarizes the described relationship between different systems and levels.

The trend-driven term *Digital Twin* summarizes the outlined requirements for a Smart Factory. A Digital Twin is a virtual image of physical, intangible objects and processes [18]. In this way, machines, products and corresponding processes can be virtually reproduced. By using sensors, it is possible to provide the Digital Twin with the same data as the actual twin in real-time. The concept of real-time data is particularly suitable for predicting the life cycle of objects as well as improving the planning and control of production [18]. The Digital Twin enriches the sensor data with object-specific information, such as existing service contracts, performance data or technical design data. Accordingly, the entire Digital Twins in one system provide a central overview of all relevant manufacturing information in real-time, which is why we defined this as part of our second requirement.

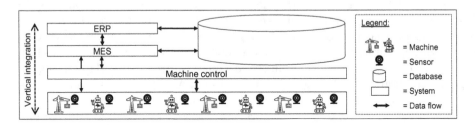

Fig. 1. Conceptual integration of data storage systems (based on [11, 16])

Requirement 2. *Data stored in machines' internal memories and data recorded by information systems should be integrated in a dynamic, scalable and cloud-based database to enable a Digital Twin.*

4.3   Machine Data Transmission

The success of Smart Factory as one Industry 4.0 scenario depends on an integrated IT infrastructure as well as standardized interfaces. Once the data has been successfully captured and stored, it is necessary to be able to transmit and share the information between different systems. In this context, interfaces represent the standardized data transport method and data structure [11]. Hence, established *eBusiness standards* (short: *standards*) and the future *IT architecture* are examined in the following.

eBusiness standards define detailed guidelines for data exchange between systems. Uniform and precise formats are needed to be interpreted by machines and systems, as machines are not able to supplement missing information [23]. Therefore, standards should be used for internal data processing between machines and systems, but also for communication between several companies. We can classify standards into categories. Technical standards, such as Extensible Markup Language (XML) or Electronic Data Interchange, form the basis for more advanced technical standards by defining the structure of data records to be transmitted clearly [23]. These standards can be further divided into identification, classification, catalog exchange, transaction and process standards. Catalog exchange and transaction standards are suitable for supporting cross-company communication. Process standards are appropriate for the technical modeling of individual company processes in a machine-readable format by using software tools. Identification standards are initially used for the cross-company unique recognition of business objects. Classification standards are useful for classifying products on the basis of the available product information [23]. Besides technical standards, functional standards define the common language between individual systems. It also opens up cross-factory or cross-company cooperation potential.

Of great importance for Industry 4.0 and Smart Factory is the Open Platform Communications Unified Architecture (OPC UA) as it improves the usability in industrial environments [11]. OPC UA is a standardized, technical interface for platform-neutral data transmission, which is being developed by the OPC Foundation [3]. Some authors [10] explicitly refer to OPC UA in the implementation recommendations for Industry 4.0, as it is able to not only transfer data, but also display the data in a machine-readable form. For this purpose, all information is represented in the OPC UA Nodes, which are divided into eight predefined classes. In this way, a common semantic vocabulary of the language is defined. While data exchange is based on standard protocols such as Transmission Control Protocol (TCP) or Hypertext Transfer Protocol Secure (HTTPS), XML or JavaScript Object Notation (JSON) can be used for representation [3].

Standards can be integrated into the overall framework of Industry 4.0 by using the Reference Architecture Model Industry 4.0 (RAMI4.0), which supports companies during the step by step transformation from a traditional factory system into a Smart Factory system. The three-dimensional model includes the integration of layers, value streams and hierarchy levels. The vertical layer represents the different perspectives within the company. The entire life cycle of objects is covered in the horizontal layer and the third dimension visualizes functional levels. As a result, the model pursues two different goals. On the one hand, missing standard solutions are identified and, on the other hand, equivalent standards are unified in order to reduce the total number of standards [1]. Following these design options, we can define requirements 3 and 4.

Requirement 3. *When using different information systems in manufacturing, technical standards need to define uniform data structures to ensure standard transmission channels.*

Requirement 4. *Functional standards should be used to define a common language between individual systems and to classify the information to be processed, especially when connecting different factories.*

A further element of machine data transmission is the companies' *IT architecture*. The basis for data transmission is provided by common bus systems. These are characterized by a uniform transmission path for several participants which are identified by the Media Access Control (MAC) [9]. Examples for popular bus systems are Ethernet, Controller Area Network (CAN) or the Universal Series Bus (USB) [9]. In some cases, the digitally stored signal must be converted into a physical signal for transmission [9]. The different bus systems are appropriate for various hierarchical levels of the IT architecture. Ethernet, for example, is not designed for real-time or small data volumes and therefore not suitable for sensors [7]. CAN, on the other hand, are optimized for small data packets for sensor information [7]. An established concept for IT architectures is the Service-Oriented Architecture (SOA). It consists of modular, task-specific systems. Based on their data and program logic, they are able to share information with other systems through standardized interfaces [16]. Web services are one option for implementing this loose connection. By using standards, they provide program functionalities online [16]. The basis for future architectures is the packaging of the individual services into one object. In this way, each micro-system preserves its own information and is able to exchange data directly with other objects or systems if required. The levels of automation become unclear or suspended. This results in flat, very flexible architectures. These are supplemented by clouds, which in turn can be used as a basis for cross-company collaborations. To become more scalable, e.g. control functionalities can be offered in the cloud [22]. In this context, the Representational State Transfer (REST) describes an architectural style for using existing web technologies for shared systems [6]. On the basis of design potentials available for IT architecture, the following two additional requirements could be identified.

Requirement 5. *A wireless or cable-connected network (e.g. bus systems) must be set up in order to transmit data, should be selected considering stability as well as speed and should accomplish the task of connecting all machines and information systems used.*

Requirement 6. *To facilitate direct data exchange between machines, network capability, a dedicated storage solution and appropriate sensor technology should be integrated, e.g. within a CPS.*

Table 1 summarizes all requirements as a basis for Smart Factories.

Table 1. Summary of requirements

No	Name	Definition
Req. 1	Sensors	For autonomous data acquisition, sensors are essential to provide comprehensive information on the characteristics, features and status of the machine and products to be manufactured
Req. 2	Data storage	Data stored in machines' internal memories and data recorded by information systems should be integrated in a dynamic, scalable and cloud-based database to enable a Digital Twin
Req. 3	Technical standards	When using different information systems in manufacturing, technical standards need to define uniform data structures to ensure standard transmission channels

(*continued*)

Table 1. (*continued*)

No	Name	Definition
Req. 4	Functional standards	Functional standards should be used to define a common language between individual systems and to classify the information to be processed, especially when connecting different factories
Req. 5	Technical connection	A wireless or cable-connected network (e.g. bus systems) must be set up in order to transmit data, should be selected considering stability as well as speed and should accomplish the task of connecting all machines and information systems used
Req. 6	Integration	To facilitate direct data exchange between machines, network capability, a dedicated storage solution and appropriate sensor technology should be integrated, e.g. within a CPS

5 Demonstration

According to Peffers et al. [19], the methodological approach of a DSR process requires the demonstration of the problem to be solved. This could involve the use of experiments, simulations, case studies or other activities. Furthermore, it is important to describe how to solve the identified problem through the development of an artifact. For the present study we demonstrate the artifact by building and demonstrating an integrated machine data exchange concept model as one dimension of Smart Factory. Figure 2 demonstrates the interaction and integration of the identified requirements within one scenario.

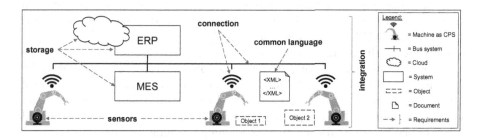

Fig. 2. Requirements for exchanging machine data

The figure illustrates three machines as CPS which are connected to the MES and ERP system via a stable bus system, which complies with requirement 5. All data acquired are stored in the cloud as dynamic database according to requirement 2. Object 2 in Fig. 2, which is described by a functional business standard conforming requirement 4, is being processed. The sensor of the CPS in the right side of Fig. 2 retrieves e.g. the status that the manufacturing process is completed as well as the status, that the machine is requesting maintenance. Therefore, the system conducted data acquisition by different sensors which meets requirement 1. These information are stored on machine level by using the short-term main memory of the PLC as one dimension of requirement 2. The CPS transmits this information to another CPS in the middle of Fig. 2. At this instance, XML was defined as the common technical standard language according to requirement 3. This document is also transferred to the MES and ERP system, which in turn initiates a further process of the third CPS. In this case, the first two CPS communicate directly with each other, whereas the third CPS received information via the MES. The last and most decisive step is the integration of all the individual components defined in requirement 6 to set a basis for an efficient Smart Factory environment.

6   Evaluation

As the evaluation is very important in the DSR process, we decided to conduct a scenario-based evaluation based on the developed requirements. By considering the current state of art in companies' factories, we show practical relevance for exchanging machine data as a basis for Smart Factory.

Studies demonstrate that over 90% of industries support their business processes with IT systems and almost 80% use a standard ERP solution [13]. This can be regarded as a basic condition for being able to store and use the acquired data. Although particularly small and medium-sized enterprises often do not possess the prerequisites or resources for such systems, we define IT architecture as a key requirement in our conceptual scenario. In addition, we identified, that standards are relevant for an efficient communication between the systems and machines, but 71% of ERP companies do not know RAMI4.0 [12]. In contrast, it appears that companies have an interest in a common uniform standard, even though standards are not mandatory. There is still a need for commitment to one standard like OPC UA, especially for a seamless communications between ERP systems and machines [12]. Standards like *eCl@ss Advanced* represent a starting point for integration [20]. Companies are also pursuing platform approaches by bundling all IoT activities, enabling them to be introduced quickly. Even though the cost of sensors has been the bottleneck for their usage in the past, they are now be used as the starting point for a wide range of data acquisition. Based on the actual situation in companies concerning machine data exchange, we can define requirements 1 (sensors), 2 (data storage) and 5 (technical connection) as basic, requirements 3 (technical standards) and 4 (functional standards) as advanced and requirement 6 (integration) as expert. Out of this categorization, we can define the state of progress towards machine data exchange as basis for a Smart Factory. If the companies' factory doesn't fulfil one of the basic requirements, implementing a Smart Factory is currently not possible. When meeting basic requirements as well as advanced requirements, we define the companies' factory as future-oriented. If all requirements are achieved, the machine data exchange complies with the requirements of a Smart Factory, which can now be further extended with additional smart functions.

7 Conclusion

Smart Factory can significantly contribute to the competitiveness of manufacturers within supply networks. Due to the increasing amount of data in combination with new information technologies such as Cloud Computing, Blockchain and Artificial Intelligence (AI), the implementation of a Smart Factory is possible today. Nevertheless, it is not implemented overall by most factories due to key problems during the integration process [25]. Attaching sensors to machines and products is not seen as a challenge today, because these objects are able to record, collect and even store all data. Through standards, intelligent machines and systems can communicate with each other and exchange data in a structured way. Based on the large amount of data, analyses can be performed to optimize system and production performance or predictive maintenance.

This work set out to build an artifact in the form of a conceptual foundation for Smart Factory as one Industry 4.0 scenario. Therefore, we sought to develop, demonstrate and evaluate a catalog of requirements for machine data exchange. The catalog should help companies to implement sustainable integrated production environments and new business models. By addressing a white spot in the current IS research, we represent a suitable starting point for future research endeavors that aim to examine requirements for other elements of Smart Factory, such as IoT, AI or Blockchain.

This research is not without limitations. It is exploratory by nature and builds upon perceptions and conclusions of the researchers. Other researchers may have derived different implications and requirements. In the future, we will continue to evaluate our theoretical requirements by practical research in different ERP systems and focus on the key enabling technologies for a Smart Factory for Industry 4.0. Therefore, a larger evaluation study with qualitative interviews could be performed to extend this initial conceptualization.

Acknowledgements. This study is based upon work funded by the German Federal Ministry of Education and Research (BMBF) within the program "Innovations for Tomorrow's Production, Services, and Work" (funding number 02K16C100) and implemented by the Project Management Agency Karlsruhe (PTKA).

References

1. Adolphs, P., et al.: Statusreport. Referenzarchitekturmodell Industrie 4.0 (RAMI4.0). VDI, Düsseldorf (2015)
2. Baheti, R., Gill, H.: Cyber-physical systems. Impact Control Technol. **12**(1), 161–166 (2011)
3. Cavalieri, S., Salafia, M., Scroppo, M.: Integrating OPC UA with web technologies to enhance interoperability. Comput. Stand. Interfaces **61**, 45–64 (2019)

4. Chen, J.H.: Simultaneous optimization of production planning and inspection planning for flexible manufacturing systems. In: Proceedings of the 9th Annual Conference on Genetic and Evolutionary Computation, pp. 1928–1935. ACM Press (2007)
5. Gill, S.: Role of CNCs and PLCs in the factory of the future. Control Eng. **65**(1), 27–28 (2018)
6. Grüner, S., Pfrommer, J., Palm, F.: RESTful industrial communication with OPC UA. IEEE Trans. Ind. Inform. **12**(5), 1832–1841 (2016)
7. Hesse, S.; Schnell, G.: Sensoren für die Prozess- und Fabrikautomation. Funktion – Ausführung – Anwendung, 7th edn. Springer Vieweg, Wiesbaden (2018)
8. Hevner, A.R., March, S.T., Park, J., Ram, S.: Design science in information systems research. MIS Q. **28**(1), 75–105 (2004)
9. Hüning, F.: Embedded Systems für IoT. Springer, Wiesbaden (2019). https://doi.org/10.1007/978-3-662-57901-5
10. Kagermann, H., Wahlster, W., Helbig, J.: Recommendations for implementing the strategic initiative INDUSTRIE 4.0. Acatech, Frankfurt (2013)
11. Kletti, J.: MES – Manufacturing Execution System. Moderne Informationstechnologie unterstützt die Wertschöpfung, 2nd edn. Springer Vieweg, Wiesbaden (2015). https://doi.org/10.1007/978-3-662-46902-6
12. Klink, P., Mertens, C., Kompalka, K.: Auswirkungen von Industrie 4.0 auf die Anforderungen an ERP-Systeme. Fraunhofer IML, Dortmund (2017)
13. Konradin Business GmbH: ERP-Studie 2011. Einsatz von ERP-Lösungen in der Industrie. Konradin Mediengruppe, Leinfelden-Echterdingen (2011)
14. Lee, J., Bagheri, B., Kao, H.: A cyber-physical systems architecture for industry 4.0-based manufacturing system. Manuf. Lett. **3**, 18–23 (2015)
15. Lucke, D., Constantinescu, C., Westkämper, E.: Smart factory - a step towards the next generation of manufacturing. In: Manufacturing Systems and Technologies for the New Frontier, pp. 115–118. Springer (2008). https://doi.org/10.1007/978-1-84800-267-8_23
16. Mertens, P.: Integrierte Informationsverarbeitung 1, Operative Systeme in der Industrie, 18th edn. Springer Gabler, Wiesbaden (2013)
17. Mertens, P., Bodendorf, F., König, W., Picot, A., Schumann, M., Hess, T.: Grundzüge der Wirtschaftsinformatik, 11th edn. Springer, Berlin (2012)
18. Negri, E., Fumagalli, L., Macchi, M.: A review of the roles of digital twin in CPS-based production systems. Proc. Manuf. **11**, 939–948 (2017)
19. Peffers, K., Tuunanen, T., Rothenberger, M.A., Chatterjee, S.: A design science research methodology for information systems research. J. Manage. Inf. Syst. **24**(3), 45–77 (2007)
20. Pethig, F., Schriegel, S. et al.: Industrie 4.0 Communication Guideline. VDMA, Frankfurt (2017)
21. Radziwon, A., Bilberg, A., Bogers, M., Madsen, E.S.: The smart factory: exploring adaptive and flexible manufacturing solutions. Proc. Eng. **69**, 1184–1190 (2014)
22. Sang, Z., Xu, X.: The framework of a cloud-based CNC system. Proc. CIRP **63**, 82–88 (2017)
23. Schleife, K., Flug, M., Stiehler, A., Dufft, N., Quantz, J.: E-Business-Standards in Deutschland. Bestandsaufnahme, Probleme, Perspektiven (2010)
24. Strozzi, F., Colicchia, C., Creazza, A., Noè, C.: Literature review on the 'Smart Factory' concept using bibliometric tools. Int. J. Prod. Res. **55**(22), 6572–6591 (2017)
25. Wang, S., Wan, J., Li, D., Zhang, C.: Implementing smart factory of industrie 4.0: an outlook. Int. J. Distrib. Sensor Netw. **12**(1), 3159805 (2016)

26. Wieringa, R.: Design Science Methodology for Information Systems and Software Engineering. Springer, Berlin (2014). https://doi.org/10.1007/978-3-662-43839-8
27. Yoon, J.S., Shin, S.J., Suh, S.: A conceptual framework for the ubiquitous factory. Int. J. Prod. Res. **50**(8), 2174–2189 (2012)
28. Zhang, Y., Zhang, G., Du, W., Wang, J., Ali, E., Sun, S.: An optimization method for shopfloor material handling based on real-time and multi-source manufacturing data. Int. J. Prod. Res. **165**, 282–292 (2015)
29. Zhang, Y., Zhang, G., Wang, J., Sun, S., Si, S., Yang, T.: Real-time information capturing and integration framework of the internet of manufacturing things. Int. J. Comput. Integr. Manuf. **28**(8), 811–822 (2014)
30. Zhong, R.Y., Dai, Q.Y., Qu, T., Hu, G.J., Huang, G.Q.: RFID-enabled real-time manufacturing execution system for mass-customization production. Robot. Comput.-Integr. Manuf. **29**(2), 283–292 (2013)
31. Zuehlke, D.: Smart factory - towards a factory-of-things. Ann. Rev. Control **34**(1), 129–138 (2010)

The Design Towards a Collaborative Subscription Service: The Case of the Finnish Newspaper Industry

Erol Kazan[1](✉) and Tuure Tuunanen[2](✉)

[1] Business IT, IT University of Copenhagen, Copenhagen, Denmark
erka@itu.dk
[2] Faculty of Information Technology, University of Jyväskylä, Jyväskylä, Finland
tuure@tuunanen.fi

Abstract. The newspaper industry is challenged with its business models. To stabilize revenues, publishers opted for digital subscriptions for generating additional revenue streams. However, digital subscriptions showcase limited success. News aggregator platforms may promise publishers a pool of paying readers. But platform fees and the loss of customer relationships enact barriers among publishers to join. This study proposes a software prototype based on design science research to address the aforementioned shortcomings by deriving design principles for a collaborative subscription service. Building on the strategic alliance, digital platform and business model literature, this research aims to identify design principles that create conducive conditions towards a collaborative subscription service among newspaper publishers.

Keywords: Digital platform · Business model · Collaboration · Prototype · Design science · Newspaper industry

1 Introduction

Newspapers are important institutional artifacts in societies as they inform and create public discourse to hold stakeholders accountable. To fulfill their tasks in the digital age, publishers expanded their distribution channels to the digital realm to serve current and future readers. In so doing, many publishers, however, are challenged to identify sustainable business models. The traditional print business continues to be a reliable revenue generator, though, many publishers exhibit early signs of decline in their growth trajectory. Thanks to the availability of ubiquitous mobile computing, online channels gained importance in monetizing news content due to revenues from online advertisements. The importance was also reflected by the publisher's investments into digital business units to leverage on these growth opportunities.

That being said, revenues from online channels have become unpredictable in the last years. With the rise of ad blockers and competition with global platforms (e.g., Facebook, Google), newspaper publishers started to compete for the same online advertisement

© Springer Nature Switzerland AG 2020
S. Hofmann et al. (Eds.): DESRIST 2020, LNCS 12388, pp. 360–366, 2020.
https://doi.org/10.1007/978-3-030-64823-7_33

spendings. To become more independent from online advertisement, publishers chose to adopt the traditional print business model in the form of digital subscriptions. Although digital subscriptions present a promising avenue for stable revenues, and resourceful publishers with broad global coverage have indeed benefited from it, smaller publishers continue to be challenged in increasing their subscriber base. To illustrate, publishers have difficulties in convincing readers to pay for digital subscriptions in the first place, as users have a limited budget for media, while similar content is freely available. Secondly, even if readers start to pay for digital subscriptions, the churn rate, which is the rate of cancelation, is considerably high. Based on these observations, existing digital newspaper subscription services portray a value mismatch between readers and publishers. Thus, presenting an avenue for improvement.

Global platform organizations (e.g., Apple) recognized the dilemma in the newspaper industry and started to offer news aggregator platforms (Apple News+), which pool content by different publishers into one service. Most publishers, however, are skeptical of this kind of services due to fears of being a commoditized and losing control over content distribution and monetization. If we consider the prevailing trend of aggregated services in different media industries, such as music (e.g., Spotify), books (e.g., Amazon Kindle) movies (e.g., Netflix), and now recently newspapers (e.g., Apple+), the question arises how to design a newspaper subscription service that addresses the concerns among publishers that reflects the needs to join a news aggregator service. This line of thinking is relevant to explore to identify sustainable subscription business models. Accordingly, this research in progress is proposing a solution (i.e., software prototype) that explores to identify business and technology aspects that facilitates positive conditions for creating a collaborative newspaper subscription service opposed to monopolistic ones (e.g., Apple News +). As such, we propose the following research question: *What are the design principles of a collaborative subscription service for the online newspaper industry?*

To answer the research question, we developed a software prototype based on the strategic alliance, digital platform, business model theories, and aiming to conduct a design science study to derive design principles that exhibit positive conditions for establishing collaborative subscription services [1–3]. These interrelated research streams are considered to be suitable to identify positive conditions for collaboration from a strategic, technical and commercial viewpoint, as well as develop test scenarios to evaluate the effectiveness of different design principles. This study contributes to the aforementioned research streams, as well as presenting a response to a call for more design science studies related to digital platforms [4]. From a practitioner viewpoint, this study could have major implications for a Nordic newspaper industry in providing insights and a strategic template for the creation of a collaborative subscription service.

2   Theoretical Background

Strategic Alliance. Organizations often team up to pool their complementary resources to achieve synergy effects such as co-creating competitive products and services. These types of organizational arrangements are synonymous with joint ventures, strategic partnerships, strategic alliances or coopetitions [1, 5], when rival organizations combine their resources to achieve shared economic benefits (e.g., efficiency) or strategic goals (e.g., market entry). Strategic alliances are difficult to create as they are subject to complex managerial processes that require compromises. This is especially a challenging endeavor for once vertically integrated organizations like newspaper publishers, which are used to control the entire value creation and capture process [5]. Likewise, the ability to join an alliance is subject to extensive scrutiny among existing alliance members, as certain resources offered by the alliance seeker could be perceived to be tradeable, potentially undermining the negotiation position [1, 5]. If we consider competitiveness in digital industries (e.g., social media, streaming services), organizations are considered to be competitive, if they possess high market reach and are able to create network effects in the form of user growth or exclusive partnerships to co-create services (e.g., attractive selection of media content) [6]. Similarly, if digital organizations lack valuable industry-specific resources (e.g., market reach, content), literature suggests the formation of digital alliances to compensate shortcomings [1]. As more digital industries embrace the logic of platform markets, strategic alliances can be considered as inter-organizational digital platforms.

Inter-organizational Digital Platforms. Digital platforms are business network promoting technology architectures [3], which orchestrate services and technology components to co-create modularized services with platform stakeholders. A common theme across platform studies is the governance and control of such platforms [7]. Like in strategic alliances, owners of digital platforms face challenges to balance the needs of different stakeholders to ensure platform attractiveness and competitiveness, while avoiding fragmentation which may cause deteriorating consequences for the entire platform [8]. Considering strategic alliances through the platform lens, inter-organizational digital platforms conduct their platform operations in a collaborative fashion to achieve conjoint benefits such as network effects (e.g., user growth). At the same time, members of collaborative digital platform face challenges. Similar to the notion of *too many chefs in the kitchen*, a shared digital platform comes along with reduced control or increased coordination costs, potentially causing drawbacks like slowing down the performance individual members and hence, the overall performance of a collaborative digital platform. As such, joining an inter-organizational digital platform requires the consideration of risks and opportunities. One way to weigh risks and opportunities for a business endeavor is through the lens of business models.

Digital Business Models. In general, digital business models can be understood through four conceptual elements: 1) value proposition (e.g., service offer), (2) value capture (e.g., pricing), (3) value architecture (e.g., platform), and lastly (4) value network (e.g., strategic alliance) [2].

Successful digital business models require the alignment of value propositions, value capture, value architecture and value network to be effective in the end. Therefore, we deem strategic alliances, digital platforms and digital business models as suitable theoretical foundations, and analytical lenses (see Fig. 1) to enquire and derive design principles for a collaborative subscription service in the newspaper industry. If we contextualize the presented literature with the logic of an online newspaper subscription services (see Table 1), the digital business model concept serves as our guiding design lens to identify avenues for innovations, determining evaluation criteria, and hence, deriving design principles for newspaper subscriptions business models.

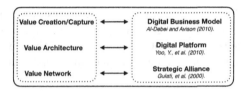

Fig. 1. Design analytical lens

Table 1. Business model dimensions of a digital subscription service

Dimension	Newspaper subscription	Value principles
Value creation	Online news articles	Valued content
Value capture	Payment plan	Attractive pricing
Value architecture	Digital platform	An effective platform architecture for delivering valued content
Value network	Publishers	A select network of strategic alliance members

3 Methodology

Our research design needs to reflect close involvement with the practice and delivery of a particular solution. Hence, we follow a design science research methodology (DSRM) that is well developed and has a decades-old tradition in Information Systems research (see Fig. 2). DSRM [9] builds on these DSR process models and suggests a way to conduct design science research in information systems. It is comprised of six phases: (1) identify the problem and motivation; (2) define the objectives; (3) design; (4) demonstrate; (5) evaluate; and (6) communicate [9].

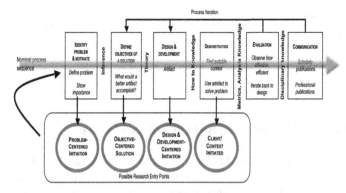

Fig. 2. *DSR Methodology*

The DSRM starts with the identification of the research problem(s) and the motivation for the research. Based on the evidence, reasoning, and inference, the process continues towards defining the objectives of a solution to solve the research problem. This process should be based upon prior knowledge or literature in the given field of research. In so doing, we utilize developed artifact (software prototype) and business model dimensions to identify areas for improvement to develop quantitative and qualitative test scenarios (see Fig. 3).

Quantitative Study: Circa 200–250 Finnish users will be invited to test the software prototype with content provided by newspaper publishers, which will assist us to collect empirical data on their 1) news consumption behavior and 2) selection of payment plans. Before testing, we will conduct a pre-study survey to investigate participants' current news media consumption patterns and their volume. In the end, the quantitative study will allow us to test different user scenarios and measure the performance of different payment plans that informs us of the second study.

Qualitative Study: The insights gathered from the quantitative study will be utilized to prompt newspaper stakeholders during a workshop. During the workshop, representatives from leading Nordic newspaper publishers (e.g., chief digital officers, business development mangers) and members from the media industry will be confronted with results from the first study and to initiate and facilitate interactive discussions. The discussions will be structured and moderated towards identifying positive conditions related to value architectures (e.g., the technical feasibility and governance of a shared architecture). Lastly, the workshop aims to identify positive conditions towards value network creation in the pre-stage (i.e., founding members) and during operation (i.e., new members).

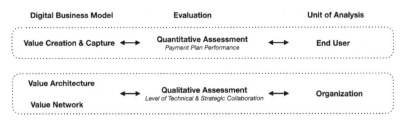

Fig. 3. Evaluation criteria

4   Prototype: Collaborative Subscription Service

Front-End Prototype (End User Facing). The first prototype is a web-based interface through which users register and access a pool of online articles based on different topics, popularity or newness. To begin with, users select a suitable payment plan to their liking or budget to access content until the end of their subscription period. Alternatively, the service supports micropayments and packages for accessing paywalled online content without a monthly digital subscription. Overall, the end-user facing prototype allows us test different payment plans to evaluate their performance (see Fig. 4).

Fig. 4. Software prototype

Back-End Prototype (Publisher Facing). The second prototype presents a database to track and record user purchases, spending and access to different newspaper articles. In so doing, the proposed system track browser activities to bill the user based on the selected payment plan. In this sense, the browser serves as a bridge between publishers and the proposed subscription service. Specifically, news articles are not hosted on the artifact itself, but the artifact sends paying readers to publishers' websites to access their content. This is different compared to existing commercial solutions (e.g., Apple News +), where content is centrally stored and accessed. At the end of the month, the content providers' monthly balance will be calculated based on various parameters (e.g., attention, time, read lines, visits) and generated revenues.

5   Conclusion

This research in progress has the goal to derive and test design principles for collaborative subscription service for the online newspaper industry. In so doing, we conceptualized and developed a software prototype that is theoretically rooted in the strategic alliance, digital platform, and business model literature [1–3]. Based on these theoretical foundations, we use the business model as our guiding design lens to derive test and evaluation scenarios for our proposed prototype. The next steps of this on-going study are tests with Amazon Turk users to identify areas of improvement in preparation for the quantitative study with Finnish readers, which allows us to collect data on usage and payment plan performance. Subsequently, the insights gained from the first study will provide insights for the second qualitative study, which involves publishers to identify positive conditions related to technical and strategic collaborations. From a practitioner viewpoint, this study could be a major contribution to Nordic newspaper industries in providing a strategic template towards collaborative subscription services.

References

1. Gulati, R., Nohria, N., Zaheer, A.: Strategic networks. Strateg. Manage. J. **21**(3), 203–215 (2000)
2. Al-Debei, M.M., Avison, D.: Developing a unified framework of the business model concept. Eur. J. Inf. Syst. **19**(3), 359–376 (2010)
3. Yoo, Y., Henfridsson, O., Lyytinen, K.: Research commentary-The new organizing logic of digital innovation: an agenda for information systems research. Inf. Syst. Res. **21**(4), 724–735 (2010)
4. de Reuver, M., Sørensen, C., Basole, R.C.: The digital platform: a research agenda. J. Inf. Technol. **33**, 1–12 (2017). https://journals.sagepub.com/doi/10.1057/s41265-016-0033-3
5. Hoffmann, W., Lavie, D., Reuer, J.J., Shipilov, A.: The interplay of competition and cooperation. Strateg. Manage. J. **39**(12), 3033–3052 (2018)
6. Eisenmann, T., Parker, G., Van Alstyne, M.: Strategies for two-sided markets. Harvard Bus. Rev. Article **84**(10), 92–101 (2006)
7. Ghazawneh, A., Henfridsson, O.: Balancing platform control and external contribution in third-party development: the boundary resources model. Inf. Syst. J. **23**(2), 173–192 (2013)
8. Boudreau, K.J.: Let a thousand flowers bloom? An early look at large numbers of software app developers and patterns of innovation. Organ. Sci. **23**(5), 1409–1427 (2012)
9. Peffers, K., Tuunanen, T., Rothenberger, M.A., Chatterjee, S.: A design science research methodology for information systems research. J. Manage. Inf. Syst. **24**(3), 45–77 (2007)

Service Science

A Digital Twin for Safety and Risk Management: A Prototype for a Hydrogen High-Pressure Vessel

Alireza Jaribion[1]([envelope]) [ID], Siavash H. Khajavi[1] [ID], Mikael Öhman[1] [ID],
Adriaan Knapen[2] [ID], and Jan Holmström[1] [ID]

[1] Department of Industrial Engineering and Management, Aalto University,
Helsinki, Finland
{alireza.jaribion,siavash.khajavi,mikael.ohman,jan.holmstrom}@aalto.fi
[2] Department of Computer Science, Aalto University, Helsinki, Finland
adriaan.knapen@aalto.fi

Abstract. The term "digital twin" refers to an emerging technology that utilizes the internet of things, software simulation, and data analytics to create a digital replica of a physical object or system. Digital twins have the potential to significantly transform condition monitoring and maintenance operations. In this research, a prototype is developed consisting of hardware and software components to enable the creation of a digital twin for an industrial application. High-pressure hydrogen vessels are industrial equipment with a high safety requirement for the storage and transfer of highly flammable hydrogen. Our prototype illustrates the effectiveness of utilizing a real-time digital twin of the hydrogen high-pressure vessel for failure risk management. The Action Design Research (ADR) is used to describe the process that led to the development of the prototype.

Keywords: Digital twin · Action design research · Risk management

1 Design of the Artifact

The prototype we present in this paper is the result of a rapid design and development effort, taking place within the context of a hackathon. Although not yet implemented, our prototype and the design process leading to it offer both practical and theoretical insights from the perspective of design science [1,2]. The practical relevance of our prototype is that it has the potential to improve the safety of an environmentally friendly energy source—saving lives in both the short and long term. By searching for a solution to our practical design problem [1]—how to improve the safety of hydrogen high-pressure vessels—we also probe the theoretically interesting problem of how to close the feedback loop between the real and the digital world. Our prototype can be described as an

Supported by Academy of Finland Project Direct Operations under Grant 323831.

S. Hofmann et al. (Eds.): DESRIST 2020, LNCS 12388, pp. 369–375, 2020.
https://doi.org/10.1007/978-3-030-64823-7_34

ensemble artifact [2], and in this paper we elaborate upon its emergence and its significance. As the prototype was developed over the course of a hackathon, the design process represents a high-paced pragmatic balancing act between technical rigor and relevance for the industry problem. In terms of Design Science methodology, we argue that the hackathon encompassed much of what can be expected from an ADR project [2]. What follows is a description of our prototype, combined with a retrospective account of the key considerations emerging throughout the design process, mapped against the ADR method stages [2].

1.1 Problem Formulation

In terms of problem formulation, industry hackathons encompass the principles of ADR. The event is initiated different companies presenting problems for which they would like to explore solutions, representing an opportunity for practice-inspired research [2]. The hackathon participants then form teams around one of the presented problems, depending on personal preferences and interests. When researchers participate in hackathons, they are bound to choose problems, which resonate with their theoretical understanding and background, ultimately resulting in a theory-ingrained artifact [2]. In our case, the interesting problem was how to improve the safety of hydrogen storage, distribution, and transportation (in accordance with applicable codes and standards (AIAA G-095-2004)).

Hydrogen is a potential energy carrier for the future [3]. After its production in plants, hydrogen is stored and then transported to the demand points. The use of high-pressure vessels is generally prevalent for the storage and transportation of hydrogen (liquid and gas); therefore, there is always a risk of explosion along its supply chain. In recent years, several incidents related to hydrogen explosions have occurred. In particular, the hydrogen explosion at the Fukushima nuclear power plant [4] caused the most severe nuclear accident since the Chernobyl disaster. Considering the financial and life losses resulting from a hydrogen explosion, it is imperative to fully understand and investigate the safety issues related to this chemical element.

1.2 Building, Intervention and Evaluation

Throughout the hackathon, the company representatives (problem owners), actively spar with the participating teams, providing instant reflection and feedback on the emerging ideas. Here the problem owner represents the organizational context, and the sparring leads to reciprocal shaping of the artifact with built-in authentic and concurrent evaluation [2]. Further, companies participate in industry hackathons to get insight in novel (often technological) solutions approaches, whereas participating teams get insight into the industry and its inherent challenges, leading to mutual learning between solution owners and participating teams [2]. In our case, throughout the hackathon, there was several such in-depth exchanges, resulting in several cycles of iterative artifact development. We set out to build a solution based on the concept of a digital twin.

Digital twins will "facilitate the means to monitor, understand, and optimize the functions of all physical assets by enabling the seamless transmission of data between the physical and virtual world [5]." In the case of hydrogen storage, distribution, and transportation, our proposed design involves applying a digital twin, whose process is illustrated in Fig. 1. The digital twin's real-time connection to hydrogen vessels provides condition monitoring. Therefore, the operator (in the control center and tanker truck) can receive more intelligent and actionable messages in the appropriate time to reduce the risk and prevent an explosion.

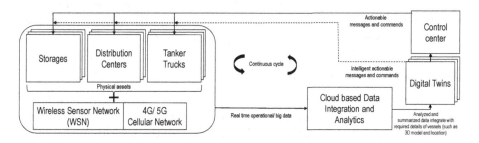

Fig. 1. Deployment of digital twin in hydrogen storage and transportation.

To monitor the status of hydrogen and to create a digital twin of a hydrogen vessel, a number of measurements are required, such as hydrogen concentration, pressure, and temperature. Moreover, the operator must track all hydrogen vessels during transportation for better decision-making. Remote systems based on sensors need to transform data to cloud by using networks; in this regard, 5G will transfer a substantial amount of data 10 times faster than 4G networks. To create the WSN considering the required measurements and 5G deployment, the proposed prototype utilizes a number of sensors and micro controllers as follows: BME680, MQ-8, Arduino MKR NB 1500, ESP8266.

The various sensors present in the hydrogen vessel send real-time measurements to an online database, which enables other devices to retrieve both the most recent measurements and historical data. A program written in Python is responsible for retrieving the latest data from the REST API, processing it using the data analytics algorithm, and making the results accessible to the operator by pushing it to the MindSphere platform. Moreover, for the data analytics, the Jaribion et al. method [6] is used to simplify the big data for the operator. By utilizing this method, the system is constantly calculating the similarity of the data collected from sensors (hydrogen concentration, pressure, and temperature) to the ideal reference point, which is set in accordance with applicable codes and standards for hydrogen maintenance. According to [6], the sensor measurements are represented by $\tilde{A}$, while the ideal reference point is represented by $\tilde{B}$, and the similarity to ideal reference point is calculated by $S(\tilde{A}, \tilde{B})$ in (1).

$$S(\tilde{A}, \tilde{B}) = \left(1 - \frac{\sum_{i=1}^{4}|a_i - b_i|}{4}\right)\left(1 - |x^*_{\tilde{A}} - x^*_{\tilde{B}}|\right) \times \frac{min\left(P(\tilde{A}), P(\tilde{B})\right) + min\left(a(\tilde{A}), a(\tilde{B})\right)}{max\left(P(\tilde{A}), P(\tilde{B})\right) + max\left(a(\tilde{A}), a(\tilde{B})\right)}$$

$$(1)$$

The analyzed data is integrated with the required details of the vessels, such as the 3D model and location, in order to create the digital twin of the hydrogen vessel. Although we used the Unity engine for this integration in the proposed prototype, the use of specialized digital twin software is recommended. By visualizing the digital twin at the control center, through an easy-to-use responsive front-end interface, the operator can monitor the hydrogen status, diagnose the fault, identify the fault location, and send actionable messages and commands to the storage unit or tanker trucks. Furthermore, the digital twin can directly and intelligently send actionable messages and commands to the storage unit, or tanker trucks without interference from the control center.

1.3   Reflection and Learning

As elaborated above, the hackathon creates an environment for mutual learning. On one hand, during the hackathon, the problem owner learns of several approaches to tackling the problem at hand. During the hackathon the different emerging artifacts are subtly shaped by the solution owner through the advice and opinions he presents to the participating teams, while the solution owner's insight into the potential of the technological or theory-ingrained approach evolves. Conversely, researchers participating in the hackathon expose themselves to a new context, which widens their perspective of the potential of their underlying theoretical and technological understanding to solve problems.

1.4   Formalization of Learning

In the fourth stage of ADR, we reflect upon the hackathon, and ask what we as researchers learned from it. Considering our solution, we note that the implementation of a WSN does not require or highly rely on existing asset instrumentation, thus allowing for fast rollout, through retrofitting with hardware and software improvements, and adjustments in currently in-use vessels. Moreover, using 4G/5G cellular networks, which leverage existing wireless communications infrastructure, allows for usage on stationary and mobile assets. In addition, cloud-based data integration and analytics bring scalability and flexibility without the need for a significant initial investment in data storage and processing. When the digital twin is created, this real-time intuitive digital representation of the asset will create situational awareness and produce actionable insight for dependent users, and the operator can then act accordingly. Overall, having a digital twin monitoring the location and status of all the vessels will provide real-time information regarding impending problems; enhance control and safety from the level of no automation to full automation; and mature digital transformation from simple control toward analytics supporting decision-making, deep learning, and predictive analytics (see Fig. 2).

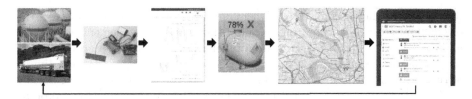

Fig. 2. The digital twin of the hydrogen vessel in action.

In terms of the three levels for generalizing learnings from ADR-projects [2], we formalize as follows: (a) The problem instance can be generalized to creating real-time situational awareness of a heterogeneous (both in terms of type and age of assets), dispersed and potentially mobile asset base. (b) The solution instance can be generalized as a digital twin of an engineering asset. Finally, we can, based on our hackathon experience—where a working prototype of the solution was produced in 48 h—state the following (c) design principles (DP):

DP1: A digital twin enables a scalability in creating situational awareness of an engineering asset base, as it accommodates asset base heterogeneity.
DP2: A digital twin enables a quick development of situational awareness of an engineering asset base, through enabling the use of existing infrastructure for data acquisition, communication, data processing and data visualization.

2   Significance to Research

The manifestation of renewable energy, such as hydrogen, requires safe storage and transportation from the production site to users. Conducting research and harnessing new technologies in this field are hence necessary [7]. Digital twin technology is among the top strategic technologies in recent years, and according to research's future predictions, "the digital twin market will reach 15 billion dollars by 2023" [5]. In the context of hydrogen storage, some articles present new mathematical methods to improve and optimize the design of high-pressure vessels [8]. However, they do not describe any procedure regarding the later use of these sensors for monitoring and fault diagnosis. Abdalla et al. [7] review and point out the safety, reliability, and cost-efficiency of materials for hydrogen storage. On the other hand, although [8] introduces the implementation of sensors during the production of vessels, and [9] discusses primary explosion protection by detecting the unintentional escape of gas in due time, neither presents any solution for improving the safety of existing vessels. Furthermore, while [10] explores the current state of the art in safety and reliability analysis for hydrogen storage and delivery technologies, the mentioned recommendations focus on encouraging companies to reduce future risks and support safe operation.

3   Significance to Practice

Hydrogen gas is highly flammable and has the highest rating of 4 on the NFPA 704, which is a standard system for the identification of the hazards of materials for emergency response [11]. Therefore, hydrogen safety, which covers the production, storage, transportation, and utilization of this element, is of great importance. Moreover, the emergence of fuel cell technology as a green alternative to internal combustion engines powered by fossil fuels signifies the timing of this research. "It is estimated that about 15–20% of all European refueling stations need to be equipped with hydrogen supply" [12]. As the global production volume of hydrogen is projected to increase over the next five years [12], the risks related to its production and handling may grow if new solutions are not adopted. Since the occurrence of large incidents creates a negative public view towards the safety and practicality of fuel cell technology, risk management of hydrogen high-pressure vessels using a digital twin can reduce the adaptation vulnerability of this fragile green technology in today's competitive market.

4   Evaluation of the Artifact

While the prototype has not been tested in the field and thus requires further development, the equipment and software successfully passed initial lab testing and functioned according to the design specification. The presented prototype was developed for a European conglomerate company during a hackathon and one of the company's managers commented on the proposed prototype as follows:

"The presented design points out to an actual topic, since our company is currently working on assuring the safety of hydrogen vessels. A group of our company experts evaluated the presented prototype as an innovative design for utilizing 5G in creation of digital twins and improving its performance. Moreover, the presented design is adoptable and scalable within the market."

References

1. Holmström, J., Ketokivi, M., Hameri, A.P.: Bridging practice and theory: a design science approach. Decis. Sci. **40**(1), 65–87 (2009)
2. Sein, M.K., Henfridsson, O., Purao, S., Rossi, M., Lindgren, R.: Action design research. MIS Q. **35**, 37–56 (2011)
3. Dagdougui, H., Sacile, R., Bersani, C., Ouammi, A.: Hydrogen Infrastructure for Energy Applications: Production, Storage, Distribution and Safety. Academic Press, Cambridge (2018)
4. Hydrogen Safety. https://en.wikipedia.org/wiki/Hydrogen_safety. Accessed 7 Feb 2020
5. Khajavi, S.H., Motlagh, N.H., Jaribion, A., Werner, L.C., Holmström, J.: Digital twin: vision, benefits, boundaries, and creation for buildings. IEEE Access **7**, 147406–147419 (2019)
6. Jaribion, A., Khajavi, S. H., Motlagh, N. H., Holmström, J.: [WiP] a novel method for big data analytics and summarization based on fuzzy similarity measure. In: 2018 IEEE 11th Conference on Service-Oriented Computing and Applications (SOCA), pp. 221–226. IEEE, Paris (2018)
7. Abdalla, A.M., Hossain, S., Nisfindy, O.B., Azad, A.T., Dawood, M., Azad, A.K.: Hydrogen production, storage, transportation and key challenges with applications: a review. Energy Convers. Manage. **165**, 602–627 (2018)

8. Moradi, R., Groth, K.M.: Hydrogen storage & delivery: review of the state of the art technologies & risk & reliability analysis. Int. J. Hydrogen Energy **44**(23), 12254–12269 (2019)
9. Burov, A.E., Burova, O.G.: Development of digital twin for composite pressure vessel. J. Phys.: Conf. Ser. **1441**(1), 012133 (2020)
10. Tzimas, E., Filiou, C., Peteves, S. D., & Veyret, J. B.: Hydrogen storage: state-of-the-art and future perspective. EU Commission, JRC Petten, EUR 20995EN (2003)
11. Cameo Chemicals. https://cameochemicals.noaa.gov/chemical/8729. Accessed 7 Feb 2020
12. Grand View Research. https://www.grandviewresearch.com/industry-analysis/hydrogen-storage-market. Accessed 7 Feb 2020

Bridging the Architectural Gap in Smart Homes Between User Control and Digital Automation

Lukas-Valentin Herm$^{(\boxtimes)}$ ⓘ, Jonas Wanner, and Christian Janiesch

Julius-Maximilians-Universität, Würzburg, Germany
{lukas-valentin.herm,jonas.wanner,
christian.janiesch}@uni-wuerzburg.de

Abstract. In today's homes, terminals such as televisions, refrigerators, washing machines, lamps, or heaters are operated separately and locally. Typically, the resident initiates actions on the terminal device manually and controls their runtime. Digitisation of the previously manual and time-consuming activities hold great potential for the ease of living. Nonetheless, so called smart home technologies have a lag of adoption. Several challenges are responsible for this, such as the fear of losing control. Current Internet of Things architectures do not overcome these challenges and are therefore identified as barriers to innovation for mass dissemination. We propose a new architectural paradigm, which will be evaluated in technical as well as social aspects to achieve a commanding coexistence of man and machine. Our approach will be equated to several well-suited publish-subscribe and request-response paradigms of the IoT spectrum to show its comparability.

Keywords: Smart home · Ambient intelligence · M2M · H2M · IoT architecture

1 Introduction

Research on smart homes has so far mainly focused on the technical exploitation of the potentials with the greatest possible degree of automation through machine-to-machine (M2M) communication [1]. However, the acceptance and adaptation by end users (here: residents), in particular in their own houses, seems much more problematic. Investigations primarily show major concerns regarding the loss of user control and a related demand for limiting the intelligent system [2]. The desired automation should offer support for better decisions [1, 2] and thus implies suitable human-to-machine (H2M) communication. Although this would achieve a better acceptance of innovation [1], it limits the potential for automation [2]. The challenge therefore lies between the discrepancies of pure M2M communication as the automation optimum and H2M communication as the ability of residents to keep control.

The findings of Russell und Norvig [3] indicate that this does not have to be a mandatory trade-off. Computers outperform people in most tasks with a focus on timeliness and data processing. Others, supposedly easy tasks for humans, pose problems [3]. A symbiosis between man and machine therefore offers optimization potential for smart homes and can offer a possible solution for users' fears. To achieve this symbiosis, there

© Springer Nature Switzerland AG 2020
S. Hofmann et al. (Eds.): DESRIST 2020, LNCS 12388, pp. 376–381, 2020.
https://doi.org/10.1007/978-3-030-64823-7_35

is a need for a suitable architectural paradigm. It should have a technical module for M2M automation that can be influenced by residents. We use a design approach to find out, which architectural model will fit with user problems and technical concerns to overcome the adaptation gap. Finally, we present an architecture based on the MQTT protocol which enables H2M and M2M real-time communication and simultaneously places the user at the center of the smart home, assisted by an integrated machine learning component.

2   Research Methodology

We use the design science research (DSR) paradigm for information systems research of Peffers et al. [4] to develop and evaluate our research approach of a user-oriented coexistence architectural model between man and machine in smart homes. Based on the recommended steps (using a combined Demonstration & Evaluation step), our research process is as follows (Fig. 1):

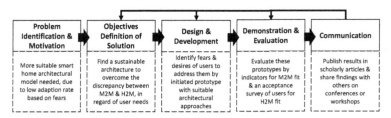

Fig. 1. Design science research steps for bridging the architectural gap

After identifying the challenges of the residents as the key factor for the low adoption rate, we defined the project's objectives in multiple iterations. Afterwards, we searched for suitable architectures to potentially overcome these problems. Within this, we decided to create an own architectural paradigm. All relevant architectural solutions will be transferred into prototypes, which we evaluate technologically regarding an M2M fit and socially regarding a H2M fit.

3   User Challenges and Architectural Approach

User Challenges. There have already been surveys on the challenges faced by residents about avoiding the adoption of smart home technologies. The most common problems seem to be compatibility with other devices [5–7], poor manageability [5, 7, 8], delivery of information to the user [7, 9, 10], willingness of the users to hand over control [9, 11–13], and security issues/reliability [5–7, 13].

Design Needs. To address these concerns a suitable architecture must consider these needs in its design. The compatibility with other devices *(CD)* requires a flexible and reactive middleware with a wide range of application interfaces. The poor manageability *(PM)* and delivery of information to the user mostly rely on an intuitive user interface and design. The backend system must always offer the power to control any smart object in the network in a way that is intuitive and free of programming. With the power to always interrupt or change machine operations, this will also solve the willingness of the users to hand over control *(WU)*. The security issues/reliability *(SIR)* should be addressed via cryptographic protocols, secure transmission protocols, and different types of quality of services.

State-of-the-Art of Architectural Approaches. We have collected suitable architectural solutions in all three paradigm types of publish-subscribe *(ps)*, request-response *(rr)* and hybrid *(h)*. This led to the following approaches, which we will evaluate for smart home usability (Table 1):

Table 1. Architectural approaches for smart home usability evaluation

Name	Source	Type	Field of use	Specific features	Solving design needs
Message Queuing Telemetry Transport for Sensor Networks *(MQTT-SN)*	[14–17]	ps	Wireless sensor networks	Supports QoS, SSL, TCP and focuses on restricted networks	CD, SIR
Event-driven Service-oriented Architecture *(EDSOA)*	[18–21]	ps	Internet of Things	Loose link between IoT device and IoT service	CD, SIR
Advanced Message Queuing Protocol *(AMQP)*	[22–24]	ps	Message-oriented middleware	Message queueing/store and forward also different security aspects	CD, SIR
Service-oriented Architecture *(SOA)*	[25, 26]	rr	Enterprise application integration	Client has control over task; manual data pulling	PM, WU, SIR
Extensible Messaging and Presence Protocol *(XMPP)*	[24, 27, 28]	h	Instant messaging	Communication via XML	PM, SIR
Service-driven Message Queuing Telemetry Transport *(SDMQTT)*	own	h	Smart home networks	Benefits from MQTT(-SN) and integrated user interaction	CD, PM, WU, SIR

Publish-subscribe architectures do not have a user-friendly interface *(WU)* and do not offer the user a H2M communication *(CD)*. Request-response architectures are not able to provide a flexible real-time middleware through manual querying of data *(CD)*. The hybrid architecture XMPP also lacks in the capability of user-oriented integration as well as real-time and flexible H2M communication *(CD, WU)*. Only our architecture is able to fulfil all of these criteria.

SQMTT. The SQMQTT is our own architectural solution and consists of four components. All (1) smart home objects must be registered to topics in a (2) stream processing broker. The broker itself routes all data equal to the MQTT-network protocol *(CD, SIR)*, despite a bidirectional forwarding of events or command requests instead of an unidirectional forwarding in its origin. This provides the user with the ability to control integrated smart home devices directly *(WU)*. This is implemented through a management module (Fig. 2).

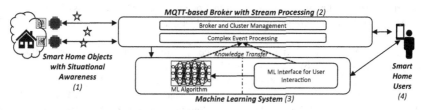

Fig. 2. Architecture of SDMQTT

The stream processing is done through complex event processing (CEP) and enables a readable rules base approach for filtering relevant events and therefore minimize the traffic load for data computation and learning. The latter is needed within a (3) machine learning system (MLS). On the one hand, the MLS is used to be able to adapt and thus continuously improve the filters in the CEP of the broker through machine learning procedures. This approach is based on similar frameworks from the IIoT sector [29]. On the other hand, it is used to evaluate service requests of smart home users or residents of the smart home more efficiently/correctly *(WU)*. It can communicate with the (4) smart home user through an interface to process and route human requests or inform the user on any events that occur *(PM)*. Therefore, a smart home user will retain controllability (H2M) with a parallel ability of an M2M-learning system. Thus, our approach can help to approach the trade-off problem mentioned by Russell und Norvig [3] in the field of smart home.

4   Evaluation and Prospects

Evaluation. In future research, we will do a technical study using applicable indicators of IoT solutions with focus on M2M fit concerning the automation potential to evaluate the architectural approaches of relevance. In addition, there will be a qualitative user acceptance survey, where we build demonstration rooms with each architectural approach to identify their acceptance with a focus on H2M fit concerning the lag of innovation diffusion. As we use a DSR approach, we plan to use the survey to identify further barriers for adoption and integrate them into our approach.

Prospects. We expect that our approaches will gather the best results in our technical and social evaluation. We assume this due to their readiness to request specific smart objects by users (request-response), while allowing a M2M-communication in parallel and thus an optimization for automation, combined with a robust controllability interruptible by users.

References

1. Wilson, C., Hargreaves, T., Hauxwell-Baldwin, R.: Smart homes and their users: a systematic analysis and key challenges. Pers. Ubiquit. Comput. **19**(2), 463–476 (2014). https://doi.org/10.1007/s00779-014-0813-0
2. Mennicken, S., Vermeulen, J., Huang, E.M.: From today's augmented houses to tomorrow's smart homes: new directions for home automation research. In: Proceedings of the 2014 ACM International Joint Conference on Pervasive and Ubiquitous Computing, pp. 105–115. ACM (2014)
3. Russell, S., Norvig, P.: Artificial Intelligence: A Modern Approach. Pearson Education Limited, Malaysia (2016)
4. Peffers, K., Tuunanen, T., Rothenberger, M., Chatterjee, S.: A design science research methodology for information systems research. J. Manage. Inform. Syst. **24**, 45–77 (2007)
5. Brush, A., Lee, B., Mahajan, R., Agarwal, S., Saroiu, S., Dixon, C.: Home automation in the wild: challenges and opportunities. In: Proceedings of the SIGCHI Conference on Human Factors in Computing Systems, pp. 2115–2124. ACM, New York, USA (2011)
6. Edwards, W.Keith, Grinter, Rebecca E.: At home with ubiquitous computing: seven challenges. In: Abowd, Gregory D., Brumitt, Barry, Shafer, Steven (eds.) UbiComp 2001. LNCS, vol. 2201, pp. 256–272. Springer, Heidelberg (2001). https://doi.org/10.1007/3-540-45427-6_22
7. Brich, J., Walch, M., Rietzler, M., Weber, M., Schaub, F.: Exploring end user programming needs in home automation. ACM Trans. Comput.-Hum. Interact. **24**, 11 (2017)
8. Davidoff, S., Lee, M., Yiu, C., Zimmerman, J., Dey, A.: Principles of smart home control. International Conference on Ubiquitous Computing, pp. 19–34. Springer, Orange County (2006)
9. Barkhuus, L., Dey, A.: Is context-aware computing taking control away from the user? Three levels of interactivity examined. International Conference on Ubiquitous Computing, pp. 149–156. Springer (2003)
10. Coskun, A., Kaner, G., Bostan, I.: Is smart home a necessity or a fantasy for the mainstream user? A study on users' expectations of smart household appliances. Int. J. Des. **12**, 7–20 (2018)
11. Dixon, C., et al.: The home needs an operating system (and an app store). In: Proceedings of the 9th ACM SIGCOMM Workshop on Hot Topics in Networks, pp. 18. ACM (2010)
12. Ball, M., Callaghan, V.: Managing control, convenience and autonomy-a study of agent autonomy in intelligent environments. Agents Ambient Intell. **12**, 159–196 (2012)
13. Yang, H., Lee, H., Zo, H.: User acceptance of smart home services: an extension of the theory of planned behavior. Ind. Manage. Data Syst. **117**, 68–89 (2017)
14. Govindan, K., Azad, A.P.: End-to-end service assurance in IoT MQTT-SN. In: 12th Annual IEEE Consumer Communications and Networking Conference (CCNC), 2015, pp. 290–296. IEEE (2015)

15. Hunkeler, U., Truong, H.L., Stanford-Clark, A.: MQTT-S—A publish/subscribe protocol for Wireless Sensor Networks. In: 3rd International Conference on Communication Systems Software and Middleware and Workshops, 2008. comsware 2008, pp. 791–798. IEEE (2008)

16. Chen, D., Varshney, P.K.: QoS support in wireless sensor networks: a survey. Int. Conf. Wireless Netw. **233**, 1–7 (2004)

17. Luzuriaga, J.E., Perez, M., Boronat, P., Cano, J.C., Calafate, C., Manzoni, P.: A comparative evaluation of AMQP and MQTT protocols over unstable and mobile networks. In: 2015 12th Annual IEEE Consumer Communications and Networking Conference (CCNC), pp. 931–936. IEEE (2015)

18. Cheng, B., Wang, M., Zhao, S., Zhai, Z., Zhu, D., Chen, J.: Situation-aware dynamic service coordination in an IoT environment. IEEE/ACM Trans. Netw. **25**, 2082–2095 (2017)

19. Lan, L., Li, F., Wang, B., Zhang, L., Shi, R.: An event-driven service-oriented architecture for the internet of things. In: 2014 Asia-Pacific Services Computing Conference (APSCC), pp. 68–73. IEEE (2014)

20. Gupta, P., Mokal, T.P., Shah, D., Satyanarayana, K.: Event-driven SOA-based IoT architecture. In: International Conference on Intelligent Computing and Applications, pp. 247–258. Springer (2018)

21. Sun, Y., Qiao, X., Cheng, B., Chen, J.: A low-delay, lightweight publish/subscribe architecture for delay-sensitive IoT services. In: 2013 IEEE 20th International Conference on Web Services (ICWS), pp. 179–186. IEEE (2013)

22. Vinoski, S.: Advanced message queuing protocol. IEEE Internet Comput. **10** (2006)

23. Kolozali, S., Bermudez-Edo, M., Puschmann, D., Ganz, F., Barnaghi, P.: A knowledge-based approach for real-time IoT data stream annotation and processing. Internet of Things (iThings). In: 2014 IEEE International Conference on, and Green Computing and Communications (GreenCom), IEEE and Cyber, Physical and Social Computing (CPSCom), IEEE, pp. 215–222. IEEE (2014)

24. Al-Fuqaha, A., Guizani, M., Mohammadi, M., Aledhari, M., Ayyash, M.: Internet of things: a survey on enabling technologies, protocols, and applications. IEEE Commun. Surv. Tutorials **17**, 2347–2376 (2015)

25. Melzer, I.: Service-orientierte Architekturen mit Web Services: Konzepte-Standards-Praxis. Springer-Verlag, New York (2010)

26. Lee, J., Lee, S.-J., Wang, P.-F.: A framework for composing SOAP, non-SOAP and non-web services. IEEE Trans. Serv. Comput. **8**, 240–250 (2015)

27. Jones, M.T.: Meet the extensible Messaging and Presence Protocol (XMPP). IBM developerWorks, Markham, ON, Canada (2009)

28. Saint-Andre, P.: Extensible Messaging and Presence Protocol (XMPP): Core. (2011)

29. Wanner, J., Herm, L.V., Hartel, D., Janiesch, C.: Verwendung binärer Daten-werte für eine KI-gestützte Instandhaltung 4.0. HMD - Praxis der Wirtschafts-informatik **56**, 1268–1281 (2019)

Designing a State-of-the-Art Information System for Air Cargo Palletizing

No-San Lee[✉], Philipp Gabriel Mazur[✉], Christian Hovestadt[✉], and Detlef Schoder[✉]

University of Cologne, Cologne Institute for Information Systems, Pohligstr. 1,
50969 Cologne, Germany
{lee,mazur,schoder}@wim.uni-koeln.de,
hovestadt@wiso.uni-koeln.de

Abstract. Palletizing in air cargo faces a large number of constraints, e.g. aviation safety and cargo handling regulations. In addition, operational, economical, and ecological goals further need to be considered. The challenge to find practicable if not optimal palletizing solutions is known as the Pallet Loading Problem (PLP) or Container Loading Problem (CLP). It defines a np-hard and highly complex problem space. In air cargo operations, there is hardly any digital support to optimize the palletizing process. As a result, desired objectives are often only met by chance, e.g. the optimal utilization of the possible loading weight, the maximum use of the available loading space, or both. The goal of this research is to report on the design and learnings from a state-of-the-art information system we built to support the manual palletizing process by considering substantially more constraints than any other system we know of. The artifact generates via heuristics optimized and practicable palletizing solutions and supports the human palletizer prior to and during the physical assembly by visualizing, monitoring and validating the generated palletizing solutions.

1 Introduction

The air cargo market is a growing sector and cargo volumes have increased by about 20% from 2014 to 2019 [1]. Looking ahead, world trade is expected to double within the next 20 years, with air cargo traffic growing at 3.6% per year, resulting in about 55% more cargo aircrafts needed for the cargo transport [2]. At the same time, the air cargo industry is facing a number of challenges. The global air transport with about 918 million metric tons of CO_2 in 2018 is responsible for roughly 2.4% of global CO_2 emissions from fossil fuel [3], putting pressure on the industry to reduce cost and optimize resources. Also, a lack of qualified personnel in air cargo operations as well as the imminent loss of expertise due to an age-related increase of leaving employees of the air cargo companies in the near future are current issues [4].

In the operational field, in particular the palletizing of air cargo, air cargo companies have to manage huge cost and time pressure. Especially, there is hardly any digital support to optimize the palletizing process and to reduce the loading time of cargo on so-called Unit Loading Devices (ULD). ULDs are standardized pallets or containers

© Springer Nature Switzerland AG 2020
S. Hofmann et al. (Eds.): DESRIST 2020, LNCS 12388, pp. 382–387, 2020.
https://doi.org/10.1007/978-3-030-64823-7_36

on or in which the cargo is positioned. The quality of a palletizing solution depends heavily on the experience and creativity of the human palletizer. If the complexity of the palletizing process increases, inexperienced palletizers mostly follow a trial-and-error approach. As a result, desired objectives are often only met by chance, e.g. the optimal utilization of the possible loading in combination with the maximum use of the available loading space within a strict time window.

In Operations Research (OR), this np-hard problem [5] is known as the Pallet Loading Problem (PLP) or Container Loading Problem (CLP). Research in this area usually seeks to find solution approaches by means of exact algorithms (e.g. integer programming [6]) or heuristics (e.g. genetic algorithms [7]). The resulting research artifacts are theoretically well understood, but often miss out constraints from reality in order to cope with the complexity. This includes in particular constraints that refer to the process of pallet and container loading. These constraints are covered in literature but not fully applied in research approaches [6–9]. One reason for the lack of practical relevance of current PLP and CLP approaches is that research approaches do not consider *all* relevant constraints [6]. Also, depending on the industrial characteristics, specific constraints may arise [10]. Within the context of air cargo, the complexity of the overall problem rises considerably due to the simultaneous consideration of strong heterogeneous cargo items, complex shapes of the ULDs and constraints based on strict aviation safety regulations. Current solutions do not reflect the entire complexity as expressed in research and practice. Consequently, a representation of reality is only inadequately achieved and there is a shortage of practicable and feasible solutions.

The goal of this research is to report on the design and learnings from a state-of-the-art information system we built to support the manual palletizing process by considering substantially more constraints than any other system we know of. The artifact generates via heuristics optimized and practicable palletizing solutions and supports the human palletizer prior to and during the physical assembly by visualizing, monitoring and validating the generated palletizing solutions.

2 Design of the Artifact

To achieve our research goal, a design-oriented approach is applied following the Design Science Research methodology introduced by Peffers et al. [11] and Hevner et al. [12]. Prior to the development of the prototype, we determined which quantitative and qualitative criteria need to be fulfilled to solve the defined problem. In collaboration with a major German air cargo company we carried out joint workshops with experts, observed the operations on-site in the cargo hub and conducted interviews with palletizers iteratively for several months.

The loading of ULDs with cargo items is started within defined time slots before the planned flight, such that, if possible, all items fit the quantity of the flight's ULDs and all safety-relevant constraints for a built-up ULD are fulfilled. The physical assembly is triggered by the supervisor's order to the palletizers and is carried out. Afterwards, the built-up ULDs are verified against the aviation safety regulations and, if met, released by the supervisor for the aircraft loading. The general process of cargo handling within an air cargo hub is described by Brandt & Nickel [8].

The palletizing process is supported by the artifact proposed here at various points. The main functions are the generation of optimized and practicable palletizing solutions and the monitoring, validation and support of physical palletizing through a user interface (UI). On a high level, the palletizing solution is calculated by a server backend (Solution Generator), while a web frontend, which is connected to the backend via REST and WebSocket APIs, guides the user through the process using multiple screens. The intended users of the artifact are the supervisor, who is responsible for the monitoring and the validation of the palletizing solutions, and the palletizer, who conducts the physical assembly. The design overview is shown in Fig. 1.

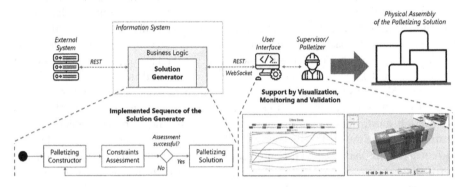

Fig. 1. Design overview of the artifact

The digitalized palletizing process starts after the information about ULDs and cargo items for a scheduled flight are present in an external cargo's booking and planning system. The consolidated information results in an input job for our artifact, composed of, e.g. flight information, cargo items and ULD characteristics. The job is sent to the Solution Generator responsible for the calculation of a palletizing solution. The practicability is achieved through the considerations of the identified constraints, including six aviation safety-relevant constraints which a ULD must fulfil to be transported by an aircraft. These are stability, floor load, maximum weight, contour, balance, and incompatibility of cargo items [10]. An optimized solution is obtained by the consideration of additional constraints, for example item orientation, stacking, no-overlap, load priorities, grouping, positioning, complete shipment [6, 8, 9], loading sequence or loading direction.

The Solution Generator calculates heuristically on the basis of an artificial intelligence a practicable solution, which in our case takes substantially more constraints into account than any other system we know of. More precisely, a genetic algorithm (GA) is applied as heuristic. GA belong, beneath neural networks and fuzzy logic, to the research field of classic computational intelligence and are chosen due to their ability of moving freely through the solution space without any contextual information except the assessment function [13]. Researchers utilize GA in this problem context [7], since they perform well if the solution space is constrained, noisy or a large number of local optima exist [14]. The goodness-of-fit of a single solution is assessed using self-defined fitness functions that can be formulated in a variable degree of complexity and sophistication. The constraints mentioned above are modeled in the heuristic as solution fitness.

Weighted and combined linearly, they form the total fitness score of a single solution. The constraints vary in the degree of satisfaction from simply modelled geometric and mechanical relationships (e.g. balance, contour) to a simulation using a real-time physics engine (e.g. stability). Mapping the constraints in the assessment function allows a flexible and expandable utilization of the heuristic. In the event of changing or tightening constraints, the modular design makes it easy to replace or add assessment functions. By considering strongly heterogeneous shapes of cargo items and ULDs as well as a wide range of relevant constraints, our design offers a comprehensive attempt in contrast to other approaches discussed in the literature.

The special features of air cargo require that a calculation can be executed for different lengths of time, since the items arrive at different intervals until shortly before departure. Since the heuristic provides better results the longer it runs, monitoring of the current solution quality is provided during the runtime of the Solution Generator. This is done by the supervisor, who can see the solution quality at the current point in time on the UI and evaluate whether it meets expected operational, economical, and ecological goals need to be considered.

The UI shows the supervisor diagrams with an overview of all constraints and the overall assessment score of the current iteration. The dynamically updated diagrams are connected to the Solution Generator by a WebSocket connection.

After termination of the Solution Generator, the palletizing solutions are released for validation by the supervisor. This validation is intended to ensure that the palletizing solutions comply with all aviation safety regulations and additional constraints and can be released to the physical assembly. The validation of the palletizing solution is based on a realistic 3D visualization. At this point, a recalculation can be initiated by the supervisor if the solution quality is insufficient.

Finally, the generated and validated palletizing solution is assigned to a palletizer for physical assembly where he/she can use the visualization as a step by step guide. The following task consists of identifying the item to be loaded next and locating the target position and rotation on the ULD. To simplify the identification of the loading items, the ID is projected onto the item as a texture within the 3D visualization.

The core of the UI is the interactive 3D WebGL-based visualization of the palletizing solution, which displays a realistic picture of the items, their loading sequence and the ULD type contour. The visualization can be explored interactively using camera operations such as rotations, zoom and panning. Interpolated color modes allow variable level of information to be displayed. On request, additional information about an item, animations of rotations and the required loading directions can be shown. The loading sequence can be fast-forwarded and rewound completely or step by step at any time.

3 Significance for Research and Practice

One of the most significant contributions to research is the implementation and evaluation of the artifact's design in order to understand and address the complexity of this research topic. Through the application and confirmation of scientifically well-founded solution approaches, found usually in OR, the artifact extends existing knowledge of research with new insights. It also facilitates the research and enables the measurement of the artifact's ability to generate innovative or creative solutions that are close to or correspond to human capabilities. This will tackle the known problems and achieve a high impact in research and practice. The results can be transferred to similar problems in other areas of cargo transport, e.g. loading of ship containers.

With an increasing number of applied constraints, the number of possible interactions between them also grows. As all relevant constraints are considered, the artifact provides the opportunity to examine the emerging dependencies between them more accurately. This goes beyond a simple cause-and-effect analysis towards the observation of a crosslinked interaction evaluation.

The artifact can also be used in the training of palletizers to increase their level of experience in palettizing within a virtual environment. By extending the artifact with a feedback component for the palletizers, e.g. in case of inconsistencies or for alternative external suggestions, the artifact can learn so that hidden, indirect knowledge is acquired and persisted.

In addition, there are also economic advantages for air cargo. The use of the artifact leads to an optimized utilization of the given space and weight capacities, which can lead to cost reduction, better calculability and a higher throughput. A better utilization of the ULDs leads to better utilization of flights or even to a reduction of flights needed, which saves fuel. In turn, fewer flights and fuel savings reduce CO_2 emissions, which is urgently needed to comply with a sustainable air cargo management.

4   Evaluation of the Artifact

For the planned evaluation, we apply the FEDS Framework for Evaluation of Design Science Research following Venable, Pries-Heje & Baskerville [15] in three consecutive setups. The first setup is performed under laboratory conditions and consists of two experiments. For this purpose, a manual palletizing with and without support of the artifact is performed in parallel. In the first experiment, palletizers without any work experience are assigned. Skilled palletizers are involved in the second experiment. Afterwards, the collected data is analyzed and compared.

The second setup includes the analysis of ULDs during the real day-to-day business. During the breakdown of ULDs on site of our collaborating air cargo company, a backward analysis of the palletizing structure is conducted and data is collected semi-automatically. The data obtained from the analysis serves as input parameters for the artifact, through which a virtual palletization is carried out. The generated palletizing solutions are compared with the original palletizing solutions from the day-to-day business and both are evaluated by experts.

The final setup includes the application of the artifact in daily operations parallel to the current palletizing process. However, there are some issues that need to be addressed in advance. For example, ensuring the required data quality for the needed input parameters, conducting necessary training and conceptualizing the artifact's measurability regarding the manual and digitalized processes and the human element.

With our research, we hope to contribute not only to design theory for PLP and CLP, but also to practically feasible solutions for palletizing processes. With the artifact we open a first big picture.

References

1. IATA: Air Freight Market Analysis - May 2019. International Air Transport Association (2019)
2. Airbus: Global Market Forecast - Cities, Airports & Aircraft - 2019–2038. Airbus S.A.S (2019)
3. Graver, B., Zhang, K., Rutherford, D.: CO_2 emissions from commercial aviation, 2018. Working Paper, International Council on Clean Transportation (2019). https://theicct.org/publicati ons/co2-emissions-commercial-aviation-2018
4. BVL: Fachkräftemangel in der Logistik – Eine Umfrage der BVL. Bundesvereinigung Logistik, Bremen (2017)
5. Karp, R.M.: Reducibility among combinatorial problems. In: Miller, R.E., Thatcher, J.W., and Bohlinger, J.D. (eds.) Proceedings of a symposium on the Complexity of Computer Computations. pp. 85–103. Springer US, Boston, MA (1972). https://doi.org/10.1007/978-1-4684-2001-2_9
6. Bortfeldt, A., Wäscher, G.: Constraints in container loading – a state-of-the-art review. Eur. J. Oper. Res. **229**, 1–20 (2013). https://doi.org/10.1016/j.ejor.2012.12.006
7. Zhao, X., Bennell, J.A., Bektaş, T., Dowsland, K.: A comparative review of 3D container loading algorithms: a comparative review of 3D container loading algorithms. Intl. Trans. Oper. Res. **23**, 287–320 (2016). https://doi.org/10.1111/itor.12094
8. Brandt, F., Nickel, S.: The air cargo load planning problem - a consolidated problem definition and literature review on related problems. Eur. J. Oper. Res. **275**, 399–410 (2019). https://doi. org/10.1016/j.ejor.2018.07.013
9. Pollaris, H., Braekers, K., Caris, A., Janssens, G.K., Limbourg, S.: Vehicle routing problems with loading constraints: state-of-the-art and future directions. OR Spectrum **37**(2), 297–330 (2014). https://doi.org/10.1007/s00291-014-0386-3
10. IATA: Cargo Handling Manual, 3rd Edition. International Air Transport Association. (2018)
11. Peffers, K., Tuunanen, T., Rothenberger, M.A., Chatterjee, S.: A design science research methodology for information systems research. J. Manag. Inform. Syst. **24**, 45–77 (2007). https://doi.org/10.2753/MIS0742-1222240302
12. Hevner, M., Park, R.: Design science in information systems research. MIS Q. **28**, 75 (2004). https://doi.org/10.2307/25148625
13. Goldberg, D.E., Holland, J.H.: Genetic algorithms and machine learning. Mach. Learn. **3**, 95–99 (1988). https://doi.org/10.1023/A:1022602019183
14. Kramer, O.: Genetic Algorithm Essentials. Springer International Publishing, Cham (2017). https://doi.org/10.1007/978-3-319-52156-5
15. Venable, J., Pries-Heje, J., Baskerville, R.: FEDS: a framework for evaluation in design science research. Eur. J. Inform. Syst. **25**, 77–89 (2016). https://doi.org/10.1057/ejis.2014.36

Designing Effective Privacy Nudges in Digital Environments: A Design Science Research Approach
Research-in-Progress

Torben Jan Barev[1]([⊠]), Andreas Janson[2], and Jan Marco Leimeister[1,2]

[1] University of Kassel, Kassel, Germany
{torben.barev,leimeister}@uni-kassel.de
[2] University of St.Gallen, St.Gallen, Switzerland
{andreas.janson,janmarco.leimeister}@unisg.ch

Abstract. When using digital technologies, various data traces are left behind for collection, storage and analysis. Innovative solutions for information systems are needed that mitigate privacy risks and foster information privacy. One mechanism to achieve this is using privacy nudges. Nudges are a concept from behavioral economics to influence individual's decisions. However, many nudges show low or at least less effects than choice architects hope for and expect. Therefore, this design science research (DSR) project focusses on developing evidence-based design principles for privacy nudges to improve their effectiveness and pave the way for more privacy sensitive IT systems. In this context, we adopt a DSR approach from Vaishnavi & Kuechler. From a theoretical perspective, we are contributing to the discussion of what drives privacy sensitive behavior. We extend generic nudge design models, making them applicable in the context of data disclosure. For practitioners, we provide guidance on how to design and implement effective privacy nudges in the user interface of digital work systems.

Keywords: Privacy nudging · Information privacy · Design science research

1 Introduction

Digital work environments are ubiquitous nowadays and the possibility to electronically acquire information about work activities as well as personal sensitive data has dramatically increased. Companies use more forms of digital work systems and implement advanced instruments such as big data analytics or artificial intelligence. With this, data can be collected, aggregated, and analyzed at a faster pace and in larger volume than ever before. This can lead to a systemic disadvantage, as an information asymmetry between the individual and the data processor exists [6]. The vulnerability to discrimination, commercial exploitation and unwanted monitoring is ubiquitous. Thus, the acceptance and adoption of modern IT systems is hindered.

The issue arising is that people value their privacy while they do not always protect it; this phenomenon is known as the Privacy Paradox [2]. As privacy is a critical antecedent

© Springer Nature Switzerland AG 2020
S. Hofmann et al. (Eds.): DESRIST 2020, LNCS 12388, pp. 388–393, 2020.
https://doi.org/10.1007/978-3-030-64823-7_37

for the acceptance of future work systems [5, 7] innovative solutions for information systems (IS) are needed that mitigate privacy risks and foster information privacy. A possible solution would embody privacy-by-design systems which are privacy enhancing technology components [10].

One mechanism to achieve this is the implementation of privacy nudges. Nudges are described as "any aspect of the choice architecture that alters people's behavior in a predictable way without forbidding any options, or significantly changing their economic incentives" [12]. Thus, privacy nudges should help users to make better privacy decisions [1]. However, some nudges emerge to have little or no impact on actual behavior [11]. Hence, in our design science research (DSR) project we are deriving evidence-based design principles that support decision architects to design effective privacy nudges. Our developed artifact should then answer the following research question: *What are key design principles for privacy nudges leading users to a more privacy friendly behavior?* To achieve our research goal, we selected an established and eminent DSPR approach that fits our purpose exactly. We follow the design science approach following Vaishnavi & Kuechler [14] (see Fig. 1).

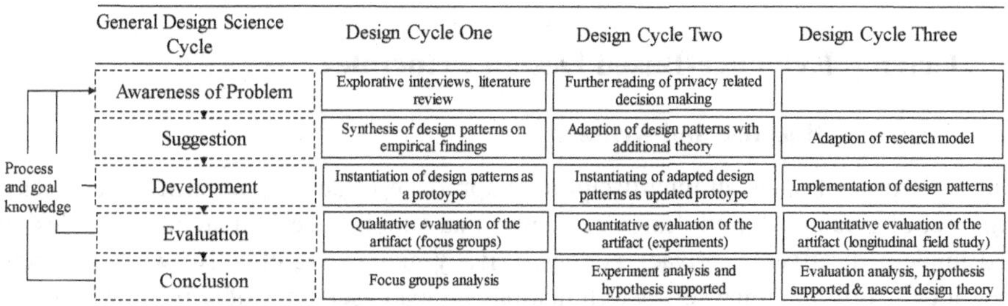

General Design Science Cycle	Design Cycle One	Design Cycle Two	Design Cycle Three
Awareness of Problem	Explorative interviews, literature review	Further reading of privacy related decision making	
Suggestion	Synthesis of design patterns on empirical findings	Adaption of design patterns with additional theory	Adaption of research model
Development	Instantiation of design patterns as a prototype	Instantiating of adapted design patterns as updated prototype	Implementation of design patterns
Evaluation	Qualitative evaluation of the artifact (focus groups)	Quantitative evaluation of the artifact (experiments)	Quantitative evaluation of the artifact (longitudinal field study)
Conclusion	Focus groups analysis	Experiment analysis and hypothesis supported	Evaluation analysis, hypothesis supported & nascent design theory

Process and goal knowledge

Fig. 1. Three consecutive design cycle and research activities.

In line with our research approach (Fig. 1), we have addressed the problem identification and motivation phase of the design science approach in this introduction. The remainder of the paper is organized to address the theoretical background of privacy nudging, the development of our design principles and evaluation. The paper closes by presenting a conclusion and contribution regarding the expected results [3, 4].

2   Related Work

2.1   Privacy Nudging

Particularly in the context of information-privacy-related decisions, human decision-making is often imperfect. Nudging is a promising approach, to enable individual users of digital systems to make decisions in line with their objectives pursued for their own data protection [5]. In digital environments, nudging typically uses design elements in the user interface to influence behavior [17]. Privacy nudges are a sub-form, describing a targeted influence on the decision-making process in order to lead people to privacy friendly decisions and guide individuals to informational self-determination [1, 9, 17].

2.2   Related Methods for Designing Nudges

To influence decisions and change behavior with nudges, various researchers proposed models of how to craft nudges [5, 8, 17]. Weinmann et al. [17] highlight for example how designers can create digital nudges and the authors developed a design cycle [17]. Another approach to provide an easier access to digital nudging is proposed by Meske and Potthoff [8] named the Digital Nudging Process Model (DINU Model). In this model the creation of digital nudging is divided into the three generic phases (1) Analyzing, (2) Designing, and (3) Evaluating including a feedback loop [11]. Linking to this, Mirsch et al. [5] proposed the Digital Nudge Design Method (DND-method) presenting a universal four-step approach of how to systematically design digital nudges [5]. These approaches tend to give mainly generic guidance of how to systematically craft digital nudges. Hence, as nudge effectiveness is highly context-dependent, these models can only serve as a scaffold. For the design and implementation of effective nudges they should be enhanced by specific characteristics of the decision environment and adapted to the privacy nudge context. On the same note, the presented models do not ensure that ethical and moral directives are thoroughly taken into account, making it prone for practitioners to design societally reprehensible nudges [18].

3   Deriving Evidence-Based Design Principles

3.1   Research Objective and Artifact

Our DSR project takes an interdisciplinary approach to develop an artifact representing a set of evidence-based design principles that support decision architects to design and implement effective privacy nudges. Privacy nudges are effective when ensuring individual's informational self-determination and lead users to a more privacy sensitive behavior. Our approach focuses on working out components of effective privacy nudges, which are assembled by the below presented design requirements. In the next step, to provide concrete guidance for nudge architects, we deduct specific design principles. Evaluating these principles in lab and real-world contexts, we generate fine granular evidence-based design principles for privacy nudges.

3.2   Design Requirements

To craft design requirements for designing effective privacy nudges, we conducted a systematic literature review and semi-structured explorative interviews with German industry representatives (n = 23). More than 50 design requirements have been collected, tested for redundancy and encapsulated to 9 tentative design requirements (Table 1). We did this in collaboration with an interdisciplinary expert group, ensuring that various perspectives are brought together. Information System (IS) knowledge, public law and IS law is brought in by two departments of a German Institute of IS Design. Ethical and philosophical knowledge is represented by an international center for ethics. Current industry knowledge for engineering future work systems is represented by two experts from a German institute for industrial engineering. After carving out the design requirements and consequential design principles, these components were condensed and simplified for easier understandability ensuring utility for choice architects.

Table 1. Design requirements for privacy nudges in digital work systems.

Design Issue	Derived requirement
Usability	DR1) Avoid slowing down work processes DR2) Ensure quick and easy decision making
Transparency	DR3) Avoid manipulation and ensure ethical standards DR4) Provide transparent information about the decision's consequences
Interaction	DR5) Avoid cognitive overload by difficult to process nudges DR6) Avoid nudges that foster distraction and stress for users
Adaptability	DR7) Consider target group's characteristics and needs
Economy	DR8) Do not endanger the company's business model DR9) implementation of privacy nudges should be cost-effective

3.3 Tentative Design Principles for Privacy Nudges

From the developed design requirements, we are now able to craft design principles for the design of privacy nudges. We conducted a systematic literature review following a methodology proposed by vom Brocke et al., as well as Webster and Watson [13, 16] and identified 38 relevant paper. To extent and validate our results we conducted an expert workshop with the same consortium as described above. The preliminary results propose design requirements that effective privacy nudges in modern work system should meet. An extract of the design principles is listed below (Table 2):

Table 2. Tentative design principles for privacy nudges.

Design requirement	Design principles
Usability	DP1) Ensuring ergonomic and simplified design DP2) Smoothly integrate Nudges into work processes DP3) Focus on relevant information for privacy friendly decision
Transparency	DP4) Give information of why and what the nudge is designed for DP5) Balance privacy and economic interest information
Interaction	DP6) Use default and framing nudges preferentially DP7) Make privacy and privacy risks tangible
Adaptability	DP8) Personalize nudges
Economy	DP9) Allow company's business model to function DP10) Ensure design and implementation costs for feasibility

Using these design principles, an exemplary privacy nudge is presented below. Here, the nudge focuses on presenting relevant information for privacy friendly decision. The nudge is personalized, framed and uses a default. It can be smoothly integrated in the user interface of a digital work system (Fig. 2).

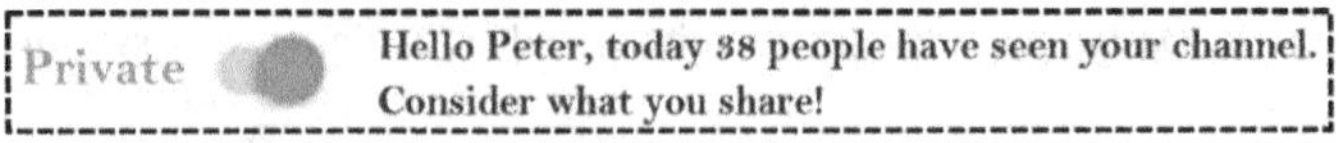

> Private   Hello Peter, today 38 people have seen your channel.
> Consider what you share!

Fig. 2. Exemplary privacy nudge developed by deploying the design principles.

For further development, we break down the developed design principles into fine granular design theory. For illustration, DP8 can be further broken down in its components of e.g. personality traits, competencies or even emotions. These components will then be empirically evaluated resulting in evidence-based design principles.

4   Evaluation and Future Outlook

We will evaluate our artifact ex post in the fourth phase of each design cycle [15] following the Framework for Evaluation in Design Science (FEDS) proposed by Venable et al. [15]. The FEDS evaluation design process consists of four steps: (1) By taking a formative evaluation approach we use empirically based interpretations to rigorously demonstrate and improve utility, quality and efficacy of our design artifact. We test how well the artifact serves its main purpose of supporting choice architects to design and implement effective privacy nudges. (2) In a first step, we take an artificial evaluation approach by introducing and educating our design principles to students with a background in IS. Having our artifact at hand, the students are required to design privacy nudges. Afterwards, we assess the effectiveness of the crafted privacy nudges. We adopt a human risk and effectiveness evaluation strategy to rigorously determine whether the benefits of the artifact will remain in real-world digital work systems over the long run or not. (3) In order to determine the properties to evaluate we adapt levels of granularity proposed by Sun and Kantor [19]. We evaluate whether the task of crafting privacy nudges was completed and whether the designed nudges have an impact on user's behavior of disclosing personal data. (4) In total, two evaluation episodes are planned with the student group. The evaluation is complemented by a naturalistic field experiment and, in the end, a summative evaluation of the artifact.

5   Contribution and Conclusion

With the artifact representing evidence-based design principles for privacy nudges, our contribution is twofold. From a theoretical perspective, our nascent design theory contributes to the discussion of what drives privacy sensitive behavior. We extend existing generic models, making them applicable in the context of data disclosure. For practitioners, we offer evaluated and specific design-directives-crafting privacy nudges. Importantly, our artifact is abstracted ensuring the adoption of our design principles to all types of privacy nudges. Even though some design principles seem promising to adapt in different applications, we can only offer evidence-based design knowledge in the environment of privacy decision making and data disclosure behavior. However, transferring and testing them in a different application environment may represent a fruitful endeavor in the future.

Acknowledgement. The research presented in this paper was funded by the German Federal Ministry of Education and Research in the context of the project Nudger (www.nudger.de), grant no. 16KIS0890K.

References

1. Acquisti, A., Sleeper, M., Wang, Y., Wilson, S., Adjerid, I., Balebako, R., et al.: Nudges for privacy and security. ACM Comput. Surv. **50**(3), 1–41 (2017)
2. Barth, S., de Jong, M.D.T.: The privacy paradox: Investigating discrepancies between expressed privacy concerns and actual online behavior – a systematic literature review. Telematics Inform. **34**(7), 1038–1058 (2017)
3. Erevelles, S., Fukawa, N., Swayne, L.: Big data consumer analytics and the transformation of marketing. J. Bus. Res. **69**(2), 897–904 (2016)
4. Cazier, J., Wilson, E., Medlin, B.: The role of privacy risk in IT acceptance. Int. J. Inform. Secur. Priv. **1**(2), 61–73 (2007)
5. Mirsch, T., Lehrer, C., Jung, R: Making digital nudging applicable: the digital nudge design method. In: International Conference on Information Systems, pp. 1–16 (2018)
6. Schwartz, P.M.: Property, privacy, and personal data. Harv. L. Rev. **117**(7) 2056 (2003)
7. Paul, P., Integrating trust in electronic commerce with the technology acceptance model: model development and validation. In: AMCIS 2001 Proceedings. vol. 159 (2001)
8. Potthoff, T.; Meske, C.: The DINU-model – a process model for the design of nudges. In: 23rd European Conference on Information Systems (ECIS), pp. 2587–2597. Portugal (2017)
9. Schöbel, S.; Barev, T.J.; Janson, A.; Hupfeld, F., Leimeister, J.M.: Understanding user preferences of digital privacy nudges – a best-worst scaling Approach. In: Hawaii International Conference on System Sciences (HICSS) (2020)
10. Spiekermann, S.: Ethical IT Innovation: A Value-Based System Design Approach, 1st edn. CRC Press, USA, Florida (2015)
11. Sunstein, C.: Nudges that fail. Behavioural. Public Policy **1**(1), 4–25 (2017)
12. Thaler, R.H., Sunstein, C.R.: Nudge. Int'l. Penguin Books, London (2009)
13. vom Brocke, J., Simons, A., Riemer, K., Niehaves, B., Plattfaut, R., Cleven, A.: Standing on the Shoulders of Giants: Challenges and Recommendations of Literature Search in Information Systems Research. In: CAIS 37 (2015)
14. Vaishnavi V. and Kuechler W.: Design science research in information systems. AISNet. In: Association for Information Systems. USA (2004)
15. Venable J.R., Pries-Heje R., Baskerville R.: FEDS: a framework for evaluation in design science research. IS Technol. **25**(1), 77–89 (2016). Springer, Berlin
16. Webster, J., Watson, R.T.: Analyzing the past to prepare for the future: writing a literature review. MIS Q. **26**(2), 13–23 (2002)
17. Weinmann, M., Schneider, C., vom Brocke, J.: Digital nudging: guiding online user choices through interface design. Commun. ACM **61**(7), (2018)
18. Weinmann, M., Schneider, C., vom Brocke, J.: Digital nudging. Bus. Inform. Syst. Eng. **58**(6), 433–436 (2016). https://doi.org/10.1007/s12599-016-0453-1
19. Sun, Y., Kantor, P.B.: Cross-Evaluation: a new model for information system evaluation. J. Am. Soc. Inf. Sci. Technol. **57**(5), 614–628 (2006)

Enabling Design-Integrated Assessment of Service Business Models Through Factor Refinement

Jürgen Anke[(⊠)] [ID]

Faculty of Computer Science/Mathematics, HTW Dresden, 01069 Dresden, Germany
juergen.anke@htw-dresden.de

Abstract. Business Model Innovation is a complex task, which requires creativity and is often performed in interdisciplinary workshop settings. To support this, practical techniques have been developed, e.g. the Business Model Canvas (BMC). It has been found that assessing financial and non-financial effects of the current business model (BM) design likely influences design decisions. However, such an assessment is difficult to integrate into the design process. Business model development tools (BMDT) are an emerging category of software, which supports business model innovation. While they have the potential to shorten the feedback cycles between the design and assessment of BMs, there is little design knowledge available on this integration. In this paper, we introduce the factor refinement approach, which establishes a link between models for the canvas-based BM design and information for their assessment on factor level. The concept is made actionable in a tool prototype, which has been found to be practically applicable in a demonstration. With that, we contribute to the design knowledge for BMDTs particularly regarding the design-integrated assessment of BMs. While our tool uses the service business model canvas, the factor refinement concept is transferable to extend other canvas-based BMDTs with assessment functionality as well.

Keywords: Service business models · Business model assessment · Business model design tools · Prototyping

1 Introduction

Smart products can sense their condition and surroundings, allow for real-time data collection, communication and feedback, and thereby enable the provision of smart services [1, 2]. Providers of such services can utilize business models to describe "the value logic of an organization in terms of creating and capturing customer value" [3]. Fostered by a service-based change in value creation [4], business models are also discussed in service research [3, 5]. Because of their characteristics, representations for service business models (SBM) differ from representations for traditional business models [5, 6]. A service-specific representation is the Service Business Model Canvas (SBMC) [5]. It is based on the well-known Business Model Canvas (BMC) [7] but

© Springer Nature Switzerland AG 2020
S. Hofmann et al. (Eds.): DESRIST 2020, LNCS 12388, pp. 394–406, 2020.
https://doi.org/10.1007/978-3-030-64823-7_38

highlights the integration of different actors within an SBM and thus, allows focusing on the co-creation in the business logic.

One of the key characteristics of component-based business model representations is their qualitative nature, which is suitable for developing and refining the business logic of an idea [5, 8]. However, to justify internal funding of innovation projects, an assessment of the planned service is required [9]. To this end, various cost items for service provision must be considered as well as savings through process improvements and revenues through additional offers to customers. Other aspects of a BM are qualitative, such as strategic relevance or non-financial benefits, especially for innovative offers. Assessing these factors in the early stages is valuable for deciding on which SBM idea should be pursued further [9]. Furthermore, it was found that determining cost and benefits has a high potential to influence BM design decisions and should, therefore, be part of an iterative BM design process [10]. To support this task, the software category "business model development tool" (BMDT) has emerged. Their functionality was recently systematized in a taxonomy by Szopinski et al. [11]. Out of the 30 tools covered, only four support both financial and non-financial assessment [11].

Nowadays, many business decisions including financial planning are performed with the help of spreadsheets like MS Excel [12]. Spreadsheets work well if the structure of the model is known and stable. However, in BM design, model elements are frequently added, removed or modified [11]. Thus, the content and structure of the spreadsheet, e.g. cell values, references, and formulas, would have to be adapted whenever changes occur, e.g. new decisions on prices, offers, cost, and quantities are made. Such a spreadsheet model evolution is an erroneous task, as the manageability of spreadsheets has found to be limited [13]. Consequently, if spreadsheets are used, the assessment will not take place before the business model is relatively stable. This delays important insights, which in turn could influence the BM design [10]. Further-more, users must develop spreadsheet models on their own and manually transfer all financially relevant information from the business model into the spreadsheet.

Therefore, the goal of this research (problem statement) is to *design a solution, which allows shortening the feedback cycle between design and assessment of service business models, as well as reducing the manual effort and sources of error associated with it.* To address this problem, we envision a web-based collaborative tool, which supports BMI for smart services by interactively capturing the design and assessment of relevant information and instantly shows the impact of changes made by the users.

2 Related Work

There are two streams of related research: (1) approaches and tools for the assessment of BMs and (2) the mapping of BMC structures to other models. Kayaoglu [14] found that there is little previous work on the assessment of BMs. He proposes a hierarchical evaluation logic, which was implemented in a software tool. It provides recommendations on how to reach a defined business state but does not support canvas-based modeling [14]. Daas et al. [15] present a system that supports BM design decisions through market analysis, success factors, and comparison of design alternatives. However, it is based on Excel and due to its high complexity, it is unlikely to be suitable for collaborative business model design. Software tools for BM stress tests are proposed by Bouwman et al. [16]. They state that "[w]hen it comes to making informed management decisions with regard to financial aspects of alternative business models, there are hardly any tools available, specifically when multiple stakeholders and financial objectives are involved" [16, p. 19]. Turetken et al. propose a "Service-dominant business model radar" as part of a BM engineering framework [10]. Although it captures cost and benefits, it is a paper-based approach for workshops, which prevents instant calculations. Jesus and da Silva advocate the combination of financial projections with the BMC to support the design of viable BMs [17]. Their canvas-based tool provides profit and loss data as well as financial indicators such as break-even point. However, it is not disclosed how the BM and calculation schemes are linked, i.e. there is no meta-model.

The second research stream deals with the mapping of (S)BMC structures to other models. This includes budget planning [18], for which some of the BMC factors are mapped to positions of a financial budget. Another purpose is the mapping of the BMC to ArchiMate [19]. The authors argue that linking the BM with the enterprise model enables better migration from as-is to to-be architectures and a more realistic cost-benefit analysis. Also, the evaluation of business models using the business case method is proposed [20]. The authors do not provide a meta-model but suggest a process in which BMC alternatives are evaluated based on data gathered before, including financial and non-financial criteria [20]. Brussee and de Groot present an online tool which uses refined basic blocks of a BMC [21]. They do provide substructures to the BMC model, but their goal is to simplify experimentation rather than to support BM assessment. The use of attributes for financial calculation in a BMC was analyzed in [22], however without details on how these were implemented. Our own work includes a meta-model that links SBMC structures to models for the assessment of SBMs [23], which is empirically grounded in 28 cases of data-driven BMs. However, this meta-model does not support non-financial assessment and has not yet been demonstrated [23]. The approach of design-integrated assessment in the area of smart services has been proposed [24], but it is also limited to financial aspects and does not provide a representation of SBMs.

In summary, we can state that BM assessment and its tool-support has been identified as a relevant problem. Only a few of the existing tools in practice [11] provide support for financial and non-financial assessment. Some academic works deal with the mapping of the BMC to other models for various purposes. To the best of our knowledge, there is no research on how to apply a meta-model in a BMDT for design-integrated assessment of service business models.

3   Research Goal and Method

Our research goal is to explore the applicability of the factor refinement concept for design-integrated assessment of service business models in BMDTs. For that, we apply the design science research (DSR) process according to Peffers et al. [25], which contains the following steps: First, the requirements for the envisioned tool are derived from the problem statement and the key concepts are defined. Second, we present the input knowledge for the solution to be designed, including an existing meta-model for a cost-benefit analysis of SBMs [23]. Third, we describe the software prototype and the rationale behind its design decisions. For its demonstration, we asked test users to complete a set of tasks using the tool prototype. Afterward, they rate a set of statements in a questionnaire to assess their experience. The discussion of results is used to derive changes for the next iteration of the tool. This paper is structured along the six core dimensions of DSR [26]. Table 1 provides an overview of these dimensions along with their use in the study at hand and the respective paper section.

Table 1. Structure of the DSR project according to [26]

Dimension	Usage in our study	Sect.
Problem	Lack of integration between the design and assessment of BM prevents short feedback cycles in the business model innovation process	1
Input knowledge	SBMC [5], tool-based financial projections of a BMC [17], meta-model for SBMC assessment [23], design-integrated assessment [24]	2
Research process	Derive Requirements from problem statement; extend existing meta-model; design and build tool prototype, demonstrate the prototype	3
Key concepts	SBMC; factor refinement; cost-benefit analysis; impact-effort matrix	4
Solution description	A web-based tool BMDT allowing the refinement of SBMC factors with assessment information based on a meta-model	5
Output knowledge	Applicability of factor refinement as an approach for design-integrated assessment of SBMs in BMDTs	6

4 Solution Design

Requirements. From the problem statement given in Sect. 1, we can derive functional requirements (FR) and quality requirements (QR) for the envisioned tool (Table 2). To enable short feedback cycles between business model design and assessment, the tool needs to capture information on both aspects (FR1, FR2). Similarly, while the relevance of financial assessment has been stated [9], some aspects cannot be quantified in monetary terms and therefore require a strategic assessment (FR3). The target groups for the use of our tool are individuals or teams (FR4), which are given the task to develop or improve service business models. This is a highly creative task [27], which calls for easily comprehensible tools (QR1-3). Similar to process modeling tools [28], high usability is expected to drive acceptance, especially for interdisciplinary teams.

Key Concepts. An SBMC is divided into three *perspectives*, namely Customer, Company and Partner [5]. In each perspective, there are the seven *dimensions* (building blocks) of the BMC as defined by Osterwalder [7]: cost structure, key activities, key resources,

Table 2. Requirements for the SBM assessment tool

ID	Requirement	Source
FR1	The tool must allow the capture of BM design decisions	[10]
FR2	The tool must allow the capture of BM assessment-relevant information	[10]
FR3	The tool must support financial and strategic assessment	[9, 11]
FR4	The tool should support collaborative work	[11, 27]
QR1	The capture of design information must be usable intuitively	[28]
QR2	The capture of assessment information must be usable intuitively	[28]
QR3	The presentation of the assessment results must be easily comprehensible	[28]

value proposition, customer segment, channel, and revenue streams. When working with an SMBC, the users adds, removes or shifts sticky notes ("Post-Its") to design the new SBM. These items are called *factors* [23]. For the assessment, this structure must be augmented with additional information. We propose the name *factor refinement* for the concept of adding assessment information to factors.

In general, qualitative and quantitative assessment criteria for BMs can be distinguished. Based on empirical data, three different types of quantitative criteria were identified in [23]: costs, revenues, and savings. In general, cost refers to the financial effort required to build and operate a service system that enables an SBM. For all effects created by the investment project at hand, monetary values must be assigned. Benefits can be either revenue or savings, e.g. through improved process efficiency. To support decision making on whether a service provider should proceed with the engineering and implementation of a new SBM or not, a simplified *cost-benefit analysis* (CBA) can be performed to assess the economic value of an investment project [29].

Several effects, especially in the relationship and channels dimensions, are qualitative, i.e. they cannot be translated directly to a countable metric. However, they could still be important for the assessment of the SBMC at hand. For example, a key activity might be real-time data analytics. If it has a high impact on a new business model and the service provider requires little effort to provide it, it is apparently beneficial. A simple instrument for a non-financial assessment is the *impact-effort matrix* (IEM) [30]. It allows prioritizing items based on a qualitative ranking of effort and impact using a qualitative rank of low, medium and high for each factor. Afterward, a consolidated score can be calculated for each dimension to allow for an overall non-financial assessment of an SBM.

Meta-model for SBMC Factor Refinements. To facilitate BM assessment through factor refinement in a BMDT, we adapt a meta-model [23] that links SBMC factors to CBA and IEM. The meta-model used for the prototype is provided as a UML class diagram (Fig. 1). Classes represent domain concepts and their attributes. Relations are expressed using associations, which can be qualified with multiplicities to show how many instances of one class can be related to another class. Compared to the original model [23], the Non-Financial class was added. It uses the QualRank enumeration to express different levels of impact and effort. Additionally, the modeling of Cost was slightly simplified by focusing only on manually added cost items. The overall results for the assessments are stored in attributes of a `Project`. They are calculated from a series of payments (represented by a set of `Project-Years`), which in turn contain derived attributes for revenue, cost, and savings.

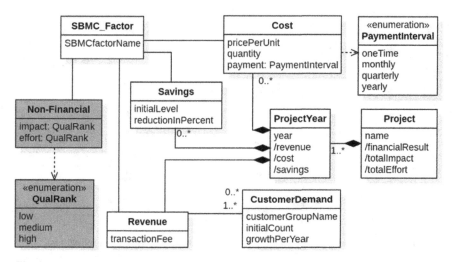

Fig. 1. Subset of the adapted meta-model from [23] (new elements are highlighted in gray)

Development of a Prototype. To demonstrate the concept of factor refinement, a working web-based proto-type[1] was implemented using Axure RP 8. Here, we present design decisions, their rationale, and reference to requirements (Table 2). For simplicity, the tool has only two main views: editor and report. Users can switch between them at any time using the two buttons at the bottom of the screen. The screen layout of the editor is identical to the SBMC, to make it easily comprehensible for those familiar with the SBMC (QR1). New factors can be added using "+"-sign, as it established in most web applications nowadays (FR1). Factors are displayed as boxes to resemble post-it notes as known from paper-based canvases (QR1). Clicking on a factor opens a dialog where users can refine the factor into either cost, revenue, savings or non-financial (FR2). Selecting one of the options allows entering further information to describe the refinement according to the meta-model (Fig. 2).

All inputs are aggregated in a reporting sheet (Fig. 3) for the focal company, i.e. the service provider. The report view contains both financial and non-financial assessment (FR2). All calculations are performed based on the data entered by the user. Financial data are shown in the categories cost, savings and revenues; and separated into one-time invest and recurring cash-flows. For each category, the total amount is shown. The factors contributing to the total amount can be shown/hidden using a plus/minus sign next to the sum (Fig. 3). The result of the non-financial assessment is displayed in a color-coded matrix, with all contributing factors listed below. We assume that this representation is familiar to users who know both the IEM and financial cases (QR3).

---

[1] Accessible at https://yc8uyf.axshare.com/sbmc_editor.html, tested with Firefox and MS Edge.

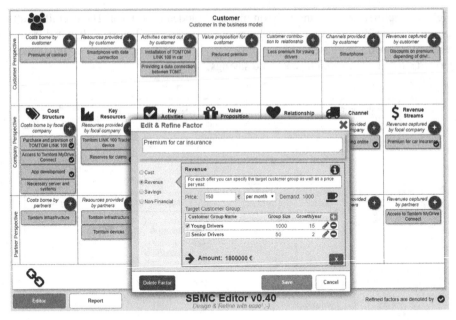

Fig. 2. The prototype showing the usage-based insurance BM and a refinement

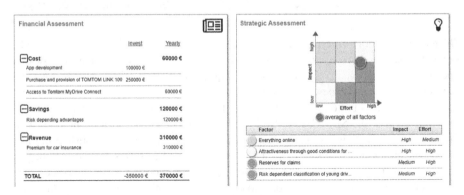

Fig. 3. Reporting view of the prototype

Being a prototype, the tool does have limited functionality. First, it does not persist any data between sessions yet. Second, there are currently no measures for collaborative work (FR4), such as users, permissions, and workspaces [11]. Finally, the reporting does not distinguish between customer, company, and partner perspectives, as the prototype is focused on the perspective of the (focal) company, i.e. the service provider. While these features are required for real-world applicability, their absence does not impede the goal of demonstrating the concept of factor refinement. Whether the approach of collecting assessment information by refining factors is intuitively usable (QR2) was not known during the design and had to be considered in the demonstration.

5   Demonstration

Case. The focus of the demonstration is to assess the feasibility and efficacy of the artifact in one case and can be seen as a "weak form of evaluation" [31]. We chose a real, anonymized case, as real cases provide higher external validity [31]. The case deals with usage-based insurance (UBI), which extends the traditional car insurance business model through data-based elements. These are gathered through sensors in the car [32]. The insurer can process data about the driving behavior to assess the risk of a specific driver and to adjust the premium. If the driver is driving carefully, the insurer offers discounts up to 25% of the monthly premium. The more aggressively the insurant drives, the less discount he or she will get. Hence, from a customer perspective, this SBM provides an opportunity to reduce the premium of the car insurance. The insurer provides a vehicle tracking device that must be installed into the car. This device is connected via Bluetooth to the customer's smartphone. All necessary data are transmitted to the insurer using a dedicated application. We consider this case as suitable, as it represents an innovative SBM to which many people can relate.

Setup. To gain an understanding of how the factor refinement approach is perceived by real users, we used the "thinking aloud" test for formative feedback. This is a method for usability testing and has successfully been applied for evaluating the work with the SBMC [33]. For the test, individual users are given a list of ten tasks, which are to be completed using the tool as proposed by [31]. Nine tasks require the refinement of factors and one refers to the interpretation of the report. As preparation, we showed the participants a short video, which introduces the SBMC, the exemplary case and the basic functions of the tool. The actual test was conducted using an online application sharing platform, which allowed us to see and hear what participants did while they processed the tasks. All sessions were recorded for further analysis. After completion of the tasks, participants were asked to fill out an online questionnaire to rate their experience. It contained a list of statements (see Table 4), to which the participants could express their opinion on a Likert scale from 1 (strongly disagree) to 5 (strongly agree).

The demonstration was conducted with 11 participants, consisting of seasoned business modeling experts and newcomers to the field, who are equally potential users. The sample included four researchers in the area of digital transformation, two practitioners with considerable experience in IT-driven BMI, and five master's students in information systems with first work experience in the IT and telco industries.

Results. To analyze the test results, a "degree of completion" indicator was defined with five levels: (1) correct perspective found, (2) correct dimension found, (3) correct factor found, (4) correct refinement type chosen, and (5) data for refinement entered correctly. The result of this analysis is provided in Table 3, along with the refinement type, which is either cost, revenue (Rev), savings (Sav) or non-financial (NF).

The results of the survey are shown in Table 4. Although the number of participants is low, we still can derive some initial findings from it. First, there is a strong indication that the tool was not only helpful for the tasks assigned to them (S2) but they also prefer it over Excel (S3) which is typically used for such tasks. Furthermore, participants indicated almost unanimously that assessment of BMs models should be tool supported (S4). Therefore, we can conclude that the efficacy and utility of the tool are considered as positive within this sample of users. This is supported by statement S5, in which

Table 3. Average degree of completion for tasks (N = 11, SD: Standard Deviation)

Task	T1	T2	T3	T4	T5	T6	T7	T8	T9
Refinement type	Cost	Cost	Rev	Rev	Cost	Cost	Sav	NF	NF
Mean	3.4	4.0	2.4	1.6	5.0	4.8	3.4	4.1	5.0
SD	1.6	1.3	2.3	2.0	0.0	0.6	1.2	1.9	0.0

respondents expressed that they understood the concept of refinement (fulfills QR2). As for the model, the results indicate that the refinement possibilities are not considered as too complex (S6). However, the results also show that at least for some users important input possibilities for the assessment were missing. Further research is required on whether this is due to a deficit of the model or usability deficits in the tool prototype. The reporting (S8-S10) is generally understood, however, there is considerable variance in the replies, which also requires further analysis.

Table 4. Statements and rating results (N = 11, SD: Standard Deviation)

General statements regarding the task		Mean	SD
S1	I understand the example case of Usage-Based Insurance (UBI)	4.6	0.6
S2	The tool helped me evaluate the UBI case	4.3	0.7
S3	I would have preferred to evaluate the business model using Excel	1.8	0.7
S4	The assessment of business models generally requires tool support	4.2	0.6
Suitability of the assessment approach		Mean	SD
S5	I have understood the concept of refining factors	4.6	0.5
S6	The possibilities for refining factors are too complex	1.7	0.4
S7	I missed important input possibilities for the assessment	2.5	1.2
Assessment results/reporting view in the tool prototype		Mean	SD
S8	I have understood the results of the financial assessment	3.9	0.8
S9	I have understood the results of the non-financial assessment	4.4	1.0
S10	I find the possibility of a non-financial assessment useful	4.5	1.2

6   Discussion

Interpretation of Results. As the results show, the highest degree of completion was achieved for tasks that referred to cost or non-financial refinements. Savings and Revenue refinements were less well understood. Some of the participants had difficulties in finding the correct factor for refinement. Misjudgments were mostly caused by insufficient knowledge on insurance terminology or problems to fully comprehend the structure of the case but also by minor bugs in the tool. Future tests should also contain tasks for the design of the SBM, not just the refinement of factors for assessment. With that, we expect users to understand the structure of the business model better than with a predefined one. **Limitations.** The results of our study are limited by several factors. First, the tool was not designed with the help of UI/UX specialists. An optimized experience would probably have helped some of the users in our sample in completing their tasks. Second, the number of participants in the demonstration was relatively low, which reduces the generalizability of results. Also choosing UBI as the case for the evaluation could have influenced the results as some of the participants might be impaired by insufficient knowledge on insurance terminology. **Next Iteration.** In the next iteration of the tool, we plan to include the modeling of offers with devices, data points, data transmission, and external services (as provided in the original meta-model [23]) to support the specifics of smart services. Furthermore, we plan to assess each perspective separately, which makes value co-creation between customer and provider as well as provider and partner transparent. **Approach for Evaluation.** The initially stated objective of shorter feedback cycles will be subject to an artifact evaluation. Employing the tool aims to improve effectiveness in the BMI process and to obtain better results. An approach, similar to [24], is to measure this in an experiment, where two groups in a workshop are given the same BMI task. The experimental group is given the tool prototype, and the control group uses Excel. After a specified time, the results are compared. Potential measures include the number of iterations, a subjective rating of utility by the participants, or a comparison of the designed business models regarding their viability by external experts.

7   Conclusion

The high complexity and qualitative nature of SBMs make their assessment difficult during design. While instruments for financial decision making, like NPV, are well established, their link to the structures of BMs is barely discussed in the literature. Furthermore, they are typically conducted using spreadsheets. These are not suitable for design-integrated BM assessment, where the level of detail is low and design changes are frequent. The integration of BM assessment into BMDTs appears to be a much more promising strategy as recognized by a taxonomy on BMDT functionality [11].

Our proposed tool targets BMI for smart services. It builds on the SBMC and thus follows a canvas-based approach, which is popular in practice [11]. It uses a meta-model that links the qualitative dimensions of the SBMC and established methods for assessing BMs. To make this link usable for BMDTs, we introduced the concept of factor refinement. It allows adding assessment-related information to each factor placed on an

SBMC. The demonstration of the tool prototype that implements this concept showed that particularly tasks regarding the refinement of factors with cost and non-financial aspects were successfully completed. The factor refinement concept has been found to be generally understood by the participants, which is the key prerequisite for ultimately achieving feedback cycle reduction between BM design and assessment.

The integrated meta-model in our approach provides a theoretical contribution as it helps researchers by promoting the understanding of assessment dependencies in SBM innovation processes. Specifically, it contributes to the body of knowledge as follows: (1) We extend the canvas-based modeling [17, 22] through an explicit meta-model of the connection between BMC elements and assessment instruments. Our approach furthermore adds non-financial assessment and support for SBMs. (2) The concept of factor refinement shows, how a meta-model can be made usable for BM assessment in BMDTs [11]. It combines canvas-based design, refinement, and instant assessment feedback and therefore transfers the idea of design-integrated assessment [24] to SBMs. (3) Our proposed solution complements the process of data collection with the business case approach for BM assessment [20]. Providing data from SBMs directly might streamline the process of comparing BM alternatives. This work provides a practical contribution for BMDT developers by demonstrating how a meta-model enables the mapping of BMs factors and assessment models can be integrated into a software tool.

Future research should focus on the interplay of meta-model and tool: First, a good balance must be found between simplicity to facilitate quick adaptations of the model and expressiveness of the result to make informed decisions on whether to pursue the service idea further. Second, the meta-model should be modularized to integrate other assessment schemes and reuse existing pricing models for external services (e.g. cloud providers) more easily. Third, it can be observed that in SBMs, factors are related to each other, e.g. the revenue of the service provider is the cost borne by the customer. By including such relations in the meta-model, designing new SBMs would be simplified. Finally, the integration and utility of an SBMC assessment tool in the overall engineering process for service business model innovation is an open question. Hence, further research is needed to understand their effectiveness for designing and managing different types of service business models [34].

References

1. Allmendinger, G., Lombreglia, R.: Four strategies for the age of smart services. Harvard Bus. Rev. **83**, 131 (2005)
2. Wuenderlich, N.V., et al.: "Futurizing" smart service. Implications for service researchers and managers. J. Serv. Mark. **29**, 442–447 (2015)
3. Fielt, E.: Business Service Management. Understanding Business Models (2011)
4. Grönroos, C.: Adopting a service business logic in relational business-to-business marketing. Otago Forum **2**, 269–287 (2008)
5. Zolnowski, A.: Analysis and Design of Service Business Models (2015)
6. Ojasalo, K., Ojasalo, J.: Adapting business model thinking to service logic. an empirical study on developing a service design tool. THE NORDIC SCHOOL, vol. 309 (2015)
7. Osterwalder, A., Pigneur, Y.: Business model generation. A Handbook for Visionaries Game Changers and Challengers. Wiley, Hoboken, NJ (2010)

8. Zott, C., Amit, R., Massa, L.: The business model. Theoretical roots, recent development, and future research. J. Manage. **37**, 1019–1042 (2011)
9. Tesch, J.F., Brillinger, A.-S., Bilgeri, D.: Internet of things business model innovation and the stage-gate process. an exploratory analysis. Int. J. Innov. Mgt. **21** (2017)
10. Turetken, O., Grefen, P., Gilsing, R., Adali, O.E.: Service-dominant business model design for digital innovation in smart mobility. Bus. Inform. Syst. Eng. **61**(1), 9–29 (2018). https://doi.org/10.1007/s12599-018-0565-x
11. Szopinski, D., Schoormann, T., John, T., Knackstedt, R., Kundisch, D.: Software tools for business model innovation: current state and future challenges. Electron. Mark. **30**(3), 469–494 (2019). https://doi.org/10.1007/s12525-018-0326-1
12. Grossman, T.A., Mehrotra, V., Özlük, Ö.: Lessons from mission-critical spreadsheets. Commun. Assoc. Inform. Syst. **20**, 60 (2007)
13. Reschenhofer, T., Matthes, F.: An empirical study on spreadsheet shortcomings from an information systems perspective. In: Abramowicz, W. (ed.) BIS 2015. LNBIP, vol. 208, pp. 50–61. Springer, Cham (2015). https://doi.org/10.1007/978-3-319-19027-3_5
14. Kayaoglu, N.: A Generic Approach for Dynamic Business Model Evaluation (2013)
15. Daas, D., Hurkmans, T., Overbeek, S., Bouwman, H.: Developing a decision support system for business model design. Electron. Mark. **23**, 251–265 (2013)
16. Bouwman, W., et al.: Business models. Tooling and a research agenda. In: Bled eCommerce Conference (2012)
17. Jesus, D.M., Mira da Silva, M.: Financial Projections based on Business Model Canvas. In: Proceedings of the 19th IBIMA Conference (2012)
18. Dudin, M.N., Kutsuri, G.N., Fedorova, I.J.'e., Dzusova, S.S., Namitulina, A.Z.: The Innovative Business Model Canvas in the System of Effective Budgeting. ASS 11 (2015)
19. Iacob, M.E., Meertens, L.O., Jonkers, H., Quartel, D.A.C., Nieuwenhuis, L.J.M., van Sinderen, M.J.: From enterprise architecture to business models and back. Softw. Syst. Model. **13**(3), 1059–1083 (2012). https://doi.org/10.1007/s10270-012-0304-6
20. Meertens, L.O., Starreveld, Eelco., Iacob, M.-E., Nieuwenhuis, B.: Creating a business case from a business model. In: Shishkov, B. (ed.) BMSD 2013. LNBIP, vol. 173, pp. 46–63. Springer, Cham (2014). https://doi.org/10.1007/978-3-319-06671-4_3
21. Brussee, R., de Groot, Peter H.T.: An online tool for business modelling and a refinement of the business canvas. In: International Conference on University Industry Interaction (2016)
22. Fritscher, B., Pigneur, Y.: computer aided business model design: analysis of key features adopted by users. In: Sprague, R.H. (ed.) Proceedings of the 47th Annual Hawaii International Conference on System Sciences, pp. 3929–3938. IEEE, Piscataway, NJ (2014)
23. Zolnowski, A., Anke, J., Gudat, J.: Towards a cost-benefit-analysis of data-driven business models. In: 13th International Conference on Wirtschaftsinformatik (2017)
24. Anke, Jürgen: Design-integrated financial assessment of smart services. Electron. Mark. **29**(1), 19–35 (2018). https://doi.org/10.1007/s12525-018-0300-y
25. Peffers, K., Tuunanen, T., Rothenberger, M.A., Chatterjee, S.: A design science research methodology for information systems research. J. Manag. Inf. Syst. **24**, 45–77 (2007)
26. vom Brocke, J., Maedche, A.: The DSR grid: six core dimensions for effectively planning and communicating design science research projects. Electron. Mark. **29**(3), 379–385 (2019). https://doi.org/10.1007/s12525-019-00358-7
27. Eppler, M., Hoffmann, F., Bresciani, S.: New business models through collaborative idea generation. Int. J. Innov. Mgt. **15**, 1323–1341 (2011)
28. Becker, J., Clever, N., Holler, J., Shitkova, M.: Towards a Usability Measurement Framework for Process Modelling Tools. In: PACIS Proceedings (2013)
29. Boardman, A.E., Greenberg, D.H., Vining, A.R., Weimer, D.L.: Cost-benefit Analysis. Concepts and Practice. Cambridge University Press, Cambridge, New York (2018)

30. Gray, D.: Impact & Effort Matrix. http://thetoolkitproject.com/tool/impact-effort-matrix
31. Johannesson, P., Perjons, E. (eds.): An Introduction to Design Science. Springer (2014)
32. Desyllas, P., Sako, M.: Profiting from business model innovation. Evidence from Pay-As-You-Drive auto insurance. Res. Policy **42**, 101–116 (2013)
33. Zolnowski, A., Böhmann, T.: Formative evaluation of business model representations - the service business model canvas. In: 22nd European. Conference on Information Systems (2014)
34. Terrenghi, N., Schwarz, J., Legner, C., Eisert, U.: Business model management: current practices, required activities and IT support. In: 13th International Conference on Wirtschaftsinformatik (2017)

Engineering Industrial Service Systems: Design and Evaluation of System-Oriented Service Delivery

Clemens Wolff[(⊠)], Niklas Kühl, and Gerhard Satzger

Karlsruhe Service Research Institute and Institute of Information Systems
and Marketing, Karlsruhe Institute of Technology, Karlsruhe, Germany
{clemens.wolff,niklas.kuehl,gerhard.satzger}@kit.edu

Abstract. Driven through ever increasing cost pressure, service
providers rely on complex information and optimization systems to
increase their operational efficiency. Those systems, however, typically
optimize from a provider perspective and, thus, neglect potential for
cost reduction on the customer side. Therefore, current approaches to
increase operational efficiency result in an inefficient resource allocation
from a system's perspective. We address this issue by designing and
evaluating a novel method—system-oriented service delivery (SOSD).
We follow a stringent Design Science Research approach and ground our
work in an analysis of current practice as well as draw upon the kernel
theories of service system engineering and mechanism design. In addition
to evaluations for effectiveness and illustration, we perform a naturalistic
evaluation capturing expert feedback on the proposed method. Thus, we
contribute a new method with high practical potential to the service system engineering discipline as well as the industrial maintenance domain.
In addition, we explore reception in industry and further improvement
areas for future design cycles to improve SOSD's implementability.

Keywords: System-oriented service delivery · Industrial
maintenance · Service system engineering.

1 Introduction

Driven by outsourcing and the ongoing servitization (i.e. the provision of services instead of products) of the manufacturing business [1], many industrial
manufacturers have outsourced their maintenance activities to third-party maintenance providers. To realize economies of scale, those maintenance providers
offer similar—if not identical—services to multiple customers and share delivery
resources (e.g. technicians) among their customers [5]. Therefore, service delivery
of customers is not independent of each other. Instead, all system participants
influence each other, resulting in a dynamic service system setting [29, 42].

© Springer Nature Switzerland AG 2020
S. Hofmann et al. (Eds.): DESRIST 2020, LNCS 12388, pp. 407–419, 2020.
https://doi.org/10.1007/978-3-030-64823-7_39

Since efficient use of resources has been identified as a competitive advantage in industrial maintenance [22], maintenance providers heavily rely on complex information and optimization systems to increase their operational efficiency [12,27]. As this work shows, current optimization models typically focus on provider-oriented metrics, thus, implement *provider-oriented service delivery (POSD)*. Whilst POSD minimizes provider costs, it neglects potential for system-wide cost optimization by considering the customer side. In detail, maintenance customers face delivery-dependent costs due to the unavailability of their production equipment [39,49]. Even though this work at hand focuses on industrial maintenance as application domain, this phenomena is also present in other domains, as, for example, Software-, Infrastructure-, or Platform-as-a-Service offerings—thus, making this a domain-independent phenomena that needs to be addressed.

Following the Design Science Research (DSR) paradigm and building on the kernel theories of mechanism design and service system engineering, this work proposes *system-oriented service delivery (SOSD)* [48] as a resource allocation and service delivery approach aiming at optimizing total system costs, i.e. the sum of the provider's as well as customers' delivery-dependent costs. In addition, we evaluate the newly proposed approach and present findings from its evaluation episodes that lay the foundation for future work to build upon.

The structure of the remainder of this work follows common practice of DSR projects: Whereas we introduce our research design in Sect. 2, Sects. 3 and 4 highlight our findings from the relevance and rigor phase. The identified design requirements are summarized in Sect. 5 before the tentative design is introduced in Sect. 6. Finally, activities and findings from the evaluation phase are described in Sect. 7 and Sect. 8 concludes this work.

2   Research Design

As overall research design, we follow the DSR paradigm and conduct a first DSR cycle—which can further be build upon in future work. As suggested by

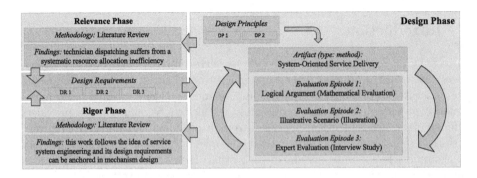

Fig. 1. Design science research approach of the first iteration

Hevner and Chaterjee [21], this cycle is characterized by three inherent phases, namely the rigor, relevance, and design phase. Within the design phase, we perform three evaluation episodes according to the Framework for Evaluation in Design Science (FEDS) [43]. Each of those evaluation episodes pursues an evaluation from a different perspective such that additional knowledge is derived. The overall research design is summarized in Fig. 1. The developed artifact of SOSD is best described as a *method*, since it consists of "actionable instructions that are conceptual" [36]. Furthermore—using the categorization of Gregor and Hevner [18]—the artifact is an *improvement*, as it is a new solution to the known problem of increased efficiency in field services.

3 Relevance Phase

To address the ever increasing cost pressure and to remain competitive, maintenance providers try to reduce their operational costs. Today, most maintenance providers pursue this through the introduction of complex information and optimization systems aimed at increasing operational efficiency [12,27]. From an academic perspective, those systems implement technician dispatching, which is the domain-specific resource allocation problem of industrial maintenance. In detail, technician dispatching is characterized by the timely assignment of spatially distributed technicians to spatially distributed maintenance tasks [46].

Optimization Objectives in Technician Dispatching: To better understand the objective functions in technician dispatching, we performed a structured literature review according to the guidelines provided by Webster and Watson [47] as well as Levy and Ellis [28]. After an initial pre-study, we decided to limit the search to the 39 peer-reviewed high quality operations research journals included in the three top categories (A+, A, B) of the JOURQUAL3 rating [44] by querying the following search term: *("technician" or "field service") and ("scheduling" or "dispatching")*. This query yielded 40 papers that were subsequently screened for relevance based on their abstract, reducing the set of relevant papers to 20. The remaining papers were then fully read and furthermore only considered relevant, if they contained a clear description of the optimization model and objective function deployed to perform technician dispatching. Through this step, three papers were removed, resulting in a set of 17 papers relevant for analysis.

Table 1 categorizes components considered relevant according to the objective functions of the identified technician dispatching optimization models. It shows that all optimization objectives are focused on provider metrics, hence, the conceptualization *provider-oriented service delivery (POSD)*. Out of the 17 optimization models presented in the papers, only two consider failure/opportunity costs of broken production equipment during resource allocation, i.e. costs occurring on the customer side. Those models were used in cases in which maintenance and technician dispatching was performed by an internal service organization, and, thus, considered relevant. Therefore, the main output of this literature

Table 1. Components of the objective function in technician dispatching

	Costs								Time-based			Others		
	Variable						Fixed							
	Travel	Outsourcing	Penalty (de-layed service)	Overtime	Failure costs (opportunity costs)	Assignment	Maintenance costs	Working	Remaining	Response time	Number tasks performed	Workload balance	Revenue
Blakeley et al. (2010) [2]	x		x									x	
Camci (2015) [6]				x			x						
Castillo-Salazar et al. (2016) [7]	x					x							
Cordeau et al. (2010) [9]										x			
Cortés et al. (2014) [10]	x		x										
Damm et al. (2016) [11]									x		x		
Froger et al. (2017) [14]			x										x
Froger et al. (2018) [15]			x										x
Hashimoto et al. (2011) [20]										x			
Iravan et al. (2017) [24]	x		x					x					
Iravan et al. (2019) [23]	x		x		x								
Kovacs et al. (2012) [26]	x	x											
Parragh and Doerner (2018) [35]	x	x											
Petrakis et al. (2012) [37]	x		x	x									
Xie et al. (2017) [50]	x	x											
Xu (2001) [51]									x		x		
Zamorano and Stolletz (2017) [52]	x		x	x									

review is that we did not find a single optimization model considering failure costs of the maintenance provider's customers—with the exception of contractually negotiated penalty payments if a service level is not met.

Identified Service Delivery Dilemma: The literature review has shown that maintenance providers implement POSD to address the ever increasing cost pressure. This approach, however, neglects delivery-dependent costs faced by customers [39,49]. Especially in reactive maintenance upon an unexpected failure, those costs are highly sensitive to the downtime duration [13,25]. Given that industrial maintenance is performed in a service system, POSD results in inefficient resource allocation from a system perspective and results in lost potential for cost savings on the customer side. Therefore, by systematically leveraging the potential for cost savings on the customer side, total costs can be reduced, thus, addressing the ever increasing cost pressure of maintenance providers.

4 Rigor Phase

In this section, we briefly introduce the kernel theories of service system engineering and mechanism design.

Service system engineering [3,4] builds on the basic understanding of service systems being complex socio-technical systems with multiple participants that enable value co-creation [29,42] and calls for "actionable knowledge for systematically designing, developing and piloting service systems" [3]. The authors further specify this by highlighting the importance of systematically engineering service architectures, service system interaction, as well as resource mobilization. Within such service systems, Satzger and Kieninger [40] argue that "partners in these systems are supposed to jointly manage the resources [...] that allow for maximization of their individual values". The implications are evident: Since industrial maintenance is performed in a service system, all system participants could benefit from jointly maximizing the system's overall value.

Mechanism design, on the other hand, is a sub-field of economic theory that is interested in engineering market mechanisms such that participants behave as desired to achieve an overall objective [31]. According to Parkes [34], such desired objectives are individual rationality (i.e. no participant is worse-off through participating), incentive compatibility (i.e. participants have an incentive to behave truthfully) and allocation efficiency (i.e. resource allocation is system-optimal). Furthermore, for a mechanism to be sustainable in the long run, it needs to be budget balanced [30]. In other words, the in- and outgoing payments of the mechanisms cancel each other out. Ideally, one designs a mechanism that fulfills all above mentioned properties, however, it has been shown that this is impossible in the presence of quasi-linear utilization functions [17]. Hence, when designing a mechanism, one must trade-off between the different objectives. The well celebrated Vickrey-Clarke-Grove mechanism [8,19,45], for example, is efficient and incentive compatible, but not budget balanced. Since technician dispatching and its generalization of resource allocation are mechanisms, mechanism design provides the theoretical background for this work. Furthermore, it gives guidelines for important properties that should be incorporated by a mechanism.

Thus, whilst the basic idea of optimizing resource allocation from a system perspective follows service system engineering, mechanism design provides concrete characteristics and requirements for an allocation mechanism.

5 Derived Design Requirements

Service delivery is based on resource allocation, which is an allocation mechanism. Thus, we aim at incorporating the desired mechanism properties, as defined by mechanism design. Since we must trade-off different mechanism properties, we argue that system efficiency, individual rationality, and budget balance are more important than incentive compatibility. Whilst system efficiency corresponds to the objective of this work, budget balance and individual rationality are mandatory for the adoption of any solution in practice. In detail, without budget balance, a mechanism cannot sustain in the long run and without individual rationality, participants would not participate in the mechanism in the first place. Whilst we acknowledge that incentive compatibility is an important property as well, we argue that it is less important than the others. To that end, however, the impact of this decision should be researched further. Thus, we derive the following design requirements (DRs) that need to be fulfilled by the tentative design:

- DR1: The developed mechanism should be system efficient
- DR2: The developed mechanism should be individually rational
- DR3: The developed mechanism should be budget balanced

6   Tentative Design

Driven by the understanding of a single holistic service system, we propose *system-oriented service delivery (SOSD)* as an overarching mechanism and novel approach for service delivery in service systems [48]. In detail, SOSD differs from POSD through two core modifications that correspond to two design principles, as shown in Table 2: system cost optimization (DP1) and a monetary compensation and benefit distribution mechanism (DP2). Whilst system efficiency (DR1) and individual rationality (DR2) are solely addressed by system cost optimization (DP1) and the monetary compensation and benefit distribution mechanism (DP2), respectively, budget balance (DR3) is jointly addressed by DP1 and DP2.

Table 2. Design principles

DP	Description	Addressed DRs
DP1	System cost optimization	DR1 & DR3
DP2	Monetary compensation and benefit distribution mechanism	DR2 & DR3

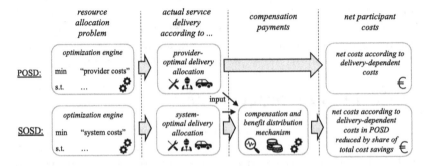

Fig. 2. System-oriented service delivery

Overall, the functioning of SOSD is depicted in Fig. 2. Given a well-defined resource allocation problem, the central planner performs resource allocation twice, once following the current allocation objective (e.g. minimize provider costs) and once following system cost optimization, i.e. minimize system costs. Whilst service is delivered according to the system-optimal resource allocation, the provider-optimal resource allocation is only required as input for the compensation and benefit distribution mechanism. In detail, to account for additional delivery-dependent costs for participants through the shift in service delivery, the compensation and benefit distribution mechanism computes payments received or made by individual participants through a three-step process: First, the monetary benefit or loss through system cost optimization is calculated for each participant (i.e. the cost difference between the provider- and system-optimal resource allocation). Second, based on those calculations, the cumulative benefits are reallocated among participants to compensate any individual losses, and, third, the remaining monetary benefit is distributed among all system participants. In other words, it ensures that no system participant has higher costs through the proposed changes, and, if the remaining monetary benefit is distributed equally, that all system participants have the same net advantage. Therefore, SOSD allows for cost reduction compared to POSD.

7 Design Evaluation

To evaluate the tentative design and gain additional knowledge on how to address the identified research objective, we conduct three evaluation episodes according to FEDS [43], as displayed in Fig. 3. Evaluation episodes one and two are dashed in the figure, since we refer to previous work by Wolff et al. [48] for them. The first evaluation episode focuses on demonstrating SOSD's superiority over POSD and the fulfillment of the derived DRs. Thus, it aims at evaluating the effectiveness of SOSD. The objective of the second evaluation episode is the illustration of SOSD. Thus, using an industrial maintenance illustrative scenario, we apply SOSD. Finally, in evaluation episode three, we evaluate SOSD from a practical perspective with regard to its usability and challenges associated to its introduction in industrial maintenance.

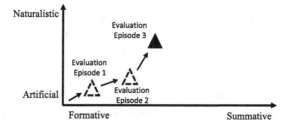

Fig. 3. Evaluation Episodes according to FEDS

7.1   Evaluation Episodes 1 and 2: Effectiveness and Illustration of SOSD

For the first and second evaluation episodes, we rely on previous work by Wolff et al. [48]. In detail, through an analytical logic argumentation [36], the authors demonstrate that SOSD is a Pareto improvement over POSD, since the costs of the entire system as well as of any individual participant in SOSD cannot exceed their costs in POSD. Therefore, SOSD is also budget balanced. Thus, the design requirements are addressed through the design principles. Furthermore, Wolff et al. [48] demonstrate the utility and applicability of SOSD in industrial maintenance using an illustrative scenario [36].

7.2   Evaluation Episode 3: Usability of SOSD

After demonstrating that SOSD is superior to POSD from a theoretical perspective, we now evaluate the usability of SOSD in industrial maintenance. To that end, we perform an interview study with experts from industry as expert evaluation [36]. In the following, we explain the applied methodology and discuss the derived findings.

Methodology: To evaluate SOSD from an industry perspective, we conducted several semi-structured expert interviews followed by a qualitative analysis [38]. To capture the perspectives of different roles within the sphere of industrial maintenance, we followed a mixed sampling approach combining the *criterion-i* and *maximum variation* sampling approaches [33]. In detail, whilst *criterion-i* emphasizes a common criterion among interviewed experts (domain expertise in this case), *maximum variation* emphasizes variation among experts (roles within industrial maintenance in this case). Furthermore, we also included one case of an IT software provider that offers an optimization engine for technician dispatching. Overall, the selection of cases and their respective role within the industrial maintenance ecosystem are displayed in Table 3. Note that for case Epsilon a group interview with two experts was conducted. The interviews were either conducted in person or via telephone. Following common practice, the interviews were summarized and categorized before the analysis [41].

Findings: Whilst all experts expressed their interest and did perceive the idea of SOSD as meaning- and useful, they also provided helpful comments as to the implementation of SOSD in practice as well as areas for further research. In the following, we highlight the most important findings, which can be divided into three main groups: delivery-dependent costs, transparency and trust among system participants, as well as computational complexity of SOSD.

First, all experts expressed their concern whether manufacturers are able to determine their costs of downtime (i.e. delivery-dependent costs in reactive maintenance) accurately. Indeed, both experts from a manufacturing case (Gamma,

Delta) acknowledged that they currently are not able to provide such information. Both stated that their companies do have cost of downtime estimates, which, however, are not incident-specific. Instead, those estimates are based on the average cost of downtime independent of the actual incident. Incident-specific costs, however, are necessary to leverage the full potential of SOSD. In addition, even if customers knew those costs accurately, in four out of five cases (Alpha, Beta, Gamma, Epsilon) the experts expressed concerns whether customers would share such sensitive data. The second group of remarks centers around trust in such service system. Whilst the experts acknowledged that value is created through collaboration and sharing benefits and losses with other participants in SOSD, they also mentioned that they would not simply trust such a system. In three out of five cases (Alpha, Delta, Epsilon), the experts explicitly mentioned the lack of trust as a reason for the failure of SOSD. That said, there also seemed to be a common understanding that transparent communication with regard to the compensation and benefit distribution mechanism is crucial. The experts stated that extensive information on whether a customer is delayed or prioritized in SOSD compared to a POSD solution would greatly increase the acceptance probability of SOSD in practice. In addition, experts of some cases (Alpha, Gamma, Epsilon) fear that some participants may behave strategically to increase their own payoff at the expense of others (e.g. through intentionally falsely providing their delivery-dependent costs). Finally, the remarks in the third group are more of a mathematical nature and were purely made by the expert of case Beta. This is no surprise, given their background in providing an optimization platform for routing in technician dispatching. In detail, the expert mentioned his concerns with regard to the mathematical complexity of SOSD. Technician dispatching is one of the most complex optimization problems to solve and for SOSD it needs to be solved twice in order to compute the compensation and benefit distribution payments, once provider- and once system-optimal. Furthermore, the expert also expressed concerns with regard to computing the hypothetical provider-optimal solution in such a highly dynamic and uncertain environment. He fears that the computed, real world system-optimal solution may not be comparable with a hypothetical provider-optimal solution.

Table 3. Overview of interviewed experts

Case	Company	Role	System role
Alpha	Component manufacturer	Head of service	Maintenance provider
Beta	Software provider	Senior consultant	Platform provider
Gamma	Manufacturer	Head of maintenance	Maintenance customer
Delta	Manufacturer	Process engineer	Maintenance customer
Epsilon	Equipment manufacturer	Service process manager & Team lead: IoT services	Maintenance provider

Overall, the interview study reveals that industry experts see great merit in SOSD, however, do not feel that it is yet ready to be implemented in practice. Thus, additional research is required. Furthermore, in order to support and justify continuous effort in the development of SOSD, estimates about possible cost savings through SOSD are necessary. Following the idea of DSR, the gained knowledge through this evaluation episode will guide further development of the tentative design in future iterations. This research has shown that it is of utmost importance to enable manufacturers to determine their delivery-dependent costs to enable the application of SOSD in industrial maintenance. In addition, this research also shows that participants fear untruthful behavior in SOSD. Thus, this should be further investigated. By investigating strategic behavior in SOSD, we also address and contribute to the challenge of lack in trust and transparency within SOSD. Finally, some algorithmic concerns should also be addressed.

8   Conclusion

In this work, we conceptualized current service delivery approaches in service systems as *provider-oriented service delivery (POSD)* and found that they are inefficient from a holistic service system perspective. Grounded in service system engineering and mechanism design, we propose *system-oriented service delivery (SOSD)* to address the previously highlighted allocation inefficiency in POSD. Our evaluation shows that the combination of system-cost optimization and the introduction of a monetary compensation and benefit distribution mechanism makes SOSD a Pareto improvement over POSD. Furthermore, based on an interview-based expert evaluation, we find that whilst experts see great merit in the idea of SOSD, they also identified challenges hindering the usability and introduction of SOSD in industrial maintenance.

With the development of SOSD, this work contributes concrete methods to its kernel theories of service system engineering and mechanism design. In addition, by outlining areas for future research associated to SOSD, this work contributes to the ongoing development of SOSD itself, to industrial maintenance—the most prominent example of the under-researched discipline of industrial services [16]— as well as to the top research priority of service delivery [32]. Even though SOSD is in an early stage, there is already one imminent managerial implication arising from it. Additional welfare can be created by overcoming organizational boundaries and by optimizing from a holistic perspective.

Evidently, this work does not come without limitations that open avenues for further research. In addition to common limitations associated to literature reviews and interview studies, we see the following main limitations of this work: First, we have demonstrated the relevance of this research through a literature-based argumentation. Whilst this is a valid approach, we believe that an interview study with experts from industry greatly improve the consideration of the application domain and yield additional design requirements grounded in practice. Second, with regard to the current evaluation episodes, we note that SOSD has not yet been evaluated from a summative perspective. Thus, this should be addressed in future work. Third, SOSD is still in a conceptual state and cannot yet be applied in practice. Therefore, additional DSR cycles gradually developing SOSD itself and increasing our understanding of the design space are necessary. For that endeavour, the findings of the expert evaluation serve as a starting point and guide future research. In addition, we should research the implications of the decision to discard incentive compatibility as a mechanism property of SOSD. Therefore, this work lays the foundation for future work to build upon in further developing SOSD.

References

1. Baines, T., Lightfoot, H., Benedettini, O., Kay, J.: The servitization of manufacturing: a review of literature and reflection on future challenges. J. Manuf. Technol. Manag. **20**(5), 547–567 (2009)
2. Blakeley, F., Argüello, B., Cao, B., Hall, W., Knolmajer, J.: Optimizing periodic maintenance operations for schindler elevator corporation. INFORMS J. Appl. Anal. **33**(1), 67–79 (2003)
3. Böhmann, T., Leimeister, J.M., Möslein, K.: Service systems engineering. Bus. Inf. Syst. Eng. **6**(2), 73–79 (2014)
4. Böhmann, T., Leimeister, J.M., Möslein, K.: The new fontiers of service systems engineering. Bus. Inf. Syst. Eng. **60**(5), 373–375 (2018)
5. Cachon, G.P., Harker, P.T.: Competition and outsourcing with scale economies. Manag. Sci. **48**(10), 1314–1333 (2002)
6. Camci, F.: Maintenance scheduling of geographically distributed assets with prognostics information. Eur. J. Oper. Res. **245**(2), 506–516 (2015)
7. Castillo-Salazar, J.A., Landa-Silva, D., Qu, R.: Workforce scheduling and routing problems: literature survey and computational study. Ann. Oper. Res. **239**(1), 39–67 (2016)
8. Clarke, E.H.: Multipart pricing of public goods. Public Choice **11**(1), 17–33 (1971)
9. Cordeau, J.F., Laporte, G., Pasin, F., Ropke, S.: Scheduling technicians and tasks in a telecommunications company. J. Sched. **13**(4), 393–409 (2010)
10. Cortés, C.E., Gendreau, M., Rousseau, L.M., Souyris, S., Weintraub, A.: Branch-and-price and constraint programming for solving a real-life technician dispatching problem. Eur. J. Oper. Res. **238**(1), 300–312 (2014)
11. Damm, R.B., Resende, M.G., Ronconi, D.P.: A biased random key genetic algorithm for the field technician scheduling problem. Comput. Oper. Res. **75**, 49–63 (2016)
12. Field, J.M., et al.: Service operations: what's next? J. Serv. Manag. **29**(1), 55–97 (2018)
13. Fox, J.P., Brammall, J.R.: Determination of the financial impact of machine downtime on the Australia post large letters sorting process. In: 9th Global Congress on Manufacturing and Management, pp. 1–7 (2008)
14. Froger, A., Gendreau, M., Mendoza, J.E., Pinson, E., Rousseau, L.M.: A branch-and-check approach for a wind turbine maintenance scheduling problem. Comput. Oper. Res. **88**, 117–136 (2017)
15. Froger, A., Gendreau, M., Mendoza, J.E., Pinson, E., Rousseau, L.M.: Solving a wind turbine maintenance scheduling problem. J. Sched. **21**(1), 53–76 (2018)
16. Gitzel, R., Schmitz, B., Fromm, H., Isaksson, A., Setzer, T.: Industrial services as a research discipline. Enterp. Model. Inf. Syst. Arch. **11**(4), 1–22 (2016)

17. Green, J.R., Laffont, J.J.: Incentives in Public Decision Making. North-Holland, Amsterdam (1979)
18. Gregor, S., Hevner, A.R.: Positioning and presenting design science research for maximum impact. MIS Q. **37**(2), 337–355 (2013)
19. Groves, T.: Incentives in teams. Econometrica **41**(4), 617–631 (1973)
20. Hashimoto, H., Boussier, S., Vasquez, M., Wilbaut, C.: A GRASP-based approach for technicians and interventions scheduling for telecommunications. Ann. Oper. Res. **183**(1), 143–161 (2011)
21. Alturki, A., Bandara, W., Gable, G.G.: Design science research and the core of information systems. In: Peffers, K., Rothenberger, M., Kuechler, B. (eds.) DESRIST 2012. LNCS, vol. 7286, pp. 309–327. Springer, Heidelberg (2012). https://doi.org/10.1007/978-3-642-29863-9_23
22. Hill, A.V.: An experimental comparison of dispatching rules for field service support. Decis. Sci. **23**(1), 235–249 (1992)
23. Irawan, C.A., Eskandarpour, M., Ouelhadj, D., Jones, D.: Simulation-based optimisation for stochastic maintenance routing in an offshore wind farm. Eur. J. Oper. Res. (2019)
24. Irawan, C.A., Ouelhadj, D., Jones, D., Stålhane, M., Sperstad, I.B.: Optimisation of maintenance routing and scheduling for offshore wind farms. Eur. J. Oper. Res. **256**(1), 76–89 (2017)
25. Kieninger, A., Berghoff, F., Fromm, H., Satzger, G.: Simulation-based quantification of business impacts caused by service incidents. In: Falcão e Cunha, J., Snene, M., Nóvoa, H. (eds.) IESS 2013. LNBIP, vol. 143, pp. 170–185. Springer, Heidelberg (2013). https://doi.org/10.1007/978-3-642-36356-6_13
26. Kovacs, A.A., Parragh, S.N., Doerner, K.F., Hartl, R.F.: Adaptive large neighborhood search for service technician routing and scheduling problems. J. Sched. **15**(5), 579–600 (2012)
27. Lehtonen, O., Holmström, J., Ala-Risku, T.: Enhancing field-service delivery: the role of information. J. Qual. Maint. Eng. **18**(2), 125–140 (2012)
28. Levy, Y., Ellis, T.J.: A systems approach to conduct an effective literature review in support of information systems research. Inf. Sci. J. **9** (2006)
29. Maglio, P.P., Vargo, S.L., Caswell, N., Spohrer, J.: The service system is the basic abstraction of service science. IseB **7**(4), 395–406 (2009)
30. Mas-Colell, A., Whinston, M., Green, J.: Microeconomic Theory. Oxford University Press, New York (1995)
31. Nisan, N.: Introduction to mechanism design (for computer scientists). In: Tardos, E., Nisan, N., Roughgarden, T., Vazirani, V.V. (eds.) Algorithmic Game Theory, pp. 209–242. Cambridge University Press, Cambridge (2007)
32. Ostrom, A.L., Parasuraman, A., Bowen, D.E., Patrício, L., Voss, C.A.: Service research priorities in a rapidly changing context. J. Serv. Res. **18**(2), 127–159 (2015)
33. Palinkas, L.A., Horwitz, S.M., Green, C.A., Wisdom, J.P., Duan, N., Hoagwood, K.: Purposeful sampling for qualitative data collection and analysis in mixed method implementation research. Adm. Policy Ment. Health **42**(5), 533–544 (2015)
34. Parkes, D.: Iterative combinatorial auctions: achieving economic and computational efficiency. Ph.D. thesis, University of Pennsylvania, Philadelphia, USA (2001). https://repository.upenn.edu/dissertations/AAI3003676/
35. Parragh, S.N., Doerner, K.F.: Solving routing problems with pairwise synchronization constraints. CEJOR **26**(2), 443–464 (2018)

36. Peffers, K., Rothenberger, M., Tuunanen, T., Vaezi, R.: Design science research evaluation. In: Peffers, K., Rothenberger, M., Kuechler, B. (eds.) DESRIST 2012. LNCS, vol. 7286, pp. 398–410. Springer, Heidelberg (2012). https://doi.org/10. 1007/978-3-642-29863-9_29
37. Petrakis, I., Hass, C., Bichler, M.: On the impact of real-time information on field service scheduling. Decis. Support Syst. **53**(2), 282–293 (2012)
38. Ritchie, J., Lewis, J.: Qualitative Research Practice, 1st edn. SAGE, London (2003)
39. Salonen, A., Tabikh, M.: Downtime costing—attitudes in Swedish manufacturing industry. In: Koskinen, K.T., et al. (eds.) Proceedings of the 10th World Congress on Engineering Asset Management (WCEAM 2015). LNME, pp. 539–544. Springer, Cham (2016). https://doi.org/10.1007/978-3-319-27064-7_53
40. Satzger, G., Kieninger, A.: Risk-reward sharing in IT service contracts–a service system view. In: 44th Hawaii International Conference on System Sciences, pp. 1–8 (2011)
41. Saunders, M., Lewis, P., Thornhill, A.: Research Methods for Business Students, 5th edn. Pearson Education, Harlow (2009)
42. Vargo, S.L., Maglio, P.P., Akaka, M.A.: On value and value co-creation: a service systems and service logic perspective. Eur. Manag. J. **26**(3), 145–152 (2008)
43. Venable, J., Pries-Heje, J., Baskerville, R.: FEDS: a framework for evaluation in design science research. Eur. J. Inf. Syst. **25**(1), 77–89 (2016)
44. VHB: VHB-JOURQUAL3 (2012). https://vhbonline.org/en/vhb4you/vhb-jourqual/vhb-jourqual-3
45. Vickrey, W.: Counterspeculation, auctions, and competitive sealed tenders. J. Finance **16**(1), 8–37 (1961)
46. Vössing, M.: Towards managing complexity and uncertainty in field service technician planning. In: 2017 IEEE 19th Conference on Business Informatics (CBI), pp. 312–319 (2017)
47. Webster, J., Watson, R.T.: Analyzing the past to prepare for the future: writing a literature review. MIS Q. **26**(2), xiii–xxiii (2002)
48. Wolff, C., Kühl, N., Satzger, G.: System-oriented service delivery: the application of service system engineering to service delivery. In: 26th European Conference on Information Systems (2018)
49. Wolff, C., Schmitz, B.: Determining cost-optimal availability for production equipment using service level engineering. In: 2017 IEEE 19th Conference on Business Informatics, pp. 176–185 (2017)
50. Xie, F., Potts, C.N., Bektaş, T.: Iterated local search for workforce scheduling and routing problems. J. Heuristics **23**(6), 471–500 (2017)
51. Xu, J., Chiu, S.Y.: Effective heuristic procedures for a field technician scheduling problem. J. Heuristics **7**(5), 495–509 (2001)
52. Zamorano, E., Stolletz, R.: Branch-and-price approaches for the multiperiod technician routing and scheduling problem. Eur. J. Oper. Res. **257**(1), 55–68 (2017)

Me, Myself and I - Supporting People with Intellectual Disabilities Towards Self-determination

Sofie Wass[1]([✉]) [iD], Lise Amy Hansen[2], and Erlend K. Stuve[3]

[1] University of Agder, Grimstad, Norway
sofie.wass@uia.no
[2] The Oslo School of Architecture and Design, Oslo, Norway
[3] Egde Consulting, Grimstad, Norway

Abstract. The transition into work is challenging for people with intellectual disabilities (ID) and there are few digital services that support this process. The transition involves several organizations and professionals that need to collaborate and coordinate their documentation and their initiatives. This prototype paper describes a self-reflective career tool designed to support young adults with ID towards self-determination and transitions into work. The users are supported through features such as mapping of interests, skills and abilities, goal setting and progress overview. The prototype of the self-reflective career tool has been evaluated formatively and is continuously redesigned and further developed. User tests have shown the importance of enabling an understanding of concepts such as skills, preferences and goals in regard to working life. The tool transfers the ownership of the information to the young adults and enables the users to identify, articulate and present their abilities in a visual and customizable manner.

Keywords: Career support · Self-determination · Intellectual disability

1 Introduction

Research confirms that in recent years there have been fewer - not more - people with ID included in Norwegian working life [1]. This sits in contrast to broad political and general public consensus in Norway that society should facilitate such work participation. Based on an Action Design Research (ADR) project [2], with the expressed aim to involve users in each stage of the innovation work, we have found that the transition from upper secondary school to working life is part of a complex context that involves many different actors with mutual dependencies. In this prototype paper, we describe the design of a self-reflective career tool for persons with ID working as a supportive vehicle to enable ownership and agency in the transition from secondary school and their next steps in life.

© Springer Nature Switzerland AG 2020
S. Hofmann et al. (Eds.): DESRIST 2020, LNCS 12388, pp. 420–425, 2020.
https://doi.org/10.1007/978-3-030-64823-7_40

2   Design of a Self-reflective Career Tool

Today people with ID are mapped and categorized in their early life - by schools, by municipalities and by careers according to their skills and abilities. However, the information is not owned nor formulated by the person him- or herself and there is a need to not only collate information, but to develop the ability to articulate preferences and perspectives particular to each person. A focus group session with a day-care center revealed the importance of individual mapping of needs. *"So, after all, there are so many things that need to be mapped out before they are suddenly put into a job. Is it a job that suits them? Is there anything he can master? Is it getting too much, is it getting too little?"* Focus group sessions with parents revealed the need to initiate work preparation earlier than today's' practice. *"I think that the last year in high school should have been better planned, that it was not so unpredictable what we went to ..."* Thus, our aim is to innovate beyond the problem situation of today, and to enable a set of actors to become proactive in their relationship to their environment [3]. Therefore, we are designing a self-reflective career tool that supports young adults with ID in self-determination and transitions into work.

The prototype comprises six main parts: (1) login and user details, (2) mapping of skills and abilities, (3) mapping of interests, (4) goal setting, (5) progress evaluation and (6) generating a CV. Most of our prototyping and testing so far have been based on number 2, 3 and 5. The aim is to find a way to enable and inspire the user to map their skills, abilities, interests and needs. Aspects of gamification and positive feedback have been tested. For example, by using a leveling system inspired by RPG games, and by giving achievement badges. The design and concept work are also based on mood words like "progress", "fun" and "inspirational" (Fig. 1).

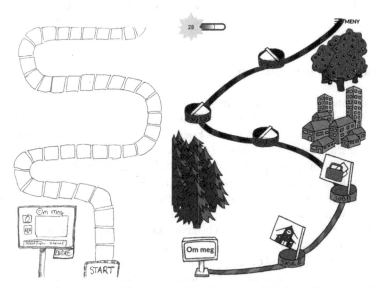

Fig. 1. Two early sketches on finding ways to visualize progress in the artifact. The white space will gradually be filled with images and icons based on the user's interests and preferences.

It is central to visualize progress to communicate what the user has achieved, what the next step is and how to reach that step. Inspired by TV and mobile games, we have been prototyping a "road" where the user has to solve different tasks to get to the next level. By mapping interests and defining goals, the "road" will be personalized by adding images and icons that are user-dependent and that the user can relate to. The user tests have shown that smiley faces combined with colors are the preferred grading of personal skills and abilities. Mapping of interests have been tested in two versions. The image in the middle shows a version where the user chooses what he/she likes or dislikes by sliding the icon to the left or the right. The image to the right shows a version where the user actively selects what he/she like or dislike (Fig. 2).

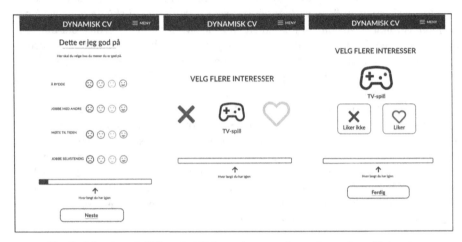

Fig. 2. Mapping of skills and abilities and two versions of mapping of interests.

3   Significance to Research

Drawing on previous research on intellectual disability and self-determination, we formulated a number of design principles to support the design of the artifact. The background for these design principles is briefly described in the following section.

ID is characterized by a limitation of cognitive functions that can be associated with learning, adaptive functioning and skills [4]. The classification of ID is by four main categories; mild, moderate, severe and profound ID. Research in disability studies reports difficulties connected to different areas depending on individual needs and abilities. However, limitations can be identified in communication skills, memory, cognitive load, reasoning, understanding and managing behavior and emotions as well as understanding of abstract concepts [5]. Thus, all these areas have to be accounted for in the design process and in the design and development of the prototype.

The design and development were influenced by theory on self-determination and the 'functional model of self-determination' which constitutes a philosophical approach that suggests that all actions are in some sense 'caused'. The term can be described as a characteristic within a person which determines the action of that person [6]. Based on literature in psychology and special education, Wehmeyer suggested an initial definition of self-determination that refers to *"the attitudes and abilities required to act as the primary causal agent in one's life and to make choices regarding one's actions free from undue external influence or interference"* [7, p. 305]. People who are causal agents are therefore able to cause things to happen in their life rather than other things causing them to act in certain ways [6]. Within disability research, self-determination has been defined within the context of Causal Agency Theory as a *"dispositional characteristic manifested as acting as the causal agent in one's life. Self-determined people (i.e., causal agents) act in service to freely chosen goals. Self-determined actions function to enable a person to be the causal agent in his or her life"* [6]. Causal Agency Theory gave us some overall aspects that are of importance for the artifact to support: volitional action (to make a conscious choice based on one's preferences), agentic action (to direct action to achieve an outcome) and action-control beliefs (to believe that one has what it takes to achieve a goal).

Our work makes two main contributions to research. Firstly, it extends previous research on self-determination [6, 7] to the design of digital artifacts. The insights from this work will be presented as design principles to share the knowledge with other researchers and designers. Secondly, the insights from the design sessions and field evaluations will support research on user involvement of persons with ID [8].

4 Significance to Practice

The self-reflective career tool supports self-determination for young person with ID, something which is essential for supporting conscious life-decisions such as self-reflection and work ambitions. The described prototype enables users to map skills and abilities, work on goal setting and view their progress towards employment. It will also support teachers, parents, potential employers and other support services in mapping the needs and abilities of the individual person. The described prototype also transfers the ownership of the information and a such the story to the individual, compared to current practice were both the information and the story is documented and owned by different institutions such as municipalities, healthcare units and work agencies. The self-reflective career tool will support transitions into work. Work participation is important for social inclusion and do not only provide an income but also impacts self-esteem, social networks, daily structure and well-being [9, 10]. The self-reflective career tool will therefore be important for young adults with ID, next-of-kin, coordinators, teachers and employers.

5 Evaluation of the Artifact

To evaluate the prototype, we have currently performed three user tests together with students with ID attending secondary school. One group (3 students) has participated in two user tests and one group (5 students) has participated in one user test. In the first test, we introduced the project during a lunch to ensure an understanding of the research and to establish trust between the students, the designer and the researchers. A paper prototype (Fig. 3) was used to carry out user tests with each student. During the test, the students were asked to complete five main tasks. They accessed the service, added information about a school they had attended and three favorite subjects, a previous internship and work tasks, and characteristics that described them as persons. As a final task, they selected among a number of predefined interests. After the user test, the students took part in an individual interview focusing on future employment, skills and abilities, personal development and decision-making. The test confirmed the relevance of the first prototype and revealed the need to clarify and support the understanding of different abstract concepts such as contact person, needs and work reference.

Fig. 3. The first user test and the paper prototype

In the second test we introduced the project during a coffee break to a new group of students and talked about future employment. As a group, we then drew out sketches of how we could visualize our individual skills and abilities. A first version of the digital prototype was then used to carry out a user test on an iPad with each student. During the test, the students were asked to complete four main tasks. They accessed the service, added their contact information, information about a school they had attended and three favorite subjects and a goal that they would like to achieve. The test gave us insights on the involvement of persons with ID in a design process. For instance, the importance of getting to know the users, stressing that the intention is not to evaluate the students but the prototype and providing continuous positive feedback.

In the third test, we visited the same group of students who participated in the first test. We started with a user test, one task was carried out on paper and one task was carried out using the first version of the digital prototype. The paper prototype focused on visualization and grading of skills and abilities and the digital prototype on mapping of interests. After the test, we discussed three different areas: leisure activities, skills and abilities and prerequisites for job satisfaction. The test revealed that smileys are the preferred way to grade skills and abilities, that students are aware of their need for adjustments in future work situations and that the artifact needs to guide users to identify and formulate individual skills and abilities.

6 Future Work

Students will be able to use the artifact on smartphones, tablets and computers. It is intended to be used both individually and together with teachers and other significant persons depending on the student's cognitive ability. We plan to further evolve the design and evaluate the artifact and the design principles through continuous user involvement, both in real settings and in a usability lab. We plan to also develop social interaction – such as teachers, parents or a career may partake in adjusting the use of the tool. A link to a screencast of the latest version of the prototype can be provided by contacting the authors.

Acknowledgement. We express our appreciation to the individuals that participated in the data collection, involved research colleagues and project partners. We like to especially thank Amanda, Marcus and Sophie for helping us to test out the prototype. The project is funded by The Research Council of Norway.

References

1. Engeland, J., Langballe, E.M.: Voksne og eldre med utviklingshemming og dagens bruk av samarbeidsfora i kommunene. https://s3.eu-west-1.amazonaws.com/ah-web-prod/docume nts/nav_-_utviklingshemning_og_bruk_av_samarbeidsfora.pdf. Accessed 5 May 2019
2. Sein, M., Henfridsson, O., Purao, S., Rossi, M., Lindgren, R.: Action design research. MIS Q. **35**(1), 37–56 (2011)
3. Dorst, K.: Frame Innovation: Create New Thinking by Design. MIT Press, Cambridge (2015)
4. WHO. https://www.who.int/classifications/icd/en/. Accessed 21 Jan 2020
5. Carulla, L.S., et al.: Intellectual developmental disorders: towards a new name, definition and framework for "mental retardation/intellectual disability. In: ICD-2011. World Psychiatry **10**(3), 175–180 (2011)
6. Shogren, K.A., Wehmeyer, M.L., Palmer, S.B., Forber-Pratt, A., Little, T.J., Lopez, S.J.: Causal agency theory: reconceptualizing a functional model of self-determination. Educ. Train. Autism Dev. Disabil. **50**(3), 251–263 (2015)
7. Wehmeyer, M.L.: Self-determination and the education of students with mental retardation. Educ. Train. Mental Retard. **27**(4), 302–314 (1992)
8. Benton, L., Johnson, H.: Widening participation in technology design: a review of the involvement of children with special educational needs and disabilities. Int. J. Child-Comput. Interact. **3**, 23–40 (2015)
9. Law, M., Steinwender, S., Leclair, L.: Occupation, health and well-being. Can. J. Occup. Ther. **65**(2), 81–91 (1998)
10. Beyer, S., Brown, T., Akandi, R., Rapley, M.: A comparison of quality of life outcomes for people with intellectual disabilities in supported employment, day services and employment enterprises. J. Appl. Res. Intellect. Disabil. **23**(3), 290–295 (2010)

Please Tell Me What to Do – Towards a Guided Orchestration of Key Activities in Data-Rich Service Systems

Fabian Hunke[(✉)], Stefan Seebacher, and Hauke Thomsen

Karlsruhe Institute of Technology, Institute of Information
Systems and Marketing, Karlsruhe, Germany
{fabian.hunke,stefan.seebacher}@kit.edu,
hauke.thomsen@student.kit.edu

Abstract. The digital transformation has led to the rise of data-rich service systems, in which organizations engage in data collection and analytics activities. Analytics-based services (ABS) are offered, enabling customers to make better decisions and providing assistance in solving more complex problems – thereby creating new customer value. The successful application of ABS requires the configuration of data and analytical models. These are usually spread across different organizational entities within the service system. Therefore, the orchestration of collaborative activities is key in creating customer value. This brings a new level of complexity for service design teams to develop new and innovative ABS solutions. This paper presents generic design knowledge that enables researchers to develop methodological assistance for these teams in the field of ABS in the future. Furthermore, it illustrates this design knowledge by presenting a canvas-based tool that offers a systematic view on the system-wide key activities required in ABS.

Keywords: Analytics-based services · Key activity orchestration · Data-rich service systems · Service design · Design science research

1 Introduction

Organizations continuously strive to harness new digital technologies in service offerings as it is an effective way to secure market position or to open up new market opportunities [1, 2]. In the wake of the ongoing digital transformation, new ways of collecting and transmitting large volumes of data are established and advances in information systems technology provide the means to analyze them [3, 4]. As a result, service systems have turned into data-rich environments that yield opportunities to create new customer value in novel service offerings [5, 6]. However, systematic approaches to leverage data and create new value propositions for customers have not been sufficiently explored and, as a consequence, organizations still experience difficulties in finding new, innovative ways to exploit these technological trends [7, 8].

The need for better guidance during service design becomes evident in the context of analytics-based services (ABS). ABS are a new type of services that builds upon

© Springer Nature Switzerland AG 2020
S. Hofmann et al. (Eds.): DESRIST 2020, LNCS 12388, pp. 426–437, 2020.
https://doi.org/10.1007/978-3-030-64823-7_41

data and applies analytical methods ("analytics") assisting customers in making better decisions and solving more complex problems [9]. The data that is used for this purpose is often distributed throughout the entire service system [10]. For instance, customers may generate data on their own mobile devices through tracking functions, which can provide a valuable basis for fitness applications [11]. Likewise, business partners may provide vital data sources, e.g. machinery data they operate in the field [12]. Similarly, analytical skills and capabilities are usually distributed across different organizational entities of the service system that have specialized in analysis and the configuration of analytical models [13]. In essence, a proper orchestration of these activities – reaching from data collection to the execution based on analytical outcomes – is necessary for creating the desired customer value and harness the benefits of digital technologies.

Service design has the potential to provide assistance in this regard. Described as a multidisciplinary approach that brings to life new service ideas, it is key to the creation of new service offerings. It provides organizations with the mindset, processes and methodological tools that enable iterative and holistic guidance to create new services [14]. Despite the rich set of methods and tools that exists for service design in general [15], dedicated support for the design of ABS remains scarce. This is particularly evident regarding the orchestration of key activities within service systems – arguably due to the fact that the field at the intersection of data, analytics and service design is still relatively new [16, 17].

Against this backdrop, the objective of this research is to *provide methodological guidance for service design teams* in developing new ABS; especially with regard to a guided orchestration of key activities within a service system. For that purpose, we propose a design science research (DSR) project that seeks to address this crucial gap in the service design literature raising the following research question: *How can we design methodological tool assistance that facilitates the orchestration of key activities in analytics-based services?*

This research should contribute to the ongoing discourse on harnessing digital technologies. First, we are able to provide insights on the design of methodological tools assisting in the service design process. We suggest a comprehensive conceptualization in form of design principles that are demonstrated and evaluated using the presented artifact. Second, we introduce a canvas-based artifact, the Key Activity Canvas. As our evaluation results suggest, the artifact provides practitioners with a viable means in purposefully orchestrating the key activities during service design.

Below, we first present the foundations of our research and review related work. This is followed by our research methodology in Sect. 3. Next, we present our findings in form of generic design knowledge, the artifact instantiation, and its evaluation. We then discuss our findings and close with a conclusion.

2 Foundations and Related Work

2.1 Using Analytics-Based Services for Creating Customer Value

Advances in information technology have led to the fact that almost every action in modern service systems generates data [18]. Sensors, for instance, allow to continuously sense machines' surroundings, condition and state in real-time [19]. Coupled with, e.g., new cloud technologies providing scalable processing power and user-friendly applications, organizations are increasingly empowered to benefit from the availability of that data through the use of analytics in providing new service offerings [4].

An early distinction of novel service offerings that occur from the proliferation of data and advances in analytics technology is made between data-as-a-service (DaaS) and analytics-as-a-service (AaaS) [13]. The former focuses on providing raw and aggregated content. The latter refers to services that utilize a variety of common analytical methods and infrastructures, which can be adapted to industry- and company-specific requirements. While this notion focuses on business-to-business applications, Huang and Rust [20], amongst others, add that data containing information about customers allow to better understand why customers make decisions and behave in a certain way; thus, creating new opportunities to provide meaningful value in new customer-facing services. Similar, smart services allow organizations to leverage sensor-equipped, connected products in the field for additional service offerings [3, 19]. Using the provided data, organizations are able to offer contextual and preemptive services to their customers [6, 21], leading to a closer relationship throughout the entire life cycle of their products.

Regardless of different concepts or terms, current research in this area consistently describes the use of data and analytics as the basis for new value propositions; either in stand-alone offerings or bundled with an existing product or service. In the scope of this research, we will not further differentiate between services that build upon data from specific sources (e.g. smart, connected objects), or a specific type of analytics (e.g. descriptive, predictive, or prescriptive). Instead, we take a broader perspective and generally refer to services, in which analytics applied to data significantly contribute to value creation as *analytics-based services*.

2.2 Service Design and the Role of Tool Assistance

Service design is described as a formalized approach that serves to develop new and innovative service offerings [14]. Referring to ABS, service design can thus serve as a means to develop new ABS. Various researchers (e.g., [22]) have developed conceptual frameworks in which they define the necessary steps for the development of new services. In essence, these processes consist of five fundamental activities [22]: 1) opportunity identification, 2) customer understanding, 3) concept development, 4) process design, and 5) refinement and implementation.

Methodological tools play a crucial role in assisting service design teams during these dedicated activities. Service design teams typically consist of multidisciplinary team members [14]. In the context of ABS, this means that members may originate from the 1) service marketing and operations, 2) information technology, or 3) data science discipline to contribute with their different backgrounds and competencies. In order to manage and channel this diversity for successful service design, various models have been proposed that are commonly referred to as visual inquiry tools [23]. These tools methodologically support service design by determining how team members (visually) frame a problem. This enables the team to refer to the same structure of the problem, thus creating a joint basis for collaboration. Often visualized in canvas-based, one-page frameworks, these artifacts also provide the opportunity to easily communicate service ideas [24].

In sum, visual inquiry tools play a crucial role in the service design process. Yet, despite their crucial role during service design, tools supporting the design of ABS still remain limited. Recent research introduces visual inquiry tools to better identify different sources that may provide data for ABS [25] or to better link data resources to value propositions [26]. Nevertheless, our review of literature unveiled a surprising lack of methodological assistance guiding the actual conceptualization of necessary activities in ABS; i.e. the orchestration of the key activities reaching from collecting data to delivering value based on analytical outcomes. Considering the complexity to configure these activities in modern, data-rich service systems, this is a crucial gap that needs to be addressed.

3   Overview of the Design Science Research Project

The objective of this research is to explore design knowledge for tools capable of supporting service design teams by guiding the orchestration of relevant key activities in ABS. We follow a design science approach as DSR can be particularly useful in the context of service design by contributing to the development of new constructs and methods [27]. Following the approach proposed by Kuechler and Vaishnavi [28], we structured our research iteratively along the five phases problem awareness, suggestion, development, and evaluation in two consecutive iterations (cf. Fig. 1).

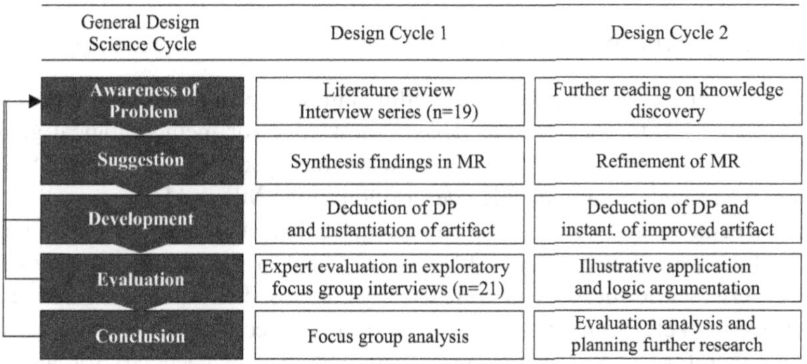

General Design Science Cycle	Design Cycle 1	Design Cycle 2
Awareness of Problem	Literature review Interview series (n=19)	Further reading on knowledge discovery
Suggestion	Synthesis findings in MR	Refinement of MR
Development	Deduction of DP and instantiation of artifact	Deduction of DP and instant. of improved artifact
Evaluation	Expert evaluation in exploratory focus group interviews (n=21)	Illustrative application and logic argumentation
Conclusion	Focus group analysis	Evaluation analysis and planning further research

Fig. 1. Overview of our consecutive design cycles and their research activities.

For the **first cycle**, we started with a literature review of relevant research in order to gain a deeper understanding of the academic discourse. Despite the focus the topic has received in research and practice [17], our review of the literature revealed a surprising lack of support for ABS design (cf. Sect. 2.2). We also conducted a series of interviews with practitioners, who are involved in the development of ABS in their organizations to obtain an understanding of the actual circumstances and issues in practice. Interview participants were purposefully sampled from an innovation management, product management, engineering, and IT background. In total, we collected 19 semi-structured interviews in which we asked the participants about current service design activities, involved actors, required competencies, and challenges they had experienced so far. The interviews were transcribed and analyzed following an abductive coding approach [29]. A detailed description of the diverse findings we revealed from this series of interviews is reported in [30]. Based on these findings, we identified a set of meta-requirements (MR) describing generic requirements that must be fulfilled by any artifact [31]. On this basis, we derived design principles (DP) that encompass generic functions and capabilities of designed artifacts [32]. We instantiated the DP in the form of an initial artifact and subsequently evaluated it in an exploratory focus group setting with practitioners [33]. The positive results of the workshop showed us that the proposed and instantiated functionalities described in the DP had a certain validity.

We started the **second cycle** with further reading on knowledge discovery in databased and data mining projects to enrich our design's conceptual foundations. Since identifying insights in data plays a central role in ABS, this appeared to be a suitable theoretical lens. We refined the existing MR and DP accordingly and instantiated a new artifact. For evaluation purposes, we illustratively applied it to a typical case of ABS within the author team [34] and used logic argumentation to better understand why the artifact works and to identify possible pitfalls during its application [35]. The results of both design cycles are presented below. An overview of the different methods conducted in each design cycle is shown in Fig. 1.

4 The "Key Activity Canvas" for Guiding Key Activity Orchestration in Data-Rich Service Systems

4.1 Meta Requirements and Design Principles

Based on two consecutive design cycles outlined in Sect. 3, we identified four MR and three associated DP to contribute to design knowledge for methodological guidance of service design teams to facilitate the orchestration of key activities in ABS. In the following, we provide a more detailed description of the MR and DP.

Located in the field of service design research, the field of application for our intended artifact is highly multidisciplinary [14]. As we had learnt from our interviews with domain experts, service design teams are usually composed of different disciplines such as 1) service marketing and operations, 2) information technology, or 3) data science. Tools must therefore be designed in such a way that all steps necessary for application can be identified even without discipline-specific knowledge. Thus, we form our first MR as: *Tools in ABS design are required to be applicable in multidisciplinary service design teams (MR1).*

Interaction plays a key role in the service system concept. As literature points out, service systems are understood as networks, in which services are co-created for mutual benefit through interaction between individuals, technology and organizations [36]. In order to take this conceptual foundation into account, tools for designing new ABS should consider all participants of a service system and be able to reflect different perspectives on the ABS under consideration. This notion forms our second MR: *Tools in ABS design are required to provide a system-based view on the ABS (MR2).*

Related application areas such as business modelling have recently seen a rapid increase in methodological tools such as the business model canvas, the value proposition canvas or the strategy alignment map [37]. Similarly, these tools also aim at improving the collaboration of (business strategy) teams. Avdiji et al. [23] emphasize that the popularity and success of these tools is due to their ability to visually frame the underlying problem by using an ontology to abstractly represent the business world to eliminate conceptual and terminological ambiguities between team members. Additionally, such an abstraction reduces complexity. Thus, our third MR becomes: *Tools in ABS design are required to use a basic abstraction that structures and visually represents the underlying problem (MR3).*

Service design projects are characterized by creative and iterative working practices. Service ideas are developed, adapted, rejected, archived and sometimes even reactivated. In order to meet these working habits, effective documentation of outcomes is critical. Ebel et al. [38] suggest providing a repository of shared material with guidelines and tutorials offering assistance on how to use it. They stress the importance for creating a shared understanding, especially among heterogenous teams. The authors propose the use of standardized templates to create, compare, and communicate ideas. This advice forms our fourth MR: *Tools in ABS design are required to use a standardized format throughout the service design project (MR4).*

We aim to design a methodological tool that facilitates service design teams to properly orchestrate the key activities within the service system of the intended ABS. ABS focus on providing meaningful value to customers by applying analytics to data. Building on seminal contributions on processes to systematically extract actionable knowledge from databases [e.g. 39], we combine MR1, MR3, and MR4 into our first DP: *Provide a basic abstraction of the required activities in the ABS according to the underlying data mining process (DP1).*

ABS require different interactions in the service system. Predominantly, organizations offering ABS interact with business partners, e.g. to share analytical capabilities, and with customers, e.g., to use customer-specific data. Thus, we combine MR2 and MR3 to form our second DP: *Provide a system-based view on the ABS by representing the organization's, customers', and business partners' perspective (DP2).*

To prevent DP1 from contradicting MR1, extra guidance should be provided to service design team members that are not familiar with data mining terminology. Thus, addressing MR1, we formulate our third DP: *Provide guidance and explanations for usage to allow an easy understanding of data mining related activities (DP3).*

4.2 Instantiation

To instantiate the DP, we decided on a canvas-based format that allows for easy evaluation of the artifact with practitioners (cf. Fig. 2). We used the activities described for data mining [39] as phases to structure the conceptual key activities of the ABS horizontally from the initial data collection to the application of the findings (cf. DP1). Secondly, we vertically subdivided each activity phase into a customer, company and partner perspective (cf. DP2). Key activities are now identified by first collecting for each phase whether and in what form these three entities can contribute to the fulfilment of the activity using post-its. This collection allows the development of alternative activity configurations in a second step. To illustrate the preferred interactions, an interaction can be illustrated in each phase by filling in the dotted arrows. To ensure that the phases remain explanatory, we added guiding questions for each subdivided phase (cf. DP3).

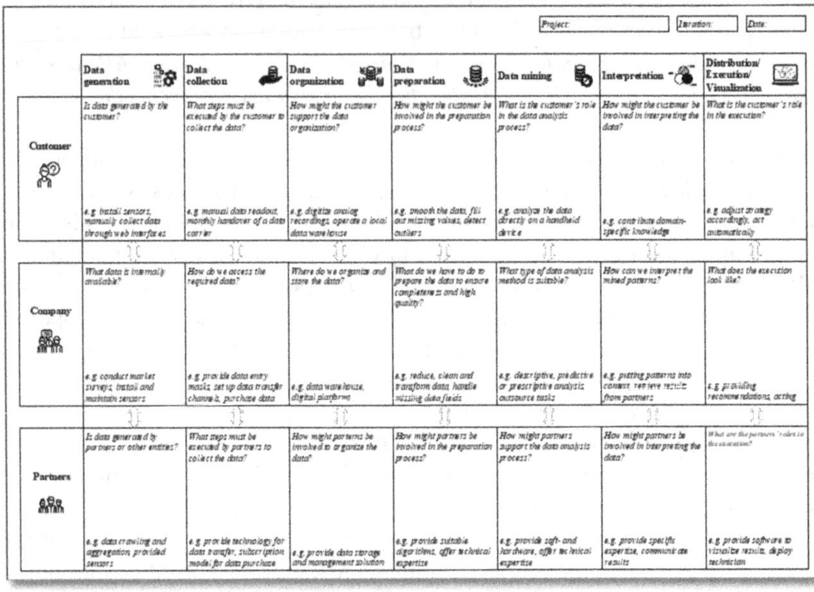

Fig. 2. Instantiation of the proposed MR and DP – the key activity canvas.

5   Demonstration and Evaluation

In order to evaluate the Key Activity Canvas and the functionality of its underlying DP, we consulted the framework for evaluation in design science (FEDS) to develop an overall strategy [35]. We decided to follow the human risk & effectiveness strategy, which should be selected "if a critical goal of the evaluation is to rigorously establish that the utility/benefit will continue in real situations" [35, p. 82]. The authors suggest starting with artificial and formative evaluations early in the project, but then progressing quickly towards naturalistic settings in summative evaluations (Fig. 3).

For that purpose, we evaluated our initial prototype at the end of design cycle 1 in a focus group workshop. We purposefully sampled the workshop participants recruiting them in their capacity as service design experts currently engaging in ABS initiatives. In total, 21 practitioners from 10 different companies across multiple industries participated in our workshop (cf. Table 1). We provided a brief introduction to our research topic and our prototype. Afterwards, we formed three groups and each group applied the prototype to a real-world case that was provided by one of the group members. Subsequently, we interviewed each group in a focus group interview according to the guidelines of Tremblay et al. [33] focusing on the demand for such a tool in their service design practices, the understandability of the instantiated design principles, and the

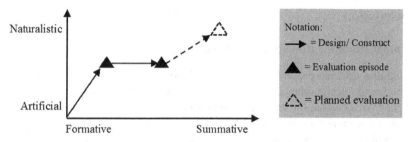

Fig. 3. Overview of the evaluation strategy and the individual evaluation episodes [35].

functionality a canvas-based prototype provides to them. In sum, we received positive feedback regarding the applicability of such a tool in service design. Regarding the functionality and understandability, we received valuable feedback, e.g., to refine the guiding questions included in the artifact.

Table 1. Overview of the workshop participants during evaluation episode one.

#	Industry	Revenue	Firm size (employees)	Participants
1	Consumer goods	<€20M	<50	2
2	Education			2
3	Fashion industry			1
4	Manufacturing	€20M–€250M	50–1.000	4
5	Public sector			3
6	Manufacturing			3
7	Education			3
8	Metal processing			1
9	Financial services	€250M–€600M	>1.000	1
10	Manufacturing			1

For the second evaluation episode, we decided to apply the refined artifact ex-post to a 'typical case' [31] of a real-world ABS use case described in [6]. The objective in this episode was to demonstrate the prototype's ability to orchestrate the activities of ABS in service systems and we used logic argumentation to evaluate the outcome's validity [40]. We plotted the canvas and filled it out with sticky notes and markers and discussed possible alternative activities the ABS could (theoretically) build upon. Particularly the opportunity to conceptualize the involvement of customers in the provision of services became evident and was accounted as an asset for service design attempts.

6 Discussion

6.1 Implications for Research and Practice

This ongoing research presents a canvas-based tool that provides service design teams with methodological guidance on how to orchestrate the relevant key activities of ABS in practice. We consider the artifact presented as an *improvement*, as it represents a new solution to a common problem [41], and as a type *method*, as it provides conceptual yet actionable instructions for practice [40]. In this section, we aim to highlight the implications that the introduction of the Key Activity Canvas raises for research and practice.

Service systems are commonly referred to as networks composed of individuals, technology, and organizations, in which services are based upon the interaction between different entities to co-create value [36]. While this basic abstraction has received wide acceptance among researchers and practitioners as a paradigm to reflect a service-dominant view on modern economies [17, 18], it provides little guidance for organizations to actually design new value propositions for its customers [5]. With the liquefaction of data throughout the service system [42] and easier access to analytics capabilities [4], service design teams are more than ever challenged to orchestrate the required system-wide ABS interactions to achieve meaningful value for its customers. The insights into our design and development process might advise researchers how to develop methodological tools guiding ABS-related design in general. *Zooming in* on visual inquiry tools and considering them in the field of ABS-design, our findings are in line with Avdiji et al. [23]. Building on their conceptual notions, our artifact (1) distinctively frames the problem of service design teams, (2) develops a shared visualization, and (3) guides the joint inquiry of service design teams. We instantiate these higher-level principles in the context of 'orchestrating key activities in data-rich service systems' and thus extend them to the specific field of ABS design. *Zooming out*, we can also refer to recent research indicating that DSR can be useful for service design research by supporting the development of new artifacts such as service design methods and tools [27]. Our work provides an illustrative example how this can be achieved and thus might advise researchers with actionable insights.

Furthermore, the introduced Key Activity Canvas illustrates the, so far, missing guidance to orchestrate key activities in data-rich service systems systematically. Reflecting the system-, analytics-, and interaction-perspective, the tool provides a viable means to foster the joint inquiry in multidisciplinary teams to orchestrate the activities of new ABS. Thus, we believe the tool immediately impacts the work of service design teams in practice.

6.2 Limitations and Future Research

Our research certainly comes with some *limitations*. First, our artifact so far lacks a summative evaluation. Although we based the current design on two design cycles, each containing an evaluation episode, the evaluations remained formative. Therefore, a subsequent design cycle is necessary to assess the extent to which the artifact meets expectations, e.g. with respect to the usefulness of the tool in service design projects under real-world conditions. Second, we note a limitation with regard to sampling the workshop participants in the first evaluation episode, which we based on a convenience sample. While we recruited the participants in their capacity as members of ABS design initiatives in their organizations, the sample predominantly represents small and medium size enterprises. Previous work emphasizes that this type of organization faces unique service design challenges that do not necessarily apply to larger organizations [e.g. 43]. Therefore, future evaluation episodes should also consider larger organizations.

These limitations, in turn, pave the way for our *future research activities* in this DSR project. To this end, we plan to conduct a third design cycle in which we aim to fine-tune our design principles based on the analysis of the evaluations previously conducted. Subsequently, we strive to carry out a field study, in which we aim to evaluate the refined artifact in a summative manner. Following Checkland [44], that evaluation episode will focus on the effects the artifact respectively its underlying design principles has on (1) efficacy, i.e. whether it supports and improves the outcomes, (2) effectiveness, i.e. whether it can be successfully used by the individuals and the team, and (3) efficiency, i.e. whether it requires an inappropriate amount of time or other resources. Ultimately, we hope to identify testable propositions that may lead to more general knowledge about the design of methodological tools that assist in designing ABS in the future.

7   Conclusion

In the wake of the digital transformation, ABS provide organizations with novel opportunities to harness digital technologies in new customer-facing services. Yet, the successful design of new service offerings is hindered by challenges like the orchestration of the key activities in ABS within the service system.

To tackle this challenge, this research derives theoretically grounded DP methodological assistance tools should generally follow. The elaborated MR and DP may serve as a knowledge base that allows to develop a new class of methodological tools dedicated to the support of ABS design in general. Additionally, we introduce the Key Activity Canvas – a novel tool for service design teams in practice that strive to develop new ABS offerings and we believe this contribution immediately impacts the work of service design initiatives in practice.

References

1. Zaki, M.: Digital transformation: harnessing digital technologies for the next generation of services. J. Serv. Mark. **33**, 429–435 (2019)
2. Vargo, S.L., Lusch, R.F.: Why "service"? J. Acad. Mark. Sci. **36**, 25–38 (2008)
3. Wuenderlich, N.V., Heinonen, K., Ostrom, A.L., Patricio, L., Sousa, R., Voss, C., Lemmink, J.G.A.M.: "Futurizing" smart service: implications for service researchers and managers. J. Serv. Mark. **29**, 442–447 (2015)
4. Fromm, H., Habryn, F., Satzger, G.: Service analytics: leveraging data across enterprise boundaries for competitive advantage. In: Bäumer, U., Kreutter, P., Messner, W. (eds.) Globalization of Professional Services, pp. 139–149. Springer, Berlin (2012). https://doi.org/10.1007/978-3-642-29181-4_13

5. Troilo, G., De Luca, L.M., Guenzi, P.: Linking data-rich environments with service innovation in incumbent firms: a conceptual framework and research propositions. J. Prod. Innov. Manag. **34**, 617–639 (2017)

6. Hunke, F., Seebacher, S., Schüritz, R., Satzger, G.: Pathways from data to value: identifying strategic archetypes of analytics-based services. In: Proceedings of 15th International Conference on Wirtschaftsinformatik (2020)

7. Schüritz, R., Seebacher, S., Satzger, G., Schwarz, L.: Datatization as the next frontier of servitization: understanding the challenges for transforming organizations. In: ICIS 2017 Proceedings, pp. 1098–1118 (2017)

8. Hunke, F., Seebacher, S., Schuritz, R., Illi, A.: Towards a process model for data-driven business model innovation. In: 19th IEEE Conference on Business Informatics, pp. 150–157 (2017)

9. Hunke, F., Engel, C., Schüritz, R., Ebel, P.: Understanding the anatomy of analytics-based services – a taxonomy to conceptualize the use of data and analytics in services. In: ECIS 2019 Proceedings, pp. 1–15 (2019)

10. Hirt, R., Kühl, N., Schmitz, B., Satzger, G.: Towards service-oriented cognitive analytics for smart service systems. In: Proceedings of 51st Hawaii International Conference on System Sciences, pp. 1622–1629 (2018)

11. Davenport, T.H., Lucker, J.: Running on data. Deloitte Rev. 5–15 (2015)

12. Vössing, M.: Redesigning service operations for the digital world: towards automated and data-driven field service planning. In: ECIS 2019 Proceedings, pp. 1–11 (2019)

13. Chen, Y., Kreulen, J., Campbell, M., Abrams, C.: Analytics ecosystem transformation: a force for business model innovation. In: 2011 Annual SRII Global Conference, pp. 11–20 (2011)

14. Joly, M.P., Teixeira, J.G., Patrício, L., Sangiorgi, D.: Leveraging service design as a multidisciplinary approach to service innovation. J. Serv. Manag. **30**, 681–715 (2019)

15. Uebernickel, F., Brenner, W., Pukall, B., Naef, T., Schindholzer, B.: Design Thinking: Das Handbuch. Frankfurter Allgem.Buch, Frankfurt (2015)

16. Williams, K., Chatterjee, S., Rossi, M.: Design of emerging digital services: a taxonomy. Eur. J. Inf. Syst. **17**, 505–517 (2008)

17. Ostrom, A.L., Parasuraman, A., Bowen, D.E., Patrício, L., Voss, C.A.: Service research priorities in a rapidly changing context. J. Serv. Res. **18**, 127–159 (2015)

18. Demirkan, H., Bess, C., Spohrer, J., Rayes, A., Allen, D., Moghaddam, Y.: Innovations with smart service systems: analytics, big data, cognitive assistance, and the internet of everything. Commun. Assoc. Inf. Syst. **37**, 733–752 (2015)

19. Beverungen, D., Müller, O., Matzner, M., Mendling, J., vom Brocke, J.: Conceptualizing smart service systems. Electron. Mark. **29**(1), 7–18 (2017)

20. Huang, M.H., Rust, R.T.: IT-related service: a multidisciplinary perspective. J. Serv. Res. **16**, 251–258 (2013)

21. Schüritz, R., Wixom, B., Farrell, K., Satzger, G.: Value co-creation in data-driven services: towards a deeper understanding of the joint sphere. In: ICIS 2019 Proceedings, pp. 1–9 (2019)

22. Kim, K.-J., Meiren, T.: New service development process. In: Salvendy, G., Karwowski, W. (eds.) Introduction to Service Engineering, pp. 253–267. Wiley, Hoboken (2010)

23. Avdiji, H., Elikan, D., Missonier, S., Pigneur, Y.: Designing tools for collectively solving ill-structured problems. In: Proceedings of 51st Hawaii International Conference on System Sciences, pp. 400–409 (2018)

24. Ciriello, R.F., Aschoff, F.R., Dolata, M., Richter, A.: Communicating ideas purposefully: toward a design theory of innovation artifacts. In: ECIS 2014 Proceedings (2014)

25. Mathis, K., Köbler, F.: Data-need fit–towards data-driven business model innovation. In: Service Design Geographies, Proceedings of ServDes, pp. 458–467 (2016)

26. Kühne, B., Böhmann, T.: Data-driven business models - building the bridge between data and value. In: ECIS 2019 Proceedings, pp. 1–16 (2019)

27. Teixeira, J.G., Patrício, L., Tuunanen, T.: Advancing service design research with design science research. J. Serv. Manag. **30**, 577–592 (2019)
28. Kuechler, B., Vaishnavi, V.: On theory development in design science research: anatomy of a research project. Eur. J. Inf. Syst. **17**, 489–504 (2008)
29. Charmaz, K.: Constructing Grounded Theory: A Practical Guide Through Qualitative Analysis. Sage, London (2006)
30. Hunke, F., et al.: Geschäftsmodelle 4.0: big data und data-analytics als Treiber für Dienstleistungsinnovation im deutschen Mittelstand. In: Stich, V., Schumann, J.H., Beverungen, D., Gudergan, G., Jussen, P. (eds.) Digitale Dienstleistungsinnovationen, pp. 167–183. Springer, Heidelberg (2019). https://doi.org/10.1007/978-3-662-59517-6_9
31. Walls, J.G., Widmeyer, G.R., El Sawy, O.A.: Building an information system design theory for vigilant EIS. Inf. Syst. Res. **3**, 36–59 (1992)
32. Baskerville, R., Pries-Heje, J.: Explanatory design theory. Bus. Inf. Syst. Eng. **2**, 271–282 (2010)
33. Tremblay, M., Hevner, A., Berndt, D.: The use of focus groups in design science research. In: Hevner, A., Chatterjee, S. (eds.) Design Research in Information Systems, pp. 121–143. Springer, Boston (2010). https://doi.org/10.1007/978-1-4419-5653-8_10
34. Patton, M.Q.: Qualitative Evaluation and Research Methods. Sage, Thousand Oaks (1990)
35. Venable, J., Pries-Heje, J., Baskerville, R.: FEDS: a framework for evaluation in design science research. Eur. J. Inf. Syst. **25**, 77–89 (2016)
36. Maglio, P.P., Vargo, S.L., Caswell, N., Spohrer, J.: The service system is the basic abstraction of service science. Inf. Syst. E-bus. Manag. **7**, 395–406 (2009)
37. Täuscher, K., Abdelkafi, N.: Visual tools for business model innovation: recommendations from a cognitive perspective. Creat. Innov. Manag. **26**, 160–174 (2017)
38. Ebel, P., Bretschneider, U., Leimeister, J.M.: Leveraging virtual business model innovation: a framework for designing business model development tools. Inf. Syst. J. **26**, 519–550 (2016)
39. Fayyad, U., Piatetsky-Shapiro, G., Smyth, P.: From data mining to knowledge discovery in databases. AI Mag. **17**, 37–54 (1996)
40. Peffers, K., Rothenberger, M., Tuunanen, T., Vaezi, R.: Design science research evaluation. In: Peffers, K., Rothenberger, M., Kuechler, B. (eds.) DESRIST 2012. LNCS, vol. 7286, pp. 398–410. Springer, Heidelberg (2012). https://doi.org/10.1007/978-3-642-29863-9_29
41. Gregor, S., Hevner, A.R.: Positioning and presenting design science research for maximum impact. MIS Q. **37**, 337–355 (2013)
42. Lycett, M.: "Datafication": making sense of (big) data in a complex world. Eur. J. Inf. Syst. **22**, 381–386 (2013)
43. Oliva, R., Kallenberg, R.: Managing the transition from products to services. Int. J. Serv. Ind. **14**, 160–172 (2003)
44. Checkland, P.: Soft systems methodology: a thirty year retrospective. Syst. Res. Behav. Sci. **11**, 11–58 (2000)

PS³ – A Domain-Specific Modeling Language for Platform-Based Smart Service Systems

Hedda Lüttenberg[✉]

Paderborn University, Paderborn, Germany
hedda.luettenberg@uni-paderborn.de

Abstract. Through progressive technological advancements, the importance and relevance of platform-based business models are proliferating. On the one hand, in the context of the internet of things, platforms enable the interactions between smart products and service providers and offer basic functionality to develop data-based smart service applications. On the other hand, multi-sided platforms efficiently network different groups of actors—for example, providers and consumers of smart service applications. In both cases, companies face the challenge of developing a complex socio-technical smart service system (SSS) comprising networked actors, smart products, and IT infrastructures, such as digital platforms. Conceptual models are established artifacts to facilitate efficient and unambiguous communication and support the development and integration of technical systems. The purpose of this paper is to design, demonstrate, and evaluate a domain-specific modeling language for the conceptual design of platform-based SSS. The presented modeling language is the first one to integrate hitherto separate research streams on SSS and digital platforms. It is demonstrated with the real case of a mechanical engineering company and evaluated conceptually.

Keywords: Smart service systems · Digital platforms · Conceptual modeling · Modeling language

1 Introduction

Propelled by the rapidly advancing digitization—the binary conversion of analogous information into a digital format [29]—physical products are increasingly capturing status, usage, and context data. By analyzing and interpreting these data, products are transforming into smart products [7]. Based on the data captured by intelligent technical systems, completely new digital services can be established [7]. Thereby, manufacturing companies are enabled to implement service-oriented business-models and offer holistic solutions, integrating goods and services to meet complex and specific customer needs [3].

Further, service providers can engage with a platform-based service system as a third-party contributor [8] to access existing resources and offer added value

© Springer Nature Switzerland AG 2020
S. Hofmann et al. (Eds.): DESRIST 2020, LNCS 12388, pp. 438–450, 2020.
https://doi.org/10.1007/978-3-030-64823-7_42

(e.g., smart service applications). Digital platforms are essential for networking involved actors [30]—including humans and technical systems [17]—and enabling interaction and information exchange [8].

However, companies face profound challenges in the design and implementation of successful platform-based smart service systems (SSS). Designers must identify and specify all relevant elements of a SSS in a complex cross-company design process [5]. They have to identify actors and their tasks for service provision and co-creation of value as well as points of interaction between these actors [4]. The designed concept of an SSS is relevant to all parties involved in the development and provision of smart service and smart products. Therefore, companies need the means to communicate their SSS concept in varying degrees of detail, depending on the phase of the development process.

In Information Systems research, conceptual models support the integration of different actors and their IT applications and enable more effective and unambiguous communication in interdisciplinary teams [3]. Therefore, to address the designer's challenges, companies can use a conceptual modeling language to design models of platform-based SSS. Several modeling languages have been proposed, most of which focus on the process of value co-creation [3,28] or the configuration of value propositions [1,25]. However, these languages do not target the design of (smart) service systems but address specific aspects of these systems. Additionally, the essential role of digital platforms is not taken into account. Today, only one approach explicitly targets modeling SSS: HUBER et al. [15] present a modeling language focusing on resources and their relationships. However, their approach limits available roles, lacks expressiveness and different levels of abstraction, and does not include platform-specific characteristics.

The objective of this paper is to develop a conceptual Domain-Specific Modeling Language (DSML) that can be used as a tool for designing, reflecting, and analyzing platform-based SSS. Furthermore, the integration of constructs from the literature on SSS and digital platforms in a meta-model enables the understanding of elements in a platform-based SSS and their relationship.

The paper proceeds as follows. In Sect. 2, SSS, digital platforms, and existing modeling approaches are discussed. In Sect. 3, the design of the DSML for platform-based SSS is explained and justified. In Sect. 4, the design, demonstration, and evaluation of the IT artifact is reported. Section 5 concludes the paper and motivates further research.

2   Related Research

2.1   Smart Service Systems

Service is "the application of specialized competencies [...] through deeds, processes, and performances for the benefit of another entity or the entity itself" [31, p. 26]. Here, service refers to the value-in-use that is co-created in interactions between service providers and service customers [31]. More specifically, *"digital service* refers to making any asset or capability applicable to others using information technology, thereby enabling digital processes of value co-creation." [6,

p. 784 (emphasis added)]. This value co-creation takes place in *service systems*, which are "configurations of people, technologies, and other resources that interact with other service systems to create mutual value" [18, p. 395].

By introducing smart products into digital service systems, *smart service* can be realized [6]. In SSS, "smart products are boundary-objects that integrate resources and activities of the involved actors[, i. e., the service provider and the service consumer,] for mutual benefit." [7, p. 12]. They "network digital competencies of the actors involved in a digital service system and/or mediate their interactions. [...] Therefore, a smart service integrates physical and digital competencies in a complex socio-technical service system." [6, pp. 784–785]. The integration and use of smart products generate distinct types of data based on which smart service can be provided [7]. In SSS, actors—comprising humans as well as technical systems [17]—perform tasks and interact with each other via different interfaces to co-create value. Digital platforms can be used to network involved actors and facilitate interaction.

2.2 Digital Platforms

Information Systems literature has defined different types of platforms, three of which are essential for modeling platform-based SSS. In the context of smart products and the internet of things (IoT), "*IoT platforms* provide the software infrastructure to enable physical 'Things' and cyber-world applications to communicate and integrate with each other" [34, p. 1194 (emphasis added)]. As smart products are essential for smart services, IoT platforms form the technical base for the implementation of SSS. By utilizing application-independent functionalities of IoT platforms, IoT applications—or smart service applications—can be developed and executed on an *application platform* [24,33].

In contrast, *digital multi-sided platforms* are not focused on the communication with or between smart products but "enable interactions between multiple groups of surrounding consumers and 'complementors'" [8, p. 163] based on functionality that is provided by a platform owner [30]. Although there is a multitude of different business models for multi-sided platforms, their structure barely differs: Multi-sided platforms exist in an ecosystem of different groups of actors and competing platforms [30]. Based on DE REUVER et al. [10] and VAN ALSTYNE et al. [30], here, a multi-sided platform is conceptualized as consisting of a platform core and a platform periphery. The platform core is provided and managed by the platform owner. Complementors can interact with that core to complement the platform with functionalities or offerings (e.g., (smart service) applications or (smart) products) that are located in the platform's periphery. Different groups of consumers can interact with the platform to find a suitable offering. Therefore, the platform matches an intent to consume with supply.

2.3 Modeling Languages for Service Systems

Modeling languages provide constructs, a meta-model representing their relationships, and graphical representations for designing models [3]. Using established modeling languages can increase the efficiency of conceptual modeling and improve the explanatory power of conceptual models through using formalized and clearly defined constructs [3]. To exploit these advantages, previous research has developed languages for modeling service that often take a business value, a business process, or an ICT perspective on service [25] (see BARROS et al. [2] for a comprehensive overview).

Modeling approaches that take a business value perspective focus on the design or configuration of value bundles (e.g., serviguration [1], e³value and e³service [25]), economic exchange in value networks [1,25], or interactions in value networks (e.g., FlexNet [4]). These approaches focus on what to offer or exchange and do not incorporate how this is done [25].

Process-centered approaches are used to model sequences of actions performed by the involved actors. General-purpose modeling languages such as Business Process Model and Notation [20] or Event-Driven Process Chains [27] are widely used but do not represent domain-specific knowledge [13]. Thus, using a DSML promises a higher integrity, clarity and comprehensibility of models [12]. Approaches that focus explicitly on service processes (e.g., Service Blueprinting [28]) are more deeply rooted in the terminology and mindset of service research. However, they often focus on business aspects, such as customer involvement but only peripherally consider technical aspects.

Languages that take an ICT perspective on service address web services, technical interfaces, and (service-oriented) architectures [16,21]. They focus on the design and provision of IT-services that differ substantially from a sociotechnical service system and are, therefore, of minor importance for this paper.

Common to these modeling languages is that they do not intend to model an entire socio-technical SSS, but focus on specific aspects. Also, technical systems—smart products and digital platforms—are not or only peripherally considered instead of including them as actors performing tasks. HUBER et al. [15] present a modeling language to model SSS that starts from a different theoretical basis comprising literature on service and IoT, but without including concepts of digital platforms. A more detailed differentiation to this modeling language is provided in Sect. 4.5.

All current modeling languages do not consider technical systems—either smart products or digital platforms—as actors that perform tasks. The modeling language presented in this paper addresses this issue and therefore takes an ICT perspective. It also adopts a business perspective by aiming to model the involved roles, the interfaces and boundary objects [7] between these roles, and tasks a role has to perform. These tasks are modeled on an abstract level and are linked, but without assigning a definite sequence to allow dynamic adaptions [15]. Therefore, the presented modeling language does not take a process-oriented view.

3   Research Approach

The purpose of this paper is to develop a DSML for platform-based SSS—called PS³—that can be used as a tool for designing and analyzing SSS. To design, demonstrate, and evaluate PS^3, I applied the design science research method, as proposed by PEFFERS et al. [23], in combination with design guidelines for DSML, as proposed by FRANK [12,13].

The design process took a problem-centered initiation focusing on overcoming current deficiencies in the design of platform-based SSS. The objective is to support designers in the development, communication, and implementation of platform-based SSS by providing a conceptual modeling language. For the design, relevant constructs for PS^3 were identified from the literature on SSS and digital platforms. The modeling language is specified by designing a meta-model and a graphical notation. As proposed by FRANK [13], I designed drafts for the meta-model and the graphical notation and applied them to model ten existing SSS (e.g., Babolat play, Tapio). The smart services were selected from different industry sectors, which are provided on different platform types to cover a broad spectrum of use cases. Based on the modeling results, PS^3 was evaluated via predefined requirements and the meta-model and the graphical notation were refined in several iterations. For demonstrating PS^3, I cooperated with a mechanical engineering company that is just starting to develop SSS and therefore requires a modeling language for their design, communication, and implementation.

4   Modeling Platform-Based Smart Service Systems

4.1   Problem Identification

Companies that intend to design and implement SSS face several challenges. They have to perform a cross-company development process [5] to identify and specify the elements of the SSS and their relationships. They must distinguish different human and non-human (groups of) actors [8] and their tasks for service provision and co-creation of value as well as points of interaction between actors [4]. Additionally, they must analyze the SSS to identify required resources and competences for the design and implementation [5]. Also, they must decide which roles to take on themselves and where partners are required. The designed concept of the SSS is relevant to all parties involved in the development and provision of smart service and smart products. Therefore, companies are in need of a conceptual model to communicate their design in varying degrees of detail, depending on the phase of the development process [5]. Additionally, designers have to take technical design decisions for which the entire SSS must be considered. They must design interfaces and boundary-objects that enable the cross-boundary integration of activities and transfer of information and knowledge [7]. They must derive requirements for the design and implementation of SSS elements, and decide for a partner's solution [5].

4.2   Definition of Objectives

In the development process of SSS, designers face several challenges for which a modeling language can provide support. By modeling a SSS, its elements are specified and their relations are defined, resulting in a comprehensive overview of interrelationships and boundaries. The identified problems designers are facing are converted into specific requirements for modeling SSS, which are supplemented by generic requirements for the design of a DSML as proposed by FRANK [13]. Therefore, the objective of this paper is to design a DSML for platform-based SSS and thereby to support companies in the design, communication, and implementation of SSS. This design objective is detailed by the following specific requirements:

R1. Mapping different roles in a SSS, incl. smart products and digital platforms. Thereby, a company can identify the required competencies and resources and decide what role(s) to take on in the service system. Also, the need for partners can be identified.
R2. Assigning tasks for value co-creation to different actors. Thereby, requirements for the technical and organizational implementation of the service system can be derived.
R3. Modeling interfaces and boundary-objects between the actors. Thereby, designers can identify and specify points of interaction and resource integration at the interfaces between actors and their activities and responsibilities.
R4. Modeling SSS on different levels of abstraction. Thereby, a designer can model a SSS idea at a higher level and detail the model during the service development process while using the model as a basis for communication.

4.3   Design and Development

The design of PS^3 is based on established constructs on SSS and digital platforms. A meta-model integrates these constructs and a graphical notation, including all constructs, makes PS^3 applicable. It took several iterations consisting of design, application, and evaluation to improve the modeling language.

Constructs. The constructs comprise sub-constructs as specialization.

Role. The literature on digital platforms distinguishes the roles of the platform owner [30], complementors [8] (also called contributors [8] or producers [30]), and customers or consumers [8,30]. The *platform owner* is responsible for the technical development of the platform and coordination of complementors [14]. Complementors provide the platform's offerings [30]. Here, the literature does not differentiate between information, applications, or physical products. In the context of SSS, two complementors are *producers* of smart products and (smart) *service providers*. The roles of the service provider and service customer are consistent with the literature on SSS [7]. The roles in a SSS can be fulfilled by one or by different organizations.

Platform. In information systems research, a plethora of platform terms exist. In the context of SSS, the three most relevant terms are focused to increase the comprehensibility of PS^3. First, *IoT platforms* are characterized by enabling communication and interaction with smart products [34]. Second, *application platforms* utilize generic functionalities and data provided by IoT platforms and provide the environment for the development and execution of (smart service) applications [24,33]. Third, *multi-sided platforms* network different groups of actors and enable their interaction [8].

Application. PORTER et al. identify four successive types of smart service enabled by smart products: Monitoring, control, optimization, and autonomy [24]. Enabled by sensors of a smart product and external data, *monitoring* of the product and its operation and usage is possible. *Control* encompasses smart service that control product functions and, therefore, enables a personalized customer experience. *Optimization* refers to an improvement of processes, performances, or the product operation. *Autonomy* describes autonomous acting of smart products or platforms, including self-x capabilities [15].

Interfaces. PAUKSTADT et al. identify three types of interfaces towards the customer: Device-based, smart product-based, and human-based [22]. *Device-based* interfaces describe clients (e.g., web applications) that can be accessed by the customer using devices (e.g., smartphones or tablets) that are not embedded in the smart product. Service delivery via the smart product is, therefore, defined as *smart product-based*. *Human-based* interfaces occur, where in addition to provision of smart service humans interact personally to co-create value in a SSS (e.g., personal consulting services).

Tasks. PS^3 does not target modeling processes, but assigning tasks to actors in the sense of (technical) design decisions. Therefore, tasks for extended data analysis and self-x capabilities, including *data preparation, analysis, altering, visualising, (remote) control, defining rules, making decisions, recommending, initiating actions,* and *performing actions* [7,15,24,26] are focused.

Data. Four different types of data are obtained by smart products: *Status data, usage data, context data,* and *location data* [7].

Smart Product. BEVERUNGEN et al. identify seven properties of smart products, of which the location, data storage and processing, and interfaces are covered by previously described constructs. A unique ID and connectivity are not included as constructs but connectivity is considered in the graphical notation of the PS^3 modeling language. Therefore, the remaining properties of smart products are *sensors* obtaining data and *actuators* performing physical actions.

Meta-model. Based on the identified constructs, a meta-model for PS^3 was designed (Fig. 1) [12,13]. The meta-model is designed as Entity Relationship Model using the Chen notation with minimum and maximum values. It depicts that two or more actors interact with each other via interfaces and perform tasks while generating or using data. To reduce the complexity, the constructs 'Smart Product', 'Role', 'Application', and 'Platform' were generalized to the construct 'Actor'. This term was inspired by the actor-network theory, since "[a] key feature of the theory is that actors are taken to include both human beings and nonhuman actors such as technological artefacts." [32, p. 468].

Graphical Notation. Since the PS^3 modeling language is intended to be applicable by companies that have no experience with modeling information systems, it should be intuitive for the proposed use. Therefore, instead of using existing

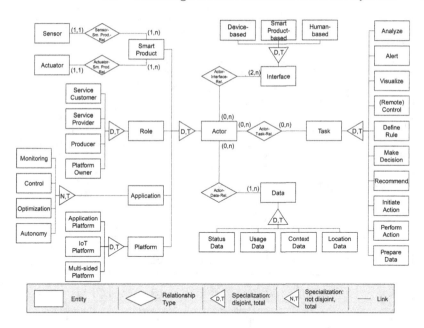

Fig. 1. Meta-model of the PS³ modeling language

abstract diagrams, e.g., Unified Modeling Language, a new notation has been designed (Fig. 2). To deal with complexity [19], PS³ provides a container as basic element structure that is used to model all elements of the SSS. This container consists of a head and a body. The head includes the graphical notation of the construct, its denotation, and a name. The body contains the specification of the element and can be omitted in early design phases, while it specified in later design phases. As proposed by MOODY, each construct corresponds to a single graphical symbol that are clearly distinguishable from each other, and their appearance suggests their meaning [19]. The symbol for generalized constructs is modified for the specialization, so that the classification is transparent. Thereby, the number of different symbols can still be cognitively manageable [19]. Also, the generalized symbol can be used if the instantiation is not yet defined.

4.4 Demonstration

The PS³ modeling language is demonstrated with the real case of a platform-based SSS established by a mechanical engineering company (MEC). This company today offers storage systems as well as maintenance and consulting services. They plan to extend their portfolio and benefit from their knowledge in a specialized field and their customers to provide smart service. They applied PS³ to model their smart service idea (see Fig. 3). Other companies that intend to use PS³ can be guided by the steps performed by MEC. In a first step, the roles were arranged. MEC takes on the role as producer in this SSS. We started

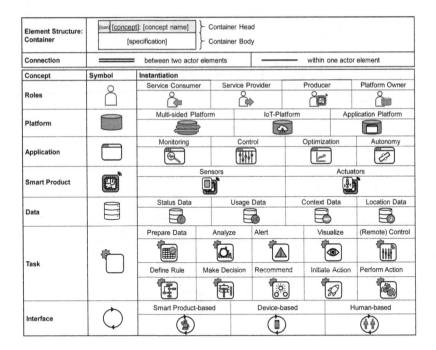

Fig. 2. Graphical notation of the PS³ modeling language

with generic roles for the platform owner and service customer. In the second step, we designed the smart product. Currently, the smart product only contains sensors that generate data and a task for data preparation. The smart product takes the role of a boundary object to integrate the service customer and the producer. MEC plans to offer a smart service for monitoring the product's condition. Therefore, in the third step, we modeled a monitoring application in the service provider's area of responsibility. The application must be implemented on an application platform. This application platform should have the ability to store product data so that several different applications can access them. MEC selected a solution for the application platform that fulfilled strategic and technical requirements. However, this application platform does not offer an integrated solution for managing and communicating with the smart products. Therefore, an additional IoT platform was added that provides this functionality. The tasks MEC has to perform on the IoT platform are currently not specified (Fig. 3).

4.5   Conceptual Evaluation and Discussion

PS³ is conceptually evaluated in terms of meeting the general and specific requirements based on multiple designed models. It fulfills all generic requirements as proposed by FRANK [13]. First, all constructs of PS³ are based on existing and known terminology from the literature on SSS and digital platforms. Second, domain-specific constructs with invariant semantics are used.

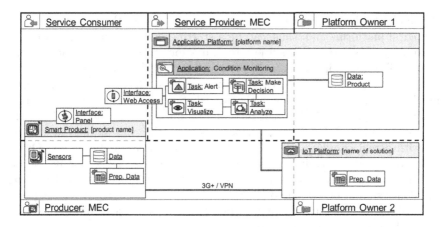

Fig. 3. Demonstration of the PS^3 modeling language

Third, the constructs allow sufficiently detailed modeling and extension mechanisms. Fourth, a clear differentiation of abstraction levels within a model is possible, since the elements are modeled in a nested manner. Fifth, the constructs are clearly assigned to relevant representations. The PS^3 modeling language also fulfills all specific requirements. First, it is possible to map different roles in a SSS. Second, tasks can be assigned to actors comprising humans (roles) and non-humans (smart products and digital platforms). Third, it is possible to model and specify interfaces and boundary objects. Fourth, by using containers, the SSS can be modeled on different levels of abstraction.

The design of PS^3 differs substantially from the modeling language presented by HUBER et al. [15]. First, the level of abstraction differs. In HUBER et al. the main constructs are *Service, Service System, Resources,* and *Relationship* while the generalized constructs for PS^3 are *Actor, Interface, Task,* and *Data.* Therefore, HUBER et al. take a global, system-centered perspective, while PS^3 takes a more detailed, actor-centered perspective. Second, there are significant differences in the resulting models. While HUBER et al. focus on modeling interrelated resources in at least two service systems for enacting service, PS^3 focuses on modeling actors in SSS and their interfaces and tasks to co-create value. Third, HUBER et al. limit available roles to service customers and participants, leaving service providers and producers of smart products unconsidered. Additionally, the language lacks the possibility of assigning detailed tasks to actors.

5 Conclusion and Outlook

This paper presents the design, demonstration, and conceptual evaluation of PS^3—a conceptual DSML for platform-based SSS—that can be used as a tool for designing and analyzing SSS. The contribution of this paper is twofold. First, PS^3 can be applied as a tool in a service engineering process to design, analyse, and communicate the concept of a platform-based SSS. Second, the presented meta-model is the first one to integrate constructs from the literature on SSS and digital platforms and, thus, can be a starting point for future research.

However, this research is subject to limitations resulting from the design of PS^3 as well as the applied research process. First, PS^3 focuses on the structure of SSS without detailing processes or interactions. At this point other modeling languages can complement the model. Second, the included constructs may be incomplete. I dealt with this issue by including a generalized notation that can be adapted for specific purposes. Third, PS^3 was applied in cooperation with a real company, but an empirical evaluation is outstanding. On the one hand, visual expressiveness and comprehensiveness of PS^3 should be analyzed [11]. On the other hand, the representational and interpretational efficiency and fidelity should be evaluated [9]. Additionally, even though MOODY's principles for designing effective visual notations [19] were addressed during the design of PS^3, their fulfillment also needs to be evaluated.

Acknowledgements. The paper presents results from the joint research project Digital Business, which is funded by the Ministry of Economic Affairs, Innovation, Digitalization, and Energy of the State of North Rhine-Westphalia, Germany (funding code: 005-1807-0107).

References

1. Baida, Z., Akkermans, H., Gordijn, J.: Serviguration. In: Sadeh, N. (ed.) Proceedings of the 5th ICEC, pp. 111–118. ACM, New York (2003)
2. Barros, A., Oberle, D. (eds.): Handbook of Service Description USDL and Its Methods. Springer, Boston, MA (2012). https://doi.org/10.1007/978-1-4614-1864-1
3. Becker, J., Beverungen, D., Knackstedt, R.: The challenge of conceptual modeling for product-service system. Inf. Syst. e-Bus Manage. **8**(1), 33–66 (2009)
4. Becker, J., Beverungen, D., Knackstedt, R., Matzner, M., Müller, O., Pöppelbuß, J.: Designing interaction routines in service networks: a modularity and social construction-based approach. Scand. J. Inf. Syst. **25**(1), 37–68 (2013)
5. Beverungen, D., Lüttenberg, H., Wolf, V.: Recombinant service systems engineering. Bus. Inf. Syst. Eng. **60**(5), 377–391 (2018)
6. Beverungen, D., Matzner, M., Janiesch, C.: Information systems for smart services. Inf. Syst. e-Bus. Manage. **15**(4), 781–787 (2017). https://doi.org/10.1007/s10257-017-0365-8
7. Beverungen, D., Müller, O., Matzner, M., Mendling, J., vom Brocke, J.: Conceptualizing smart service systems. Electron. Mark. **29**(1), 7–18 (2017). https://doi.org/10.1007/s12525-017-0270-5
8. Boudreau, K.J., Hagiu, A.: Platform rules: multi-sided platforms as regulators. In: Gawer, A. (ed.) Platforms, Markets and Innovation, pp. 163–191. Edward Elgar Publishing (2009)
9. Burton-Jones, A., Wand, Y., Weber, R.: Guidelines for empirical evaluations of conceptual modeling grammars. J. Assoc. Inf. Syst. **10**(6) (2009)
10. de Reuver, M., Sørensen, C., Basole, R.C.: The digital platform: a research agenda. J. Inf. Technol. **33**(2), 124–135 (2017)

11. Figl, K.: Comprehension of procedural visual business process models. Bus. Inf. Syst. Eng. **59**(1), 41–67 (2017)

12. Frank, U.: Some guidelines for the conception of domain-specific modelling languages. In: Nüttgens, M., Thomas, O., Weber, B. (eds.) Enterprise modelling and information systems architectures, pp. 93–106. GI e.V, Bonn (2011)

13. Frank, U.: Domain-specific modeling languages: requirements analysis and design guidelines. In: Reinhartz-Berger, I., Sturm, A., Clark, T., Cohen, S., Bettin, J. (eds.) Domain Engineering, p. 133. Springer, Berlin, Heidelberg (2013). https://doi.org/10.1007/978-3-642-36654-3_6

14. Gawer, A., Cusumano, M.A.: Platform leadership: How Intel, Microsoft, and Cisco drive industry innovation. HBS Press, Boston (2002)

15. Huber, R.X.R., Püschel, L.C., Röglinger, M.: Capturing smart service systems: development of a domain-specific modeling language. Inform. Syst. J. **29**(6), 1207–1255 (2019)

16. Kohlborn, T., La Rosa, M.: SOA approaches. In: Barros, A., Oberle, D. (eds.) Handbook of Service Description, pp. 111–133. Springer, Boston (2012). https://doi.org/10.1007/978-1-4614-1864-1

17. Latour, B.: Science in Action: How to Follow Scientists and Engineers Through Society. Harvard University Press, Cambridge (1987)

18. Maglio, P.P., Vargo, S.L., Caswell, N., Spohrer, J.: The service system is the basic abstraction of service science. Inf. Syst. e-Bus. Manage. **7**(4), 395–406 (2009)

19. Moody, D.: The "physics" of notations: toward a scientific basis for constructing visual notations in software engineering. IEEE Trans. Softw. Eng. **35**(6), 756–779 (2009)

20. OMG: about the business process model and notation version 2.0.2 (2014)

21. Papazoglou, M.P.: Web Services: Principles and Technology. Pearson, Harlow (2008)

22. Paukstadt, U., Strobel, G., Eicker, S.: Understanding services in the era of the internet of things: A smart service taxonomy. In: Proceedings of the 27th European Conference on Information Systems (ECIS). Stockholm & Uppsala, Sweden (2019)

23. Peffers, K., Tuunanen, T., Rothenberger, M.A., Chatterjee, S.: A design science research methodology for information systems research. J. Manage. Inform. Syst. **24**(3), 45–77 (2007)

24. Porter, M.E., Heppelmann, J.E.: How smart, connected products are transforming competition. Harv. Bus. Rev. **92**(11), 64–88 (2014)

25. Razo-Zapata, I.S., Gordijn, J., de Leenheer, P., Wieringa, R.: e³ service: a critical reflection and future research. Bus. Inf. Syst. Eng. **57**(1), 51–59 (2015)

26. Rizk, A., Bergvall-Kåreborn, B., Elragal, A.: Towards a taxonomy for data-driven digital services. In: Bui, T. (ed.) Proceedings of the 51st HICSS (2018)

27. Scheer, A.W.: Wirtschaftsinformatik: Referenzmodelle für industrielle Geschäftsprozesse. Berlin, Heidelberg, 6, durchgesehene auflage edn. (1995)

28. Shostack, L.G., Kingman-Brundage, J.: How to design a service. In: Congram, C.A., Friedman Margaret L. (eds.) The AMA Handbook of Marketing for the Service Industries, pp. 243–261 (1991)

29. Tilson, D., Lyytinen, K., Sørensen, C.: Digital infrastructures: the missing is research agenda. Inf. Syst. Res. **21**(4), 748–759 (2010)

30. Van Alstyne, M.W., Parker, G.G., Choudary, S.P.: Pipelines, platforms, and the new rules of strategy. Harv. Bus. Rev. **94**(4), 54–62 (2016)

31. Vargo, S.L., Lusch, R.F.: Why "service"? J. Acad. Mark. Sci. **36**(1), 25–38 (2008)

32. Walsham, G.: Actor-network theory and IS research: current status and future prospects. In: Lee, A.S., Liebenau, J., DeGross, J.I. (eds.) Information Systems and Qualitative Research. ITIFIP, pp. 466–480. Springer, Boston (1997). https:// doi.org/10.1007/978-0-387-35309-8_23
33. Wortmann, F., Flüchter, K.: Internet of things. Bus. Inf. Syst. Eng. **57**(3), 221–224 (2015)
34. Yang, H., Kumara, S., Bukkapatnam, S.T., Tsung, F.: The internet of things for smart manufacturing: a review. IISE Trans. **51**(11), 1190–1216 (2019)

SISA News: Software to Support the Swedish Information Systems Community

Jonas Sjöström$^{(\boxtimes)}$

Uppsala University, Campus Gotland, 62167 Visby, Sweden
jonas.sjostrom@im.uu.se

Abstract. This paper reports on the design, adoption, and continued use of the SISA News software. The software draws ideas from news syndication, the community of practice concept, 'leaky knowledge in organizations, and microservice architectures. It provides a news flow for the Swedish information systems community through RSS, Facebook, and the web. The news flow aggregates information systems news from 18/20 Swedish IS departments. We evaluate the software through a multi-level community detection analysis from 24+ months of news consumption among 100 Swedish information systems researchers.

Keywords: News syndication · Research · Community · Leaky knowledge · Software · Design science research

1 Introduction

DeSanctis [6] expresses the importance of the information systems (IS) social life as follows: "The social life of the IS research community is its future. How we attract and retain members, and the nature of our scholarly discourse with one another, will be the ultimate determinants of the legitimacy of the field." (p. 394).

Improved transparency between departments, and stronger social relations, are likely to promote collaboration and may thus facilitate ideation and, ultimately, joint research and education activities. Funding agencies and academic institutions recognize the growing importance of collaboration to increase quality of research and higher education. For example, the Swedish government's latest proposition for research funding [9] strongly focuses on collaboration – nationally and internationally, and between academia and practice. Similarly, research-funding agencies around the world increasingly require consortia consisting of several universities and industrial or public sector partners.

In addition to adhering to funding requirements, IS researchers and teachers are part of a community of practice [6] and often operate in concert with colleagues at other universities. The establishment of high-impact research environments may depend on successful collaboration with external peers [17, 20]. On the education side, as demonstrated by the AIS curriculum guideline efforts [22], and the activities and outlets provided by the AIS special interest group on education, there is also a great interest among IS scholars to collaborate on curricular and didactical issues.

© Springer Nature Switzerland AG 2020
S. Hofmann et al. (Eds.): DESRIST 2020, LNCS 12388, pp. 451–456, 2020.
https://doi.org/10.1007/978-3-030-64823-7_43

We also see a need for IS researchers to improve communication to practice, not only in terms of publications [21], but through an increased transparency between society and ongoing IS research.

In this paper, we report on a design science research (DSR) initiative to promote interaction between Swedish IS departments, communication and to the public. The empirical context is the Swedish IS academy (SISA) – a community of Swedish IS academics founded in 2010. SISA aims at "creating and building on common interest regarding research information to students, practitioners, other academic disciplines, research funding organizations, politicians and civil servants." [18]. 20 IS departments in Sweden are SISA members, taking turns to chair the network. The chairing department organizes the annual meeting, typically two days of lectures and workshops around current topics and concerns, followed by a closing board meeting. SISA also awards the best Ph.D. thesis each year, as well as awarding pedagogical achievements every second year.

At the SISA annual meeting in 2017, the participants explored how to expand collaboration further through new initiatives. One suggestion concerned the opportunity to strengthen the community through the use of collaborative tools and social media. The proposition was that a joint news outlet could benefit the Swedish IS community. Such a tool, we anticipated, would increase awareness among the community's members about what is taking place at other departments. This paper presents the resulting 'SISA News' software as well as its use in the community over 24 + months.

2   The SISA News Software

IS – as an academic discipline – has previously been addressed from a community of practice (CoP) point of view [5, 11]. Despite the discussed crisis in IS [2], the field has a pragmatic legitimacy building on its social life, i.e., well established publication outlets and conferences, and a long tradition of providing IS competence to practice through research and education [6]. Hoadley and Kilner [10] articulate four purposes for content-sharing in a CoP: Attracting new members through immediate value, socializing new members, stimulating conversation, and motivating members to contribute to the community.

News syndication has been quite extensively studied in an organizational context, e.g., in relation to topic-specific interest communities [3], news syndication for pedagogics in higher education, and social networking/community building [12], as well as higher education institutions use of social media to interact with their community [4, 8]. Other studies include social media use by non-profit organizations [14, 23] and more general studies of social media for community of practice [e.g., 24, 25] and work on social media strategies [15]. We have, however, not been able to identify a study focusing the impact of news syndication to deliver aggregated content into a *distributed* community of practice, such as SISA.

Our work also relates to the idea of 'leaky knowledge' [13] in a social media setting. We consider the design work at hand as a case of designing 'leaky knowledge'. By design, the news is published for IS scholars. The leakiness facilitates actors at the various universities to pick up on what is going on at each other's departments, which may affect their course of action in their home organization.

News syndication and its technical standards (RSS/Atom) highly influenced the design. The use of existing RSS feeds, and other HTTP-based sources and services, resonated well with the concept of a microservices architecture [1, 7, 16]; that is, small, loosely coupled components that interact via a lightweight protocol.

The artifact presentation (Fig. 1) shows how the RSS/Atom standard and the microservices concepts were implemented in the design work.

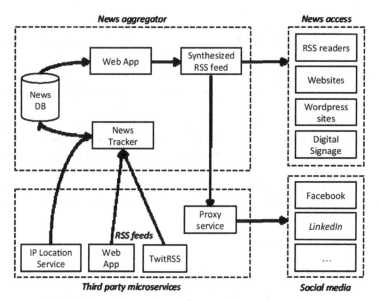

Fig. 1. Conceptual architecture for the SISA News software.

The core of the software is the *news tracker*, which periodically pulls source feeds (RSS and Twitter feeds through the proxy service TwitRSS). Some source feeds are filtered through a basic keyword matching mechanism to only include IS news. The news items are stored in the *news database*. The web app publishes a *synthesized feed* – 'SISA news'. Another third-party service is used to pull news from the aggregated feed and push it into social media channels. Also, following [19], we built in logging features into the design to facilitate evaluation of how people accessed news. The logging depends on a third-party IP location service to lookup location information from an IP address. The IP address is then discarded, to comply with privacy regulations.

From January 1, 2018, the news were available on a Facebook page[1], integrated into the SISA web site [18], or by subscribing to the RSS feed using a standard RSS reader[2]. 18/20 Swedish IS departments are included in the aggregated news.

---

[1] https://www.facebook.com/SvenskaInformationssystemakademin/.

[2] http://gotlab.im.uu.se/News/GetRssFeed?feedName=SISA.

3 Evaluation

Here we present one out of several evaluation activities that has taken place: A cross-regional analysis of news reads, based on log data. Each time a person clicks a news item, the software logs a time stamp, the news item id, and the country and region of the newsreader.

Our data is based on the period January 1, 2018–January 27, 2020. In average, one news article per day was posted. Almost 8000 new articles were clicked. A 'click' means that someone has clicked a news item summary to access the full article. We thus consider a click to be a news read. However, we assume that many people have also seen summaries without clicking them, e.g., in the Facebook flow. Thus the news service may also have 'leaked' knowledge that we do *not* account for here. The Facebook page has 100 followers, which corresponds to approximately 1/3 of all IS staff at the 20 Swedish IS departments.

In order to better understand the structural properties of network interactions, we employed a network analysis using R. We performed a community detection analysis to understand if there were clustering among the regions, i.e., high degrees of news reads within groups of regions as compared to interactions in the entire country (Fig. 2). The *multi-level community detection* analysis strategy was selected following recommendations on appropriateness of various clustering algorithms in different contexts of analysis [26].

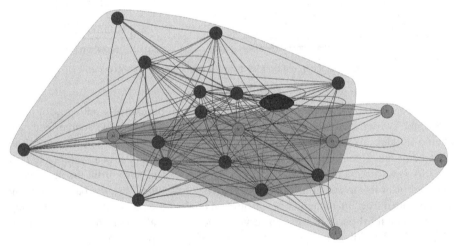

Fig. 2. Regional network interactions and identified clusters. Each edge represents a region.

The multi-level algorithm works iteratively to determine how to cluster the nodes to maximize the modularity score. The modularity score increases when there are many interactions within the clusters (*cohesion* in software engineering terms), and fewer between clusters (*coupling* in software engineering terms). Since multi-level clustering requires an undirected graph, we converted the directed network graph to an undirected one by summing the news reads from X → Y with the ones from Y → X *et cetera*.

Each vertice thus represents the total number of news reads *between* two regions. The multi-level clustering revealed three clusters in the network, with a modularity score of **0.1**. If modularity is 1, all interactions occur within the clusters. The modularity in this case is thus is very low, showing that the clustering is weak and there is a high degree of interaction between all regions – thus matching the goals of SISA to increase transparency and interactions between departments across the country.

4 Conclusions

We have presented the SISA News software; drawing from needs of the Swedish IS community, and reported on its use over 24+ months. Using a multi-level community detection algorithm we have shown that news consumption occurs across all regions, albeit with a few very week clusters. Also, the log data reveals a continued use of the software. Other evaluation efforts – focusing the perceived value of the software among stakeholders – have been conducted but are not reported here due to space limitations. Future work will present more thorough evaluations as well as theoretical contributions of the DSR project as a whole.

The SISA News software is a novel hybrid design, drawing from ideas of news syndication to improve sharing within a community of practice. Also, the innovativeness of the software lies within its built-in evaluation support, allowing for a near real-time monitoring of how knowledge 'leaks' between different parts of the community. Further, we have shown that a low-cost app based on news syndication has been adopted and continually used within a large subset of the Swedish IS community, with only minor promotion efforts. The significance to practice lies in the potential application of the concept in other communities around the world.

References

1. Akenine, D., et al.: Boken om IT-arkitektur. Hoi Förlag AB (2014)
2. Benbasat, I., Zmud, R.W.: The identity crisis within the IS discipline: defining and communicating the discipline's core properties. MIS Q. 183–194 (2003)
3. Buns, A.: Gatewatching, not gatekeeping: collaborative online news. Media Int. Aust. Inc. Cult. Policy. **107**(1), 31–44 (2003)
4. D'Andrea, V., Gosling, D.: Improving Teaching And Learning In Higher Education: A Whole Institution Approach: A Whole Institution Approach. McGraw-Hill Education (UK) (2005)
5. Desanctis, G.: The Social life of information systems research * a response to Benbasat and Zmud' s Call for returning to the IT artifact the IS community of practice. J. Assoc. Inf. Syst. **4**(7), 360–376 (2003)
6. DeSanctis, G.: The social life of information systems research: a response to Benbasat and Zmud's call for returning to the IT artifact. J. Assoc. Inf. Syst. **4**(1), 16 (2003)
7. Dragoni, N., Giallorenzo, S., Lafuente, A.L., Mazzara, M., Montesi, F., Mustafin, R., Safina, L.: Microservices: yesterday, today, and tomorrow. Present and Ulterior Software Engineering, pp. 195–216. Springer, Cham (2017). https://doi.org/10.1007/978-3-319-67425-4_12
8. Forkosh-Baruch, A., Hershkovitz, A.: A case study of Israeli higher-education institutes sharing scholarly information with the community via social networks. Internet High. Educ. **15**(1), 58–68 (2012)

9. Hellmark Knutsson, H.: Kunskap i samverkan-för samhällets utmaningar och stärkt konkurrenskraft (2016)
10. Hoadley, C.M., Kilner, P.G.: Using technology to transform communities of practice into knowledge-building communities. ACM Siggr. Bull. **25**(1), 31–40 (2005)
11. Klein, H.K., Hirschheim, R.: The structure of the IS discipline reconsidered: implications and reflections from a community of practice perspective. Inf. Organ. **18**(4), 280–302 (2008)
12. Lee, M.J.W., et al.: RSS and content syndication in higher education: subscribing to a new model of teaching and learning. EMI. Educ. Media Int. **45**(4), 311–322 (2008)
13. Leonardi, P.M.: The social media revolution: sharing and learning in the age of leaky knowledge. Inf. Organ. **27**(1), 47–59 (2017)
14. Lovejoy, K., Saxton, G.D.: Information, community, and action: how nonprofit organizations use social media. J. Comput. Commun. **17**(3), 337–353 (2012)
15. Mergel, I.: Designing a social media strategy to fulfill your agency's mission. Publ. Manag. **42**(1) 26 (2013)
16. Newman, S.: Building Microservices: Designing Fine-Grained Systems. O'Reilly Media Inc. (2015)
17. Nunamaker, J.F., et al.: Creating high-value real-world impact through systematic programs of research. MIS Q. **41**, 2 (2017)
18. SISA: Svenska Informationssystemakademin.s http://sisa-org.se
19. Sjöström, J., Kruse, L.C., Haj-Bolouri, A., Flensburg, P.: Software-embedded evaluation support in design science research. In: Chatterjee, S., Dutta, K., Sundarraj, R.P. (eds.) DESRIST 2018. LNCS, vol. 10844, pp. 348–362. Springer, Cham (2018). https://doi.org/10.1007/978-3-319-91800-6_23
20. Sjöström, J., et al.: The origin and impact of ideals in eHealth research: experiences from the U-CARE research environment. JMIR Res. Protoc. **3**, 2 (2014)
21. Te'eni, D., et al.: Stimulating dialog between information systems research and practice. Eur. J. Inf. Syst. **26**(6) 541–545 (2017)
22. Topi, H., et al.: IS 2010: Curriculum guidelines for undergraduate degree programs in information systems. Commun. Assoc. Inf. Syst. **26**(1) 18 (2010)
23. Waters, R.D., et al.: Engaging stakeholders through social networking: how nonprofit organizations are using Facebook. Publ. Relat. Rev. **35**(2), 102–106 (2009)
24. Wenger, E.: Communities Of Practice: A Brief Introduction (2011)
25. Wenger, E.: Communities of practice and social learning systems: the career of a concept. Soc. Learn. Syst. Commun. Pract. **3**, 179–198 (2010)
26. Yang, Z., et al.: A comparative analysis of community detection algorithms on artificial networks. Sci. Rep. **6**, 30750 (2016)

System-Wide Learning in Cyber-Physical Service Systems: A Research Agenda

Dominik Martin[1]([⊠]), Niklas Kühl[1], Johannes Kunze von Bischhoffshausen[2], and Gerhard Satzger[1]

[1] Karlsruhe Institute of Technology, Kaiserstraße 89, 76131 Karlsruhe, Germany
martin@kit.edu
[2] Trelleborg Sealing Solutions Germany GmbH, Schockenriedstr. 1, 70565 Stuttgart, Germany

Abstract. The rapid development in sensor technology as well as in communication mechanisms exponentially grows the amount of data that is permanently gathered via products, machines, or assets within Cyber-Physical Systems. While this data offers enormous potential for creating additional value by generating valuable insights or creating innovative services, these opportunities are often times not exploited: Especially in complex value creation networks, only individual actors tend to have access to the collected data and they hardly share it with other network members. In our conceptual work, we target a three-fold contribution: First, we develop a framework for system-wide learning that structures data-based collaboration with other actors in a complex value creation network based on IoT, a Cyber-Physical Service System. Second, we systematically develop five individual research questions that need to be addressed to realize viable solutions. And thirdly, we conceptualize a research design to address this research agenda in future steps.

Keywords: System-wide learning · Cyber-Physical Service System · Industrial Internet of Things · Research agenda

1 Introduction

Sensor technology has become a key driver of developments like "Industry 4.0" or the "Internet of Things" (IoT) in general [1]. Large numbers of machines and products are equipped with sensors to constantly monitor their condition, log usage data or trigger control processes. In addition, other technological advances (e.g., high speed communication, robotics, Artificial Intelligence) contribute to ample opportunities to improve companies' internal efficiency and to conceive and capture new opportunities for innovation and technology-enabled value (co-)creation.

Nevertheless, purely technical systems have some shortcomings compared to humans [2]. People as a part of several complex systems like the universe, society, etc. are able to perceive the context of their environment and to link it to other information and learned knowledge [3]: So, a human inside a room may perceive the lighting condition and sounds of raindrops on the roof and translate it into the information that it may be

© Springer Nature Switzerland AG 2020
S. Hofmann et al. (Eds.): DESRIST 2020, LNCS 12388, pp. 457–468, 2020.
https://doi.org/10.1007/978-3-030-64823-7_44

raining outside. Combined with other stored information and learned knowledge, this may advise him to carry an umbrella when leaving to not get soaking wet.

In contrast, we often observe narrow and isolated IoT applications that are primarily targeted to exploit short-term business potential [4, 5]. As these local solutions bear the disadvantage of ignoring the context—the "big picture"—a huge potential is left untapped.

As a consequence, there is an urgent need for 'system thinking' [6] in the industrial applications of IoT [5]. For example, suppliers in complex value chains often have no access to data of the end product, although integrated sensors do produce ample data. So, in complex systems like an aircraft, condition monitoring for individual components could be achieved in cooperation with the supplier who has the necessary domain knowledge but (today) no access to the data [7]. In the research areas of ubiquitous computing, the ability of technical systems to collect context information has been addressed for quite some time, but obviously there is a lack of practical implementation in industry [8].

In order to address this issue, this article develops an understanding of Cyber-Physical Service Systems (CPSS) as a special (sensor-based) type of Service System. In a conceptual analysis we then target three contributions: First, we develop a framework for system-wide learning in CPSS. Second, we identify five key research questions that need to be solved within this framework to systematically advance the exploitation of (so far) hidden IoT value creation potentials. Thirdly, we draw on Design Science Research to propose a research design to address these questions in future work.

We will proceed as follows: We first position our work and report on relevant literature for theoretical and practical motivation. We then continue to define *Cyber-Physical Service Systems* and relate to other concepts in the field. With the definition at hand, we introduce the concept of *system-wide learning* and develop relevant research questions along the way. Finally, we conclude with a short summary, limitations as well as the outlook for future research.

2   Related Work and Positioning

To approach our endeavor, we choose Design Science Research (DSR) as a research paradigm, as we favor a strong focus on artifact design and rigor evaluation. As stressed by Hevner (2007) [9], both, the knowledge base and research contribution (rigor cycle) as well as the practical aspects of the application domain of the to-be-designed artifact (relevance cycle) need to be taken into account.

Our first insights on the rigor cycle show that complex value creation structures around an in-core Cyber-Physical System aiming to create additional value through services have so far been insufficiently researched [10, 11]. It has been found that the unification of characteristics of Service System research with the more technical properties of Cyber-Physical Systems is a fundamental prerequisite for the purposeful development of a concept for system-wide learning within such complex socio-technical systems [8, 12].

The term system-wide learning appears in literature in several contexts (e.g., education [13] or healthcare [14]). Generally speaking, system-wide learning wants to clearly differentiate itself from learning in isolated entities. System-wide considerations are able to generate valuable insights which would not be possible with a singular view. The approach of system-wide learning in the context of this work aims to leverage data within complex systems to generate added value through a holistic view. Precisely this increase in value and meaning of data is addressed by the information value chain [15]. This describes different degrees of maturity of data, information and knowledge up to wisdom, which enable differently founded decisions in each phase [16].

With regard to the relevance cycle, there is a significant need to bring 'systems thinking' [6] into industrial IoT applications [5]. Udoh and Kotonya (2017) [17] complain in addition to the hesitant development of IoT solutions in general, that there is a lack of frameworks to address heterogeneity in IoT systems. Furthermore, the identification of roles of involved stakeholders [17] as well as the enrichment of data with metadata is also insufficiently addressed [18]. Ramakrishnan et al. (2014) and Sukode et al. (2015) [19, 20] emphasize generally inadequate sensor availability and propose using secondary sources of information to collect necessary contextual information. Similarly, Sukode et al. (2015) [20] stress the need for context discovery, context sharing, and context reasoning research.

As a preliminary result from both cycles, we derive the overall, design-focused, research question (RQO): *How can system-wide learning be enabled in complex Service Systems that are directly related to a Cyber-Physical System?*

3   Cyber-Physical Service Systems

In the course of ongoing servitization, the concept of Service Systems as "value-co-creation configurations of people, technology, value propositions connecting internal and external service systems, and shared information (e.g., language, laws, measures, and methods)" [21, p. 18] has emerged. The central goal of such a system is to create value through the collaboration of service clients and service providers in more or less complex arrangements (i.e., individual persons can form a Service System, but also entire economies) [22]. While the concept of a Service System particularly emphasizes the need for information, it does not make a concrete statement about its origin. The concept of Cyber-Physical Systems offers exactly this missing building block. However, in contrast to Mikusz (2015) [23], who equates Cyber-Physical Systems and Service Systems, we follow the common notion of Cyber-Physical Systems in literature and do not see them as an exclusive prerequisite for value co-creation. Rather we see them as an integral part that can foster co-creation when embedded in a is a Service System. It is obvious that today's technical systems are able to provide an enormous amount of potentially usable data through communication channels [8, 12].

In order to uncover these potentials, we propose to combine the characteristics of Service Systems and Cyber-Physical Systems (CPS). We, therefore, define the concept of Cyber-Physical Service Systems (CPSS) as a subset of Service Systems: Cyber-Physical Service Systems are Service Systems that center around one or more Cyber-Physical System(s) with the target of creating value. Thus, the data of these Cyber-Physical Systems is an essential building block for innovative services [24, 25]. Figure 1 schematically illustrates the structure of a Cyber-Physical Service System. An embedded system can gather data by means of sensor technology, which is usually processed on the edge device itself by software artifacts [26]. The collected data triggers control tasks that can affect the physical environment through an actuator [11]. Enriching the embedded systems with communication mechanisms creates a Cyber-Physical System [27]. These communication mechanisms enable the transfer of data from the CPS to cyberspace and, thus, allow interaction with humans [26]. Due to the lack of specification of the Service System concept, where the information used for value creation through services actually comes from and, moreover, due to the potential of CPS to generate that information, we propose the definition of CPSS as a CPS embedded within a Service System.

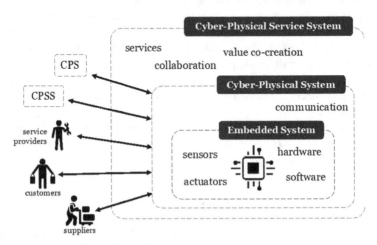

Fig. 1. Cyber-Physical Service System structure

4   System-Wide Learning in CPSS and Open Research Questions

With the development of advanced sensor technology and the decline in hardware costs an increasing number of machines and products has been equipped with sensors to acquire data on assets behavior [28–30]. Theoretical and applied research either focuses on developing smart materials equipped with sensors or on the implementation of single-purpose sensor technology into assets, machines or components in order to be able to monitor a component's condition [31, 32]. Especially for very complex assets (i.e., aircraft engines, production machines, wind turbines), the reliability of each individual component is of enormous importance.

However, in many cases it is either technically not feasible or uneconomic to continuously monitor the components or parts of interest with dedicated sensors [33]. For instance, it is not possible to incorporate sensor technology into a part of interest—such as i.e., a seal—due to, for instance, technical reasons or unreasonable expenses [34]. In contrast to this isolated approach, where only a local solution is developed for an individual component of an entire system, we propose to address the problem holistically. Leveraging context information from surrounding components or the entire system can enrich the data available for a single system component. By learning from this additional data, conclusions can be drawn about a component even if it cannot be observed directly due to a lack of physical sensors. So instead of physical sensors, virtual sensors based on environmental data can be used to create additional value.

The information value chain (Fig. 2; also known as DIKW hierarchy) aims to depict ways to generate insights or value from data by following five steps [15, 16]: Data, Information, Knowledge, Wisdom, Decision. At each of these steps, the different degrees of value and meaning of data provide specific opportunities from holistically perceiving CPSS. In the following sections, we discuss open questions and possible approaches with regard to our proposed system-wide learning framework (Fig. 3) by referring to the information value chain.

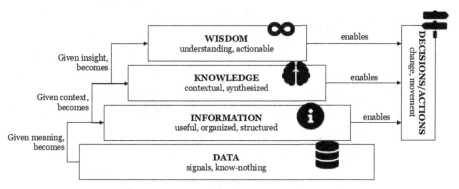

Fig. 2. Information value chain based on Rowley (2007) [16]

4.1 Data

Data represents raw facts and properties of objects, events and their environment. They are a product of observation, however, are of no use until they are in a useable (i.e., relevant) form [15, 16]. For instance, the characters "101" are meaningless unless its specific meaning is inferred or known. Raw data is an essential foundation for value creation in Cyber-Physical Service Systems. Therefore, it is absolutely crucial that there is a sufficient amount of data of acceptable quality that can be used for system-wide learning.

In modern technical systems, data is usually collected for different reasons. Either they serve for documentation purposes or as a basis for rule-based decision-making. In addition, not only data generated by technical systems is of value, but also manual user input or context data. Therefore, the amount and kind of data being collected is usually driven by historical decisions or generally by the system design. Due to a potentially diverse supplier structure of complex systems, the origin of the data and its sovereignty is often not with only one company. Therefore, incentive strategies within a CPSS are necessary to provide data access to all interested stakeholders [35, 36]. The technical requirements for the transferability of data must be ensured by means of suitable interfaces.

The decision as to which data should be collected in which areas of the system should therefore not be a historical or isolated decision. Rather, the design of a CPSS must already be adapted to the requirements with regard to the data to be collected.

Thus, a uniform architecture of the underlying CPSS is crucial for the applicability of system-wide learning. Therefore, the research question (RQ1) arises: *How must a CPSS architecture be designed to capture data needed for system-wide learning?*

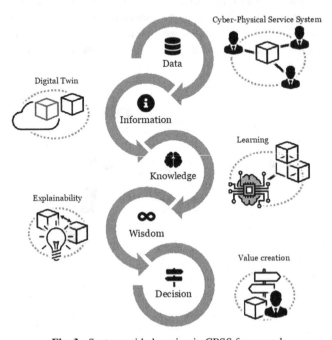

Fig. 3. System-wide learning in CPSS framework

4.2 Information

Information is contained in descriptions, answers to questions that begin with such words as who, what, when and how many. Information systems generate, store, retrieve and process data from which information is inferred [16]. For instance, a temperature value observed by a temperature sensor is meaningful only by additional metadata such as the temperature unit and time of sensing [18]. Thus, information is organized and structured data in a useful and understandable form. Information emerges due to its extension by a certain meaning.

The central question is, therefore, how reality in a CPSS can be transformed into a digital representation in a usable and structured form, including all components and facets. This requires an underlying unified architecture of a digital twin, which models different parts of the system, like components, assets, processes as well as the entire system itself [37]. The distinction between gathering of raw data and its enrichment with meta-data (meaning) driven by the design of a corresponding digital representation is an important aspect. While the architecture of a CPSS terminates the available amount of data, its meaning, structure and usefulness are dependent on its virtual form. A digital twin represents this virtual counterpart of an asset or CPSS, which companies can leverage to digitally mirror and manage it throughout the entire life cycle [38]. Research on digital twins is currently still too isolated and application specific. Therefore, holistic thinking, stronger standardization in the areas of data acquisition as well as a general architecture of such digital representations of CPSS are strongly required [38, 39].

Thus, the second research question (RQ2) is: *How do digital twins of all CPSS components have to be modeled to represent a structured digital representation of reality?*

4.3 Knowledge

Knowledge is the result of the transformation of information into instructions. It can be obtained either by transmission from another who has it, by instruction, or by extracting it from experience [16]. Although information alone is already useful for a number of questions, however, additional knowledge can be created by adding relationships and patterns.

In order to determine connections, patterns and relationships between separate system components and their effects on others, the applications of machine learning methods seem suitable [34]. Humans use their experiences and skills to learn and to draw conclusions from different information sources. By using suitable machine learning methods, this human characteristic can be modeled. From the mere presence of different information about certain processes and contexts new knowledge can be created, which is encapsulated in the form of models.

Further interesting aspects need to be explored in this context (i.e., CPSS): Most importantly how generalizable knowledge can be generated from available information by means of machine learning techniques. As a foundation, it is necessary to identify ways to integrate data /information that is not trivial to be collected (e.g., missing labels for classification /regression), but still present in a systemic context [37]. Furthermore, the application-related /domain-specific knowledge of people (e.g., physical interactions, implicit knowledge, etc.) should be considered for integration [40].

The core aspects of this phase, thus, are the application of machine learning at various system levels of a CPSS (components, assets, processes, entire system) to generate knowledge as well as the integration of non-trivial context information and application-related knowledge. The third research question (RQ3) can be, therefore, formulated as follows: *How can digital twins be supplemented by contextual information and application-oriented knowledge in order to achieve a complete representation of the real system properties and interconnections?*

4.4 Wisdom

Rowley (2007) [16] defines wisdom as the ability to increase effectiveness. Wisdom adds value, which requires the mental function that we call judgement. This includes ethical and aesthetic values which are inherent to the actor and, furthermore, are unique and personal.

Thus, wisdom arises from knowledge through understanding of all relationships and, therefore, represents actionable, integrated and applied knowledge. In order to make the knowledge created in the previous phase explainable or interpretable, it is necessary to identify meaningful ways to model knowledge by machine learning, which can be made explainable or interpretable [41]. Furthermore, it has to be investigated, how individual data (sources) impact the performance of machine learning models for the generation of knowledge [42].

In addition, the need for explainability of machine learning models is a topic of acute social relevance. The black-box problem poses people with difficulty in making decisions based on knowledge generated by unintelligible machine learning processes [43]. Accordingly, the enrichment of artificially created knowledge by additional explanations is essential for the applicability of this knowledge. Based on the interpretability of models, it is also possible to evaluate the importance of individual data sources in order to obtain a certain estimation of the value of individual data.

The fourth research question (RQ4), thus, is: *How can patterns and interconnections of knowledge within a CPSS be made explainable and interpretable for humans, in order to form a solid basis for decisions and actions?*

4.5 Decisions /Action

Decision making is basically the most interesting and most important part of the information value chain, as in the absence of action, capturing, understanding, leveraging, etc. of data it is of little use. The creation of actual tangible value proceeds in this final phase. Decisions can be made on the basis of information, knowledge and wisdom. Due to the different level of maturity and value of data in each particular phase, decisions and actions can be taken on different levels. Exclusively data is not sufficient as a basis for decision-making, as the corresponding necessary context is missing.

Thus, rather abstract questions arise, e.g., 'how generated wisdom can be used in order to enable value-creation within a CPSS?' or 'which services can be designed based on wisdom?'

The core of this phase is thus the harnessing of the generated wisdom, which leads to the fifth research question (RQ5): *How can existing wisdom within a CPSS be used in order to enable value co-creation of services?*

5   Research Agenda

To address these derived research questions with Design Science Research (DSR), we recommend applying the methodology of Hevner and Chatterjee (2010) [44] with design cycles according to Kuechler, William Vaishnavi (2012) [45] and evaluation strategies according to Venable et al. (2016) [46]. We propose to conduct design research in five consecutive phases with a mixed evaluation strategy.

The first phase aims to set ground for our proposed framework of system-wide learning in CPSS and, thus, focuses on the identification of problems regarding the general design and architecture of Cyber-Physical Service Systems (RQ1). In three subsequent phases, several design cycles according to Kuechler, William Vaishnavi (2012) [45] for the development of methods to overcome these problems (RQ2, RQ3, RQ4) can be performed. In each of these phases, the method design and development are also guided by using the Design Science Research methodology assessing feasibility, usability and efficiency. The fifth phase focuses on applicability and usability (RQ5) of the developed knowledge of the preceding phases, which can be evaluated by an interview study with practitioners.

In all five phases, we propose to refer to different use cases from practice. Finally, we recommend evaluating the overall design science project (RQO) according to Venable et al. (2016) [46] (see Fig. 4) to verify organizational impacts of the developed framework by a case study [47]. Venable et al. (2016) [46] propose a framework to characterize individual DSR evaluation episodes by two dimensions. One dimension represents the functional purpose of the evaluation (formative vs. summative) while the other dimension describes the evaluation paradigm (artificial vs. naturalistic).

With the increasing complexity of the research subject and the need to build on existing research, the evaluation purpose drifts from formative to summative. While a mainly formative approach is applicable for the first evaluation episode (RQ1) in order to be able to react appropriately during the development of the artifact, a verification of the success of the artifact as quickly as possible is a suitable strategy for the final episode (RQ5). Furthermore, the evaluation paradigm arises from the nature of the artifact itself. While in the case of RQ1 and RQ5, the artifacts' efficacy in their real environment is of primary interest, RQ2, RQ3 and RQ4 will be evaluated more artificially, since these are mainly of a technical nature.

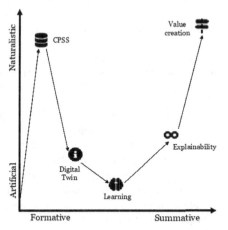

Fig. 4. Overall evaluation strategy according to Venable et al. (2016) [46]

6   Conclusion and Outlook

Due to embedded sensors and interconnectedness, machines and products produce large amounts of data which is often only used for a specific purpose. The entire potential of this already existing data is therefore far from being exploited. We, therefore, propose a novel framework to address these uncovered potentials. System-wide learning is a framework that leverages data that is already gathered to enable (new) value co-creation. To do so, the five-step framework describes the phases from the design of Cyber-Physical Service Systems and digital twins for data acquisition and enhancement to a necessary context, learning through the use of machine learning techniques, the conception of explainability, and the overall goal of value creation. For each of these steps, explicit research questions are provided. For this purpose, we present a research agenda, which proposes the development of corresponding artifacts in five consecutive phases and the evaluation of them with suitable methods. At the same time, we are already presenting results from the first phase. A systematic literature review depicts a need for a clear definition of Service Systems, which especially lie around a Cyber-Physical System: Cyber-Physical Service Systems.

Limitations of our work are the so far sparse results from a first relevance cycle building only on literature and a few expert interviews, which shows the necessity of such a framework. Moreover, due to the nature of a research agenda, this work in its current state is conceptual and the proposed framework does not provide concrete results for all five phases. Overall, an interesting research topic that has extraordinary practical relevance lies ahead.

References

1. Lu, Y.: Industry 4.0: a survey on technologies, applications and open research issues. J. Ind. Inf. Integr. **6** 1–10 (2017)
2. Checkland, P.B.: Information systems and systems thinking: time to unite? Int. J. Inf. Manage. **8**, 239–248 (1988)
3. Abowd, G.D., Dey, A.K., Brown, P.J., Davies, N., Smith, M., Steggles, P.: Towards a better understanding of context and context-awareness. In: Gellersen, H.-W. (ed.) HUC 1999. LNCS, vol. 1707, pp. 304–307. Springer, Heidelberg (1999). https://doi.org/10.1007/3-540-48157-5_29
4. Lydon, B.: IoT requires 'systems thinking. https://www.isa.org/intech/201802talk/
5. Lee, I., Lee, K.: The Internet of Things (IoT): applications, investments, and challenges for enterprises. Bus. Horiz. **58**, 431–440 (2015). https://doi.org/10.1016/j.bushor.2015.03.008
6. Hicks, J.R.: The Foundations of Welfare Economics (1939)
7. Schüritz, R., Satzger, G.: Patterns of data-infused business model innovation. In: Proceedings of CBI 2016: 18th IEEE Conference on Business Informatics, pp. 1–10 (2016)
8. Chen, T., Tsai, H.R.: Ubiquitous manufacturing: current practices, challenges, and opportunities. Robot. Comput. Integr. Manuf. **45**, 126–132 (2017)
9. Hevner, A.R.: A three cycle view of design science research a three cycle view of design science research. Scand. J. Inf. Syst. **19**, 1–6 (2007)
10. Monostori, L., Kádár, B., Bauernhansl, T., Kondoh, S., Kumara, S., Reinhart, G., Sauer, O., Schuh, G., Sihn, W., Ueda, K.: Cyber-physical systems in manufacturing. Cirp. Ann. **65**, 621–641 (2016)
11. Möstl, M., Schlatow, J., Ernst, R., Dutt, N., Nassar, A., Rahmani, A., Kurdahi, F.J., Wild, T., Sadighi, A., Herkersdorf, A.: Platform-centric self-awareness as a key enabler for controlling changes in CPS. Proc. IEEE **106**, 1543–1567 (2018)

12. Martin, D., Hirt, R., Kühl, N.: Service systems, smart service systems and cyber- physical systems—what's the difference? towards a unified terminology. In: 14th Internationale Tagung Wirtschaftsinformatik 2019, Siegen, Germany, February 24-27, pp. 17–31 (2019)
13. Knapp, M.S.: How can organizational and sociocultural learning theories shed light on district instructional reform? Am. J. Educ. **114**, 521–539 (2008)
14. Taitz, J., Genn, K., Brooks, V., Ross, D., Ryan, K., Shumack, B., Burrell, T., Kennedy, P.: System-wide learning from root cause analysis: a report from the new south wales root cause analysis review committee. Qual. Saf. Heal. Care. **19**, 1–5 (2010)
15. Ackoff, R.: From Data to Wisdom, pp. 170–172 (1989)
16. Rowley, J.: The wisdom hierarchy: representations of the DIKW hierarchy. J. Inf. Sci. **33**, 163–180 (2007). https://doi.org/10.1177/0165551506070706
17. Udoh, I.S., Kotonya, G.: Developing IoT applications: challenges and frameworks. IET Cyber-Phys. Syst. Theor. Appl. **3**, 65–72 (2017)
18. Patel, P., Cassou, D.: Enabling high-level application development for the Internet of Things. J. Syst. Softw. **103**, 62–84 (2015). https://doi.org/10.1016/j.jss.2015.01.027
19. Ramakrishnan, A.K., Preuveneers, D., Berbers, Y.: Enabling self-learning in dynamic and open IoT environments. Procedia Comput. Sci. **32**, 207–214 (2014)
20. Sukode, S., Gite, P.S., Agrawal, H.: Context Aware Framework in IoT: A Survey. Int. J. Adv. Trends Comput. Sci. Eng. 4, 1–9 (2015)
21. Maglio, P.P., Spohrer, J.: Fundamentals of service science. J. Acad. Mark. Sci. **36**, 18–20 (2008). https://doi.org/10.1007/s11747-007-0058-9
22. Spohrer, J., Maglio, P.P., Bailey, J., Gruhl, D.: Steps toward a science of service systems. Computer. Long. Beach. Calif. **40**, 71–77 (2007). https://doi.org/10.1109/MC.2007.33
23. Mikusz, M.: Towards a conceptual framework for cyber-physical systems from the Service-Dominant logic perspective. In: 2015 American Conference on Information System AMCIS 2015, pp. 1–13 (2015)
24. Wan, J., Zhang, D., Zhao, S., Yang, L., Lloret, J.: Context-aware vehicular cyber-physical systems with cloud support: architecture, challenges, and solutions. IEEE Commun. Mag. **52**, 106–113 (2014). https://doi.org/10.1109/MCOM.2014.6871677
25. Peters, C., et al.: Emerging digital frontiers for service innovation. Commun. Assoc. Inf. Syst. **39**, 136–149 (2016)
26. Gunes, V., Peter, S., Givargis, T., Vahid, F.: A survey on concepts, applications, and challenges in cyber-physical systems. KSII Trans. Internet Inf. Syst. **8**, 4242–4268 (2014)
27. Poovendran, R.: Cyber-physical systems: close encounters between two parallel worlds. In: Proceedings of the IEEE. pp. 1363–1366 (2010)
28. Civerchia, F., Bocchino, S., Salvadori, C., Rossi, E., Maggiani, L., Petracca, M.: Industrial Internet of Things monitoring solution for advanced predictive maintenance applications. J. Ind. Inf. Integr. **7**, 4–12 (2017)
29. Macskassy, S.A., Provost, F.: A brief survey of machine learning methods and their sensor and IoT applications. Int. Conf. Inf. Intell. Syst. Appl. 172–175 (2017)
30. Gubbi, J., Buyya, R., Marusic, S., Palaniswami, M.: Internet of Things (IoT): a vision, architectural elements, and future directions. Futur. Gener. Comput. Syst. **29**, 1645–1660 (2013). https://doi.org/10.1016/j.future.2013.01.010
31. Uluyol, O., Parthasarathy, G., Foslien, W., Kim, K.: Power curve analytic for wind turbine performance monitoring and prognostics. In: Annual Conference of the Prognostics and Health Management Society, pp. 1–8 (2011)
32. Hodge, V.J., Keefe, S.O., Weeks, M., Moulds, A.: Wireless Sensor Networks for Condition Monitoring in the Railway Industry: A Survey. IEEE Trans. Intell. Transp. Syst. **16**, 1088–1106 (2015). https://doi.org/10.1109/TITS.2014.2366512

33. Thompson, A.J., Yang, G.-Z.: Tethered and implantable optical sensors. In: Yang, Guang-Zhong (ed.) Implantable Sensors and Systems. LNCS, pp. 439–505. Springer, Cham (2018). https://doi.org/10.1007/978-3-319-69748-2_6

34. Martin, D., Kühl, N.: Holistic system-analytics as an alternative to isolated sensor technology: a condition monitoring use case. In: Proceedings of the 52nd Annual Hawaii International Conference on System Sciences (HICSS-52), Grand Wailea, Maui, Hawaii, January 8–11 2019, pp. 1005–1012 (2019)

35. Du, T.C., Lai, V.S., Cheung, W., Cui, X.: Willingness to share information in a supply chain: A partnership-data- process perspective. Inf. Manag. **49**, 89–98 (2012)

36. Enders, T., Martin, D., Sehgal, G.G., Schüritz, R.: Igniting the spark: overcoming organizational change resistance to advance innovation adoption – the case of data-driven services. In: Nóvoa, H., Drăgoicea, M., Kühl, N. (eds.) IESS 2020. LNBIP, vol. 377, pp. 217–230. Springer, Cham (2020). https://doi.org/10.1007/978-3-030-38724-2_16

37. Stephant, J., Charara, A., Meizel, D.: Virtual sensor: Application to vehicle sideslip angle and transversal forces. IEEE Trans. Ind. Electron. **51**, 278–289 (2004)

38. Dietz, M., Pernul, G.: Digital Twin: empowering enterprises towards a system-of-systems approach. Bus. Inf. Syst. Eng. **62**(2), 179–184 (2019). https://doi.org/10.1007/s12599-019-00624-0

39. Uhlemann, T.H.J., Lehmann, C., Steinhilper, R.: The digital twin: realizing the cyber-physical production system for industry 4.0. Procedia CIRP. **61**, 335–340 (2017)

40. Valdés-Pérez, R.E.: Principles of human—computer collaboration for knowledge discovery in science. Artif. Intell. **107**, 335–346 (1999)

41. Gilpin, L.H., Bau, D., Yuan, B.Z., Bajwa, A., Specter, M., Kagal, L.: Explaining explanations: an overview of interpretability of machine learning. In: 2018 IEEE 5th International Conference on Data Science and Advanced Analytics, pp. 80–89 (2018)

42. Enders, T.: Exploring the value of data - a research agenda. In: Satzger, G., Patrício, L., Zaki, M., Kühl, N., Hottum, P. (eds.) Exploring Service Science, pp. 274–286. Springer International Publishing, Cham (2018). https://doi.org/10.1007/978-3-030-00713-3_21

43. Adadi, A., Berrada, M.: Peeking inside the black-box: a survey on explainable artificial intelligence (XAI). IEEE Access. **6**, 52138–52160 (2018)

44. Hevner, A.R., Chatterjee, S.: Design Research in information Systems: Theory and Practice (2010)

45. Kuechler, W., Vaishnavi, V.: A framework for theory development in design science research: multiple perspectives. J. Assoc. Inf. **13**, 395–423 (2012)

46. Venable, J., Pries-Heje, J., Baskerville, R.: FEDS: A framework for evaluation in design science research. Eur. J. Inf. Syst. **25**, 77–89 (2016)

47. Yin, R.K.: Case Study Research: Design and Methods, 4th edn. Thousand Oaks, CA Sage (2009)

Author Index

Printed in the United States
By Bookmasters